PROTOCOL SPECIFICATION, TESTING, AND VERIFICATION, IX

PROTOCOL SPECIFICATION, TESTING, AND VERIFICATION, IX

Proceedings of the IFIP WG 6.1 Ninth International Symposium on
Protocol Specification, Testing, and Verification
Enschede, The Netherlands, 6–9 June, 1989

Edited by

ED BRINKSMA
GIUSEPPE SCOLLO
CHRIS A. VISSERS

University of Twente
Tele-Informatics Group
Department of Informatics TW/RC
Enschede, The Netherlands

1990

NORTH-HOLLAND
AMSTERDAM · NEW YORK · OXFORD · TOKYO

ELSEVIER SCIENCE PUBLISHERS B.V.
Sara Burgerhartstraat 25
P.O. Box 211, 1000 AE Amsterdam, The Netherlands

Distributors for the United States and Canada:
ELSEVIER SCIENCE PUBLISHING COMPANY INC.
655 Avenue of the Americas
New York, N.Y. 10010, U.S.A.

ISBN: 0 444 88343 6

Printed in The Netherlands.

Preface

This year's edition of the IFIP Working Group 6.1 International Symposium on Protocol Specification, Testing, and Verification is the ninth in a series of annual meetings. By now these have become well-established events for all researchers and practitioners that take an interest in the application of formal methods to the design, description, analysis, implementation and testing of open systems. As such they not only are a regular meeting place for many who are active in this area, but also provide an excellent orientation point for newcomers.

The steady growth of the interest of the topic of the Symposium is clearly reflected in its history. Started as a closed workshop in 1981, the transition to an open symposium was made in Zürich in 1987, which proved to be a great success. This year the Symposium was held at the University of Twente in Enschede, The Netherlands. Approximately 170 people participated in the Symposium and the Tutorial Day. A record number of 94 papers were submitted, testifying to the vitality of the research activities in this field.

Out of the submitted papers the programme committee selected 26 for presentation at the Symposium. Because of the considerable number of good submissions this task was not easy, and a number of interesting contributions had to be rejected. Three invited presentations were included in the programme, which were selected to add some new flavours to the usual menu. They ranged from a technical topic (real-time specification), via an emerging topic (Open Distributed Processing), to a political topic (EEC research policy).

To stimulate the professional interaction between the participants two short workshop sessions were organized on 'Approaches to Protocol Implementation Using Formal Methods' and 'Graphics and Interactive Interfaces for FDTs'. Both in these workshops and in the regular Symposium sessions, the atmosphere could be described as 'lively', with ample participation of the critical audience. We think that this attitude signifies that the future of this series of Symposia looks bright, and that we may look forward to new, successful editions in the years to come.

Ed Brinksma
Giuseppe Scollo
Chris A. Vissers

June, 1989

Contents

Session 1: System Specification

Invited Presentation:

Session 2: Process Algebra Applications

Session 3: Conformance Testing

Session 4: Specification Language Transformation

Invited Presentation:

Session 5: Transition System Applications

Session 6: Tool Environments

Session 7: Verification by State Space Exploration

Session 8: Temporal Logic Applications

Acknowledgements

We wish to thank all the reviewers who have helped us with great efficiency to evaluate the large number of submitted papers. The members of the Programme Committee are thanked for their share in the reviewing process, as well as for chairing the Symposium sessions and workshops. In particular we wish to mention Michel Diaz, Rudolf Jan Heijink, Björn Pehrson, Rainer Prinoth, Juan Quemada, and Robin Sharp for attending the Programme Committee meeting in March, and helping us to put together the Final Programme.

Marie-Bernadette Stevens and Linda van der Zaag of the International Conference and Study Centre "Drienerburght", and our secretary Wilma Hiddink, were responsible for the local organization, and are to be credited for the smooth organization of much of the non-technical work. Many members of our department helped out with the installation of equipment and all sorts of errands.

Several organizations kindly agreed to sponsor the Symposium. The Netherlands PTT Research, APT Nederland BV, Philips Telecommunication and Data Systems, and the University of Twente are thanked for their generous financial support. The loan of equipment by SUN Microsystems Nederland for the demonstration of software tools is highly appreciated.

We are grateful to all the people and organizations above, and all others who have devoted their time, their skills, and their enthusiasm to make this year's Symposium a success.

Ed Brinksma
Giuseppe Scollo
Chris A. Vissers

Programme Committee and Invited Speakers

Programme Committee

Programme Chair:

Ed Brinksma	*University of Twente, Enschede, Netherlands*
Giuseppe Scollo	*University of Twente, Enschede, Netherlands*
Chris Vissers	*University of Twente, Enschede, Netherlands*

Sudhir Aggarwal	*Bellcore, Morristown, USA.*
Gregor v. Bochmann	*University of Montreal, Canada*
Tommaso Bolognesi	*CNUCE, Pisa, Italy*
André Danthine	*University of Liège, Belgium*
Piotr Dembinsky	*Warshaw, Poland*
Michel Diaz	*LAAS du CNRS, Toulouse, France*
Rudolf Jan Heijink	*Research Neher Laboratories, Leidschendam, Netherlands*
Luigi Logrippo	*University of Ottawa, Canada*
Björn Pehrson	*SICS, Stockholm, Sweden*
Rainer Prinoth	*GMD, Darmstadt, FRG.*
Juan Quemada	*ETSI Telecomunicacion, Madrid, Spain*
Dave Rayner	*National Physical Laboratory, Teddington, UK*
Harry Rudin	*IBM Research Laboratory, Zurich, Switzerland*
Krishan Sabnani	*AT&T Bell Laboratories, Murray Hill, USA*
Robin Sharp	*Technical University of Denmark, Lyngby, Denmark*
Deepinder Sidhu	*University of Maryland, USA*
Norio Shiratori	*Tohoku University, Sendai, Japan*
Ken Turner	*University of Stirling, UK*

Invited Speakers

Willem Paul de Roever and Jozef J.M. Hooman	*Technical University Eindhoven, Netherlands*
Joost J. van Griethuysen	*Philips International, Eindhoven, Netherlands*
Jean-Jacques Lauture	*CEC, Brussels, Belgium*

Referees

P.D. Amer	*University of Delaware, Newark, USA.*
R. Alderden	*University of Twente, Enschede, Netherlands*
B. Berthomieu	*LAAS du CNRS, Toulouse, France*
S.A. Black	*Hewlett Packard Laboratories, Bristol, UK*
T.P. Blumer	*Phoenix Tech. ltd., Cambridge, USA*
S. Budkowski	*BULL S.A., Les Clayes s/s Bois, France*
F. Caneschi	*TECSIEL, Pisa, Italy*
I. Castellani	*INRIA Sophia Antipolis, France*
A.R. Cavalli	*CNET, Issy les Moulineaux, France*
V. Chari	*Marben, Paris, France*
J.P. Courtiat	*LAAS du CNRS, Toulouse, France*
E.L. Cusack	*British Telecom, Ipswich, UK*
P. van Eijk	*University of Twente, Enschede, Netherlands*
R.A. Fleming	*Hewlett Packard Laboratories, Bristol, UK*
D. Freestone	*British Telecom, Ipswich, UK*
M. Gouda	*University of Texas, Austin, USA*
J.F. Groote	*CWI, Amsterdam, The Netherlands*
M.C.B. Hennessy	*University of Sussex, Brighton, UK*
D. Hogrefe	*University of Hamburg, FRG*
G. Holzmann	*AT&T Bell Laboratories, Murray Hill, USA*
G. Karjoth	*IBM Research Laboratory, Zurich, Switzerland*
J. Kroon	*Research Neher Laboratories, Leidschendam, Netherlands*
J. van de Lagemaat	*University of Twente, Enschede, Netherlands*
S.S. Lam	*University of Texas, Austin, USA*
L. Lamport	*DEC, Palo Alto, USA*
R. Langerak	*University of Twente, Enschede, Netherlands*
P. Linington	*University of Kent, Canterbury, UK*
J. Linn	*NITS, Gaithersburg, USA*
M.T. Liu	*Ohio State University, Columbus, USA*
A. Lombardo	*University of Catania, Italy*
L. Mackert	*IBM Research Laboratory, Heidelberg, FRG*
F. Marso	*University of Liège, Belgium*
J. de Meer	*GMD-Fokus, Berlin, FRG*
C. Morgan	*Oxford University, Oxford, UK*
E. Najm	*INRIA, Rocquencourt, France*
R. De Nicola	*IEI, Pisa, Italy*
I. Niemegeers	*University of Twente, Enschede, Netherlands*
J. Pachl	*University of Waterloo, Canada*
S. Palazzo	*University of Catania, Italy*
G. Pappalardo	*University of Newcastle upon Tyne, UK*
A. Rensink	*University of Twente, Enschede, Netherlands*

M. Sajkowski	*SOI - Politechnika Poznanska, Poznan, Poland*
R. Saracco	*CSELT, Turin, Italy*
B. Sarikaya	*Concordia University, Montreal, Canada*
J. Schot	*University of Twente, Enschede, Netherlands*
J. Sifakis	*LGI/IMAG, Grenoble, France*
M. van Sinderen	*University of Twente, Enschede, Netherlands*
S.A. Smolka	*SUNY, Stonybrook, USA*
R.L. Tenney	*University of Massachusetts, Boston, USA*
H. van Thienen	*University of Nijmegen, Netherlands*
M. Thomas	*University of Glasgow, UK*
J. Tretmans	*University of Twente, Enschede, Netherlands*
H. Ural	*University of Ottawa, Canada*
F. Vogt	*University of Hamburg, FRG*
S. Vuong	*University of British Columbia, Vancouver, Canada*
C. West	*IBM Research Laboratory, Zurich, Switzerland*

Session 1:

System Specification

Protocol Specification, Testing, and Verification, IX
E. Brinksma, G. Scollo and C.A. Vissers (Editors)
Elsevier Science Publishers B.V. (North-Holland)

Signalling System No. 7
The Network Layer

I. J. Hayes*, M. Mowbray†and G. A. Rose*

Abstract

The paper formally specifies message streams, routing and rerouting within CCITT's Signalling System No 7, using the Z specification language. The paper advocates the use of several related views (projections) to specify complex systems. Multiple projections provide a useful technique for separation of concerns. Three views are presented:

- an External View – a service view, concerned with the identification of individual correctly sequenced message streams from origin to destination without routing detail.
- a Sectional Stream View – a refinement of the external view which identifies the route of a stream as a sequence of sections, each a signalling point and an outgoing linkset. This view is the basis for rerouting.
- a Network View – a specification of overall network connectivity (topology) accommodating the totality of streams. Routing labels are added to messages to identify streams.

The stream and network views are then related for consistency of connectivity (e.g., that stream routes are consistent with current link availability) and consistency of projection (the projection of the totality of messages in the network with respect to a particular routing label is consistent with the corresponding stream view).
The paper does not discuss service-primitive or protocol-unit details, congestion control, or management or test procedures.

1 Introduction

The CCITT Recommendation with respect to the Network Layer within Signalling System No 7 [2] necessarily addresses many issues : it uses various descriptive styles with different levels of formality. In parts, the distinction between specification and implied implementation is not made. The overall network behaviour is highly parallel and complex: it is difficult to comprehend such gross behaviour from service-primitive and field-format details, state identification numbers, etc..

This paper confines its attention to message routing and rerouting using formal methods. It does not address link activation/deactivation, congestion control, management or test procedures; nor does it contain the syntax/formats of primitives or protocol units. The goal of the paper is to demonstrate that by focussing on several views or projections of overall behaviour, the number of current concerns can be controlled: this facilitates comprehension.

*Key Centre for Software Technology, University of Queensland, Australia.
†Overseas Telecommunications Commission, Australia.

The Network Layer provides services which enable a User Part to send message sequences between not necessarily adjacent signalling points in identifiable streams. Messages are confined to streams by routing labels and there are no dependencies across streams within the network. Streams are conceptually concurrent, although an implementation may merge them arbitrarily. The paper specifies streams at two levels of abstraction: the more abstract level is an External Stream View as seen by the User Part; the less abstract level is a Sectional Stream View which refines the external view by modelling the route as a chain of sections. The paper then presents a global Network View which accommodates the multiplicity of streams. Finally, the stream and network views are related by identifying the individual links on a stream's route and equating the stream's attributes to corresponding projections of the network's attributes. The individual link detail corresponds to that of the most abstract specification of the Link Layer [1, 3]. The formal specifications are written in the Z notation, developed at Oxford University. Reference[3] includes an overview of the Z notation and bibliographic references.

2 An External Stream View

The External Stream View captures the essential service information with respect to one stream at the UserPart–Network interface: it is devoid of routing, signalling link, and other network details.

SPC is the set (type) of signalling-point codes; the codes identify a network's potential signalling points. The *SPC* of an origin point is called an origin-point code and the *SPC* of a destination is called a destination-point code.

$$SPC \mathrel{\widehat{=}} 0 \,..\, 16383$$

Between any two signalling points there can be sixteen streams of communication. A stream selector is used to distinguish streams between the same two signalling points; the stream selectors are taken from the set *SLS*. (In order to keep our notation consistent with that used in [2], the name *SLS*, which is derived from Signalling Link Selector, has been used. At the network level, signalling link selectors determine the individual signalling links within the linksets of a route. At this more abstract level, however, signalling link selectors identify streams, within which message sequencing is respected, from a given origin point to a given destination point.) Provision for multiple streams from an origin to a destination enables parallelism in the network to be exploited – parallelism, however, is deferred to a later view.

$$SLS \mathrel{\widehat{=}} 0 \,..\, 15$$

MSG is the set of all signalling messages. We do not define its structure.

For a single message stream we record, at a particular stage, the messages actually sent by the application at the origin (*MsgsSent*) and the messages actually delivered (*MsgsDelivered*) to the application at the destination. This is shown in figure 1 and formalised by schema *STREAM_ext*.

STREAM_ext

$MsgsSent, MsgsDelivered : \mathrm{seq}\ MSG$
$MsgsDelivered \subseteq MsgsSent$

(In Z, a sequence is modelled as a function having as domain a contiguous set of natural numbers $(1 \,..\, n)$. The subset relation on sequences is equivalent to " is a prefix of ".)

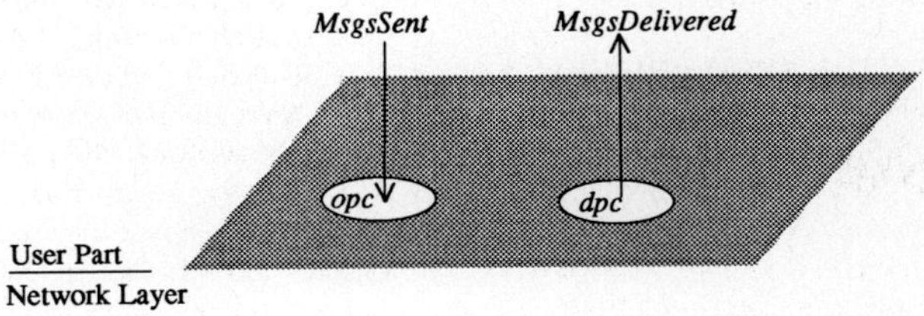

Figure 1: External Stream View

2.1 Initialisation

$$STREAM\_ext\_INIT \triangleq [STREAM\_ext \mid MsgsSent = \langle\,\rangle]$$

Since *MsgsDelivered* is a prefix of *MsgsSent*, this implies *MsgsDelivered* = ⟨ ⟩ (the empty sequence).

2.2 Stream Identification

A stream is uniquely identified by a combination of origin and destination point codes and a stream selector. We will refer to such a combination as a *routing label.* (Again the term *routing label* is chosen for consistency with [2], but at this level of abstraction we are not concerned with the particular route used by a stream.)

```
RTG_LAB ________________________________________
| opc, dpc : SPC
| sls : SLS
|_______________________________________________
```

opc and *dpc* identify a message's origin and destination point codes respectively and *sls* completes the identification of the stream.

For each routing label there is possibly a stream.

```
STREAMS_EXT ____________________________________
| Stream_ext : RTG_LAB ⇸ STREAM_ext
|_______________________________________________
```

Schema *STREAMS_EXT* provides for a multiplicity of streams. The domain of *Stream_ext* identifies the streams instantiated at a particular time. (The symbol ⇸ denotes a partial function.) In particular, *STREAMS_EXT* imposes no cross constraints between streams, so that streams may be sensibly studied in isolation.

3 A Sectional Stream View

The sectional stream view models a stream's path from origin to destination as a chain of sections, one corresponding to each signalling point on route, except for the destination point. A section then is an abstraction for a signalling point and its ongoing linkset (the set of all physical links directly connecting a pair of signalling points).

3.1 Sections

Figure 2 illustrates a section. *MsgsRecd* and *MsgsOut* represent the messages received and output from the section respectively. *MsgsInSect* represents the messages within a section (i.e., stored in the corresponding signalling point and on the ongoing link – details hidden in this view).

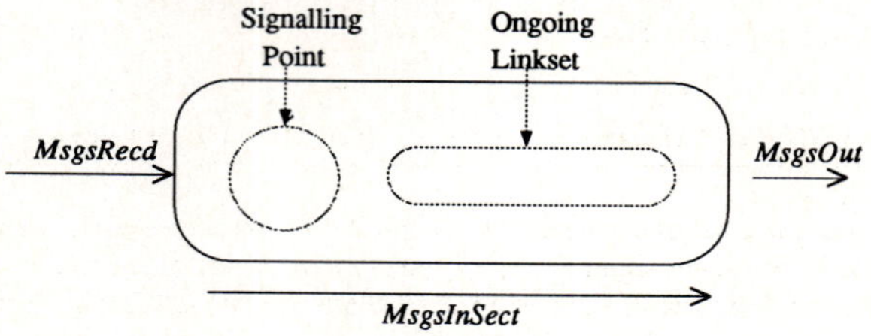

Figure 2: A Section

SECTION

$$MsgsRecd, MsgsOut, MsgsInSect : \mathrm{seq}\ MSG$$

$$MsgsRecd = MsgsOut \frown MsgsInSect$$

Symbol $\frown$ denotes sequence concatenation (note the order of the sequences – messages in *MsgsOut* precede messages in *MsgsInSect*).
A route is a non-empty sequence of signalling points with no duplicates.

$$ROUTE \mathrel{\widehat{=}} \{s : \mathrm{seq}_1\ SPC \mid \forall i, j : \mathrm{dom}\ s \bullet i \neq j \Rightarrow s\ (i) \neq s\ (j)\}$$

Figure 3 shows the chain of sections constituting the route from origin to destination. This sectional stream view is formalised by the schema STREAM_sect below.

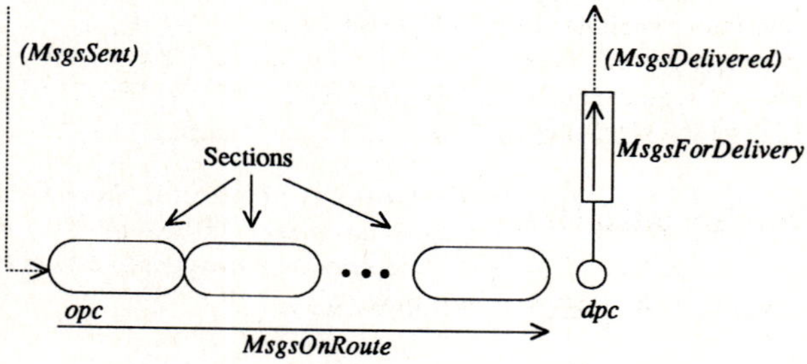

Figure 3: Sectional Stream View

$$
\begin{array}{l}
\textit{STREAM\_sect} \\
\hline
\quad Route : ROUTE \\
\quad Section : SPC \twoheadrightarrow SECTION \\
\quad MsgsOnRoute, MsgsForDelivery : \mathrm{seq}\ MSG \\
\hline
\quad \mathrm{dom}\ Section = \mathrm{ran}\ (\mathrm{front}\ Route) \\
\quad \forall p : 1 \mathinner{\ldotp\ldotp} \#Route - 2 \bullet \\
\qquad Section\ (Route\ (p)).MsgsOut = Section\ (Route\ (p+1)).MsgsRecd \\
\quad MsgsOnRoute = {}^\frown/\ \mathrm{rev}\{i : 1 \mathinner{\ldotp\ldotp} \#Route - 1 \bullet i \mapsto Section(Route(i)).MsgsInSect\} \\
\quad \exists s : \mathrm{seq}\ MSG \bullet s \frown MsgsForDelivery = Section\ (Route\ (\#Route - 1)).MsgsOut \\
\hline
\end{array}
$$

The route of a stream is a sequence of distinct signalling points from origin to destination. A section is associated with each signalling point on route, except the destination, by function *Section.* The sections join end-to-end so that the output of one is the input to the next. *MsgsOnRoute* is the concatenation of the *MsgsInSect* of the total span of sections supporting the given stream. *MsgsForDelivery* represents those messages output from the final section and not yet delivered to the destination. (# denotes cardinality and the • appearing in the final construct indicates set restructuring, e.g.,$\{n : \mathbb{N} \bullet n^2\}$ denotes {0,1,4,9,...}. Symbol ${}^\frown/$ denotes distributed concatenation: it concatenates a sequence of sequences. Function rev reverses a sequence.)

Theorem

$$
\begin{array}{l}
\textit{STREAM\_sect}; \\
MsgsSent, MsgsDelivered : \mathrm{seq}\ MSG \mid \\
\quad MsgsSent = Section\ (Route\ (1)).MsgsRecd \\
\quad MsgsDelivered \frown MsgsForDelivery = Section\ (Route\ (\#Route - 1)).MsgsOut \\
\vdash \\
\textit{STREAM\_ext}
\end{array}
$$

The proof relies on the fact that *MsgsOut* of the last section is a prefix of (includes equal to) *MsgsSent* (the remainder being *MsgsOnRoute*) and *MsgsDelivered* is a prefix of *MsgsOut* of the last section (the remainder being *MsgsForDelivery*). That is, if the input to the first section is the message sequence sent to the network, and the output from the last section becomes the message sequence delivered via messages awaiting delivery, then the sectional stream view implies the external stream view.

3.2 Section Initialisation

$$\textit{SECTION\_INIT} \triangleq [\textit{SECTION} \mid MsgsRecd = \langle\,\rangle]$$

SECTION_INIT implies that *MsgsOut* must also be empty.

$$
\begin{array}{l}
\textit{STREAM\_sect\_INIT} \triangleq \textit{STREAM\_sect} \mid \\
\quad Section\ (Route\ (1)).MsgsRecd = \langle\,\rangle
\end{array}
$$

That is, the first and by implication each succeeding section is an instance of *SECTION_INIT*.

3.3 Rerouting Operations

At the linkage level of detail, if traffic intended for a failed link out of signalling point P cannot be redirected to an alternative link in the same linkset, rerouting is required. Figure 4 illustrates rerouting from P to Q via a signalling point not previously on the route. This implies selection of an alternative linkset from P for the particular destination. At the sectional level, the section corresponding to P couples to a new empty section which in turn couples to P's old successor Q. Operation *INSERT_SECT* specifies this alternative routing.

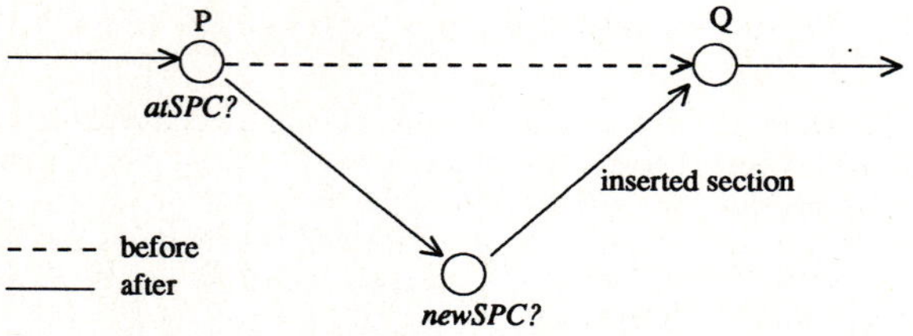

Figure 4: Section Insertion

INSERT_SECT

$$\Delta STREAM\_sect$$
$$atSPC?, newSPC? : SPC$$

$$atSPC? \in \operatorname{ran} \ \operatorname{front} \ Route$$
$$newSPC? \notin \operatorname{ran} \ Route$$
$$\exists \, pre, post : \operatorname{seq} \ SPC \bullet$$
$$\quad Route = pre \frown \langle atSPC? \rangle \frown post \land$$
$$\quad Route' = pre \frown \langle atSPC?, newSPC? \rangle \frown post$$
$$\exists \, SECTION \bullet$$
$$\quad MsgsRecd = Section\ (atSPC?).MsgsOut \land$$
$$\quad MsgsInSect = \langle \rangle$$
$$\quad Section' = Section \cup \{newSPC? \mapsto \theta SECTION\}$$
$$\theta STREAM\_sect' \setminus (Route', Section') = \theta STREAM\_sect \setminus (Route, Section)$$

($\Delta STREAM\_sect$ above is defined as $STREAM\_sect \land STREAM\_sect'$. Z distinguishes the value of a state variable after an operation by priming it – priming a schema name, primes each of its constituent state variables. Conjoining two schemas, merges the declarations and conjoins the two predicates. The final predicate states that all components of $STREAM\_sect'$ and $STREAM\_sect$ are equal except for *Route* and *Section*.)

When a failed link becomes available, the normal route may be restored by removing the section inserted above. As a preliminary, messages in the previously-inserted section must have reached Q before route restoration in order to retain message sequencing (i.e., to prevent new messages sent directly from P to Q from overtaking old messages sent via the detour). This is illustrated in Figure 5 and specified by operation *REMOVE_SECT*.

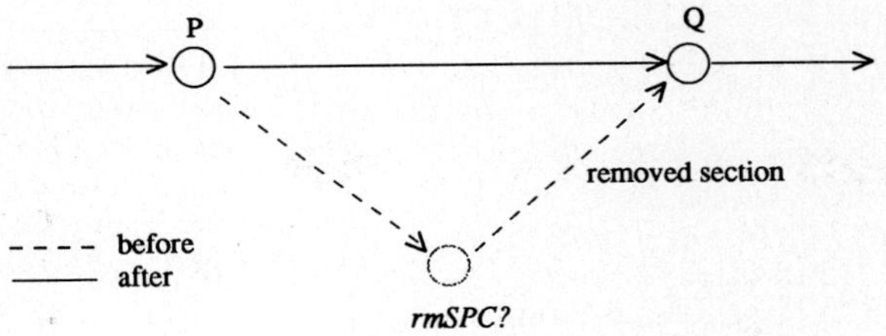

Figure 5: Section Removal

REMOVE_SECT

$$\begin{array}{|l}
\Delta STREAM_sect \\
rmSPC? : SPC \\
\hline
rmSPC? \in \operatorname{ran} (\operatorname{front} (\operatorname{tail} Route)) \\
Section\ (rmSPC?).MsgsInSect = \langle\rangle \\
Route' = \operatorname{squash}\ Route \rhd \{rmSPC?\} \\
Section' = \{rmSPC?\} \lhd Section \\
\theta STREAM_sect' \setminus (Route', Section') = \theta STREAM_sect \setminus (Route, Section)
\end{array}$$

(Symbol $\rhd$ denotes range subtraction; function squash converts a $\mathbb{N} \nrightarrow X$ function to a sequence of X; and $\lhd$ denotes domain subtraction.) At the sectional level of abstraction, rerouting which conforms to the above operations only modifies *Route* and *Section* and in such a way that *MsgsOnRoute* remains invariant.

3.4 Multiple Streams

For each stream we have a stream sectional view. The route taken by the sections must be from the origin of the stream to its destination.

STREAMS_SECTIONS

$$\begin{array}{|l}
Stream_sect : RTG_LAB \nrightarrow STREAM_sect \\
\hline
\forall lab : \operatorname{dom} Stream_sect \bullet \\
\quad \operatorname{let} route \mathrel{\widehat{=}} Stream_sect\ (lab).Route \bullet \\
\quad\quad lab.opc = route\ (1) \\
\quad\quad lab.dpc = route\ (\#route)
\end{array}$$

This multiplicity of sectional streams is now related to the multiplicity of external streams (*STREAMS_EXT*).

STREAMS_EXT_STREAMS_SECTIONS

STREAMS_EXT
STREAMS_SECTIONS

dom *Stream_ext* = dom *Stream_sect*
$\forall$ *lab* : dom *Stream_ext* $\bullet$
  $\exists$ *STREAM_ext*; *STREAM_sect* $\bullet$
    STREAM_ext = *Stream_ext* (*lab*)
    STREAM_sect = *Stream_sect* (*lab*)
    MsgsSent = *Section* (*Route* (1)).*MsgsRecd*
    MsgsDelivered $\frown$ *MsgsForDelivery* =
      Section (*Route* (#*Route* − 1)).*MsgsOut*

The correspondences established between external and sectional streams are consistent with the Theorem in section 3.1.

4 A Network View

The network view specifies the connectivity of the network under consideration, i.e., describes its signalling links and signalling points. This view is stream-independent in that it accommodates a multiplicity of streams, i.e., many of its attributes (state variables) merge corresponding attributes of individual streams.

4.1 The Signalling Links

SLC is the set of all signalling link codes; the codes identify links within a given linkset.

SLC $\triangleq$ 0 . . 15

A signalling link is identified by the ordered signalling point pair it directly connects and its *SLC*.

SL

From, *To* : *SPC*
slc : *SLC*

From $\neq$ *To*

The reverse of a signalling link is the link with transposed ends and the same *SLC*.

ReverseSL : *SL* $\rightarrowtail$ *SL*

ReverseSL (*sl*1) = *sl*2
$\Leftrightarrow$ (*sl*1.*To* = *sl*2.*From* $\wedge$ *sl*1.*From* = *sl*2.*To* $\wedge$ *sl*1.*slc* = *sl*2.*slc*)

As links in the network carry messages for a number of streams we need to tag each message with its stream identification (routing label).

RMSG

RtgLab : *RTG_LAB*
Msg : *MSG*

SL_INFO

MsgsIn, *MsgsOut*, *MsgsOn* : seq *RMSG*

MsgsIn = *MsgsOut* $\frown$ *MsgsOn*

SL_INFO is a stream-independent view of a signalling link corresponding to the most abstract level of the Link Layer.

4.2 The Signalling Points

The external and sectional stream views focussed attention on the origin and destination signalling points and on the intervening signalling points of an individual stream. Here, attention is directed to the network's totality of signalling points. Figure 6 shows the message sequences associated with a signalling point. A signalling point receives messages (*MsgsRecd*)

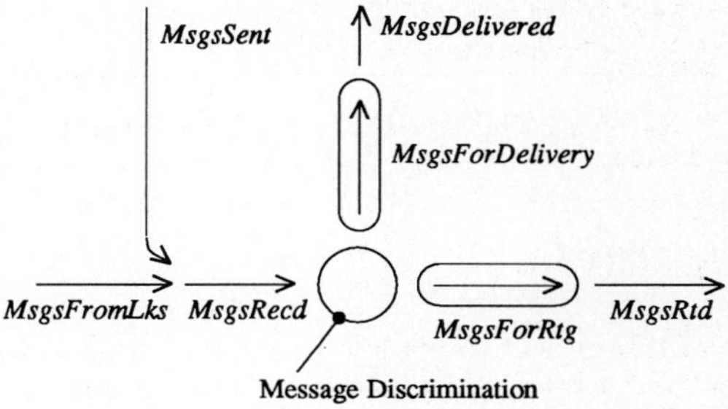

Figure 6: Signalling Point Messages

from incoming linksets (*MsgsFromLks*) and from the Application (*MsgsSent*). The messages from the two sources are distinguished by their origin point codes. The destination point code distinguishes between received messages destined for the signalling point and those that are not. Messages for the signalling point become delivered messages (*MsgsDelivered*) via a messages for delivery queue (*MsgsForDelivery*). Ongoing messages become routed messages (*MsgsRtd*) via a messages for routing queue (*MsgsForRtg*). Schema *SP_INFO* below formalises these requirements.

SP_INFO ___

$spc : SPC$
$MsgsFromLks, MsgsSent, MsgsRecd, MsgsForDelivery,$
$MsgsDelivered, MsgsForRtg, MsgsRtd : \mathrm{seq}\ RMSG$

---

let
$O\_RMSG \mathrel{\widehat{=}} \{RMSG \mid RtgLab.opc = spc\}$
$D\_RMSG \mathrel{\widehat{=}} \{RMSG \mid RtgLab.dpc = spc\}$
$\bullet$
$MsgsRecd \upharpoonright O\_RMSG = MsgsSent$
$MsgsRecd \upharpoonright (RMSG - O\_RMSG) = MsgsFromLks$
$MsgsDelivered \frown MsgsForDelivery = MsgsRecd \upharpoonright D\_RMSG$
$MsgsRtd \frown MsgsForRtg = MsgsRecd \upharpoonright (RMSG - D\_RMSG)$

(Symbol $\upharpoonright$ above indicates sequence range restriction.)

4.3 The Network

The network comprises the signalling links and signalling points. The network's current mapping of signalling link selectors to signalling link codes within each active linkset is also associated with the network because it applies to all streams using the linkset.

$$
\begin{array}{l}
\textit{NETWORK} \\
\hline
NwkSL, AvailSL : \mathbb{P}\, SL \\
Adjacent, Linked : SPC \leftrightarrow SPC \\
SLinfo : SL \twoheadrightarrow SL\_INFO \\
SPinfo : SPC \twoheadrightarrow SP\_INFO \\
SelectSLC : (SPC \times SPC) \twoheadrightarrow (SLS \rightarrow SLC) \\
\hline
AvailSL \subseteq NwkSL \\
\forall\, sl : NwkSL \bullet ReverseSL\,(sl) \in NwkSL \\
Adjacent = \{from, to : SPC \mid \exists\, sl : NwkSL \bullet from = sl.From \land to = sl.To\} \\
Linked = \{from, to : SPC \mid \exists\, sl : AvailSL \bullet from = sl.From \land to = sl.To\} \\
\mathrm{dom}\ SLinfo = AvailSL \\
\mathrm{dom}\ SPinfo = \mathrm{dom}\ Adjacent \\
\forall\, p : \mathrm{dom}\ SPinfo \bullet SPinfo\,(p).spc = p \\
\mathrm{dom}\ SelectSLC = Linked \\
\forall\ (spc1, spc2) : Linked; f : SLS \rightarrow SLC \bullet SelectSLC\ (spc1, spc2) = f \\
\quad \Rightarrow \{SL \mid From = spc1 \land To = spc2 \land slc \in \mathrm{ran}\ (f)\} \subseteq AvailSL \\
\hline
\end{array}
$$

(Symbol $\leftrightarrow$ indicates a binary relation.) A network comprises a set of signalling links (*NwkSL*), a subset of which (*AvailSL*) is available. Moreover, the network's links are symmetric, i.e., each link has an associated reverse link. A pair of signalling points are *Adjacent* iff they are directly connected by some link, and *Linked* iff at least one directly connecting link between them is available. The symmetry of *NwkLS* implies that *Adjacent* is a symmetric relation. Only available signalling links have defined signalling link information. Signalling point information is retained for all signalling points.

SelectSLC selects the particular *SLC* within a given linkset for a given *SLS*. The linkset must include an available link and all *SLS* values must be mapped onto available links. Selection of links within a given linkset therefore depends on *SLS* only. (The linksets on route for a stream are determined by its routing label at the sectional stream level via *Route*, i.e., adjacent signalling points on *Route* identify linksets.)

With respect to network operations, it is necessary to specify operations, such as "retrieve messages", which do not distinguish individual streams, and demonstrate that the effect of these operations, or sequences thereof, on a particular stream corresponds to an operation, or operation sequence, within the sectional stream view. Such demonstrations require the relationship between the stream and network states, the topic of Section 5.

5 Relating Stream and Network Views

In order to relate stream and network views, we need to be able to extract the sequence of messages constituting a given stream (with a given routing label) from a sequence of tagged messages. *Select* performs this function.

$$
\begin{array}{|l}
Select : (\text{seq } RMSG) \times RTG\_LAB \rightarrow \text{seq } MSG \\
\hline
\forall rms : \text{seq } RMSG;\ lab : RTG\_LAB \bullet \\
\quad Select\ (rms, lab) = \\
\qquad \text{squash } \{i : \text{dom } rms \mid rms\ (i).RtgLab = lab \bullet i \mapsto rms\ (i).Msg\}
\end{array}
$$

The specification now relates the underlying connectivity and state information of the network to the multiplicity of streams. This relationship requires that for every stream,

- the stream and restricted network views agree at the origin and destination points,
- signalling points along each sectional stream's route be linked (i.e., be directly connected by an available signalling link),
- the state variables of associated signalling points (restricted) and sections agree,
- the link associated with each section be identified,
- the state variables of the identified link and associated section agree, e.g., that the link's *MsgsOut*, restricted to messages belonging to the stream under consideration, be identical to the section's *MsgsOut*, and
- the state variables of signalling points and links paired within each section agree.

$$
\begin{array}{|l}
\multicolumn{1}{l}{STREAMS\_NETWORK} \\
\hline
STREAMS\_EXT\_STREAMS\_SECTIONS \\
NETWORK \\
\hline
\forall lab : \text{dom } Stream\_sect \bullet \\
\quad Select\ (SPinfo\ (lab.opc).MsgsSent, lab) = Stream\_ext\ (lab).MsgsSent \\
\quad Select\ (SPinfo\ (lab.dpc).MsgsDelivered, lab) = Stream\_ext\ (lab).MsgsDelivered \\
\quad \text{let } stream \mathrel{\widehat{=}} Stream\_sect\ (lab) \bullet \\
\qquad Select\ (SPinfo\ (lab.dpc).MsgsForDelivery, lab) = stream.MsgsForDelivery \\
\qquad \forall spc : \text{ran front } stream.Route \bullet \\
\qquad\quad spc\ \underline{Linked}\ (Next\ (Route)\ (spc)) \\
\qquad\quad \text{let} \\
\qquad\qquad\quad spinfo \mathrel{\widehat{=}} SPinfo\ (spc) \\
\qquad\qquad\quad section \mathrel{\widehat{=}} Section\ (spc) \\
\qquad\quad \bullet \\
\qquad\qquad\quad Select\ (spinfo.MsgsRecd, lab) = section.MsgsRecd\ \wedge \\
\qquad\qquad\quad \exists SL \bullet \\
\qquad\qquad\qquad From = spc \wedge To = Next\ (Route)\ (spc)\ \wedge \\
\qquad\qquad\qquad slc = SelectSLC\ (From, To)\ (lab.sls)\ \wedge \\
\qquad\qquad\qquad \text{let } slinfo = SLinfo\ (SL) \bullet \\
\qquad\qquad\qquad\qquad Select\ (slinfo.MsgsOn \frown spinfo.MsgsForRtg, lab) = \\
\qquad\qquad\qquad\qquad\quad section.MsgsInSect\ \wedge \\
\qquad\qquad\qquad\qquad Select\ (slinfo.MsgsOut, lab) = section.MsgsOut\ \wedge \\
\qquad\qquad\qquad\qquad Select\ (slinfo.MsgsIn, lab) = Select\ (spinfo.MsgsRtd, lab) \\
\hline
\end{array}
$$

(Function *Next*, the definition of which is omitted, returns *spc*'s successor on *Route*.)

6 Conclusions

A network carrying a multiplicity of message streams between various origin and destination points is highly concurrent and therefore inherently complex. The complexity, however, may be managed by focussing on individual message streams and by describing the streams at two levels of abstraction. The more abstract view captures the primary intent of the network—to faithfully transfer a message sequence from origin to destination. The less abstract view adds routing detail by identifying a stream's signalling transfer points and therefore its linksets, but does not identify individual links. It is proved that the less abstract view is a valid refinement of the more abstract view.

Having specified streams generally, they are identified by tags (routing labels) on their constituent messages. It is noted that streams may share signalling points and links without loss of identity (uniqueness of routing labels). Overall network behaviour is then implied by insisting that at every signalling point and on every link the projection (restriction) of the overall behaviour with respect to a particular routing label (stream) is consistent with the specification of the stream. This avoids an attempt to construct explicitly a model of overall behaviour, say by arbitrarily, but fairly, merging a multiplicity of streams.

The paper illustrates the advantage of introducing an intermediate abstract structure, namely "section", comprising a signalling point and an ongoing linkset – a combination which may not arise normally in real-world discourse about networks. Generally, formal methods support abstraction, including projections: the paper shows through example that comprehension and specification is facilitated by careful choice of the level(s) of abstraction, e.g., re-routing at the sectional level. Choice of appropriate abstractions is a key aspect of formal description techniques.

The paper does not consider network liveness. However, established liveness properties of individual links together with, the fact that message retrieval from links does not imply regression of messages already received from a link suggest a suitable formal approach which could be based on the present model. The model also appears suitable for studies in more complex situations involving reverse transmission along a previous link in the event of an intended transition point becoming inaccessible.

7 Acknowledgements

The initiative and financial and technical support of the Overseas Telecommunications Commission (OTC) Australia is acknowledged. We thank Roger Duke, Paul King, Anthony Lee and Graeme Smith for their technical comments, and Paul Bakker and Wendy Johnston for their assistance with the preparation of the paper.

References

[1] *CCITT Recommendation Q.703, Specification of Signalling Link No.7, vol. VI fascicle VI.7.* Geneva, 1985.

[2] *CCITT Recommendation Q.704, Specification of Signalling Link No.7, vol. VI fascicle VI.7.* Geneva, 1985.

[3] R. Duke, I. Hayes, P. King, and G. Rose. Protocol verification and specification using Z. In *Protocol Specification, Testing, and Verification VIII*, pages 33–46, North Holland, 1988.

Protocol Specification, Testing, and Verification, IX
E. Brinksma, G. Scollo and C.A. Vissers (Editors)
Elsevier Science Publishers B.V. (North-Holland)
IFIP, 1990

Functional specification for an ISDN switching system: an experience using Estelle.[1]

Marc Phalippou

CNET LAA/SLC/EVP, BP-40, F-22301 LANNION Cedex, FRANCE
E-mail: (X.400) phalippou@LANNION.CNET.ATLAS.FR
(uucp) phalippou@cnetlu.inria.fr

Abstract: *FDTs are considered as potential candidates for the specification of the functional architecture of an ISDN switching system. This particular application requires specific possibilities from the language: the top-down approach which is used for designing such a complex system implies the use of an abstract and flexible view of data, and needs some structuring facilities for the stepwise refinement process of the program. We show here how both problems, in spite of their apparent difficulty, can be elegantly solved in Estelle using dynamic features.*

Keywords: *entity/relationship model, Estelle, Formal Description Techniques, functional specification, ISDN.*

1 Introduction

A strong requirement for a wide acceptance of a language is its adequacy to describe what is in designers' minds. Formal Description Techniques do not depart from this rule; and only a concrete experience in their use can make us appreciate if the constructs of a particular language do correspond to the needs of its users.

This paper relates some of the conclusions of a work that has been done in CNET for the Esprit project Sedos Estelle Demonstrator. In order to evaluate Estelle and the Estelle Workstation which has been developped in this project, this language was used to model some part of an ISDN prototype switching system, called CERAME. This modelling took place at an early stage of the software development cycle, the functional specification, which gives a quite abstract view of the system. At this stage, the main problems which appear are the description of a unified and high-level view of data, and the decomposition of the control part automaton into logically coherent smaller units which will be refined later.

We analyse which requirements on FDTs are needed for their use in this particular context, and we show how some attractive features, especially the constructs related to the dynamic instantiation and release of modules, allow to model in a "natural" way different parts of the abstract specification: we found in Estelle primitives in order to describe data based on the entity/relationship model, and we used the dynamic modules in order to introduce a structure in the behaviour of a "flat" automaton.

Our purpose is not to argue about the respective advantages and drawbacks of different FDTs as regards ease of use or abstraction power: a sensible answer to such a question can only result from the analysis of the experience of many users. But our experiment shows that we must beware of too definitive (although widespread) ideas: in this particular case,

[1]This work has been supported by ESPRIT project P1265 "Sedos Estelle Demonstrator"

Estelle, which is often qualified of "low level" specification language, is well adapted for the description of "high level" structures, including data (this is sometimes rashly considered its weakpoint).

This paper is organized as follows: part 2 is an introduction to the CERAME ISDN experiment and to the Sedos Estelle Demonstrator project, which outlines the objectives of the work which is discussed here; part 3 analyses the possibility to describe "high level" data structures with Estelle, and part 4 deals with the structuring possibilities offered by the dynamic constructs of the language.

2 The framework of our study

2.1 ISDN

In the telecommunications area, ISDN (Integrated Service Digital Network) is the backbone on which all the future services will rely in the next decades. The telecommunications world is currently switching massively from analogic to digital technology; whereas in traditional telephone networks voice was the main business and data transfer was a mere peripheral source of income, the move to integrated digital technology will make use of the same network investments for all kinds of services.

Among the basic services to be provided to ISDN users, we can list the establishment of end to end digital communications, with a choice between circuit or packet switching, and additional facilities such as call forwarding, nuisance call trap or double call. Possibilities to make remote watching or control by exchanging single messages, at low cost, will be offered too. This digital network will require a great amount of software, for the handling of the numerous communication protocols and the switching functions which will be provided (and not to speak of the many "value-added" applications which will be developed on top of the ISDN communication facilities!).

The CERAME team from CNET Lannion is currently involved in the design and the experimentation of switching systems for the next generation of ISDN [LER87]. They have developed a prototype of this switching system in order to test the interconnection of the numerous communication protocols involved and also the new facilities provided to the users of the network. For this purpose, they used a quite formal software development procedure, going from informal requirements to code generation through functional analysis and organic analysis. But although they have defined a semi-formal language for the functional analysis, they did not make use of a standard formal description technique.

The study whose results are described here was concerned with the modelling of the double-call facility. This feature allows a telephone subscriber to manage two simultaneous calls from its telephone, with the possibility to switch as he wants from one call to the other (these can be either outgoing or incoming calls). The double-call module of the CERAME prototype must handle all the actions involved in this process, and ensure the coherence of the various data linked to them.

2.2 Sedos Estelle Demonstrator

One purpose of the Esprit project P1265 is to promote the use of Estelle [ISO87] as a formal specification language. In this framework, an Estelle workstation (EWS) has been developped, which includes a syntactical editor, a compiler which generates intermediate code, from which implementation code can be derived, and an interactive simulator for debugging (cf. [AYA89]). A second step of the project is to develop various applications belonging to different fields (computer networks, telecommunication protocols, industrial networks) with the objective of evaluating both the interests of the workstation and the adequacy of Estelle language to these various application domains.

CNET was responsible for the ISDN application, in which Estelle was evaluated as a potential candidate for the *functional specification step* of CERAME software development. The particularities of this context are:

- the software to describe is made of switching related functions, and not communication protocols, for which Estelle (among others FDTs) has often been used.
- it is a high level description, and what has to be modelled is a function-data architecture, where the function part is structured according to the different functional elements, while the data part follows the entity/relationship model introduced by Chen [CHEN76].

The work performed consists in the specification in Estelle of a particular part of the ISDN architecture (the double-call facility) which includes most of the programming concepts which are used in CERAME (see [SED88],[SED89]). The main difficulty lies in the fact that the functional specification already exists, based on a function/data approach; the challenge here is to *use the same model* (which corresponds to the needs of the users) and to describe it with a standard FDT.

3 A high level description of data

3.1 Pascal data types

Contrary to other FDTs such as Lotos or SDL which provide means to specify data based on the abstract data type theory, the Estelle data part is based on Pascal data types. Although those are of an easy use, since they correspond to widespread programming concepts, shared by many different languages, they can nevertheless be charged with several drawbacks:

- the number of data types is predefined, by means of elementary types (integers, enumerations) and constructions (arrays, records). More liberty is sometimes needed in the way to design data, for instance for defining set relationships between types.
- data must be stored in variables, which can only be accessed by their names, and not by their content.
- dynamic allocation of variables and release of memory space is not provided by built-in constructs of the language, but must be handled "manually" with pointers: some data structures as simple as lists or queues need some non-trivial manipulations.
- Pascal data types correspond to a particular implementation of data in the computer, and in this sense they can be considered as an overspecification of the intentions of their users: the semantics of "integer" should not depend on the particular computer which is used! Let us remark that this drawback disappears in Estelle, in which integers and real numbers are considered in their mathematical sense ([ISO87], 8.2.1).

Due to these limits, it is difficult, using only Estelle data constructs, to represent an abstract model such as the following one.

3.2 The entity/relationship model

This model has been introduced in order to give a unified view of data. The world is made of different *entities*, which are "things" which can be distinctly identified (for instance a specific person, or an event). A *relationship* is an association among entities (for instance "father-son" is a relationship between two "person" entities). The main relevant concepts in the frame of our application are the following:

- A *domain* is the set of values that can be taken by a particular *attribute*. It corresponds to the Estelle notion of "type".

- An *attribute* is the smallest piece of information which has its own meaning in the model. The value of an attribute is an element of its domain. For instance, attributes of the entity "people" are "name", "age".

- An *entity* is a class of objects which is characterized by a list of attributes. It is a concept which has its own meaning in the system. The definition of an entity must be self-contained, with no reference to other entities or relationships. Two different entities (classes) cannot share any attribute name. Thus an attribute (given by its name) cannot belong to more than one entity.

- Each *instance* (i.e. every individual object in the class) of an entity must be distinguished from the others: for this reason, one particular attribute, named *key*, allows to access without ambiguity one particular instance of this entity.

- A *relationship* is a class of objects which define a link between one or several entities. It allows to introduce attributes which have a meaning only for this particular relationship, and not for the associated entities considered separately. A relationship instance is identified either by one particular key (for instance the key of one of its related entities) or by the union of several keys.

We can notice that the above concepts are similar to the ones used in object-oriented languages: entities and relationship are *classes*, and their instances are *objects*. This formalism has many advantages: natural description of the handled data, which helps to the design of the data model by providing natural coherence and avoiding redundancies; rigorous approach due to the independent treatment of the different parameters of entities and relationships; data description model different from the actual implementation, which is important to design general specifications without implementation choices; and ease of use due to a graphical formalism (see figure 1: this figure represents the entities and relationships which are handled by the double-call facility).

3.3 Estelle description of the model

It results from the previous considerations that *Pascal data types are not suited* for a natural description of entities and relationships, since dynamic aspects are important here, together with the possibility to search an object in the database trough its content (attributes) rather than through its name. So a solution consisting of (chained) record structures will not be appropriate, since primitive functions for database management would have to be designed.

On the contrary, Estelle provides the concept of *module instances* which can be created and released by primitive language instructions. Such structures can model easily entities and relationships. Since an entity is only a "box" in which data are stored, these modules will have a very simple behaviour (`body part`) with nothing in it. The information stored inside an entity or a relationship (the attributes) is defined by several Pascal variables which are grouped in a record structure, which represents the content of the object. Since it must be visible from the outside, it is declared as an `exported` variable. So the declaration of an entity type is:

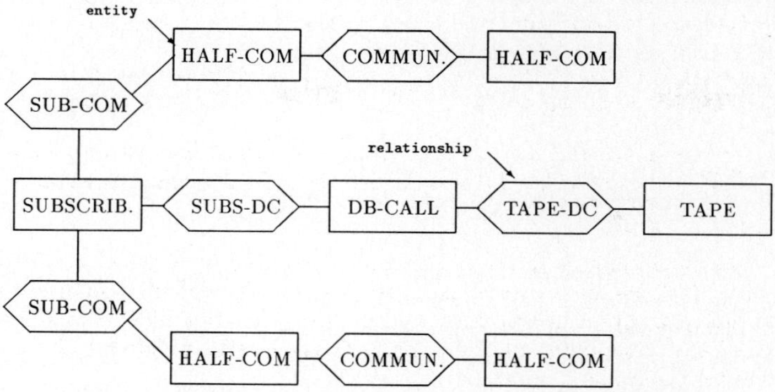

NB: the Estelle graphical representation is very similar;
each one of the above boxes corresponds to a module instance.

Figure 1: Entity/relationship model: graphical formalism

```
MODULE double_call_M;
   EXPORT attributes: attributes_t;
END;

BODY double_call_B FOR double_call_M;
END;
```

where `attributes_t` has been previously declared, for instance for the entity *double_call*:

```
attributes_t = RECORD
                  double_call_id  : 0..255;
                  com_identifier  : array [1..2] of identifier_t;
                  local_state     : array [1..2] of state_t;
                  distant_state   : array [1..2] of state_t;
               END;
```

An advantage of this approach is to provide an easy way to design database access primitives. The creation of a new entity is made by an `init` statement followed by the initialization of the attributes:

```
INIT double_call_I WITH double_call_B;
double_call_I.attributes.double_call_id := 10;
double_call_I.attributes.com_identifier[1] := a11;
double_call_I.attributes.com_identifier[2] := a12;
double_call_I.attributes.local_state[1] := on_hold;
...
```

Removing an object from the database is made with the `release` instruction. Let us remark that *only one* `double_call` *entity module variable is declared in the program.* The different double_call entities are initialized using this same entity variable, and then they constitute module instances which can be accessed only by their content (they have no name to distinguish them); the *key* distinguishes a unique object, but search is also allowed on other criteria, and may return several objects as its result. *So Estelle provides a mechanism for search by content* which cannot be found in Pascal, LDS ... Access to these modules is made with Estelle search statements such as:

```
PROVIDED EXIST x:double_call_M SUCHTHAT x.attributes.double_call_id = 10
```

or

```
FORONE x:double_call_M
SUCHTHAT x.attributes.double_call_id = 10 DO ...
OTHERWISE ...
```

These database management functions are introduced in our model as transitions of a "database" module, which is the father module of all entities and relationships modules. We can notice that the distinction between *classes* and *instances* of objects is similar in Estelle and in the entity/relationship model. Finally, as it is explained in figure 1 the resulting structure of the database in Estelle is very close (from a graphical point of view) to the graphical entity/relationship representation. This can constitute an argument in favor of the use of Estelle since the designer will have a minimum translation effort to perform.

3.4 Further comments

This example shows a complementarity between Pascal data types, which are used to model some aspects of the database (the most basic elements, the attributes), and the Estelle higher level structures which handle higher parts of the model. Since data are modelled with modules, there is a great homogeneity in the resulting specification between the control part and the data part: it is a standard point of view, advocated by Milner and Hoare, that there should be no difference between processes and objects (see [HOA85] p.65).

One could wonder if abstract data types would allow a better modelling of entity/relationship concepts. In this particular case, it would result in more modelling work, since we should have to define all the operations on the database which are here built-in constructs of the Estelle language (not to speak of redefining all Pascal data-types which are used for the attributes!). Moreover, in this example we cannot say that Estelle generates overspecification since we are specifying a data model which is not related with some kind of implementation. The difference lies rather in the fact that the Estelle description is more *operational* while an abstract data type description would be more *functional*.

4 Transition oriented versus structured specification

4.1 Need for structuring

The title of this section makes reference to [BOCH87] where the authors compare two different programming styles, which can be represented by the small CSP examples:

```
[ c1 --> a1
  []
  c2 --> a2
  []
  c3 --> a3
]

transition oriented
```

```
[ c1 --> [ c11 --> a11
           []
           c12 --> a12
         ]
  []
  c3 --> a3
]

structured
```

The first style is called *transition oriented*. It consists in defining the behaviour of a particular module as a "flat" automaton, as a list of all possible transitions. The state of the automaton is defined by the value of the different variables of the program, and is used in the guard of the transitions for defining which transition can occur in which state, while the body of the transition indicates the new state which is reached. Such a program does not impose any kind of ordering as regards the execution of the different transitions: at each moment there is an undeterministic choice between all enabled (possible) transitions.

Such a programming style is quite natural for specifying systems which are initially designed as finite state automata, since the translation is trivial. Anyway, some readibility problems may appear if the size of the module is too big: for instance, the double-call module of our CERAME specification has about 250 transitions, which corresponds roughly to 3000 lines of Estelle. If no additional structure is given to such a module, it is difficult to understand at a first glance the behaviour of the automaton; moreover, bugs are likely to happen and to be difficult to understand.

Another programming style, called *structured programming* is introduced in the above referenced paper. The idea is that the logical structure of a module can be described explicitely through "control structures" and so it is no more hidden in the particular structure of the transition system. Classical Pascal instructions (`if ... then ... else, while ... do ...,-etc`) are used together with the choice statement `select`. This way of programming should be preferred for big modules: it is a standard point of view among programmers that structure and order are better than chaos and disorder for the readability of programs. The problem in our particular case is that Estelle is based on the transition oriented style and *does not directly provide any facility for structuring* the behaviour of a module.

4.2 Behaviour of the double-call

Let us have a look into the behaviour of the double-call module which we plan to structure. We can imagine it as a two-level system: at the higher level, external modules can send requests to the double-call module. Depending on the current state of the system, a particular "transition" of the double-call facility will be activated, and then the current state will be updated. This is a standard automaton behaviour. But in our particular application a second detail level must be described in order to specify the behaviour of the system: each one of the above mentioned "transitions" is in fact a (deterministic) automaton, which sends messages and then waits for answers before the next transition. So a higher level transition is composed of more elementary transitions, which can be message handling, data access or function calls.

In Estelle a transition can not "embody" other transitions. The way the upper level transitions are used is very similar to a subroutine call: they are activated, they perform some actions, and then they terminate and the "main" level can resume its computation. But in Estelle subroutines cannot include transitions nor message handling: they are pure Pascal subroutines. Nevertheless, it seems interesting to emphasize the natural structure of the double-call; in fact the two transition levels correspond to different time scales. The upper level transitions specify the interaction between users and the system, and the average time between two events is in the range of one second. On the contrary, the second level transitions model the inner behaviour of a computer, so the duration of a sequence of such transitions should not exceed one millisecond. It is important to be able to detect immediately this structure when looking at the specification.

4.3 The adopted solution

Again the dynamic constructs of Estelle provide a means for a concise solution to this problem. Since the only Estelle structure which can include smaller transitions is a module, each one

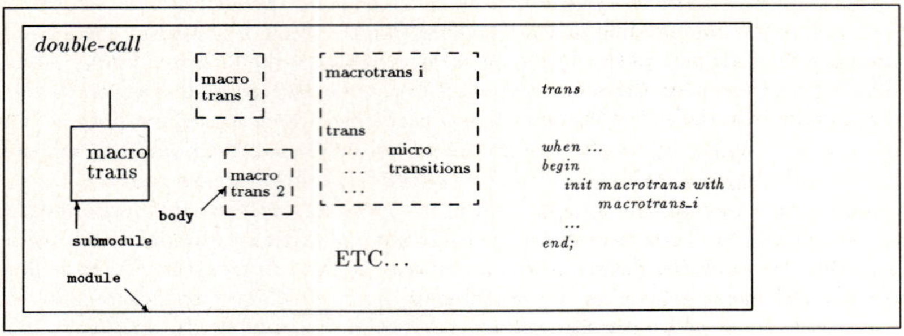

Figure 2: Structured specification: graphical view

```
BODY double_call_B  FOR double_call_M;
   CHANNEL father_son(father,son);
      BY son: end_of_execution(returned_parameter1: type1; ... );
   IP to_son: father_son(father);
   STATE  ... ,waiting, ...;

   MODULE macrotrans_M (parameter1: type2; parameter2: type3);
      IP to_father: father_son(son); ...
   END;

   BODY macrotrans_B_1 FOR macrotrans_M;
       STATE ...
       INITIALIZE ...
       TRANS ...   TRANS ...
       TRANS  FROM ... TO terminated
              BEGIN
                 OUTPUT to_father.end_of_execution(value1, value2);
              END;
   END;
          ... {other macrotrans bodies}
   MODVAR
      macrotrans: macrotrans_M;
   INITIALIZE  ...
   TRANS ...
      FROM ... TO waiting                             {subroutine call}
      BEGIN
         INIT macrotrans WITH macrotrans_B_1(value3, ... );
         CONNECT macrotrans.to_father TO to_son;
         ...
      END;

      FROM waiting TO ...                             {end of subroutine}
      WHEN to_son.end_of_execution
      BEGIN
         RELEASE macrotrans;
         ...
      END;
END;
```

Figure 3: Structured specification: program skeleton

of the higher level transitions corresponds to the activation of a module. From the higher level point of view, these modules are some kind of subroutines. The module header contains information about the parameters which are given to the subroutine during the activation. In fact, in our particular case, the same module header is used for every transition, and a single module variable is initialized with different bodies depending on the different transitions.

So the entire double-call facility is made of one "father" module with a child `macrotrans` module for modelling the subroutine. An channel makes a link between an internal interaction point of the father module and an external interaction point of its child. The subroutine call corresponds to an `init` statement of the child module. During the subroutine processing, the father module is in a waiting state in which it cannot accept any interaction except the "end of computation" message from its child module on the internal interaction port. The Estelle program skeleton can be seen in figure 3 and its graphical representation in figure 2.

It is clear that the introduction of the structure may be thought as inelegant at a first glance since we must introduce in the specification a few objects which are not part of the system to be modelled and which are here only to replace some missing constructions of the language. Anyway we feel it is worth doing this little effort since the resulting specification becomes much easier to manipulate: a top-down approach allows to design first the main level, and then all the different `macrotrans` modules. Moreover, those are now independent and can be validated separately.

5 Conclusion

The purpose of this paper was to relate our experience in applying a FDT for the specification of an ISDN switching system, which is a particular example of a complex open system. For such a high level specification, we had to model some concepts which are beyond the standard scope of application of these languages (protocols).

Our conclusion is that some features of Estelle, related to the dynamic manipulation of module instances, are well adapted to describe some concepts where dynamism plays an important role; surprisingly, such an abstract data model as the entity/relationship model appeared to be easy to describe with a language like Estelle, often considered "implementation oriented". However, our difficulties for structuring the double-call module point out some missing constructs of the language, which can be replaced only with a relatively large effort.

So this study leads to a similar conclusion as [DIN87], i.e. to encourage further applications of Formal Description Techniques to the design of switching systems; as far as CNET is concerned, several teams are working in this direction: for instance, among other issues, the EWS has been used for writing an Estelle description of the level 2 of the LAP-D, or for interfacing TCP-IP onto X25. These "real size" studies should demonstrate clearly the benefits we can expect from FDTs.

Acknowledgements

I am grateful to the anonymous referees whose comments were helpful to enhance some parts of this paper. I am also grateful to Roland Groz who carefully reviewed the successive versions of this paper.

References

[AYA89] Ayache J.M., Berrocal J., Budkowski S., Diaz M., Dufau J., Druilhe A.M., Echevarria N., Groz R., Huybrechts M., *Presentation of the Sedos Estelle Demonstrator project*, The Formal Description Technique Estelle, North-Holland, 1989.

[BOCH87] Bochmann G., Verjus J.P., *Some comments on transition-oriented versus structured specifications of distributed algorithms and protocols*, IEEE Transactions on Software Engineering, April 1987.

[CHEN76] Chen Peter Pin-Shan, *The Entity-Relationship Model—Toward a Unified View of Data*, ACM Transactions on Database Systems, Vol. 1, No. 1, March 1976, Pages 9–36.

[DIN87] Dinsenmeyer I., Louvet O., Groz R., *Utilisation de techniques de description formelle (TDF) pour la spécification de logiciels de commutation*, Annales des Télécommunications, 42, 7-8, 1987.

[HOA85] Hoare C.A.R., *Communicating Sequential Processes*, Prentice-Hall International Series in Computer Science, Englewood Cliffs, NJ, 1985.

[ISO87] *Estelle, a formal description technique based on an extended state transition model*, ISO DIS 9074, March 1987.

[LER87] Le Roux A., Dauphin J.L., Laurens J., *ISDN Packed Switching: from Experimentation to System Integration*, International Switching Symposium, proceedings, Phoenix, Arizona, March 1987.

[SED88] *Telecommunication application–Preliminary report*, Deliverable R241, Esprit Project 1265 Sedos Estelle demonstrator, July 1988.

[SED89] *Application au domaine des Télécommunications–Rapport intermédiaire*, Deliverable R242, Esprit Project 1265 Sedos Estelle demonstrator, March 1989.

Protocol Specification, Testing, and Verification, IX
E. Brinksma, G. Scollo and C.A. Vissers (Editors)
Elsevier Science Publishers B.V. (North-Holland)
IFIP, 1990

Formal Specifications of Telephone Systems in LOTOS

M. Faci, L. Logrippo, B. Stépien

University of Ottawa
Protocols Research Group
Department of Computer Science
Ottawa, Ontario, Canada K1N 6N5
E-mail: lmlsl@acadvm1.uottawa.ca

Abstract. It is shown that the OSI Formal Description Technique LOTOS can be appropriately used for the formal specification of telephone systems. A methodology quite similar to the one currently well-established for OSI protocols and services can be applied. We discuss the preliminary results of an ongoing project in this direction. We provide a small, didactically-oriented specification of a simple telephone system, and we discuss its structure.

1. INTRODUCTION AND MOTIVATION

LOTOS [ISO1], the Language of Temporal Ordering Specifications, has been conceived in the framework of OSI standardization as a tool for the formal description of OSI services and protocols. In fact, most examples of LOTOS specifications found in the literature today relate to this type of application. It is our contention, however, that the concepts of LOTOS are general enough to make the language useful for a wide range of applications.

Intent of this paper is to show that LOTOS is appropriate for telephone systems (TS) specifications. We feel that this is practically important, given the greater market importance of telephone networks with respect to packet-switching networks, and the fact that, in the long range, these two types of networks are expected to become integrated. In this context, it is also not without importance the fact that the CCITT has been studying LOTOS as a possible successor for its Specification and Description Language (SDL) [ST], which today is the most commonly used language for the formal specification of standard telephony procedures.

During the past few years, our group has been involved in two feasibility studies addressed to this application area. In the course of these studies, we have produced telephone system specifications covering different sets of functionalities, and written in different styles (the first study used the language described in the 1985 DP). We report here on some results of this ongoing project.
The example chosen for this paper is a simple POTS (Plain Old Telephone System)

specification. Its size is kept intentionally small, to make it possible to explain it almost completely in the paper. All the important functions of POTS are described. We hope that this paper can be useful as an introduction to the use of LOTOS in telephony.

To the best of our knowledge, this is the first paper that discusses this subject. This is not to say, however, that the problem of formally specifying telephone systems is a new one. We mentioned above that the CCITT has developed the language SDL for this purpose. Zave [Z] has written a well-known paper presenting a formalism for describing distributed systems, especially protocols and telephone systems. These are only two of the best known techniques in the literature.

2. SPECIFICATIONS OF TELEPHONE SYSTEMS IN LOTOS

A not unexpected observation that we made at the beginning of our work was that several concepts originally developed for the description of data communications protocols and services are also very appropriate for the description of telephone systems. One such concept is the concept of service provider [VL]. The sample specification we give in this paper is the specification of a POTS service provider, that is, the system as seen from a user's perspective, without concern for its internal functioning.

There are, however, important differences between telephone system specifications and service and protocol specifications, especially of the type that have been specified in LOTOS so far. Telephone specifications are dominated by the connection and disconnection phases, where the connection is established or released and a number of housekeeping functions is performed. Such functions include: (1) maintaining the list of busy numbers, (2) checking whether the telephone is in use or not, and (3) generating busy signals. The "data exchange" phase has a minimal importance, and in fact it is even impossible to portray faithfully, because in POTS data are not discrete.

Another type of element that cannot be dealt with in LOTOS at the present stage are timing aspects. These are important in TS specifications, however as it is currently standardized LOTOS is unable to specify time delays faithfully. Some research has been done in this area, and some proposals exist [Q][BR]. However in this paper we wanted to use only standard LOTOS. We are looking forward to progress in this important issue.

3. PROBLEMS OF SPECIFICATION STYLES IN TS SPECIFICATIONS

Vissers, Scollo and van Sinderen [VSV] identified four main styles for writing LOTOS specifications, viz. the monolithic style, the state-oriented style, the resource-oriented style and the constraint-oriented style. Each one of these styles has its own uses in TS specifications, and of course they can be mixed in a specification.

The specification style used in the example of this paper could probably best be characterized constraint-oriented, because no internal functioning of the telephone system is described.

4. THE STRUCTURE OF THE POTS SPECIFICATION

In this section, we will present the design methodology of our specification, explain its structure, and discuss our solutions to some key design decisions. But first, an informal description of POTS is in order. The complete LOTOS specification is presented later in section 4.4.

4.1 The Informal Description

First, we introduce the terminology that we will use throughout this paper. *System* refers to the local telephone branch exchange. A *telephone* consists of a *Caller* side and *Receiver* side. Each telephone is identified by a unique number, which we call the *telephone number* (or simply *number*). A number may be connected to more than one telephone *extension*. Each extension has a *handset* which the user picks up before dialing the number of another user, or answering a ring. This is the case where we may find one telephone extension in the kitchen, another one in the bedroom, and possibly a third one in the garden. Only one extension may be used at a time.

The POTS requirements are that the system must allow for an arbitrary number of users to access the telephone system and communicate with each other. The telephone system works in the following manner. The first user, the *caller*, picks up the handset. This results in a signal, called *originate*, being sent to the telephone network. If no other extension for the same number is in use, the network responds by sending a tone signal to the user. The *caller* is now in a position to dial the number of the second user, the *receiver*. When the *caller* completes dialling the number, the telephone network checks if the *receiver* number is free, and if so, a *ring* signal is sent to the second telephone. If the second user does not pick up the handset to answer, the *caller* will eventually hang up and both telephones are free. However, if the *receiver* picks up the handset, the telephone stops ringing and the two parties engage in a conversation. When the conversation is finished, either party may hang up. The first user who hangs up makes his telephone free to make or receive other calls. The second telephone remains busy until the user hangs up.

4.2 The Architecture of the Specification

LOTOS makes it possible to describe the behavior of systems in a stepwise fashion, moving from one abstraction level to another. This is a powerful technique since, at each level, it helps the designer in capturing a complete and precise behavior of the (sub)system before considering lower level details. This principle, which has inspired our specification to a large degree, has become well established in the area of service and protocol specifications[ISO2, T]. Using this principle within the framework of the constraint-oriented specification style, we were able to identify three types of constraints:

(1) *Local constraints* are used to enforce the appropriate sequence of events at each telephone, and are different according to whether the telephone is a caller or a receiver. Therefore local constraints are represented by the processes *Caller* and *Receiver* and an instance of one of these is associated with each telephone existing in the system.

(2) *End-to-End* constraints are related to each connection, and enforce the appropriate sequence of actions between telephones in a connection. For example, ringing at the receiver must necessarily follow dialling at the caller. Process *Controller* enforces these constraints.

(3) *Global constraints* are system-wide constraints. In our specification we identified one main *value* constraint, which is the fact that at any time, a number is used at most once. This constraint is enforced by the process *Check_In_Use*.

The notions of local, end-to-end, and global constraints are well-known in the area of service specifications [BO, ISO2]. One of our objectives is to show that LOTOS makes it possible to express these constraints quite naturally.

The top level behavior, lines 87 to 89 in the specification, is composed of two processes, *Connections* and *Check_In_Use*. These two processes synchronize through gate *Ctl*. This structure reflects the behavior of the system we wish to model. Stated informally, we want to create as many *connections* as necessary provided that neither the calling number nor the called number is already in use. *Check_In_Use*, which we will describe later, satisfies a global constraint by keeping track of free and busy numbers and passing the resulting *Status* (through gate *Ctl*) to the *Connections* process.

The behavioral expression of the process *Connections* is composed of two processes: *Single_Connection* interleaved with the process *Connections* itself. This creates the desired effect of having an arbitrary number of connections existing simultaneously. Note the action *i* (line 94, in the specification) before the recusive call to *Connections*. It is needed to prevent the interpreter from looping endlessly, by attempting to provide an infinite number of potential connections. The process *Single_Connection* is viewed as the composition of three processes: *Caller*, *Receiver* and *Controller*. The conceptual notion of modeling the transmitter (*Caller*) side and the receiver (*Receiver*) side by two interleaved processes is quite natural; it works that way in real life, as well. The caller and the receiver of the same telephone do not need to exchange any information. However, both the *Caller*(line 98) of one side and the *Receiver*(line 100) of the other side must synchronize with the *Controller*(line 103).

4.3 Descriptions of Processes

In this section we will give the details of those processes which we feel will contribute significantly to the understanding of the specification, discuss the constraints that were imposed on them, and finally, present our solution to the hang up phase which proved to be a challenging part of the problem.

A set of nine synchronization signals are used in the specification. These are : *Originate, Connect, DisInd, Disconn, Dial, Ring, CircBusy, Offhook, Tone, Send_Voice,* and *Rec_Voice*. Of these, only three signals, *Originate*, *Dial* and *Disconn* are used to specify the global constraints (see the predicate *NoConstraint*, lines 63 and 303). The global constraints are enforced by the process *Check_In_Use*, defined at lines 274 and onward . The result of this process' synchronization (with the *Controller*) is a *Status* value which is passed to the *Controller*. Synchronization on *Originate* produces two results: (1) if the number is not already in use, *Ok* is passed to the *Controller* and the number itself is added to the list of busy numbers, (2) if the number is already in use, *Busy* is passed to the *Controller* and the list of busy numbers remains unchanged. Synchronization on *Dial* produces two results as well: (1) if the number is not already in use, *Ok* is passed to the *Controller* and the number itself is added to the list of busy numbers, (2) if the number is already in use, *Busy* is passed to the *Controller* and the list of busy numbers remains unchanged. Finally, synchronization on *Disconn* results in removing the number from the list of busy numbers and the status is not important in this case. In the first two cases, *Originate* and *Dial*, the status is important because the *Controller* uses it to carry out its actions further.

In addition to synchronizing with *Check_In_Use*, the *Controller* (line 194 and onward) synchronizes with the *Caller* and the *Receiver* using all signals. It is responsible for detecting an *Originate* signal, sending the *Tone* to the originating *Caller*, detecting *Circ_Busy* signals, forwarding a *Ring* signal to the *Receiver* process, establishing the connection for the

Voice exchange, and *Disconn*ecting both parties at the end of the conversation. It is also responsible for handling hang ups by either communicating side. Note that to enable the *Controller* to detect which telephone is sending an *Offhook* signal, we have chosen to have the user enter the number of the telephone he/she is using. The alternative solution would require the *Controller* to provide the number by searching through the list of free numbers and associating it with the telephone from which the *Offhook* signal is received (this could be specified by using the *choice* construct). From a specification point of view, this would only complicate the logic of the *Controller* process.

The *Caller* process gets the number from the user (line 109), forwards the *Originate* signal to the *Controller*, then depending on whether the number is free or busy, one of two actions is carried out. If the number is busy (another person is already talking to your father using the extension upstairs), then you must hang up and the *Caller* process stops. On the other hand, if your number is free, a subprocess, *Dialing*, is instantiated to accomplish the following actions: get the *Tone* from the *Controller*, get the called number from the user, forward it to the *Controller* and then return the called number to the *Caller*. The *Caller* will then synchronize its actions with *Check_In_Use* to instantiate one of two subprocesses: *Normal_Connection*, if the called number is not in use, or *Number_Is_Busy*, if the called number is already in use. Process *Normal_Connection* instantiates process *Talking* which establishes *Voice*. Note that the user is also given the option to hang up any time, even during the normal connection phase. This is handled by the *User_Disconnect* process.

The *Receiver* (lines 152 and onward) process is blocked until the *Controller* reaches the corresponding synchronization point. This happens when the *Receiver* is ready to *Ring*. The *Receiver* then continues with the rest of its actions, which are to synchronize on *Offhook*, *Connect* and then instantiate another process, *Talking*, which handles the *Voice* exchange. Again, note that the *Receiver* may hang up at any time after he has answered (*Offhook*) the telephone. Handling the hang up is carried out by another instance of the same process, *User_Disconnect*. Other details are left to the reader as an exercise.

The most challenging feature of the design turned out to be the handling of the hang up phase. For a hang up situation, we distinguish three different cases: (1) the caller hangs up before dialling the called number. This is the simplest case, since at this point the connection has not been established yet, and the only housekeeping required is the removing of the caller number from the busy list. (2) the caller hangs up after the second telephone starts ringing. This is the most complex case, since the two telephones have already been connected, and a hang up at this point requires disconnecting both telephones and removing both numbers from the list of busy numbers. Finally, (3) either the caller or the called hangs up after the called has picked up the telephone handset. This case is similar to the first one except that a hang up by either side forces the other side to eventually hang up. The first case is handled by process *C_Abort_Call*. Cases (2) and (3) are handled by process *Disconnection*.

4.4 The LOTOS specification

In this section we present the complete LOTOS specification of the POTS system. It allows an arbitrary number of telephone users to use the telephone network and communicate with each other, in pairs.

```
specification Telephone_System [Usr]:noexit

 (* Abstract Data Types  Definitions *)

library Boolean, NaturalNumber endlib

type Stat_Sort is Boolean
    sorts Stat_Sort
    opns
      Ok    :-> Stat_Sort
      Busy  :-> Stat_Sort
      _eq_: Stat_Sort,Stat_Sort -> Bool
    eqns
      forall x: Stat_Sort
        ofsort  Bool
        x eq x = true;
        Ok eq Busy = false;
        Busy eq Ok = false;
endtype

type Natset is NaturalNumber
    sorts Natset
    opns
      empty: -> Natset
      add:   Nat, Natset -> Natset
      remove:   Nat, Natset -> Natset
      isin : Nat, Natset -> Bool
      notin: Nat, Natset-> Bool
    eqns
      forall x,y: Nat, s: Natset
      ofsort Natset
         add(x,add(x,s)) = add(x,s);
         remove(x,add(x,s)) = s;
         not(x eq y) =>
         remove(x,add(y,s)) =
                     add(y,remove(x,s));
      ofsort Bool
         isin(x,empty) = false;
         isin(x,add(y,s)) =
                     (x eq y) or (isin(x,s));
         isin(x,remove(x,s)) = false;
         not(x eq y) =>
         isin(x,remove(y,s)) = isin(x,s);
         notin(x,s) = not(isin(x,s));
endtype

type signal is Boolean
    sorts  Sig_Sort
    opns
      Originate:-> Sig_Sort
      Offhook:->  Sig_Sort
      Hang_Up:->  Sig_Sort
      Connect:-> Sig_Sort
      Disind: -> Sig_Sort
      Disconn:-> Sig_Sort
      Voice:-> Sig_Sort
      Rec_Voice:-> Sig_Sort
      Send_Voice:-> Sig_Sort
      Ring:-> Sig_Sort
      Dial:-> Sig_Sort
      Tone:-> Sig_Sort
      Circ_Busy:-> Sig_Sort
      NoConstraint: Sig_Sort -> Bool
    eqns
      forall x,y :Sig_Sort
      ofsort Bool
         NoConstraint(Originate) = false;
         NoConstraint(Connect) = true;
         NoConstraint(Disind) = true;
         NoConstraint(Disconn) = false;
         NoConstraint(Dial) = false;
         NoConstraint(Ring) = true;
         NoConstraint(Circ_Busy) = true;
         NoConstraint(Offhook) = true;
         NoConstraint(Tone) = true;
         NoConstraint(Voice) = true;
         NoConstraint(Rec_Voice) = true;
         NoConstraint(Send_Voice) = true;
endtype(*signal*)

(*---------------------------------------*)
(*      Behavioral Expression           *)
(*---------------------------------------*)

behaviour
   hide Ctl in
   (     Connections[Usr,Ctl]
    |[Ctl]|
        Check_In_Use[Ctl])
where
   process Connections[Usr,Ctl]:noexit:=
   ( Single_Connection[Usr,Ctl]
      |||
    i; Connections[Usr,Ctl])
   where
      process Single_Connection[Usr,Ctl]:
              noexit:=
     ( (  Caller[Usr,Ctl]
         |||
          Receiver[Usr,Ctl]
        )
      |[Ctl]|
      Controller[Ctl]
     )
     where

     process Caller[Usr,Ctl]:noexit:=
        (
          Usr ? Number:Nat ! Offhook;
          (
            Ctl ! Number ! Originate ? Status: Stat_Sort;
            ( ( ( Dialing[Usr,Ctl](Number)
                  >>
                    accept Number :Nat in
                    Normal_Connection[Usr,Ctl](Number)
                    []
                    Number_Is_Busy[Ctl](Number)
                )
                [> User_Disconnect[Usr,Ctl](Number)
            )
```

```
          []
          ( Ctl ? Busynumber: Nat ! Circ_Busy ! Busy;
            Usr ! Number ! Hang_Up;
            stop
          ))))

   where

      process Dialing[Usr,Ctl](Num:Nat):exit(Nat) : =
      ( Ctl ! Num ! Tone ! Ok;
        Usr ? Cnum: Nat ! Dial;
        Ctl ! Cnum ! Dial ? Cstat: Stat_Sort;
        exit(Num)
      )
      endproc (* Dialing *)

      process Normal_Connection [Usr,Ctl]
              (Num:Nat):  noexit:=
      ( Ctl ! Num ! Connect ! Ok;
        Talking[Usr,Ctl](Num)
      )
      endproc (* Normal_Connection *)

      process Number_Is_Busy[Ctl]
              (Num:Nat):noexit:=
      ( Ctl ? Busynumber: Nat ! Circ_Busy ! Busy;
        stop
      )
      endproc (* Number_Is_Busy *)
   endproc (* Caller *)

   process Receiver[Usr,Ctl]:noexit:=
   ( Ctl ? Callednumber:Nat ! Ring ! Ok;
     exit(Callednumber)
     [>
      ( Ctl ? Callednumber:Nat ! Disind ! Ok;
        Ctl ! Callednumber ! Disconn ! Ok;
        stop)
   )
   >>   accept Callednumber:Nat in
     ( Usr ! Callednumber ! Offhook ;
       (
         Ctl ! Callednumber ! Connect ! Ok;
         Talking[Usr,Ctl](Callednumber)
         [> User_Disconnect[Usr,Ctl](Callednumber)
       ))
   endproc (* Receiver *)

   process Talking[Usr,Ctl](Num:Nat):noexit:=
   ( Ctl ! Num ! Rec_Voice ! Ok;
     Usr ! Num ! Voice;
     Talking[Usr,Ctl](Num)
     []
     Usr ! Num ! Voice ;
     Ctl ! Num ! Send_Voice ! Ok;
     Talking[Usr,Ctl](Num)
   )
   endproc (* Talking *)


   process User_Disconnect[Usr,Ctl](Num:Nat):
   noexit:=
   ( Usr ! Num  ! Hang_Up;
     Ctl ! Num  ! Disconn ? Status:Stat_Sort;
     stop
    []
     Ctl ! Num  ! Disind  ! Ok;
     Ctl ! Num  ! Disconn ! Ok;
     Usr ! Num  ! Hang_Up;
     stop
   )
   endproc (* Caller_Disconnect *)

   process Controller[Ctl]:noexit:=
   ( Ctl ? Number: Nat ! Originate
         ? Status: Stat_Sort;
     ( ( ( Ctl ! Number ! Tone ! Status;
           Ctl ? Callednumber: Nat  ! Dial ?
                 Calledstatus: Stat_Sort;
           exit(Number,Callednumber,Calledstatus)
           [> C_Abort_Call[Ctl](Number)
         )
         >>
         accept  Number, Callednumber: Nat,
                 Calledstatus:Stat_Sort in
         Complete_Call[Ctl] (Number, Callednumber,
                                     Calledstatus)
       )
       []
       ( Ctl ! Number ! Circ_Busy ! Status;
         stop
       )))
   where

      process C_Abort_Call[Ctl](Number:Nat):
              noexit:=
      ( Ctl ! Number ! Disconn ! Ok;
        stop
      )
      endproc

      process Complete_Call[Ctl]
      (Number: Nat, Callednumber:Nat,
      Calledstatus: Stat_Sort) :  noexit:=
      ( ( Ctl ! Callednumber ! Ring ! Calledstatus;
          Ctl ! Callednumber ! Connect ! Calledstatus;
          Ctl ! Number ! Connect ! Calledstatus;
          Calling[Ctl](Number,Callednumber)
          [>
           Disconnection[Ctl](Number, Callednumber)
        )
       []
       ( Ctl ! Callednumber ! Circ_Busy ! Calledstatus;
         Ctl ! Number ! Disconn ! Busy;
         stop
       ))
      where
```

```
              process Calling[Ctl](N:Nat,C:Nat):noexit:=
              ( ( Ctl ! N ! Send_Voice ! Ok;
                  Ctl ! C ! Rec_Voice ! Ok;
                  Calling[Ctl](N,C)
                )
               []
                ( Ctl ! C ! Send_Voice ! Ok;
                  Ctl ! N ! Rec_Voice ! Ok;
                  Calling[Ctl](N,C)
                )
              )
              endproc (* Calling *)

      process Disconnection[Ctl]
      (Number:Nat, Callednumber:Nat): noexit:=
              ( ( Ctl ! Number ! Disconn ! Ok;
                  Ctl ! Callednumber ! Disind ! Ok;
                  Ctl ! Callednumber ! Disconn ! Ok;
                  stop
                )
               []
                ( Ctl ! Callednumber ! Disconn ! Ok;
                  Ctl ! Number ! Disind ! Ok;
                  Ctl ! Number ! Disconn ! Ok;
                  stop
                )
              )
              endproc (* Disconnection *)
          endproc (* Complete_Call *)
        endproc (* Controller *)
      endproc (* Single_Connection *)
    endproc (* Connections*)

    process Check_In_Use[Ctl]:noexit:=
    (
      Checking[Ctl](empty)
    )
    where

      process Checking[Ctl](Inuse:Natset):noexit:=
      (
        Ctl ? Number:Nat ! Originate ! Ok
                [notin(Number,Inuse) ];
        Checking[Ctl](add(Number,Inuse))
       []
        Ctl ? Number:Nat ! Originate ! Busy
        [isin(Number,Inuse)];
        Checking[Ctl](Inuse)
       []
        Ctl ? Number:Nat ! Dial ! Ok
                [notin(Number,Inuse) ];
        Checking[Ctl](add(Number,Inuse))
       []
        Ctl ? Number:Nat ! Dial ! Busy
        [isin(Number,Inuse)];
        Checking[Ctl](Inuse)
       []
        Ctl ? Number:Nat ! Disconn ? Status: Stat_Sort;
        Checking[Ctl](remove(Number,Inuse))

       []
         Ctl ? Number:Nat ? Signal: Sig_Sort
               ? Status:Stat_Sort [ NoConstraint(Signal) ];
        Checking[Ctl](Inuse)
      )
      endproc (* Checking *)
    endproc (* Check_In_Use *)
endspec
```

5. LOTOS AND SDL

Since SDL is a standard language for specifying telephone systems, we had hoped to close this paper by a comparison between our specification and a similar one written in SDL. Unfortunately, we were not successful in locating such work. However, the following general remarks can be made:

(1) Only state-oriented specifications are possible in SDL. In particular, the constraint-oriented style, along with the type of modularization presented in this paper, are not possible.

(2) SDL modules, called "blocks", communicate by means of queues, so modularity in SDL cannot be as fine-grained as in LOTOS.

(3) Explicit time can be modeled in SDL, but not in LOTOS as currently defined. Time aspects are an important part of telephone system specifications, but could not be taken into account in our specification.

6. CONCLUSION

We have shown that LOTOS is appropriate for specifying the observable behavior of telephone systems. Of course, nowadays, telephones are much more complex than the ones described in this paper, however features such as Call transfer, Hold, Conference call, Call forward, etc. can be treated by extending the basic mechanism described here. By writing and debugging LOTOS specifications of such systems during the design phase, telephone system designers can give precise descriptions and validate their designs before reaching the implementation stage. Implementors are then presented with a validated and precise specification of the system, which would contribute greatly towards the quality of the final product. In the final steps, the behavior of the implementation can be compared with the behavior of the specification, by using formal or informal testing methods[GL].

ACKNOWLEDGMENTS.

Funding sources for our work include the National Sciences and Engineering Research Council of Canada, the Telecommunications Research Institute of Ontario (Design of Validation Environments project), Bell-Northern Research and the Canadian Department of Communications. We are indebted to Raymond Aubin and Boumezbeur Rezki for preliminary work leading to this paper.

REFERENCES

[BO] Bochmann, G. V. A General Transition Model for Protocols and Communication Services. IEEE Trans. Comm., 28 (1980) 643-650.

[BR] Brinksma, E. On the Design of Extended LOTOS, A Specification Language for Distributed Systems. Doctoral Dissertation, Universiteit Twente (NL), 1988.

[GHL] Guillemot, R., Haj-Hussein, M., and Logrippo, L. Executing Large LOTOS Specifications. Proceedings of the VIII International Symposium on Protocol Specification, Verification, and Testing, Atlantic City, N.J., 1988.

[GL] Guillemot, R., and Logrippo, L. Derivation of Useful Execution Trees from LOTOS by Using an Interpreter. Proceedings of the FORTE 88 International Conference,

Stirling, UK, 1988.

[ISO1] International Organization for Standardization, Information Processing Systems, Open Systems Interconnection. IS 8807: LOTOS: A Formal Description Technique Based on the Temporal Ordering of Observational Behavior (1988).

[ISO2] ISO/IEC JTC1/SC6 N4870, Formal Description of ISO 8072 (Transport Service) in LOTOS (working draft), 1988.

[M] Milner, R. A Calculus of Communicating Systems. Lecture Notes in Computer Science No.92 (Springer-Verlag) 1980.

[Q] Quemada, J., and Fernandez, A. Introduction of Quantitative relative Time in LOTOS. In: Rudin, H., and West, C.H. Protocol Specification, Testing, and Verification, VII. North-Holland, 1987, 105-121.

[Q1] Quemada, J., Pavon, S., and Fernandez, A. Transforming LOTOS Specifications with LOLA - The Parameterized Expansion. Proceedings of the FORTE 88 International Conference, Stirling, UK, 1988.

[ST] Saracco, R., and Tilanus, P. (eds.) SDL '87 - State of the Art and Future Trends. North-Holland, 1987.

[T] Turner, K. Constraint-oriented style in LOTOS. University of Stirling, 1988.

[T1] Turner, K.J. An Architectural Semantics for LOTOS. In: Rudin, H., and West, C.H. Protocol Specification, Testing, and Verification, VII. North-Holland, 1987, 15-28.

[VL] Vissers, C. A., and Logrippo, L. The Importance of the Service Concept in the Design of Data Communications Protocols. In Diaz, M. (ed.) Protocol Specification, Testing, and Verification, V. North-Holland, 1986.

[VSV] Vissers, C.A., Scollo, G., and van Sinderen, M. Architecture and Specification Style in Formal Descriptions of Distributed Systems. Proceedings of the VIII International Symposium on Protocol Specification, Verification, and Testing, Atlantic City, N.J., 1988.

[Z] Zave, P. The Distributed Alternative to Finite-State-Machine Specifications. ACM Trans. on Prog. Lang. and Systems, Vol. 7, No. 1, Jan. 1985, PP. 10-36.

Invited Presentation:

Design and Verification in Real-time Distributed Computing: an Introduction to Compositional Methods

Protocol Specification, Testing, and Verification, IX
E. Brinksma, G. Scollo and C.A. Vissers (Editors)
Elsevier Science Publishers B.V. (North-Holland)

Design and verification in real-time distributed computing: an introduction to compositional methods*

J.J.M. Hooman
W.P. de Roever

Dept. of Mathematics and Computing Science
Eindhoven University of Technology
P.O. Box 513, 5600 MB Eindhoven, The Netherlands
e-mail: mcvax!eutws1!wsinjh and mcvax!eutws1!wsinwpr

Abstract

Formal methods for the specification and verification of real-time systems can be considered from the viewpoint of expressibility (which properties can be specified), specification language (real-time temporal logic, first order assertions with time as explicit parameter), and programming features (time-out, communication mechanism, concurrency). We stress compositional methods, i.e. methods in which the specification of a compound program can be inferred from specifications of its constituents without reference to the internal structure of those parts. This allows programming with such parts via their specifications rather than through their fully worked out code, thus separating the use of those parts as modules from their implementation. Therefore compositionality enables verification during the process of (top-down) design - the derivation of correct programs - instead of the more familiar a posteriori verification based on already completed program code. We extend these compositional methods to real-time distributed computing. Compositional reasoning during top-down development is illustrated by an example concerning a watchdog timer.

1 Introduction

Numerous methods have been given for the specification and verification of (real-time) distributed programs. These methods can be considered from several viewpoints:

- The class of programs to which the method does apply: For instance, concurrent programs may communicate in many different ways; via shared variables or via message passing. We can distinguish between synchronous message passing—both sender and receiver wait until a partner is available—and asynchronous communication with many variations of buffering.
- The form of the correctness formulae used to specify and verify programs: Several methods use invariants, e.g. expressed in Temporal logic, or Hoare-triples (i.e. a program with pre- and post-condition) using first order logic.
- The properties which can be expressed: Real-time properties (expressing timing requirements, e.g. "communication every 5 time units"), safety properties (which can be falsified in finite time, e.g. "communication within 10 time units", or "nontermination"), or liveness properties (e.g. "eventually a communication will take place").

*This work was supported by ESPRIT Project 937: Debugging and Specification of Ada Real-Time Embedded Systems (DESCARTES).

- Is the method only applicable to complete program code or is it possible to verify design steps during the process of program development?

In this paper we concentrate on the last point, especially for real-time distributed message passing. We illustrate in section 3 the development from a-posteriori methods (which require the complete program text) towards compositional methods (supporting verify-while-design). Compositionality can be considered as a repercussion of hierarchical, structured, program derivation on specification and verification formalisms for (real-time) concurrent processes. A separation of concerns is proposed, implying a separation of the use of (and the reasoning about) a module from its implementation.
This leads to the following definition of *compositionality* for proof methods:

> Properties of a compound programming language construct (such as sequential composition and parallel composition) can be deduced from specifications for its constituent parts without any further information about the internal structure of these parts.

In general, compositional program specification and verification dictates, as a principle, that all aspects of program execution which are required to define the meaning of a compound construct from its constituents must be explicitly addressed in semantics and assertion language alike. In *semantics* because, otherwise, no compositional semantics can be defined, since compositionality in semantics requires that the meaning of a compound statement is a function of the meaning of its parts (the guiding principle of denotational semantics). In *specification languages* because, otherwise, no compositional verification rules can be formulated in which the specification of a compound construct should follow from specifications of its constituent parts without knowledge about their internal structure (the internal structure often providing implicit information which has not been explicitly stated in the specification as in [OG76,AFR80]). The rationale for this principle is that one must be able to specify the behaviour of a module in isolation, i.e., without any implicit prior assumption regarding the environment within which it ultimately functions. Hence, all assumptions which are needed regarding the environment—because these influence the behaviour of a module—must be made explicit as parameters (in the semantics and specification of that module alike) for only then one can abstract away from the remaining aspects (such as inner syntactic structure).

In case of shared variable communication this compositionality principle implies that when defining the behaviour of a module any change of a shared variable by the environment must be explicitly expressed as an assumption of that module regarding its environment. This is worked out in Aczel's model for shared variable semantics as cited in [dR85]. Similarly, when considering distributed communication via input/output-statements the specification of, e.g., an input statement in one module requires explicit expressibility of assumptions regarding a corresponding output statement in another module. In case one abstracts away from blocking behaviour only assumptions regarding the value communicated must be expressible. If blocking behaviour is a focus of interest, as in the present paper, this is again an assumption regarding program execution which must be stated explicitly; i.e. one has to state the effect of no communication partner being available in the assertion language and one must be able to express the assumption that no partner is available in the assertion language.

When timing behaviour of a statement is considered, all factors concerning the execution of this statement which influence that timing behaviour must be expressible. E.g. in the present paper we make the maximal progress assumption with respect to distributed i/o-communication: no communication statement should wait for communication when its partner is also ready to communicate. This aspect of timing behaviour requires, indeed, that one must be able to express when a partner is waiting to communicate. For, otherwise, maximal progress would not be expressible within the semantics, and hence timing behaviour of i/o-statements could not be characterized. In this real-time context, the introduction of priorities for processes on a single processor implies conceptually that certain statements which are ready to execute will not be executed on account of their lower priority and because at most one action can be executed at a time on a uniprocessor. Modelling the timing behaviour of such statements requires that the semantics, and hence the specification language, contains primitives to state explicitly when a statement is executing and when it is requesting processor time with a certain priority. These aspects of reasoning formally about real-time and scheduling by means of priorities are addressed technically in section 3.4 and illustrated in section 4.

In section 2 we describe a real-time programming language with synchronous message passing and two types of parallel composition; one for parallel programs executing on a single processor and one for concurrent programs each executing on its own processor. In section 3 we give an example of a classical non-compositional method. We indicate how a compositional proof system (i.e. rules and axioms relating programs and specifications) can be achieved, and how such a method can be extended to reason about real-time properties. Compositional reasoning is illustrated, in section 4, by an example of a watchdog timer with several stages of development and using both notions of parallelism. Part of this example can also be found in [HW89] using real-time temporal logic. In section 5 we sketch the development of the field, leading to a description of the state of the art and the place of our work therein.

2 A Real-Time Programming Language

We consider a real-time programming language which is akin to OCCAM [Occ88] and based on real-time variations of CSP [Hoa78] for which a formal denotational semantics has been given in [KSR+88]. A program in our language can have the following form:
$\ll S_{11} \,|||\, \cdots \,|||\, S_{1n_1} \gg \,\|\, \cdots \,\|\, \ll S_{m1} \,|||\, \cdots \,|||\, S_{mn_m} \gg$
where $\|$ expresses concurrent execution of the programs $\ll S_{i1} \,|||\, \cdots \,|||\, S_{in_i} \gg$, each on its own processor. The parallel operator $|||$ expresses that the programs involved are executed on a single processor. The brackets $\ll$ and $\gg$ indicate that no other processes are executed on a particular processor. Actions of parallel processes on a single processor are interleaved, on the basis of priorities assigned to statements. A statement **prio** p (S) assigns priority p to statement S. Statements without such an explicit priority have priority 0. A higher

number corresponds to a higher priority. There are two *primitive statements*:

- **skip** which does not take any execution time, and
- assignment $x := e$ which takes a certain execution time.

Processes communicate and synchronize by synchronous message passing via unidirectional channels which connect exactly two processes. Let D be a channel name, then our language contains the following *IO-statements*:

- **D!e** Output: send the value of expression e through channel D as soon as a corresponding input command is available.
- **D?x** Input: receive a value via channel D and assign this value to the variable x. Similar to the output command, this statement has to wait for a corresponding partner before a (synchronous) communication can take place.

In general, a processor can be either at a *scheduling* point or at a *nonscheduling* point. The priority of a statement is only considered at scheduling points; then a statement can only execute if there are no other statements with a higher priority on the same processor which request processor time. In case of equal priorities a nondeterministic choice is made (to abstract from specific scheduling policies). The execution of a statement at a *nonscheduling point* can not be interrupted, not even by requesting statements with a higher priority. A statement requests processor time until it has the highest priority; then a primitive statement can start executing at a scheduling point. An IO-statement with highest priority either waits for a partner (allowing lower priorities to execute) or starts the communication if a partner is available. In this paper only the start and termination points of primitive and IO-statements are considered to be scheduling points.

Furthermore, our syntax contains the following *composite commands*:

- Sequential composition $S_1; S_2$.
- A guarded command $[b_1; IO_1 \rightarrow S_1 [] \cdots [] b_n; IO_n \rightarrow S_n [] b; \mathbf{delay}\, d \rightarrow S]$, with IO_i denoting an IO-statement. It is executed as follows: first wait until an IO-command of the open guards (i.e. for which the boolean b_i evaluates to true) can be executed and then continue with the corresponding S_i. If the delay guard is open (b evaluates to true) and no IO-guard can be taken within d time units, then S is executed. This makes it possible to model a *time-out*, i.e. to restrict the waiting period for certain communications.

  Example 2.1 Consider $[D?x \rightarrow S_1 [] \mathbf{delay}\, 5 \rightarrow S_2]$; if the D-communication can not be executed within 5 time units then the delay-branch is taken and S_2 requests execution time. Note that in guards with a boolean expression equivalent to *true* this boolean is often omitted. ∎

- An iteration statement $*$**G** repeats the execution of guarded command G as long as at least one of the guards is open. When none of the guards is open $*G$ terminates.

2.1 Basic Timing Assumptions

In order to determine the real-time behaviour of programs, we have to make assumptions about the execution time of atomic statements and the overhead associated with composite constructs. Moreover, bounds must be given on how long a process is allowed to wait with the execution of a primitive statement when a processor is available, and with the execution of an IO-statement when processor and communication partner are available. In this work we assume *maximal progress* which means that a process never waits unnecessarily; if execution can proceed it will do so immediately. Note that there are two reasons for a process to wait:

- Wait to execute an IO-statement because no communication partner is available. By the maximal progress assumption, two statements $D!e$ and $D?x$ are not allowed to wait simultaneously if both can execute on their processor.
- Wait to execute an atomic statement because the processor is not available. The maximal progress constraint implies that if a processor is idle, then no statement on that processor requests execution time.

Throughout this paper we use $\equiv$ to express syntactic equality.

3 Compositionality and Real-Time

In section 3.1 we explain the principles of traditional non-compositional methods. The development towards compositional proof systems based on Hoare triples is described in section 3.2. Extensions of these formulae with invariants are discussed in section 3.3. Since none of the methods described in the sections 3.1— 3.3 can express timing behaviour of programs, we do not use the operator $|||$ nor the brackets $\ll$, $\gg$ in these sections. In section 3.4 the compositional method based on explicit assumption-commitment reasoning is adapted to real-time.

3.1 Non-Compositional Methods

Classical verification methods for parallel processes, such as [OG76] for shared variable communication and [AFR80,LG81] for synchronous message passing, consist of two stages. First a *local* correctness proof is given for each of the sequential processes by associating assertions with locations in the program. In the second, *global*, stage a consistency check is applied to the local proofs:

- For shared variables this is the *interference freedom* test which verifies that assertions in the proof of one process remain valid under actions of other processes.
- For communication via message passing the *cooperation* test is applied to verify correctness of assertions attached to locations after input- and output-statements.

Such methods are not compositional because at parallel composition they require the complete program text, annotated with assertions, of the constituent processes.

As an example, we consider in more detail the method of Apt, Francez and de Roever [AFR80] for synchronous message passing. This method is based on *Hoare triples*, that are correctness formulae of the form $\{p\}\ S\ \{q\}$ with the following meaning: if we start program S in a state satisfying assertion p (the pre-condition) and if S terminates then assertion q (the post-condition) holds for the termination state. E.g. $\{x = 5\}\ x := x + 1\ \{x = 6\}$.

First we indicate how a proof system can be formulated to derive such Hoare triples for sequential programs. With $q[e/x]$ denoting textual substitution of e for each free occurrence of x in assertion q, we have the following assignment axiom:

Axiom 3.1 (assignment) $\{q[e/x]\}\ x := e\ \{q\}$

Example 3.1 With this axiom we can derive $\{x = 5\}\ x := x + 1\ \{x = 6\}$ because $(x = 6)[x + 1/x]$ equals $x + 1 = 6$, which is equivalent to $x = 5$. ∎

Furthermore the proof system contains rules for compound constructs. For instance, sequential composition is modelled by the following rule:

Rule 3.1 (sequential composition) $\dfrac{\{p\}\ S_1\ \{r\},\ \{r\}\ S_2\ \{q\}}{\{p\}\ S_1; S_2\ \{q\}}$

By such a rule the formula below the line can be derived from the formulae above the line. Soundness of the rule is proven by showing that validity of the formulae above the line implies that the formula below the line is valid. Note that this rule is compositional because the formula for $S_1; S_2$ is derived without using the structure of S_1 or S_2. To strengthen pre-conditions and weaken post-conditions, the proof system contains the following rule:

Rule 3.2 (consequence) $\dfrac{p \rightarrow p_1,\ \{p_1\}\ S\ \{q_1\},\ q_1 \rightarrow q}{\{p\}\ S\ \{q\}}$

To illustrate the rule for parallel composition in [AFR80], we consider the proof of $\{y = 3\}\ B?x\ ;\ x := x + 1\ ;\ E!(x + 2)\ \|\ B!y\ ;\ E?y\ ;\ y := y + 2\ \{x = 4 \wedge y = 8\}$.

In the first stage we attach assertions to all locations in the program text of the two processes, leading to so called *proof outlines*:
$\{true\}\ B?x\ \{x = 3\}\ ;\ x := x + 1\ \{x = 4\}\ ;\ E!(x + 2)\ \{x = 4\}$, and
$\{y = 3\}\ B!y\ \{y = 3\}\ ;\ E?y\ \{y = 6\}\ ;\ y := y + 2\ \{y = 8\}$.
In this stage only the post-conditions of assignments are verified: from the assignment axiom we obtain $\{x = 3\}\ x := x + 1\ \{x = 4\}$ and $\{y = 6\}\ y := y + 2\ \{y = 8\}$. Observe that the post-conditions of the input statements $B?x$ and $E?y$ express assumptions about the values sent by the communication partner.

These assumptions are verified in the second stage by means of the *cooperation* test.[1] In general, this test requires that for $\{p_1\}\ D?x\ \{q_1\}$ and $\{p_2\}\ D!e\ \{q_2\}$ in the proof outlines of two processes we have to prove $\{p_1 \wedge p_2\}\ D?x\ \|\ D!e\ \{q_1 \wedge q_2\}$, which is equivalent to $\{p_1 \wedge p_2\}\ x := e\ \{q_1 \wedge q_2\}$. In our example this leads to the proof obligations:
$\{true \wedge y = 3\}\ B?x\ \|\ B!y\ \{x = 3 \wedge y = 3\}$ and
$\{y = 3 \wedge x = 4\}\ E?y\ \|\ E!(x + 2)\ \{y = 6 \wedge x = 4\}$ which are easy to prove.

After the verification of the first two stages we obtain the conjunction of all pre-conditions from the sequential processes as the pre-condition of the complete program and the conjunction of the post-conditions as the final post-condition. In our example this leads to

[1]In the full method of [AFR80] auxiliary variables and a global invariant are used to make the method complete, i.e. to guarantee that any valid Hoare triple can be proven.

pre-condition $true \wedge y = 3$ and post-condition $x = 4 \wedge y = 8$ which are equivalent to the required conditions.

3.2 Towards Compositionality

In this section we discuss how a compositional proof method can be obtained for programs which communicate via synchronous message passing. First the cooperation test from [AFR80] is removed by disallowing implicit assumptions in the post-conditions of IO-statements. The local proof of a sequential program should be valid in any arbitrary environment. To derive a required (valid) post-condition for the complete program, we use a *history variable* h which denotes the communication history of the complete program. A (communication) *history* is a sequence of records (D, v) where D is a channel name and v a value. E.g. $<(D,5),(E,6),(B,8),(E,0)>$ is a history expressing four communications: first one via channel D with value 5, then a communication via E with value 6, etc. Let $<>$ denote the empty sequence. History variable h does not appear in the program, but it is updated implicitly in the semantics of IO-statements. This leads to the following formulae:

- For an output command e.g. $\{h =<(D,5)>\}\ E!6\ \{h =<(D,5),(E,6)>\}$.
- For an input statement $D?x$ we can only express in the post-condition that there exists a value which is communicated via D and assigned to x. For instance, $\{h =<>\}\ D?x\ \{\exists v : h =<(D,v)> \wedge x = v\}$.

Example 3.2 Consider the parallel composition of $D!5$ and $D?x$, using Hoare triples $\{h =<>\}\ D!5\ \{h =<(D,5)>\}$ and $\{h =<>\}\ D?x\ \{\exists v : h =<(D,v)> \wedge x = v\}$.
Suppose the pre- and post-condition after parallel composition are obtained by taking the conjunction of, resp., pre- and post-conditions of the sequential programs. Then
$\{h =<>\}\ D!5 \parallel D?x\ \{h =<(D,5)> \wedge \exists v : h =<(D,v)> \wedge x = v\}$.
Since the post-condition implies $v = 5 \wedge x = v$, and hence $x = 5$, the consequence rule leads to $\{h =<>\}\ D!5 \parallel D?x\ \ \{x = 5\}$. By a so called *substitution rule* (not given in this paper), we could substitute $<>$ for h in the pre-condition, thus obtaining pre-condition *true*. ∎

Example 3.2 suggests the following rule: $\dfrac{\{p_1\}\ S_1\ \{q_1\},\ \{p_2\}\ S_2\ \{q_2\}}{\{p_1 \wedge p_2\}\ S_1 \| S_2\ \{q_1 \wedge q_2\}}$

Example 3.3 Consider again $S_1 \equiv B?x\,;\, x := x+1\,;\, E!(x+2) \parallel S_2 \equiv B!y;\, E?y;\, y := y+2$.
First derive the following Hoare triples: $\{h =<>\}\ B?x\ \{\exists v_1 : h =<(B,v_1)> \wedge x = v_1\}$,
$\{\exists v_1 : h =<(B,v_1)> \wedge x = v_1\}\ x := x+1\ \{\exists v_1 : h =<(B,v_1)> \wedge x = v_1+1\}$, and
$\{\exists v_1 : h =<(B,v_1)> \wedge x = v_1+1\}\ E!(x+2)\ \{\exists v_1 : h =<(B,v_1),(E,v_1+3)> \wedge x = v_1+1\}$.
By two applications of the sequential composition rule we obtain:
$\{h =<>\}\ B?x\,;\ x := x+1\,;\ E!(x+2)\ \{\exists v_1 : h =<(B,v_1),(E,v_1+3)> \wedge x = v_1+1\}$.
Similarly, $\{h =<> \wedge y = 3\}\ B!y;\, E?y;\, y := y+2\ \{\exists v_2 : h =<(B,3),(E,v_2)> \wedge y = v_2+2\}$.
Then the parallel composition rule above leads to

$$\{h =<> \wedge y = 3\}\ S_1\|S_2\ \{\ \exists v_1 : h =<(B,v_1),(E,v_1+3)> \wedge x = v_1+1 \wedge \exists v_2 : h =<(B,3),(E,v_2)> \wedge y = v_2+2\}.$$

The post-condition implies $v_1 = 3 \wedge v_2 = v_1+3 \wedge x = v_1+1 \wedge y = v_2+2$, which leads to

$x = 4 \wedge y = 8$. Thus, by the consequence rule, $\{h =<> \wedge y = 3\}\ S_1 \| S_2\ \{x = 4 \wedge y = 8\}$. (Again $h =<>$ in the pre-condition can be removed by the substitution rule.) ∎

Although this works nicely for two processes, the next example shows that there is a problem if more than two processes are involved.

Example 3.4 Consider $S_1 \equiv B!0\ ;\ E?x \ \|\ S_2 \equiv B?y\ ;\ D!(y+1) \ \|\ S_3 \equiv D?z\ ;\ E!(z+1)$. Following the previous example, we could first prove:
$\{h =<>\}\ S_1\ \{q_1 \equiv \exists v_1 : h =< (B,0),(E,v_1) > \wedge x = v_1\}$, and
$\{h =<>\}\ S_2\ \{q_2 \equiv \exists v_2 : h =< (B,v_2),(D,v_2+1) > \wedge y = v_2\}$. But then the conjunction of q_1 and q_2 implies *false* whereas $S_1 \| S_2 \| S_3$ terminates and hence does not satisfy post-condition *false*. ∎

The problem is that h denotes the global history of the complete program—e.g. consisting of three processes—whereas each of the processes in isolation can only describe the history on its own channels. A possible solution is to give each process its own history variable, and to combine these local history variables at parallel composition. Zwiers [Zwi88], however, shows that concise and simple rules for parallel composition can be formulated if each process uses projections of global history variable h onto its own channels. Such a projection expresses the view of a particular process on the global history. Formally, the *projection* of h onto a set of channel names *cset*, notation h_{cset}, denotes the sequence obtained from the history denoted by h by removing all records with channel name not in *cset*. E.g. if $h =< (B,0),(D,1),(E,3) >$ then $h_{\{D\}} =< (D,1) >$, $h_{\{D,E\}} =< (D,1),(E,3) >$, and $h_{\{F\}} =<>$. Henceforth we write h_D, h_{DE}, and h_F instead of, resp., $h_{\{D\}}$, $h_{\{D,E\}}$, and $h_{\{F\}}$.

At parallel composition of S_1 and S_2 we require that the post-condition of S_i only refers to h via projections on the channels occurring in S_i, for $i = 1,2$. If, moreover, the post-condition of S_1 (resp. S_2) does not refer to program variables of S_2 (resp. S_1), then the following rule for parallel composition is sound:

Rule 3.3 (parallel composition) $$\frac{\{p_1\}\ S_1\ \{q_1\},\ \{p_2\}\ S_2\ \{q_2\}}{\{p_1 \wedge p_2\}\ S_1 \| S_2\ \{q_1 \wedge q_2\}}$$

Observe that this is a compositional rule because a Hoare triple for $S_1 \| S_2$ can be derived without knowing the internal structure of S_1 and S_2. Recall that Hoare triples are not sufficient to formulate the cooperation test but that proof outlines are required. In the rule above this test is replaced by a simple syntactic check on the Hoare triples for the parallel components.

Except for bottom-up verification such a rule can be used for top-down development. Therefore, consider $\{p\}\ S\ \{q\}$ as a specification for a program S. Suppose we decide to implement S as $S_1 \| S_2$. Then S_1 and S_2 can be implemented independently, using specifications $\{p_1\}\ S_1\ \{q_1\}$ and $\{p_2\}\ S_2\ \{q_2\}$ provided $p \rightarrow p_1 \wedge p_2$, $q_1 \wedge q_2 \rightarrow q$ and certain requirements on the post-conditions hold.

3.3 Extensions of Hoare Triples

A Hoare triple is perfectly suited to describe the observable behaviour of a sequential program which is given by initial and final state. For a parallel program also the communication behaviour on its external channels is observable. Hence a specification of a parallel component should express this communication interface. Note, however, that a specification $\{p\}\ S\ \{q\}$ has an important limitation: it only specifies the behaviour of S if S terminates. All non-terminating computations of S satisfy such a specification trivially. Thus the post-condition can not be used to express the communication interface. Therefore, a Hoare triple is extended with an invariant, called *commitment* in this paper, which must hold throughout the computation. This leads to a formula $C : \{p\}\ S\ \{q\}$ where commitment C describes the communication interface of S during its execution. The success of such formulae in many applications is based on a simple rule for parallel composition in which, besides conjunctions for pre- and post-conditions, also the conjunction of commitments can be taken.

Yet the framework explained so far is not satisfactory. In the form of the specification of a process there is no separate component describing the behaviour of its environment, whereas in general the behaviour of a process depends heavily on its environment. Especially when specifying so called reactive processes [HP85], which have an intensive relation with their environment, we want to specify a process relative to explicit assumptions about its environment. Therefore the specification formula is extended with a second invariant, called *assumption*, which expresses assumptions about the environment and by which we can strengthen post-condition and commitment. This leads to formulae $(A, C) : \{p\}\ S\ \{q\}$, where

A is an **assumption** describing the expected behaviour of the environment of S, and
C is a **commitment** which is guaranteed by process S itself, as long as the environment does not violate the assumption.

The general idea is that assumption and commitment reflect the communication interface between parallel components (and hence do not contain program variables), whereas pre- and post-condition facilitate the reasoning at sequential composition.

In the following examples, $seq_1 \preceq seq_2$ expresses that sequence seq_1 is an initial prefix of sequence seq_2.

Example 3.5 Now assumptions about the values sent by the environment can be expressed explicitly. For instance, $h_D \preceq < (D,3) >$, which expresses that the history of channel D is a prefix of $< (D,3) >$, can be used as an assumption as follows:
$(h_D \preceq < (D,3) >, true) : \{true\}\ D?x\ \{x = 3\}$.
This assumption can be used for a commitment about the next communication:
$(h_D \preceq < (D,3) >, h_B \preceq < (B,4) >) : \{true\}\ D?x\ ;\ B!(x+1)\ \{x = 3\}$. ∎

A proof system for these assumption-commitment based formulae has been given in [Hoo89]. In this paper we discuss mainly the proof obligations for assumptions and commitments at parallel composition. Consider the parallel composition $S_1 \| S_2$, and assume assumption-commitment pairs (A_1, C_1) for S_1 and (A_2, C_2) for S_2. Which conditions have to be verified to obtain a pair (A, C) for $S_1 \| S_2$? Consider assumption A_2 of S_2:

- A_2 may contain assumptions about joint channels of S_1 and S_2 which connect these two processes; these assumptions must be justified by commitment C_1 of S_1.

- A_2 may contain assumptions about external channels of S_2. These assumptions are maintained in the new network assumption A for $S_1 \parallel S_2$.

This leads to the following proof obligation: $A \wedge C_1 \rightarrow A_2$. Similarly for A_1: $A \wedge C_2 \rightarrow A_1$.

To obtain a sound rule with these implications, the meaning of a formula (A_i, C_i) : $\{p_i\}$ S_i $\{q_i\}$ has to be defined carefully. A simple implication between A_i and C_i would with the implications above and $A \equiv \mathit{true}$ lead to circular reasoning, e.g. $A_1 \rightarrow C_1 \rightarrow A_2 \rightarrow C_2 \rightarrow A_1$. Therefore in defining the meaning of $(A_i, C_i) : \{p_i\}\ S_i\ \{q_i\}$ we require that if p_i holds in the initial state then 1) C_i holds initially, and 2) C_i holds after every communication provided A_i holds after all preceeding communications. This inductive step inside the meaning of formulas is sufficient to avoid circularity (see [MC81]).

As in Rule 3.3 we can take the conjunction of pre-conditions and post-conditions and also of commitments, provided 1) the assertions A_i, C_i, p_i and q_i of S_i refer only to h via projections on the channels, and 2) p_i and q_i do not refer to program variables of the other process. (Program variables are not allowed in A_i and C_i.) With these constraints, the following rule for parallel composition is valid:

Rule 3.4 (par. comp. A-C)
$$\frac{(A_1, C_1) : \{p_1\}\ S_1\ \{q_1\},\ (A_2, C_2) : \{p_2\}\ S_2\ \{q_2\} \quad A \wedge C_1 \rightarrow A_2,\ A \wedge C_2 \rightarrow A_1}{(A, C_1 \wedge C_2) : \{p_1 \wedge p_2\}\ S_1 \| S_2\ \{q_1 \wedge q_2\}}$$

Example 3.6 Consider $S_1 \equiv B?x\,;\ x := x+1\,;\ E!(x+2) \parallel S_2 \equiv D?y\,;\ B!y\,;\ E?y\,;\ y := y+2$. Then for S_1 and S_2 we can derive
$(A_1 \equiv h_B \preceq <(B,3)>\,,\ C_1 \equiv h_E \preceq <(E,6)>) : \{h_{BE} = <>\}\ S_1\ \{x = 4\}$, and
$(A_2 \equiv h_D \preceq <(D,3)> \wedge h_E \preceq <(E,6)>, C_2 \equiv h_B \preceq <(B,3)>) : \{h_{BDE} = <>\}\ S_2\ \{y = 8\}$.
Since S_1 and S_2 communicate with each other via the channels B and E, we take for $S_1 \| S_2$ the assumption about the remaining channel: $A \equiv h_D \preceq <(D,3)>$.
Then $A \wedge C_1 \rightarrow A_2$ and $A \wedge C_2 \rightarrow A_1$, thus the parallel composition rule leads to
$(A, C_1 \wedge C_2) : \{h_{BDE} = <>\}\ S_1 \| S_2\ \{x = 4 \wedge y = 8\}$. ∎

3.4 Extension to Real-Time

In this section we discuss the extension of compositional methods, in particular the assumption/commitment formalism described in the previous section, to real-time specifications containing timing requirements.

We express the timing behaviour of a program from the viewpoint of an external observer with his own clock. Thus at the level of reasoning there is a conceptual global clock. Since our global clock is not incorporated in the distributed system itself, it does not impose any synchronization upon processes. In the specification a special variable *time* is introduced which refers to this external clock. E.g. if an assignment takes between 3 and 5 time units, then $\{x = 5 \wedge \mathit{time} = 2\}\ x := x + 1\ \{x = 6 \wedge 5 < \mathit{time} < 7\}$. In this paper we assume that *time* ranges over a dense time domain which includes the natural numbers with the standard ordering $<$, e.g. the rational numbers.

To express the communication behaviour of a program, our assertion language contains primitives to express when a communication via a certain channel takes place, and which value is transmitted. Recall from section 2 that the maximal progress assumption imposes certain constraints on waiting before a communication takes place. As already explained in section 1, this implies that we must be able to express when a process is waiting to communicate via a particular channel. In this paper we use the following primitives:

- *comm via D at t with value v*, to denote that a communication via channel D with value v takes place at t.
- *wait to D! at t*, to denote that a process is waiting to send a message via D at t.
- *wait to D? at t*, to denote that a process is waiting to receive via D at t.

Note that, in general, communication takes a certain period of time, and hence there will be an interval of points at which a process is communicating via a particular channel with a certain value. With these primitives the *maximal progress* constraint can be expressed as follows, for every channel D;

Axiom 3.2 (MP) $\forall t : \neg(\textit{wait to } D?\textit{ at } t\ \wedge \textit{wait to } D!\textit{ at } t\ )$

Furthermore we will later use the following axiom which excludes that a program is simultaneously waiting to communicate and communicating on the same channel:

Axiom 3.3 (Excl) $\forall t : \neg[(\textit{wait to } D?\textit{ at } t\ \vee \textit{wait to } D!\textit{ at } t\ ) \wedge \textit{comm via } D \textit{ at } t]$

The following abbreviations are frequently used:

- $\textit{comm via } D \textit{ at } t \equiv \exists v : \textit{comm via } D \textit{ at } t \textit{ with value } v$
- $\textit{(wait to) comm via } D! \textit{ at } t \equiv \textit{comm via } D \textit{ at } t \vee \textit{wait to } D! \textit{ at } t$
- $\textit{wait to } D! \textit{ during } (t_0, t_2) \equiv \forall t_1, t_0 < t_1 < t_2 : \textit{wait to } D! \textit{ at } t_1$
- $\textit{wait to } D! \textit{ at } t \textit{ Until comm via } D \equiv$

  $\forall t_1 \geq t : \textit{wait to } D! \textit{ at } t_1 \vee\ \exists t_2\ \forall t_1, t \leq t_1 < t_2 : \textit{wait to } D! \textit{ at } t_1 \wedge \textit{comm via } D \textit{ at } t_2$

From these definitions we derive the following lemma.

Lemma 3.1 $\textit{wait to } D! \textit{ at } t \textit{ Until comm via } D \rightarrow \textit{(wait to) comm via } D! \textit{ at } t$

Example 3.7 Consider processes P_1 and P_2 with specifications
$\{p_1\}\ P_1\ \{\textit{wait to D? at 5 Until comm via D}\}$ and
$\{p_2\}\ P_2\ \{\textit{wait to D! at 5 Until comm via D}\}$.
Then the rule for parallel composition leads to the following post condition for $P_1 \parallel P_2$: $\textit{wait to D? from 5 Until comm via } D \wedge \textit{wait to D! from 5 Until comm via } D$. Now the maximal progress requirement implies that there is no point of time with waiting for input and waiting for output via channel D. Hence the D communication must start at time 5. ▮

Considering uniprocessor implementations with scheduling based on priorities, again our assertion language must be extended to achieve compositionality. Recall from section 2 that in this case we have to express when a process is executing and when it requests processor time with a certain priority. Therefore we introduce the following predicates:

- $\textit{exec}(t, \infty)$ which is true when the process is executing at a non-scheduling point t.
- $\textit{exec}(t, p)$, for $p \neq \infty$, which is true when the process is executing at a scheduling point t with priority p.
- $\textit{req}(t, p)$ which is true when the process requests processor time at t with priority p.

Furthermore, a priority is associated with waiting for a communication:

- *(wait to) comm via D! at t with prio p*

The following general axiom expresses that if a statement is executing with a certain priority, then no IO-statement is waiting to communicate or communicating with a lower priority:

Axiom 3.4 (Prio) $exec(t, p_1) \wedge p_1 > p_2 \rightarrow \neg(wait\ to)\ comm\ via\ D!\ at\ t\ with\ prio\ p_2$

In the assumption/commitment formalism, we can now express in the assumption when the environment of a process is waiting to communicate. With such an assumption we can determine when the communication must take place, and derive the termination time in the post-condition (assume the communication takes 1 time unit):

$$\begin{aligned}(A \ &\equiv\ (wait\ to)\ comm\ via\ D!\ at\ 5 \wedge \forall t, 3 \leq t < 5 : \neg comm\ via\ D\ at\ t,\\ C \ &\equiv\ \forall t, 3 \leq t < 5 : wait\ to\ D?\ at\ t \wedge \forall t, 5 < t < 6 : comm\ via\ D\ at\ t) :\\ &\{time = 3\}\ D?x\ \{time = 6\}\end{aligned}$$

Note that, due to the maximal progress constraint, a communication takes place as soon as both process and environment are ready for input and, resp., output.

When adding timing primitives to the assertion language, Rule 3.4 for the parallel composition $S_1 \| S_2$ has to be adapted slightly. Therefore observe that in the post-conditions q_1 and q_2 of, resp., S_1 and S_2 the special variable *time* denotes the termination time of, resp., S_1 and S_2. Since these termination times will be different in general (and then $q_1 \wedge q_2$ could implies *false*), we substitute logical variables t_1 (resp. t_2) for *time* in assertion q_1 (resp. q_2) before the conjunction is taken. Hence Rule 3.4 is adapted as follows: replace $q_1 \wedge q_2$ in the post-condition of $S_1 \| S_2$ by q, and add to the conditions above the line $q_1[t_1/time] \wedge q_2[t_2/time] \wedge time = max(t_1, t_2) \rightarrow q$ because the parallel construct terminates if both processes have terminated.

Example 3.8 Consider the following specifications (**action** d is used to represent an internal actions which takes d time units and assume communications take one time unit):

$$\begin{aligned}(A_1 \ &\equiv\ (wait\ to)\ comm\ via\ B?\ at\ 2 \wedge \forall t, 0 \leq t < 2 : \neg comm\ via\ B\ at\ t \wedge\\ &\quad (wait\ to)\ comm\ via\ D?\ at\ 6 \wedge \forall t, 3 \leq t < 6 : \neg comm\ via\ D\ at\ t,\\ C_1 \ &\equiv\ \forall t, 2 < t < 3 : comm\ via\ B\ at\ t \wedge wait\ to\ D!\ at\ 3\ Until\ comm\ via\ D \wedge\\ &\quad [\forall t : (\exists v : comm\ via\ D\ at\ t\ with\ value\ v) \rightarrow v = 5]) :\\ &\quad \{time = 0\}\ S_1 \equiv \ll B!1\ ;\ D!5\ ;\ \mathbf{action}\ 2 \gg\ \{time = 9\},\ \text{and}\end{aligned}$$

$$\begin{aligned}(A_2 \ &\equiv\ wait\ to\ D!\ at\ 3\ Until\ comm\ via\ D \wedge\\ &\quad [\forall t : (\exists v : comm\ via\ D\ at\ t\ with\ value\ v) \rightarrow v = 5],\\ C_2 \ &\equiv\ (wait\ to)\ comm\ via\ D?\ at\ 6 \wedge \forall t, 3 \leq t < 6 : \neg comm\ via\ D\ at\ t \wedge\\ &\quad \forall t, 6 < t < 7 : comm\ via\ D\ at\ t) :\\ &\quad \{time = 0\}\ S_2 \equiv \ll \mathbf{action}\ 6\ ;\ D?x \gg\ \{time = 7 \wedge x = 5\}\end{aligned}$$

Take for $S_1 \| S_2$ the following assumption: $A \equiv (wait\ to)\ comm\ via\ B?\ at\ 2 \wedge \forall t, 0 \leq t < 2 : \neg comm\ via\ B\ at\ t$, then clearly: $A \wedge C_1 \rightarrow A_2$ and $A \wedge C_2 \rightarrow A_1$. The parallel composition rule leads to $(A, C_1 \wedge C_2) : \{time = 0\}\ S_1 \| S_2\ \{time = 9 \wedge x = 5\}$. ∎

For the uniprocessor parallel composition $|||$ we follow the same scheme, with some changes to deal with the *exec* and *req* primitives. Observe that the commitments C_1 and C_2 in general express different properties of these predicates. Therefore rename *exec* in C_1 and C_2 by, resp., predicates e_1 and e_2. Since $S_1 ||| S_2$ executes iff S_1 or S_2 executes, we add the property $exec \leftrightarrow e_1 \vee e_2$, which is an abbreviation of $\forall p \, \forall t : exec(t,p) \leftrightarrow e_1(t,p) \vee e_2(t,p)$. Similar changes are made for the *req* predicate. This leads to the following conditions for deriving a pair (A, C) for $S_1 ||| S_2$ from pairs (A_1, C_1) for S_1 and (A_2, C_2) for S_2:

- $A[e_1/exec, r_1/req] \wedge C_1[e_2/exec, r_2/req] \wedge (e_1 \vee e_2 \leftrightarrow exec) \wedge (r_1 \vee r_2 \leftrightarrow req) \rightarrow A_2$, and $A[e_1/exec, r_1/req] \wedge C_2[e_2/exec, r_2/req] \wedge (e_1 \vee e_2 \leftrightarrow exec) \wedge (r_1 \vee r_2 \leftrightarrow req) \rightarrow A_1$

- $C_1[e_1/exec, r_1/req] \wedge C_2[e_2/exec, r_2/req] \wedge (e_1 \vee e_2 \leftrightarrow exec) \wedge (r_1 \vee r_2 \leftrightarrow req) \rightarrow C$

4 Example Watchdog Timer

To illustrate our formalism with an example, consider the network pictured in Fig. 1. Process

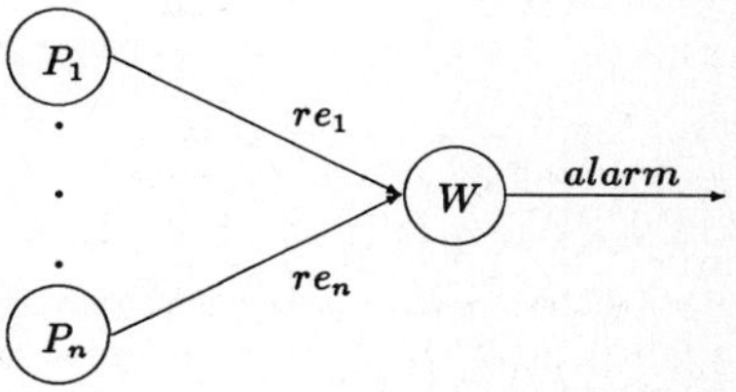

Figure 1: Watchdog Timer Network

W is a "watchdog" process: its job is to ensure that processes $P_1, \ldots, P_n$ are functioning properly. Each P_i indicates that it is functioning by sending a reset-signal on channel re_i at least every v_i (say) time units. Process W is always ready to receive signals on any re_i. If there is no communication on a particular re_k for v_k or more time units, then, within K (say) time units, W sends a warning on channel *alarm*. In section 4.1 we give a specification for process W. Given specifications for the P_i, we prove for $P_1 \| \cdots \| P_n \| W$ that one of the P_i is not functioning correctly iff W tries to send on channel *alarm*. This is verified using our proof system without knowing the implementations of $P_1, \ldots, P_n$ and W. To demonstrate program design from a specification, in section 4.2 W is implemented as a parallel composition $W_1 \| \cdots \| W_n \| S$ and we show which specifications for W_i and S are sufficient to derive the specification of W. Next W_i and S are, independently, implemented, satisfying the corresponding implementations. In section 4.3, we show that P_i can be implemented as $\ll$ **prio** 2 (B_i) $|||$ **prio** 1 $(WH_i) \gg$ where B_i performs the real task of P_i and WH_i is a watchdog handler which sends signal via re_i as long as B_i is functioning properly.

In this example we concentrate on the assumption-commitment reasoning. Henceforth all specifications have pre-condition $time = 0$ and post-condition *true*.

4.1 Specification of the Watchdog Timer

In this section we give a formal specification for the watchdog timer W which tries to communicate via channel *alarm* at a certain point of time only if, for some k, there was a previous period of at least v_k time units during which W is waiting for input via one of the re_i. Furthermore, if there is a waiting period for input via re_k of v_k time units, then, for some constant K, W starts waiting to output on channel *alarm* until the actual communication takes place. Hence we specify W as follows.

$$\begin{aligned}
(A^W &\equiv \textit{true}, \\
C_0^W &\equiv [\textit{wait to } re_k? \textit{ during } (t_2 - v_k, t_2) \rightarrow \\
&\quad \exists t_0 \leq t_2 + K : \textit{wait to alarm! at } t_0 \textit{ Until comm via alarm}] \wedge \\
C_1^W &\equiv [(\textit{wait to}) \textit{ comm via alarm! at } t_1 \rightarrow \\
&\quad \exists k\, \exists t_0 \leq t_1 : \textit{wait to } re_k? \textit{ during } (t_0 - v_k, t_0)]) : W
\end{aligned}$$

By convention, free variables in such a specification (e.g. t_1 and t_2) are universally quantified.

We prove that W tries to send a message via *alarm* iff there is an error in one of the processes P_i. Therefore we use the following specification for the P_i, using a predicate $error_i$ which represents some erroneous behaviour of P_i. For all i:

$$\begin{aligned}
(A^{P_i} &\equiv \textit{true}, \\
C^{P_i} &\equiv [error_i \leftrightarrow \exists t\, \forall t_1, t - v_i < t_1 < t : \neg(\textit{wait to}) \textit{ comm via } re_i! \textit{ at } t_1\ ]) : P_i
\end{aligned}$$

This asserts that there is an error in P_i iff there exists a period of v_i time units during which P_i is neither communicating via re_i nor waiting to communicate via re_i. Given our specifications for $P_1, \ldots, P_n$ and W, we try to prove that $P_1 \| \cdots \| P_n \| W$ has commitment $\exists k : error_k \leftrightarrow \exists t : (\textit{wait to}) \textit{ comm via alarm! at } t$. We can apply parallel composition n times and obtain $(\textit{true}, C_1^W \wedge C_2^W \wedge \bigwedge_{i=1}^n C^{P_i}) : \ldots P_1 \| \cdots \| P_n \| W \ldots$
First prove $\exists k : error_k \leftarrow \exists t : (\textit{wait to}) \textit{ comm via alarm! at } t$.

$$\begin{aligned}
& && \exists t : (\textit{wait to}) \textit{ comm via alarm! at } t \\
\rightarrow\ & \{C_1^W\} && \exists t\, \exists k\, \exists t_0 \leq t : \textit{wait to } re_k? \textit{ during } (t_0 - v_k, t_0) \\
\rightarrow\ & \{\text{definition}\} && \exists k\, \exists t_0\, \forall t_1, t_0 - v_k < t_1 < t_0 : \textit{wait to } re_k? \textit{ at } t_1 \\
\rightarrow\ & \{\text{MP, Excl}\} && \exists k\, \exists t_0\, \forall t_1, t_0 - v_k < t_1 < t_0 : \neg \textit{wait to } re_k! \textit{ at } t_1 \wedge \neg \textit{comm via } re_k \textit{ at } t_1 \\
\rightarrow\ & \{\text{definition}\} && \exists k\, \exists t_0\, \forall t_1, t_0 - v_k < t_1 < t_0 : \neg(\textit{wait to}) \textit{ comm via } re_k! \textit{ at } t_1 \\
\rightarrow\ & \{C^{P_k}\} && \exists k : error_k
\end{aligned}$$

Next we try to prove $\exists k : error_k \rightarrow \exists t : (\textit{wait to}) \textit{ comm via alarm! at } t$.
From $\exists k : error_k$ we obtain, by C^{P_k}, $\exists k \exists t \forall t_1, t - v_k < t_1 < t : \neg(\textit{wait to}) \textit{ comm via } re_k! \textit{ at } t_1$. Thus $\exists k\, \exists t\, \forall t_1, t - v_k < t_1 < t : \neg \textit{comm via } re_k \textit{ at } t_1$, but with the current specification of W nothing can be derived from this. The specification of W only expresses how W should behave if it does something on any of the channels. But then W need not do anything; even the simple program **skip** would satisfy its specification. Therefore we modify the specification for W as follows:

$$
\begin{aligned}
(A^W &\equiv \mathit{true}, \\
C_1^W &\equiv [(\mathit{wait\ to})\ \mathit{comm\ via\ alarm!\ at}\ t_1 \rightarrow \\
&\qquad \exists k\, \exists t_0 \le t_1 : \mathit{wait\ to\ re_k?\ during}\ (t_0 - v_k, t_0)] \wedge \\
C_2^W &\equiv [\exists t\, \forall t_1, t - v_k < t_1 < t : \neg \mathit{comm\ via\ re_k\ at}\ t_1 \rightarrow \\
&\qquad \exists t_0 \le t + K : \mathit{wait\ to\ alarm!\ at}\ t_0\ \mathit{Until\ comm\ via\ alarm}]) : W
\end{aligned}
$$

Note that C_0^W follows from C_2^W. Now the proof proceeds as follows, for all k,

$$
\begin{array}{lll}
 & & \mathit{error}_k \\
\rightarrow & \{C^{P_k}\} & \exists t\, \forall t_1, t - v_k < t_1 < t : \neg(\mathit{wait\ to})\ \mathit{comm\ via\ re_k!\ at}\ t_1 \\
\rightarrow & \{\text{definition}\} & \exists t\, \forall t_1, t - v_k < t_1 < t : \neg \mathit{comm\ via\ re_k\ at}\ t_1 \\
\rightarrow & \{C_2^W\} & \exists t_0 \le t + K : \mathit{wait\ to\ alarm!\ at}\ t_0\ \mathit{Until\ comm\ via\ alarm} \\
\rightarrow & \{\text{Lemma 3.1}\} & \exists t_0 : (\mathit{wait\ to})\ \mathit{comm\ via\ alarm!\ at}\ t_0
\end{array}
$$

This reasoning allows us to verify properties of $P_1 \| P_2 \| \cdots \| P_n \| W$ (and to discover incompleteness of the specification) using the specifications for the components, without knowing the implementations of these processes.

4.2 Implementing the Watchdog Timer

Next we implement process W as a parallel composition, $W \equiv W_1 \| \cdots \| W_n \| S$, where each W_i is a watchdog timer for process P_i. W_i signals process S via channel al_i as soon as there is no communication on re_i for at least v_i time units. Process S waits for a signal on any of the al_i's; after receipt of a signal it tries to send a message on *alarm* (see Fig. 2).

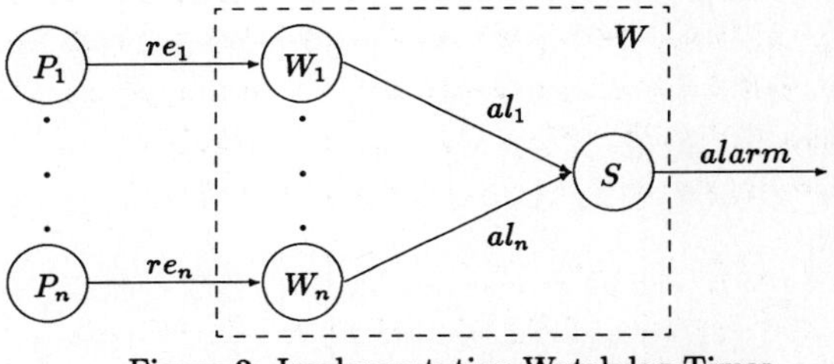

Figure 2: Implementation Watchdog Timer

We prove that the following specifications for W_i and S are sufficient to derive the specification for W. The specification for W_i expresses that W_i tries to communicate via al_i only if it has been waiting to communicate via re_i during a period of v_i time units. On the other hand, if there is a period of v_i time-units during which no communication via re_i occurs, then W_i will try to communicate via al_i within a certain time bound K_i.

$$
\begin{aligned}
(A^{W_i} &\equiv \mathit{true}, \\
C_1^{W_i} &\equiv [(\mathit{wait\ to})\ \mathit{comm\ via\ al_i!\ at}\ t_1 \rightarrow \\
&\qquad \exists t_0 \le t_1 : \mathit{wait\ to\ re_i?\ during}\ (t_0 - v_i, t_0)] \wedge \\
C_2^{W_i} &\equiv [\exists t\, \forall t_1, t - v_k < t_1 < t : \neg \mathit{comm\ via\ re_i\ at}\ t_1 \rightarrow \\
&\qquad \exists t_0 \le t + K_i : (\mathit{wait\ to})\ \mathit{comm\ via\ al_i!\ at}\ t_0]) : W_i
\end{aligned}
$$

Let K_S be a constant (e.g. denoting the maximum duration of a communication). The specification for S asserts that it tries to send a message via *alarm* only if there was a preceding communication via one of the al_k. If S does not try to communicate nor communicates via one of the al_k at a certain point of time, then within K_S time units it will wait to communicate via alarm until the actual communication can be performed.

$$
\begin{aligned}
(A^S &\equiv \textit{true}, \\
C_1^S &\equiv [(\textit{wait to})\ \textit{comm via alarm}!\ \textit{at}\ t_1 \rightarrow \exists k\, \exists t_0 \leq t_1 : \textit{comm via}\ al_k\ \textit{at}\ t_0] \wedge \\
C_2^S &\equiv [\neg\ \textit{wait to}\ al_k?\ \textit{at}\ t_2 \rightarrow \\
&\qquad \exists t_0 \leq t_2 + K_S : \textit{wait to alarm}!\ \textit{at}\ t_0\ \textit{Until comm via alarm}]) : S
\end{aligned}
$$

We show that $W_1 \| \cdots \| W_n \| S$ satisfies the specification of W. We can take, by repeated application of the parallel composition rule, the conjunction of commitments: $\bigwedge_{i=1}^{n}(C_1^{W_i} \wedge C_2^{W_i}) \wedge C_1^S \wedge \wedge C_2^S$. This implies C_1^W as follows:

$$
\begin{aligned}
& && (\textit{wait to})\ \textit{comm via alarm}!\ \textit{at}\ t_1 \\
\rightarrow\ & \{C_1^S\} && \exists k\, \exists t_3 \leq t_1 : \textit{comm via}\ al_k\ \textit{at}\ t_3 \\
\rightarrow\ & \{\text{definition}\} && \exists k\, \exists t_3 \leq t_1 : (\textit{wait to})\ \textit{comm via}\ al_k!\ \textit{at}\ t_3 \\
\rightarrow\ & \{C_1^{W_k}\} && \exists k\, \exists t_3 \leq t_1 \exists t_0 \leq t_3 : \textit{wait to}\ re_k?\ \textit{during}\ (t_0 - v_k, t_0) \\
\rightarrow\ & \{t_0 \leq t_3 \leq t_1\} && \exists k\, \exists t_0 \leq t_1 : \textit{wait to}\ re_k?\ \textit{during}\ (t_0 - v_k, t_0)
\end{aligned}
$$

Next we prove C_2^W.

$$
\begin{aligned}
& && \exists t\, \forall t_1, t - v_k < t_1 < t : \neg \textit{comm via}\ re_k\ \textit{at}\ t_1 \\
\rightarrow\ & \{C_2^{W_k}\} && \exists t_2 \leq t + K_k : (\textit{wait to})\ \textit{comm via}\ al_k!\ \textit{at}\ t_2 \\
\rightarrow\ & \{\text{definition}\} && \exists t_2 \leq t + K_k : \textit{wait to}\ al_k!\ \textit{at}\ t_2 \vee \textit{comm via}\ al_k!\ \textit{at}\ t_2 \\
\rightarrow\ & \{\text{MP, Excl}\} && \exists t_2 \leq t + K_k : \neg\ \textit{wait to}\ al_k?\ \textit{at}\ t_2 \\
\rightarrow\ & \{C_2^S\} && \exists t_2 \leq t + K_k\, \exists t_0 \leq t_2 + K_S : \textit{wait to alarm}!\ \textit{at}\ t_0\ \textit{Until comm via alarm} \\
\rightarrow\ & \{\text{calculus}\} && \exists t_0 \leq t + K_k + K_S : \textit{wait to alarm}!\ \textit{at}\ t_0\ \textit{Until comm via alarm}
\end{aligned}
$$

Hence the specification of W can be derived provided $K_k + K_S \leq K$.
The processes W_i and S can be implemented as: $W_i \equiv *[re_i? \rightarrow \textbf{skip} [] \textbf{delay}\ v_i \rightarrow al_i!]$, and $S \equiv [[]_{i=1..n}\, al_i? \rightarrow alarm!]$. With the proof system given in [Hoo89] it can be shown that these programs meet the specifications given earlier, provided: K_S is greater than the maximum duration of a communication via al_i, and K_i is greater than the overhead for a guarded command to start the execution of the delay branch in case of a time-out.

4.3 Watchdog Handlers on a Uniprocessor

In this section we give a possible implementation of the processes P_i. We assume that each P_i is executed on a single processor and that it has to perform a certain task given by a program B_i. When B_i is executing continuously for at least v_i time units this is considered to be an error. For instance, if B_i models a keyboard handler then an error indicates that there is no time left to store characters in a buffer. Such errors can be detected by a watchdog handler WH_i which executes in parallel with B_i on the same processor and which tries to send signals via channel re_i. We prove that if WH_i has a lower priority than B_i, then WH_i will try to send via re_i at least once every v_i time units iff no error occurs in B_i. Given the specifications for B_i and WH_i below, we show that $\ll$ **prio** 2 (B_i) ||| **prio** 1 $(WH_i) \gg$ satisfies the specification of P_i given earlier.

Suppose **prio** 2 (B_i) satisfies the following specification, where the assumption expresses that if any other statement on the same processor executes at a nonscheduling point (with priority ∞), then within a constant time K_c no statement in the environment is executing or some statement executes with a priority lower than 2.

$$\begin{aligned}
(A^{B_i} &\equiv exec(t,\infty) \rightarrow \exists t_1, t < t_1 \leq t + K_c : \neg exec(t_1,p) \vee (exec(t_1,p) \wedge p < 2),\\
C_1^{B_i} &\equiv [error_i \rightarrow \exists t\, \forall t_1, t - v_i < t_1 < t : exec(t_1,2)] \wedge\\
C_2^{B_i} &\equiv [\exists t\, \forall t_1, t - v_i < t_1 < t : exec(t_1,p) \rightarrow error_i]) :\\
&\quad \textbf{prio } 2\ (B_i)
\end{aligned}$$

The specification for the watchdog handler **prio** $1(WH_i)$ commits that it will not execute continuously at nonscheduling points for more than K_c time units (hence satisfying A^{B_i}) and if it waits to communicate, then it waits with priority 1. Finally, if it does not communicate nor waits to communicate via re_i, then it is not executing but requesting processor time.

$$\begin{aligned}
(A^{WH_i} &\equiv true,\\
C_1^{WH_i} &\equiv A^{B_i} \wedge\\
C_2^{WH_i} &\equiv [(wait\ to)\ comm\ via\ re_i!\ at\ t_1 \rightarrow (wait\ to)\ comm\ via\ re_i!\ at\ t_1\ with\ prio\ 1] \wedge\\
C_3^{WH_i} &\equiv [\neg(wait\ to)\ comm\ via\ re_i!\ at\ t_2 \rightarrow \neg exec(t_2,p) \wedge req(t_2,p)]) :\\
&\quad \textbf{prio } 1\ (WH_i)
\end{aligned}$$

To derive the specification for P_i, we first prove

$$\begin{aligned}
(A^i &\equiv \forall t\, \forall p : \neg exec(t,p),\\
C_1^i &\equiv [error_i \rightarrow \exists t\, \forall t_1, t - v_i < t_1 < t : \neg(wait\ to)\ comm\ via\ re_i!\ at\ t_1\ ] \wedge\\
C_2^i &\equiv [\exists t\, \forall t_1, t - v_i < t_1 < t : \neg(wait\ to)\ comm\ via\ re_i!\ at\ t_1 \rightarrow\\
&\qquad (error_i \vee \exists t\, \forall t_1, t - v_i < t_1 < t : \neg exec(t_1,p) \wedge req(t_1,p))]) :\\
&\quad \textbf{prio } 2\ (B_i) \mid\mid\mid \textbf{prio } 1\ (WH_i)
\end{aligned}$$

In this formula, assumption A^i expresses that no other statement is executing on the same processor. To derive this specification, first consider assumption A^{B_i} and prove:
$A^i[e_1/exec] \wedge C_1^{WH_i}[e_2/exec] \wedge (e_1 \vee e_2 \leftrightarrow exec) \rightarrow A^{B_i}$.
From $A^i[e_1/exec]$ which equals $\forall t\, \forall p : \neg e_1(t,p)$, we obtain $e_2 \leftrightarrow exec$. Then it is easy to see that $C_1^{WH_i}[e_2/exec] \wedge (e_2 \leftrightarrow exec) \rightarrow A^{B_i}$. For the commitments we have to prove:
$(C_1^{B_i} \wedge C_2^{B_i})[e_1/exec] \wedge C_2^{WH_i} \wedge C_3^{WH_i}[e_2/exec, r_2/req] \wedge (e_1 \vee e_2 \leftrightarrow exec) \wedge (r_1 \vee r_2 \leftrightarrow req) \rightarrow (C_1^i \wedge C_2^i)$. First consider C_1^i:

$$\begin{aligned}
& error_i\\
\rightarrow\ & \{C_1^{B_i}[e_1/exec]\}\ \ \exists t\, \forall t_1, t - v_i < t_1 < t : e_1(t_1,2)
\end{aligned}$$

$$\begin{array}{lll}
\to & \{e_1 \to exec\} & \exists t\,\forall t_1, t - v_i < t_1 < t : exec(t_1, 2) \\
\to & \{\text{Prio}\} & \exists t\,\forall t_1, t - v_i < t_1 < t : \neg(wait\ to)\ comm\ via\ re_i!\ at\ t_1\ with\ prio\ 1 \\
\to & \{C_2^{WH_i}\} & \exists t\,\forall t_1, t - v_i < t_1 < t : \neg(wait\ to)\ comm\ via\ re_i!\ at\ t_1
\end{array}$$

Next prove C_2^i:

$$\begin{array}{lll}
 & & \exists t\,\forall t_1, t - v_i < t_1 < t : \neg(wait\ to)\ comm\ via\ re_i!\ at\ t_1 \\
\to & \{C_3^{WH_i}[e_2/exec, r_2/req]\} & \exists t\,\forall t_1, t - v_i < t_1 < t : \neg e_2(t_1,p) \wedge r_2(t_1,p) \\
\to & \{\neg e_2 \to \neg exec \vee e_1, r_2 \to req\} & \exists t\,\forall t_1, t - v_i < t_1 < t : (\neg exec(t_1,p) \vee e_1(t_1,p)) \wedge req(t_1,p) \\
\to & \{\text{calculus}\} & \exists t\,\forall t_1, t - v_i < t_1 < t : e_1(t_1,p) \vee \\
 & & \exists t\,\forall t_1, t - v_i < t_1 < t : (\neg exec(t_1,p) \wedge req(t_1,p)) \\
\to & \{C_2^{B_i}[e_1/exec]\} & error_i \vee \exists t\,\forall t_1, t - v_i < t_1 < t : \neg exec(t_1,p) \wedge req(t_1,p)
\end{array}$$

Now given the specification for **prio** 2 (B_i) ||| **prio** 1 (WH_i), the rule for $\ll \ldots \gg$-introduction allows us to drop the assumption $A^i \equiv \forall t\,\forall p : \neg exec(t,p)$, because the brackets express that no other processes are executing on the same processor. Furthermore, the commitment is extended with $\forall t\,\forall p : req(t,p) \to exec(t,p)$ expressing that statements are requesting execution time only if the processor is busy executing an other statement. Observe that with this assertion $\neg exec(t_1,p) \wedge req(t_1,p)$ in C_2^i implies $false$, and thus leads to: $\exists t\,\forall t_1, t - v_i < t_1 < t : \neg(wait\ to)\ comm\ via\ re_i!\ at\ t_1 \ \to error_i$

Hence we obtain the following specification for P_i:

$$\begin{array}{lll}
(A^{P_i} & \equiv & true, \\
C^{P_i} & \equiv & [error_i \leftrightarrow \exists t\,\forall t_1, t - v_i < t_1 < t : \neg(wait\ to)\ comm\ via\ re_i!\ at\ t_1\ ]) : \\
 & & \ll \textbf{prio}\ 2\ (B_i)\ |||\ \textbf{prio}\ 1\ (WH_i) \gg
\end{array}$$

This is exactly the specification which has been used in section 4.1.

It can be shown that **prio** 1 $(*[re_i! \to$ **skip**$])$ is a possible implementation of **prio** 1 (WH_i), provided K_c is greater than the maximum duration of a communication via re_i.

5 State of the Art and Conclusion

In particular for concurrent programs communicating via message passing, one can observe a development from non-compositional proof methods which require the (final) program text for their application, such as [AFR80,LG81], towards compositional theories, e.g. [CH81, Sou84,Zwi88] (see [HdR86] for an overview of this development). Whereas these methods verify only safety properties, with linear temporal logic [Pnu77,MP82] also liveness (progress) properties can be verified. Compositional proof systems for temporal logic have been given in [BKP84,NDGO86].

All these methods are not designed to verify and specify real-time properties. Now an obvious approach towards a verification theory for real-time programs is to adapt and extend an already existing method which does not incorporate any notion of time. For instance, in traditional linear temporal logic safety and liveness properties are expressed by means of a qualitative notion of time (e.g. "eventually", "henceforth", "until"). In order to express real-time constraints, extensions of this logic have been proposed [Koy89,BH81,SL87] which also includes a quantitative notion of time (e.g. "eventually within 5 time units", "always after 7 time units"). These extensions have been applied to the specification of real-time communication properties of a transmission medium [KVR83] and the verification of local area network protocols [SPE84]. A compositional proof theory for real-time distributed message passing using an assertion language based on real-time temporal logic has been given in [HW89].

Similarly, real-time extensions have been formulated for other methods. Zwarico and Lee [ZL85] have adapted Hoare's trace model [Hoa85] (with one invariant and a satisfaction relation) to real-time. Nested parallelism is not allowed in their programming language, a restricted version of sequential composition is used, and there is no explicit mechanism for expressing time constraints. A review of formal description techniques for real-time systems can be found in [JG88].

In this paper we have discussed a compositional proof system for real-time distributed message passing in which assumptions can be made about the behaviour of the environment in the style of [MC81,ZREB84]. This formalism has been used for the top-down design of a watchdog timer, thus illustrating the verify-while-develop paradigm. The main idea of the method is that suitable assumptions about the environment reduce the immense number of possible behaviours of complex real-time systems. Although not dealing with real-time, Misra and Chandy [MC81] have used the advantages of assumptions in the hierarchical design and verification of distributed processes with message passing. They proposed a rule for parallel composition and demonstrated their method on several examples. In [ZREB84] these ideas are formalized, resulting in a compositional proof system for assumption/commitment based specifications. The examples in [Oss83] show that the Misra-Chandy method is easy to use and leads to simple and natural correctness proofs. Pandya [Pan88] extends this formalism to asynchronous communication and progress properties.

Our method can be extended to various other communication mechanisms such as several versions of asynchronous communication and broadcast. For instance, we are working on a real-time communication protocol for channels which can loose, reorder and duplicate messages but which satisfy certain real-time constraints such as a maximum message lifetime. We realize, however, that numerous programming language concepts are not treated. This leaves us with a wealth of non-real-time methods which are possible candidates for ramification with real-time.

References

[AFR80] K.R. Apt, N. Francez, and W.P. de Roever. A proof system for Communicating Sequential Processes. *TOPLAS*, 2:359–385, 1980.

[BH81] A. Bernstein and P.K. Harter, Jr. Proving real-time properties of programs with temporal logic. In *Proc. 8th Symposium on Operating System Principles*, pages 1–11, 1981.

[BKP84] H. Barringer, R. Kuiper, and A. Pnueli. Now you may compose temporal logic specifications. In *Proc. 16th Symposium on Theory of Computing*, pages 51–63, 1984.

[CH81] Zhou Chao Chen and C.A.R. Hoare. Partial correctness of Communicating Sequential Processes. In *Proc. IEEE Int. Conf. on Distr. Computing Systems*, pages 1–12, 1981.

[dR85] W.P. de Roever. The quest for compositionality - a survey of assertion-based proof systems for concurrent programs, Part I: concurrency based on shared variables. In *Proc. IFIP Working Conference 1985: The role of abstract models in computer science*, pages 181–207. North-Holland, 1985.

[HdR86] J. Hooman and W.P. de Roever. The quest goes on: a survey of proof systems for partial correctness of CSP. In *Current Trends in Concurrency*, pages 343–395. LNCS 224, 1986.

[Hoa78] C.A.R. Hoare. Communicating Sequential Processes. *CACM*, 21(8):666–677, 1978.

[Hoa85] C.A.R. Hoare. *Communicating Sequential Processes.* Prentice-Hall, 1985.

[Hoo89] J. Hooman. Compositional specification and verification of distributed real-time systems. Technical report, Eindhoven Univ. of Technology, The Netherlands, 1989.

[HP85] D. Harel and A. Pnueli. On the development of reactive systems. *Logics and Models of Concurrent Systems*, pages 477–498. NATO, ASI-13, 1985.

[HW89] J. Hooman and J. Widom. A temporal-logic based compositional proof system for real-time message passing. In *Parallel Architectures and Languages Europe.* LNCS, 1989.

[JG88] M. Joseph and A. Goswami. Formal description of real-time systems: a review. Research Report RR129, Department of Computer Science, Univ. of Warwick, 1988.

[Koy89] R. Koymans. *Specifying Message Passing and Time-Critical Systems with Temporal Logic.* PhD thesis, Eindhoven Univ. of Technology, The Netherlands, 1989.

[KSR+88] R. Koymans, R.K. Shyamasundar, W.P. de Roever, R. Gerth, and S. Arun-Kumar. Compositional semantics for real-time distributed computing. *Information and Computation*, 79(3):210–256, 1988.

[KVR83] R. Koymans, J. Vytopyl, and W.P. de Roever. Real-time programming and asynchronous message passing. In *Proc. 2nd PODC*, pages 187–197, 1983.

[LG81] G.M. Levin and D. Gries. A proof technique for Communicating Sequential Processes. *Acta Informatica*, 15:281–302, 1981.

[MC81] J. Misra and K.M. Chandy. Proofs of networks of processes. *IEEE Transactions on Software Engineering*, 7(7):417–426, 1981.

[MP82] Z. Manna and A. Pnueli. Verification of concurrent programs: a temporal proof system. In *Foundations of Computer Science IV, Distributed Systems: Part 2*, volume 159 of *Mathematical Centre Tracts*, pages 163–255, 1982.

[NDGO86] V. Nguyen, A. Demers, D. Gries, and S. Owicki. A model and temporal proof system for networks of processes. *Distributed Computing*, 1(1):7–25, 1986.

[Occ88] INMOS Limited. OCCAM *2 Reference Manual*, 1988.

[OG76] S. Owicki and D. Gries. An axiomatic proof technique for parallel programs. *Acta Informatica*, 6:319,340, 1976.

[Oss83] M. Ossefort. Correctness proofs of communicating processes: Three illustrative examples from the literature. *TOPLAS*, 5(4):620–640, 1983.

[Pan88] Paritosh Pandya. Compositional verification of distributed programs. Technical Report CS-88/3 (Ph.D. Thesis), Tata Institute of Fundamental Research, Bombay, India, 1988.

[Pnu77] A. Pnueli. The temporal logic of programs. In *Proc. 18th FOCS*, pages 46–57, 1977.

[SL87] A.U. Shankar and S.S. Lam. Time-dependent distributed systems: proving safety, liveness and real-time properties. *Distributed Computing*, 2:61–79, 1987.

[Sou84] N. Soundararajan. Axiomatic semantics for CSP. *TOPLAS*, 6(4):647–662, 1984.

[SPE84] D.E. Shasha, A. Pnueli, and W. Ewald. Temporal verification of carrier-sense local area network protocols. In *Proc. 11th POPL*, pages 54–65, 1984.

[ZL85] A. Zwarico and I. Lee. Proving a network of real-time processes correct. In *Proc. IEEE Real-Time Systems Symposium*, pages 169–177, 1985.

[ZREB84] J. Zwiers, W.P. de Roever, and P. van Emde Boas. Compositionality and concurrent networks: soundness and completeness of a proofsystem. Technical Report 57, Univ. of Nijmegen, The Netherlands, 1984.

[Zwi88] J. Zwiers. *Compositionality, Concurrency and Partial Correctness: Proof theories for networks of processes and their relationship.* LNCS 321, 1988.

Session 2:

Process Algebra Applications

Protocol Specification, Testing, and Verification, IX
E. Brinksma, G. Scollo and C.A. Vissers (Editors)
Elsevier Science Publishers B.V. (North-Holland)

A Verification Method for LOTOS Specifications and its application

Norio Shiratori, Hiroaki Kaminaga, Kaoru Takahashi, and Shoichi Noguchi

Research Institute of Electrical Communication
Tohoku University
2-1-1, Katahira, Aoba-ku, Sendai, 980 Japan

This paper proposes a verification method for the observational equivalence between two systems specified in LOTOS. Here, LOTOS is an FDT (Formal Description Technique) developed within ISO for OSI (Open Systems Interconnection). We first introduce two equivalence relations based on the observational equivalence, and discuss the properties based on the observational equivalence. Then, we give an effective verification method for the observational equivalence. As an application of the proposed method, an example verifying the consistency between the service definition and the protocol specification of a simple communication protocol is given.

1. Introduction

As communication systems are developing and getting more complicated, informal specifications of communication protocols are causing an increasingly large number of errors or undesired behaviours. To facilitate the design of correct protocols, several Formal Description Techniques (FDTs) have been developed and employed. FDTs play important roles at each stage of protocol design and implementation [1] [2] . LOTOS (Language of Temporal Ordering Specification) [3]-[5] is an FDT developed within ISO particularly for the Open Systems Interconnection (OSI) computer network architecture. LOTOS provides a formally well-defined basis for verification. The verification of two systems specified in LOTOS, for example the verification of consistency between the service definition and the protocol specification of a communication protocol, can be considered using the notion of *observational equivalence.*

In this paper, we propose a verification method for the observational equivalence between two systems specified in LOTOS. We first introduce two equivalence relations based on the weak bisimulation equivalence which is defined in [3], (1) a *k*-weak bisimulation equivalence and (2) a quasi-strong bisimulation equivalence. Then, using these two equivalence relations, we show that we can easily check the weak bisimulation equivalence between two systems specified in LOTOS. Also, we give an effective verification method for bisimulation equivalence. In this method, we first transform LOTOS specifications into their labelled transition systems, which are the models of the system specifications. Secondly, we transform the labelled transition systems into *reduced normal forms.* A reduced normal form is a labelled transition system which preserves the equivalence and has the least number of states and transitions. Finally, we check the isomorphism between the reduced normal forms. Two LOTOS specifications whose reduced normal forms are isomorphic are observationally equivalent.

In Section 2, we summarize the outline of LOTOS, especially the concepts concerning observational equivalence. In Section 3, we discuss the equivalence in LOTOS. In Section 4, we introduce a reduced normal form of a finite transition system and give a transformation procedure. In Section 5, we give a simple example of verification. Finally, Section 6 is the conclusion of this paper and also gives some indications about future work.

2. Preliminaries [3] - [5]

In this section, the concepts of LOTOS used in this paper are summarized.

2.1. The main features of LOTOS

In LOTOS a distributed and concurrent system is described in terms of a set of interacting *processes*. A process is an abstract entity that is able to perform *internal events* and communicates with other processes via *events* at communication points called *gates*. An event is an elementary unit of synchronization among processes. The static picture of a process can be imagined as that of a black box capable of communication with other processes. The mechanisms inside this box are not observable. Thus, all events occurring inside a process (i.e. internal events) are unobservable and denoted by **i**. In LOTOS, processes can be defined by the temporal relations between events in the externally observable behaviour of processes, and they are expressed by *behaviour expressions*. The formation rules of the behaviour expressions are essential parts of LOTOS, and are based on a modification of the Calculus of Communicating Systems (CCS) [6]. In the case that an event involves exchange of data, the description of data structures and value expressions is based on the algebraic specification of abstract data types (ADTs) [7] - [10] .

LOTOS has the following two models ; (a) *labelled transition systems* as models for behaviour expressions, and (b) *many sorted algebras* as models for data types. The behaviour expression is not dependent upon the way data types are interpreted. In this paper, we mainly discuss about the behaviour expressions and the labelled transition systems.

A behaviour expression is produced by applying an operator to other behaviour expressions. There are several operators in LOTOS to describe behaviour expressions as follows.

(i) *action prefix* (denoted by ';')

The behavior of $a;B$ is considered to be the event a followed by the behaviour of B, where B is a behaviour expression.

(ii) *choice* (denoted by '[ ]')

The behavior of $B1$ [ ] $B2$ will be the behaviour of either $B1$ or $B2$, where $B1$ and $B2$ are behaviour expressions.

(iii) *inaction* (denoted by '**stop**')

stop means that a process can execute no event.

(iv) *parallel composition* (denoted by '$|[g_1, g_2, \cdots g_n]|$')

The behavior of $B1 |[g_1, g_2, \cdots g_n]| B2$ will be a composition in which $B1$ and $B2$ must synchronize with respect to the gates $g_1, g_2, \cdots g_n$.

(v) In addition to the four operators listed above, there are operations such as *hiding, instantiation, guarding, enabling, disabling, successful termination.*

2.2. A labelled transition system

Formal models of the LOTOS specifications (behaviour expressions) are labelled transition systems.

[Definition 1]

A labelled transition system LTS is a 4-tuple $\langle S, A, T, s_0 \rangle$, where

(a) S is a non-empty set, whose elements are referred to as *states* ;

(b) A is a set, whose elements are referred to as *events* (or *actions*) ;

(c) T is a set of *transition relations*, which contains precisely one relation $-a\rightarrow \subseteq S\times S$ for each $a\in A$;

(d) $s_0\in S$ is *the initial state of* LTS.

An element of a transition relation is called *a transition*.

If S and A are finite, LTS is called *a finite labelled transition system*. □

[Definition 2]

Two labelled transition systems with identical event sets $LTS1=\langle S_1, A, T_1, s_{01}\rangle$ and $LTS2=\langle S_2, A, T_2, s_{02}\rangle$ are *isomorphic* if there exists a one-to-one function $f: S_1\rightarrow S_2$ such that :

(a) $s_{11}-a\rightarrow s_{12}$ if and only if $f(s_{11})-a\rightarrow f(s_{12})$ for all $a\in A$, $s_{11}, s_{12}\in S_1$;

(b) $f(s_{01}) = s_{02}$. □

Isomorphic classes of labelled transition systems can be assumed as rudimentary models for the behaviour of communicating processes. In a labelled transition system, states (depicted by nodes) are labelled by behaviour expressions, and transitions (depicted by arcs) are labelled by events. The axioms and inference rules of the operational semantics of LOTOS [3] allow the construction of the transition relations. Therefore, we can build a labelled transition system from a given behaviour expression by applying axioms and inference rules to the behaviour expression.

2.3. Equivalence in LOTOS

Equivalence in LOTOS is called *observational equivalence*. The idea of observational equivalence, originally proposed in [6] for CCS " agents ", is that two processes are considered equivalent whenever we cannot distinguish them by any finite external observation. External observations are formalized by the observable sequence relation ' $=\Rightarrow$ '.

[Definition 3]

Let $LTS=\langle S, A, T, s_0\rangle$ be a labelled transition system.

(a) Let $s, s'\in S$, $a_1, \cdots, a_n\in A$ and t denote a string $a_1\cdots a_n$ of events. The relation $-t\rightarrow$ is defined as the obvious extension of the transition relation to event sequences :

$s-t\rightarrow s'$ if and only if there exist $s_0,\cdots,s_n\in S$ such that $s=s_0-a_1\rightarrow s_1, \cdots,$ $s_{n-1}-a_n\rightarrow s_n=s'$. In particular, $s-\varepsilon\rightarrow s$ for n=0, where ε is the empty string.

(b) Let $s,s'\in S$, $a_1,\cdots,a_n\in A-\{\mathrm{i}\}$ and t denote a string $a_1\cdots a_n$ of observable events, and let i^n denote a sequence of n ($n\geqq 0$) i-events. The relation $s=t\Rightarrow s'$ is defined as follows :

$s=t\Rightarrow s'$ if and only if there exist a sequence $\mathrm{i}^{m_0} a_1 \mathrm{i}^{m_1} \cdots a_n \mathrm{i}^{m_n}$ of events such that $s-\mathrm{i}^{m_0} a_1 \mathrm{i}^{m_1}\cdots a_n \mathrm{i}^{m_n}\rightarrow s'$. This implies that $s=\varepsilon\Rightarrow s'$ whenever $s-\mathrm{i}^n\rightarrow s'$, and that $s=\varepsilon\Rightarrow s$ for any s. □

By using the observable sequence relation, the notion of weak bisimulation is defined. The theory of bisimulation was originally proposed by Park [17], and includes observational equivalence as a special case.

[Definition 4]

Let $LTS1=\langle S_1, A, T_1, s_{01}\rangle$ and $LTS2=\langle S_2, A, T_2, s_{02}\rangle$ be labelled transition systems and let $S=S_1\cup S_2$. A relation $\mathbf{R}\subseteq S\times S$ is *a weak bisimulation relation* if for every pair $(s_1, s_2)\in\mathbf{R}$ and every string $t\in(A-\{\mathrm{i}\})^*$ of observable events :

(a) whenever $s_1=t\Rightarrow s_1'$, for some $s_2'\in S$: $s_2=t\Rightarrow s_2'$ and $(s_1', s_2')\in\mathbf{R}$;

(b) whenever $s_2=t\Rightarrow s_2'$, for some $s_1'\in S$: $s_1=t\Rightarrow s_1'$ and $(s_1', s_2')\in\mathbf{R}$. □

[Definition 5]

Let $B1$ and $B2$ be behaviour expressions, and let $LTS1=\langle S_1, A, T_1, s_{01}\rangle$ and $LTS2=\langle S_2, A, T_2, s_{02}\rangle$ be their labelled transition systems, respectively. Let $S=S_1\cup S_2$. Two states s_1 and s_2 *are weak bisimulation equivalent*, written $s_1\approx s_2$, if there exists a weak bisimulation relation $\mathbf{R}\subseteq S\times S$ such that $s_1\mathbf{R}s_2$. $LTS1$ and

LTS2 are weak bisimulation equivalent, written $LTS1 \approx LTS2$, if $s_{01} \approx s_{02}$. $B1$ and $B2$ *are weak bisimulation equivalent*, written $B1 \approx B2$, if and only if $LTS1 \approx LTS2$. □

3. Properties of the weak bisimulation equivalence

In this section, we discuss the properties of the weak bisimulation equivalence. All proofs are omitted for lack of space. The weak bisimulation equivalence is also discussed in [3] and [12].

3.1. A k-weak bisimulation equivalence

Although a labelled transition system is finite, if it contains *a loop*, the set of its event sequences is not finite. In this case, we can not easily check the equivalence based on the definition of weak bisimulation equivalence. So we introduce an equivalence relation which restricts the length of a string of observable events.

[Definition 6]

Let $LTS = \langle S, A, T, s_0 \rangle$ be a labelled transition system and k be a positive integer. A relation $\mathbf{R}_k \subseteq S \times S$ is *a k-weak bisimulation relation* if for every pair $(s_1, s_2) \in \mathbf{R}_k$ and every string $t \in (A - \{\mathbf{i}\})^*$ of observable events such that $|t| \leqq k$:

(a) whenever $s_1 = t \Rightarrow s_1'$, for some $s_2' \in S$: $s_2 = t \Rightarrow s_2'$ and $(s_1', s_2') \in \mathbf{R}_k$;

(b) whenever $s_2 = t \Rightarrow s_2'$, for some $s_1' \in S$: $s_1 = t \Rightarrow s_1'$ and $(s_1', s_2') \in \mathbf{R}_k$,

where $|t|$ is the length of the string t (i.e. the number of events in t). In particular, for $k=1$ $s_1 = t \Rightarrow s_1'$ means $s_1 = a \Rightarrow s_1'$ ($a \in A - \{\mathbf{i}\}$) or $s_1 = \varepsilon \Rightarrow s_1'$. □

[Definition 7]

Let $LTS1 = \langle S_1, A, T_1, s_{01} \rangle$ and $LTS2 = \langle S_2, A, T_2, s_{02} \rangle$ be labelled transition systems, and let $S = S_1 \cup S_2$ and k be a positive integer. Two states s_1 and s_2 are *k-weak bisimulation equivalent*, written $s_1 \approx^{(k)} s_2$, if there exists a k-weak bisimulation relation $\mathbf{R}_k \subseteq S \times S$ such that $s_1 \mathbf{R}_k s_2$. $LTS1$ and $LTS2$ are *k-weak bisimulation equivalent*, written $LTS1 \approx^{(k)} LTS2$, if $s_{01} \approx^{(k)} s_{02}$. □

k-weak bisimulation equivalence has the following property.

[Proposition 1]

Let k be a positive integer. Two labelled transition systems $LTS1$ and $LTS2$ are k-weak bisimulation equivalent if and only if $LTS1$ and $LTS2$ are $k+1$-weak bisimulation equivalent. □

Proposition 1 means that $LTS1 \approx^{(1)} LTS2$ iff $LTS1 \approx^{(2)} LTS2$, $LTS1 \approx^{(2)} LTS2$ iff $LTS1 \approx^{(3)} LTS2$, ……. Hence, the following theorem holds.

[Theorem 2]

Let k be a positive integer. Two labelled transition systems $LTS1$ and $LTS2$ are k-weak bisimulation equivalent if and only if $LTS1$ and $LTS2$ are weak bisimulation equivalent. □

In particular, for $k=1$ we have the following corollary.

[Corollary 3]

Two labelled transition systems $LTS1$ and $LTS2$ are 1-weak bisimulation equivalent if and only if $LTS1$ and $LTS2$ are weak bisimulation equivalent. □

By corollary 3, we can check a weak bisimulation equivalence between two labelled transition systems by using the definition of 1-weak bisimulation equivalence.

3.2 A quasi-strong bisimulation equivalence

In this subsection, we introduce a definition of the equivalence which is not based on the events' sequence but based on any single event including the internal event **i**.

[Definition 8]

Let $LTS1 = \langle S_1, A, T_1, s_{01} \rangle$ and $LTS2 = \langle S_2, A, T_2, s_{02} \rangle$ be labelled transition systems. A relation $\mathbf{Q}\subseteq S\times S$ is *a quasi-strong bisimulation relation* if for any pair $(s_1,s_2)\in\mathbf{Q}$ and any $a\in(A-\{\mathrm{i}\})\cup\{\lambda\}$:

(a) whenever $s_1-a\rightarrow s_1'$ then, for some $s_2'\in S$: $s_2-a\rightarrow s_2'$ and $(s_1',s_2')\in\mathbf{Q}$;

(b) whenever $s_2-a\rightarrow s_2'$ then, for some $s_1'\in S$: $s_1-a\rightarrow s_1'$ and $(s_1',s_2')\in\mathbf{Q}$,

where $s-\lambda\rightarrow s'$ means $s-\mathrm{i}\rightarrow s'$ or $s=s'$. □

[Definition 9]

Let $B1$ and $B2$ be behaviour expressions, and let $LTS1=\langle S_1, A, T_1, s_{01}\rangle$ and $LTS2=\langle S_2, A, T_2, s_{02}\rangle$ be their labelled transition systems, respectively. Two states s_1 and s_2 *are quasi-strong bisimulation equivalent*, written $s_1\sim s_2$, if there exists a quasi-strong bisimulation relation $\mathbf{Q}\subseteq S\times S$ such that $s_1\mathbf{Q}s_2$, where $S=S_1\cup S_1$. $LTS1$ and $LTS2$ *are quasi-strong bisimulation equivalent*, written $LTS1\sim LTS2$, if $s_{01}\sim s_{02}$. $B1$ and $B2$ *are quasi-strong bisimulation equivalent*, written $B1\sim B2$, if and only if $LTS1\sim LTS2$. □

A quasi-strong bisimulation equivalence is a little different from the strong equivalence of [6] and the strong bisimulation equivalence of [12]. A quasi-strong bisimulation equivalence is weaker than the strong bisimulation equivalence. Namely, two behaviour expressions are quasi-strong bisimulation equivalent if they are strong bisimulation equivalent, but not vice versa. For example, the following behaviour expressions are quasi-strong bisimulation equivalent, but not strong bisimulation equivalent to each other.

$B1 = a;b;\mathbf{stop}[\,]a;\mathrm{i};b;\mathbf{stop}$, $B2 = a;b;\mathbf{stop}[\,]\mathrm{i};a;b;\mathbf{stop}$,

$B3 = a;(b;\mathbf{stop}[\,]\mathrm{i};b;\mathbf{stop})$, $B4 = a;b;\mathbf{stop}$.

Quasi-strong bisimulation equivalence is a sufficient condition for *1*-weak bisimulation equivalence between two labelled transition systems, but it is not a necessary condition. We transform a labelled transition system so that we can check the *1*-weak bisimulation equivalence between two labelled transition systems by using the quasi-strong bisimulation equivalence.

[Definition 10]

Let $LTS=\langle S, A, T, s_0\rangle$ be a labelled transition system. *The Q-closure of LTS* is a labelled transition system $LTS'=\langle S, A, T\cup T', s_0\rangle$ such that
$T'=\{-a\rightarrow \mid\ =\varepsilon\Rightarrow-a\rightarrow=\varepsilon\Rightarrow$ in LTS, following Definition 3(b) $\}$. □

The Q-closure of a labelled transition system has the following property.

[Proposition 4]

Let $LTS=\langle S, A, T, s_0\rangle$ be a labelled transition system and let $LTS'=\langle S, A, T\cup T', s_0\rangle$ be the Q-closure of LTS. Two states s_1 and s_2 are quasi-strong bisimulation equivalent in LTS' if and only if s_1 and s_2 are *1*-weak bisimulation equivalent in LTS. □

To determine whether two states are quasi-strong equivalent or not, for the case where LTS is finite, we define the following relation according to [6].

[Definition 11]

Let S be a finite set of states and A be a finite set of events. Then, a family of relations $\mathbf{Q}^{(n)}\subseteq S\times S$ is defined inductively as follows.

For any $(s_1,s_2)\in S\times S$:

$s_1\mathbf{Q}^{(0)}s_2$ is always true, and

$s_1\mathbf{Q}^{(n+1)}s_2$ if for all $a\in(A\text{-}\{\mathrm{i}\})\cup\{\lambda\}$

(a) whenever $s_1-a\rightarrow s_1'$, for some $s_2'\in S$: $s_2-a\rightarrow s_2'$ and $s_1'\mathbf{Q}^{(n)}s_2'$;

(b) whenever $s_2-a\rightarrow s_2'$, for some $s_1'\in S$: $s_1-a\rightarrow s_1'$ and $s_1'\mathbf{Q}^{(n)}s_2'$. □

Since S and A are finite, there exist $\mathbf{Q}^{(m)}$ such that $\mathbf{Q}^{(0)}\supsetneq\mathbf{Q}^{(1)}\supsetneq\cdots\supsetneq\mathbf{Q}^{(m)}=\mathbf{Q}^{(m+k)}$ for all $k(\geqq 1)$. Each is an equivalence relation. For $\mathbf{Q}^{(m)}$, the following proposition holds.

[Proposition 5]

Let $LTS1=\langle S_1, A, T_1, s_{01}\rangle$ and $LTS2=\langle S_2, A, T_2, s_{02}\rangle$ be labelled transition systems and let $\mathbf{Q}$ be a quasi-strong bisimulation relation such that $s_{01}\mathbf{Q}s_{02}$. For any two states s_1 and s_2, $s_1\mathbf{Q}s_2$ if and only if $s_1\mathbf{Q}^{(m)}s_2$. □

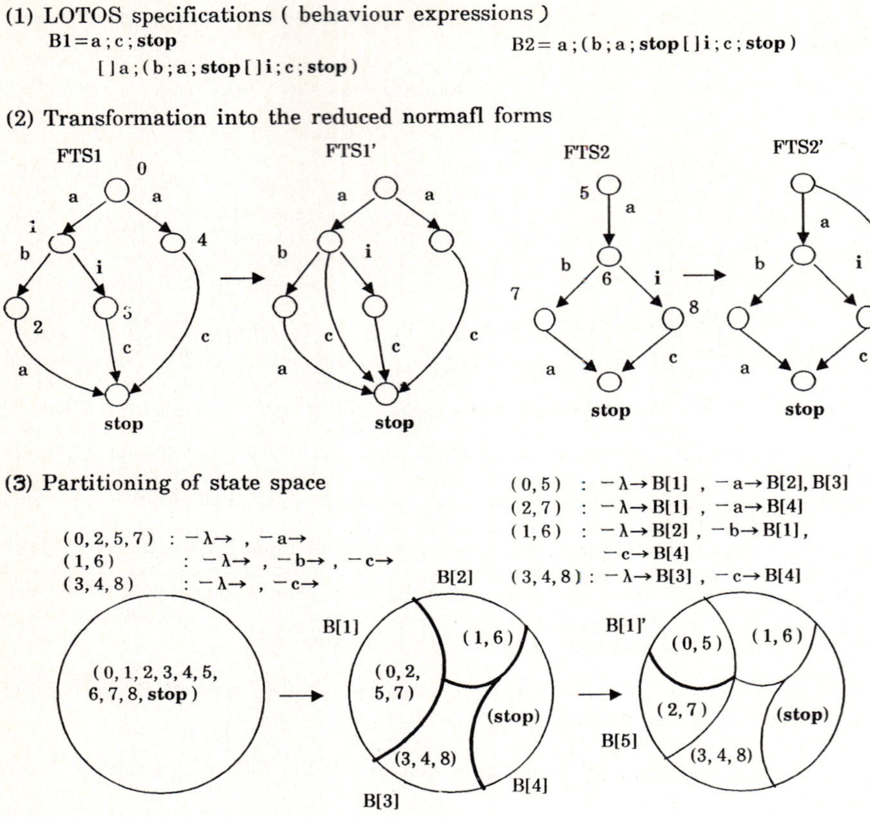

Fig. 1 An example of the verification of the weak bisimulation equivalence

If not $s_1 \mathbf{Q} s_2$, then *not* $s_1 \mathbf{Q}^{(n)} s_2$ for some $\mathbf{Q}^{(n)}$ $(0 \leqq n \leqq m)$.

[An example of the verification]

In **Fig.1**, we give a simple example of the verification of the weak bisimulation equivalence. At first, two behaviour expressions *B1* and *B2* are transformed into their labelled transition systems *FTS1* and *FTS2*. Secondly, *FTS1* and *FTS2* are transformed into their Q-closures *FTS1'* and *FTS2'*. Then the state space of *FTS1'* and *FTS2'* are partitioned into the equivalence classes based on the relation $\mathbf{Q}^{(n)}$ as follows. The relation $\mathbf{Q}^{(0)}$ gives the initial partition п={ *S* (= { 0, 1, 2, 3, 4, 5, 6, 7, 8, **stop** }) }. The block *S* is split into *B[1]*, *B[2]*, *B[3]* and *B[4]* by the relation $\mathbf{Q}^{(1)}$. Then the relation $\mathbf{Q}^{(2)}$ partitions *B[1]* into *B[1]'* and *B[5]*. The relation $\mathbf{Q}^{(3)}$ partitions no more blocks. Hence $\mathbf{Q}^{(2)} = \mathbf{Q}^{(3)} = \cdots$ $(m=2)$ and the final partition is п'= { *B[1]'*, *B[2]*, *B[3]*, *B[4]*, *B[5]* }. *FTS1'* and *FTS2'* are quasi-strong bisimulation equivalent since two initial states '0' and '5' belong to the same equivalence class in the final partition п'. Thus, *FTS1* and *FTS2* are *1*-weak bisimulation equivalent and also weak bisimulation equivalent. Finally two behaviour expressions *B1* and *B2* are concluded to be weak bisimulation equivalent.

4.The reduced normal form of a finite transition system

4.1. The reduced normal form of a finite labelled transition system

Theories of equivalénces allow us not only to prove the equivalence relation between two behaviour expressions, but also to replace complex behaviour expressions with simpler, equivalent ones. Based on this fact, we present a method which does not check directly the equivalence relation between two original finite labelled transition systems, but does it after transforming transition systems into their reduced normal forms.

[Definition 12]

Let *FTS* be a finite labelled transition system. *The reduced normal form of FTS* is a finite labelled transition system which is weak bisimulation equivalent to *FTS* and has the least number of states and transitions. □

We have the following properties on the reduced normal form.

[Proposition 6]

If a finite labelled transition system *FTS* is in the reduced normal form, no two distinct states s_1 and s_2 in *FTS* are weak bisimulation equivalent. □

[Proposition 7]

Let *FTS* be a finite labelled transition system. If a finite labelled transition system *FTS'* is weak bisimulation equivalent to *FTS* and has the least number of transitions, *FTS'* is the reduced normal form of *FTS*. □

[Theorem 8]

Let *FTS1* and *FTS2* be two finite labelled transition systems and FTS_1' and FTS_2' be the reduced normal forms of *FTS1* and *FTS2*, respectively. FTS_1' and FTS_2' are isomorphic if and only if *FTS1* and *FTS2* are weak bisimulation equivalent. □

4.2. Construction of the reduced normal form

In this subsection, we give a procedure to transform any finite labelled transition system into its reduced normal form.

Let $FTS = < S, A, T, s_0 >$ be a given finite labelled transition system. At first, we transform *FTS* into its Q-closure *FTS'*. Next, we apply the Partitioning Algorithm defined below to partition state space *S* to quasi-strong bisimulation equivalent classes *S'*. Then, we construct a new finite labelled transition system *LTS"* based on *S'*. Finally, we delete transitions while preserving the weak bisimulation equivalence to *LTS"*.

(1) Partitioning Algorithm of state space

The partitioning algorithm of state space is an application of the Algorithm 4.5 in [11]. We use the following notations.

For $E \subseteq A-\{i\}$ and $B \subseteq S$,

$T^{-1}(E, B) = \{s \mid \text{for all } a \in E(\neq \emptyset),\ s - a \rightarrow s' \text{ and } s' \in B\}$,

$T^{-1}(\emptyset, B) = \{s \mid \text{for all } a \in A-\{i\}, \text{ there is no } s' \in B \text{ such that } s - a \rightarrow s'\}$.

The number of elements in a set *S* is denoted by $\| S \|$.

Now we have an algorithm.

- Input : A set of n elements *S*, an initial partition $\pi = \{S\} = \{B[1]\}$, and a set of transition relations $T \cup T'$.
- Output: A partition $\pi' = \{B[1], B[2], \cdots, B[q]\}$, where each block *B[i]* is a set of states which are quasi-strong equivalent to each other.

[Algorithm]

```
begin
    WAITING ←{1} ;
    q←1 ;
    for each E such that T⁻¹(E,B[1]) ≠ ∅ do
```

```
begin
   q ← q+1 ;
   create a new block B[q] ;
   B[q] ← T⁻¹(E,B[1]) ;
   add q to WAITING ;
end
while WAITING is not empty do
begin
   select and delete any integer i from WAITING ;
   for each E such that T⁻¹(E,B[i]) ≠ ∅ do
      begin
       INVERSE ← T⁻¹(E,B[i]) ;
       for each j such that B[j] ∩ INVERSE ≠ ∅ and B[j] ⊈ INVERSE do
          begin
             q ← q+1 ;
             create a new block B[q] ;
             B[q] ← B[j] ∩ INVERSE ;
             B[j] ← B[j] − B[q] ;
             if j is in WAITING then add q to WAITING
             else
                if ||B[j]|| ≦ ||B[q]|| then
                   add j to WAITING
                else add q to WAITING
          end
      end
end
end
```

□

The difference between this algorithm and Algorithm 4.5 is that $T \cup T'$ is a set of relations $\{ -a\rightarrow \subseteq S \times S,\ a \in A \}$ here, whereas in Algorithm 4.5 it is just a mapping from S to S. We handle this by defining T^{-1} as above. The correctness of this algorithm can be checked in a manner similar to Algorithm 4.5. and it is omitted here.

(2) Construction of a new finite labelled transition system

We construct a finite labelled transition system $FTS''=\langle S', A, T', s_0' \rangle$, where

(a) $S'=\{[s] \mid s \in S$ is a representative element of the class $[s]$ obtained by the Partitioning Algorithm$\}$

(b) $T'=\{[s]-a\rightarrow[s'] \mid s-a\rightarrow s'\}$

(c) $s_0'=[s_0]$ is the initial state of FTS''.

(3) Reduction of transitions

In general, FTS'' obtained in (2) is the Q-closure of its reduced normal form. If there exist distinct transitions $s-a\rightarrow s'$ and $s=a\Rightarrow s'$ in FTS'', then delete the transition $s-a\rightarrow s'$, where $s,s' \in S'$ and $a \in A$.

A brief example is shown in **Fig.2**. (e) is the reduced normal form of (a).
The reduced normal form of a labelled transition system has the following significance.

(i) It is used to check the weak bisimulation equivalence effectively ;
(ii) it is suitable for computer processing ;
(iii) it is very useful to avoid needlessly long specifications ;
(iv) it offers effective measures for conformance testing.

5. An example of the verification

In this subsection, we give a simple example of the specifications of service definition and protocol specification and their verification. Two processes *T-service* and *T-protocol* are modeled as shown in **Fig.3**, and their LOTOS specifications are given in the appendix.

T-service is a service definition provided to users *ti* and *ta*. Service primitives of *T-service* and their temporal relations are depicted in **Fig.4**(a). *T-service* is a

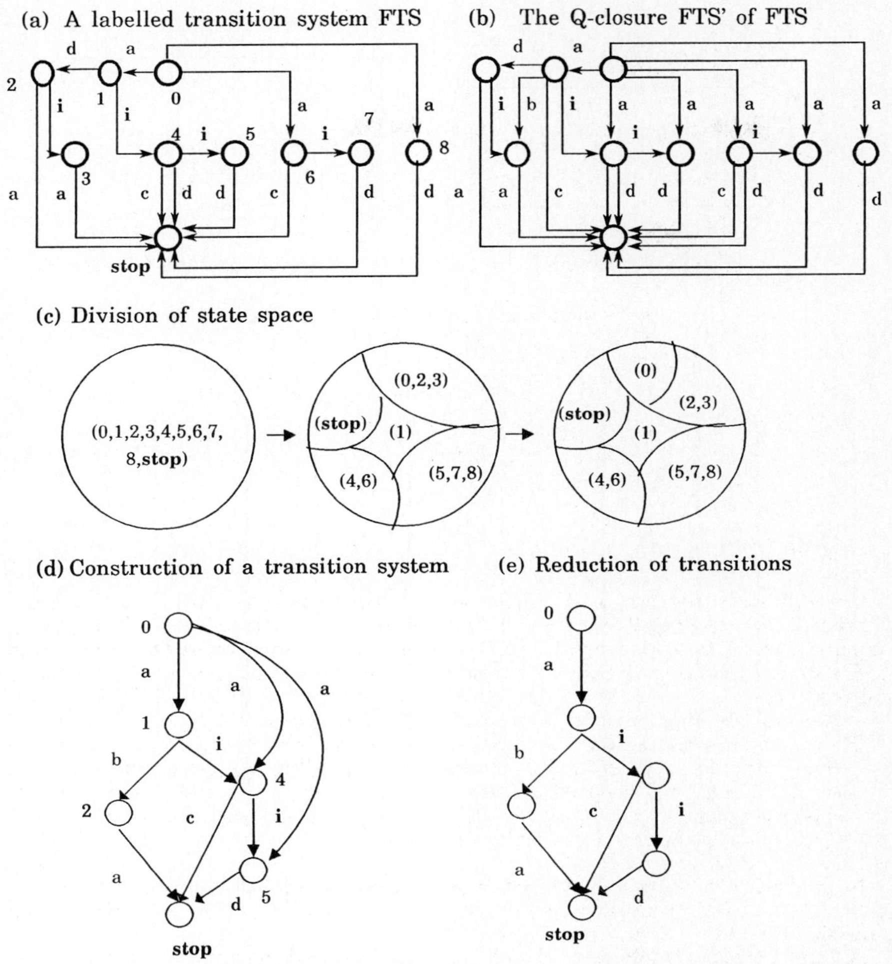

Fig.2 An example of transformation into the reduced normal form

composition of three *TS*s, and each *TS* is assumed to be a buffer of unit capacity. *T-protocol* is composed of *TN*, *NT* and *N-service*. Service primitives of *N-service* and their temporal relations are depicted in **Fig.4**(b). *TN* and *NT* are protocol entities and provide service for users above (*ti* and *ta*) by using *N-service*. They are interfaces between *N-service* and users above . Events occurring at gate *t1*, *t2* in *T-service* and *n1*, *n2*, *n3*, *n4* in *T-protocol* are made unobservable. Equivalence between *T-service* and *T-protocol* is verified by observing the behaviours at gate *ti* and *ta*. Both *T-service* and *T-protocol* are transformed to the reduced normal form shown in **Fig.5** by using the method of the previous section. Thus *T-service* and *T-protocol* are weak bisimulation equivalent.

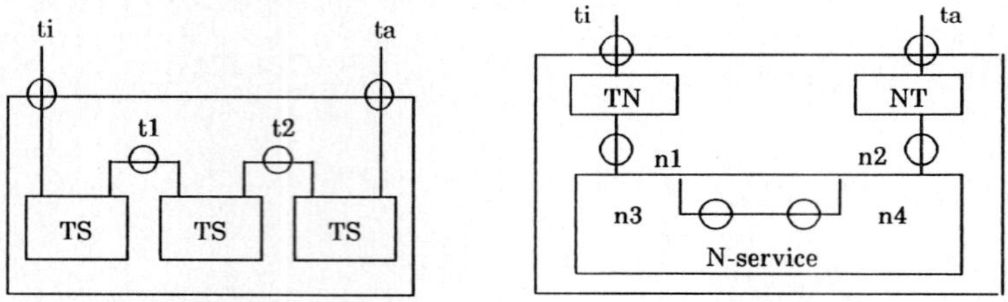

(a) T-service (b) T-protocol

Fig.3 Models of T-service and T-protocol

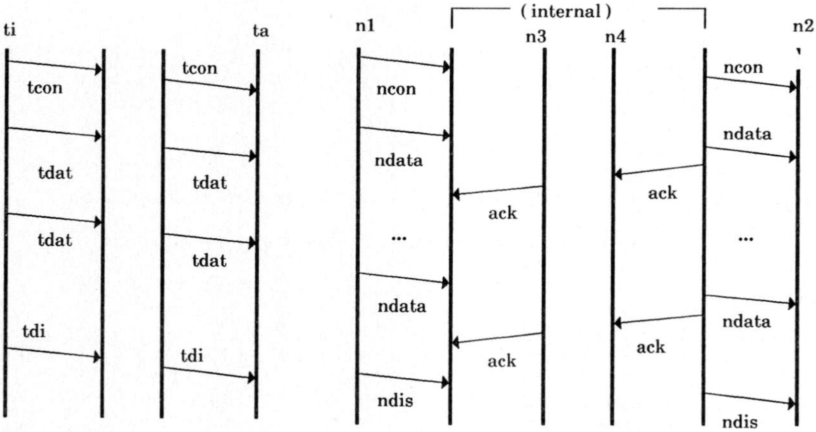

(a) T-service (b) N-service

Fig.4 Events in T-service and N-service

6. Conclusions

In this paper, we have proposed a verification method for LOTOS specifications, for the case where the corresponding labelled transition systems are finite. Although we did not discuss data types, these methods are available for the verification of LOTOS specifications independently of data type descriptions. We are now developing the prototype verification system using the proposed method. Our final goal is to construct a protocol design system based on these methods which ensures the correctness of specifications. For this purpose, the following further researches have to be done:

(i) an effective method to apply reduction rules to behaviour expressions and labelled transition systems in the course of constructing a labelled transition system is to be devised,

(ii) a mechanism to interpret the abstract data types needs to be developed,

(iii) an extension of the proposed verification method to some of the classes which have infinite system states should be carried out.

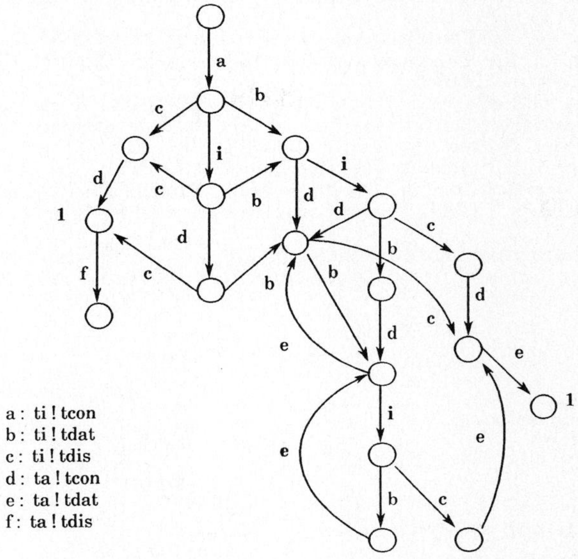

Fig.5 The reduced normal form of T-service and T-protocol

REFERENCES

[1] G.V.Bochmann and C.A.Sunshine : " Formal Methods in Communication Protocol Design ", IEEE Trans. Commun. vol.COM-28, no.4, pp.624-631, (1980) .

[2] C.A.Vissers, R.L.Tenney and G.V.Bochmann : " Formal Description Techniques ", Proceedings of the IEEE, vol.71, no.12, pp.1356-1362, (1983) .

[3] ISO : " Information processing systems - open systems interconnection, LOTOS - a formal description technique based on the temporal ordering of observational behaviour ", ISO/TC97/SC21 DIS 8807, (1987) .

[4] E. Brinksma : " An Introduction to LOTOS ", in Protocol Specification, Testing and Verification VII, North-Holland (1987) .

[5] T.Bolognesi and Ed Brinksma : " Introduction to the ISO Specification Language LOTOS ", Computer Networks and ISDN Systems vol.14, North-Holland, (1987) .

[6] R.Milner : " A Calculus of Communicating Systems " , Lecture Notes in Computer Science, vol.92, Springer-Verlag, (1980) .

[7] H.Ehrig and B.Mahr : " Fundamentals of Algebraic Specification 1 : Equations and Initial Semantics ", EATCS Monographs on Theoretical Computer Science, Springer Verlag (1985) .

[8] J.A.Goguen, J.W.Thatcher and E.G.Wagner : " An Initial Algebra Approach to the Specification,Correctness and Implementation of Abstract Data Types ", in Current Trends in Programming Methodology IV, Prentice Hall, (1978) .

[9] J.V.Guttag, E.Horowitz and D.R.Musser : " Abstract Data Types and Software Validation ", CACM, vol.21, no.12, pp.1048-1064, (1976) .

[10] D.R.Musser : " Abstract Data Type Specification in the AFFIRM System ", IEEE Trans. Software Eng., vol.SE-6, no.1, pp.24-32, (1980) .

[11] A.V.Aho, J.E.Hopcroft and J.D.Ullman : The design and analysis of computer algorithms, Addison-Wesley , (1974) .

[12] T.Bolognesi and S.A.Smolka : " Fundamental Results for the Verification of Observational Equivalence : a Survey ", in Protocol Specification, Testing and Verification VII , North-Holland (1987) .

[13] V.Carchiolo, A.Faro, O.Mirabella, G.Pappalardo and G.Scollo : " A LOTOS

Specification of the PROWAY Highway Service", IEEE Trans. Comput. vol.C-35, no.11, pp.949-968, (1986).
[14] E.Najm : "A Verification Oriented specification in LOTOS of The Transport Protocol", in Proc. of the 7th International Workshop on Protocol Specification, Testing and Verification (1987).
[15] E.Brinksma, G.Scollo and C.Steenbergen : "LOTOS Specifications, their Implementations and their Tests", in Proc. of the 6th International Workshop on Protocol Specification, Testing and Verification (1986).
[16] C.A.Sunshine, D.H.Tompson, R.W.Erickson, S.L.Gerhart and D.Schwabe : "Specification and Verification of Communication Protocols in AFFIRM Using State Transition Models", IEEE Trans. Software Eng., vol.SE-8, no.5, pp.460-489, (1982).
[17] D.Park : "Concurrency and Automata on Infinate Sequences", Proc, 5th GI Conference, Lecture Notes in Computer Science, vol.104, Springer-Verlag, (1981).

APPENDIX

(a) T-service

```
specification
      T-service [ ti, ta ]
  type      TS__primitives is
    sorts   ts__primitives
    opns    tcon, tdata, tdis :  → ts__primitives
  endtype
behaviour
    hide t1, t2 in
( TS [ti,t1] | [t1] | TS [ t1, t2 ] | [ t2 ] | TS [ t2, ta ] )
    where
    process TS[t1,t2] : noexit :=
Connection-phase [t1,t2] >> Data-phase [t1,t2 ]
        where
        process
            Connection-phase [ t1, t2 ] :=
                    t1! tcon ; t2! tcon ; exit
        endproc
        process Data-phase[t1,t2] : noexit :=
         t1! tdata ; t2! tdata ; ( Data-phase [ t1,
            t2 ] [ ] Termination-phase [ t1, t2 ] )
         where
            process
                Termination-phase [ t1, t2 ] :=
                    t1! tdis ; t2! tdis ; stop
            endproc
        endproc
    endproc
endspec
```

(b) T-protocol

```
specification
      T-protocol [ ti, ta ]
  type      TP__primitives is
    sorts   tp__primitives
    opns    tcon, tdata, tdis, ncon, ndata, ndis,
                     ack :  → tp__primitives
  endtype
behaviour
    hide n1, n2, n3, n4 in ( TN [ti, n1] | [n1] |
  N-service [n1, n2, n3, n4] | [n2] | NT [n2, ta] )
    where
      process
        TN [ ti, n1 ] : noexit := TNC-phase
           [ ti, n1 ] >> TND-phase [ ti, n1 ]
        where
        process
            TNC-phase [ ti, n1 ] :=
                    ti! tcon ; n1! ncon ; exit
        endproc
  process
    TND-phase [ ti, n1 ] : noexit :=
        ti! tdata ; n1! ndata ; ( TND-phase
        [ ti, n1 ] [ ] TNT-phase [ ti, n1 ] )
        where
         process
           TNT-phase [ ti, n1 ] : noexit :=
                ti! tdis ; n1! ndis ; stop
         endproc
   endproc
endproc
process
   N-service [ n1, n2, n3, n4 ] :=
       NSC-phase [ n1, n2, n3, n4 ]
         >> NSD-phase [ n1, n2, n3, n4 ]
   where
    process
       NSC-phase [ n1, n2, n3, n4 ] :=
             n1! ncon ; n2! ncon ; exit
    endproc
    process
  NSD-phase [ n1, n2, n3, n4 ] : noexit :=
  n1! ndata ; n2! ndata ; n4! ack ; n3! ack
      ; ( NSD-phase [ n1, n2, n3, n4 ]
       [ ] NST-phase [ n1, n2 ] )
     where
     process
       NST-phase [ n1, n2 ] : noexit :=
n1! ndis ; n2! ndis ; stop
     endproc
    endproc
endproc
process
   NT [ n2, ta ] : noexit :=
NTC-phase [ n2, ta ] >> NTD-phase [ n2, ta ]
   where
    process
    NTC-phase [ n2, ta ] :=
        n2! ncon ; ta! tcon ; exit
    endproc
    process
   NTD-phase [ n2, ta ] : noexit :=
        n2! ndata ; ta! tdata ; ( NTD-
phase [ n2, ta ] [ ] NTT-phase [ n2, ta ] )
    where
      process
     NTT-phase [ n2, ta ] : noexit :=
        n2! ndis ; ta! tdis ; stop
      endproc
    endproc
  endproc
endspec
```

Protocol Specification, Testing, and Verification, IX
E. Brinksma, G. Scollo and C.A. Vissers (Editors)
Elsevier Science Publishers B.V. (North-Holland)

Stepwise Refinement of Layered Protocols by Formal Program Development

Terry Stroup*
Universität Erlangen
Informatik VII
Martensstraße 3
8520 Erlangen, F.R.G.

Norbert Götz
Universität Erlangen
Informatik VII
Martensstraße 3
8520 Erlangen, F.R.G.

Michael Mendler
Laboratory for Foundations of Computer Science
University of Edinburgh
Edinburgh EH9 3JZ, U.K.

Abstract

The techniques of *Formal Program Development* are used to implement a standardized protocol by stepwise refinement and to verify selected properties of the resulting implementation. The technique, which makes extensive use of parametrized (or generic) modules, permits the verification to exhibit exactly the same modular structure as the program, thereby assuring code and proof the same degree of perspicuity, reusability and ease of maintenance. Though the technique worked quite well on the chosen example, larger standardized protocols are insufficiently structured to permit structured proofs of their properties. We explore the use of modern software technology to design large protocols more amenable to tractable analysis.

1 Introduction

Despite the long and enviably successful tradition of verifying standardized protocols [Rud], their implementation remains astonishingly expensive and fraught with unexpected difficulties. It is not unusual for the marketable implementation of a stable standard to bind large quantities of manpower for years at a time and require the redesign of significant portions of the alleged standard before it indeed supports communication between heterogeneous components. Though there is widespread agreement among developers of protocols, amply documented by the literature on protocol specification, that Formal Descriptions are necessary to permit careful validation, there has been comparatively little discussion of how classes of real protocols might be structured so as to be readily comprehended, genuinely verified and reliably implemented. In particular, neither the composition of protocols from reusable modules nor their stepwise refinement from high-level descriptions has received adequate attention in the literature.

Recent research in *Formal Program Development* [ST88b] has concentrated on the design of independent Formal Description Techniques, with their associated programming and verification styles, that permit the orthogonal design of

- algorithms and data types,
- interactions among processes and
- interconnections of parametrized modules.

Adequate theories have been developed, especially for algebraic programming styles, that permit languages to be designed and implemented in which each of these three language components can be redesigned or exchanged outright, without affecting the others. This has the practical advantage, for example, that CCS (Calculus of Communicating Systems [Mil89]), a language for describing process interactions, can be combined with an arbitrary sequential programming notation to yield a language for sequential processes that communicate via a handshake mechanism. Similarly, EML (Extended Meta-Language [ST85]), a language for composing large modules from parametrized component modules, is designed to permit the composition of either highly abstract specifications in an arbitrary logical formalism or of executable code in a concrete programming language. In fact, this flexibility permits EML to support not only the modular structuring of both a program and its verification, but its refinement, step by step, from an abstract specification to executable code.

We have tested such orthogonally designed languages quite successfully in the implementation and verification, though not of course in the design, of a standardized protocol, the *Application Control Service Element*

*This research was sponsored in part by the "Projekt für flexibel automatisierte Produktionssysteme (PAP)"

(ACSE) [ISOb] of the ISO Application Layer. Our experiment had three overriding objectives. We wanted first and foremost to ensure an intimate correspondence between the structure of the program and that of the verification. Further, we wanted to use techniques that permit arbitrary predicates in a powerful logic for specification purposes. And finally, the result was to be a provably correct, executable version of the protocol, not merely an elegant but sterile abstraction.

In the next section we explain at an intuitive level how a metalanguage for interconnecting parametrized modules may be used to implement layered protocols by means of stepwise refinement. We outline how the modules language supports a verification with precisely the same modular structure, because it is organized arround exactly the same constructions, as the resulting program. In section 3 we demonstrate these techniques using the first two (of thirteen) refinement steps for ACSE as a concrete example. The example supports a comparison in section 4 with related work and a discussion of additional methods that we have explored elsewhere [SMG89] for the correct implementation of verifiable protocols.

We shall assume a passing acquaintance with the algebraic specification of data types and with process algebras; both are familiar in protocol specifications from the growing body of work on LOTOS [BB87]. The notation we have used is a mild variation on ML [HMM86] as extended by Sannella and Tarlecki in [ST85] with an embedded version of CCS called PFL (*Parallel Functional Language*) [Mit]. ([Wik87] is an elementary account of ML and [Har86] provides an advanced introduction.) We chose to work with Extended ML because of its generality, its solid theoretical foundation and because of its proximity to ML, a language we find congenial to careful software-development. We wish to emphasize however, that our methods pertain to any suitably designed language, and could be applied in any situation in which adequate tools for Formal Program Development are available; [Han88] and [LL88] describe two such systems and refer to a baker's dozen more.

2 Stepwise Refinement

2.1 Specifications and their Implementations

The central concept in program verification is the *meaning* of a program or of a specification. It is useful for a general account of specification and verification to regard the meaning of a program or specification as consisting of the set of all assertions that it entails. Depending on the logical machinery with which the inferences are drawn, various classes of assertions can be expressed and investigated. Temporal properties are most readily expressed and handily investigated, for example, in a temporal logic; epistemic logics are better suited to deal with such properties as information exchange or concensus among distributed agents. For our investigations we have used many-sorted first-order logic with equality.

Having construed the meaning of programs and specifications as comprising everything that can be inferred from them, we can give a very general account of verification, stepwise refinement, modularization and other concepts important in the systematic development of software. This level of generality has numerous advantages. It facilitates, for example, a dispassionate comparison of specific Formal Description Techniques [San88], or, in a more technical vein, it supports broadly applicable programming methodologies [ST88b].

A program P *satisfies* a specification S or is *correct* with respect to its specification, written $S \rightsquigarrow P$, if everything that can be inferred from S can also be inferred from P; i.e. the meaning of S is contained in that of P. Whatever is true of P, but not of S, is an *implementation detail* of P.

A *verification* that P indeed implements S, i.e. that $S \rightsquigarrow P$, consists of proving that the meaning of the specification is in fact contained in that of the program. A good way to show this is by proving, using the logical machinery at hand, that the assertions in S follow from those in the description of P.

Because verifications can become lengthy and even complicated, the work involved should be supported by a machine and of course even automated, whenever this is possible. But even with automated support, any program sufficiently large, and its verification, must be broken into smaller chunks that can be pieced together to yield the desired overall result. It is expedient, both for the success of the verification and for the reusability of the parts, to ensure that proof and program exhibit exactly the same structure.

Two techniques have proved effective in achieving the required structuring. The first is gradual *refinement*, step by step, from a very high-level description to an executable description, i.e. a program. Each step in the refinement comprises a *design decision*: a choice is made, say of an algorithm or of a data structure, that adds an implementation detail to the design achieved so far. Given a chain $S_1, \ldots, S_n$ of refinements, the task of verifying that the final, executable specification S_n meets its highest-level specification S_1 can be broken into a chain of verifications that S_{i+1} is correct with respect to S_i, i.e. $S_i \rightsquigarrow S_{i+1}$. (We shall then say that S_{i+1} *implements* S_i, even though common usage often holds that S_n is "the" implementation.) Thus a sequence $S_1 \rightsquigarrow S_2 \rightsquigarrow \ldots \rightsquigarrow S_n$ of refinements is one way of factoring an implementation and its verification into manageable pieces.

The second successful technique involves factoring a specification into parts that can be composed to fulfil the original specification; in symbols $S \rightsquigarrow S' \otimes S''$. If the operator $\otimes$ is such that the component specifications S' and S'' may be refined independently, we will call them *modules*. The *independent* refinement simply means that if $S' \rightsquigarrow T'$ and $S'' \rightsquigarrow T''$ then $S \rightsquigarrow T' \otimes T''$, assuming (as we do here) that $\otimes$ can be applied at both levels of abstraction. If the refinement process involves such modularizations, we obtain a refinement tree, say

$$S_1 \rightsquigarrow \left\{ \begin{array}{l} S_2 \rightsquigarrow \left\{ \begin{array}{l} S_4 \rightsquigarrow S_6 \\ \odot \\ S_5 \rightsquigarrow S_7 \end{array}\right. \\ \otimes \\ S_3 \rightsquigarrow \left\{ \begin{array}{l} \Delta \\ S_8 \rightsquigarrow S_9 \end{array}\right. \end{array}\right.$$

(with binary operators $\otimes$ and $\odot$ and unary operator Δ) that embodies the *structure* of the program. Now if S_2, say, has been refined to $S_4 \odot S_5$ we must show, as with the simple refinement chain, that the composition of S_4 with S_5 by means of $\odot$ indeed fulfils S_2. Further refinements need not however take the whole of $S_4 \odot S_5$ into account; instead the smaller specifications S_4 and S_5 may be refined independently.

A *design strategy* attempts to arrange the sequence of design decisions in such a way that a suitable implementation results. A programming language that supports a design strategy from high-level specifications all the way to an executable program should support a verification that each refinement step is indeed correct. We will call a verification that respects both the modular and the refinement structure of a program a proof *along the structure.*

We attempt to show in the following that such structuring techniques can be applied to the verification of protocols. A technically meticulous and highly readable introduction to the essence of specification and verification and associated concepts, such as stepwise refinement, is to be found in [TM87]. A mathematically more general presentation of similar ideas, which guided the present work, is [ST88b]. It turns out that the latter, fully general theory of specification and verification actually requires, as [ST88a] demonstrates, definitions in some respects more complicated than we have suggested. Our informal exposition distorts that theory slightly to permit simpler, proof-theoretic explanations of model-theoretic intentions.

The utility of (Semi-) Formal Program Development in industrial practice is argued convincingly in [Gog86].

2.2 The Structure of ISO Protocols

The ISO Reference Model structures communications software by dividing it into layers, each of which performs a specific task in the communication. Each of the layers can be depicted as in Figure 1.

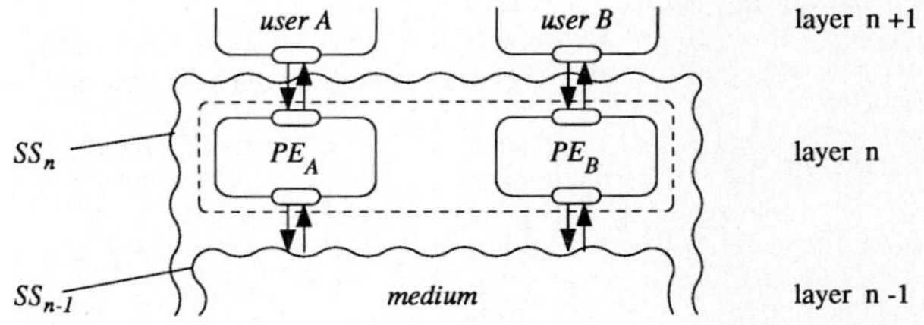

Figure 1: Structure of an ISO Layer

Users communicate with one another using the layer beneath them as a (virtual) medium, whose duties are performed on an individual machine by a *protocol entity* connected with the user via the so-called *service access point.* The nth layer consists (for two machines) then of two such entities that take on communications chores from the $(n+1)$th layer through the respective service access points and discharge their task using the simpler or less convenient services of the $(n-1)$th layer as a medium, which may of course perform its chores in similar fashion. Communications are exchanged in the form of precisely defined messages, called *service elements.* It is important for the modularity of the scheme that the users notice nothing of this recursive decomposition of their medium. All they see of the medium's behavior is the flow of transactions (i.e. service elements) through the wavy line enclosing layers 1 through n.

In this refinement scheme the description of the medium from the point of view of its users is called the *service specification* SS_n of the nth layer. The *protocol specification* describes the behavior of the protocol entities (PE_A, PE_B) of the nth layer; this description presupposes a medium that fulfils the service specification SS_{n-1} of the $(n-1)$th layer. A clear, functional criterion for the correctness of the protocol entities can be formulated as in [vB80]:

> ...the entities executing a given protocol together with the underlying medium actually provide the specified communication service to the user entities in the layer above.

That means of course that the specification SS_n is implemented by composing PE_A and PE_B with SS_{n-1}. This composition can be expressed quite naturally using CCS as in [Par87]; we choose to motivate essentially the same idea using refinements of specifications as follows. If we designate the composition (i.e. the arrows in Figure 1) by $(\|)$ we get a refinement tree as follows, assuming as in our definition of modules that this composition allows independent refinements:

$$\ldots \rightsquigarrow SS_n \rightsquigarrow \begin{cases} PE_A & \rightsquigarrow \ldots \\ (\|) & \\ SS_{n-1} & \rightsquigarrow \ldots \\ (\|) & \\ PE_B & \rightsquigarrow \ldots \end{cases}$$

This ISO Trident provides a handy model with which to explain how the modules language in ML is used to support stepwise modular refinement.

A (service) *specification*, say of the Application Layer, in which our example protocol ACSE resides, and a (protocol) specification of ACSE's implementing entity are written schematically in EML as follows:

```
signature A_LAYER = {                    signature ACSE_PE = {
    type  . . .                              type  . . .
    val   a_layer : beh                      val   acse_pe : beh
    axiom . . .     }                        axiom . . .     }
```

where **A_LAYER** and **ACSE_PE** name the type of objects being specified, **type** declares the sorts involved in specifying such an object, **val** declares the operators, be they constants or functions, over the declared sorts, and **axiom** postulates something of one or more of the declared operators. The protocol entity contains, for example, a nullary operation **acse_pe**, whose type is **beh**, for "behavior," the type assigned to CCS processes in ML. If **PE** is an object of type **ACSE_PE**, i.e. **PE : ACSE_PE**, we can select its process component using the familiar notation **PE.acse_pe**, which is thus of type **beh**. (We are taking liberties with the syntax of EML here and simplifying some details of the program that need not be explained as yet.)

A *specification-building operation* **Mk_A_Layer** that constructs an **A_LAYER** from two ACSE protocol entities, or **ACSE_PE**s, and a **P_LAYER**, each specified by a corresponding **signature** statement, should be a function

$$\texttt{Mk\_A\_Layer} : \quad \texttt{ACSE\_PE} \times \texttt{P\_LAYER} \times \texttt{ACSE\_PE} \longrightarrow \texttt{A\_LAYER}$$

The description of this function is thus a parametrized version of the specification **A_LAYER** that constructs **A_LAYER**'s various sorts and operations from the sorts and operations in its arguments. For instance, the **acse_pe** is constructed using ML's built-in operator **||** defined on the basic sort **beh**. All of this is written using an EML **functor**

```
functor Mk_A_Layer ( PE1 : ACSE_PE,
                     PL  : P_LAYER,
                     PE2 : ACSE_PE )  :  A_LAYER  =  {

   a_layer  =  PE1.acse_pe  ||  PL.p_layer  ||  PE2.acse_pe
   }
```

A verification along the functor **Mk_A_Layer** must show that applying it to arbitrary arguments that satisfy their respective specifications, **ACSE_PE** and **P_LAYER**, yields a result that satisfies the axioms postulated in the specification **A_LAYER**. At this stage of the verification we assume, for example, of any **PE : ACSE_PE** and any **PL : P_LAYER** that their respective components **acse_pe** and **p_layer** are indeed CCS processes with the specified behaviors. (Subsequent stages must of course justify the assumption.) We may thus use the metatheory of CCS to show that their parallel composition yields an **a_layer** component that satisfies the axioms in **A_LAYER**. This verification would justify specializing the general assertion

$$SS_n \rightsquigarrow PE_A (\|) SS_{n-1} (\|) PE_B,$$

to

$$\texttt{A\_LAYER} \rightsquigarrow \texttt{Mk\_A\_Layer(ACSE\_PE, P\_LAYER, ACSE\_PE)}.$$

Thus EML functors embody the design decisions in a refinement step. Furthermore, their semantics guarantees the modularity of the component specifications: further refinements of each component are guaranteed by the compiler to be unaffected by design decisions in the refinements of any other component.

Our next design decision is to refine an ACSE protocol entity, the **acse_pe** component of which is a CCS process, to an output automaton, since this is the form in which ISO protocol standards are formulated. (We could of course decide to implement the protocol entities in some other way, which the ISO explicitly permits, but we would then have to show that our implementation exhibits the same behavior as the one based on the automata in the standard.) The ISO standard calls the automaton an Association Control Protocol Machine or ACPM [ISOa]. Our functor, **Mk_ACSE_pe**, should thus construct an **ACSE_PE** by means of an **ACPM**. If we again show that the body of the functor builds an object satisfying the 'output' specification from one satisfying the 'input' specification, i.e. if we provide a verification along the construction, we have shown the second refinement step correct:

$$\texttt{ACSE\_PE} \rightsquigarrow \texttt{Mk\_ACSE\_pe(ACPM).}$$

By means of further refinement steps, each incorporating a concrete design decision, we have implemented ACSE all the way down to executable ML code and verified some of its properties [SMG89]. We illustrate these techniques in greater detail in the next section.

3 The Refinement of ACSE

In this section we aim to show how stepwise modular refinement applies to a simple standardized protocol, ACSE. We will describe the Application Layer, in which ACSE resides, as a CCS process and then refine it into a (small) system of processes; these will be refined in turn. For these two steps we will sketch verifications of which details may be found in [SMG89]. In this brief exposition we merely hint at the remaining refinements; again, details are provided elsewhere. We begin by establishing some useful notation for CCS and then provide a first specification of the A-Layer using this notation.

3.1 Some CCS Notation

We will find some specialized CCS notation useful for our specifications with PFL, which diverges in details, inessential for our purposes, from the classical formulation in [Mil89].

Communication between CCS agents occurs by exchanging messages over so-called *ports*. Let $\mathcal{P}$ be an arbitrary but fixed set, possibly infinite, of ports. We assign each $p \in \mathcal{P}$ a set of messages $\mathcal{N}_p$, called its *type*, that may be transmitted on it. The exchange of a message v on port p consists then of the synchronous occurrence of two *events*, $(\bar{p}, v)$, which offers the communication of v, and (p, v), which accepts the communication of v, each on the port p, where $p \in \mathcal{P}$ and $v \in \mathcal{N}_p$. These two events combine by definition to form the single, non-observable event τ, which does not synchronize with any other event. Ports are unidirectional: information flows only in one direction along them from one agent to the other.

Thus we have introduced, in part tacitly, the following notations:

- $\mathcal{B}$ — processes or agents
- $\mathcal{P}$ — ports
- $\mathcal{N}_p$ — for $p \in \mathcal{P}$ messages on port p
- $\mathcal{E}$ — events
- $\mathcal{I} \subseteq \mathcal{E}$ — input events
- $\mathcal{O} \subseteq \mathcal{E}$ — output events
- $\tau \in \mathcal{E}$ — internal, non-observable event

We have, in addition, already determined the structure of events:

$$\begin{aligned} \mathcal{I} &:= \{(p,v) \mid p \in \mathcal{P}, v \in \mathcal{N}_p\} \\ \mathcal{O} &:= \{(\bar{p},v) \mid p \in \mathcal{P}, v \in \mathcal{N}_p\} \end{aligned} \qquad \mathcal{E} := \mathcal{I} \uplus \mathcal{O} \uplus \{\tau\}$$

The *behavior* of a CCS process is described, according to its operational semantics, by a transition relation $\delta \subseteq \mathcal{B} \times \mathcal{E} \times \mathcal{B}$: $(P, e, Q) \in \delta$ means that the process $P \in \mathcal{B}$ is transformed by the event $e \in \mathcal{E}$ into the process $Q \in \mathcal{B}$. We extend δ as usual to sequences of events $\mathcal{E}^*$ and write $P \xrightarrow{s} Q$ for $P, Q \in \mathcal{B}$ and $s = s_1 s_2 \cdots s_n \in \mathcal{E}^*$.

Taking $\mathcal{E}_0 := \mathcal{E} \setminus \{\tau\}$ to be the set of observable events, we define for $P, Q \in \mathcal{B}$ and $t \in \mathcal{E}_0{}^*$ an *observable* transition to be

$$P \overset{t}{\Longrightarrow} Q \quad \overset{\text{def}}{\Longleftrightarrow} \quad \exists s \in \mathcal{E}^*.\ P \xrightarrow{s} Q \wedge \pi(s) = t,$$

where $\pi : \mathcal{E}^* \to \mathcal{E}_0{}^*$ is the uniquely determined (monoid) homomorphism that deletes all occurrences of τ in $s \in \mathcal{E}^*$.

We will also need a relation $port \subseteq \mathcal{E}_0 \times \mathcal{P}$, which obtains just when the event e indeed occurs on the port p:

$$port(e,p) \quad \overset{\text{def}}{\Longleftrightarrow} \quad \exists v \in \mathcal{N}_p.\ e = (p,v) \vee e = (\bar{p},v).$$

We can now express the fact that a process $P \in \mathcal{B}$ has an observable transition involving a communication event on port $p \in \mathcal{P}$ using the following predicate $ready \subseteq \mathcal{B} \times \mathcal{P}$:

$$ready(P,p) \quad \overset{\text{def}}{\Longleftrightarrow} \quad \exists Q \in \mathcal{B}.\, \exists e \in \mathcal{E}_0.\ P \overset{e}{\Longrightarrow} Q \wedge port(e,p)$$

Next we define a relation $is\_input\_port \subseteq \mathcal{B} \times \mathcal{P}$, which characterizes the input ports $p \in \mathcal{P}$ of a process $P \in \mathcal{B}$, i.e. those ports that are used only in input events:

$$\begin{aligned} is\_input\_port(P,p) \quad \overset{\text{def}}{\Longleftrightarrow} \quad & \forall Q \in \mathcal{B}.\, \forall s \in \mathcal{E}_0{}^*.\forall e \in \mathcal{E}_0. \\ & P \overset{es}{\Longrightarrow} Q \wedge port(e,p) \quad \Rightarrow \quad e \in \mathcal{I}. \end{aligned}$$

Finally the binary infix predicate $observation\_at\_ports \subseteq \mathcal{E}_0{}^+ \times \mathcal{P}^+$, defined for nonempty sequences $s_1 s_2 \cdots s_m \in \mathcal{E}_0{}^+$ and $p_1 p_2 \cdots p_n \in \mathcal{P}^+$ of observable events and ports as

$$\begin{aligned} & s_1 s_2 \cdots s_m \ observation\_at\_ports \ p_1 p_2 \cdots p_n \\ & \overset{\text{def}}{\Longleftrightarrow} \quad \forall 1 \leq i \leq m.\, \exists 1 \leq j \leq n.\ port(s_i\,,\, p_j), \end{aligned}$$

expresses that all the ports at which the events s_i occur are among the ports p_j.

3.2 The A-Layer as a CCS Process

To keep our discussion simple we restrict our attention to the case of an A-Layer serving only two users via two service access points. This is the fundamental situation on which more complicated communication structures can be built. We begin by determining how the users ($user_1$, $user_2$) are connected to the A-Layer (Figure 2) and the types of messages they will exchange. Since the communication between the users and the service

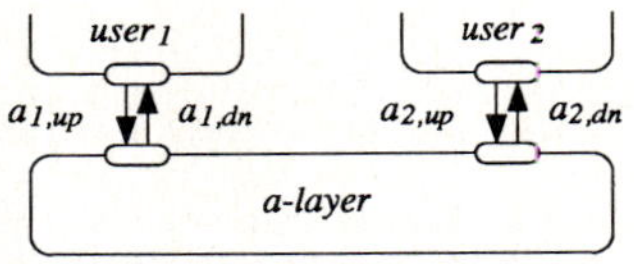

Figure 2: The A-Layer as CCS Process

provider is bidirectional, whereas CCS ports are unidirectional, we shall need a port for each direction. These we shall designate $a_{1,up}$, $a_{1,dn}$, $a_{2,up}$, $a_{2,dn}$.

Note that we do not yet impose any structure on these messages; that will be done in due time. For now it suffices to assume a single type of messages, the type $A\_Message$ of A-Layer messages, that subsumes all of the service elements on any port. (We avoid naming this set "service element", reserving that designation, as does the ISO, for messages with a certain structure. When the messages assume such structure in a later refinement step, they will be so designated.)

With the notation at hand we can specify certain static properties of the A-Layer. It should consist of a process a_layer parametrized by four ports, each capable of transmitting A-Messages.

Process: $a\_layer : \mathcal{P} \times \mathcal{P} \times \mathcal{P} \times \mathcal{P} \longrightarrow \mathcal{B}$

Ports: $a_{1,up}, a_{2,up}, a_{1,dn}, a_{2,dn} \in \mathcal{P}$
$\mathcal{N}_{a_{1,up}} = \mathcal{N}_{a_{2,up}} = \mathcal{N}_{a_{1,dn}} = \mathcal{N}_{a_{2,dn}} \ := \ A\_Message$

This part of the specification will be reflected in ML, because of its static nature, using typing information.

We are now ready to specify dynamic properties of the A-Layer, for example deadlock freedom. We shall say that the A-Layer process is *deadlock free* if at all times some communication event is possible at each of its service access points, i.e. if the A-Layer process cannot arrive in some state in which it neither emits nor accepts messages at one of its service access points. We can express this as follows in the meta-theory of CCS:

Deadlock Freedom:

$$\begin{aligned} \forall P \in \mathcal{B}.\, \forall t \in \mathcal{E}_0{}^*.\ \ \text{a\_layer} \overset{t}{\Longrightarrow} P \ \Rightarrow \quad & (\,\text{ready}(P, a_{1,up}) \vee \text{ready}(P, a_{1,dn})\,) \\ \wedge \ & (\,\text{ready}(P, a_{2,up}) \vee \text{ready}(P, a_{2,dn})\,) \end{aligned}$$

This is of course not the only property we could formulate using the predicates available to us, nor is this property in isolation by any means an adequate specification of the services provided by ACSE. Any adequate specification would have to require further properties, formalized versions of requirements to be found in [ISOb], which could also be formulated in similar predicates. We will however assume without loss of generality that this is the only property of ACSE that needs to be verified.

3.3 The A-Layer as an ML Specification

Even at this level of abstraction we can already formulate the A-Layer as an ML specification, despite the fact that we have not yet fixed any details of the protocol entities or of the underlying communications medium. These details will be added in later refinement steps.

Before we proceed with our specification, we must point out how CCS is embedded (under the name *Parallel Functional Language* or PFL [Mit]) in ML. Processes and ports in PFL are special, predefined ML data types: there is a type **beh** (*behavior*) for processes, i.e. elements of $\mathcal{B}$, and a data type α **chan** (*channel*) for ports, i.e. elements of $\mathcal{P}$, whose message type is α. Message types, i.e. instantiations of the type variables α in the port type α **chan**, can be any elementary or arbitrarily complex derived type.

For the sake of clarity and to demonstrate the possibilities for modularization in ML, we will separate the specification of the A-Layer's message type *A_Message* from that of the process *a_layer*. The following specification **A_MESSAGE** will be incorporated into the specification **A_LAYER** as a subspecification.

```
signature A_MESSAGE = {
  type A_Message
  val is_ok, is_up, is_dn : A_Message -> bool
     .
     . (axioms)
     .
  }
```

This signature specifies the type **A_Message** and several unary predicates i.e. subsets over that type. A more specific characterisation of these sets is provided by the (suppressed) axioms.

We formulate the specification of the A-Layer as an ML signature **A_LAYER**.

```
signature A_LAYER = {
  structure A : A_MESSAGE
  val a_layer : A.A_Message chan * A.A_Message chan *
                A.A_Message chan * A.A_Message chan   -> beh

  axiom (A_Layer_live) :
    forall a1_up, a1_dn, a2_up, a2_dn : A.A_Message chan.
    forall P : beh.
    forall t : (A.A_Message * A.A_Message chan) list.
      if a_layer(a1_up, a1_dn, a2_up, a2_dn) == t ==> P
      then ( ready(P, a1_up) orelse ready(P, a1_dn) ) andalso
           ( ready(P, a2_up) orelse ready(P, a2_dn) )
      else true
    .
    . (further axioms)
    .
  }
```

The declaration `structure A : A_MESSAGE` ensures that any structure satisfying the specification **A_LAYER** will contain a substructure satisfying the specification **A_MESSAGE**. By means of the identifier **A** for this substructure, we can refer to its components; **A.A_Message** designates for example the message type.

With `val a_layer : A.A_Message chan * ... -> beh` we declare the process **a_layer** to be a function of four ports of type **A.A_Message**. This function is thus a generic process parametrized over its four connecting ports (**a1_up**, **a1_dn**, **a2_up**, **a2_dn**). Note that this parametrization, which permits us to create numerous processes that share the same code, corresponds to renaming in CCS.

This representation provides the basis for a more general design of an A-Layer that supports more than two or even an unbounded, i.e. dynamically varying, number of users. Such a design could, for example, use control processes to survey and administer service access points. These control processes could dynamically create, via repeated applications of the function **a_layer**, as many instances of the A-Layer process as there are dialogues, using whatever ports are appropriate to hook up the users. Further details on how to implement dynamic creation and interconnection of CCS processes in the language PFL can be found in [Mit].

The axiom **(A_Layer_live)** is a direct encoding in ML of the deadlock freedom property formulated in the last section.

3.4 First Refinement: The Functor Mk_A_Layer

Having specified the external form of the A-Layer in **A_LAYER**, we turn our attention to its internal structure by constructing it from more primitive components. As we have already explained, we shall compose two **ACSE_PE**s and a **P_LAYER** to build an **A_LAYER** using the functor **Mk_A_Layer**.

We begin with a specification of the P-Layer, which, apart from the axioms governing its behavior, bears a superficial resemblance to the A-Layer. (The resemblance is only superficial because, apart from the axioms and names, the substructures for the messages localize significant differences in imported modules.)

```
signature P_LAYER = {
  structure P : P_MESSAGE
  val p_layer : P.P_Message chan * P.P_Message chan *
                P.P_Message chan * P.P_Message chan   -> beh

  axiom (P_Layer_input) :
    forall p1_up, p1_dn, p2_up, p2_dn : P.P_Message chan.
      is_input_port( p_layer(p1_up, p1_dn, p2_up, p2_dn) , p1_dn)
    andalso
      is_input_port( p_layer(p1_up, p1_dn, p2_up, p2_dn) , p2_dn)

  axiom (P_Layer_live) :
    forall p1_up, p1_dn, p2_up, p2_dn : P.P_Message chan.
    forall P : beh.
    forall t : (P.P_Message * P.P_Message chan) list.
      if p_layer(p1_up, p1_dn, p2_up, p2_dn) == t ==> P
      then ready(P, p1_dn) andalso ready(P, p2_dn)
      else true
    .
    . (further axioms)
    .
}
```

The axioms will be explained in the next section, where we can better contrast them with those above and yet a third set of axioms, to be presented shortly. Note that we have again relegated the details of the P-Layer's messages to a substructure.

```
signature P_MESSAGE = {
  type P_Message
  val is_ok, is_up, is_dn : P_Message -> bool
    .
    . (axioms)
    .
}
```

The protocol entities that communicate by means of the P-Layer are pictured in Figure 3. They exchange

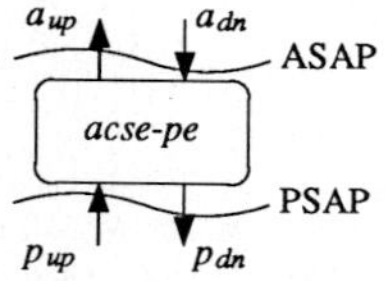

Figure 3: ACSE Protocol Entity

A-Messages via an *Application Service Access Point* (ASAP) with the user of ACSE's services and P-Messages via a *Presentation Service Access Point* (PSAP) with the underlying medium. Their specification, whose axioms are again explained in the next section, as a (generic) CCS process is therefore based on both of the specifications **A_MESSAGE** and **P_MESSAGE**:

```
signature ACSE_PE = {
  structure A : A_MESSAGE
  structure P : P_MESSAGE
  val acse_pe : A.A_Message chan * A.A_Message chan *
                P.P_Message chan * P.P_Message chan   -> beh

  axiom (ACSE_PE_live):
    forall ai_up, ai_dn : A.A_Message chan.
    forall pi_up, pi_dn : P.P_Message chan.
    forall P : beh.
    forall t : (A.A_Message * A.A_Message chan) list.
```

```
      if acse_pe(ai_up, ai_dn, pi_up, pi_dn) == t ==> P
      then ready(P, ai_up) orelse ready(P, pi_dn) orelse
           ( ready(P, ai_dn) andalso ready(P, pi_up) )
      else true

  axiom (ACSE_PE_bounded):
    exists N >= 0.
    forall ai_up, ai_dn : A.A_Message chan.
    forall pi_up, pi_dn : P.P_Message chan.
    forall P, Q : beh.
    forall t, u : (A.A_Message * A.A_Message chan) list.
      if acse_pe(ai_up, ai_dn, pi_up, pi_dn) == t ==> P andalso
         P == u ==> Q                               andalso
         u observation at ports [ai_up, pi_dn]
      then size(u) <= N
      else true
    .
    . (further axioms)
    .
  }
```

The only remaining question is how we are to piece together objects that satisfy the respective specifications **P_LAYER** and **ACSE_PE** to satisfy the specification **A_LAYER**. The following functor provides an answer, though we are of course obliged to show this in a formal verification:

```
functor Mk_A_Layer ( E1 : ACSE_PE,
                     PL : P_LAYER,
                     E2 : ACSE_PE
                     sharing structure E1.A = E2.A
                                   and E1.P = E2.P = PL.P
                   ) : A_LAYER =  {

  structure A = E1.A
  fun a_layer(a1_up , a1_dn , a2_up , a2_dn) =
      let val p1_up = pfl_newport() and p1_dn = pfl_newport()
          and p2_up = pfl_newport() and p2_dn = pfl_newport()
      in
      E1.acse_pe (a1_up , a1_dn , p1_up , p1_dn) ||
      PL.p_layer (p1_up , p1_dn , p2_up , p2_dn) ||
      E2.acse_pe (a2_up , a2_dn , p2_up , p2_dn)
      end
  }
```

The functor accepts as input three parameter structures: **E1** and **E2** for the protocol entities whose signatures are **ACSE_PE**, and **PL** for the P-Layer whose signature is **P_LAYER**. In addition, the declaration **sharing structure E1.A = E2.A and structure E1.P = E2.P = PL.P** forces the substructures **A** and **P** in the two instances of **ACSE_PE**, i.e. in the the two protocol entities **E1** and **E2**, and in the **P_LAYER**, **PL**, to be identical.

The functor heading shows *which* components are to be composed; the body of the functor shows *how* they are to be composed. The body begins by declaring **structure A = E1.A** which incorporates the substructure for messages required by the specification **A_LAYER**. Although we have done this by taking the appropriate substructure from **E1**, we could have used **E2** as well, because of the sharing condition. In declaring the process **a_layer** we have generated four local ports by means of **pfl_newport()**; using these ports we then bind the A-Layer together with the P-Layer. Because these declarations are local, they cannot be refered to outside the process **a_layer**. This is another way of encoding CCS's hiding operator in ML. We use this hiding mechanism in preference to the one already mentioned, in order to permit the A-Layer to contain a generic process *a_layer* that can generate as many pairs of protocol entities as are needed. Thus if we were to write the functor in CCS it would (ignoring the parametrization with ports and the sharing condition) look like this:

$$a\_layer := (E_1.acse\_pe \parallel PL.p\_layer \parallel E_2.acse\_pe) \setminus \{p_{1,up}, \ldots, p_{2,dn}\}.$$

Note in passing that **pfl_newport()** has a side-effect: each time it is invoked it yields a new port different from all previous ports. Since this is the only point in the specification where such non-functional behavior occurs, it is not difficult to keep it from affecting the verification.

3.5 Verification along the Functor Mk_A_Layer

Now we must fulfil our obligation to verify that the construction of an A-Layer from three more elementary components is indeed correct. We proceed in general as follows. First, we hypothesize some desirable properties of the components. These properties are then formulated as axioms and incorporated into the components' specifications. Second, we prove that any objects satisfying those properties fulfil the specification of the result, when they are composed as in the body of the functor. This can be proved, if at all, by showing that the axioms of the result specification follow from the assumptions (our hypotheses) in the argument specifications under the laws governing the compositions in the body of the functor. The mathematical underpinning for a rigorous version of this appealingly simple strategy is erected in [ST88a], [ST88b] and [ST89].

Once these two steps have been performed, the components must be designed and verified with respect to the newly completed specifications. This top-down strategy can of course be modified in obvious ways to accomodate standard components or bottom-up design or other reasonable variations as well.

We must find (plausible) assumptions for the objects in **P_LAYER** and **ACSE_PE** such that `(A_Layer_live)` follows from their composition using `Mk_A_Layer`. Good engineering practice requires that this property of the resulting process `a_layer` be easily proved without imposing excessive restrictions on the P-Layer and the protocol entities. This is accomplished essentially by reducing the liveness requirement `(A_Layer_live)` to liveness requirements, `(ACSE_PE_live)` and `(P_Layer_live)`, for the entities and the P-Layer.

`(ACSE_PE_live)` requires the protocol entity, regardless of its state, to offer an output on one of its ports `ai_up` or `pi_dn`, or to accept input on *both* input ports `ai_dn` and `pi_up`. (Our specification does not in fact state that `ai_up` and `pi_dn` are the output ports nor that `ai_dn` and `pi_up` are the input ports, because the formal proof makes no use of this fact. Our intuitive explanation of the proof is facilitated though by the use of this information, which we could formulate in axioms if we wanted.) This axiom is weaker than the requirement that the protocol entity always be ready to perform input or output on each port. According to `(ACSE_PE_live)`, the entity may leave one of the service access points unattended so long as it is emitting output. The length of output sequences is however bounded by a second axiom, `(ACSE_PE_bounded)`, to prevent inputs from being postponed indefinitely. (The (infix) predicate `observation at` asserts that its first argument `u` is a sequence of events at the listed ports, `ai_up` and `pi_dn`.)

Of the P-Layer we require via `(P_Layer_live)` a somewhat stronger liveness property than of the protocol entities. We expect that the P-Layer always be willing to accept an input at each of the ports `p1_dn` and `p2_dn`. (Note that `p1_dn` and `p2_dn` are indeed required by `(P_Layer_input)` to be input ports.) In reality this liveness property is only guaranteed by the P-Layer for specific messages. A more realistic liveness property could be obtained by distinguishing control information, such as a disconnect request, from data. This could be done for example by splitting the P-Layer's input ports each into two ports, one for each type of information.

`(P_Layer_live)` is also a stronger liveness property than that to be proved of the A-Layer: the A-Layer has the choice, at each of its service access points, whether to offer an input or an output event, whereas the P-Layer is constrained always to offer input events.

It can in fact be shown that this is a necessary requirement in order to prove `(A_Layer_live)`, if we assume that the protocol entity has finite buffering capacity, i.e. that it cannot store arbitrarily long input sequences before emitting an output.

Proof (Sketch)

Due to limited space we merely sketch the proof here; formal details may be found in the appendix to [SMG89].

We choose a service access point, say $a_{1,up}$, $a_{1,dn}$, and show that the A-Layer, no matter what its state, either emits a message on $a_{1,up}$ or accepts a message on $a_{1,dn}$. This can be reduced to the following two properties:

1. The protocol entity can always be brought by means of an appropriate sequence of output events on $p_{1,dn}$ into a state from which it either emits a message on $a_{1,up}$ or offers an input event on $a_{1,dn}$.

2. The P-Layer is always able to accept any sequence of inputs on $p_{1,dn}$.

(1) can be shown from `(ACSE_PE_live)` and `(ACSE_PE_bounded)`: According to `(ACSE_PE_live)` there is always an output event on $p_{1,dn}$, if the protocol entity does not currently offer an event on either $a_{1,up}$ or $a_{1,dn}$. Since the same argument applies again following the output on $p_{1,dn}$, we can only continue to emit messages on $p_{1,dn}$, until we reach the bound required by `(ACSE_PE_bounded)` to exist. Then the entity must offer an input event, which according to `(ACSE_PE_live)` means that input is possible on *both* inputs, in particular on $a_{1,dn}$.

We infer (2) from `(P_Layer_live)` and `(P_Layer_input)` as follows. According to `(P_Layer_input)`, $p_{1,dn}$ is an input port. Now `(P_Layer_live)` asserts that the P-Layer is always prepared to accept some input at each access point, in particular at $p_{1,dn}$. But CCS agents as implemented in the language PFL accept arbitrary messages at a given port, so long as the message indeed belongs to the port's type, so that if the P-Layer accepts some sequence, it must accept arbitrary (correctly typed) sequences.

□

3.6 Second Refinement: The Functor Mk_ACSE_pe

ACSE's protocol entities are specified in [ISOa] as output automata called Association Control Protocol Machines (ACPM). Rather than incorporate the ISO's specification all at once into our implementation of ACSE, we have postponed specific design decisions as much as possible by starting with the most abstract view of the ACPM consistent with the standard. At this stage of the refinement, we specify only that the ACPM is an output automaton (actually a Mealy automaton), but do not specify its state space or its transition and output functions. These details we leave for subsequent design decisions.

```
signature ACPM = {
  structure A : A_MESSAGE
  structure P : P_MESSAGE
  datatype In  = a_in  of A.A_Message | p_in  of P.P_Message
  datatype Out = a_out of A.A_Message | p_out of P.P_Message
  type State
  val init
  val next_state : In * State -> State
  val output     : In * State -> Out
     .
     . (axioms)
     .
  }
```

Since the protocol entity processes messages from both the A and P Layers, the automaton's input and output sets (`In`, `Out`) are declared to be the disjoint union of **`A_Message`** and **`P_Message`**. In ML, this is done using the type constructors (`a_in`, `p_in`, `a_out`, `p_out`). These can then be used to distinguish the two kinds of input and output.

Now to complete this refinement we need a functor that constructs an **`ACSE_PE`** from an **`ACPM`**.

```
functor Mk_ACSE_pe (M : ACPM) : ACSE_PE = {
  structure A = M.A
  structure P = M.P

  fun acse_pe (a_up , a_dn , p_up , p_dn) =
      let fun read (state) =
                 ( a_dn inp msg =>
                        write (M.output    (M.a_in(msg), state),
                               M.next_state(M.a_in(msg), state))
                 )
               + ( p_up inp msg =>
                        write (M.output    (M.p_in(msg), state),
                               M.next_state(M.p_in(msg), state))
                 )
          and write (M.a_out(msg), state) =
                 ( a_up out msg => read(state) )
            | write (M.p_out(msg), state) =
                 ( p_dn out msg => read(state) )
      in
          read (M.init)
      end
  }
```

In order to explain this functor we must again consider the syntax of PFL. The CCS process $\bar{\alpha}e.B$, which emits the value of an expression e on port α, transforming into the process B is written `a out e => B`. The process $\beta x.B$, which reads a value x on port β, transforming into the process B is written `b inp x => B`. Alternative behaviors are composed (as in classical CCS) using `+`.

The process **`acse_pe`** is defined in the functor **`Mk_ACSE_pe`** by mutual recursion of the locally declared processes **`read`** and **`write`**. It starts in the state **`M.init`** and reads a message **`msg`** on one of the two ports **`a_dn`** or **`p_up`**. This message is converted, using the type constructors **`a_in`** or **`p_in`** from the signature **`ACPM`**, to a message of type **`In`**. The result is then of correct type to be used by the function **`M.output`** to compute an output message of type **`Out`** that depends on the current state. The function **`next_state`** computes, in similar fashion, the automaton's new state. These results are the arguments to **`write`**, which emits the message on the port **`a_up`** or **`p_dn`**, depending on whether the message is of the form **`M.a_out(msg)`** or **`M.p_out(msg)`**. Finally the process is ready to read a message in the new state.

We have thus completed the second refinement step. Using the functor **`Mk_ACSE_pe`** we can convert an automaton described by means of a state space and transition and output functions into a CCS process. It is important to note that the type **`beh`** does not occur in the signature **`ACPM`** of the parameter to **`Mk_ACSE_pe`**. That means that further refinements are conventional *sequential* refinements, free of CCS processes.

3.7 Verification along the Functor Mk_ACSE_pe

Now we would have to verify that **Mk_ACSE_pe** constructs an object that satisfies the specification **ACSE_PE**, into which we incorporated the axioms **(ACSE_PE_live)** and **(ACSE_PE_bounded)** in the course of the last refinement step. It turns out that both **(ACSE_PE_live)** and **(ACSE_PE_bounded)** follow without further assumptions from the body of the functor. In particular, we need not find further properties of **ACPM** that permit us to verify **Mk_ACSE_pe**.

Thus we have verified deadlock freedom without having to consider the refinements all the way down to executable code. Despite this degree of remoteness from the final implementation, it is assured to be free of deadlock if further sequential refinements are verified against their respective specifications.

3.8 Overview

Figure 4 displays (most of) the entire structure of our implementation of ACSE. Functors are ovals and specifications are rectangles.

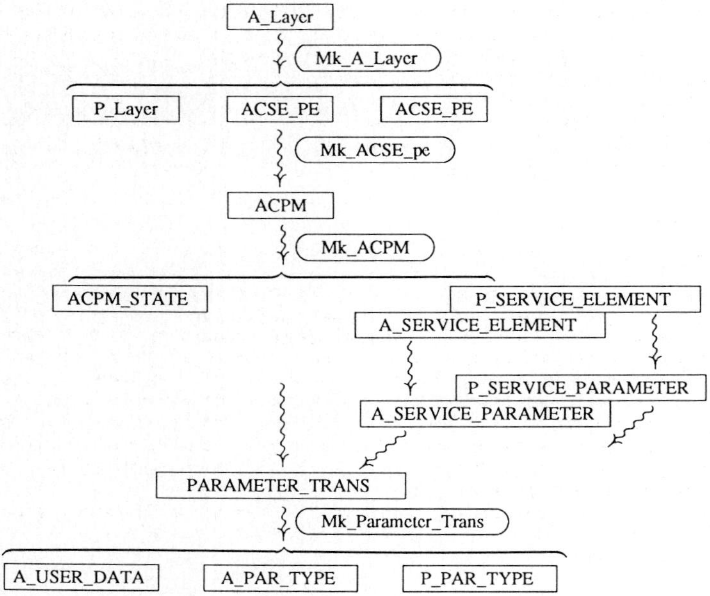

Figure 4: Overview

The figure makes clear that a verification of deadlock freedom succeeds at a fairly high level of abstraction. Further refinements, if shown correct with respect to the specifications **ACPM** and **P_LAYER**, are guaranteed to be free of deadlock, without our having to verify this property anew. This is not surprising for properties, such as deadlock freedom, that can be formulated without regard to the protocol's function. On the other hand, the functional properties we have investigated elsewhere tend to require verification to deeper levels of the diagram.

The principal difficulty we encountered in dealing with functional properties had little to do with our implementation of ACSE but rather with formulating a formal specification of ACSE in the first place. The final authority concerning ACSE's function should be its service specification [ISOb] and the functional properties of ACSE's implementing protocol entities depend on a P-Layer whose function should be governed by its service specification [ISOc]. Any formal verification of ACSE's functional properties requires a formalization of functional properties specified in these two documents. Both are vague, and occasionally inconsistent, so that ascertaining whether they indeed required a given property to hold, usually posed impenetrable difficulties.

4 Conclusion

4.1 Related Work

Two lines of work are closely related to our own, the algebraic specification of protocols using LOTOS and the stepwise refinement of distributed implementations from service specifications using modular decomposition, a relatively recent development.

The first is most thoroughly presented in [CFM*86], where a LOTOS specification of a standardized transport protocol is investigated: it is shown, using algebraic transformations, that an implementation using appropriate protocol entities indeed fulfils the service specification. This work resembles ours in its use of an algebraic style for the specification, in its effort to structure the protocol's parts and in its aim to specify and verify a broad spectrum of properties. Apart from the use in [CFM*86] of a very different, but highly successful verification strategy, the main technical differences lie in our use of generic modules to support the formal concord between proof and program, and in our use of a more expressive logic.

It also deserves mention that the result of our stepwise refinement is a compiled ML program, not an abstract specification awaiting final implementation before it can be used. As verification technology comes of age, it will become ever more important to ensure, as our implementation in fact does, that the final product, the executable code itself, functions as intended.

Stepwise refinement of protocol implementations from their service descriptions is emphasised in recently published work by Li and Maibaum [LM88]. They derive Stenning's protocol, using a temporal logic, by a sequence of refinements from a global (i.e. non-distributed) description. They illustrate techniques, certain to become important in the design of distributed systems, of gradually decoupling a service specification into a web of local entities that together perform the specified service. They deal therefore with a fundamental issue that we have here ignored (see however [SMG89]): the systematic design of protocols. Since they verify each step of the refinement, they also arrive at a demonstrably correct implementation. Their techniques are amenable to the same kind of explicit structuring, using a modules language, that we have presented here.

4.2 Prospects

The success or failure of a specific Formal Program Development, such as that of ACSE, depends intimately on the freedom to structure the software during the evolving implementation. Despite oracular service specifications, our techniques sufficed to verify some of ACSE's properties, but the verification was hampered by deficient structure in the protocol entity's official description [ISOa], which is merely a tabular presentation of a finite state machine. Our decision to implement the protocol entities using this machine precluded further structuring and forced the verification to consist of an unstructured examination of numerous cases. For large protocols described similarly, the verification strategy we followed would be infeasible.

That does not however mean that our techniques could not be used to *design* (or redesign) large protocols from scratch. Much theoretical work remains to be done to support design strategies that refine distributed implementations step by step from monolithic descriptions. Interesting strategies are presented in [Old85]. Recent developments in the Testing Theory of distributed agents, for which [Hen88] is an excellent introduction, also bode well for the systematic design of distributed systems [Hen89].

We are also exploring the possibility of developing distributed software by means of gradual refinement [SMG89]. In the case of ACSE, we could depict the crucial refinement as follows:

$$ACSE_{SS} \rightsquigarrow \cdots \rightsquigarrow \left\{ \begin{array}{c} ACSE_{PS} \\ \textcircled{\scriptsize$\|$} \\ P\text{-}Layer_{SS} \\ \textcircled{\scriptsize$\|$} \\ ACSE_{PS} \end{array} \right.$$

where *SS* and *PS* are meant to suggest specifications similar in intent to current service and protocol specifications, but more highly structured. The service specification $ACSE_{SS}$ would be at a very high level of abstraction: it would deal only with the individual services provided, describe their allowed interactions, and prescribe reactions to exceptional circumstances, all using global information.

Our research suggests that such service descriptions can be made clear, concise and exoteric. (The last property is essential for acceptance by users without special training.) We are also convinced that it will be comparatively easy to verify such properties as liveness and correct functionality at this level of abstraction; the verified refinement from $ACSE_{SS}$ would then ensure that the distributed description on the right has these properties as well. Once the protocol entities of type $ACSE_{PS}$ have been designed, and are known to fulfil their intended function (because the refinement steps were verified), they may be treated as specifications of ordinary sequential programs, to be further refined by whatever design decisions seem best suited to the task. These final implementations by various programs in various languages would indeed ensure open communication among heterogeneous components, assuming they were developed even by semi-formal analogues of the techniques we have illustrated.

Acknowledgements. We wish to thank Thomas Amrhein and Uwe Nestmann for patient discussions and two anonymous referees for calling our attention to numerous oversights and in one case for trenchant criticism and astute questions.

References

[BB87] Tommaso Bolognesi and Ed Brinksma. Introduction to the ISO specification language LOTOS. *Computer Networks and ISDN Systems*, 14(1):25–29, January 1987.

[CFM*86] V. Carchiolo, A. Faro, O. Mirabella, G. Pappalardo, and G. Scollo. A LOTOS specification of the PROWAY highway service. *IEEE Transactions on Computers*, C-35(11):949–968, November 1986.

[Gog86] Joseph A. Goguen. Reusing and interconnecting software components. *IEEE Computer*, 19(2):16–28, February 1986.

[Han88] H. Hansen. The ACT-System: experiences and future enhancements. In *Recent Trends in Data Type Specification*, pages 113–130, Springer, LNCS 332, 1988.

[Har86] Robert Harper. *Introduction to Standard ML*. Technical Report ECS-LFCS-86-14, University of Edinburgh, November 1986.

[Hen88] Matthew Hennessy. *Algebraic Theory of Processes*. MIT, 1988.

[Hen89] Matthew Hennessy. Observing processes. In J. W. de Bakker, W.-P. de Roever, and G. Rozenberg, editors, *REX School/Workshop on Linear Time, Branching Time and Partial Order in Logic and Models for Concurrency, Noordwijkerhout 1988*, pages 173–200, Springer, LNCS 354, 1989.

[HMM86] Robert Harper, David MacQueen, and Robin Milner. *Standard ML*. Technical Report ECS-LFCS-86-2, University of Edinburgh, March 1986.

[ISOa] *Information Processing Systems — Open Systems Interconnention — Protocol Specification for the Association Control Service Element.* ISO/TC97/SC21 8650: 1987 (E).

[ISOb] *Information Processing Systems — Open Systems Interconnention — Service Definition for the Association Control Service Element.* ISO/TC97/SC21 8649: 1987 (E).

[ISOc] *Information Processing Systems — Open Systems Interconnention — Connection Oriented Presentation Service Definition.* ISO 8822 proof G.

[LL88] Thomas Lehmann and Jacques Loeckx. The specification language of OBSCURE. In *Recent Trends in Data Type Specification*, pages 131–153, Springer, LNCS 332, 1988.

[LM88] D.-H. Li and Thomas S. E. Maibaum. A top-down step-wise refinement methodology for protocol specification. In *CONCURRENCY*, pages 197–221, Springer, LNCS 335, 1988.

[Mil89] Robin Milner. *Communication and Concurrency*. Prentice Hall, 1989.

[Mit] Kevin Mitchell. An introduction to PFL. In: Foundation of Concurrent Programming, A five day course prepared by the LFCS, University of Edinburgh, December 15–19, 1986.

[Old85] Ernst-Rüdiger Olderog. Specification-oriented programming in TCSP. In K. R. Apt, editor, *Logics and Models of Concurrent Systems*, pages 397–435, NATO ASI Series, Vol. F13, Springer, 1985.

[Par87] Joachim Parrow. *Verifying a CSMA/CD-protocol with CCS*. Technical Report ECS-LFCS-87-18, University of Edinburgh, January 1987.

[Rud] Harry Rudin. Beitrag auf der Diskussionssitzung der Informationstechnischen Gesellschaft (ITG) im VDE: *System- und Anwendungssoftware in der Nachrichtentechnik*, 19.–20.03.1987 in Arnoldshain/Taunus.

[San88] Donald Sannella. *A Survey of Formal Software Development Methods*. Technical Report ECS-LFCS-88-56, University of Edinburgh, July 1988.

[SMG89] Terry Stroup, Michael Mendler, and Norbert Götz. *Implementierung und Verifikation eines Standardprotokolls*. Arbeitsberichte des IMMD, Universität Erlangen, forthcoming 1989.

[ST85] Donald Sannella and Andrzej Tarlecki. Program specification and development in Standard ML. In *12th Symposium on Principles of Programming Languages*, pages 67–77, ACM, 1985.

[ST88a] Donald Sannella and Andrzej Tarlecki. Specifications in an arbitrary institution. *Information and Control*, 76:165–210, 1988.

[ST88b] Donald Sannella and Andrzej Tarlecki. Toward formal development of programs from algebraic specifications: Implementations revisited. *Acta Informatica*, 76(3):233–281, 1988.

[ST89] Donald Sannella and Andrzej Tarlecki. *Toward Formal Development of ML Programs: Foundations and Methodology (preliminary version).* Technical Report ECS-LFCS-89-71, University of Edinburgh, February 1989.

[TM87] Wladyslaw M. Turski and Thomas S. E. Maibaum. *The Specification of Computer Programs.* Addison-Wesley, Reading, Massachusetts, 1987.

[vB80] Gregor v. Bochmann. A general transition model for protocols and communication services. *IEEE Transactions on Communications*, COM-28(4), 1980.

[Wik87] Aake Wikström. *Functional Programming Using Standard ML.* Prentice Hall, 1987.

Protocol Specification, Testing, and Verification, IX
E. Brinksma, G. Scollo and C.A. Vissers (Editors)
Elsevier Science Publishers B.V. (North-Holland)

A testing theory for LOTOS using deadlock detection

Rom Langerak
Department of Computer Science
University of Twente
PO box 217 7500 AE Enschede The Netherlands
uucp: mcvax!utinu1!infrl

Abstract

Testing equivalence and reduction preorder are not always satisfactory formal notions of implementation in the sense that they sometimes identify too many processes. In order to provide a suitable observational discrimination between processes a testing language is defined that has a construct for the detection of deadlock. With the help of this testing language a testing theory is developed that gives rise to several new implementation relations. Existing notions are placed in this framework, which leads to a simple relation between different preorders and associated equivalences.

0. Introduction

The specification, implementation, and analysis of complex distributed systems (such as OSI systems [ISOa]) calls for the application of formal methods. Amongst the formal description techniques that have been developed to this end are the so-called process algebraic languages, e.g. CCS [Mil], CSP [Hoa], ACP [Ba,BeKl1] and LOTOS [BoBr,ISOb]. The underlying semantics of these languages can be described by labelled transition systems.
An important semantical issue in this approach is the notion of equivalent behaviour: when can two specifications be said to be equivalent in the sense that they describe the same behaviour? Many equivalence relations have been proposed, e.g. observation equivalence [Abr,Mil], bisimulation equivalence [Pa], testing equivalence [DeNHe,BrSc], failure equivalence [BeKl2,BroRo] and refusal equivalence [Ph]. Furthermore, there is the related issue of conformance: when can a process be said to be a valid implementation of a given specification? Since in practical situations a formal description of an implementation might be not available, an answer to this question has to take into account some notion of testing. A very promising approach is provided by [BrScSt,Br1,Br2]. Two hierarchical notions of implementation are captured by preorder relations, called *reduction* and *extension*; these relations both give rise to the same equivalence relation, called *testing equivalence*. This equivalence is very similar to e.g. failure equivalence. By disregarding the robustness of an implementation a so-called *conformance relation* is obtained. An algorithm is given, which derives from a specification a test suite by means of a *canonical tester* [Br1,Br2]. This canonical tester is a specification of a system which tests whether an implementation conforms to its specification. The derivation algorithm has been implemented in a functional language [Eer].
However, it could be argued that the notions of reduction and testing equivalence do not always match our intuition satisfactorily. Testing equivalence sometimes identifies processes which could be discriminated by a finer, still suitable notion of testing. In this paper we will develop this notion by extending LOTOS with a language construct that can detect deadlock. This construct bears some similarity to the priority operator of [Ba,BaBeKl]. We will develop a testing theory based on this notion of testing that is strongly related to the notions of refusal testing [Ph] and failure trace equivalence [Ba]. We will use a basic version of LOTOS, i.e. without value passing, for describing processes. We will only consider finite LOTOS processes in this paper.

The organisation of this paper is as follows: section 1 discusses some drawbacks of testing equivalence. In section 2 the testing language TLOTOS is developed. Section 3 describes the testing theory induced by TLOTOS . In section 4 the testing theory is connected to the concept of failure traces. Section 5 describes another notion of testing in connection with the concept of generalized failure. Generalized failure semantics takes place strictly between failure and failure trace semantics. Section 6 places several notions of testing in a hierarchical framework. Section 7 discusses related work, and section 8 contains conclusions and directions for further research.

1. Weaknesses of reduction and testing equivalence

We will discuss two examples, both coming from the realm of vending machines, in which it is shown that the notions of reduction and testing equivalence are not completely satisfactory. For the definitions of reduction and testing equivalence we refer to [Br1,Br2]. We repeat the notations: Let B_1 and B_2 be processes. B_1 **te** B_2 means that B_1 and B_2 are testing equivalent. B_1 **red** B_2 means that B_1 is a reduction of B_2; this can be interpreted such as that B_1 is a valid implementation of B_2. We will adopt a different notation for **te** and **red**, in order to obtain more uniformity in the notation for other equivalences and preorders. Testing equivalence is also known in the literature as *failure* equivalence [BeKl2,BroRo]. We will therefore denote **te** by $\approx_F$ and **red** by $\leq_F$.

Example 1.1 Suppose we have a coffee dispenser in which you have to insert two coins before collecting a cup of coffee. However, you should not insert the second coin too quickly, or you are left with nothing. This dispenser can be modelled by:

$B_1 =$

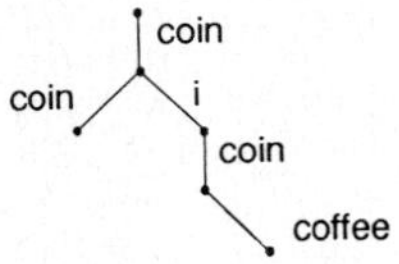

Now take the following machine in which you insert two coins and get nothing:

$B_2 =$

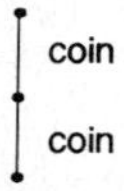

Rather surprisingly, $B_2 \leq_F B_1$. With B_2, no matter how long you wait before entering the second coin, you will never get coffee, and still it is considered a valid implementation of B_1! This anomaly results from the assumption that an internal event will eventually occur, when no event is offered. This interpretation is, though not generally agreed upon, widespreadly accepted; failure preorder and equivalence appear to be not in accordance with this interpretation.

◊

Even without (explicit) internal actions there could arise a problem, as the next example illustrates.

Example 1.2. Consider these coffee and tea dispensers:

$B_1 =$

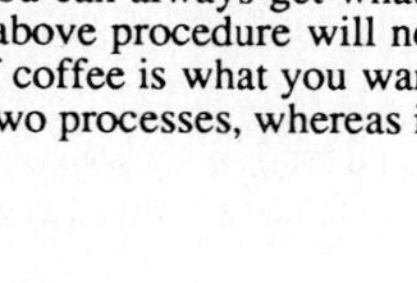

$B_2 =$

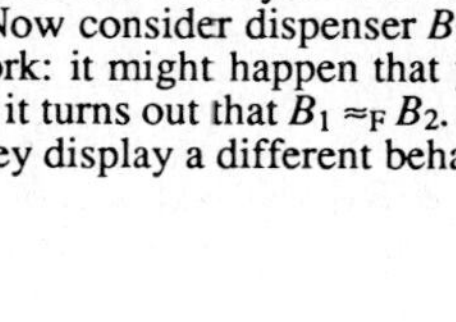

Suppose you want to obtain coffee from machine B_1. First insert a coin, then try the coffee button. If it doesn't work, hit the machine, and try again: this time you will be successful. So with dispenser B_1 you can always get what you want. Now consider dispenser B_2. Obviously, with this dispenser the above procedure will not always work: it might happen that you will have to settle for tea, even if coffee is what you want. However, it turns out that $B_1 \approx_F B_2$. So testing equivalence identifies the two processes, whereas intuitively they display a different behaviour.

◊

When we look at example 1.2 we can see that we have endowed the user of the dispenser with the ability to take a certain course of action on the basis of the detection of a deadlock: if the coffee button refuses, then hit the machine. This kind of procedure is not expressible in LOTOS, since LOTOS has no construct for the detection of deadlocks. This means we have to leave the assumption that the observer of a LOTOS process is another LOTOS process. Therefore, in the next section we will define the language TLOTOS (Testing LOTOS) which does have the ability to detect deadlocks. With the application of this testing language we will be able to discriminate between the two processes B_1 and B_2 of example 1.2. With TLOTOS we will also be able to reject B_2 as an implementation of B_1 in example 1.1.
In this paper we will only consider *finite* processes. With "finite" we mean that the process does not have arbitrarily long traces, i.e. the trace length is bounded (we will not worry about whether a process is finitely branching). Infinite processes cause problems when they contain so-called *divergences* (infinite or arbitrarily long chains of internal actions). Divergences have been dealt with in different ways. In [Hoa] divergence is considered to be a specification error and is identified with a special CHAOS process. In [DeNHe] and [Ph] divergence is given a less harsh but comparably special treatment. Since divergence arises quite naturally in the practice of specification these approaches are not completely satisfactory. The testing equivalence of [BrSc] deals with divergence in a natural and "fair" manner, but as a consequence the testing equivalence relation is not a congruence relation w.r.t. the hiding operator. This is not satisfactory because of the important role of the hiding operator in the specification practice, especially in the context of OSI [ISOa].
Because of these problems, and for the sake of clarity of exposition, we will defer the treatment of infinite processes to a later stage of research and consider in this paper finite processes only.

2. The testing language TLOTOS

For the definitions of labelled transition system and Basic LOTOS we refer to [BrScSt,Br2].We define the language TLOTOS by the syntax of table 1 and axioms and inference rules of table 2.
We assume the existence of a countable set of *labels* or *observable actions* L. In table 1 and 2, B, B_1 and B_2 stand for TLOTOS behaviour expressions, and X stands for a countable set of TLOTOS behaviour expressions.

Name	**Behaviour Expression**
inaction	**stop**
action prefix	$a;B \quad (a\in L)$
	$\mathbf{i};B$
deadlock detection	$\theta;B$
successful termination	**pass**
choice	$B_1[]B_2$
generalized choice	ΣX

Table 1. TLOTOS syntax

Name	**Axioms and inference rules**
inaction	no rules
action prefix	$a;B\ -a\rightarrow B \quad (a\in L)$
	$\mathbf{i};B\ -\tau\rightarrow B$
deadlock detection	$\theta;B\ -\theta\rightarrow B$
successful termination	$\mathbf{pass}\ -\gamma\rightarrow \mathbf{stop}$
choice	$g\in L\cup\{\gamma,\theta,\tau\}$:
	$B_1\ -g\rightarrow B_1' \vdash B_1[]B_2\ -g\rightarrow B_1'$
	$B_2\ -g\rightarrow B_2' \vdash B_1[]B_2\ -g\rightarrow B_2'$
generalized choice	$g\in L\cup\{\gamma,\theta,\tau\}$:
	$B\ -g\rightarrow B' \vdash \Sigma\,\{B\}\cup X\ -g\rightarrow B'$

Table 2. Axioms and inference rules of TLOTOS

We have γ as the special label that represents the successful termination of a TLOTOS process. Notice that in LOTOS this role is played by the special δ label. In TLOTOS δ is treated as an ordinary label so from now on we always assume $\delta\in L$. In TLOTOS a process does not have to

terminate after observing a δ; in particular, we want to be able to observe a γ after it, in order to know that the test has been successful.
The deadlock detection label θ (from θανατος, death) could be considered as a label with lowest priority; θ may only happen if the system would otherwise be in a deadlock. The operator by which this is achieved and the role of θ will be made clearer further on.
The γ and θ labels are reserved; they may not occur in a LOTOS process.
Now we can use TLOTOS to specify a test process for a LOTOS process; what we still need is a way to apply a test process to a process. We will therefore define a new *test composition* operator $\|_\theta$ which is similar to the LOTOS composition operator, but differs in the following: a θ may only occur if there would be a deadlock otherwise, so:
- the state is stable, i.e. has no τ-derivation;
- no observable action, other than θ, can occur.

Suppose we have a LOTOS process P and a TLOTOS test process T. If the label set of P is given by $L(P)$ we assume $L(P) \subset L$ (the inclusion is proper since $\delta \in L$). Applying T to P is denoted by $P \|_\theta T$. We define the test composition operator by table 3.

Syntax: $P \|_\theta T$
Inference Rules:
1. $P \text{-}\tau\!\rightarrow P' \;\vdash P \|_\theta T \text{-}\tau\!\rightarrow P' \|_\theta T$
2. $T \text{-}\tau\!\rightarrow T' \;\vdash P \|_\theta T \text{-}\tau\!\rightarrow P \|_\theta T'$
3. $T \text{-}\gamma\!\rightarrow \mathbf{stop} \;\vdash P \|_\theta T \text{-}\gamma\!\rightarrow \mathbf{stop}$
4. $P \text{-}a\!\rightarrow P', T \text{-}a\!\rightarrow T', a \in L \;\vdash P \|_\theta T \text{-}a\!\rightarrow P' \|_\theta T'$
5. $\neg(\exists p \in L \cup \{\tau, \gamma\} : P \|_\theta T \text{-}p\!\rightarrow), T \text{-}\theta\!\rightarrow T' \;\vdash P \|_\theta T \text{-}\theta\!\rightarrow P \|_\theta T'$

Table 3. Syntax and inference rules of the test composition operator

We will show instances of the application of TLOTOS in the next two examples.

Example 2.1. Let B_1 and B_2 be the processes of example 1.1. Now consider the following test process:
T = *coin* ; θ ; *coin* ; *coffee* ; **pass**
Now it is not hard to see that $B_1 \|_\theta T$ can only lead to a successful termination:
$B_1 \|_\theta T$ –*coin*→–τ→–θ→–*coin*→–*coffee*→–γ→ **stop**, because the θ will only happen after the τ has happened. However, for B_2 we find that $B_2 \|_\theta T$, after the observation –*coin*→–θ→–*coin*→, is in a deadlock. So with the help of T, we are able to reject B_2 as an implementation of B_1.
◊

Example 2.2. Let B_1 and B_2 be the two processes of example 1.2. Now consider the following test process:
T = *coin* ; (*coffee* ; **pass**
[] θ ; *bang* ; *coffee* ; **pass**)
Now it is easy to check that $B_1 \|_\theta T$ can only terminate successfully, whereas $B_2 \|_\theta T$ might deadlock, after the observation –*coin*→–θ→–*bang*→. So with T, we can distinguish the process B_1 from B_2.
◊

It could be asked whether the ability of TLOTOS to detect a deadlock is realizable in practice. We mention two possibilities of tackling this test implementation problem:
- it might be possible to monitor the internal activity of a system in order to be able to conclude the stability of a system in a given state. When in a stable state the system refuses certain actions, it can be concluded that the system deadlocks w.r.t. these actions.
- it could be possible to postulate a maximum response time for a given system; after the maximum response time, the system is assumed to be in a stable state. The rejection of possibly correct systems that fail to meet the response time criterium would have its justification in the fact that such systems could be considered to be of no practical avail.

Notice that in the testing theory of [Br1,Br2], there is exactly the same problem concerning the feasibility of deadlock detection. Our proposal for a testing language does in fact not consist of an extension of the *kind* of observation that is being made, but only on the *use* that is made of the result of the observation. In the testing theory of [Br1,Br2], after a trace, a deadlock is observed, and after that, nothing is observed anymore. In our testing proposal, after the observation of a deadlock for some actions, still other actions can be observed. The kind of observation being made

is the same in both cases; therefore we think testing with TLOTOS is just as feasible as testing with LOTOS.
In [Ba,BaBeKl] so-called *priorities* are introduced. Priorities are specified by a partial order on the label set. In this approach, our θ label could be considered to have a priority that is lower than the priority of any other label, i.e. the partial order is given by
$\forall p \in L \cup \{\tau, \delta\}: \theta < p$. The priority operator of [Ba,BaBeKl] is however not defined for processes with internal actions.

3. Testing theory for TLOTOS.

In this section we develop a testing theory for testing with TLOTOS in the same spirit as the theory of [Br1,Br2]. Most of the concepts and notations are borrowed from or inspired by [Br1,Br2].

Definition 3.1.

- A *test* is a TLOTOS process; the set of all tests is called *TEST*.
- Let $\sigma \in (L \cup \{\theta, \gamma\})^*$, T a test and P a LOTOS process, then a derivation $P \parallel_\theta T = \sigma \Rightarrow P' \parallel_\theta T'$ is a *test run* of P and T; a test run is *completed* if $P' \parallel_\theta T' \sim$ **stop**.
- A completed test run $P \parallel_\theta T = \sigma \Rightarrow P' \parallel_\theta T'$ is *successful* if $\sigma = \sigma'\gamma$ for some $\sigma' \in (L \cup \{\theta\})^*$; a completed test run *fails* if it is not successful.

◊

We will use the convention that "process" means "LOTOS process" unless stated otherwise. Now for a test and a process P, there are three possibilities: all completed test runs are successful, some are successful and others fail, and all completed runs fail. In order to express these situations, we introduce the following definition:

Definition 3.2. Let T be a test and P a process. We define the following notations:

- P **may** $T \Leftrightarrow$ there is a successful run of P and T;
- P **~~may~~** $T \Leftrightarrow$ there is no successful run of P and T;
- P **must** $T \Leftrightarrow$ all completed runs of P and T are successful;
- P **~~must~~** $T \Leftrightarrow$ not all completed runs of P and T are successful.

◊

We are now ready to discuss the problem of what to consider as a valid implementation for a given specification. Suppose we have a specification process P_{spec} and an implementation process P_{imp}. There are two intuitively natural demands on P_{imp}:

- The behaviour that P_{imp} exhibits must be *allowed* by P_{spec}; this means that if P_{imp} has a successful run with any given test T, there must also be a successful run of P_{spec} and T.
- The behaviour that P_{spec} *prescribes* must be exhibited by P_{imp}; this means that if P_{spec} has only successful runs with any given test T, also P_{imp} must have only successful runs with T.

We will denote the fact that a process P_{imp} is a valid implementation of a specification P_{spec} by $P_{imp} \leq_{FT} P_{spec}$. The subscript FT stands for *failure trace*, for reasons which will be made clear later on. The above considerations lead to the following definition:

Definition 3.3. Let P_{imp} and P_{spec} be processes. We define the relation $\leq_{FT}$ by

$$P_{imp} \leq_{FT} P_{spec} \;\Leftrightarrow\; \forall T \in TEST: (P_{imp}\ \mathbf{may}\ T \Rightarrow P_{spec}\ \mathbf{may}\ T) \wedge (P_{spec}\ \mathbf{must}\ T \Rightarrow P_{imp}\ \mathbf{must}\ T)$$

◊

Proposition 3.4. The relation $\leq_{FT}$ is a preorder, i.e. a reflexive and transitive relation.
Proof: follows immediately from the definition of $\leq_{FT}$.

◊

Since $\leq_{FT}$ is a preorder, we can use it to define an equivalence relation in a standard way.

Definition 3.5. Let P_1 and P_2 be processes. Then we define the relation $\approx_{FT}$ by

$$P_1 \approx_{FT} P_2 \;\Leftrightarrow\; (P_1 \leq_{FT} P_2) \wedge (P_2 \leq_{FT} P_1) \;\Leftrightarrow$$
$$\forall T \in TEST: (P_1\ \mathbf{may}\ T \Leftrightarrow P_2\ \mathbf{may}\ T) \wedge (P_1\ \mathbf{must}\ T \Leftrightarrow P_2\ \mathbf{must}\ T)$$

◊

Proposition 3.6. Let P_1 and P_2 be processes. Then $P_1 \leq_{FT} P_2 \Rightarrow P_1 \leq_F P_2$
Proof: This follows easily from the fact that $\exists P': P = \sigma \Rightarrow P' \not= a \Rightarrow$ for all $a \in A$, with $\sigma = a_1 \ldots a_n$, is equivalent to P **may** T, with
$T = a_1 ; \ldots ; a_n ;(\Sigma \{ a ; \mathbf{stop} \mid a \in A \} [] \theta ; \mathbf{pass})$

◊

Corollary 3.7. Let P_1 and P_2 be processes. Then $P_1 \approx_{FT} P_2 \Rightarrow P_1 \approx_F P_2$

◊

The following lemma and theorem show that it is not necessary to deal with the **must** concept, and that the notion of **may** is sufficient to define the $\leq_{FT}$ relation.

Lemma 3.8. Let P_2 and P_1 be processes, and T a test. Then the following holds:
$(P_2$ **must** $T \wedge P_1$ **must** $T) \Rightarrow (\exists T' \in TEST$: P_2 **may** $T' \wedge P_1$ **may** $T')$.

Proof: If P_1 **must** T, then for some σ, $P_1 \Vert_\theta T = \sigma \Rightarrow P_1' \Vert_\theta T_1 \sim$ **stop**, with $\sigma \neq \sigma'\gamma$ for all σ'.
Now change T into T', by first replacing all occurrences of **pass** in T with **stop**, and changing state T_1 into T_1' by adding a branch: θ ; **pass**, such that $T_1' -\theta\rightarrow$ **pass**. We will show that this resulting T' is the desired test:
P_1 **may** T', because $P_1 \Vert_\theta T' = \sigma \Rightarrow P_1' \Vert_\theta T_1'$, after which only a θ can happen, followed by a γ, so P_1 and T' have a successful test run.
P_2 **may** T', because either $P_2 \Vert_\theta T'$ will not reach a state $P_2' \Vert_\theta T_1'$, and this is the only way to terminate successfully, or it will reach a state $P_2' \Vert_\theta T_1'$, but now a θ will not happen. For if a θ would happen, this would imply that θ was the only event that could possibly happen, but this would imply that
$P_2 \Vert_\theta T = \sigma \Rightarrow P_2' \Vert_\theta T_1 \sim$ **stop**, contrary to the assumption that P_2 **must** T.

◊

Theorem 3.9. Let P_1 and P_2 be processes. Now the following holds:
$(P_1 \leq_{FT} P_2) \Leftrightarrow (\forall T \in TEST$: P_1 **may** $T \Rightarrow P_2$ **may** $T)$

Proof: The $\Rightarrow$ part follows immediately. For the $\Leftarrow$ part, we have to prove that
$(\forall T \in TEST$: P_1 **may** $T \Rightarrow P_2$ **may** $T) \Rightarrow (\forall T \in$: P_2 **must** $T \Rightarrow P_1$ **must** $T)$, and this follows from lemma 3.8 by contraposition.

◊

Sofar, we assumed our tests to be in the set *TEST* of all TLOTOS processes. This set, however, is rather large, and contains many processes that are uninteresting or unattractive in the light of testing, e.g. processes that do never terminate successfully, or contain internal nondeterminism. We will show that a smaller, attractive set of tests is sufficient to assess the $\leq_{FT}$ relation.

Definition 3.10. Let L be a set of labels. We define the set *WSEQTEST* of all *weakly sequential tests* as the smallest subset of *TEST* that satisfies:

1. **pass** $\in$ *WSEQTEST*
2. if $T \in WSEQTEST$, then for all $a \in L$, a ; $T \in WSEQTEST$
3. if $T \in WSEQTEST$, then for all $A \subseteq L$, $\Sigma\{$ a; **stop** $\mid a \in A\}$ [] θ ; $T \in WSEQTEST$

◊

Lemma 3.11 Let T be a test. There exists a set $WSEQ(T)$ of weakly sequential tests, such that for all processes P:
$(P$ **may** $T) \Leftrightarrow (\exists T' \in WSEQ(T)$: P **may** $T')$

Proof: Let $\sigma = a_1a_2...a_n\gamma$ be the trace of a potentially successful run of T. Now
$T'_\sigma = a_1$; ... a_n ; **pass** is a TLOTOS process. Suppose for a state p of T'_σ, with $T'_\sigma - a_1..a_i \rightarrow p$, holds: $p-\theta\rightarrow$; p corresponds to a unique state p' of T, namely the state p' of T that has been visited during the execution of the successful run of P and T, for which $T = a_1..a_i \Rightarrow p'$ with $p' - \theta \rightarrow p''$ where p'' has also been visited. Define $A \subseteq L$ by $\{a \in L \mid p' -a\rightarrow \}$ and add to state p the branch Σ { a ; **stop** $\mid a \in A\}$, so that now $p -a\rightarrow$ for all $a \in A$. Repeat this for all such states p and call the resulting process T_σ. Now let $WSEQ(T)$ be the set of all possible T_σ processes; we will prove that for $WSEQ(T)$ the theorem holds.
$\Leftarrow$: if there is a $T_\sigma \in WSEQ(T)$ such that P **may** T_σ, then σ is also a successful run of P and T, so P **may** T.
$\Rightarrow$: suppose P **may** T. Then there is a successful run σ of P and T; σ is of course a potentially successful run of T, so $T_\sigma \in WSEQ(T)$. It is easy to check that σ is also a successful run of P and T_σ, so P **may** T_σ.

◊

The set *WSEQTEST* is nice, but not as nice as possible. Take for instance the test
$T_1 = (a$; **stop**) [] θ ; ((b ; **stop**) [] θ ; T'). Here we see that for the creation of T_1 according to definition 3.10, two successive applications of step 3 are needed. If we look at process
$T_2 = (a$; **stop** [] b ; **stop**) [] θ ; T', we see that only one application of step 3 is needed, whereas for all P, $(P$ **may** $T_1) \Leftrightarrow (P$ **may** $T_2)$, as can be seen quite easily. In general, if we have $T_1 = \Sigma\{x$; **stop** $\mid x \in A\}$ [] θ ; (Σ {x ; **stop** $\mid x \in B\}$ [] θ ; T'), then for test
$T_2 = \Sigma\{x$; **stop** $\mid x \in A \cup B\}$ [] θ ; T', $(P$ **may** $T_1) \Leftrightarrow (P$ **may** $T_2)$ for all processes P. Define the set of *sequential tests SEQTEST* as the set of all weakly sequential tests for which step 3 of definition

3.10 is never applied consecutively. By repeated application of the above procedure, we see that to each weakly sequential test T_1 there corresponds a unique sequential test T_2 such that (P **may** T_1) $\Leftrightarrow$ (P **may** T_2). This proves the following corollary:

Corollary 3.12 Let T be a test. There exists a set $SEQ(T)$ of sequential tests, such that for all processes P:
(P **may** T) $\Leftrightarrow$ ($\exists T' \in SEQ(T)$: P **may** T')

◊

Theorem 3.13 Let P_1 and P_2 be processes. Then
($P_1 \leq_{FT} P_2$) $\Leftrightarrow$ ($\forall T \in SEQTEST$: P_1 **may** $T \Rightarrow P_2$ **may** T).
Proof: The $\Rightarrow$ part is trivial. The $\Leftarrow$ part follows from theorem 3.9 and corollary 3.12.

◊

4. Failure traces

In this section, we will link the testing theory of section 3 to the concept of *failure trace*. Failure traces are informally defined in [Ba].

Definition 4.1. A *failure trace* f is a string of the form $f = A_0a_1A_1a_2...a_nA_n$, $n \geq 0$, with
- $a_i \in L$, $1 \leq i \leq n$
- $A_i \subseteq L$ or $A_i = \varepsilon$, $0 \leq i \leq n$ (ε is the neutral element w.r.t. concatenation).

◊

Definition 4.2. Let P be a process, and let $\sigma = a_1a_2...a_n$ be a trace of P. This means that
$\exists P_0, P_1, ..., P_n$: $P \xrightarrow{\tau^{k0}} P_0 \xrightarrow{a_1\tau^{k1}} P_1 \xrightarrow{a_2\tau^{k2}} ... P_{n-1} \xrightarrow{a_n\tau^{kn}} P_n$, for some $k0,...,kn \geq 0$
Now if f is a failure trace $f = A_0a_1A_1...a_nA_n$, for which the following holds:
- if $P_i \xrightarrow{\tau}$ then $A_i = \varepsilon$ ($0 \leq i \leq n$)
- if $\neg(P_i \xrightarrow{\tau})$ then $A_i = \varepsilon$ or $A_i \subseteq (L\text{-}out(P_i))$ ($0 \leq i \leq n$), where $out(P) = \{g \in L \mid P \xrightarrow{g}\}$,

we call f a *failure trace of* P. The set of all failure traces of P is denoted by $FTr(P)$.

◊

So we get a failure trace of a process P by taking a trace of P, and then optionally put at those places in the trace that correspond to a stable state a refusal set of that state. Notice that for all processes P, $\varepsilon \in FTr(P)$.

Example 4.3. Suppose $L = \{a, b, c, \delta\}$ and P is the process
$P = a$; (b ; **stop** [] **i** ; c ; **stop**). Failure traces of P are e.g. $a\{a,b,\delta\}$, $\{\}ab\{a,b,c,\delta\}$ and $\{b,c,\delta\}a\{a,b,\delta\}c\{a,b,c,\delta\}$. The failure trace $a\{\}b$ is not a failure trace of P, since the state from which b might happen is not stable.

◊

We now show that there is a bijection between failure traces and sequential tests.
Let T be a sequential test, then we recursively define the failure trace $f = ftr(T)$ by
1. ftr(**pass**) = ε
2. $ftr(a\,;T') = a\,ftr(T')$
3. $ftr(\Sigma\{\,a$; **stop** $\mid a \in A\}$ [] θ ; $T') = A\,ftr(T')$

Since for a sequential test T, step 3 will never be applied consecutively, $ftr(T)$ as defined above is indeed a failure trace.
Let f be a failure trace, then we recursively define the sequential test $T = st(f)$ by
1. $st(\varepsilon)$ = ***pass***
2. $st(af') = a\,; st(f')$
3. $st(Af') = \Sigma\{\,a$; **stop** $\mid a \in A\}$ [] θ ; $st(f')$

By induction on the structure of the definitions of ftr and st, it is easily seen that, for all failure traces f, $ftr(st(f)) = f$, and for all tests T, $st(ftr(T)) = T$. So there is a bijection between failure traces and sequential tests.

Theorem 4.4. Let P be a process, T a sequential test and f a failure trace, with $T = st(f)$ or, equivalently, $f = ftr(T)$. Then
(P **may** T) $\Leftrightarrow$ ($f \in FTr(P)$)
Proof: by induction on the structure of T and f:
1. $f = \varepsilon$ and T = **pass**: trivial, since for all processes P, P **may pass** and $\varepsilon \in FTr(P)$.
2. $f = af'$ and $T = a\,; T'$, with $f' = ftr(T')$:
P **may** $a\,; T' \Leftrightarrow \exists P_0, P_1, k0, k1$: $P \xrightarrow{\tau^{k0}} P_0 \xrightarrow{a\tau^{k1}} P_1 \wedge P_1$ **may** $T' \Leftrightarrow$
$\exists P_0, P_1, k0, k1$: $P \xrightarrow{\tau^{k0}} P_0 \xrightarrow{a\tau^{k1}} P_1 \wedge f' \in FTr(P_1) \Leftrightarrow af' \in FTr(P)$

3. $f = Af'$ and $T = \Sigma\{a\,;\,\mathbf{stop} \mid a \in A\}\ []\ \theta\,;\,T'$, with $f' = ftr(T')$:
P **may** $\Sigma\{a\,;\,\mathbf{stop} \mid a \in A\}\ []\ \theta\,;\,T' \Leftrightarrow$
$\exists P_0, k0$: $P -\tau^{k0}\rightarrow P_0 \wedge A \subseteq (L\text{-}out(P_0)) \wedge \neg P_0\text{-}\tau\rightarrow \wedge P_0$ **may** $T' \Leftrightarrow$
$\exists P_0, k0$: $P -\tau^{k0}\rightarrow P_0 \wedge A \subseteq (L\text{-}out(P_0)) \wedge \neg P_0\text{-}\tau\rightarrow \wedge f' \in FTr(P_0)$
$\Leftrightarrow \quad Af' \in FTr(P)$, where $out(P)=\{g \in L \mid P\text{-}g\rightarrow\}$.

◊

Corollary 4.5. Let P_1 and P_2 be processes. Then
$(P_1 \leq_{FT} P_2) \Leftrightarrow (FTr(P_1) \subseteq FTr(P_2))$

◊

5. Generalized failures.

When we consider the difference between failure and failure trace equivalence this difference consists of two aspects:

1. Failure trace equivalence distinguishes between processes like B_1 and B_2 of example 1.2. This difference is relevant to an observer who can make decisions on the basis of the observation of a refusal of an event.
2. Failure trace equivalence distinguishes between processes like B_1 and B_2 of example 1.1. This difference is relevant to an observer with the ability to wait until a process has reached a stable state.

Even if one is not interested in the first aspect, it could very well be the case that the second aspect is still relevant. So it could be asked whether there is a notion stronger than failure semantics that agrees with failure trace semantics on the second aspect (waiting until stability) while discarding the second aspect (observing a refusal).
In answer to this question, we define a new preorder and associated equivalence that have position between the preorders and equivalences of respectively failure traces and failures.
We do this by restricting the set of sequential tests to a set $TEST_{GF}$; the subscript GF stands for *generalized failure*, which will be made clear later on.

Definition 5.1. Let L be a set of labels. We define the set $WTEST_{GF}$ as the smallest subset of $TEST$ that satisfies:
1. $\mathbf{pass} \in WTEST_{GF}$
2. if $T \in WTEST_{GF}$, then for all $a \in L$, $a\,;\,T \in WTEST_{GF}$
3. if $T \in WTEST_{GF}$, then $\theta\,;\,T \in WTEST_{GF}$
4. $\Sigma\{a\,;\,\mathbf{stop} \mid a \in A\}\ []\ \theta\,;\,\mathbf{pass} \in WTEST_{GF}$ for all $A \subseteq L$

◊

Notice that a θ can not occur in a choice, except in the final stage of the observer. In this way the θ performs in fact the role of a delay process: wait until the process has reached a stable state. In practical implementations such delay processes (e.g. timers) may play an important role; therefore we think that general failure semantics might be a useful refinement of failure semantics.

Analogously to the definition of *SEQTEST*, we define the set $TEST_{GF}$ as the set of all tests in $WTEST_{GF}$ for which step 3 and 4 of definition 5.1 are never applied consecutively. In order to keep the notation uniform, we will from now on denote *SEQTEST* by $TEST_{FT}$ (where again the subscript FT stands for failure trace). We give the following definition:

Definition 5.2. Let P_1 and P_2 be processes. The preorder $\leq_{GF}$ is defined by
$(P_1 \leq_{GF} P_2) \Leftrightarrow (\forall T \in TEST_{GF} : P_1$ **may** $T \Rightarrow P_2$ **may** $T)$
and the equivalence relation $\approx_{GF}$ by
$(P_1 \approx_{GF} P_2) \Leftrightarrow (P_1 \leq_{GF} P_2 \wedge P_2 \leq_{GF} P_1)$

◊

We will call $\leq_{GF}$ and $\approx_{GF}$ *generalized failure* preorder and equivalence, respectively. The next theorem and corollary show that generalized failure preorder takes a position between failure trace preorder and failure preorder.

Theorem 5.3. Let P_1 and P_2 be processes. Then
(i) $P_1 \leq_{FT} P_2 \Rightarrow P_1 \leq_{GF} P_2$
(ii) $P_1 \leq_{GF} P_2 \Rightarrow P_1 \leq_{F} P_2$

Proof: (i) follows from the fact that $TEST_{GF} \subset TEST_{FT}$.

(ii) follows from the fact that $\exists P'$: $P = \sigma \Rightarrow P' \not= a \Rightarrow$ for all $a \in A$ is equivalent to P **may** T, with (suppose $\sigma = a_1 ... a_n$)
$T = a_1 ; ... ; a_n ; \Sigma\{ a ; \mathbf{stop} \mid a \in A \} [] \theta ; \mathbf{pass}$, and $T \in TEST_{GF}$.

◊

Corollary 5.4. Let P_1 and P_2 be processes. Then
(i) $P_1 \approx_{FT} P_2 \Rightarrow P_1 \approx_{GF} P_2$
(ii) $P_1 \approx_{GF} P_2 \Rightarrow P_1 \approx_F P_2$

◊

The next definition defines generalized failures; this concept plays the same kind of role as failure traces for failure trace preorder and equivalence.

Definition 5.5. Let P be a process, and let (σ, A) be a failure of P, with $\sigma = a_1 ... a_n$ and $A \subseteq L$. This means that
$\exists P_0, P_1, ..., P_n$: $P - \tau k0 \rightarrow P_0 - a_1 \tau k1 \rightarrow P_1 ... - a_n \tau kn \rightarrow P_n$, for some $k0, ..., kn \geq 0$,
with $P_n \not= a \Rightarrow$ for all $a \in A$. Now a string $x_1 a_1 x_2 a_2 .. x_n a_n X$, for which the following holds:
- if $P_{i-1} - \tau \rightarrow$ then $x_i = \varepsilon$ $(1 \leq i \leq n)$
- if $\neg(P_{i-1} - \tau \rightarrow)$ then $x_i = \varepsilon$ or $x_i = \varnothing$
- $X = A$ or $X = \varepsilon$

will be called a *generalized failure* of P. The set of all generalized failures of P is denoted by $GF(P)$.

◊

Notice that a generalized failure is a special case of a failure trace. There is a bijection between tests from $TEST_{GF}$ and generalized failures.
Let $T \in TEST_{GF}$, then we recursively define the generalized failure $gf(T)$ by
1. $gf(\mathbf{pass}) = \varepsilon$
2. $gf(a ; T') = a\ gf(T')$
3. $gf(\theta ; T') = \varnothing\ gf(T')$
4. $gf(\Sigma\{ a ; \mathbf{stop} \mid a \in A\} [] \theta ; \mathbf{pass}) = A$

Conversely, let g be a generalized failure, then we recursively define $t(g) \in TEST_{GF}$ by
1. $t(\varepsilon) = \mathbf{pass}$
2. $t(ag') = a ; t(g')$
3. $t(\varnothing g') = \theta ; t(g')$
4. $t(A) = \Sigma\{ a ; \mathbf{stop} \mid a \in A\} [] \theta ; \mathbf{pass}$

It is not hard to see that t and gf define a bijection between tests from $TEST_{GF}$ and generalized failures. The next theorem corresponds to corollary 4.5.

Theorem 5.6. Let P_1 and P_2 be processes. Then
$(P_1 \leq_{GF} P_2) \Leftrightarrow (GF(P_1) \subseteq GF(P_2))$
Proof: Omitted. Very similar to the proof of theorem 4.4.

◊

Example 5.7. Let P_1 and P_2 be the processes $P_1 = a ; \mathbf{stop} [] \mathbf{i} ; b ; \mathbf{stop}$ and $P_2 = \mathbf{i} ; b ; \mathbf{stop} [] \mathbf{i} ; (a ; \mathbf{stop} [] b ; \mathbf{stop})$. Then P_1 and P_2 are not generalized failure equivalent, since $GF(P_2)$ contains the generalized failure $\varnothing a$ and $GF(P_1)$ does not.

◊

6. Other equivalences and preorders.

In this section, we will deal with three other preorders and associated equivalences. Two of them, failure preorder and trace preorder, are already familiar; the third, complete trace preorder, is a simple extension of trace preorder.

Definition 6.1. Let L be a set of labels. We define the set $TEST_F$ by
1. $\mathbf{pass} \in TEST_F$
2. if $T \in TEST_F$, then for all $a \in L$, $a ; T \in TEST_F$
3. $\Sigma\{a ; \mathbf{stop} \mid a \in A\} [] \theta ; \mathbf{pass} \in TEST_F$ for all $A \subseteq L$

◊

Now if we define the relation $\leq_F$ in the usual manner, i.e.
$(P_1 \leq_F P_2) \Leftrightarrow (\forall T \in TEST_F$: P_1 **may** $T \Rightarrow P_2$ **may** $T)$,
we can see that $\leq_F$ is the failure preorder (see the proof of proposition 3.6). If we denote the set of failures of a process P by $F(P)$, this means that
$(P_1 \leq_F P_2) \Leftrightarrow (F(P_1) \subseteq F(P_2))$.

Definition 6.2. Let L be a set of labels. We define the set $TEST_T$ by
1. **pass** $\in TEST_T$
2. if $T \in TEST_T$, then for all $a \in L$, $a ; T \in TEST_T$

◊

If we define the relation $\leq_T$ in the usual manner, i.e.
$(P_1 \leq_T P_2) \Leftrightarrow (\forall T \in TEST_T$: P_1 **may** $T \Rightarrow P_2$ **may** $T)$,
we can see that $\leq_T$ is the trace preorder. If we denote the set of traces of a process P by $Tr(P)$, this means that
$(P_1 \leq_T P_2) \Leftrightarrow (Tr(P_1) \subseteq Tr(P_2))$.

We can replace the notion of trace by that of *complete trace*, which is a trace which cannot be extended further, and define complete trace preorder and equivalence. For example, the processes $P_1 = a$; b ; **stop** and $P_2 = a$; **stop** [] a ; b ; **stop** are trace equivalent, but not complete trace equivalent since P_2 has a complete trace a which P_1 has not.

Definition 6.3. Let L be a set of labels. We define the set $TEST_{CT}$ by
1. **pass** $\in TEST_{CT}$
2. if $T \in TEST_{CT}$, then for all $a \in L$, $a ; T \in TEST_{CT}$
3. $\Sigma\{a$; **stop** $\mid a \in L\}$ [] θ ; **pass** $\in TEST_{CT}$

◊

If we define the relation $\leq_{CT}$ in the usual manner, i.e.
$(P_1 \leq_{CT} P_2) \Leftrightarrow (\forall T \in TEST_{CT}$: P_1 **may** $T \Rightarrow P_2$ **may** $T)$,
we can see that $\leq_{CT}$ is the complete trace preorder. If we denote the set of complete traces of a process P by $CTr(P)$, this means that
$(P_1 \leq_{CT} P_2) \Leftrightarrow (CTr(P_1) \subseteq CTr(P_2))$.

It is important to notice that we have defined $\leq_T$ and $\leq_{CT}$ by using only **may** in the definitions. Using also the **must** notion in the respective definition allows to discriminate between processess that are trace or complete trace equivalent but not failure equivalent (so theorem 3.8 does not hold for $TEST_T$ or $TEST_{CT}$).

We summarize our results. We have defined several subsets of $TEST$, which are in the following relation to each other:
$TEST_T \subset TEST_{CT} \subset TEST_F \subset TEST_{GF} \subset TEST_{FT} = SEQTEST \subset TEST$
We can define five preorders in the following general way:
$(P_1 \leq_X P_2) \Leftrightarrow (\forall T \in TEST_X$: P_1 **may** $T \Rightarrow P_2$ **may** $T)$
with associated equivalences:
$(P_1 \approx_X P_2) \Leftrightarrow (P_1 \leq_X P_2 \wedge P_2 \leq_X P_1)$
The five preorders have the following properties:
$(P_1 \leq_T P_2) \Leftrightarrow (Tr(P_1) \subseteq Tr(P_2))$ (trace)
$(P_1 \leq_{CT} P_2) \Leftrightarrow (CTr(P_1) \subseteq CTr(P_2))$ (complete trace)
$(P_1 \leq_F P_2) \Leftrightarrow (F(P_1) \subseteq F(P_2))$ (failure)
$(P_1 \leq_{GF} P_2) \Leftrightarrow (GF(P_1) \subseteq GF(P_2))$ (generalized failure)
$(P_1 \leq_{FT} P_2) \Leftrightarrow (FTr(P_1) \subseteq FTr(P_2))$ (failure trace)
Because of the inclusion ordering of the test sets, the following holds:
$\leq_{FT} \Rightarrow \leq_{GF} \Rightarrow \leq_F \Rightarrow \leq_{CT} \Rightarrow \leq_T$
and thus
$\approx_{FT} \Rightarrow \approx_{GF} \Rightarrow \approx_F \Rightarrow \approx_{CT} \Rightarrow \approx_T$

The next example shows that the inclusions are strict.

Example 6.4. Consider the following four processes: $B_1 = c$; **stop** [] a ; b ; **stop**, $B_2 = c$; **stop** [] a ; **stop** [] a ; b ; **stop**, $B_3 = c$; **stop** [] a ; **stop** [] **i** ; a ; b ; **stop** and $B_4 = c$; **stop** [] **i** ; a ; **stop** [] a ; b ; **stop**.
Now the following holds: $\approx_t$ identifies all four processes, $\approx_{ct}$ identifies just B_2, B_3 and B_4, $\approx_f$ identifies just B_3 and B_4, and $\approx_{gf}$ identifies none of the processes. For a comparison of $\approx_{gf}$ and $\approx_{ft}$, take B_1 and B_2 of example 1.2 : $\approx_{gf}$ identifies these processes, but $\approx_{ft}$ does not.

◊

We see that the testing theory of TLOTOS allows us to place different notions of implementation and equivalence into a nice and unifying structure.

7. Related work

We have started our work by pointing out some drawbacks of the related notions of failure equivalence [BeKl2, BroRo] and testing equivalence [DeNH, BrScSt]. In [GeBo] this criticism is illustrated by an example which is similar to our examples. However, in order to solve the problem, recourse is there taken to the introduction of an explicit time domain, which has a profound effect on the underlying language model. We have proposed a solution by concentrating on the observational power of the testing language, leaving the language model intact.

This approach bears a similarity to the work of [Abr] who establishes a hierarchy of equivalence notions by studying several strong notions of testing; an important motivation for this is the theoretical result that observation equivalence can be formally defined as a testing equivalence. Our motivation lies in connecting implementation notions with the problem of conformance testing: what tests should be applied in order to ascertain that an implementation conforms to its specification? Therefore we have restricted ourselves to a testing language that can reasonably be expected to be realizable in practice.

It turns out that failure trace equivalence as defined in section 5 corresponds to the failure trace equivalence informally defined in [Ba] and to the refusal equivalence of [Ph] (when restricted to finite processes). We will not give a proof of the latter but point out the similarity of our set SEQTEST with the set of L-tests in [Ph] together with the correspondence of our theorem 3.9 to proposition 3.16.(a) in [Ph]. To our knowledge there is no counterpart in the literature to our concept of generalized failure equivalence.

The ready trace equivalence of [BaBeKl] is strictly finer than failure trace equivalence. This means that testing for ready trace preorder asks for a stronger testing framework than that provided by TLOTOS.

Our testing theory is similar in vein to [BrScSt]. The theory developed there is used in [Br1] to develop a so-called canonical tester; it is shown in [Br2] that the concept of canonical tester can be used as a basis for the derivation of conformance test suites. Our work can be seen as a preliminary to linking up with this theory of test suite derivation. It is to be expected that different application areas will ask for different implementation concepts, and so for different conformance tests. The testing theory of TLOTOS provides a key to understanding both the relation between these different notions of implementation as well as the relation between an implementation notion and its conformance tests. Future work will concentrate on the automatic derivation of test suites for each implementation notion.

8. Conclusions

It appears that testing equivalence and reduction preorder are not always satisfactory; sometimes they seem to identify too many processes. In order to solve this problem, we have defined the testing language TLOTOS. The main new feature in this language is a construct for the detection of deadlock. With this language we are able to specify test processes that cannot be specified in LOTOS. In this way we can discriminate processes that could not be discriminated by LOTOS test processes. Since the observational prerequisites of TLOTOS are in fact already implied by the testing notion of reduction, we think that the theory of testing with TLOTOS is not more or less realistic than the theory of testing with LOTOS.

We have defined a hierarchy of five test sets; each test set gives rise to a preorder and associated equivalence. Each preorder defines in fact a behaviour of LOTOS processes in terms of a context which is formed by a specific set of tests. The inclusion hierarchy of the test sets carries over to the preorders; it turns out that TLOTOS forms a unifying framework for dealing with different notions of equivalent behaviour.

The deadlock detection feature has been designed with testing in mind. However, it could be seen as a possible enhancement to LOTOS, since there are useful processes that cannot be specified without it. This would call for notions of behaviour of TLOTOS processes which have not been investigated and are for further study.

Three other important problems are to be solved yet.

Firstly, we have only considered *finite* LOTOS processes. Infinite processes pose problems because of the emergence of divergences. The extension of our notions to infinite processes is likely to pose a challenging problem, viz. one has to see how much can be done by making certain assumptions about performance constraints on implementations.

Secondly, it would be nice if a canonical tester for each preorder could always be designed for any specification. The canonical tester of [Br1,Br2] is a tester for conformance, which is a weaker relation than reduction. However, we have found a way (not in this paper) of extending this

canonical tester to cover reduction. Also for trace and complete trace preorder it seems to be not too hard to design a canonical tester. Experience with examples for the other preorders has convinced us that this problem can be solved, but more work remains to be done.
Thirdly, this approach still has to be extended to full LOTOS processes with value expressions.

Acknowledgements

The author wishes to thank his colleagues in the Conformance Testing Group and Giuseppe Scollo for stimulating discussions. Special thanks go to Ed Brinksma for patiently correcting wild conjectures and shallow reasoning.

References

[Abr] S. Abramsky, Observational Equivalence as a Testing Equivalence, Th. Comp. Sc. 53 (1987), pp. 225-241.

[Ba] J.C.M.Baeten, Procesalgebra, Kluwer (1986) (in Dutch).

[BaBeKl] J.C.M.Baeten, J.A.Bergstra, J.W.Klop, Ready trace semantics for concrete process algebra with priority operator, Computer Journal Vol 30, n. 6 (1987), pp. 498-506.

[BeKl1] J.A.Bergstra, J.W.Klop, Algebra of communicating processes with abstraction, Theoretical Computer Science 37 (1985) pp. 77-121 .

[BeKl2] J.A.Bergstra, J.W.Klop, Failure semantics with fair abstraction, CWI report CS-R8609, Centre for Mathematics and Computer Science, Amsterdam (1986).

[BoBr] T.Bolognesi, E.Brinksma, Introduction to the ISO Specification Language LOTOS, Computer Networks and ISDN Systems 14 (1987), pp. 25-59.

[Br1] H.Brinksma, On the existence of canonical testers, memorandum INF-87-5, University of Twente, NL, (January 1987).

[Br2] H.Brinksma, A theory for the derivation of tests, in: Proceedings of the Eighth International Conference on Protocol Specification, Testing and Verification, ed. S. Aggarwal, (North Holland, Amsterdam, 1988).

[BroRo] S.D. Brookes and A.W. Roscoe, An Improved Failures Model for Communicating Sequential Processes, Proc. NSF-SERC Seminar on Concurrency, Springer-Verlag LNCS 197 (1985).

[BrScSt] E.Brinksma, G.Scollo, C.Steenbergen, LOTOS Specifications, their implementations and their tests, in: G.v.Bochmann, B.Sarikaya, Proc. IFIP 6.1 Sixth International Workshop on Protocol Specification, Testing and Verification, St.Jovite, Canada, (North Holland, Amsterdam, 1987), pp. 349-360.

[DeNHe] R. De Nicola, M.C.B. Hennessy, Testing Equivalences for Processes, Th. Comput. Sci. 34 (1984), pp. 83-133.

[Eer] H.Eertink, The implementation of a testderivation algorithm, M.Sc. Thesis, memorandum INF-87-36, University of Twente, NL, (November 1987).

[GeBo] R.Gerth, A.Boucher, A Timed Failures Model for Extended Communicating Processes, in: Proceedings of 14th ICALP, ed. T. Ottmann, LNCS 267, (Springer-Verlag, Berlin, 1987), pp. 95-114.

[Hoa] C.A.R.Hoare, Communicating Sequential Processes, Prentice-Hall International (1985).

[OSI] ISO, Information Processing Systems, Open Systems Interconnection, Basic Reference Model, IS 7498, 1983.

[ISOa] ISO, Information Processing Systems, Open Systems Interconnection, Basic Reference Model, IS 7498, 1983.

[ISOb] ISO, Information Processing Systems, Open Systems Interconnection, LOTOS - A Formal Description Technique Based on the Temporal Ordering of Observational Behaviour, IS 8807, January 1989.

[Mil] R. Milner, A Calculus of Communicating Systems, LNCS 92, (Springer-Verlag, Berlin, 1980).

[Pa] D.Park, Concurrency and Automata on Infinite Sequences, Proc. 5th GI Conference, LNCS 104 pp. 167-183, 1981

[Ph] I.Phillips, Refusal testing, Theoretical Computer Science (1987) 50 pp. 241-284 .

Session 3:

Conformance Testing

Protocol Specification, Testing, and Verification, IX
E. Brinksma, G. Scollo and C.A. Vissers (Editors)
Elsevier Science Publishers B.V. (North-Holland)
IFIP, 1990

Design and Implementation of a Ferry Clip Test System

S. T. Chanson, B. P. Lee, N. J. Parakh and H. X. Zeng[1]

Department of Computer Science
University of British Columbia
Vancouver, B.C., CANADA.

Abstract

The Ferry Clip concept has been proposed as a general approach to realize protocol test methods. This paper describes the design and implementation of a Ferry Clip based Test System for protocol testing. By structuring the system into a specialized set of modules, the effort required to test different protocol implementations can be reduced considerably. Implementation issues encountered in building the system under different hardware/software environments are also discussed.

Abbreviations

ASP	Abstract Service Primitive
CPU	Central Processing Unit
FCP	Ferry Control Protocol
FCTS	Ferry Clip based Test System
FSM	Finite State Machine
FTMP	Ferry Transfer Medium Protocol
INET	Internet
IPC	Interprocess Communication
ISO	International Standards Organization
ITL	Idacom Test Language
LMAP	Lower Mapping Module
LT	Lower Tester
MPT	Multi-port Protocol Tester
OSI	Open Systems Interconnection
PDU	Protocol Data Unit
PT	Protocol Tester
PTE	Protocol Testing Environment
SAP	Service Access Point
SUT	System Under Test
TM	Test Manager
TTCN	Tree and Tabular Combined Notation
UT	Upper Tester

1 Introduction

Open Systems Interconnection (OSI) requires conformance testing of protocol implementations. Conformance testing involves determining whether a given protocol implementation conforms to the specification as defined by the standards to which it purports to adhere. The purpose of conformance testing is to increase the probability that different protocol implementations can interwork together. Conformance testing can be done in test centers for certification purposes or by the implementors during protocol development for diagnostic purposes. Since diagnostic testing is performed by the vendor, all the available *service access*

[1] H.X.Zeng is with the Chengdu Institute of Computer Application, Academia Senica, People's Republic of China.

points (SAPs) may be used, including those the vendor does not wish to expose to the outside world. Hence, diagnostic testing allows a higher degree of control and observation of the *implementation under test* (IUT).

The *International Standards Organization* (ISO) has defined a set of abstract test methods for the conformance testing of computer protocols [6]. The Ferry Clip concept [2] [3] [4] is a test approach to realize those test methods and is a generalization of the Ferry Concept as defined by Zeng [1]. The main idea is to transport test data transparently from the *system under test* (SUT) to the test system thus allowing both the *upper tester* (UT) and the *lower tester* (LT) to reside in the test system (see Figure 1). This simplifies the synchronization between the UT and the LT and reduces the amount of software that must reside in the SUT [1] [3]. A Ferry Clip system consists of two major components, an Active Ferry Clip which resides in the test system, and a Passive Ferry Clip which resides in the SUT (see Figure 1). The two ferries use the services of the *ferry control protocol* (FCP) [4] to transfer test data between the *Test Manager* (TM) in the test system and an external IUT residing in the SUT. The FCP provides a standard interface on top of some existing protocol such as X.25 which actually transfers the test data, and which we shall call the *ferry transfer medium protocol* (FTMP). Once the FCP is standardized, the ferry clip test system can be used to test different IUTs with little change required to the test system. This is in contrast to an ad hoc scheme where the entire test system or at least a major portion of it has to be rewritten to test different IUTs.

One of our main goals was to study the design and implementation issues involved in building a *Ferry Clip based Test System* (FCTS) on various hardware and software architectures. Emphasis was placed on structuring the FCTS so as to minimize the amount of code that would have to be rewritten to test different IUTs or use different FTMPs.

As of this date, we have implemented the system on three different environments - Unix, MPT and OSI-PTE. Unix is a popular operating system which runs on many different mainframes and workstations; MPT [12] is a general-purpose protocol tester manufactured by Idacom Electronics; and the OSI-PTE is a sophisticated test system currently being developed at the University of British Columbia. This paper will focus on the design and experience gained in the implementation for the MPT environment with a brief description of the other two. In this paper the terms Active Ferry and Active Ferry Clip as well as the terms Passive Ferry and Passive Ferry Clip are used interchangeably. Following the introduction, section 2 describes a model for structuring the Active and Passive Ferry Clips. Section 3 briefly describes the role of the TM in an FCTS, and a model for structuring an *encoder/decoder* (E/D) in a modular fashion. Section 4 discusses the implementation of the FCTS in the MPT environment with a brief mention of the other two. Section 5 describes some of the protocols that have been tested by the FCTS and section 6 concludes the paper.

2 Structuring the Ferry Clips

2.1 The Active Ferry Clip

The functions performed by the Active Ferry are independent of the particular IUT being tested. Hence, changing the IUT has no effect on the Active Ferry. However, since the Active Ferry uses the services of an underlying FTMP, part of its code is FTMP specific. Nevertheless, a considerable portion of the Active Ferry's functions such as fragmenting, reassembly and buffering of test data are operations that are independent of the FTMP.

To minimize the change to the Active Ferry when a different FTMP is used, it was decided to structure the Active Ferry into two modules (see Figure 2(a)) as follows.

1. The Active Ferry Finite State Machine Module (Active Ferry FSM)

   All functions of the Active Ferry that are independent of the FTMP are incorporated into this module. The main function of this module is to implement the Active Ferry's protocol state machine - hence its name. Specifically, fragmenting and reassembly of test data packets as well as buffering of test data to be sent to the Passive Ferry are performed by this module.

   The Active Ferry FSM interacts with the Test Manager module and the *Lower Mapping Module* (LMAP) through single interfaces by means of *abstract service primitives* (FM-ASPs and FT-ASPs respectively - see figure 2). These are discussed in [4] and listed in Appendix C. The state table of the Active Ferry is given in Appendix A.

2. The Active Ferry Lower Mapping Module (Active Ferry LMAP)

   This module contains all the code that is dependent on the particular FTMP. Specifically, it maps the Active Ferry ASPs (namely the FT-ASPs) into the ASPs or commands specific to the FTMP being used. The complexity of this mapping and hence the corresponding size of the LMAP module depends on the FTMP as well as the interface it provides.

   By localizing the code specific to the FTMP in this module, it is possible to change the FTMP by simply rewriting this module. No change to any other part of the Active Ferry is required. A library of LMAP modules corresponding to different FTMPs can be set up. Thus, the problem of configuring the Active Ferry to use a particular FTMP supported by the SUT is reduced to simply selecting an appropriate Active Ferry LMAP module from the library.

2.2 The Passive Ferry Clip

The chief goal in designing a Passive Ferry is to keep it small and compact so that it may be possible to implement it in a SUT with memory limitations. The Passive Ferry's code depends on the IUT as well as on the FTMP being used. Once again, our aim was to structure the

Passive Ferry to facilitate the replacement of both the FTMP and the IUT. Hence, it was decided to structure the Passive Ferry into three modules (see Figure 2(b)) as follows.

1. Passive Ferry Finite State Machine Module (Passive Ferry FSM)

   This module contains all the functions of the Passive Ferry that are independent of the IUT and FTMP. It implements the Passive Ferry protocol state machine as described in [4] and listed in Appendix B. Fragmentation, reassembly and the buffering of test data packets (see section 4.1.3) are performed by this module.

   The Passive Ferry FSM interacts with the FTMP via a set of Ferry ASPs (FT-ASPs) and with the IUT Interface module (described below) via another set of ASPs (FD-ASPs) as described in [4] and listed in Appendix C.

2. Passive Ferry Lower Mapping Module (Passive Ferry LMAP)

   This module contains the code for all the Passive Ferry functions that are specific to a particular FTMP, but independent of the IUT. It maps the Passive Ferry ASPs (FT-ASPs) into the ASPs specific to the FTMP being used. Hence, it is the only module that needs to be modified in the Passive Ferry when the FTMP is replaced by a new one.

3. IUT Interface Module

   This module contains all the code specific to the IUT. The Passive Ferry interfaces with the IUT through its upper and/or lower SAPs. Some data conversion is usually necessary to convert the data received by the Passive Ferry in a ferry *protocol data unit* (PDU) into the format used by the IUT. This format is often implementation dependent and therefore unique to each IUT; hence this module needs to be rewritten or modified for each new IUT.

2.3 The Ferry Transfer Medium Protocol

In order to make the FCP simple and easy to implement, certain requirements have to be placed on the FTMP. Since the FCP cannot handle lost, mangled or out of sequence packets it is necessary that the FTMP guarantees end-to-end error free delivery of data and does not resequence data packets (i.e., Transport functionality according to the OSI/RM terminology[2]). The protocol used as the FTMP may be connection-oriented or connectionless, and either stream (e.g., Unix INET stream sockets [5]) or packet (e.g., X.25 [8]) oriented.

2.4 Requirements on the System Under Test

In order to use the Ferry Clip approach the SUT should satisfy the following requirements. It must provide a communication medium for the transfer of information to and from the test

[2]However, in the case that the tester and the SUT are directly connected, Data Link or Network functionality is sufficient.

system. Furthermore, the IUT must provide an interface through which the Ferry Clip can be attached. Ideally both the upper and lower IUT interfaces are exposed thereby allowing maximum degree of control and observation; this is, for example, often possible in diagnostic testing. However, the Ferry Clip can be used even if only one of the interfaces is exposed, as demonstrated by our testing of X.25 packet layer in the MPT environment.

2.5 The Ferry Control Protocol

The purpose of the FCP is to provide a transparent, error-free service between the two ferries independent of the FTMP. The FCP defines ASPs (see appendix C) for connection and disconnection of the ferry channel and the transfer of data between the two ferries. It also defines ASPs to communicate between the TM and Active Ferry FSM module, and the Passive Ferry FSM and IUT Interface modules. Special control ASPs are defined to perform functions such as looping back of data sent from the Active to the Passive Ferry so as to test the ferry channel. Further details of the FCP may be found in [4].

3 The Test Manager and Encoder/Decoder

3.1 The Test Manager

The TM is that component of the FCTS that oversees the operation of the system. It reads and executes the test script and logs all incoming and outgoing data exchanges for future analysis. Furthermore, it is the responsibility of the TM to continue or abort the execution of a test script if an abnormal condition is detected.

The TM communicates with the Active Ferry through the E/D module (see Figure 1). Communication between the TM and the Active Ferry is via the set of FM-ASPs (see Appendix C). The test data is encoded by the E/D module so as to make it easy for the IUT Interface to convert the test data into a form that the IUT accepts. Similarly, data received by the Active Ferry is sent to the TM through the E/D module so that it can be converted into a format the TM understands.

With the Ferry Clip approach, events for both SAPs of an IUT can be specified in the same test script. Furthermore, since both the UT and LT can be merged together within the TM on the test system, the synchronization problems between the UT and LT do not occur in a FCTS.

The Ferry Clip concept could be extended to incorporate multiple Ferry Clips inside the SUT. Interaction and synchronization between different IUTs could be specified in a single test script. This could prove to be a useful feature for testing a protocol stack, allowing observation of the protocol exchanges at various layer boundaries.

3.2 The Encoder/Decoder

The encoding/decoding function can be done either at the Active or the Passive Ferry. It is done at the Active Ferry in our design to reduce the size and complexity of the software on the SUT.

A portion of the E/D may have to be rewritten for each IUT, since different implementations of the same protocol may provide different interfaces. For example, we have tested two implementations of the X.25 packet layer, one of which provides an upper interface using X.213 ASPs and another a proprietary interface.

To facilitate replacement of the E/D, the interface it provides to the TM and Active Ferry modules should be clear and concise and the E/D itself should be well structured.

The E/D module was subdivided into two parts: the primitive specification and the encoding/decoding parts. Different implementations of the same protocol might require the same primitives to be encoded differently. Hence, it should be possible for the encoding/decoding part to be replaced independently of the primitive specification part.

The primitive specification part defines the primitives available and their parameters. It describes what the TM is allowed to send and receive. The encoding/decoding part is called by the primitive specification part. It does the actual transformation from primitives to PDUs or whatever representation the IUT requires.

The primitive specification part should be defined as completely as possible. It should include all possible primitives and all the parameters for the primitives, even those that are not supported by the particular IUT. The encoding/decoding part could choose to ignore those parameters in the primitive specification part which are not supported by a particular IUT. In this way, when a different IUT has to be tested, only the encoding/decoding part needs to be changed.

To reduce the effort in replacing the E/D module, encoding and decoding formats could be specified externally instead of being coded into the E/D module. One possible solution is to build an interpreter that would accept PDU specifications in some format similar to that of the PDU definition part of TTCN-GR [14]. The primitives, parameter names for each primitive, parameter length and the allowable range for each parameter could be listed in the PDU definition part. Each IUT would now have its own PDU definition part from which its E/D could be automatically generated.

4 Implementation of the Ferry Clip based Test System

One of our main goals was to study the issues involved in implementing a FCTS in different environments. Three different environments were chosen. Interesting design and implementation issues were encountered in all the environments. Certain parts of the system such as the buffering scheme used were dictated by the environment. However, the proposed scheme for structuring the ferries (described in sections 2 and 3) was used consistently and proved to be extremely useful in all the environments in which the FCTS was built.

4.1 The Idacom MPT Environment

The MPT368.2 [12] is a portable *protocol tester* (PT) manufactured by Idacom Electronics. It runs a proprietary operating system with a built in Forth interpreter and contains three Motorola 68000 CPUs, two of which are available for implementing the FCTS. Even though memory is partitioned between the three CPUs, a CPU can access another CPU's memory partition. Communication between the CPUs is via inter-CPU messages. The operating system is event driven. Events are triggered by an incoming frame, a keyboard entry, a timer expiration or an inter-CPU message.

Two protocol testers were used - one for the test system and the other for the SUT. The two PTs were connected via an RS-232C serial cable. The TM, E/D and Active Ferry were implemented as a single process on one CPU of the test system. The Passive Ferry and IUT reside on different CPUs in the SUT.

4.1.1 The Test Manager and Encoder/Decoder

Keyboard events are processed immediately. Frame events are passed to the Active Ferry for further processing by the Active Ferry LMAP module. Timeout events as well as decoded test data packets received from the Passive Ferry are placed in the TM's event queue.

The test language used is an enhanced version of *Idacom test language* (ITL) [13]. It is a state-based language which has the control and expression evaluation features of Forth. Each state defined in the test script is associated with a list of events expected to be received, the corresponding action to be taken for each event, and an optional state change command. An example of a test script written in ITL and the corresponding test log generated are given in Figures 3(a) and 3(b) respectively.

A Forth procedure is defined in the E/D for each primitive that can be sent. Invoking this procedure either from the keyboard or from the test script would cause a corresponding primitive to be sent via the ferry. Decoded primitives received from the IUT via the ferry become events on the TM's event queue.

When the TM calls the E/D to send test data to the IUT, the E/D module does not return to the TM until the Active Ferry accepts the packet. The E/D module will invoke the FTMP to clear the output packets if the buffers of the Active Ferry become full.

Multiple E/D modules can be compiled on top of the test system. Different E/D modules for different layers can mix and match in order to do multi-layer protocol testing.

4.1.2 The Active Ferry Clip

The Active Ferry was structured into two modules - Active Ferry FSM and LMAP. The Active Ferry FSM module maintains a finite set of buffers. The buffers are used to store packet fragments before they are accepted by the FTMP for transmission to the Passive Ferry.

Fragmentation and reassembly of data packets is required since the FTMP places a limit on the maximum size of a packet it will accept. The Active Ferry accepts data packets of arbitrary size from the TM and fragments it so that each fragment can fit into an FTMP packet. The packet fragments are reassembled at the Passive Ferry. The Passive Ferry performs similar fragmentation of data packets received from the IUT before transmitting them to the Active Ferry.

The underlying FTMP could refuse to accept data from the Active Ferry FSM once the FTMP's local buffers fill up. Since the Active Ferry buffers have finite capacity, some mechanism is needed to inform the Test Manager when its local buffers are full. The scheme used is described below.

When the Test Manager sends a packet to the Active Ferry for transmission to the Passive Ferry, the Active Ferry FSM calculates how many packet fragments will result when the data packet is fragmented. If there are enough buffers to store all the fragments, the data packet is accepted, fragmented and stored in the Active Ferry FSM buffers for later transmission to the Passive Ferry. Otherwise, the Test Manager is informed that the packet cannot be accepted in which case the Test Manager simply retries at a later time. The Active Ferry FSM attempts to send as many data fragments as it can to the Active Ferry LMAP module, thereby clearing the buffers as soon as possible for more packets from the Test Manager. In this fashion, a fast Test Manager will not swamp a slow Active Ferry with data.

A special service primitive called FM-FLUSH was introduced. Its specific purpose is for the Test Manager to call the Active Ferry periodically, instructing it to send any waiting data thereby clearing the Active Ferry FSM buffers.

From our experience in using Unix INET stream sockets and X.25 as the FTMP, we observed that the flow control schemes used by different protocols and the methods for accessing them vary a great deal. For example, with Unix INET domain sockets there was no convenient way to query the protocol for the status of the socket buffers. A "write" operation to the socket would have to be made. The operation would block if the socket buffers were full (it would fail if the "write" operation was made non-blocking). In our version of X.25 Packet Layer, it was possible to query the status of its buffers before a "write" operation was issued.

For uniformity and to minimize the code that needs to be rewritten for different FTMPs, it was decided to implement a simple flow control scheme at the Ferry protocol level. The scheme is independent of the flow control facilities offered by the underlying FTMP. The tradeoff is that the functionality of the Active and Passive Ferries increases, thereby increasing the size of their code. Hence, the flow control scheme should be simple and compact.

The scheme used was as follows. The "reserved bits" in the control field of a FY-CNTL PDU [4] were used to implement two additional control functions, namely "flow control on" and "flow control off". When the Passive Ferry discovers its local buffers have filled past a certain "high-water mark" it sends a "flow control on" control message to the Active Ferry. The Active Ferry then ceases to send any further data to the Passive Ferry. However, it continues to accept data packets sent to it by the Passive Ferry, thereby allowing the Passive Ferry to clear its buffers. When the Passive Ferry's local buffers clear below a "low-water mark", it sends a "flow control off" control message to the the Active Ferry, informing it to resume sending data packets.

The "high-water mark" must be chosen carefully. This is because before the "flow control on" message gets to the Active Ferry, data may still be sent to the Passive Ferry which must be ready to accept them. Hence, the "high-water mark" must be chosen so that there will still be enough space in the Passive Ferry's local buffers to accept data until the "flow control on" message gets to the Active Ferry. The additional buffers required can usually be estimated quite easily as follows:

E = Maximum packet delay from Passive to Active Ferry.
B = Baud rate of the line.
P = Maximum number of bits in a packet fragment.
N = Number of buffers required above the "high-water mark".

$$N = \lceil B \times E/P \rceil$$

Generally, there is no problem in estimating "N". Only in the case of long haul networks where the end-to-end delay has a high degree of variance does "E" become tricky to estimate. Overestimating "E" simply results in some buffer space not being used sometimes, but underestimating it could result in overflowing the Passive Ferry's local buffers.

4.1.3 The Passive Ferry

The Passive Ferry was implemented on one of the two available CPUs in the SUT. The other available CPU was used to run the IUT. The structuring was done in this manner so that the Passive Ferry would not interfere with the operation of the IUT. The Passive Ferry was structured into three modules - Passive Ferry FSM, LMAP and the IUT Interface module. The IUT Interface module resided on the same CPU as the IUT. Communication between the Passive Ferry FSM and the IUT Interface modules was by means of inter-CPU messages.

Three sets of buffers were maintained in the Passive Ferry. The first set was to store data packets received from the Active Ferry before they could be worked on. The other two sets of buffers were used to store packets to be sent to the Active Ferry - one set for data packets and the other for control packets. The reason for separating the "data" and "control" buffers was so that higher priority could be given to packets in the control buffer. This would ensure that a "flow control on" control message could be sent before any waiting data packets.

4.1.4 The Lower Mapping Module

The LMAP module resided in the same CPU as the Passive Ferry FSM module. Communication between these two modules was achieved via the FT-ASPs (Appendix C).

In the MPT version of X.25, the user specifies the frames and packets to be generated. For example, a "SABM" command would send across a SABM frame, and a "CALL" would send a "call request" packet to the peer entity. It is LMAP's responsibility to map the FT-ASP's into the MPT X.25 commands and vice-versa. For example, an FT-CONNreq requires the Active Ferry LMAP module to send a SABM frame and wait for a UA frame after which it must send a CALLreq packet and wait for a CALLcnf packet before returning a FT-CONNcnf to the Active Ferry FSM module. This is complicated further by the fact that other frames and packets could be received by the Active Ferry LMAP module during the process of setting up the link. These must be handled by the LMAP module. With this interface, the mapping between the Ferry ASPs and the FTMP commands is not trivial. To best realize this mapping it was decided to implement the LMAP module as a finite state machine.

In the OSI-PTE version of the Test System, the X.25 used as the FTMP provides the user with a set of X.213 ASPs [9]. As an example, the user could invoke the N_CONNreq ASP to set up a network connection. If the peer entity accepts the connection, a N_CONNcnf ASP would be returned to the user. With this interface, there is a one-to-one mapping between the Ferry and FTMP ASPs. In this case, the LMAP module is very simple, and constitutes only a small portion of the overall size and complexity of the Active and Passive Ferries. An example of the mapping between the connection oriented Network service primitives (X.213) and the Ferry service primitives can be found in [4].

4.1.5 The IUT Interface Module

In the MPT environment, the IUT interface was placed together with the IUT on a single CPU. The IUT Interface was compiled on top of the IUT, and was divided into three parts: the Passive Ferry interface, an input handler and an output handler for each layer.

The Passive Ferry interface is essentially an arbiter for incoming events. Several handlers are installed in the interface for event handling. Simple message passing IPC is used to communicate between the Passive Ferry FSM and the IUT interface. The Passive Ferry FSM can send two type of messages to the IUT interface, namely initialize-IPC and incoming-packet.

When the Passive Ferry has a packet for the IUT, it sends the connection point ID and a buffer address with the incoming-packet message. The handler specified in the connection point ID is then called to send the packet to the correct SAP of the IUT. In this implementation, only one handler, the input handler was installed. It simply puts the packet into the IUT's buffer, and frees the buffer allocated by the Passive Ferry by replying to the incoming message.

Whenever the IUT has output, the output handler is invoked. It simply allocates a common buffer and messages the Passive Ferry to handle the packet.

The entire IUT interface was implemented in about 150 lines of Forth code.

In the three environments in which the FCTS was built, the test system and the SUT had the same CPU architecture. Hence, the basic data types had the same representation on both the test system and the SUT. A more general situation would be where the test system and the SUT have different architectures. In such an environment the representation of even the basic data types could differ. It would be useful to adopt some standard data representation such as ASN.1 [11]. This would save considerable amount of work which would otherwise have to be performed to convert between different data types. We estimate that the amount of work necessary to use ASN.1 is comparable with that performed to implement the system in the OSI-PTE environment, namely 2 or 3 days. However, the advantage in using ASN.1 is that little or no change would be needed to the E/D and the IUT Interface modules when testing different implementations of the same protocol.

4.2 The Unix Environment

Unix is a powerful and widely used operating system. The Unix environment used to develop the FCTS consisted of a pair of SUN 3/50 workstations connected via an ethernet local area network. Each workstation ran a version of Unix BSD 4.2 (Sun/OS 3.2).

The FCTS was implemented as a set of three processes. The Test Manager, E/D and Active Ferry were structured into a single process running on one workstation. The Passive Ferry and IUT were implemented as two processes running on the other workstation.

Communication between the ferries was achieved using Unix stream sockets in the internetwork domain [5]. This particular type of socket was chosen since it best fits the FTMP requirements (see section 2.3).

The main problem in the design was devicing a method to prevent a deadlock occurring between the Active and Passive Ferries. If both the Active and Passive Ferries send data to a socket whose buffers are full, both will block and wait for the other to clear the socket buffers. This problem was solved by making the write operation performed by the Active Ferry to the socket non-blocking. Hence, the Active Ferry could always clear a blocked Passive Ferry's buffers, thereby preventing the deadlock from occurring.

4.3 The OSI-PT Environment

The OSI-PTE [15] [16] is a new environment for the implementation and testing of computer protocols designed to run on an Idacom PT. It is a realization of the OSI Reference Model [7] within a single operating system process for efficiency. Besides providing an operating environment which is close to the OSI reference model, the OSI-PTE also allows the incorporation of a Test Manager into the test system. The system supports all test methods suggested by ISO as well as passive monitoring, logging and analysis capabilities.

The OSI-PTE is an event driven system. Each protocol is structured as a single or a group of protocol entities. Communication between protocol entities is through an event-posting scheme whereby one protocol entity posts an event to another protocol entity. The important events are incoming service primitives from the upper or lower SAPs and timer expiry events.

When a protocol entity receives a service primitive event, it also receives the parameters that correspond to that service primitive. Overall the system resembles the OSI Reference Model much more closely than the other two environments discussed.

Only the Passive Ferry was built in this environment. The IUT Interface was sub-divided into a "lower" and an "upper" IUT Interface which performed the mappings for the lower and upper SAPs of the IUT respectively. The Passive Ferry consisted of three entities, namely the Passive Ferry FSM, the Lower and the Upper IUT Interfaces. The FTMP (X.25) and the IUT were in turn independent protocol entities. The Active Ferry and TM on the MPT were used in conjunction with the Passive Ferry built in the OSI-PTE environment to test an implementation of the Transport protocol in the OSI-PTE environment.

5 IUT

5.1 The NULL IUT

The simplest IUT possible is a protocol which returns data sent to it without altering the data in any way. Our version of the NULL IUT simply returns test data received by its upper SAP through its lower SAP and vice versa.

The NULL IUT allows the IUT interface to be tested. This is not the same as using the ferry *loopback mode* which only tests the FTMP as no data is sent to the IUT. Hence, it is useful to use a NULL IUT to confirm that the IUT Interface is functioning correctly before testing the actual IUT.

5.2 Some IUTs That Were Tested

The FCTS is not restricted by the fact that a particular IUT may only present the tester with a single SAP. Greater control and observation of the IUT could be achieved if both SAPs are accessible, but the IUT can still be tested through a single SAP.

Two versions of the X.25 packet layer have been used as the IUT, one in the Unix environment and the other in the MPT environment. In addition an implementation of the Transport protocol was also tested in the OSI-PTE environment.

The Unix version of the X.25 packet layer was a single Unix process that allowed the tester to connect to it through a Unix socket. The IUT Interface was fairly trivial since little format change was required to bring the data in a FY-DATA PDU into the form the IUT required. Access was possible to both the upper and lower SAPs of the IUT.

In the MPT environment, the X.25 packet layer IUT ran on a single CPU in the MPT . The IUT Interface was once again quite simple since the E/D module encoded the test data in a format that the IUT could accept. However, the Packet layer IUT for the MPT does not have a clearly defined upper SAP, since it was taken from a reference emulation of X.25 designed to work with a test responder. We chose not to test the upper SAP at all, and were able to adapt existing test scripts with minimal modifications. A sample test script and the corresponding test log are given in Figure 3.

6 Conclusions

This paper has presented some interesting issues encountered in building a Ferry Clip based Test System (FCTS). A method was presented for structuring the Active and Passive Ferry Clips so as to reduce the effort required to test different IUTs as well as to use different FTMPs. An FTMP independent flow control scheme as well as the use of a standard data representation scheme such as ASN.1 was also suggested to increase the portability of the FCTS. Other implementation issues encountered and their proposed solutions can be found in [17] and [18].

The FCTS has been developed on three different environments as part of the UBC/Idacom research project to develop the next generation of protocol test systems. Our experience has convinced us that the Ferry Clip approach is a powerful and useful technique for protocol testing. This technique has been submitted to ISO and has replaced the Ferry Concept in Annex B of ISO DP9646-4 [6].

Acknowledgement

The authors would like to acknowledge the financial support from the Natural Sciences and Engineering Research Council of Canada and Idacom Electronics in this work, and useful discussions with Dr. Dave Rayner.

References

[1] H. X. Zeng and D. Rayner, *The impact of the ferry concept on protocol testing*, in Diaz, M. (ed.), Protocol Specification, Testing, and Verification V, p.533-544, North-Holland, 1986.

[2] H. X. Zeng, X. F. Du and C. S. He, *Promoting the "Local" Test Method with the New Concept "Ferry Clip"*, Proceedings of the 8th IFIP Symposium on Protocol Specification, Testing and Verification, Atlantic City, June 1988.

[3] H. X. Zeng. Q. Li, X. F. Du and C. S. He, *New Advances in Ferry Testing Approaches*, Journal of Computer Networks and ISDN Systems, 15,1 (1988).

[4] H. X. Zeng, S. T. Chanson and B. R. Smith, *On Ferry Clip Application in Protocol Testing*, to appear in Journal of Computer Networks and ISDN Systems, 1989.

[5] S. Sechrest, *An Introductory 4.3BSD Interprocess Communication Tutorial*, MT XINU Manual, 4.3BSD with NFS, Programmer's Supplementary Documents, Volume 1, PS1, 1986.

[6] ISO/TC 97/SC 21 N, 2nd DP 9646, *Conformance Testing Methodology and Framework*, 1987.

[7] CCITT Draft Recommendation X.200, *Reference Model of Open System Interconnection for CCITT Applications*, 1988.

[8] CCITT Draft Recommendation X.25, *Interface Between DTE and DCE Terminals Operating in Packet Mode*, 1988.

[9] CCITT Draft Recommendation X.213, *Network Service Definition for OSI for CCITT Applications*, 1988.

[10] CCITT Draft Recommendation X.223, *Use of X.25 to Provide OSI Connection-Mode Network Service*, 1988.

[11] G. V. Bochmann and C. S. He, *Ferry Approaches to Protocol Testing and Service Interfaces*, Proceedings of the 2nd International Symposium on Interoperable Information Systems, Tokyo, Japan, November 1988.

[12] IDACOM Electronics Ltd., *MPT368.2 User Manuals - Forth Programming*, November 1987.

[13] B. R. Smith *ITL - IDACOM Test Language - Language Specification* , Version 1.0, UBC-IDACOM Project Documentation, 7 October 1988.

[14] ISO Working Document DP 9646-3, *The Tree and tabular Combined Notation*, 12 July 1988.

[15] R. I. Chan, *OSI PT Environment*, Version 1.32, UBC-IDACOM Project Documentation, 21 September 1988.

[16] R. I. Chan et el., *A Software Environment for OSI Protocol Testing Systems*, Proceedings of the 9th IFIP Symposium on Protocol Specification, Testing and Verification, Enschede, The Netherlands, June 1989.

[17] N. J. Parakh, *The Implementation of a Ferry Clip Test System*, M.Sc. thesis, Department of Computer Science, University of British Columbia, 1989.

[18] B. P. Lee, *Portability Issues in Designing a Test System*, M.Sc. thesis, Department of Computer Science, University of British Columbia, 1989.

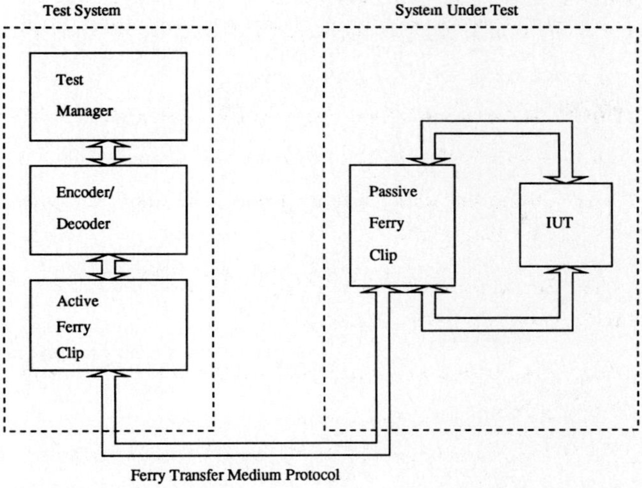

Figure 1 - Schematic Diagram of Ferry Test System

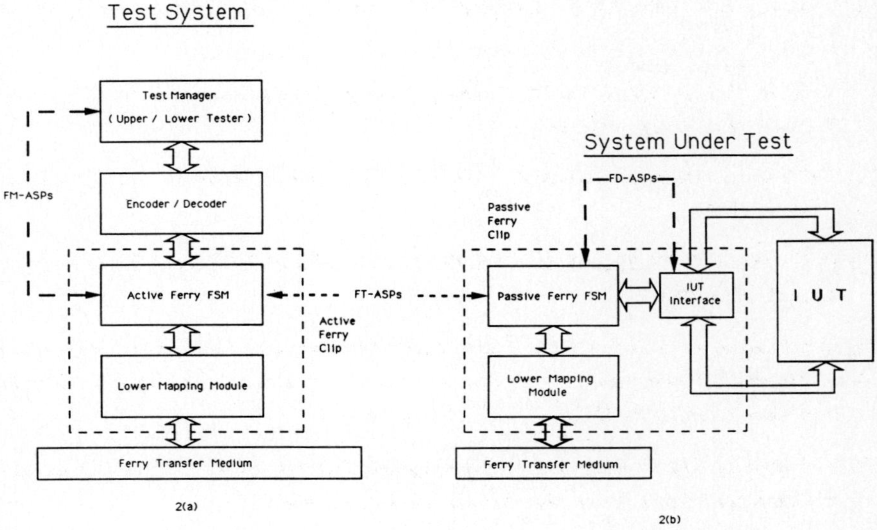

Figure 2 - The Ferry Clips

```
( SAMPLE FERRY CLIP ITL TEST SCRIPT                                        )
(                                                                          )
( PURPOSE : Send a Restart Request, expect a Restart Confirm.              )
(           Send a Call Request, expect a Call Confirm.                    )
(           Send a Clear Request, expect a Clear Confirm.                  )
(                                                                          )
( ENTER FUNCTION KEY CF1 TO START THE TEST                                 )


( Initialize Test Manager )
TCLR

( State 0 : Wait for CNTL-F1 to be pressed, then send Ferry Connect Request )
0 STATE{ FK_CF1 ACTION{
                    PRINT_TIME
                    " TEST STARTING" BTYPE WCR 20 COUNTER1 !
                    F_CONN 1 NEW_STATE
                 }ACTION
  }STATE

( State 1 : Wait for Ferry Connect Confirm, send Restart Request )
1 STATE{  F_CONN_CONF 1 ?RX ACTION{
                              PKT:RESTART
                              2 NEW_STATE
                           }ACTION
       OTHER_EVENT         ACTION{
                              " VERDICT : " RTYPE " INCONCLUSIVE" YTYPE WCR
                              TM_STOP
                           }ACTION
  }STATE

( State 2 : Wait for Restart Confirm, send Call Request )
2 STATE{ RESTARTcnf 1 ?RX ACTION{
                            PKT:CALL 3 NEW_STATE
                         }ACTION
       OTHER_EVENT       ACTION{
                            " VERDICT : " RTYPE " FAILED" RTYPE WCR
                            F_DISC TM_STOP
                         }ACTION
  }STATE

( State 3 : Wait for Call Confirm, send Clear Request )
3 STATE{ CALLcnf 1 ?RX ACTION{
                         PKT:CLEAR
                         4 NEW_STATE
                      }ACTION
       OTHER_EVENT    ACTION{
                         " VERDICT : " RTYPE " FAILED" RTYPE WCR
                         F_DISC TM_STOP
                      }ACTION
  }STATE

( State 4 : Wait for Clear Confirm, send Ferry Disconnect Request )
4 STATE{ CLEARcnf 1 ?RX ACTION{
                          F_DISC
                          " VERDICT : " RTYPE " PASSED" BTYPE WCR
                          " TEST FINISHED" BTYPE WCR TM_STOP
                       }ACTION
       OTHER_EVENT     ACTION{
                          F_DISC
                          " VERDICT : " RTYPE " FAILED" RTYPE WCR
                          " TEST FINISHED" BTYPE WCR TM_STOP
                       }ACTION
}STATE
```

Figure 3(a) - Sample ITL Test Script

<u>Result of Test Script</u>

```
PRESS CF1 TO START
OCTOBER 13 1988          17 : 39 : 45
TEST STARTING
SEND FERRY CONNECT
RECV FERRY CONNECT CONFIRM
SEND LOWER SAP PKT:RESTARTreq
RECV LOWER SAP PKT:RESTARTcnf
SEND LOWER SAP PKT:CALLreq
RECV LOWER SAP PKT:CALLcnf
SEND LOWER SAP PKT:CLEARreq
RECV LOWER SAP PKT:CLEARcnf
SEND FERRY DISCONNECT
VERDICT : PASSED
TEST FINISHED
```

Figure 3(b) - Test Log

State	Event	Action	Next State
idle	FM-CONN req FM-DISC req	FT-CONN req none	connecting idle
	FM-CNTL req FD-DATA req	FM-DISC ind	idle
	FT-DISC ind FT-ERROR ind	none FT-DISC req	idle
connecting	FM-DISC req	FT-DISC req	idle
	FT-CONN cnf FT-DISC ind FT-ERROR ind	FM-CONN cnf FM-DISC ind EXCEPTION	connected idle idle
connected	FM-DISC req	FT-DISC req	idle
	FM-CNTL req FD-DATA req	FT-DATA req(FY-CNTL) FT-DATA req(FY-DATA)	connected
	FT-DATA ind	P1: FD-DATA ind P2: control actions	connected
	FT-DISC ind FT-ERROR ind	FM-DISC ind EXCEPTION	idle

Notes:

- In any state, the action and transition taken for events not listed in the table are the same as those listed for the FT-ERROR ind event, *e.g.* if an FM-CNTL req is received in the *connecting* state, the EXCEPTION action should be taken and the state should change to *idle*.
- EXCEPTION indicates the dual actions FT-DISC req and FM-DISC ind.
- P1 (predicate 1) – the FT-DATA received is an FY-DATA PDU.
- P2 (predicate 2) – the FT-DATA received is an FY-CNTL PDU; action is to process FY-CNTL flag bits and generate FM-CNTL cnf.

Appendix A - State Table for Active Ferry

State	Event	Action	Next State
idle	FT-CONN ind	P1: FT-CONN rsp P2: FT-DISC req	connected idle
	FT-DISC ind FT-ERROR ind	none FT-DISC req	idle
	FD-DATA req	none	idle
connected	FT-DISC ind FT-ERROR ind	none FT-DISC req	idle
	FT-DATA ind	P3: FT-DATA req (loop back) P4: FD-DATA ind P5: control actions	connected
	FD-DATA req	P6: FT-DATA req(FY-DATA) P3: none	connected

Notes:

- In any state, the action and transition taken for events not listed in the table are the same as those listed for the FT-ERROR ind event.
- P1 (predicate 1) – the incoming FT-CONN ind is acceptable.
- P2 – the incoming FT-CONN ind is unacceptable.
- P3 – the passive ferry clip is in loop-back mode.
- P4 – received data is FY-DATA PDU and the passive ferry clip is not in loop-back mode.
- P5 – received data is FY-CNTL PDU and the passive ferry clip is not in loop-back mode. Perform appropriate control actions and generate FY-CNTL (using FT-DATA req) back to active ferry.
- P6 – the passive ferry clip is not in loop-back mode.

Appendix B - State Table for Passive Ferry

FT-CONNECT request	(FT-CONN req	[test system only]
FT-CONNECT indication	(FT-CONN ind)	[SUT only]
FT-CONNECT response	(FT-CONN rsp)	[SUT only]
FT-CONNECT confirm	(FT-CONN cnf)	[test system only]
FT-DISCONNECT request	(FT-DISC req)	
FT-DISCONNECT indication	(FT-DISC ind)	
FT-DATA request	(FT-DATA req)	
FT-DATA indication	(FT-DATA ind)	
FT-ERROR indication	(FT-ERROR ind)	

FT-ASPs

FM-CONNECT request	(FM-CONN req)
FM-CONNECT confirm	(FM-CONN cnf)
FM-DISCONNECT request	(FM-DISC req)
FM-DISCONNECT indication	(FM-DISC ind)
FM-CONTROL request	(FM-CNTL req)
FM-CONTROL confirm	(FM-CNTL cnf)

FM-ASPs

FD-DATA request	(FD-DATA req)
FD-DATA ind	(FD-DATA ind)

FD-ASPs

Appendix C - Ferry Control Protocol ASPs

Protocol Specification, Testing, and Verification, IX
E. Brinksma, G. Scollo and C.A. Vissers (Editors)
Elsevier Science Publishers B.V. (North-Holland)

ON TEST SEQUENCE GENERATION FOR PROTOCOLS

Wendy Y. L. Chan, Son T. Vuong** and M. Robert Ito**

*Department of Electrical Engineering
**Department of Computer Science

The University of British Columbia
Vancouver, BC
CANADA V6T 1W5

ABSTRACT

This paper presents preliminary findings obtained from an ongoing study on the generation of conformance test sequences for communication protocols. A method for generating test sequences for the control structure of protocols is first presented, followed by the proposal of a hybrid technique to generate test sequences that separately cover both the control and data flow aspects of protocols. The control structure of a protocol is assumed to be modelled by a finite state machine (FSM). The goal is to separately provide state-identification capabilities to those input/output pairs (I/Os) that lack them. During testing, each I/O is thus capable of assuming dual roles: as a test for the transition that it occurs in and as a means of verifying the correctness of the state transition that occurred during the previous transition test. A minimal tour that traverses each I/O pair at least once is now capable of detecting both transition and transfer errors. The concept of unique input/output (UIO) sequences previously developed for another test generation procedure is applicable here. This method is combined with a data flow oriented method, called static data flow analysis, to produce test sequences which test the control and data flow aspects of protocols separately. The resulting hybrid technique is directly applicable to protocols specified in Estelle.

I. INTRODUCTION

A communication protocol is a set of rules which defines all possible interactions amongst communicating entities. Conformance testing is a procedure applied to protocols implemented within these entities to ensure the implementations conform to their respective specifications.

One problem in conformance testing that is gaining recognition from the research community is test sequence generation; particularly, sequences generated from the formal specification of protocols. The formal specification language of interest in this paper is Estelle [ISO88]. Recent work on test generation has been done by Sarikaya [Sari87] and Ural [Ural87], both of whom emphasize the data flow aspect of protocols and both of whom work from normal form Estelle specifications [Sari86]. These differ from other studies such as [Sari82], [Aho88] and [Sabn85], where only the control structure of the protocol, modelled as a finite state machine, is considered.

An Estelle specification of a protocol essentially combines a finite state machine (FSM) model for the control structure with a set of Pascal statements for the data flow aspect of the protocol. A test sequence generated from an Estelle specification should thus cover both control and data flows. This paper presents a method to generate test sequences to cover the FSM portion of the specification. It then proposes a hybrid method, which is a combination of the control flow testing method and a data flow oriented method, used in software testing, to generate sequences that cover the control flow as well as the data flow of protocols. The data flow method is static data flow analysis [Rapp85], which was first used by Ural in [Ural87] for protocol testing, but his work did not explicitly take control flow testing into consideration.

This paper is divided into two parts. The first part begins with a brief introduction to FSM models and ends with a presentation of the test sequence generation method developed for FSMs. A succinct presentation of Estelle begins the second part, which ends with a discussion of the hybrid test generation technique. Materials presented in this paper are preliminary results obtained so far in the study. The paper thus concludes with a discussion of the various problems that remain to be solved.

II. FINITE STATE MACHINE MODELS

A deterministic FSM can be represented as a directed graph, G=(N,E), where N is a finite set of nodes and E is a set of edges. The nodes represent the states of the machine, while the edges represent transitions between states. A state transition is caused by an input. An output may or may not result; it is a function of the present state and input, and it is typically externally visible unless it is a null output. Each edge is identified by the input and output operations (I/O) that occur inside the represented transition. Figure 1a illustrates an example of an FSM graph representation.

A protocol typically has an upper and a lower interface via which inputs and outputs are transmitted. These inputs and outputs are merged into a single set of inputs and a single set of outputs in the FSM model of the protocol. In this paper, some assumptions are made about these models: they are minimal, completely specified and strongly connected. Inputs not specified for a particular state are assumed to be ignored by the protocol implementation; that is, no output is generated and the implementation remains in its present state. This *Completeness Assumption* turns incompletely specified FSMs into completely specified FSMs. In this paper, testing is applied only to the I/Os explicitly specified in the transition table. The FSM is assumed to have an initial state from which all other states can be reached. Upon startup, the implementation is assumed to be in its initial state. Every state in the model is assumed to be reachable from every other state. Figure 2a shows an example of the control structure of the Class 0 Transport Protocol modelled as an FSM.

During conformance testing, the protocol implementation under test (IUT) is treated as a black box. A sequence of test inputs are fed to the IUT and the outputs are observed to determine whether the IUT behaves exactly according to its specification. A test sequence refers to the sequence of test inputs as well as the corresponding sequence of outputs expected from the IUT. The fault detection capability of a test rests upon the design of the test sequence. As we will see later, the hybrid technique generates test sequences aimed at capturing particular types of errors. These errors may occur in the control flow or in the data flow of the IUT. The process of test sequence generation generally has two stages. The first stage is concerned with the fault detection capability of the test sequence while the second stage is concerned with optimizing the resulting test sequence.

III. TEST SEQUENCE GENERATION FOR FSMS

The test sequence generation method is developed with two simple goals in mind: to detect transition errors and to detect transfer errors in an FSM.

An edge with an incorrect output operation has a transition error. A transition error is generally observable, which makes it easy to detect. Any method that traverses each transition in an FSM at least once is capable of detecting transition errors. One example is the well-known transition tour method [Nait81].

An edge with an incorrect starting state or ending state has a transfer error. Since states are not directly observable, these errors are relatively more difficult to detect. It was shown in [Sari82] that the transition tour method cannot detect transfer errors. Other methods which produce longer sequences, such as those in [Gone70], [Chow78] and [Sabn85], are capable of detecting transfer errors. These errors are detected by appending a special sequence of test inputs to each transition test to specifically verify that the final state, at which the previous transition test ended, is correct. This special input sequence causes a sequence of outputs which distinguishes or identifies a state.

It follows that if each transition were visibly unique to a particular state such that no two states would generate the same output in response to an input, then each I/O becomes a "signature" to its starting state; that is, it is unique to its starting state and is thus capable of identifying the starting state. Each transition test input, I1, can then be followed by any test input, I2, specified for its final state and the output in response to I2 would be capable of verifying the correctness of the state transition caused by I1. This implies pairs of transition-test input and final-state-verification input can be concatenated and merged so that each test input assumes dual roles: for testing the next transition and for identifying the final state for the previous transition test.

In general, however, identical inputs for different starting states may generate identical outputs. Since these I/Os lack the capability for state-identification, their deficiencies can be supplemented by concatenating state signatures with their executions during testing, thereby providing the state-identification function separately.

A *concatenated state signature*, CSS, is a sequence of I/Os which may be of length one or longer. It is different from a *state signature* or a *simple I/O* (SIO) [Hsie71], which is an I/O unique to its starting state and which may or may not end at the same starting state. An CSS is not only unique to its starting state, its final state must also be identical to its starting state. The reason why it must end at its starting state is because of its application as an added state-identification function during testing. It is ideally inserted in front of the I/O that requires it during testing; hence, its starting state must be identical to the final state of the previous transition test, which is the same as the starting state of that I/O, and its ending state must also be identical to that starting state, to allow the transition test for that I/O to follow.

The uniqueness requirement for the CSSs can be satisfied by SIOs or unique I/O (UIO) sequences [Sabn85]; while the ending state requirement is satisfied by concatenating paths to those SIOs or UIO sequences that end at states different from their starting states. The concatenated sequence remains unique since its first portion is unique. This also suggests that FSMs that possess SIOs or UIO sequences also possess CSSs; and an SIO which ends at the same state it started from can thus be used as an CSS. Since SIOs are UIO sequences of length one, UIO sequences will be used to refer to both types of I/Os from now on.

The algorithm for finding UIO sequences in [Sabn85] can be used to find the first portion of the CSS, while Dijkstra's algorithm [Aho74] computes the shortest path for the second portion. Since a state may have more than one UIO sequence, this implies more than one CSS may exist, the shortest of which would be chosen. The chosen CSS for each state for Example 1 is *a/x a/x* for state 1, *b/y b/x c/z b/x* for state 2, *b/x a/z b/x* for state 3, *b/x c/y a/z* for state 4 and *a/z a/x* for state 5. Their concatenations to those I/Os that require them are reflected in the revised graph representation shown in Figure 1b, where appropriate edge labels have been updated accordingly. In this example, only b/y from state 2, as well as a/z and c/z from state 5 do not require the CSSs. For the Class 0 Transport Protocol, since each input produces output(s) unique to its starting state, no CSS is required.

Recall that CSSs are appended to only those I/Os that cannot identify their own starting states. During testing, SIOs are themselves used as state signatures since they are unique to their starting states; in this sense, a test sequence may contain more than one signature which identify the same state. This differs from many methods, where each state is identified by only one sequence. A minimal tour that traverses the revised graph in Figure 1b is as follows:

a/x a/x a/x a/x a/x b/x b/y b/x a/z b/x b/x c/z a/x a/x c/y b/x c/y a/z b/x b/x a/z b/x c/y a/z b/x c/y a/z a/x c/z a/x a/x b/x b/y b/x c/z b/x a/x c/z

This tour is by no means unique. An algorithm such as the Rural Chinese Postman tour [Aho88] can be used to find the minimal tour. Note that the last input is needed to verify the final state for the last transition test, while the first input should ideally be able to verify that the initial state is indeed state 1. The following extracts each transition test from the tour and lists the state-verification sequence(s) used for its final state. Both states 2 and 5 use two different signatures for its verification.

transition a/x from state 1: a/x.a/x to verify final state 1
transition b/x from state 1: b/y and b/y.b/x.c/z.b/x to verify final state 2
transition b/y from state 2: b/x.a/z.b/x to verify final state 3
transition b/x from state 3: c/z to verify final state 5
transition c/z from state 5: a/x.a/x to verify final state 1
transition c/y from state 1: b/x.c/y.a/z to verify final state 4
transition b/x from state 4: b/x.a/z.b/x to verify final state 3
transition c/y from state 3: a/z to verify final state 5
transition a/z from state 5: b/x.c/y.a/z to verify final state 4
transition a/x from state 4: c/z to verify final state 5
transition a/x from state 2: c/z to verify final state 5

The above sequence can be shortened to 36 I/Os by eliminating the state-verification step for the second transition test for c/z from state 5, which was there only to bring the machine to state 1; its final state was already verified the first time it was visited. The same goes for the second transition test for b/x from state 1; its purpose was to bring the machine to state 2. Its first appearance was already verified by b/y near the beginning of the sequence. This further reduces the sequence to a length of 32. The following summarizes the steps taken to generate the minimal sequence:

Step 1: Determine the minimal tour from the original graph representation, ensure that each transition is covered at least once.
Step 2: Identify the set of transitions, T, whose final states are verifiable by the subsequent I/Os; that is, identify the SIOs and gather their preceding transitions into T.
Step 3: One by one, append a CSS to each I/O whose preceding transition test is not in T, add that transition test to T.

The procedure first checks for all those transition tests whose final states can be verified with the shortest signatures possible, then it adds CSSs only for verifying the final states of those transition tests that still need verification. Each transition test is verified only once by keeping track of them in T.

A note of interest is in the application of the CSSs. When an CSS is appended to each transition test, the CSS functions as the "status message" feature discussed in [Aho88], which verifies the final state of each transition test. A minimal tour with CSSs functioning as "status messages" is as follows for Example 1:

a/x a/x a/x a/x a/x b/x b/y b/x c/z b/x b/y b/x a/z b/x b/x a/z a/x c/z a/x a/x c/y b/x c/y a/z b/x b/x a/z b/x c/y a/z a/x a/z b/x c/y a/z a/x a/z a/x c/z a/x a/x b/x b/y b/x c/z b/x a/x a/z a/x

The tour can be shortened by requiring that final-state-verification be performed only once for each transition, instead of performing it every time a transition is traversed. For Example 1, the length of the tour would be shortened to 43. This is obtained by removing the CSSs for the second c/z and b/x from the above sequence.

It should be noted that because tests are performed only for those I/Os that are explicitly specified for the FSM, extra edges in a test machine are not detected by these tests. Two types of extra edges can be identified: those whose input labels appear elsewhere in the same FSM graph, and those whose input labels do not appear anywhere else on the same graph. For the first type of extra edges, we can account for them by gathering the set of inputs specified for the whole graph and generating tests to cover this set of inputs for each state that exists on the graph. The completeness assumption, if used, is thus verified as well. Hence, for Example 1, all of *a*, *b* and *c* would be fed to states 1, 2, 3, 4 and 5 during test, instead of just those inputs indicated on the graph. For the second type of extra edges, everything else "under the sun" would have to be used as inputs; which is obviously impossible.

IV. ESTELLE

Estelle is a formal description technique developed within the International Organization for Standardization [ISO88] for the specification of communication protocols and services. Facilities in Estelle [Budk87, Tenn88] allow the specification of a hierarchy of modules. Parent modules may dynamically create and destroy child modules. Modules contain abstract message interfaces or interaction points that can be connected to form communication channels. These channels can be dynamically connected and disconnected by the parent modules. Messages or interaction primitives may be exchanged across these channels, enabling communications among modules. The control structure of the modules is based on an extended finite state machine model. A state change in a module occurs if the criteria expressed in a set of clauses are met. These criteria include conditions expressed in a predicate, as well as the reception of messages, or inputs, from other modules. A state change may be accompanied by a set of actions performed by the module, one of which may be an output operation in the form of a message transmitted to other modules. Each set of actions is collectively identified as a transition.

An Estelle specification may be simplified to a form that is more easily represented by a set of directed graphs. The simplified form of an Estelle specification is known as its normal form [Sari86]. Conditional and loop statements are eliminated in the normal form specification (NFS). Modules are combined into one single module and state sets are expanded into the respective states they represent. An NFS displays the two types of flows explicitly. Control flow is identified by changes in the state variable, while data flow is identified by operations on protocol variables, input primitive parameters and output primitive parameters. These operations are specified within each transition. [Ural87] provides an example of an NFS of the Class 0 Transport Protocol, part of which is reproduced here in the Appendix. Each transition is identified by a number. State transitions are indicated using the keywords FROM and TO. Inputs and outputs are preceded by the keywords WHEN and OUT respectively. The PROVIDED clause indicates the predicate condition that must be satisfied before a state transition can take place. Operations within each transition body are expressed in Pascal statements. There may be zero or more output operations in a transition, while there may not be more than one input operation. In this paper, transitions with outputs but no inputs are concatenated with the appropriate transitions that have inputs but no output. These are treated as one transition. For example, transitions *tdatr/-* and *-/dt* in Figure 2a are treated as one transition *tdatr/-.-/dt*; the same is done for transitions *dt/-* and *-/tdati*.

V. HYBRID TEST SEQUENCE GENERATION TECHNIQUE

Since the normal form of Estelle more clearly displays both the control flow and data flow of a protocol, the following discussion makes use of the normal form of Estelle.

Since an Estelle specification describes the control flow as well as the data flow of a protocol, a test sequence generated from such a specification should cover both flows. Here, the control flow test generation method is combined with a data flow oriented test method, called static data flow analysis, to form a hybrid technique that generates sequences which separately cover both flows. This implies errors that can occur in the FSM that represents the control flow or in the Pascal statements specifying the data flow can be captured. Ural [Ural87] was the first to apply static data flow analysis to the generation of test sequences for protocols specified in Estelle. Part of his work in [Ural87] is repeated here to illustrate the data flow oriented test method and to combine it with the control flow test method presented in section III to form the hybrid approach.

Two sets of directed graphs can be generated from an Estelle specification. One graph is for the FSM model of the control flow. For the data flow, it is desirable to display the interactions amongst the input primitive parameters, protocol variables and output primitive parameters. To do this systematically, a technique called static data flow analysis is borrowed from software testing and applied here. Static data flow analysis originated in compiler optimization [Hech77]. It was applied to test data selection for software testing in [Rapp85] and is now generally accepted as a structural testing strategy [Weis85]. Essentially, data flow analysis tracks input variables through a program until they are ultimately used to produce output values. Associations between the definition of, or the assignment of a value to, a variable and the usage of that variable are identified and examined during testing. In here, the effects of input primitive parameters on output primitive parameters are of particular interest. The relationship between input and output primitive parameters can also be determined and specified in a formalism such as the External Behavior Expression [Wu89], EBE, to aid the process of test generation.

A data flow path for a particular parameter or variable refers to the sequence of I/Os, or transitions, where the first transition contains the definition of the parameter or variable while the last transition contains the usage of that parameter or variable. These two transitions are connected by a sequence of transitions based on the control structure. A data flow path of length one is a path embodied within the same transition; that is, the usage of a variable immediately follows the definition of that variable within the same transition. This kind of flow paths is covered during the transition testing portion of control flow testing. Data flow paths which extend from one transition to another require that the particular sequence of transitions be examined during testing. This sequence may or may not already be covered during control flow testing. This type of flow path is referred to as "inter-transitional" data flow path from now on. The construction of "inter-transitional" data flow paths requires identifying the transition at which the definition occurs, the transition at which the usage occurs, and connecting these two transitions with a path based on the control structure. The path must be executable and it must be free of any re-definition of the variable; that is, the definition is *live* in the connecting path. Here, the variables defined by the input primitive parameters and constants are tracked until they are used either for computational purposes or as predicates. When computations eventually lead to the definition of output primitive parameters, these are observed to verify that the computations are indeed correct. Predicate uses, however, may or may not be verifiable. Table 1 lists the definitions, usages as well as their respective connecting paths for the protocol variables in Example 2. The definitions and usages are extracted from the NFS given in the Appendix. They are a subset of the set of definitions and usages identified in [Ural87]. These are the inter-transitional definition-usage pairs. The data flow paths for each variable is generated according to the control flow graph shown in Figure 2a. Both live and executable requirements for the paths are user-determined in this paper. The minimal connecting path is used here. The live requirement resulted in no connecting path being derived for the variables *in.buffer* and *out.buffer*, each of which is re-defined in the same transition its usage appears in. Most of the definitions are assigned from input primitive parameters, and most of the usages define output primitive parameters. Tracking these protocol variables thus traces the effects of input primitive parameters on output primitive parameters across different transitions. The predicate uses of *qts.estimate* in this case can be observed by verifying their final states.

In the hybrid method, the control flow graph is first constructed from the Estelle specification. For the Class 0 Transport Protocol, its control flow graph is illustrated in Figure 2a. Although the predicate clauses are not represented in the graph, they play a part in the control flow. The control flow test generation method presented in section III is then applied to this graph, yielding the following sequence of I/Os:

tcreq/tdind cr/dr tcreq/cr dr/ndreq,tdind tcreq/cr dr/ndreq,tdind tcreq/cr cc/tccon tdatr/-.-/dt dt/-.-/tdati tdreq/ndreq tcreq/cr cc/tccon ndind/tdind cr/tcind tdreq/dr cr/tcind tcres/dr,tdind cr/tcind tcres/cc nrind/tdind tcreq/tdind

The predicate clauses are considered by the user during the sequence generation process to ensure the final sequence is executable. Only those clauses involving protocol variables need to be considered; those involving input primitive parameters can be dealt with directly by selecting the appropriate values for input during testing.

Following control flow, data flow is considered next. The derived data flow paths are added to the control flow graph. This is illustrated in Figure 2b, which is a combination of Figure 2a and the paths listed in Table 1. Each path is denoted by an edge labelled with the corresponding concatenated sequence of transitions. Some new edges may be added here. For Figure 2b, an edge is added from state IDLE to DATA to accommodate two new paths. The resulting flow graph is referred to as an "extended" flow graph (EFG). A minimal tour of the EFG in Figure 2b is obtained, which ensures each data flow path is visited at least once. The resulting sequence is as follows:

cr/tcind.tdreq/dr cr/tcind.tdreq/dr cr/tcind.tcres/dr,tdind cr/tcind.tcres/dr,tdind cr/tcind.tcres/cc nrind/tdind cr/tcind.tcres/cc ndind/tdind

To observe the effect of the predicate usages in this example, the final state can be verified. Since each I/O is a "signature" to its starting state, any I/O specified for the final state can be used for this purpose; otherwise, CSSs would have to be appended to the appropriate data flow paths. The above sequence is appended to the control flow test sequence derived earlier, forming the following sequence which covers both control flow and data flow.

tcreq/tdind cr/dr tcreq/cr dr/ndreq,tdind tcreq/cr dr/ndreq,tdind tcreq/cr cc/tccon tdatr/-.-/dt dt/-.-/tdati tdreq/ndreq tcreq/cr cc/tccon ndind/tdind cr/tcind tdreq/dr cr/tcind tcres/dr,tdind cr/tcind tcres/cc nrind/tdind tcreq/tdind cr/tcind.tdreq/dr cr/tcind.tdreq/dr cr/tcind.tcres/dr,tdind cr/tcind.tcres/dr,tdind cr/tcind.tcres/cc nrind/tdind cr/tcind.tcres/cc ndind/tdind

In essence, the sequence generated from the hybrid technique tests the control flow of the protocol first, then it tests the data flow. If both flows were tested simultaneously using just the EFG to obtain the final test sequence, then the resulting sequence would be longer than if two sequences were generated separately and concatenated together. The reason is because simultaneous testing requires that each data flow is also able to identify its starting state, in case it follows a transition test for control flow testing. This implies more CSSs might be required, adding to the length of the final sequence. Hence, it is desirable to complete control flow testing prior to data flow testing in this case. However, the final sequence can be further reduced by examining the control flow portion and eliminating those data flow paths that are already covered from the data flow portion. The above sequence can thus be further reduced to a length of 29. Normally, additional reduction can be achieved by using the methods for reducing the control flow test sequence mentioned in section III; however, for this particular example, each I/O is already an SIO, hence, no CSSs are required. The resulting sequence is optimized.

The first portion of the final test sequence is specifically for detecting transition and transfer errors that can occur in the control flow structure. The second portion of the sequence is for detecting data flow anomalies by tracking through the flow of input primitive parameters and protocol variables, and observing the output primitive parameters that reflect their uses. Some definitions such as *to.t.addr* and *from.t.addr* in the input primitive *tcreq* in transition *tcreq/tdind* do not reach their uses. This transition is not specifically included as part of the data flow to be examined, but it is included in the control flow part of the test, and its adherence to the predicate requirement is verified by observing its final state, which is done in the control flow part of the test. The data flow requirement imposed here is that every usage of a variable must be preceded by its definition, and the usage is observed whenever possible. Every definition does not necessarily reach a use in an Estelle specification, the *definition live* requirement for each path connecting a definition-usage pair weeds out these definitions. Predicate clauses involving protocol variables are considered in both control flow and data flow sequences. They must be considered in control flow to ensure executability of the final sequence. Since they also represent uses of variables previously defined, they must also be observed and verified, whenever possible, during data flow testing.

The following is the concatenation of another control flow test sequence with the same data flow test sequence, where the former is obtained from using the CSSs as "status message" features.

tcreq/tdind tcreq/tdind tcreq/tdind cr/dr tcreq/tdind tcreq/cr dr/ndreq,tdind.tcreq/cr dr/ndreq,tdind tcreq/tdind tcreq/cr dr/ndreq,tdind.tcreq/cr dr/ndreq,tdind tcreq/tdind tcreq/cr dr/ndreq,tdind.tcreq/cr cc/tccon tdatr/-.-/dt tdatr/-.-/dt tdatr/-.-/dt dt/-.-/tdati tdatr/-.-/dt tdreq/ndreq tcreq/tdind tcreq/cr dr/ndreq,tdind.tcreq/cr cc/tccon tdatr/-.-/dt ndind/tdind tcreq/tdind cr/tcind tdreq/dr.cr/tcind tdreq/dr tcreq/tdind cr/tcind tdreq/dr.cr/tcind tcres/dr,tdind tcreq/tdind cr/tcind tdreq/dr.cr/tcind tcres/cc tdatr/-.-/dt nrind/tdind tcreq/tdind cr/tcind.tdreq/dr cr/tcind.tdreq/dr cr/tcind.tcres/dr,tdind cr/tcind.tcres/dr,tdind cr/tcind.tcres/cc nrind/tdind cr/tcind.tcres/cc ndind/tdind

The CSSs chosen for the states are as follows: *tcreq/tdind* for IDLE, *dr/ndreq,tdind.tcreq/cr* for WFCC, *tdreq/dr.cr/tcind* for WFTR and *tdatr/-.-/dt* for DATA. This sequence can again be reduced by verifying the final state only once for each transition test, and by using the method outlined above for reducing the data flow portion. The reduced sequence has a length of 49.

The order in which the sequences are derived and concatenated are not restricted to control flow followed by data flow, as was done above. If the set of data flow paths cover most of the control flow paths, then optimization can be achieved by eliminating control flow paths based on the generated data flow sequence. The ordering thus rests on the nature of the specification. More than one minimal final sequence may exist.

VI. CONCLUSIONS

A hybrid technique is suggested which combines two test sequence generation methods to yield a test sequence that separately covers both the control and data flow aspects of protocols specified in Estelle. The control flow portion of the protocol is tested first, followed by the data flow portion. This method differs from others in that it considers the possible errors that may occur in the control flow as well as those that may occur in the data flow of a protocol implementation, and it generates sequences aimed at capturing these errors.

While conformance testing typically treats the implementation as a black box, the design process for the test sequence does not have to treat the given specification as a black box. The types of errors that can be captured during testing depends on the test sequence used. If certain errors are known to be possible beforehand, then the test can be designed to specifically capture these errors. In this case, the possible errors that can occur in the control structure are transition and transfer errors, the test sequence is thus designed to capture these errors. Since data flow anomalies may occur at the data flow portion of the protocol, the test sequence is also designed to detect these anomalies if they exist.

For control flow testing, a sequence generation method is presented which adds state-identification capabilities to those I/Os that lack them. More than one sequence, or state signature, may be used during testing to verify a particular final state. When an CSS is concatenated to each transition test, it functions as a "status message" feature that is absent, but desirable, in most protocols. Length of test sequences are reduced when state-verification is performed only once for each transition, rather than each time the transition appears.

Shortly following the completion of this paper, the authors observed a slight problem with the usage of UIOs for state verification during testing and suggested that an added UIO-verification procedure precede any use of the UIOs to ensure that they are also unique in the implementation. The details of this finding can be found in [Chan89]. This implies the UIO-verification procedure must be included as part of the control flow testing procedure proposed in this paper. Without the UIO-verification procedure, the fault coverage of tests based on UIOs may be less than that based on distinguishing sequences [Chan89].

Deriving the control flow and data flow test paths constituted the first stage of the test sequence generation process, which focuses on the achievable fault coverage. The EFG then captures these paths graphically to facilitate the optimization stage that followed.

Future work is required in four different areas. The first is a closer scrutiny of some of the proposed algorithms. For instance, by requiring that each transition test be verified only once during control flow testing and that duplicated paths be removed, how can the EFG, displaying both control and data flows, be used in the search of the minimal final sequence? The second is in estimating the minimal fault-coverage required of protocol test sequences and the fault-coverage achieved so far. Other testing methods may need to be added to the hybrid technique to increase its fault-coverage, such as boundary-interior path testing. This method essentially imposes weights on certain edges, requiring them to be traversed more than once. The third is an examination of the role of the predicate clauses in the Estelle specification. Those clauses which involve protocol variables are the ones of concern here. In this paper, they were treated in both control and data flow testing, but the pros and cons of treating them as added constraints to control flow testing remain to be examined. Finally, there is the old undecidable problem of path executability. Not every path selected would be executable. Although the user can weed out the inherently unexecutable paths, other paths may require a particular sequence or repetition of transitions, or specific input values. This suggests perhaps the subsequent test data selection process need to be combined with test sequence generation, to ensure the executability of paths by imposing specific values to be used during testing.

ACKNOWLEDGEMENT

The authors gratefully acknowledge the support from Natural Sciences and Engineering Council of Canada and Idacom Electronics Limited in the form of an University and Industry Cooperative Research Grant.

REFERENCES

[Aho74] Aho, A.V., Hopcroft, J.E. and Ullman, J.D., The Design and Analysis of Computer Algorithms, Addison-Wesley, Reading, MA, 1974, pp. 207-209.

[Aho88] Aho, A.V., Dahbura, A.T., Lee, D. and Uyar, U.M., "An Optimization Technique for Protocol Conformance Test Generation Based on UIO Sequences and Rural Chinese Postman Tours," *Preliminary Proceedings, Eighth International Symposium on Protocol Specification, Testing, and Verification,*, Atlantic City, N.J., 1988.

[Budk87] Budkowski, S. and Dembinski, P., "An Introduction to Estelle: A Specification Language for Distributed Systems," *Computer Networks and ISDN Systems,* vol 14., 1987, pp. 3-23.

[Chan89] Chan, W.Y.L., Vuong, S.T. and Ito, M.R., "An Improved Protocol Test Generation Procedure Based On UIOs," - submitted for publication, March 1989.

[Chow78] Chow, T., "Testing Software Design Modeled by Finite-State Machines," *IEEE Transactions on Software Engineering,* vol SE-4, no. 3, 1978, pp. 178-187.

[Gone70] Gonenc, G., "A Method for the Design of Fault Detection Experiments," *IEEE Transactions on Computers,* vol. C-19, no. 6, June 1970.

[Hech77] Hecht, M.S., Flow Analysis of Computer Programs, New York: North-Holland, 1977.

[Hsie71] Hsieh, E.P., "Checking Experiments for Sequential Machines," *IEEE Transactions on Computers,* vol. C-20, no. 10, Oct. 1971, pp. 1152-1166.

[ISO88] ISO/TC97/SC21/WG1/Subgroup B, "Estelle - A Formal Description Technique Based on an Extended State Transition Model," IS 9074, 1988.

[Nait81] Naito, S. and Tsunoyama, M., "Fault Detection for Sequential Machines by Transition Tours," *Proceedings of IEEE Fault Tolerant Computing Conference,* 1981.

[Rapp85] Rapps, S. and Weyuker, E.J., "Selecting Software Test Data Using Data Flow Information," *IEEE Transactions on Software Engineering,* vol. SE-11, no. 4, April 1985, pp. 367-375.

[Sabn85] Sabnani, K.K. and Dahbura, A.T., "A New Technique for Generating Protocol Tests," *Proceedings of 9th Data Communications Symposium,* IEEE Computer Society Press, Sept. 1985, pp. 36-43.

[Sari82] Sarikaya, B. and Bochmann, G.v., "Some Experience with Test Sequence Generation for Protocols," *Protocol Specification, Testing and Verification,* C. Sunshine (Ed.), North-Holland, 1982, pp. 555-567.

[Sari86] Sarikaya, B. and Bochmann, G.v., "Obtaining Normal Form Specifications for Protocols," *Computer Network Usage: Recent Experiences,* L. Csaba, K. Tarnay and T. Szentivanyi (Eds.), North-Holland, 1986, pp. 601-612.

[Sari87] Sarikaya, B., Bochmann, G.v., and Cerny, E., "A Test Design Methodology for Protocol Testing," *IEEE Transactions on Software Engineering,* vol. SE-13, no. 5, May 1987, pp. 518-531.

[Tenn88] Tenney, R.L., "A Tutorial Introduction to Estelle," invited paper, *First International Conference on Formal Description Techniques,* at the University of Stirling, Sept. 1988.

[Ural87] Ural, H., "Test Sequence Selection Based on Static Data Flow Analysis," *Computer Communications,* vol. 10, no. 5, Oct. 1987, pp. 234-242.

[Weis85] Weiser, M.D., Gannon, J.D. and McMullin, P.R., "Comparison of Structural Test Coverage Metrics," *IEEE Software, Mar. 1985, pp. 80-85.*

[Wu89] Wu, J. and Chanson, S.T., "A New Approach to Test Sequence Derivation Based on External Behaviour Expression (EBE)," Technical Report 89-3, Department of Computer Science, The University of British Columbia, Vancouver, BC, Canada, January 1989.

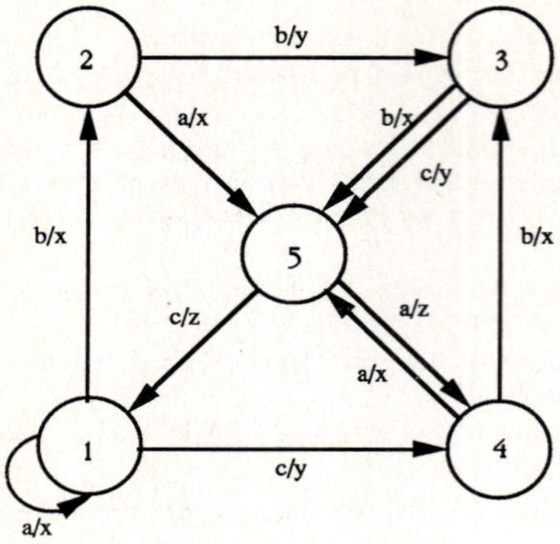

Figure 1a. A graph representation of a finite state machine. (Example 1)

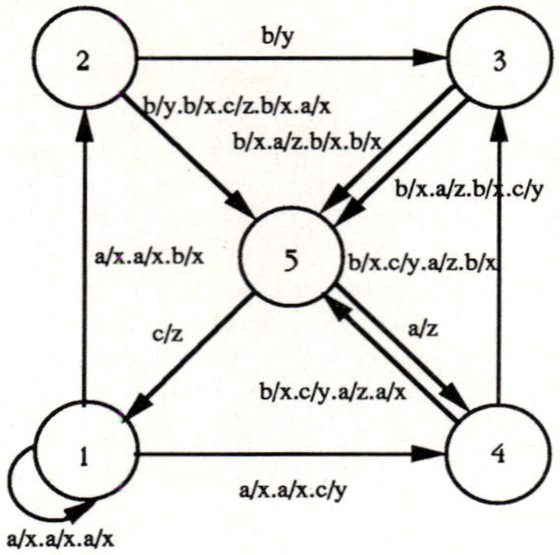

Figure 1b. Modified flow graph with CSSs for Example 1.

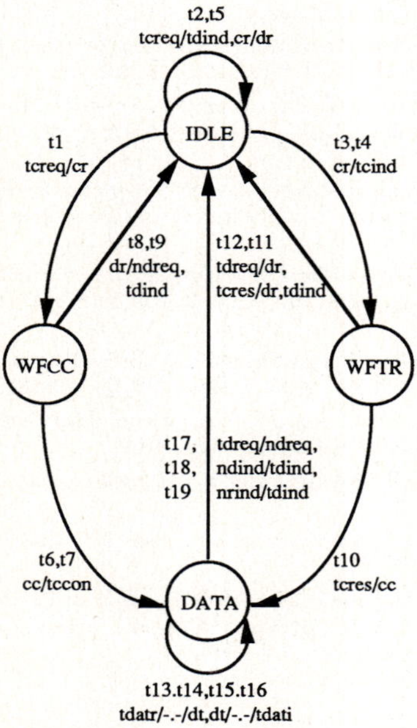

Figure 2a. Finite state machine representation for control structure of Class 0 Transport Protocol. (Example 2)

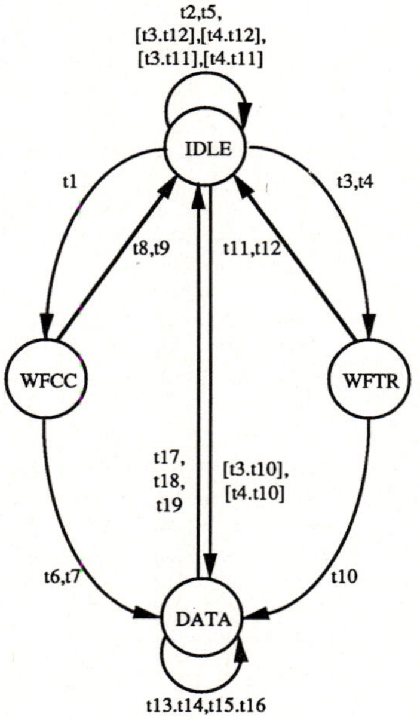

Figure 2b. Extended flow graph for Class 0 Transport Protocol. (Data flow paths are in brackets.)

Table 1. Data flow paths for extracted definition-usage pairs.

protocol variable	definition	usage	path
calling.t.addr	t3,t4	t10	t3.t10, t4.t10
called.t.addr	t3,t4	t10	t3.t10, t4.t10
remote.refer	t3,t4	t10, t11, t12	t3.t10, t4.t10 t3.t11, t4.t11 t3.t12, t4.t12
tpdu.size	t3,t4	t10	t3.t10, t4.t10
qts.estimate	t3,t4	t10, t11	t3.t10, t4.t10 t3.t11, t4.t11
in.buffer	t6, t7, t10	t15.t16	none
out.buffer	t6, t7, t10	t13.t14	none

APPENDIX NFS for OSI Class 0 Transport Protocol

```
.....
WHEN tcreq (to.t.addr, from.t.addr,
            qts.req)
FROM idle
PROVIDED tcreq.in.qts.req <> ok
TO idle
t2: BEGIN
    tdind.out.ts.disc.reason :- ...;
    tdind.out.ts.user.reason :- ...;
    output tdind(ts.disc.reason,
                 ts.user.reason);
    END;

WHEN cr (source.ref,option,calling.t.addr,
         called.t.addr, max.tpdu.size)
FROM idle
PROVIDED cr.in.max.tpdu.size - nil
      and cr.in.option - ok
TO wftr
t3: BEGIN
    remote.refer :- cr.in.source.ref;
    tpdu.size :- cr.in.max.tpdu.size;
    calling.t.addr :- cr.in.calling.t.addr;
    called.t.addr :- cr.in.called.t.addr;
    qts.estimate :- ...;
    tcind.out.to.t.addr :- called.t.addr;
    tcind.out.from.t.addr :- calling.t.addr;
    tcind.out.qts.pro :- qts.estimate;
    output tcind(to.t.addr,from.t.addr,
                 qts.pro);
    END;
```

```
WHEN cr (source.ref, option,calling.t.addr,
         called.t.addr, max.tpdu.size)
FROM idle
PROVIDED cr.in.max.tpdu.size <> nil
      and cr.in.option - ok
TO wftr
t4: BEGIN
    remote.refer :- cr.in.source.ref;
    tpdu.size :- ...;
    calling.t.addr :- cr.in.calling.t.addr;
    called.t.addr :- cr.in.called.t.addr;
    qts.estimate :- ...;
    tcind.out.to.t.addr :- called.t.addr;
    tcind.out.from.t.addr :- calling.t.addr;
    tcind.out.qts.pro :- qts.estimate;
    output tcind(to.t.addr,from.t.addr,
                 qts.pro);
    END;
.....

WHEN cc (max.tpdu.size)
FROM wfcc
PROVIDED cc.in.max.tpdu.size <> nil
TO data
t6: BEGIN
    qts.estimate :-...;
    tccon.out.qts.res :- qts.estimate;
    in.buffer :- nil;
    out.buffer :- nil;
    output tccon(qts.res);
    END;
```

```
WHEN cc (max.tpdu.size);
FROM wfcc
PROVIDED cc.in.max.tpdu.size <> nil
TO data
t7: BEGIN
      qts.estimate :- ...;
      in.buffer :- nil;
      out.buffer :- nil;
      tccon.out.qts.res :- qts.estimate;
      output tccon(qts.res);
      END;
......
```

```
WHEN tcres (qts.req)
FROM wftr
PROVIDED tcres.in.qts.req <- qts.estimate
TO data
t10: BEGIN
      local.refer :- ...;
      cc.out.dest.refer :- remote.refer;
      cc.out.source.ref :- local.refer;
      cc.out.calling.t.addr :- calling.t.addr;
      cc.out.called.t.addr :- called.t.addr;
      cc.out.max.tpdu.size :- tpdu.size;
      in.buffer :- nil;
      out.buffer :- nil;
      output cc(dest.refer,source.ref,
                calling.t.addr,called.t.addr,
                max.tpdu.size);
      END;
```

```
WHEN tcres (qts.req)
FROM wftr
PROVIDED tcres.in.qts.req > qts.estimate
TO idle
t11: BEGIN
      dr.out.dest.refer :- remote.refer;
      dr.out.disconnect.reason :- ...;
      dr.out.add.clear.reason :- ...;
      tdind.in.ts.disc.reason :- ...;
      output dr(dest.refer,
                disconnect.reason,
                add.clear.reason);
      output tdind(ts.disc.reason);
      END;
```

```
WHEN tdreq (ts.user.reason)
FROM wftr
TO idle
t12: begin
      dr.out.disconnect.reason :- ...;
      dr.out.add.clear.reason :-
          tdreq.in.ts.user.reason;
      dr.out.dest.refer :- remote.refer;
      output dr(dest.refer,
                disconnect.reason,
                add.clear.reason)
      END;
```

```
WHEN tdatr (tsdu.fragment)
FROM data
TO data
t13: BEGIN
      insert(out.buffer,
             tdatr.in.tsdu.fragment);
      END;
```

```
FROM data
PROVIDED out.buffer <> nil
TO data
t14: BEGIN
      remove(out.buffer, dt.out.user.data);
      output dt(user.data);
      END;
```

```
WHEN dt (user.data)
FROM data
TO data
t15: BEGIN
      insert(in.buffer, dt.in.user.data);
      END;
```

```
FROM data
PROVIDED in.buffer <> nil
TO data
t16: BEGIN
      remove(in.buffer,
             tdati.out.tsdu.fragment);
      output tdati(tsdu.fragment);
      END;
.....
```

Protocol Specification, Testing, and Verification, IX
E. Brinksma, G. Scollo and C.A. Vissers (Editors)
Elsevier Science Publishers B.V. (North-Holland)

Protocol Conformance Testing Using Multiple UIO Sequences

Y.-N. Shen† *F. Lombardi*† *A. T. Dahbura*‡

ABSTRACT

This paper presents new results for automatically generating conformance test sequences for communication protocols by means of *Unique Input/Output (UIO)* sequences [6] and the *Rural Chinese Postman Algorithm* [10]. The contribution of this paper is to show that if *multiple* minimum-length UIO sequences are computed for each state of the FSM specification then the length of the resulting test sequence is significantly reduced without an appreciable increase in the time needed to compute the sequence. An algorithm for optimal assignment of the multiple UIO sequences is given which is based on network flow and is polynomial in the number of states and transitions of the FSM.

I. Introduction

Test generation for conformance testing has been widely advocated for ensuring that protocol implementations are consistent with their specifications [1]. In recent years, several approaches have been developed for protocol conformance test generation [1]-[10]; these techniques are based upon traditional finite automata theory and usually assume a *Mealy machine* model of a finite-state machine (FSM) [3].

The approach of [5] assumes a minimal strongly connected and deterministic Mealy machine. The test sequence is generated by an approximation algorithm which guarantees that each transition of the specified FSM is traversed at least once. An optimization algorithm for the same approach, based on the so-called *Chinese Postman Problem* in graph theory [12], was proposed in [7] for finding a *minimum-cost* test sequence which traverses each transition of the FSM at least once.

In [6,10], the use of *Unique Input/Output (UIO)* sequences is proposed for the purpose of testing a protocol implementation. A UIO sequence provides a natural and practical means for verifying that the protocol implementation is in a given expected state. It was shown in [8],[9] that the use of UIO sequences yields a significant improvement in effectiveness over approaches such as that given in [5]. The UIO sequence approach was combined with the *Rural Chinese Postman Algorithm* in [10] to provide a robust, compact test sequence for protocol conformance testing. Practical experience has shown a 3-to-1 reduction in test length over ad hoc methods with an unforetold improvement in detection capabilities and test sequence derivation time.

The objective of this paper is to extend the basic results of [6,10] for the automatic testing of communication protocols. The novelty of the proposed approach is that it derives *multiple* minimum-length UIO sequences for each state in the specified FSM, as opposed to the approach given in [10], which was more restrictive in that exactly one UIO sequence is generated for each state. The result is a substantial reduction (4%-37%) in the length of the test sequences required for protocol conformance testing with no noticeable increase in the time required to generate the test sequence.

---

† Texas A&M University, Department of Computer Science, College Station, TX 77843-5464.

‡ AT&T Bell Laboratories, 600 Mountain Avenue, Murray Hill, New Jersey 07974-2070.

This research was supported in part by grants from AT&T and NATO.

This paper is organized as follows. Section II reviews the Rural Chinese Postman/UIO sequence approach and introduces the relevant notation and terminology. Section III discusses the motivation for selecting multiple UIO sequences and provides an example. In Section IV, an algorithm is given for determining the optimal assignment of multiple UIO sequences. Section V describes the results of the technique for actual and simulated protocols.

II. Preliminaries

A protocol can be specified as a *deterministic finite-state machine (FSM)* [2], where $S=\{s_1, \cdots, s_n\}$ is a finite set of states, $I=\{i_1, \cdots, i_\alpha\}$ is a finite set of inputs (stimuli), and $O=\{o_1, \cdots, o_\beta\}$ is a finite set of outputs. The next state *(NS)* and the output *(O)* functions are given by the two mappings NS: $S \times I \rightarrow S$ and Z: $S \times I \rightarrow O$, respectively. Machines of this form, whose output is a function of the current state and the applied input, are commonly called *Mealy* machines [3].

An FSM is represented by a directed graph $G=(V, E)$, where the set $V=\{v_1, \cdots, v_n\}$ represents the set of specified states, S, of the FSM and a directed edge (v_i, v_j) with label $L=a_k/o_l$ (denoted as $(v_i, v_j; L)$) represents a transition from state s_i to state s_j with input a_k and output o_l in the FSM. There is a *cost* associated with each edge $(v_i, v_j; L)$ which usually is time taken to realize the corresponding transition in the FSM. The fact that the FSM is deterministic implies that for each vertex v_i, there are no two edges leaving v_i with identical input labels. An example of a graph representation of an FSM is shown in Figure 1.

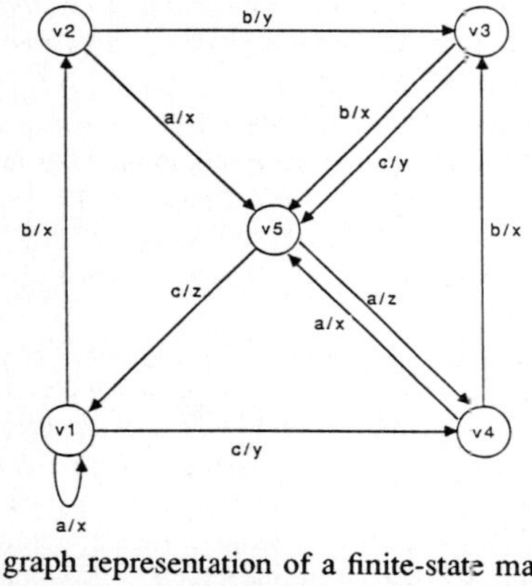

Figure 1. A graph representation of a finite-state machine (FSM). All edges are of equal cost and reset edges are not shown.

An FSM implementation can be tested using an approach commonly referred to as a *checking experiment* [3], which is an input/output sequence pair $(i_1/o_1),(i_2/o_2)...$ such that the response of the implementation to $i_1,i_2,...$ is $o_1,o_2,...$ if and only if the implementation behaves according to its specification. A checking experiment tests the implementation of an FSM for the correctness of every specified transition; that is, it verifies that each specified input for state s_i, $i=1,...,n$, in the implementation produces the expected output and takes the implementation to the expected state.

In the past, checking experiments were based on the existence of an input sequence called a *distinguishing sequence*, which produces a distinct output sequence for each initial state of the FSM [2],[3]. Unfortunately, only a very limited number of FSMs have a distinguishing sequence [2,3]. A new approach was proposed in [6], based on the concept of *Unique Input/Output (UIO)* sequences: a UIO sequence for a state s_i is a specified input/output sequence of minimum length $UIO_i = (a_{k_1}/o_{l_1}) \cdots (a_{k_r}/o_{l_r})$ with initial state s_i such that there is no $s_j \neq s_i$ for which UIO_i is a specified input/output sequence for initial state s_j [6]. For example, a set of minimum-length UIO sequences for the FSM shown in Figure 1 is given in Table I.

STATE	UIO SEQUENCE
v1	b/x a/x
v2	b/y
v3	b/x c/z
v4	b/x c/y
v5	c/z

Table I. The UIO sequences for the FSM of Figure 1.

In practice, nearly all FSMs have UIO sequences for each state [8,9,10]; furthermore, the length of a UIO sequence is never more than that of a distinguishing sequence (if a distinguishing sequence exists) and in practice, is usually less. A breadth-first search algorithm for determining a set of minimum-length UIO sequences for an FSM is given in [6].

Once a set of minimum-length UIO sequences is found, it is desired to compute a minimum-cost test sequence which checks the correctness of each transition of the FSM. To check the correctness of a transition from state s_i to state s_j with input/output a_k/o_l, the implementation is put into state s_i, input a_k is applied and the output is checked to verify that it is o_l, and the new state of the FSM implementation is checked to verify that it is s_j by applying the input sequence for UIO_j and verifying that the resulting output sequence is that which is expected; this process is denoted as $TEST(v_i,v_j;a_k,o_l)$.

The procedure described in [8] computes the minimum-cost test sequence which contains the subsequence $TEST(v_i,v_j;a_k/o_l)$ for each transition of the FSM. In the resulting test

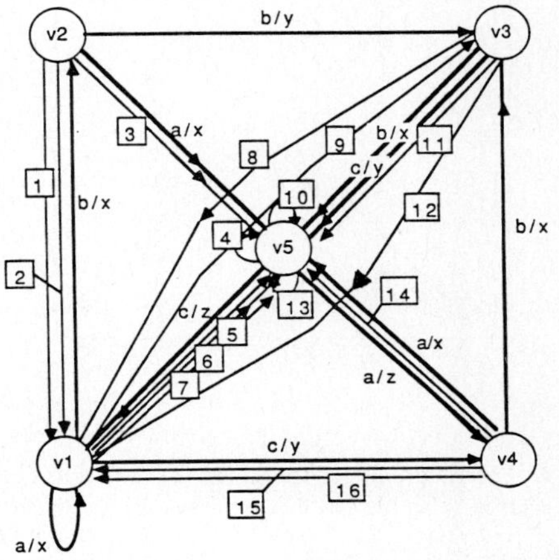

1. b/y b/x c/z
2. a/x c/z
3. ri/null b/x a/x
4. a/z b/x c/y
5. ri/null b/x a/x
6. a/x b/x a/x
7. c/y b/x c/y
8. b/x c/z
9. b/x b/y
10. c/z b/x a/x
11. ri/null b/x a/x
12. c/y c/z
13. ri/null b/x a/x
14. ri/null b/x a/x
15. b/x b/x c/z
16. a/x c/z

Figure 2. The graph G' for the graph of Figure 1 (bold edges represent edges in E and fine edges represent edges in E_C).

sequence, no two subsequences are overlapped. The method consists of constructing a directed graph $G'=(V',E')$ from G such that $V'\equiv V$ and $E'\equiv E\cup E_C$, where

$$E_C=\{(v_i,v_k;L_l)\bullet UIO_j:(v_i,v_j;L_l)\in E \text{ and } TAIL(UIO_j)=v_k\},$$

where $TAIL(UIO_j)$ is defined as the final state of the sequence UIO_j. For example, the graph G' is derived for the graph G of Figure 1 and is shown in Figure 2. The problem of finding the minimum-cost test sequence which tests each transition of the FSM is equivalent to finding a Rural Chinese Postman tour [10] of G' over E_C; that is, a minimum-cost tour which begins at the vertex of G' representing the designated *start state* of the FSM, traverses each edge in E_C at least once, and returns to the vertex representing the start state. The edges in E may or may not be traversed.

The Rural Chinese Postman Problem on G' can be solved in two steps [13]:

1) Construct a directed graph $\hat{G}^*=(\hat{V}^*,\hat{E}^*)$ from G', where $\hat{V}^*\equiv V'$, each edge in E is included in $\hat{E}^*$ zero or more times, and each edge in E_C is included in $\hat{E}^*$ at least once, such that the total cost of edges in $\hat{E}^*$ is minimum and the in-degree of each vertex $v_i\in\hat{V}^*$ is equal to its out-degree ($\hat{G}^*$ is therefore *symmetric*). The graph $\hat{G}^*$ is called a *rural symmetric augmentation* of G'. For example, the graph $\hat{G}^*$ of the graph G' of Figure 2 is shown in Figure 3.
2) Find an *Euler tour* [11] of the resulting graph $\hat{G}^*$, that is, a tour of $\hat{G}^*$ which traverses each edge of $\hat{E}^*$ exactly once. Since $\hat{G}^*$ is symmetric, such a tour is guaranteed to exist [13]. An Euler tour consisting of 55 input/output pairs for the graph $\hat{G}^*$ shown in Figure 3 is given in Table II.

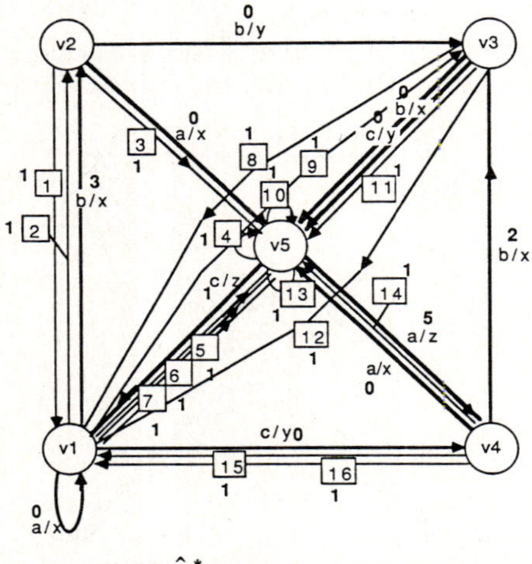

Figure 3. The graph $\hat{G}^*$ of the graph G' shown in Figure 2 (values correspond to the number of times each edge is used).

For a vertex $v_i\in G'$, let

$$d_{in}^{E_C}(v_i) = |\{(v_j,v_i;L_k):(v_j,v_i;L_k)\in E_C\}| \text{ and let}$$

$$d_{out}^{E_C}(v_i) = |\{(v_i,v_j;L_k):(v_i,v_j;L_k)\in E_C\}|.$$

The *index* $\xi(v_i)$ of a vertex $v_i\in G'$ is defined as the difference between the number of edges in E_C into v_i and the number of edges in E_C out of v_i:

$$\xi(v_i)=d_{in}^{E_C}(v_i) - d_{out}^{E_C}(v_i).$$

ri/null	b/x b/y	c/y c/z	a/x b/x a/x
a/z b/x c/y	c/z b/x a/x	ri/null b/x a/x	a/z
a/x c/z	c/y b/x c/y	a/z	b/x
b/x c/z	b/x	b/y b/x c/z	b/x
a/x c/z	b/x	ri/null b/x a/x	a/z
b/x	ri/null b/x a/x	a/z	b/x b/x c/z
ri/null b/x a/x	a/z	ri/null b/x a/x	c/z

TOTAL= 55 input/output pairs

Table II. An optimal conformance test sequence for the FSM shown in Figure 1 (read from left to right).

If $\xi(v_i)=0$ for all $i=1, \cdots, n$ then no edges in E need be included in $\hat{E}^*$ in Step 1) of the above procedure; however, if $\xi(v_i)\neq 0$ then some edges in E must be replicated for $\hat{G}^*$ to be symmetric. The optimal number of replications for each edge such that the resulting tour is of minimum cost is computed by means of a minimum-cost, maximum-flow algorithm [14] on a graph $G_F = (V_F, E_F)$ constructed from G' as follows. Let $V_F \equiv V' \cup \{s, t\}$, where s and t are the *source* and *sink* of of G_F, and let

$$E_F = E \cup \{(s, v_i): v_i \in C\} \cup \{(v_j, t): v_j \in D\},$$

where $C \subset V_F$ ($D \subset V_F$) is the set of vertices in G' with positive (negative) indices. For simplicity, self-loops in E are omitted in E_F, and when there exist multiple edges between v_i and v_j in G', only an edge of minimum cost (in E) is included in E_F. Since there are no multiple edges in G_F, edge labels are omitted. Let each edge (s, v_i) have cost zero and *capacity* [11] $\gamma(s, v_i) \equiv \xi(v_i)$, and let each edge (v_j, t) have cost zero and capacity $\gamma(v_j, t) \equiv -\xi(v_j)$. The remaining edges in E_F have the same cost in G_F as in G' and have infinite capacity. The graph G_F for the graph G' of Figure 2 is shown in Figure 4.

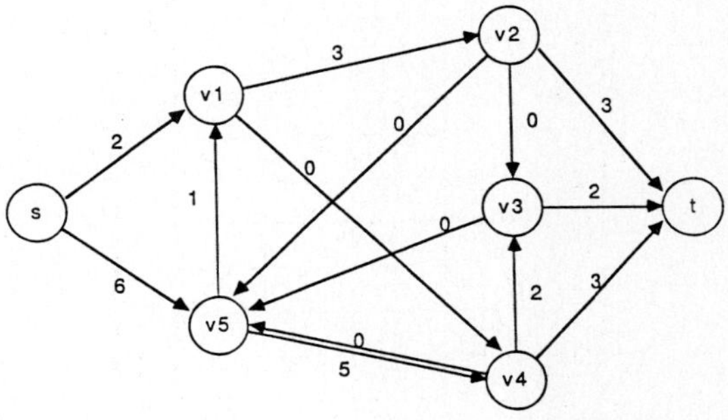

Figure 4. The graph G_F of the graph G' shown in Figure 2 and a minimum-cost maximum flow.

Given a minimum-cost maximum flow F on G_F, define a function χ on E':

$$\chi(v_i, v_j; L_i) = \begin{cases} 1, & \text{if } (v_i, v_j; L_i) \in E_C; \\ F(v_i, v_j; L_i), & \text{if } (v_i, v_j; L_i) \in E. \end{cases}$$

It was shown in [10] that the function χ forms a minimum-cost rural symmetric augmentation of G'. A minimum-cost maximum flow of G_F for the graph G' of Figure 1 is given in Figure 4. There are eight units of flow in the minimum-cost maximum flow depicted, and a total of 11 edge replications in E. Thus, since the total cost of the edges in E_C is 43, the cost of the test sequence is 55 (including an initial reset input), as shown in Table II.

III. Using Multiple UIO Sequences to Decrease Test Sequence Cost

As described in the previous section, the edges of E in G' must be replicated in order to generate a Rural Chinese Postman tour; the cost of the tour is equal to the total cost of the edges in $\hat{E}^*$.

The approach presented in [10] is such that only one G' can be generated from G, since exactly one UIO sequence per state is computed. Therefore, the value for $\xi(v_i)$, $i=1,...,n$, is fixed and is usually not equal to zero. This means that more edge replications occur, leading to an increased cost of the test sequence.

As an example, consider the graph G' shown in Figure 2. There are six edges in E_C into v_5 and no edges in E_C leaving v_5 (not including self-loops); hence, $\xi(v_5)=6$. Similarly, $\xi(v_1)=2$, $\xi(v_2)=-3$, $\xi(v_3)=-2$, and $\xi(v_4)=-3$.

A key observation is that there may exist several minimum-length UIO sequences for a given state; for example, for the FSM shown in Figure 1 there exist four UIO sequences for v_1: $UIO_1^1=\{b/x,a/x\}$, $UIO_1^2=\{a/x,b/x\}$, $UIO_1^3=\{c/y,b/x\}$, and $UIO_1^4=\{a/x,c/y\}$. The set of minimum-length UIO sequences for the other states of the FSM of Figure 1 is given in Table III. A judicious choice of UIO sequences for each edge test could reduce the length of the overall test sequence. For example, consider using UIO_1^3 in place of UIO_1^1 for the transitions going into state v_1; this will reduce the number of edges in E_C going into v_5 while increasing the number of edges in E_C going into v_3. Thus, $\xi(v_5)$ is reduced while $\xi(v_3)$ is increased. Therefore, the number of augmented edges for the symmetric graph $\hat{G}^*$ is reduced and so is the cost of the resulting test sequence.

STATE	UIO SEQUENCE	TAIL
v1	b/x a/x	v5
	a/x b/x	v2
	c/y b/x	v3
	a/x c/y	v4
v2	b/y	v3
v3	b/x c/z	v1
	b/x a/z	v4
v4	b/x c/y	v5
v5	c/z	v1
	a/z	v4

Table III. The complete set of minimum-length UIO sequences for the FSM shown in Figure 1.

The new graph G' using the UIO sequences of Table III is shown in Figure 5. Note that UIO_1^2 is used to test transition $(v_1,v_1;a/x)$ (shown as edge 2) and UIO_1^3 is used to test the transition $(v_1,v_1;ri/null)$ (shown as edge 13). Therefore, *multiple UIO sequences for each state are used.*

The new indices for the vertices of the new graph G' shown in Figure 5 are as follows: $\xi(v_1)=\xi(v_2)=\xi(v_3)=0$; $\xi(v_4)=-1$; and $\xi(v_5)=1$. A rural symmetric augmentation $\hat{G}^*$ of the graph G' of Figure 5 is given in Figure 6. The resulting Euler tour is given in Table IV; the

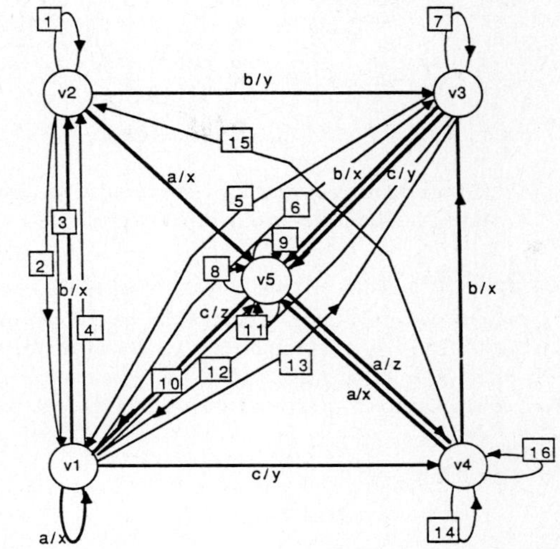

1. ri/null a/x b/x
2. b/y b/x c/z
3. a/x c/z
4. a/x a/x b/x
5. b/x c/z
6. b/x c/z
7. ri/null c/y b/x
8. a/z b/x c/y
9. c/z b/x a/x
10. c/y b/x c/y
11. ri/null b/x a/x
12. c/y c/z
13. ri/null c/y b/x
14. a/x a/z
15. ri/null a/x b/x
16. b/x b/x a/z

Figure 5. An alternative graph G' (bold edges represent edges in E and fine edges represent edges in E_C).

cost of the new test sequence is only 45, yielding a reduction of 20% over the sequence given in Table II.

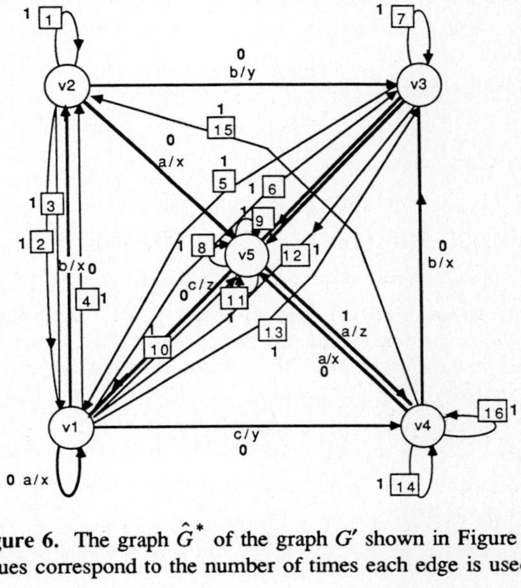

Figure 6. The graph $\hat{G}^*$ of the graph G' shown in Figure 5 (values correspond to the number of times each edge is used).

ri/null	a/x a/x b/x	ri/null a/x b/x	b/y b/x c/z
b/x b/y	ri/null c/y b/x	b/x c/z	ri/null c/y b/x
c/y c/z	c/y b/x c/y	a/z b/x c/y	c/z b/x a/x
ri/null b/x a/x	a/z	a/x a/z	b/x b/x a/z
ri/null a/x b/x	a/x c/z		

TOTAL= 45 input/output pairs

Table IV. A lower-cost conformance test sequence for the FSM shown in Figure 1 (read from left to right).

IV. An Algorithm for Optimal Multiple UIO Sequence Assignment

In the previous section, it was seen that a reduction in the amount of variation among the indices of the vertices in G' leads to a corresponding reduction in the total cost of the test sequence. In the ideal case, G' is symmetric, so that no augmentation is needed; when this happens, no edges from E are included in $\hat{G}^*$ and the cost of the test sequence is simply the cost of the edges in E_C.

Let the *degree* of G' be defined as

$$\Delta(G')=\sum_{i=1}^{n} |\xi(v_i)|,$$

and let there be $r_j>0$ minimum-length UIO sequences with distinct tail states for state s_j. The *multiple UIO sequence assignment problem* is as follows:

> Given G and a set $MUIO_j=\{UIO_j^1, \ldots, UIO_j^{r_j}\}$ for v_j, $j=1,\ldots,n$, find an element $UIO_j^{\alpha} \in MUIO_j$ for each edge $(v_i,v_j;L)\in E$ such that $\Delta(G')$ is minimized.

Let the in-degree and out-degree of vertex v_i in G be denoted as $d_{in}^E(v_i)$ and $d_{out}^E(v_i)$, respectively. Note that the number of edges in E_C which leave v_i in G' is exactly $d_{out}^E(v_i)$ and does not vary. Consider vertex v_j with in-degree $d_{in}^E(v_j)$ in G. Exactly $d_{in}^E(v_j)$ UIO sequences from $MUIO_j$ must be assigned to the edges going into v_j; each edge $(v_i,v_j;L)\in E$ generates an edge $(v_i, v_k)\in E_C$, where $k=TAIL(UIO_j^{\alpha})$ for some $UIO_j^{\alpha}\in MUIO_j$. Therefore, the multiple UIO sequence assignment problem is to assign an appropriate value of α for each $(v_i,v_j;L)\in E$ such that $\Delta(G')$ is minimized.

Given G, let $G_M=(V_M, E_M)$ be a directed graph such that

$$V_M \equiv \{s,t\} \cup V_X \cup V_Y,$$

where $V_X=\{x_1,\ldots,x_n\}$ and $V_Y=\{y_1,\ldots,y_n\}$; let

$$E_M \equiv E_S \cup E_T^- \cup E_T^+ \cup E^*,$$

where $E_S=\{(s,x_i):x_i\in V_X\}$, $E_T^-=\{(y_j,t):y_j\in V_Y\}$, $E_T^+=\{(y_j,t):y_j\in V_Y\}$, and

$$E^*=\{(x_i,y_j)\text{:there exists } UIO_i^{\alpha} \text{ such that } TAIL(UIO_i^{\alpha})=v_j\}.$$

An edge $(y_j,t)\in E_T^-$ is denoted as $(y_j,t)^-$ and an edge $(y_j,t)\in E_T^+$ is denoted as $(y_j,t)^+$. As an example, the graph G_M, constructed from the graph G of Figure 1 and the set of minimum-length UIO sequences of G shown in Table III, is given in Figure 7.

Let each edge $(s,x_i)\in E_S$ have cost zero and capacity $\gamma(s,x_i)=d_{in}^E(v_i)$; let each edge $(y_j,t)\in E_T^-$ have cost -1 and capacity $\gamma(y_j,t)=d_{out}^E(v_j)$; let each edge $(y_j,t)\in E_T^+$ have cost +1 and infinite capacity; finally, let each edge $(x_i,y_j)\in E^*$ have cost zero and infinite capacity.

A *flow* F on G_M is a function $F: E_M \rightarrow Z^+$, where Z^+ is the set of non-negative integers, satisfying the following conditions:

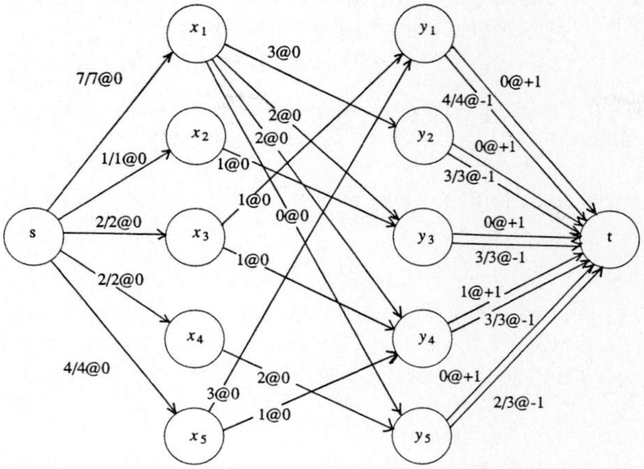

$C(F^*) = 14$

Figure 7. The graph G_M for the FSM of Figure 1 and the set of multiple UIO sequences of Table III. A minimum-cost maximum flow is shown.

(1) for each vertex $x_i \in V_X$,

$$F(s,x_i) = \sum_{(x_i,y_j) \in E^*} F(x_i,y_j);$$

(2) for each vertex $y_j \in V_Y$,

$$F(y_j,t)^- + F(y_j,t)^+ = \sum_{(x_i,y_j) \in E^*} F(x_i,y_j);$$

(3) for each edge $(s,x_i) \in E_S$, $F(s,x_i) \leq \gamma(s,x_i)$; and,

(4) for each edge $(y_j,t)^- \in E_T^-$, $F(y_j,t)^- \leq \gamma(y_j,t)^-$.

The *cost* of the flow F is:

$$C(F) = \sum_{(y_j,t)^+ \in E_T^+} F(y_j,t)^+ - \sum_{(y_j,t)^- \in E_T^-} F(y_j,t)^-.$$

Given a minimum-cost maximum flow F^* on G_M, the *multiple UIO sequence assignment procedure* for constructing G' is as follows:

> For each $v_j \in V$, assign to each edge $(v_i,v_j) \in E$ exactly one UIO sequence $UIO_j^\alpha \in MUIO_j$ such that each UIO_j^α in $MUIO_j$ is used exactly $F^*(x_i,y_j)$ times, where $(x_i,y_j) \in E^*$ is the edge in G_M which represents UIO_j^α.

For the minimum-cost maximum flow F^* of the graph G_M shown in Figure 7, $F^*(x_1,y_5)=2$; therefore, UIO_1^1 is assigned to two edges going into vertex v_1 in G: $(v_5,v_1;c/z)$ and $(v_5,v_1;ri/null)$. Similarly, since $F^*(x_1,y_2)=3$, UIO_1^2 is assigned to three edges going into vertex v_1 in G: $(v_2,v_1;ri/null)$, $(v_4,v_2;ri/null)$, and $(v_1,v_1;a/x)$. Finally, since $F^*(x_1,x_3)=2$, UIO_1^3 is assigned to two edges going into vertex v_1: $(v_3,v_1;ri/null)$ and $(v_1,v_1;ri/null)$. The procedure is identical for the other vertices of G.

Note that since there exist edges of infinite capacity from each $x_i \in V_X$ to some $y_j \in V_Y$ and from each $y_i \in V_Y$ to t, $F^*(s,x_i) = \gamma(s,x_i) = d_{in}^E(v_i)$ for each $x_i \in V_X$. This guarantees that each edge in G is assigned a UIO sequence.

Theorem 1: If F^* is a minimum-cost maximum flow F^* on G_M and G' is constructed from F^* using the multiple UIO sequence assignment procedure then

$$C(F^*) = \Delta(G') - |E|.$$

Proof: Since F^* is a maximum flow of minimum cost, the values of flow for the edges in E_T^- and E_T^+ are as follows:

Class 1:

if $\sum_{x_i \in V_X} F(x_i, y_j) > d_{out}^E(v_j)$ for $y_j \in V_Y$ then

$$F(y_j, t)^+ = \sum_{x_i \in V_X} F(x_i, y_j) - d_{out}^E(v_j)$$

$$\text{and } F(y_j, t)^- = d_{out}^E(v_j);$$

Class 2:

if $\sum_{x_i \in V_X} F(x_i, y_j) \le d_{out}^E(v_j)$ for $y_j \in V_Y$ then

$$F(y_j, t)^+ = 0$$

$$\text{and } F(y_j, t)^- = \sum_{x_i \in V_X} F(x_i, y_j).$$

This is so because, since the cost of flow through edges in E_T^- is negative, any maximum flow of minimum cost will maximize the flow through those edges and use the edges of E_T^+ only when necessary.

Let the vertices in V_Y be partitioned into two sets, O and U, where O (U) is the set of vertices in Class 1 (Class 2) above. Note that, by the multiple UIO sequence assignment procedure,

$$d_{in}^{E_C}(v_j) = \sum_{x_i \in V_X} F(x_i, y_j)$$

and $d_{out}^{E_C}(v_j) = d_{out}^E(v_j)$.

From the definitions given above,

$$C(F^*) = \sum_{(y_j,t)^+ \in E_T^+} F(y_j, t)^+ - \sum_{(y_j,t)^- \in E_T^-} F(y_j, t)^-$$

$$= \sum_{y_j \in O} (F(y_j,t)^+ - F(y_j,t)^-) + \sum_{y_j \in U} (F(y_j,t)^+ - F(y_j,t)^-)$$

$$= \sum_{y_j \in O} \left\{ \left[\sum_{x_i \in V_X} F(x_i, y_j) - d_{out}^E(v_j) \right] - d_{out}^E(v_j) \right\} + \sum_{y_j \in U} \left\{ \left[- \sum_{x_i \in V_X} F(x_i, y_j) \right] - d_{out}^E(v_j) + d_{out}^E(v_j) \right\}.$$

$$= \sum_{y_j \in O} (d_{in}^{E_C}(v_j) - d_{out}^{E_C}(v_j)) + \sum_{y_j \in U} (d_{out}^{E_C}(v_j) - d_{in}^{E_C}(v_j)) - \sum_{y_j \in V_Y} d_{out}^E(v_j)$$

$$= \sum_{y_j \in V_Y} | d_{in}^{E_C}(v_j) - d_{out}^{E_C}(v_j) | - |E|$$

$$= \Delta(G') - |E|. \quad \square$$

Theorem 2: If F^* is a minimum-cost maximum flow on G_M then the corresponding assignment of UIO sequences to the edges of G is such that the degree $\Delta(G')$ of G' is minimized.

Proof: Assume that F^* is a minimum-cost maximum flow on G_M such that the corresponding assignment of UIO sequences to the edges of G forms a graph G'_1 of degree $\Delta(G'_1)$, but there exists a different assignment of UIO sequences to the edges of G such that the corresponding graph G'_2 is of degree $\Delta(G'_2) < \Delta(G_1)$.

From G'_2, construct a flow F' on G_M, where (O,U) is a partition of the vertices of V_Y and:

1) $F'(x_i,y_j)$ is the number of times $UIO_i^\alpha \in MUIO_i$ such that $v_j = TAIL(UIO_i^\alpha)$ is used;
2) $F'(s,x_i) = \gamma(s,x_i) = d_{in}^{E}(v_i)$ for each $x_i \in V_X$; and,
3) for each vertex $y_j \in V_Y$:

$$\text{if } d_{in}^{E_c}(v_j) > \gamma(y_j,t)^- = d_{out}^{E}(v_j) \text{ then let } y_j \in O \text{ and}$$
$$F'(y_j,t)^+ = d_{in}^{E_c}(v_j) - d_{out}^{E}(v_j)$$
$$\text{and } F'(y_j,t)^- = d_{out}^{E}(v_j);$$
$$\text{if } d_{in}^{E_c}(v_j) \le \gamma(y_j,t)^- = d_{out}^{E}(v_j) \text{ then let } v_j \in U \text{ and}$$
$$F'(y_j,t)^+ = 0$$
$$\text{and } F'(y_j,t)^- = d_{in}^{E_c}(v_j).$$

By construction, F' is a valid flow on G_M and since $F'(s,x_i) = \gamma(s,x_i)$ for each $(s,x_i) \in E_S$, F' is a maximum flow.

The cost of F' is:

$$
\begin{aligned}
C(F') &= \sum_{(y_j,t)^+ \in E_T^+} F'(y_j,t)^+ - \sum_{(y_j,t)^- \in E_T^-} F'(y_j,t)^- \\
&= \sum_{y_j \in O} (F'(y_j,t)^+ - F'(y_j,t)^-) + \sum_{y_j \in U} (F'(y_j,t)^+ - F'(y_j,t)^-) \\
&= \sum_{y_j \in O} \left[\left[d_{in}^{E_c}(v_j) - d_{out}^{E}(v_j) \right] - d_{out}^{E}(V_j) \right] + \sum_{y_j \in U} \left[\left[-d_{in}^{E_c}(v_j) \right] - d_{out}^{E}(v_j) + d_{out}^{E}(v_j) \right]. \\
&= \sum_{y_j \in O} (d_{in}^{E_c}(v_j) - d_{out}^{E_c}(v_j)) + \sum_{y_j \in U} (d_{out}^{E_c}(v_j) - d_{in}^{E_c}(v_j)) - \sum_{y_j \in V_Y} d_{out}^{E}(v_j) \\
&= \sum_{y_j \in V_Y} \left| d_{in}^{E_c}(v_j) - d_{out}^{E_c}(v_j) \right| - |E| \\
&= \Delta(G'_2) - |E|.
\end{aligned}
$$

By Theorem 1,

$$C(F^*) = \Delta(G'_1) - |E| > \Delta(G'_2) - |E| = C(F'),$$

contradicting the assumption that F^* is a minimum-cost maximum flow. □

It was shown in [6] that a single minimum-length UIO sequence for state s_i can be computed by means of a breadth-first search (BFS) algorithm; this is feasible since the length of UIO sequences in actual protocols has been found to be in most cases of length no more than five. Therefore, computing the set of *all* minimum-length UIO sequences for a given state does not add noticeably to the computation time. A minimum-cost maximum flow on G_M can be computed by a variety of different algorithms such as minimum-cost augmentations, scaling, or partial scaling [10],[14]. The most practical to implement require in the worst case $O(|E^*|^2 \log n)$ operations.

V. Results of Multiple UIO Sequence Approach

The technique of generating multiple UIO sequences per state, constructing the graph G_M, computing a minimum-cost maximum flow on G_M, and assigning UIO sequences to edges accordingly, was performed on a number of FSM specifications and yielded favorable results, shown in Table V.

FSM	$\|V\|$	$\|E\|$	$\|I\|$	$\|O\|$	$\|E_C\|$	Cost of Tour Single UIO	Cost of Tour Multiple UIO	SAVINGS
FSM.1	50	916	50	50	1832	2426	1836	24.3%
FSM.2	20	620	50	50	1240	1769	1240	30.0%
FSM.3	50	771	20	20	2131	2790	2169	22.3%
FSM.4	50	199	10	5	592	826	645	21.9%
FSM.5	50	100	5	5	351	616	598	2.9%
X.25	14	134	28	14	366	474	452	4.6%

Table V. Lengths of test sequences generated using single and multiple UIO sequences for sample FSMs.

Specifications *FSM.* 1 through *FSM.* 5 are randomly generated FSMs with varying parameters for number of states, number of edges, number of possible inputs, and number of possible outputs. For example, *FSM.* 1 has 50 states, 916 transitions, 50 possible inputs, and 50 possible outputs. Note that not all inputs are specified for each state. By generating a single UIO sequence per state, the resulting tour is of cost 2426 of which the cost of the scenarios (that is, the edges in the set E_C) is 1832. Therefore, the cost of the extra transitions used is 590. However, when *multiple* UIO sequences are generated per state and a corresponding assignment of edges to UIO sequences is produced, the cost of the tour is reduced to 1836, so that only four extra transitions are traversed in addition to the scenarios, for a savings of 24.3%.

The final specification considered, *X.* 25, models the core behavior of the CCITT Recommendation X.25 protocol for access to packet switched data networks [15]. The graph consists of 14 states and 134 transitions; the cost of the tours which are generated using single and multiple UIO sequences per state are 474 and 452, respectively, for a savings of 4.6%. Intuitively, the difference is savings between *X.* 25 and *FSM.* 1 is due to the lower number of transitions per state which lead to other states in *X.* 25, yielding less flexibility in the choice of UIO assignments.

VI. Conclusions and Discussion

In this paper, a technique has been introduced for reducing the execution time of test sequences for protocol conformance testing which are generated using the UIO sequence- Rural Chinese Postman method described in [10]. Because *multiple* UIO sequences are generated per state, an appropriate assignment of edges to UIO sequences decreases the number of transitions required in the resulting tour. An algorithm for producing such an assignment by means of network flow techniques has been given; both real and randomly generated FSMs have been studied as test cases and indicate that the savings in reducing the length of the tour is substantial.

Several issues remain open. First, the assignment of edges to UIO sequences which minimizes $\Delta(G')$ may not, in theory, minimize the length of the tour. This is because there is no guarantee on the cost of the set of edges which are augmented to produce $\hat{G}^*$; for example, one multiple UIO sequence assignment may lead to two edges of unit cost being replicated to form $\hat{G}^*$ while an "optimal" assignment may lead to the replication of a single edge of high cost. In this study, however, no such situation was ever encountered.

In [10] it was shown that a sufficiency condition for the Rural Chinese Postman algorithm given there to be valid is that the edge-induced subgraph of edges in E_C be a *weakly connected* spanning subgraph of G'; that is, that the underlying undirected subgraph formed by making the edges of E_C undirected is connected. It is possible that this condition is not met when multiple UIO sequences are used, even if the reset capability and/or self-loop properties, as described in [10], are present. If the edge-induced subgraph formed by the edges of E_C is not weakly connected then various simple heuristics can be used to make it weakly connected, such as 1) adding edges in E to E_C until E_C is weakly connected, or 2) making minor changes to the assignment of edges to UIO sequences until E_C is weakly connected. Such actions will usually slightly increase the cost of the tour.

Acknowledgements

The authors are grateful to Anup Sharma for providing the results given in Table V.

References

[1] G.V. Bochmann and C.A. Sunshine, "A survey of formal methods," in *Computer Networks and Protocols*, P.E. Green (Ed.). New York: Plenum Press, 1983 (pp. 561-578).

[2] F.C. Hennie, "Fault detection experiments for sequential circuits," *Proc. 5th Ann. Symp. Switch. Theory and Logical Design*, pp. 95-110, 1964.

[3] Z. Kohavi, *Switching and Finite Automata Theory*. New York: McGraw-Hill, 1978.

[4] G. Gonenc, "A method for the design of detection experiments," *IEEE Trans. Comput.*, vol. C-19, no. 6, pp. 551-558, June 1970.

[5] S. Naito and M. Tsunoyama, "Fault detection for sequential machines by transition tours," in *Proc. 11th. IEEE Fault Tolerant Comput. Symp.*, IEEE Computer Soc. Press, pp. 238-243, 1981.

[6] K.K. Sabnani and A.T. Dahbura, "A protocol test generation procedure," *Computer Networks*, vol. 15, no. 4, pp. 285-297, 1988.

[7] M.U. Uyar and A.T. Dahbura, "Optimal test sequence generation for protocols: the Chinese postman algorithm applied to Q.931," in *Proc. IEEE Global Telecommunications Conference*, pp. 68-72, 1986.

[8] D. Sidhu and T. Leung, "Fault coverage of protocol test methods," in *Proc. IEEE INFOCOM '88*, pp. 80-85, March 1988.

[9] B. Wang and D. Hutchinson, "Protocol testing techniques," *Computer Communications*, vol. 10, no. 2, pp. 79-87, April 1987.

[10] A.V. Aho, A.T. Dahbura, D. Lee, and M.U. Uyar, "An optimization technique for protocol conformance test generation based on UIO sequences and rural Chinese postman tours," in *Protocol Specification, Testing, and Verification, VIII*, S. Aggarwal and K.K. Sabnani (Eds.). New York: Elsevier North-Holland, 1988 (pp. 75-86).

[11] J.A. Bondy and U.S.R. Murty, *Graph Theory With Applications*. New York: Elsevier North Holland, 1976.

[12] M.-K. Kuan, "Graphic programming using odd or even points," *Chinese Math.*, vol. 1, pp. 273-277, 1962.

[13] J. Edmonds and E.L. Johnson, "Matching, Euler tours and the Chinese postman," *Mathematical Programming*, vol. 5, pp. 88-124, 1973.

[14] R.E. Tarjan, *Data Structures and Network Algorithms*. Philadelphia, PA: Society for Industrial and Applied Mathematics, 1983.

[15] CCITT Recommendation X.25, in CCITT Orange Book, vol. VIII. 2 (Public data networks, 1977).

Protocol Specification, Testing, and Verification, IX
E. Brinksma, G. Scollo and C.A. Vissers (Editors)
Elsevier Science Publishers B.V. (North-Holland)

THE CO-OP METHOD FOR COMPOSITIONAL DERIVATION OF CONFORMANCE TESTERS.

Clazien D. WEZEMAN

Formal Methods Group
Research and Technology/Information Services Standards Division
British Telecom
St Vincent House
1, Cutler Street
Ipswich, United Kingdom

A new method is presented for the derivation of conformance testers T(S) from labelled transition systems S where internal transitions may be included. This method, named the CO-OP method, is shown to lead to the construction of optimized canonical testers. It is applied to basic LOTOS behaviour expressions, giving the possibility of compositional derivation of testers; i.e. a tester T(B1*B2) can be constructed from the attributes of the testers T(B1) and T(B2), where * is any basic LOTOS operator. Furthermore, using the results of this application, it is shown why in many cases a tester for a combined process B=B1*B2 is not equivalent to the combination of the testers for its components; i.e. T(B1*B2)≠T(B1)*T(B2).

Introduction.

As a result of the recent increase in the use of formal methods for the specification of complex distributed systems there is a need for systematic methods to derive tests from such specifications. Tests are needed to determine whether implementations conform to their specifications. The aim of this paper is to present a new method for deriving such tests from process specifications written in languages that can be interpreted in terms of labelled transition systems where internal transitions may be included [Brinksma,87].

In the literature two main approaches can be found to the construction of a tester T(S) from a specification S. The first one, elaborated in [Brinksma,87], uses a model of processes (failure trees) identifying processes that are testing equivalent. This leads to the development of a complete algorithm that constructs canonical testers T(S) that are unique up to testing equivalences. The second one is the syntactical approach explored in [Freestone,88], [Steenbergen,86] and [Pitt,87]. Here tests are derived directly from specifications' syntaxes. Some rules are given to transform basic LOTOS choice specifications into test suite specifications by rewriting only. Also some preliminary work is done investigating the possibility of deriving testers for combined specifications from the combination of their testers.

The new method for derivation of canonical testers presented in this paper is based on the approach of [Pitt,87] and [Freestone,88]. The method is named the CO-OP method after its main components, the sets named Compulsory(B) and Options(B). It is developed for process specifications written in languages that can be interpreted in terms of labelled transition systems where internal transitions may be included. The result is applied to basic LOTOS [ISO IS8807,88]. It is shown how to derive the attributes that are needed for the construction of a tester for a combined process B1*B2 from the attributes of the testers of its components B1 and B2. This allows testers to be derived compositionally, i.e. testers for processes B1*B2 can be derived from the attributes used in the construction of the testers for its components B1 and B2. Furthermore it gives an insight in the problems that arise trying to construct a tester T(B1*B2) directly as T(B1)*T(B2).

The rest of this paper is organized as follows. In section 1 we give a general framework of the definitions and concepts used. In section 2 we present the CO–OP method. In section 3 we apply the method to basic LOTOS and in section 4 we show using the results of this application that $T(B1*B2) \neq T(B1)*T(B2)$ for many basic LOTOS operators *. Finally in section 5 we draw some conclusions.

1. General framework.

This paper considers process specifications that can be written as labelled transition systems where internal, unobservable actions may be included. Such systems allow formal, unambiguous representations of complex processes. Examples of languages whose expressions can be interpreted in terms of labelled transition systems are CCS [Milner,80], SCCS, CSP [Hoare,85] and LOTOS [ISO IS8807,88]. In this paper we concentrate on LOTOS. This language is choosen, as it has recently become an international standard and is expected to be widely used in the formal specification of industrial systems, e.g. communication protocols. We restrict ourselves to basic LOTOS, i.e. LOTOS without value passing. To visualize labelled transition systems we (sometimes) use tree representation.

Definition 1.1 (*labelled transition system [Brinksma,88]*)
A *labelled transition system TS* is defined as a 4–tuple $TS=\langle S,L,T,s_0\rangle$ with
- S is a (countable) non–empty set of states;
- L is a (countable) set of observable actions;
- $T=\{-\mu\text{->}\subseteq S\times S \mid \mu\in L\cup\{\tau\}\}$ is a set of binary relations on S, the transitions;
- $s_0 \in S$ is the initial state of TS.

We use the following notation for transitions and sets of observable and unobservable actions that are relevant within labelled transition systems. It is identical to the notation in [Brinksma,88].

L	denotes the alphabet of observable actions; a,b,c,... denote its elements.
L*	denotes the set of strings over L; σ, σ_1,.. denote its elements; ε is the empty string.
L'	denotes $L\cup\{\tau\}$, i.e. the set of observable events extended with the invisible action τ. Variables over this set are denoted by μ, μ_1,...

Capital letters B,P,Q,R,.. are used to range over states; states may be identified with processes, interpreting a state as the initial state of a process.

$P-\mu_1..\mu_n\text{->}Q$	stands for: there exist P_i with $0\leqslant i\leqslant n$ such that $P=P_0-\mu_1\text{->}..-\mu_n\text{->}P_n=Q$.
$P-\mu_1..\mu_n\text{->}$	stands for: there exist Q such that $P-\mu_1..\mu_n\text{->}Q$.
$P\not-\mu_1..\mu_n\text{->}$	stands for: not $P-\mu_1..\mu_n\text{->}$.
$P=\varepsilon\text{=>}Q$	stands for: $P-\tau^n\text{->}Q$ ($n\geqslant 0$; $P-a^0\text{->}Q$ iff $P=Q$).
$P=a\text{=>}Q$	stands for: there exist P_1,P_2 such that $P=\varepsilon\text{=>}P_1-a\text{->}P_2=\varepsilon\text{=>}Q$.
$P=a_1..a_n\text{=>}Q$	stands for: there exist P_i with $0\leqslant i\leqslant n$ such that $P=P_0=a_1\text{=>}P_1=a_2\text{=>}..=a_n\text{=>}P_n=Q$. This is also denoted by $P=\sigma\text{=>}Q$, with $\sigma=a_1...a_n$.
$P=\sigma\text{=>}$	stands for: there exist Q such that $P=\sigma\text{=>}Q$.
$P\neq\sigma\text{=>}$	stands for: **not** $P=\sigma\text{=>}$.
Tr(P)	is used to denote $\{\sigma\in L^* \mid P=\sigma\text{=>}\}$; the *trace set* of P.
out(P)	is used to denote $\{a\in L \mid P=a\text{=>}\}$.
P=a1..an->Q	stands for: there exist P_1 such that $P=a_1..a_{n-1}\text{=>}P_1-a_n\text{->}Q$.

The syntax, axioms and inference rules of basic LOTOS behaviour expressions are given in table 1.2. For each behaviour expression of the language these rules generate a labelled transition system. Although the syntax of basic LOTOS allows infinite series of internal events, in this paper we deal only with finite processes without infinite series of internal events. Also the enabling operator is omitted in this paper.

Name	Syntax	Axioms or Inference Rules
inaction	**stop**	none
action prefix		
−unobservable	**i**; B	⊢ i; B−τ−>B
−observable	a; B	a∈L ⊢ a; B−a−>B
choice	B1[]B2	B1−a−>B1' ⊢ B1[]B2−a−>B1' B2−a−>B2' ⊢ B1[]B2−a−>B2'
parallel composition		
−general case	B1 |[g1,..,gn]| B2	B1−a−>B1', a∉{g1,..,gn,δ} ⊢ B1 |[g1,..,gn]| B2−a−>B1' |[g1,..,gn]| B2 B2−a−>B2', a∉{g1,..,gn,δ} ⊢ B1 |[g1,..,gn]| B2−a−>B1 |[g1,..,gn]| B2' B1−a−>B1', B2−a−>B2', a∈{g1,..,gn,δ} ⊢ B1 |[g1,..,gn]| B2−a−>B1' |[g1,..,gn]| B2'
−pure interleaving	B1|||B2	B1−a−>B1' ⊢ B1|||B2−a−>B1'|||B2 B2−a−>B2' ⊢ B1|||B2−a−>B1|||B2'
−full synchronization	B1||B2	B1−a−>B1', B2−a−>B2' ⊢ B1||B2−a−>B1'||B2' B1−τ−>B1' ⊢ B1||B2−τ−>B1'||B2 B2−τ−>B2' ⊢ B1||B2−τ−>B1||B2'
disabling	B1[>B2	B1−a−>B1', a≠δ ⊢ B1[>B2−a−>B1'[>B2 B1−δ−>B1' ⊢ B1[>B2−δ−>B1' B2−a−>B2' ⊢ B1[>B2−a−>B2'
successful termination	**exit**	**exit**−δ−>stop
hiding	B\(g1,...,gn)	B−a−>B', a∈{g1,..,gn} ⊢ B\(g1,..,gn)−τ−>B'\(g1,..,gn) B−a−>B', a∉{g1,..,gn} ⊢ B\(g1,..,gn)−a−>B'\(g1,..,gn)

Note: B\g1,..,gn is a short notation for ***hide*** *g1,..,gn* ***in*** *B.*

Table 1.2. *Axioms and inference rules for basic LOTOS behaviour expressions.*

The objective of conformance testing is to establish whether an implementation under test (IUT) conforms to its specification. To be able to decide this, a formal notion of conformance is needed. We use the notion of conformance given in [Brinksma,88] formalized using the notation above as follows:

Definition 1.3. (*conformance*)
Let B1 and B2 be processes.
B1 **conf** B2 iff ∀σ∈Tr(B2). ∀A⊆L.
if ∃B1'. ∀a∈A. B1=σ=>B1'≠a=>
then ∃B2'. ∀a∈A. B2=σ=>B2'≠a=>

Definition 1.3 expresses that B1 conforms to B2 if B1 contains no unexpected deadlocks with respect to traces in B2. However it does allow B1 to possess traces not specified in B2. For example, consider figure 1.4 where B1 **conf** B2, even though B1 has a trace (c) that is not included in B2. It is not the case that B3 **conf** B2, since B3=ε=>B3↛b−>, but **not** ∃B2'.B2'=ε=>B2'↛b−>.

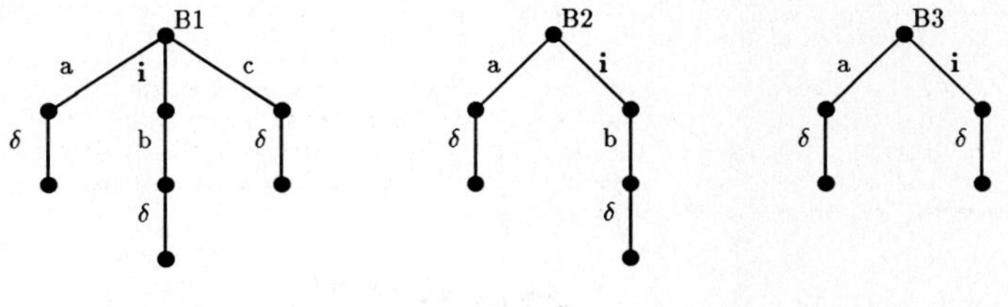

figure 1.4.

We regard a conformance tester as a (LOTOS) process running concurrently with, and communicating with, the IUT. This is an abstraction of the implemented tester. For the conformance tester we use the concept of a general canonical tester as given in [Brinksma,87]. The basic idea of a canonical tester T(S) is that (i) it is capable of exploring all and only traces in S, and (ii) that P conforms to S iff every deadlock between P and the tester T(S) can be explained by the tester having reached a terminal state.

Definition 1.5. (*general canonical tester*)
Let S be a process. A (general) canonical tester of the process specification S (in LT(L)) is a process T(S) with
(i) Tr(T(S))=Tr(S); and
(ii) for all processes P, for all $\sigma \epsilon L^*$. P **conf** S iff
$P \| T(S) = \sigma => \approx$ **stop** implies $T(S) = \sigma => \approx$ **stop**

Running a canonical tester T(S) concurrently with an IUT once, it will only test one trace in S. Unless S consists of one trace only, it cannot be decided whether the IUT conforms to S. To test conformance the tester should be rerun until it has tested all traces in S. We define a test case to be an irreducible reduction [Brinksma,87] of T(S) and a test suite to be a set of test cases. [Brinksma,87] shows that the test suite containing all and only test cases of T(S) has equivalent testing power to T(S); i.e. this test suite can test all and only traces of S, and an IUT conforms to S if and only if every deadlock between a test case and the IUT can be explained by the test case having reached a terminal state.

Because definition 1.3 is used as the notion of conformance, this tester does not include any robustness tests; i.e. it does not test the implementation against an environment that behaves incorrectly. Although robustness tests would complement this work, they would have to be based on a different notion of conformance.

If T(B1) is a canonical tester for process B1 and B1 is testing equivalent [LOTOS IS8807,88] to B2 then T(B1) is a canonical tester for B2. We use $\sim_{te}$ to denote testing equivalence.

2. The CO–OP method.

Based on ideas found in [Steenbergen,86], [Pitt,87] and [Freestone,88], in this section we show how test cases can be derived from process specifications. Also we give an expression for the behaviour of a tester after interaction in an event. Next we introduce the CO–OP method, which is built using these concepts. We prove that it gives canonical testers and give rules to eliminate redundant information contained in its outputs. We then show its working in an example.

2.1. Initial behaviour.

The initial behaviour of a tester, i.e. its behaviour up to and including the first external event in each of its branches, is determined by the initial behaviours of its test cases. These initial behaviours have to be derived from the initial behaviour of the specification of the process under test.

[Steenbergen,86] presents some interesting ideas on the derivation of the initial behaviour of test cases from processes where two different kinds of branches are mixed – some branches start with an internal event (i–branches) and some without (e–branches). The work recognizes that for a process B defined as the process tree shown in figure 2.1.

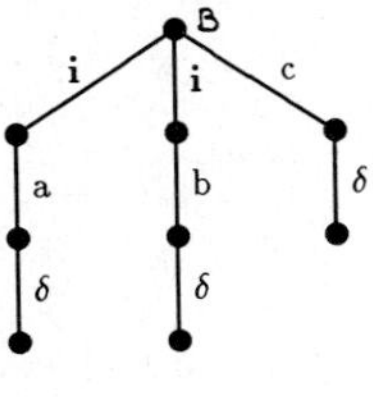

figure 2.1.

B can make an internal transition into one of two states: one where it will accept only *a*, the other where it will accept only *b*. To test an implementation of B, each test case should offer a choice between *a* or *b*. A process that does not offer the possibility of interacting in *a* or *b* may deadlock with a conforming implementation and thus will not a proper test case. Also, in constructing a test case one or more of the events that appear in the e-branches may be used: in figure 2.1 event *c*. A canonical tester for B of figure 2.1 should consist of the test cases t1 = a; δ [] b; δ and t2 = a; δ [] b; δ [] c; δ .

[Pitt,87] and [Freestone,88] deal with process specifications in a standard form where there are no choice expressions with both i-branches and e-branches. Choice expressions with e-branches are preceded by internal events. Consider for example process B in figure 2.2.

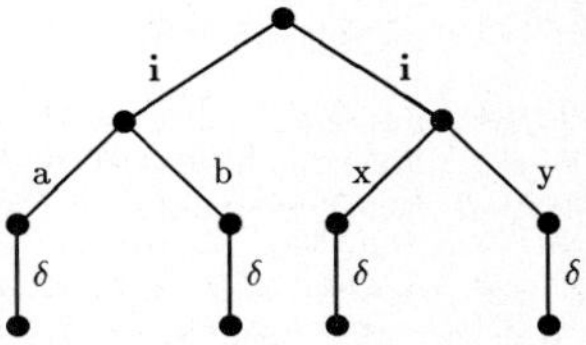

figure 2.2.

B can do an internal transition into one of two states: one where it will accept only *a* or *b*, one where it will accept only *x* or *y*. Pitt concludes that each test case for process B should offer at least one element from each of the two sets {a,b} and {x,y}. For specifications in this standard form, there exists a set M of sets M_i of events, such that in each test case at least one element of each set $M_i \epsilon M$ should be used. Each set $M_i \epsilon M$ corresponds to a state that can be reached by B by making an internal transition. Notice that from these states no internal transition can be performed. In figure 2.2, M = { {a,b}, {x,y} }, and test cases for B are t1 = a; δ [] x; δ, t2 = b; δ [] x; δ, t3 = a; δ [] y; δ and t4 = b; δ [] y; δ.

Labelled transition systems are not restricted to the forms considered by Steenbergen and Pitt. In general, both i-branches and e-branches may appear and also choice expressions with both i-branches and e-branches after internal events. An example of a process including all these features is illustrated in figure 2.3.

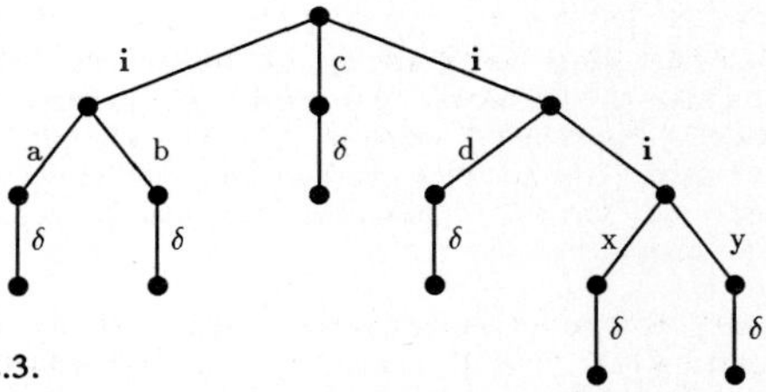

figure 2.3.

Notice that B can do an internal transition and enter a state where it can interact only in events of the set {x,y} and from where it cannot do an internal transition. Each test case for B should offer the possibility of interacting in at least one of these events. Similarly each test case must also offer the possibility of interacting in at least one of the events of the set {a,b}. In addition a test case may include any of the external events that can be performed from states that can do both internal and external events (*c* or *d*).

We define a *stable* state as a state which will accept only external events and cannot do an internal event. If process B can internally move to a stable state Q then each test case should have the possibility of interacting in at least one of the events *y* such that Q–y–>. Test cases that cannot interact in any of these events may deadlock with a correct implementation of B. A test suite containing such a test case is thus not a canonical tester for B.

We define an *unstable* state as a state that can do an internal event. If P is an unstable state which can be reached from B, then the events *x* for which P–x–> may be included in test cases. To cover all possible traces of B in a canonical tester for B for all $a \in out(B)$ there should be at least one test case which can interact in *a*.

The discussion above leads us to the definition of two sets *Compulsory(B)* and *Options(B)* specifying the compulsory and optional elements of test cases for B.

Definition 2.4. (*Compulsory(B)*)
Let B be a labelled transition system.
Compulsory(B) = { comp⊆L(B) ∣ ∃B'. B=ε=>B'-/i-> and comp = { x∈L(B) ∣ B'-x->} }

Definition 2.5. (*Options(B)*)
Let B be a labelled transition system.
Options(B) = { x∈L(B) ∣ ∃B'. B=ε=>B'-i-> and B'-x-> }

Compulsory(B) is a set of sets of events. For each stable state B' for which B=ε=>B' holds, Compulsory(B) contains a set *comp* with the external events that can be performed from B'. In each test case at least one element of each set–element of Compulsory(B) *must* be used.

Options(B) is a set of events. For each unstable state B' for which B=ε=>B' holds, this set contains all external events that can be performed from B' without making any internal transitions before doing so. Elements of Options(B) *may* be used in test cases.

We follow [Pitt,87] by defining orth(M) to be the set of all sets which can be formed by choosing precisely one member from each element of the set M. Also we define the following notation.

$$\underset{a \in V}{[]}\ a = x_1 \ [] \ x_2 \ [] \ \ldots \ [] \ x_n \qquad \textit{where } V = \{x_1, x_2, \ldots, x_n\}$$

Test cases for a process B can begin in one of the two following ways.

$$T1 = \underset{a \in V}{[]}\ a; \ldots \qquad\qquad T2 = (\underset{a \in V}{[]}\ a; \ldots)\ []\ option; \ldots$$

where V∈orth(Compulsory(B)) and option∈Options(B)

Test cases with an initial behaviour as given by T1 or T2 we call *basic test cases*. They contain the minimum number of interaction possibilities. Other test cases can be constructed combining basic test cases by the choice operator; i.e. if t1,t2,..,tm are basic test cases then tn=t1[]t2[]...tm is a test case. The complete conformance test suite consists of the union of the set of basic test cases with the set of test cases that can be constructed combining (basic) test cases with the choice operator.

The discussion above does not cover processes B where ∃B'. B=ε=>B'≈**stop**. Here B can move internally to a state where it will not accept any $a \in out(B)$. For such processes the empty set will be an element of Compulsory(B) and the construction of test cases of type T1 and T2 fails. Although in most cases the occurrence of deadlock is a design fault testers have to be able to deal with deadlocking processes. All test cases should have the ability to deadlock. Basic test cases of the following forms cover the point.

T3 = **i**; **stop** T4 = **i**; **stop** [] a; ... *for some a∈out(B)*

Notice that the initial behaviour of all test cases is completely defined by the sets Compulsory(B) and Options(B). We show later that the set of test cases constructed above has equivalent testing power to the initial behaviour of the canonical tester.

2.2. Subsequent behaviour.

For any process B, the behaviour of the tester after interaction in an event is fully dependent on the behaviour of B after interaction in this event. If there is more than one state B' with B=a->B' then, after interaction in *a*, it is not known to the tester which transition has been chosen within the process under test. The behaviour of B after interaction in *a* can then be seen as a non-deterministic choice. This can be illustrated by the basic LOTOS choice process B for which the following equation holds.

B = a; B1 [] a; B2 []...[] a; Bn $\sim_{te}$ a; (i; B1 [] i; B2 []...[] i; Bn)

The behaviour of B after interaction in ***a*** is testing equivalent to the non-deterministic choice expression (i; B1 [] i; B2 []...[] i; Bn).

[Steenbergen,86] uses this testing equivalence approach to rewrite processes where there is more than one B' such that B=a->B' to processes where there is only one such B'. This means that the set Compulsory(B) and Options(B) as defined in the previous section will need amendment. We want to affect the construction of these sets and also the structure of the process under test as little as possible. Therefore we do not rewrite the specification of the process replacing all branches starting with the same external event by one single branch starting with that event. Instead we define the behaviour expression *B* ***after*** *a* giving the (possible non-deterministic) behaviour of process B after interaction in ***a***. A tester for B after interaction in *a* will then be T(B) **after** *a* = T(B **after** *a*).

Definition 2.6. *(B* ***after*** *a)*
Let B be a labelled transition system. Let $a \in out(B)$. The behaviour of B after interaction in *a* is specified by:

B **after** a = $\left(\underset{B_i \in AS_a(B)}{[]} \text{ i; } B_i \right)$ *where* $AS_a(B)$ = { B' | B=a->B' } □

2.3. The CO-OP method.

So far we have given rules to derive the initial behaviour of test cases and the behaviour of a tester after interaction in an event from the process specification. The next step in the construction of a conformance tester is to organise these concepts into a general normal form for a canonical tester. The result of this organisation is the *CO-OP method*, a method for the derivation of conformance testers from labelled transition systems, defined as follows.

Algorithm 2.7. *(CO-OP method)*
Given a labelled transition system B, its conformance tester T(B) can be constructed (recursively) as follows:

(1) Construct the sets Compulsory(B) and Options(B).
(2) Construct for all $a \in out(B)$ the specification B **after** a.
(3) Construct the conformance tester T(B) as:

If $\emptyset \notin$ Compulsory(B)
Then T(B) = $\underset{V \in orth(Compulsory(B))}{[]}$ i; $\left(\underset{a \in V}{[]} \text{ a; T(B } \textbf{after} \text{ a)} \right)$
[] $\left(\underset{option \in Options(B)}{[]} \text{ option; T(B } \textbf{after} \text{ option)} \right)$
Else T(B) = **i; stop**
[] $\left(\underset{a \in out(B)}{[]} \text{ a; T(B } \textbf{after} \text{ a)} \right)$ □

The significance of the CO-OP method is that it produces canonical testers, as theorem 2.8 states.

Theorem 2.8. Let B be a process described as a labelled transition system. T(B) constructed following algorithm 2.7 is a general canonical tester for B.

Proof: The proof is based on Brinksma's failure tree method [Brinksma,88]. This method states that for a specification S, its canonical tester T(S) is a process with F(T(S))=F(S)', for certain given F and F'. For T(B) constructed following the CO-OP method it can be proved that F(T(B))=F(B)' [Wezeman,88]. T(B) is thus a canonical tester for B. □

Basic test cases can be derived from T(B) by pruning all or all but one of the e–branches, pruning all but one of the i–branches, and subsequently removing the internal event. All other test cases can be constructed by combining basic test cases with the choice operator. The initial behaviour of these test cases is identical to that of the test cases of section 2.1.

The set of basic test cases constructed following the ideas above may contain redundant elements; i.e. it may contain test cases t1, t2 and t3 such that t3 = t1[]t2. Here t3 is redundant as a basic test case because it can be constructed combining two other basic test cases by the choice operator. It can be removed from the basic test cases without loss of information since t3 and any test case based on t3 can also be constructed from t1[]t2.

To remove redundant basic test cases we introduce $orth_c$(M), a subset of orth(M). $Orth_c$(M) is orth(M) minus exactly the sets in orth(M) that can be formed by the union of other sets in orth(M). If orth(Compulsory(B)) is replaced by $orth_c$(Compulsory(B)) in definition 2.7 then this redundancy problem no longer exists: there are no $OM_1, OM_2, OM_3 \in orth_c$(Compulsory(B)) with corresponding basic test cases t1,t2,t3 such that t3=t1[]t2.

More redundant basic test cases can be removed by applying the following rules:

Rule 2.9. **if** $\exists$comp1, comp2$\in$Compulsory(B). comp1$\subseteq$comp2 **and** comp1$\neq\emptyset$
then Options(B) := Options(B) $\cup$ {comp2–comp1};
Compulsory(B) := Compulsory(B) – {comp2}.

Rule 2.10. **if** $\exists$op$\in$Options(B), comp$\in$Compulsory(B). op$\in$comp
then Options(B) := Options(B) – op

The application of rules 2.9 and 2.10 and the use of $orth_c$() instead of orth() in algorithm 2.7 does not affect the total set of test cases specified by T(B). This is stated formally in theorem 2.11 below.

Theorem 2.11. Let B be a process described as a labelled transition system. T(B) constructed following algorithm 2.7 but with application of rule 2.9 and 2.10 and the use of $orth_c$ instead of orth is a general canonical tester for B.

Proof: As in proof 2.7. It can be proved that the use of rules 2.9 and 2.10 and of $orth_c$ do not influence the construction of F(T(B)) and thus that still F(T(B))=F(B)' [Wezeman,88]. This implies that T(B) is a canonical tester for B. □

The working of the CO–OP method and the use of $orth_c$() and rules 2.9 and 2.10 is illustrated in the following example.

Example 2.12. Consider a process given by the folllowing process tree.

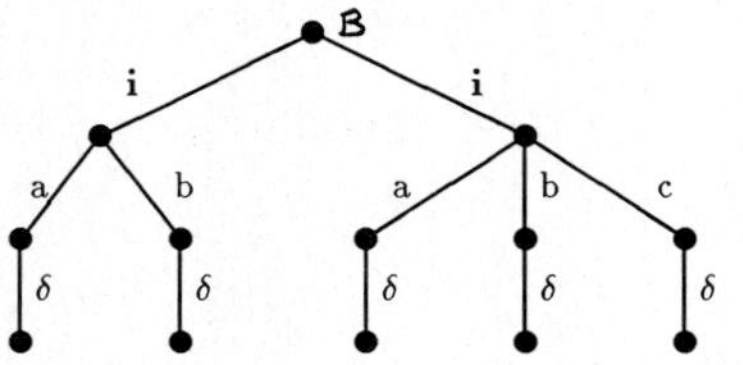

Options(B) = $\emptyset$;
Compulsory(B) = { {a,b},{a,b,c} }
Orth(Compulsory(B)) =
{ {a}, {b}, {a,b}, {a,c}, {b,c} }
$Orth_c$(Compulsory(B)) =
{ {a}, {a,c}, {b}, {b,c} }

Following the CO–OP method the canonical tester for B would be:

T(B) = i; a; δ [] i; b; δ
[] i; (a; δ [] c; δ)
[] i; (b; δ [] c; δ)

Application of rule 2.9 gives a simpler canonical tester, specifying the same set of test cases.

T(B) = i ; a; δ [] i ; b; δ [] c ; δ □

3. Application of CO–OP method to basic LOTOS.

The CO–OP method can be applied to any specification written in a formal language that allows interpretation of its expressions by a system of labelled transition systems. In this section we apply it to basic LOTOS expressions. This is done so that a tester T(B) for a process B=B1*B2 can be constructed from the attributes used in the construction of T(B1) and T(B2), for any basic LOTOS operator *, thus giving the possibility of compositional derivation of conformance testers.

3.1. Initial behaviour for basic LOTOS behaviour expressions.

Table 1.2 gave rules that generate labelled transition systems for each basic LOTOS behaviour expression. Following these rules and using definitions 2.4 and 2.5 the sets Compulsory(B) and Options(B) can be constructed for any behaviour expression B. Furthermore for a process B=B1*B2, where * is any basic LOTOS operator, it is possible to derive these sets using those of B1 and B2. Table 3.1 shows how this can be done.

behaviour expression B	**Compulsory(B)**	**Options(B)**
a; B1	{ {a} }	$\emptyset$
i; B1	C(B1)	O(B1)
B1 [] B2	(**if** B1–i–> **then** C(B1)) $\cup$ (**if** B2–i–> **then** C(B2)) $\cup$ (**if** B1-/i–> **and** B2-/i–> **then** { $c_1 \cup c_2 \mid c_1 \in C(B1),\ c_2 \in C(B2)$ })	O(B1) $\cup$ O(B2) $\cup$ (**if** B1-/i–> **and** B2–i–> **then** el(C(B1))) $\cup$ (**if** B1–i–> **and** B2-/i–> **then** el(C(B2)))
B1 || B2	{ $c_1 \cap c_2 \mid c_1 \in C(B1),\ c_2 \in C(B2)$ }	(O(B1) $\cap$ out(B2)) $\cup$ (O(B2) $\cap$ out(B1))
B1 ||| B2	{ $c_1 \cup c_2 \mid c_1 \in C(B1),\ c_2 \in C(B2)$ }	O(B1) $\cup$ O(B2)
B1 |[g1,..,gn]| B2	{ $c_1 - g^* \cup c_2 - g^* \cup (c_1 \cap c_2 \cap g^*) \mid$ $c_1 \in C(B1),\ c_2 \in C(B2)$ }	O(B1)–g* $\cup$ O(B2)–g* $\cup$ (O(B1) $\cap$ out(B2) $\cap$ g*) $\cup$ (O(B2) $\cap$ out(B1) $\cap$ g*)
B1\g*	{ $c_1 \mid c_1 \in C(B1)$ **and** $c_1 \cap g^* = \emptyset$ } $\cup$ { $c_j \mid \exists g_j \in out(B1) \cap g^*.$ $c_j \in C((B1$ **after** $g_j)\backslash g^*)$ }	O(B1)–g* $\cup$ { op $\mid \exists g_j \in out(B1) \cap g^*.$ op $\in O((B1$ **after** $g_j)\backslash g^*)$ } $\cup$ { op $\mid \exists c_1 \in C(B1).$ $c_1 \cap g^* \neq \emptyset$ **and** op $\in c_1 - g^*$ }
stop	{ {} }	$\emptyset$
exit	{ {δ} }	$\emptyset$
(B1)	C(B1)	O(B1)
B1 [> B2	**if** B2–i–> **then** C(B2) **else** { $c_1 \cup out(B2) \mid c_1 \in C(B1)$ }	O(B1) $\cup$ O(B2) $\cup$ (**if** B2–i–> **then** out(B1))

Notation: C(B) = Compulsory(B), O(B) = Options(B),
g* = {g1,...,gn},
el(M) = { $x \mid \exists Mi \in M.\ x \in Mi$ },
out(B) = { $x \mid x \in$ Options(B) or $x \in$ el(C(B)) } = { x $\mid$ B=x–> }

Table 3.1. *Compulsory and Options for basic LOTOS behaviour expressions.*

For some basic LOTOS syntax elements, the construction of Compulsory(B1*B2) and Options(B1*B2) depends on the occurrence of internal events so that B1–i–> or B2–i–>. Since information on the stability of processes is lost in the construction of the sets Compulsory() and Options(), it is not possible to derive these sets for B1*B2 from the sets for B1 and B2 only. Therefore we introduce a new boolean attribute *unstable(B)*. Its value is *true* iff B–i–>. For each behaviour expression B, unstable(B) can be derived from the values of this attribute for its components using table 3.2.

<table>
<tr><th>behaviour expression</th><th>unstable(B)</th></tr>
<tr><td>a; B1</td><td>false</td></tr>
<tr><td>i; B1</td><td>true</td></tr>
<tr><td>B1 [] B2</td><td>unstable(B1) ∨ unstable(B2)</td></tr>
<tr><td>B1 || B2</td><td>unstable(B1) ∨ unstable(B2)</td></tr>
<tr><td>B1 ||| B2</td><td>unstable(B1) ∨ unstable(B2)</td></tr>
<tr><td>B1 |[g1,..,gn]| B2</td><td>unstable(B1) ∨ unstable(B2)</td></tr>
<tr><td>B1\(g1,...,gn)</td><td>unstable(B1) ∨ ({g1,...,gn}∩out(B1) ≠ ∅)</td></tr>
<tr><td>stop</td><td>false</td></tr>
<tr><td>exit</td><td>false</td></tr>
<tr><td>(B1)</td><td>unstable(B1)</td></tr>
<tr><td>B1 [> B2</td><td>unstable(B1) ∨ unstable(B2)</td></tr>
</table>

Table 3.2. *Unstable(B) for basic LOTOS behaviour expressions.*

The attributes Compulsory(B), Options(B) and unstable(B) completely define the initial behaviour of a tester for B and for any combined process B1*B2 their values can be derived from the values of these attributes for its components B1 and B2.

3.2. Subsequent behaviour for basic LOTOS behaviour expressions.

<table>
<tr><th>behaviour expression B</th><th>condition</th><th>B after a (defined for a∈out(B) only)</th></tr>
<tr><td>a; B1</td><td>–</td><td>i; B1</td></tr>
<tr><td>i; B1</td><td>a∈out(B1)</td><td>B1 after a</td></tr>
<tr><td>B1 [] B2</td><td>a∈out(B1)∩out(B2)</td><td>B1 after a [] B2 after a</td></tr>
<tr><td></td><td>a∈out(B1)−out(B2)</td><td>B1 after a</td></tr>
<tr><td></td><td>a∈out(B2)−out(B1)</td><td>B2 after a</td></tr>
<tr><td>B1 || B2</td><td>a∈out(B1)∩out(B2)</td><td>(B1 after a) || (B2 after a)</td></tr>
<tr><td>B1 ||| B2</td><td>a∈out(B1)∩out(B2)</td><td>((B1 after a) ||| B2) [] (B1 ||| (B2 after a))</td></tr>
<tr><td></td><td>a∈out(B1)−out(B2)</td><td>(B1 after a) ||| B2</td></tr>
<tr><td></td><td>a∈out(B2)−out(B1)</td><td>B1 ||| (B2 after a)</td></tr>
<tr><td>B1 |[g1,..,gn]| B2</td><td>a∈{g1,...,gn}</td><td>(B1 after a)|[g1,...,gn]|(B2 after a)</td></tr>
<tr><td></td><td>a∈(out(B1)∩out(B2))−g*</td><td>((B1 after a) |[g1,...,gn]| B2)
[] (B1 |[g1,...,gn]| (B2 after a))</td></tr>
<tr><td></td><td>a∈out(B1)−(out(B2)∪g*)</td><td>(B1 after a) |[g1,...,gn]| B2</td></tr>
<tr><td></td><td>a∈out(B2)−(out(B1)∪g*)</td><td>(B2 after a) |[g1,...,gn]| B1</td></tr>
<tr><td>B1\(g*)</td><td>a∈out(B1)−g*</td><td>(B1 after a)\g*
[] ($[]_{g_i \in out(B1) \cap (g^*)}$ ((B1 after g_i)\(g*)) after a)</td></tr>
<tr><td>stop</td><td>–</td><td>not defined as out(B) is empty</td></tr>
<tr><td>exit</td><td>a=δ</td><td>i; stop</td></tr>
<tr><td>(B1)</td><td>a∈out(B1)</td><td>(B1 after a)</td></tr>
<tr><td>B1 [> B2</td><td>a∈out(B2)−out(B1)</td><td>B2 after a</td></tr>
<tr><td></td><td>a∈out(B1)−out(B2), a≠δ</td><td>(B1 after a) [> B2</td></tr>
<tr><td></td><td>a∈out(B1)−out(B2), a=δ</td><td>B1 after a</td></tr>
<tr><td></td><td>a∈out(B1)∩out(B2), a≠δ</td><td>(B2 after a) [] (B1 after a [> B2)</td></tr>
<tr><td></td><td>a∈out(B1)∩out(B2), a=δ</td><td>(B1 after a) [] (B2 after a)</td></tr>
</table>

Table 3.3. *B **after** a for basic LOTOS behaviour expressions.*

Table 3.3 lists for each basic LOTOS syntax element the expression B **after** a. Again this is done in a compositional way: for B=B1*B2 the expression B **after** a is defined in terms of B1 **after** a and B2 **after** a only, where * is any basic LOTOS operator. Notice that B **after** a is defined for $a \epsilon out(B)$ only.

In table 3.3 **(hide** g1,...,gn **in** B1) **after** *a* is given by a recursive expression. This expression terminates because we have assumed throughout this paper that processes do not contain infinite series of internal events.

Notice that, for some behaviour expressions B, in the expression *B* ***after*** *a* the first internal event is removed. This is done for those expressions where B_i ***after*** *a* is used in the expression B **after** a, for some component B_i of B. Since each branch of Bi **after** a is ensured to start with an internal event, the expression B **after** a of table 3.3 is equivalent to the one that would have been constructed following definition 2.6.

3.3. The CO–OP method.

For basic LOTOS processes the CO–OP method becomes:

Algorithm 3.4. *(CO–OP method for basic LOTOS specifications)*
Given a basic LOTOS specification B, its conformance tester T(B) can be constructed as follows:

(1) Construct the sets Compulsory(B) and Options(B) as follows.
  (a) If B is a composition of other basic LOTOS expressions, combined by a basic LOTOS operator so that B=B1*B2: construct the sets Compulsory() and Options() and evaluate unstable() for the components B1 and B2 separately;
  (b) Construct Compulsory(B), Options(B) following table 3.1 and using the results of step (1a). Evaluate unstable(B) using table 3.2 and the result of step (1a);
  (c) Rewrite Options(B) and Compulsory(B) following rules 2.9 and 2.10;

(2) Construct the expression B **after** a for each $a \epsilon out(B)$ as follows:
  (a) If B=B1*B2 where * is a basic LOTOS operator: construct expressions B1 **after** a and B2 **after** a separately;
  (b) Construct B **after** a using table 3.3 and the results of step (2a);

(3) Construct the tester T(B) as:

If $\emptyset \not\epsilon$ Compulsory(B)
Then T(B) = [] i; ([] a; T(B **after** a))
$\qquad\qquad a \epsilon V$
$\qquad V \epsilon Orth_c(Compulsory(B))$
$\qquad$ [] ([] option; T(B **after** option))
$\qquad\qquad option \epsilon Options(B)$
Else T(B) = **i** ; **stop**
$\qquad$ [] ([] a; T(B **after** a))
$\qquad\qquad a \epsilon out(B)$ □

Theorem 3.5. Let B be a basic LOTOS behaviour expression. T(B) constructed following algorithm 3.4 is a general canonical tester for B.

Proof: Interpret B as a labelled transition system and apply proof of theorem 2.8. □

The attributes used in the construction of a canonical tester for B are: unstable(B), Compulsory(B), Options(B) and B **after** a. The first three completely define the initial behaviour of T(B); the last one defines its behaviour after interaction in any $a \epsilon out(B)$. For each composed behaviour expression B=B1*B2 its tester T(B) can be constructed from the attributes used in the construction of the testers of its components B1 and B2, where * is a basic LOTOS operator. In this sense, the CO–OP method is a method for compositional derivation of tests. It is in the line of the syntactical approach of [Pitt,87] and [Freestone,88] in that testers can be derived directly from specification syntaxes.

The following example illustrates the working of the method.

Example 3.6. Consider a process B = B1 || B2 as follows.

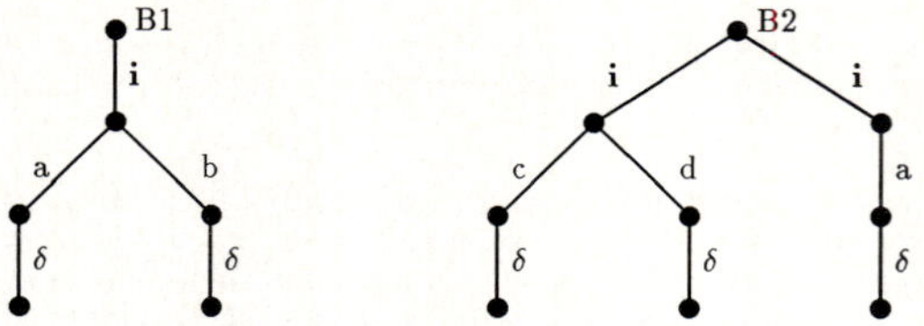

The sets Compulsory() and Options() for B1 and B2 are as follows:

Compulsory(B1) = { {a,b} }   Compulsory(B2) = { {c,d}, {a} }
Options(B1) = ∅   Options(B2) = ∅

Compulsory(B1||B2) and Options(B1||B2) can now be defined following table 3.1. We find:

Compulsory(B1||B2) = { {}, {a} }   Options(B1||B2) = ∅

Since Compulsory(B1||B2) contains the empty set the test suite for B1||B2 will be:

T(B1||B2) = i ; **stop** [] a ; δ □

4. Compositional testers.

The application of the CO–OP method to LOTOS gives compositional testers in the sense that testers T(B1*B2) can be constructed from the attributes used in the construction of T(B1) and T(B2). A question that arises is whether it is possible to construct T(B1*B2) direct from T(B1) and T(B2) and whether preservation of structure is possible; i.e. can T(B1*B2) be constructed as T(B1)*T(B2) or as a simple derivation of this product?

As a result of investigations based on the use of the CO–OP method we may conclude that the possibilities of constructing T(B1*B2) as T(B1)*T(B2) or a process derived from that, are fairly minimal. This is due to two factors.

(i) The initial behaviour of T(B1)*T(B2) is formed using some combination of the orth–products of the sets Compulsory() of B1 and B2. For a canonical tester T(B1*B2) constructed following the CO–OP method however we find that first the sets Options() and Compulsory() for B1 and B2 are combined into those for B1*B2 following table 3.1 and using table 3.2. The initial behaviour of T(B1*B2) is then formed using the orth–product of Compulsory(B1*B2). This may lead to T(B1)*T(B2) containing test cases that are not in T(B1*B2) and vice versa.

Removing or adding test cases from T(B1)*T(B2) can be done by removing or adding branches. However, in many cases it cannot be decided which branches to add or remove without further information on B1 and B2 such as the exact structure of Compulsory() and unstable() for B1 and B2. This information cannot be retrieved from T(B1)*T(B2) since here the orth–products of the sets Compulsory() are used and the value unstable() is not available at all.

(ii) The nondeterministic behaviour of a canonical tester after interaction in an event is in many cases not reflected in T(B1)*T(B2).

An example illustrating problems of the first sort is the parallel process given by the following trees.

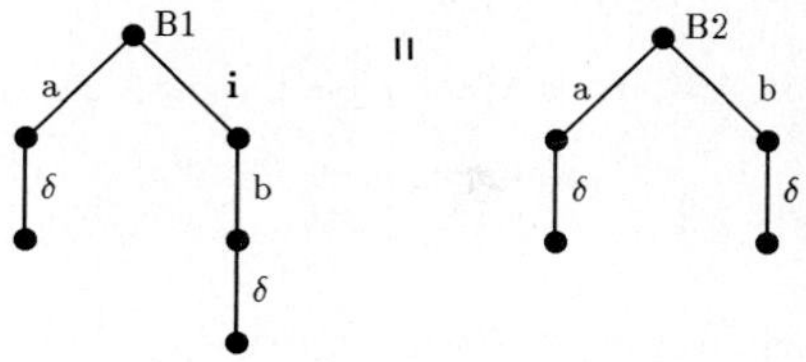

figure 4.1.

The process T(B1)||T(B2) is very different from the canonical tester T(B1||B2):

T(B1)||T(B2) = (a; δ [] i; b; δ) || (i; a; δ [] i; b; δ)
= i; a; δ [] i; b; δ [] i; (a [] b)
= i; a; δ [] i; b; δ [] i; **stop**

T(B1||B2) = i; b; δ [] a; δ

T(B1)||T(B2) contains a deadlocking branch and a branch *i; a; δ* that are not in T(B1||B2). They cannot be removed from T(B1)||T(B2) without further information on the exact structure of the sets Compulsory(B1) and Compulsory(B2), information that cannot be retreived from T(B1) and T(B2). T(B1||B2) thus cannot be derived from T(B1)||T(B2) only.

Problems of the second type may occur in fully interleaved processes. For processes B=B1|||B2 the initial behaviour of T(B1)|||T(B2) is identical to that of T(B1|||B2). Since B1 and B2 are fully interleaved one would expect that a tester for the combination can be derived easily from T(B1)|||T(B2). However if B1|||B2 can reach a state B1'|||B2' from where both B1' and B2' can both do event *a*, then after interaction in this event the tester for the combination must proceed as T(i; B1' **after** a [] i; B2' **after** a) which is not equivalent to T(B1' **after** a) ||| T(B2' **after** a).

Similar problems arise for the other basic LOTOS operators. Further investigation on this subject is left for future research projects.

5. Conclusions.

This paper has presented a method for the systematic derivation of canonical testers from processes specified by labelled transition systems. Rules have also been given for removing redundancy from its products. The method has been applied to basic LOTOS, allowing derivation of canonical testers from specifications in this language directly from their syntax. This means that a tester T(B1*B2) can be constructed from the attributes used in the construction of T(B1) and T(B2).

Furthermore the analytic concepts underlying the CO-OP method (particularly Compulsory, Options and the orth function) have proved useful in investigating the feasibility of the construction of T(B1*B2) directly from T(B1)*T(B2), where * is any basic LOTOS operator. Unfortunately it appears not to be possible to construct T(B1*B2) in this way.

This paper has presented the CO-OP method for general LTS and for basic LOTOS. It can be applied to specifications written in any language that allows interpretation of its expressions in terms of such specifications. The sets Compulsory(B), Options(B) and the expression B **after** a should then be defined for each syntax element B of these languages.

Further work in this area would usefully include examination of ways of pruning the set of basic test cases even further, including metrics to indicate the importance of certain test cases, including infinite processes and extending the LOTOS application to full LOTOS including value passing. We hope to report on some of these issues in the future.

Acknowledgements.

The work presented in this paper formed part of an M.Sc. project carried out within British Telecom Research and Technology under supervision of the department of Informatics of the University of Twente, The Netherlands. It was performed under FORMAP, a collaborative project between British Telecommunications plc and General Electric Company plc, within the UK Alvey programme (SE/051).

My thanks go to Ed Brinksma of the University of Twente and to David Freestone of BT for their many detailed and helpful criticisms.

Acknowledgement is made to the Director, Research and Technology of British Telecom for permission to publish this paper.

REFERENCES.

[Brinksma,86] E.Brinksma, G.Scollo, Formal notions of implementation and conformance in LOTOS, Memorandum INF 86-13, University of Twente, NL, March 1986.

[Brinksma,87] E.Brinksma, On the existence of canonical testers, Memorandum INF-87-5, University of Twente, NL, 1987

[Brinksma,88] E.Brinksma, A theory for the derivation of tests, in Proc. IFIP WG6.1 Eighth International Symposium on Protocol Specification, Testing, and Verification, Atlantic City, USA, June 1988.

[Freestone,88] D.Freestone, D.Pitt, A formal approach to conformance testing, 1988, submitted for publication.

[Hoare,85] C.A.R. Hoare, Communicating sequential processes, Prentice Hall Int, GB, 1985.

[ISO IS8807,88] ISO IS 8807, LOTOS, a formal description technique based on the temporal ordering of observational behaviour, NL, July 1988.

[Pitt,87] D.H.Pitt, A formal approach to conformance testing, FORMAP WP B69, GB, 1987.

[Steenbergen,86] C.Steenbergen, Conformance testing of OSI systems, Memorandum INF-86-24, University of Twente, NL, August 1986.

[Wezeman,88] C.D.Wezeman, The CO-OP method for compositional derivation of conformance testers, M.Sc.Thesis, University of Twente, NL, August 1988.

Session 4:

Specification Language Transformation

Protocol Specification, Testing, and Verification, IX
E. Brinksma, G. Scollo and C.A. Vissers (Editors)
Elsevier Science Publishers B.V. (North-Holland)

A MULTI-PROCESSOR ESTELLE-TO-*C* COMPILER TO PROTOTYPE DISTRIBUTED ALGORITHMS ON PARALLEL MACHINES*

Claude JARD, Jean-Marc JEZEQUEL

I.R.I.S.A. Campus de Beaulieu
F-35042 RENNES CEDEX, FRANCE
E-mail : jard@irisa.fr, jezequel@irisa.fr

Abstract. This paper presents a first attempt to generate parallel code from Estelle descriptions. We have dealt with a simple context in which only a static subset of Estelle and an homogeneous target machine are considered. We begin to present and justify the concept of experimentation on distributed algorithms for which our Estelle compiler has been designed. Then we discuss how the Estelle constructs are mapped onto *C* structures and how they are interpreted by a distributed runtime kernel. A technical annex gives an idea of the current version of the tool, named Echidna.

1 Introduction

1.1 The experimentation concept to analyse distributed algorithms

Everybody is aware that correct distributed algorithm design and implementation is still a very difficult exercise. So, as well in research laboratories as in software companies, people agree about the necessity of validating the specification before implementing the distributed algorithm.

Validation tools are quite different in their forms and their abilities, but they always accept in input a formal description of the considered distributed algorithm (or protocol). They output data, which can be viewed as confidence levels on some properties of the algorithm.

For short, we can say that the designer may attack his algorithm by three complementary techniques. We list here their advantages and major drawbacks :

- the formal properties verification : it gives a definite answer about validity, but existing methods only can actually analyse simplified models of the considered protocol. This forces the distributed algorithm to be described at an high abstraction level, so its formal verification leaves open the problem of properties preservation during its refinement course.
- the protocol simulation, using a simulated (and centralized) environment : it can deal with more refined models of the algorithm and efficiently detect errors on a subset of the possible algorithm behaviours. The main difficulty in such a case is to describe formally and simulate the execution environment. This one is generally very simplified, because it wouldn't be realistic (nor interesting) to take into account all the parameters of a real system, as for example, the exact influence of message size on transmission delays, or the action durations (which are not computable without execution).
- the observation and test of the protocol prototype implementation : here, the execution environment is a real one. But as there is a lack of tools to observe a distributed system as a whole, it will be difficult to validate actually the protocol. Moreover, the prototype behaviour may closely depend on implementation choices (e.g. non-determinism resolution). So, it will also be difficult to generalize from the observation to the possible protocol behaviours.

*This work has been partially supported by the French program on parallelism of the CNRS/C^3, and within the ADP research team of the IRISA laboratory.

It appears clearly that those approaches are much more complementary than in competition, and that an advised designer would try to use all of them. To help him, we propose to define and justify an intermediate technique, called experimentation, to fill the gap between simulation and prototype implementation.

Experimenting aims at observing the algorithm execution in a real environment (i.e. on a real distributed system) while allowing the larger subset of possible behaviours to occur.

Some parameters do not need to be simulated anymore as they are provided by the underlying system. If this distributed system is general enough, providing a controled environment, we will be able to transpose some aspects of the experimental behaviours to any other system, more or less modulus the experimentation machine. Some experimental results about particular algorithms, called synchronizers, running on the Intel iPSC hypercube confirm this point of view [3].

Another advantage of experimention on parallel machines is that we can fully use the power of such machines, to make it feasible to validate large distributed algorithms made of few thousand processes.

But, as we are on a real distributed system, we have to set up special techniques to perform distributed observation and measurement acquisition.

1.2 The Echidna project : tools for experimentation

The Echidna project aims at providing tools to prototype distributed algorithms on parallel machines. It provides an Estelle compiler for multi-processor machines and a set of software tools to observe the behaviours of the distributed algorithm under experimentation.

The formal description models the distributed system as a whole : we only consider closed systems. Since we are not interested in producing code for heterogeneous networks (as in [14] or [12] for example), we can work on the full algorithm, where remote communication belongs to the formal model. This allows us to produce executable parallel code directly.

Having a rather good experience in studying Formal Description Techniques for protocols, we chose the Estelle language, now an ISO standard [1], to describe our distributed algorithms. As communicating automata is the natural semantics of loosely coupled distributed systems, Estelle is particularly well suited for our purpose. On the other hand, Estelle is a superset of the ISO Pascal, with some ADA concepts (class-instance mechanism, kind of modularity ...). This allows efficient compilers producing efficient code.

Numerous works have been done around Estelle concerning automated verification, simulation or prototype implementation (see the survey [4]). Several Estelle tools have been developed in the U.S. (NBS compiler), Canada, Europe, where two EEC projects (Esprit Sedos and Sedos-demo [7]) aim at building an Estelle Work-Station.

So, with the very same formal description, we will be able to verify, simulate, or even implement a distributed algorithm : we are ensured to work on the very same object.

Our contribution to that research area is to be able to translate automatically Estelle descriptions into parallel executable code for distributed systems in order to perform experimentation. In the framework of experimentation, the target parallel machine must be general purpose, powerful and with an easily customizable environment. Our machine model consists in a set of sites (processors or machines) only communicating by message passing through an end to end reliable communication network. There is no loss of messages. They are exchanged within a finite but unpredictable delay, and the communication channels are FIFO queues.

Different machines may implement this abstract experimentation station model. We have focussed our development on the Intel iPSC hypercube supercomputer (64 80386-processors with 4-MBytes of memory each, see [8] for a more detailled presentation), since it has been available in our laboratory for two years. We have also been interested in networks of SUN-workstations (above TCP/IP) and PC's, and we are now investigating the Transputer world through the Floating Point Systems T-40 hypercube machine held in Grenoble (France) and the T-node supercomputer.

For portability reasons, we decided to generate *C* code, all the considered machines having an efficient *C* compiler (which was not the case for Pascal). Mapping Pascal constructs of Estelle into

C is a tedious task but this allows to generate a compact code which can be easily interfaced with other programs and libraries.

The purpose of this article is to present a first attempt to generate parallel code from Estelle descriptions. We have dealt with a simple context in which only a static subset of Estelle and an homogeneous target machine (same processors and compilers) are considered. We present how the Estelle constructs are mapped onto C structures and how they are interpreted by a Distributed RunTime Kernel (DRTK). Tools for distributed observation are under development and will be the core of an other presentation (some ideas were presented in [10]). We give in annex an example of a short Estelle program, its C translation and the current version manual of the compiler (which begins to be widely used by parallel programmers). A detailed version of this paper is available as a french technical report [11].

2 The computation model

2.1 Our Estelle model

We present here our considered Estelle subset. We assume that full Estelle is known to the readers (see [5] and [6] for presentations).

A system is either a set of parallel sub-systems running asynchronously, or a set of tasks. Asynchronous parallelism is required between physical sites. It is the Estelle programmer's responsability to define mapping of processes on physical sites : if the first parameter of a module is an integer, it is interpreted as the node identifier where the process must be run, the actual *placement* being done during task creation (initialisation)[1].

We do not consider the dynamic part of Estelle : the system architecture remains unchanged after initialisation. So there are two classes of modules : the structuring modules (refinements) which have no transition part and disappear after the configuration phase, and the real processes (leaves) which perform transitions but without dynamic statements like init, connect, detach ... Several Estelle concepts may then be simplified : sharing variables between children of a module becomes impossible, and distinction between processes and activities is irrelevant.

Such a static subset has already been considered in Veda [9] and Xesar [13] tools and seems to suit well for the context of experimentation. It considerably simplifies our parallel implementation. Implementing full Estelle would be an interesting project in using Estelle as a programming language for parallel machines.

The last semantic restriction is the delay clause, which is not implemented. But, we have built a global time service to timestamp events for observation. This global time may be used to implement the delay clause if necessary.

There are other (syntactic) restrictions : embedding procedures and transitions is not allowed. We reject Estelle particularities as "any" < *type* > and the famous "...", and we do not handle module variable manipulation through *all, exist, suchthat* constructs. This is not essential restrictions and they will disappear when integrating our compiler to an Estelle workstation.

The compiler translates the formal description into a set of data structures (expressed in the C programming language), which fully describe the specification constants, types, channel definitions, module specifications and their associated body definitions. Those data structures are then compiled by the local C compiler, and linked with the DRTK to be loaded and run on the target distributed system.

The DRTK allows the execution of an Estelle program on a distributed system (see figure 1). It consists of three parts : the scheduler, the Estelle runtime and the system interface. We detail their features in the following sections.

2.2 The Distributed Driver

The entry point of the executable code is on each node the *main()* function, whose text is:

[1]Each node is supposed to own a unique identity (a positive integer), and one node owns the identity 0. A centralised machine is assumed to be node 0 of a one node network.

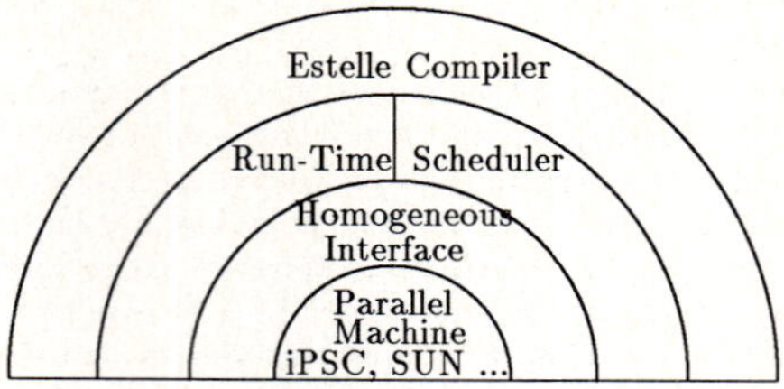

Figure 1: The Echidna compiler

```
main(){
   int seed,duration;
   getOptions();
   init(seed);
   configuration();
   startScheduler(duration);
   terminate(0);
}
```

getOptions() parses the command line to find options and parameters for the execution of the protocol, such as the duration of the execution, the seed for the random generator (in order to achieve reproductible experiments), or an alternate behaviour for the scheduler...

init() realises the general initialisation of the experiment.

configuration() is an external function, generated by the compiler. Upon invocation, it creates the root task of the Estelle specification and run its *initialize* part, which creates its child modules and recursively initialize them. When this resulting tree structure is achieved, only the leaf tasks that must be run on a node are actually set up in the active process list of this node to be scheduled by the local scheduler.

In the distributed execution of an Estelle specification, there are two levels of parallelism:

- inter-nodes parallelism which is the real parallelism of the machine (the distributed driver runs in parallel on each site)
- intra-node parallelism or pseudo-parallelism: the parallelism simulated by a local scheduler.

startScheduler() actually starts the task scheduling, according to the policy selected on the command line by the user, within deterministic or non-deterministic and synchronous or asynchronous. So the scheduler performs on each node the following simplified algorithm:

Repeat Until EndofExperiment

- Accept remote messages from outside (if some);
- For each process of this node, select first firable transition or choose at random one transition of all fireable transitions of maximal priority;
- For each process (or only for a subset of them if asynchronousity is simulated), fire the chosen transitions (if any);

end repeat

2.3 The Estelle Runtime

The aim of the Estelle Runtime is to build a virtual machine allowing the execution of an Estelle program, above the *C* runtime of the real machine. It provides the Estelle and Pascal primitive functions and objects that do not exist in the *C* programming language: set manipulation, error detection and recovery, good random generator (for non-determinism), process manipulation ...

Furthermore, the runtime recognizes remote communications in order to route them through the network: when a message (interaction) is sent on an interaction point (ip), which is connected to an ip located on an other node, the message is routed by the underlying network (supposed to be FIFO without any loss nor alteration of messages) to the destination node. There, the function *AcceptRemoteMessages*() invocated at each iteration of the scheduler, will accept the message and queue it at the destination ip.

This runtime is made of 1000 lines of *C*, and is easily portable on every machine where a classical *C* compiler is available.

2.4 The Interface with the System

The aim of this module is to provide an implementation of the parallel machine model (as defined in section 1.2), building an homogeneous interface with the underlying distributed system, whichever it is. It deals with remote communications, local clock, I/O and node identifiers.

If the real distributed system is close enough to the model, this module can be quite short (100 lines of *C* for the *iPSC/2*). But if not so close, this interface will be more complex, as for example with a SUN network (TCP/IP above *ethernet*), where we had to develop a software package from the *socket* concept.

Anyway only this part of the DRTK is to be adapted for each system, so the Echidna tool still remains easily portable.

When there is only one node, Echidna appears as an Estelle simulator which can be run on small computers (like PC).

3 The *C* representation of Estelle objets

3.1 The Estelle specification

The Estelle specification is a kind of black box without any external interaction.

If we look inside this black box during an execution, we can see some objects which interact each others:

- the tasks (or process), made of the association of a body to a module.
- the interactions points (ip), which are the interfaces between tasks and the outside world.
- the messages, or interactions, that tasks exchange on channels linking their ip's.
- the transitions, which are atomic guarded actions that can be performed by the tasks.

We will now describe in some details how those objects are represented with the *C* programming language.

3.2 The tasks

A task is made of a specification (*module*) and a *body*. The module is created upon declaration within its nesting module (its *father*). When the father module initialize its children, it provides them a *body* (see below the Estelle instruction *init*).

At run time, a task is represented by a control block which stores:

- some private data for the DRTK: process number, node identifier, activity state, transition descriptor list...
- the module ip's descriptors
- the child module descriptors (pointers to control blocks)
- the local variables of the process, including the main state of the automaton.
- the parameters transmited at initialisation time.

The *C* representation of this control block is implemented by the following generic type:

```
typedef struct context {
  ker_workspace kw; /*private space for the DRTK (invisible)*/
  union for all modules type of {
    list of (ip *)  lip;
    union for all the possible bodies of each module of {
       list of (struct context *) lt;
       list of (local variables) lv;
       list of (parameters) lpar;
    }
  }
} context;
```

3.3 The interaction points

The interaction points are the interfaces between tasks. They are used in a generic fashion and implemented as a DRTK private type. They are only known in the generated code as predefined descriptors.

An interaction point is made of:

- a unique ip identity over the whole system
- the node identity where the ip is located
- a pointer to its connected ip, if this ip is located on the same node.
- the unique identity of its corresponding ip
- the node identity where the corresponding ip is located
- a pointer to the task owner of the ip
- an unbounded queue storing messages received at this ip

The DRTK provides primitives to create ip's, to release them (when owner tasks are not initialised on this given node), to attach and connect them. The ip's which remain on a node after the configuration step are stored in a global list. Upon reception of an external message, this list will be searched in order to find out the destination ip. The size of an ip queue is only limitated by the available memory.

3.4 The messages

Messages are the interactions exchanged between tasks through their ip's. A message is made of:

- a static block holding:
  - the total size of the message
  - the destination ip identity
  - the message type
- a varying block, generated by the compiler to store the message parameters

The DRTK provides primitives to manage messages: create, delete, copy, local or remote send, add to an ip queue, and accept remote messages.

3.5 The transitions

An Estelle transition is a $< condition, action >$ pair. A *condition* is made of a (possibly empty) clause list, within *when* (message available on an ip), *provided* (boolean condition on the first message on the queue or on any local variable of the task), *from* (condition on the main control state of the automaton), *delay* (specifying a time constraint for the firing of the transition) and *priority* (relative priority with respect to the other transitions of the *same task*).

An *action* is an optional change of the automaton main control state, followed by a compound Pascal statement, where specific Estelle instructions may take place (*e.g.* message sending...).

The Estelle langage makes it possible to gather different transitions under the same text (that we call meta-transition) with the *any* clause. An Estelle transition will be referenced by the number of its meta-transition and a key identifying this transition within its meta-transition. This key looks like an access to a multi-dimensional array, and allows to set up the values for the indexes of the *any* clauses of the meta-transition.

We have chosen to generate only two *C* functions for each such meta-transition: evaluation and launch of the transition. Those functions take as parameters the task control block descriptor, and the transition identifying key.

Guard Evaluation The guard evaluation function starts setting up some temporary variables corresponding to the *any* clauses indexes, according to the parameter key. Then, it uses the functions provided by the DRTK to test the specified clauses. If they are all verified, it returns the priority of the transition, else it returns the value -1.

If we have a spontaneous transition without priority clause, the guard evaluation function is simply a NOP function which returns the minimal priority.

The *initialize* part of a module is represented by such a spontaneous transition, fired only once during the initialisation step of the task.

Transition firing The *action* part is translated in a *C* function, which, as the guard evaluation function, starts setting up *any* clauses indexes. Then it performs the associated compound Pascal statement, including the optional control state change.

4 The generated code

4.1 Non-Pascal instructions translation

First, let us see how instruction that appears within guards are translated:

When This clause is found in guards to test if a given message is available on an ip, and to open visibility on its parameters. It is translated within a guard evaluation function to:

```
{
# define ActualParameter_1 = m_in → FormalParameter_1
                    ...
# define ActualParameter_n = m_in → FormalParameter_n
   msg * m_in;
   if (((m_in = get_msg(ipDescriptor)) == NIL) ||
      (m_in → msg_kind != WantedType)) return(-1);
   /* tests on message parameters as specified */
}
```

From, Provided Those clauses allow to test the main control state of the automaton and any other local variable of the task. They are directly translated to proper *C* tests.

Priority As described above, the priority is computed and returned by the guard evaluation function.

Delay This clause is not currently implemented.

Any The unfactorisation of this kind of meta-transition is implemented as described in the previous paragraph.

Following instructions can only be found in the *action* parts of transitions.

Init This module initialisation instruction associates a body to the considered module instance. Here is its syntax:

$$init < ModuleInstance > with < body > (parameters)$$

It is translated to the following *C* block:

```
if (mk_proc(& context,Site,ContextSize,TransitionList,
                SubModuleNumber,ipNumber) == OnThisNode) {
    context → FormalParameter1 = ActualParameter1;
        ...
    context → FormalParametern = ActualParametern;
    init_proc(context);/*fire the task initialisation transition*/
}
```

Connect and Attach *Connect* allows a module to realise the connection between its sub-modules ip's, and *Attach* to link up a sub-module ip with a nesting module ip. Those instructions are implemented with direct invocations of corresponding DRTK primitives.

Output This instruction allows a task to send a message on one of its ip. Here is its syntax:

$$output < ipName > . < InteractionName > (MessageParameters)$$

It is translated to a *C* block which creates a message with the right tag selector, then assigns message parameters, and actually sends out the message on the selected ip:

```
{
  msg * m;
  m = mk_msg(MessageSize);
    m → FormalParameter1 = ActualParameter1;
        ...
    m → FormalParametern = ActualParametern;
  send_msg(ipDescriptor,m);
}
```

To This instruction allows to modify the main state of the automaton. It is translated to a straight assignment on a local variable of the task called *State*, whose type is *enum*.

All The instruction *all i : LowBound..UpperBound do < instruction >* is a non-directivist loop, without previous declaration of the loop index. We implement it with a classical *C* loop.

Trace This instruction is our only extension to the Estelle language (which does not have any input/output instructions). Its syntax is the same as *writeln* in Pascal, but its semantic is specially designed within the experimentation context [2].

4.2 The generated code structure

The code generated by our compiler has the following form:

```
# include < echidnak.h > /* External declarations from the DRTK */
# define ( list of constants declared with Estelle keyword const )
typedef ( list of types declared with Estelle keyword type )
typedef struct {
  msg_type msg_kind;
  union {
      /* on the parameters of each possible message type */
        } u;
} msg;

typedef union s_context {
  ker_workspace kw; /* private space for the DRTK (invisible)*/
  union for all modules type of {
    list of (ip *) lip;
    union for all the possible bodies of each module of {
      list of (struct context *) lt;
```

```
        list of (local variables) lv;
        list of (parameters) lpar;
      }
    }
} context;


/* Here is the code for meta-transitions, for i := 1 to n */
int guard_i(a, p)
    int a; context * p; /* a is used to set up ANY-clause variables */
{
    /* test to perform guard evaluation */
    if firable return (priority) else return (-1);
}
int action_i(a, p)
    int a; context * p; /* a is used to set up ANY-clause variables */
{
    /* code to fire the transition */
}

/* Definition of variables to be exported to the DRTK */
/* The array transition[] gives the correspondance between a */
/* meta-transition text and its absolute number for the DRTK */
int (* transition[])() = {
        guard_1, action_1,
        ...
        guard_n, action_n
};
/* The array transany[] gives the variation bound for the */
/* any key for each transition */
int transany[n] = { nany_1, ..., nany_n };

void configuration()
{
    /* realise the nesting module creation (the specification) */
    /* and call its initialisation transition */
}
```

4.3 Pascal translation

On the syntactic level, the Pascal and *C* languages only differ in minor ways. The situation is worse on the semantic level.

Our translation is very similar to the public program PtoC written by Per Bergsten of the university of Gothenburg in Sweden.

Here is a list of the main problems we have encountered and their solutions :

- constants : number aliases are simply *define*d but string constants are converted to static character arrays, in order to avoid unnecessary duplication of strings in the object code.
- types and variables : integer subranges are mapped onto standard *C* arithmetic types according to a short table in the translator (scanned topdown until an enclosing subrange is found).

  C-arrays have peculiar semantics. Pascal arrays are encapsulated in a *struct* with a single member named *a*.

  Records and their variants are translated into C *struct* and *union* definitions. Artificial names (*u* and *v_xxx*) must be supplied for all record variants.

  The problem of recursive types as pointer types is solved by introducing a name (*s_xxx*) for the record type.

  Set types are translated in arrays of words. The first member gives the size of the set and the others hold the bits. The maximum handled size is 2048 elements.

- statements : the only parts that require special care are *with* and *for* statements. The with-statement is translated into nested compound statements, where pointer variables, referencing the corresponding records are declared and initialized. In order to evaluate once the record address, the accessible record fields are renamed within the scope of the with-statement.

  The for-statement requires that the loop boundaries are evaluated exactly once and must be exited when the upper bound has been reached. For that reason, the upper/lower bounds are held in local variables and a conditional break statement is added to the end of the loop.
- expressions : when the operands are sets, the expression is converted into a function call.

  The lower bound of the index type must be substracted when indexing.

  Pointer references and var parameters are handled by prefixing the expression with an asterisk. The special case of dereferencing followed by selection is also recognized.

4.4 Variables accesses and renaming

In order to generate reentrant code for transitions, the variables of Estelle bodies must be accesses through references to a process context. We have chosen a simple way to do this using the *C*-preprocessor : before generating the transitions of the given module body, the variables strings are *define*d to be references through a context pointer to the union structure coding all the Estelle bodies. They are *undefi*ned when the transitions are generated.

Renaming is necessary since the block structure of the Estelle description is partially destroyed in the generated code. We chose to rename an user identifier only if its string is declared several times in the source text. In that case, it is prefixed by a unique number identifying its scope.

To prevent clashes of identifiers with the DRTK, the user identifiers are written with an initial uppercase letter, while the *C* identifiers and keywords begin by a lowercase character.

5 Implementation of the compiler

The compiler is written in Pascal and is seven thousand lines long. Parsing is performed using a left recursive descent of procedures. It consists of three major procedures that performs successively the conversion of the Estelle source program into a parse tree, some necessary transformations to prepare *C* generation, and the final traversal of the tree that prints the coresponding *C* constructs.

They are augmented by a set of procedures that maintain internal dynamical data structures (table for identifiers and strings, a multi-level symbol table, the parse tree...)

Full Estelle is parsed : the considered subset is defined by filtering. Most semantics checks are performed, either statically during parsing, or dynamically during execution. There is no other limitation on this subset: length of Estelle identifiers, number of messages, modules, interaction points (multiple dimension arrays of modules and ips are handled) and even the size of the specification are only limitated by the available memory. The compiler is quite fast (100 lines/s on a Sun), and can easily be run on a PC.

6 Conclusion

Validating a distributed algorithm is also experimenting it in order to better understand its real behaviour and performances, highlighting some phenomena generally non observable by verification nor by simulation.

The *ECHIDNA* tool implements this complementary approach of validation. *ECHIDNA* is now available for the Intel Hypercubes *iPSC/1* and *iPSC/2*, for Transputer based FPS-T40 Hypercube, for Sun Workstations Networks (with TCP/IP), Gould and PC. We are planning to make it also available for Apollo Workstations and other Transputer Networks (as for example the T-node machine).

As the input language for *ECHIDNA* is ISO Estelle, one can use a formal description of a distributed algorithm to run not only experimentation but also verification and simulation. Thus we are sure that the same distributed algorithm is studied during the three parts of the validation process. This approach proved itself useful for some real problems, as for example the synchronizers study led at the IRISA, or the MAC/TR atomic fault resistant diffusion protocol validation (DELTA 4 Esprit Project): *ECHIDNA* allowed to get interesting measurements to compare real efficiency of different algorithm versions.

Furthermore the *ECHIDNA* ability to directly produce code for distributed systems makes Estelle a good choice as a high level parallel programming language for parallel machines (where there exist usually only *C* and Fortran environments). So, beyond validation activities, the main application fields considered for *ECHIDNA* are massive simulations, distributed systems and algorithms teaching, study and analyse, and even parallel prototype implementations.

If this interest for Estelle as a true parallel language is confirmed in the future, we think that it would be interesting to implement a full Estelle compiler for distributed systems.

References

[1] IS 9074. Estelle *: a Formal Description technique based on an Extented State Transition Model.* ISO TC97/SC21/WG6.1, 1989.

[2] M. Adam, Ph. Ingels, C. Jard, J.-M. Jézéquel, and M. Raynal. Experimentation on parallel machines is helpful to analyse distributed algorithms. In *Proceedings of the Workshop on Parallel and Distributed Algorithms, Bonas, France*, North Holland, September 1988.

[3] M. Adam, Ph. Ingels, and M. Raynal. *Algorithmes Distribués synchrones et systèmes répartis asynchrones : concepts, mises en œuvre et expérimentations.* Rapport de Recherche RR-0862, INRIA, Centre IRISA, Rennes, July 1988. 27 p.

[4] G.V. Bochmann. Usage of protocol development tools : the results of a survey. In 7th *IFIP International Workshop on Protocol Specification, Testing, and Verification, Zurich, Suisse*, North Holland, May 1987.

[5] S. Budkowski and P. Dembinski. An introduction to Estelle: a specification language for distributed systems. *Computer Networks and ISDN Systems*, 14:3–23, 1987.

[6] J.-P. Courtiat, P. Dembinski, R. Groz, and C. Jard. Estelle : un langage ISO pour les algorithmes distribués et les protocoles. *Technique et Science Informatique*, 6(2), 1987.

[7] C. Diaz, M. Vissers and J.-P. Ansart. Sedos: software environment for the design of open distributed systems. In *Proceedings of the Esprit '85 week*, North Holland, 1985.

[8] M. Heath. The hypercube: a tutorial overview. In Michael T. Heath, editor, *Hypercube Multiprocessors 1986*, pages 7–11, Oak Ridge National Laboratory, 1986.

[9] C. Jard, R. Groz, and J.F. Monin. Development of VEDA : a prototyping tool for distributed algorithms. In *IEEE Trans. on Software Engin.*, March 1988.

[10] C. Jard and J.-M. Jézéquel. Outils pour l'expérimentation d'algorithmes distribués sur machines parallèles. In *Actes du Colloque C^3 d'Angoulème*, GRECO C^3/CNRS, December 1988.

[11] C. Jard and J.-M. Jézéquel. *Un compilateur Estelle multi-processeurs pour l'expérimentation d'algorithmes distribués sur machines parallèles.* Technical Report 453, IRISA University of Rennes, January 1989.

[12] J.L. Richard and T. Claes. A generator of C-code for Estelle. In M. Diaz, JP. Ansart, JP. Courtiat, P. Azéma, and V. Chari, editors, *The Formal Description Technique Estelle, results of the ESPRIT Sedos Project.*, North Holland, 1989.

[13] J.L. Richier, C. Rodriguez, J. Sifakis, and J. Voiron. Verification in XESAR of the sliding window protocol. In 7th *IFIP International Workshop on Protocol Specification, Testing, and Verification, Zurich, Suisse*, North Holland, May 1987.

[14] S. Vuong, A. Lau, and R. Chan. Semi-automatic implementation of protocols using an Estelle-C compiler. *IEEE Transactions on Software Engineering*, SE-14(3):384–393, March 1988.

ANNEX **Mon Jun 5 13:44:01 1989** **1**

```
{ A game of life in parallel }
specification life; default individual queue;
const Nx = 40; Ny = 25; Nx_1 = 39; Ny_1 = 24;              { Nx * Ny processes }
type  cx = 0 .. Nx_1; cy = 0 .. Ny_1; Neigh = (N, E, S, O);     { 2-D grid  }
      state_typ = boolean;
channel news (caller, called); by caller : changed;
   module cel activity (id : integer; initial_state : state_typ);
       ip I : array [Neigh] of news (caller);          { ! changed (st)     }
          R : array [Neigh] of news (called);          end;
   body algo for cel;
   var env, my_state : state_typ;
   initialize begin my_state := initial_state; env := false end;
   trans provided (my_state <> env) begin              { alternate state    }
              my_state := not my_state;                { broadcast the change }
              trace (id, ord(my_state));               { tracing            }
              all v : Neigh do  output I [v]. changed  end;
   trans any c : Neigh do when R [c]. changed begin env := not env end;
   end;
modvar C : array [cx,cy] of cel;
initialize var gx : cx; gy : cy; begin
       gx := Nx div 2; gy := Ny div 2;                 { seed }
       all x : cx do all y : cy do
              init C [x,y] with algo (y*Nx + x, (x = gx) and (y = gy));
       all u : cx do all v : cy do begin
              connect C [u,v]. I [N] to C [u,(v+1) mod Ny]. R [S];
              connect C [u,v]. R [N] to C [u,(v+1) mod Ny]. I [S];
              connect C [u,v]. I [O] to C [(u+1) mod Nx,v]. R [E];
              connect C [u,v]. R [O] to C [(u+1) mod Nx,v]. I [E] end end;
end.
```

Snapshot of this algorithm execution on the *iPSC/2*, coupled to a graphical tool

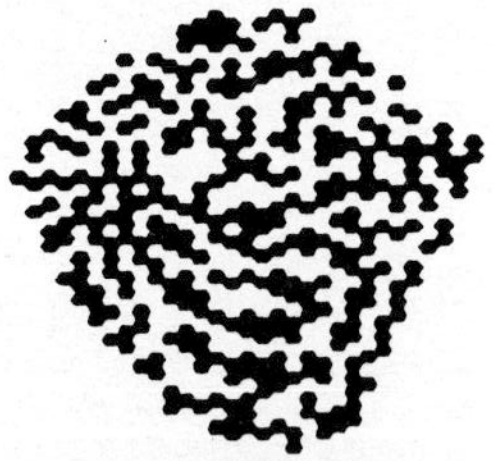

EC(1) *** ECHIDNA PROJECT *** EC(1)

NAME

ec, Estelle compiler for Unix and iPSC; ECHIDNA project.

SYNOPSIS

ec [-sngifcCtG] [-m file] [-l file] [-o object_file] [estelle_file]

DESCRIPTION

The ec program translate an Estelle formal description to C data structures, and then compile and link them with a system dependant kernel, to produce code for various architectures (see below).
If an error is found in the source, your favourite editor (as defined in the environment variable EDITOR, or vi otherwise) is invoked on the errored line. When you leave it, compilation is resumed.
If no argument is given, the last version of this page is displayed.

OPTIONS

```
-s  Target system is the sun (default).
-n  Target system is a network of Sun (TCP/IP)
-g  Target system is the Gould: produce code for the Gould
-i  Target system is the iPSC.
-f  Target system is the FPS-T20
-m  Link with an extra object or C file module, endding with .o or .c
      (can be repeted)
-l  Link with a library file, generaly beginning with "l"
      (can be repeted)
-c  Perform only Estelle to C translation.
-C  Perform C compilation and link with the kernel.
-t  Don't produce extra-code to check index range validity.
-G  Debug option for use with dbx.
-o object_file : Names the executable program "object_file".
```

USAGE

You can provide the following optional parameters to your executable Estelle program:

```
  -dxxxx  The duration 'nnnn' of the execution in seconds
      (default=0 means infinity)
  -sxxxx A seed (integer) xxxx for the random generator
  -u  Prevent the bufferisation of trace output
  -q  Make execution quiet : no header nor warning displayed
  -a  Simulate an asynchronous execution of processes  within a node
  -D  Select a deterministic semantic for the execution: the first
        firable transition of a process is actually fired, priorities
        are ignored.
```

To load and run your program, see system specific instructions.
For exemple:

```
- On a Sun, enter:       program_name [arg1 ..[argn]]
- On a Sun network:      getsun sun1 sun2 ..sunN
                         loadsun "program_name [arg1 ..[argn]]"
- On the ipsc/2:         getcube [cubesize] #see ipsc manual
                         load program_name [arg1 ..[argn]]
- On the Gould, rlogin gould; cd directory and like on a Sun.
```

If no execution duration is specified, a <CTRL C> must be entered to stop the program, and remaining processes should be killed.

BUGS

- unrecognized parameters on command-line are ignored

Bugs and others problems are to be reported to:

```
  J-M Jezequel TB105 IRISA poste 537 e-mail: jezequel@irisa.fr
or:
  C. Jard      TB107 IRISA poste 538 e-mail: jard@irisa.fr
```

```
/*
@(#) 5/2/89(ADP-IRISA) --ECHIDNA Compiler-- Version 2.93
*/
/*
**  Code derived from specification Life
*/
        /* Kernel declarations */
# include "echidnak.h"
        /* User   constants */
# define Nx 40
# define Ny 25
# define Nx_1 39
# define Ny_1 24
        /* User   types */
typedef char  Cx;
typedef char  Cy;
typedef enum { N, E, S, O }   Neigh;
typedef Boolean  State_typ;
        /* User type for interactions */
typedef enum {  Changed } msg_type;
typedef struct {
  msg_type  msg_kind;
  union {
        /* Channel News */
    struct {
      int  dummy;
    }  m_Changed;
  } u;
} msg;
        /* User type for process contexts */
typedef union s_context {
        /* Block module of Life */
# define nbports_Life         0
  struct {         ,
    union {
        /* Local vars of Life */
# define nbsons_Life      1000
      struct {
        struct { struct { union s_context *  a[Ny_1 + 1]; }  a[Nx_1 + 1]; }  v_i3_C;
      }  Life;
    } u;
  }  Life;
        /* Block module of Cel */
# define nbports_Cel         8
  struct {
    struct { address  a[4]; }  I;
    struct { address  a[4]; }  R;
    union {
        /* Local vars of Algo */
# define nbsons_Algo  0
      struct {
        State_typ  v_Env, v_My_state;
        Integer  v_Id;
        State_typ  v_Initial_state;
      }  Algo;
    } u;
  }  Cel;
} context;
        /* User procedures and transitions */
# define numlt_Life  1
# define nbt_Life  1
# define numlt_Algo  2
# define nbt_Algo  3
        /* Transitions for Life */
# define i3_C  p->Life.u.Life.v_i3_C
# define guard_1  nop
```

```
int action_1(a,p)
 int  a;
 context  * p;
 {
 Cx  Gx;
 Cy  Gy;

 Gx = Nx / 2;
 Gy = Ny / 2;
 {
   Cx  X;
   Cx  b1 = 39,
     b2 = 0;

   if (b1 >= b2)
     for (X = b1; ; X--) {
       {
         Cy  Y;
         Cy  b3 = 24,
           b4 = 0;

         if (b3 >= b4)
           for (Y = b3; ; Y--) {
             if (mk_proc(&i3_C.a[index(X, 0, 39 )].a[index(Y, 0, 24 )],
             numlt_Algo, nbt_Algo, nbsons_Algo, nbports_Cel)) {
             i3_C.a[index(X, 0, 39 )].a[index(Y, 0, 24 )]->Cel.u.Algo.v_Id = Y * Nx +
             i3_C.a[index(X, 0, 39 )].a[index(Y, 0, 24 )]->Cel.u.Algo.v_Initial_state
             (void)init_proc( i3_C.a[index(X, 0, 39 )].a[index(Y, 0, 24 )]);
             }
             if (Y == b4) break;
           }
       }
       if (X == b2) break;
     }
 }
 {
   Cx  U;
   Cx  b5 = 39,
     b6 = 0;

   if (b5 >= b6)
     for (U = b5; ; U--) {
       {
         Cy  i15_V;
         Cy  b7 = 24,
           b8 = 0;

         if (b7 >= b8)
           for (i15_V = b7; ; i15_V--) {
             { if ((i3_C.a[index(U, 0, 39 )].a[index(i15_V, 0, 24 )] == (context *)0)
             i3_C.a[index(U, 0, 39 )].a[index((i15_V + 1) % Ny, 0, 24 )] == (context *
             connect_ip(&(i3_C.a[index(U, 0, 39 )].a[index(i15_V, 0, 24 )]->Cel.I.a[in
             &(i3_C.a[index(U, 0, 39 )].a[index((i15_V + 1) % Ny, 0, 24 )]->Cel.R.a[in
             { if ((i3_C.a[index(U, 0, 39 )].a[index(i15_V, 0, 24 )] == (context *)0)
             i3_C.a[index(U, 0, 39 )].a[index((i15_V + 1) % Ny, 0, 24 )] == (context *
             connect_ip(&(i3_C.a[index(U, 0, 39 )].a[index(i15_V, 0, 24 )]->Cel.R.a[in
             &(i3_C.a[index(U, 0, 39 )].a[index((i15_V + 1) % Ny, 0, 24 )]->Cel.I.a[in
             { if ((i3_C.a[index(U, 0, 39 )].a[index(i15_V, 0, 24 )] == (context *)0)
             i3_C.a[index((U + 1) % Nx, 0, 39 )].a[index(i15_V, 0, 24 )] == (context *
             connect_ip(&(i3_C.a[index(U, 0, 39 )].a[index(i15_V, 0, 24 )]->Cel.I.a[in
             &(i3_C.a[index((U + 1) % Nx, 0, 39 )].a[index(i15_V, 0, 24 )]->Cel.R.a[in
             { if ((i3_C.a[index(U, 0, 39 )].a[index(i15_V, 0, 24 )] == (context *)0)
             i3_C.a[index((U + 1) % Nx, 0, 39 )].a[index(i15_V, 0, 24 )] == (context *
             connect_ip(&(i3_C.a[index(U, 0, 39 )].a[index(i15_V, 0, 24 )]->Cel.R.a[in
             &(i3_C.a[index((U + 1) % Nx, 0, 39 )].a[index(i15_V, 0, 24 )]->Cel.I.a[in
             if (i15_V == b8) break;
```

```
          }
        }
        if (U == b6) break;
      }
    }
}

# define nany_1  1
        /* Transitions for Algo */
# define Id  p->Cel.u.Algo.v_Id
# define Initial_state  p->Cel.u.Algo.v_Initial_state
# define Env  p->Cel.u.Algo.v_Env
# define My_state  p->Cel.u.Algo.v_My_state
# define guard_2  nop
int action_2(a,p)
  int  a;
  context  * p;
  {
  My_state = Initial_state;
  Env = False;
}

# define nany_2  1
int guard_3(a,p)
  int  a;
  context  * p;
  {
  if (  (My_state != Env))
  )
  return(0);
  return(-1);
}
int action_3(a,p)
  int  a;
  context  * p;
  {
  My_state = (Boolean)(!My_state);
  (void)sprintf(cbuf,"%10d%10d\n", Id, (unsigned)(My_state)),update();
  {
    Neigh  i9_V;
    Neigh  b9 = 3,
      b10 = 0;

    if ((int)(b9) >= (int)(b10))
      for (i9_V = b9; ; i9_V = (Neigh)((int)(i9_V)-1)) {
        /* Send message Changed */
        {
          msg * m_out;
          m_out = (msg *) mk_msg(sizeof(msg_type) + sizeof(m_out->u.m_Changed));
          m_out->msg_kind = Changed;
          send_msg(p->Cel.I.a[index((int)(i9_V), 0, 3 )], m_out);
        }
        if (i9_V == b10) break;
      }
  }
}

# define nany_3  1
int guard_4(a,p)
  int  a;
  context  * p;
  {
# define i10_C  ( a)
  msg  *m_in;
  if (((m_in = get_msg(p->Cel.R.a[index((int)(i10_C), 0, 3 )])) == (msg *)NIL) ||
  (m_in->msg_kind != Changed)) return(-1);
  return(0);
  return(-1);
# undef  i10_C
}
int action_4(a,p)
  int  a;
  context  * p;
  {
  msg  *m_in;
# define i10_C  ( a)
  m_in = (msg *)get_msg(p->Cel.R.a[index((int)(i10_C), 0, 3 )]);
  Env = (Boolean)(!Env);
  rm_msg(p->Cel.R.a[index((int)(i10_C), 0, 3 )]);
# undef  i10_C
}

# define nany_4  4
# undef Id
# undef Initial_state
        /* Transition accesses */
int (* transition[])() = {
  guard_1, action_1,
  guard_2, action_2,
  guard_3, action_3,
  guard_4, action_4
};
int transany[4] = {nany_1, nany_2, nany_3, nany_4};
        /* Main configuration */
void configuration()
{ context * p; address root;
  (void)mk_proc(&root, -1,
  sizeof(p->Life.u.Life),
  numit_Life, nbt_Life, nbsons_Life,0);
  setup_proc( init_proc( root ));
}
/*
**  End of program code
*/
```

Protocol Specification, Testing, and Verification, IX
E. Brinksma, G. Scollo and C.A. Vissers (Editors)
Elsevier Science Publishers B.V. (North-Holland)

Combining ASN.1 support with the Lotos language

Gregor v. Bochmann and Michel Deslauriers

Université de Montréal, dépt. informatique
C.P. 6128, Succ. A, Montréal
Canada

The ASN.1 notation is widely used for the definition of OSI Application layer protocols. Formal description techniques (FDT's) have been developed for writing complete formal specifications of OSI protocols and services. This paper discusses various approaches for relating ASN.1 and FDT specifications in the case of the Lotos FDT. Using an abbreviated notation for commonly used data structures in Lotos, the paper presents a translation approach between ASN.1 and Lotos which can be used to relate ASN.1 definitions of PDU's and the data type definitions used in the corresponding Lotos protocol specification. It can also be used as a basis for combining ASN.1 and Lotos tools, as demonstrated by an experimental system which is described.

1. Introduction

The OSI protocol standards of the so-called Application layer are specified using the ASN.1 notation [ASN1] for the definition of the parameters and data structures of the protocol data units (PDU's). This relatively formal notation allows the definition of complex data structures in relatively compact form. It is also associated with a coding scheme [ASN1 C] which is normally used as transfer syntax for the exchange of PDU's between different OSI end- systems.

Several formal description techniques (FDT's) have independently been developed for writing formal specifications of OSI protocols and services. It is therefore important to clearly define a correspondence between ASN.1 and appropriate constructs in the FDT's in order to be able to define the correspondence between the OSI protocol standard written partly in the ASN.1 notation and a formal specification of the same protocol written in an FDT. This paper discusses these issues in detail for the FDT Lotos [Loto 87,Bolo 87]; similar considerations also apply to the other FDT's (a system for Estelle is described in [Boch 89]).

A clearly defined correspondence between ASN.1 and an FDT is also important in relation to FDT support tools. Formal specifications can be used, in conjunction with automatic or semi- automatic tools, during the design, implementation and testing phases of protocols (for a survey, see [Boch 87c]). In the case of OSI application layer protocols, it is therefore desirable that the FDT-related tools can be combined with ASN.1 tools which provide support for the ASN.1 coding scheme.

This paper discusses the issues involved in the translation of ASN.1 definitions into Lotos data type definitions. It also presents a tool which allows for the translation between ASN.1-encoded PDU's and corresponding Lotos data values which are used during the execution of Lotos specifications. The paper is organized as follows. Section 2 provides a discussion of what aspects of a protocol can be defined by ASN.1 and Lotos; it also mentions some difficulties related to these langugages and identifies three approaches for the integration of ASN.1 and Lotos. One of the appoaches, based on a translation from ASN.1 into Lotos, is pursued within the remaining part of the paper.

A possible translation scheme from ASN.1 into the Lotos data types is described in Section 3. In this context, an abbreviated notation for common data structures, similar to the one described in [Scol 87], is suggested. The ASN.1-Lotos tool, presented in Section 4, is based on this translation. It can be combined with existing Lotos tools in such a manner that the latter effectively communicate through the exchange of ASN.1-encoded PDU's. Some conclusions are given in Section 5.

2. Data types in Lotos and ASN.1

The Lotos language has two relatively independent parts : (1) a specification language for defining the temporal ordering of interactions, related to CCS [Miln 80], and (2) a specification language for defining abstract data types, based on ACT ONE [Ehri 85]. The discussions in this paper are related to the latter part, and are relatively independent of the former.

In general, it is useful to distinguish the following aspects of data types. These aspects are distinguished by most specification languages, including object-oriented languages; but most languages do not address all of these aspects.

(a) Sets of values: each data type is usually associated with one or more sets of values, called sorts in Lotos. For instance, the set of natural numbers is associated with the Lotos type NaturalNumber, contained in the standard library.

(b) Notation for defining constant values belonging to a sort: while a notation for constant values of predefined data types is usually given by the language, it is also important to foresee a notation for defining constants of user-defined data types.

(c) Operations and their signatures: each type defines a number of operations that may be invoked. The signature of an operation defines the number of arguments, and for each argument the expected sort, as well as the sort of the result argument, if any.

(d) Behavior of the operations: this aspect defines the result obtained by the operation for a particular set of arguments. It may also define restrictions on the order in which different operations may be executed.

(e) Coding of values: if data values are exchanged over a communication link, the coding of the data values for transmission must be defined. In the case of implementation languages, the coding of values in memory must also be defined; however, this aspect is usually compiler dependent, and not part of the language definition.

The abstract data type part of Lotos includes constructs for defining the four aspects (a), (b), (c) and (d). Constants are defined in the form of operations (aspect (c)) which have no arguments. The behavior aspect (d) is defined in terms of assertions, in the form of equations involving constants, variables and other operations. Depending on the style of writing, these equations may be in a form directly executable through a rewriting formalism. It is in this behavior aspect that various specification languages exhibit large differences. For instance, most object-oriented languages provide for an algorithmic definition of the actions to be performed when an operation of an object is to be executed.

The ASN.1 abstract notation [ASN1] is mainly a language for defining data sorts (aspect (a)). It also includes a notation for defining data values (aspect (b)). However, it includes no notation for defining operations and the behavior of operations. On the other hand, the associated coding convention [ASN1 C] defines the coding aspect (e). This is one of its main benefits.

We conclude from the above discussion that ASN.1 is largely incomplete as a specification language; however, since it provides the ASN.1 coding convention used for OSI Application layer protocols, it provides a very useful addition to the FDT's developed for formal OSI specifications. In fact, none of Estelle [BudK 87], Lotos nor SDL [Sara 87] include such a feature. On the other hand, the data sort aspect (a) of ASN.1 is redundant with corresponding facilities in the respective FDT's. Therefore, the integration of ASN.1 with an FDT requires a careful study and comparison of the data sort aspects of the two languages. After a short discussion of certain difficulties with Lotos and ASN.1 type definition facilities, we discuss in the following several approaches to an integration of the two languages.

The following difficulties have been identified in relation to the abstract data types of Lotos :

(1) The ACT ONE notation lacks constructs for defining common data structures such as Pascal record types; therefore specifications often include some lengthy parts that define such structures using the basic facilities provided by the language. A proposal for including some abbreviated notations for such common data structures is presented in [Scol 87]. In section 3 we introduce similar abbreviations.

(2) The Lotos type checking scheme is very rigid. It does not allow for property inheritance, commonly used in object-oriented languages, nor does it allow a simple use of generic types.

The following difficulties have been identified in relation to the ASN.1 notation :

(1) There is no clear distinction between the aspects (a), (b) and (e) within the so-called abstract notation [ASN1] which is used to define data types. This is further discussed in Section 3.

(2) ASN.1 has no formal definition; some aspects of the notation are not very clearly defined. This makes a comparison with other languages difficult.

In view of an integration between ASN.1 and Lotos, there seem to be the following possible approaches :

(1) Translation approach : this approach assumes that the ASN.1 definitions of OSI Application layer protocols are translated into corresponding Lotos data type definitions, which must be integrated into a complete formal specification of the protocol written in standard Lotos. This approach is pursued in the subsequent sections of this paper. It can also be taken for the integration of ASN.1 with Estelle [Boch 89] or SDL.

(2) Addition approach : in this approach, the Lotos language is extended to accept, in addition to the ACT ONE data type definitions, also ASN.1 type definitions to be used for the PDU's. Although this approach seems superficially simple, it also requires the definition of the ASN.1 notation in terms of the ACT ONE notation, as with the translation approach above. This is necessary to allow the use of elements of the PDU's within the formal specification of the protocol. This approach has been used for the combination of ASN.1 and Estelle [Hase 87].

(3) Substitution approach : this approach, and the following one, start from the premise that the existing data type facilities of Lotos are not satisfactory and should be replaced by some other data type definition facility. A proposal for the substitution of the ACT ONE part of Lotos by a data type facility based on ASN.1 is presented in [Alve 87].

(4) New development approach : the substitution approach implies an important change of the Lotos language. Such an important change may be an occasion for defining a partially new

language which includes not only features from Lotos and ASN.1, but also some useful aspects of object-oriented languages [Boch 89g].

3. Translation of ASN.1 into ACT ONE

This section describes a possible translation of ASN.1 specifications into corresponding data type definitions in ACT ONE. It is important to note that several such translations can be defined each of them preserving the ASN.1 semantics. Once a translation is defined, an automatic translation tool can be constructed (see for example Section 4), which can be used to translate a given ASN.1 specification of an Application layer protocol into corresponding ACT ONE definitions.

It is important to note that the automatic translation described here is only useful if the resulting type definitions can be integrated into a complete protocol specification written in Lotos (such as those written for the Transport and Session protocols) which can be used in protocol engineering activities, such as protocol validation, protocol implementation or testing. Such a complete Lotos specification cannot be obtained automatically, but must be written by people. Therefore it is important that the ACT ONE definitions resulting from the translation of ASN.1 PDU definitions be easily readable.

Therefore, the translation discussed below should not only be evaluated in respect to the question of whether the ASN.1 semantics is preserved by the translation, but also in respect to the question of whether the resulting ACT ONE specifications are suitable for incorporation into complete specifications of OSI Application layer protocols.

3.1. Coding-related information

Certain information included in ASN.1 definitions is related to the coding aspect (see (e) in Section 2). This information is not required for the description of the logical behavior of the protocol entity, and is therefore not represented in the ACT ONE definitions obtained by the translation. Instead, this information may be included in the form of comments, in order to make the correspondence with the original ASN.1 definition more intuitive. We note that the coding-related information is taken into account by the ASN.1 support tool described in Section 4. It seems also possible to completely describe the ASN.1 encoding in ACT ONE [Azco 87]. However, it is questionable whether such an approach can lead to reasonably efficient coding and decoding routines.

The following ASN.1 information is coding-related :

(1) The presence and numerical values of TAG's.

(2) The distinction between SEQUENCE and SET; they only differ in respect to the question whether the order of the elements, in the coded representation, is relevant for the semantics or not.

(3) The IMPLICIT indication.

3.2. Abbreviated notations

As mentioned above, it seems to be useful to add to Lotos certain abbreviated notations for defining data structures commonly found in protocol specifications. The translation described in this section was developed in two stages, first a translation into an extended ACT ONE including a set of abbreviations, similar to those described in [Scol 87], and then the translation for the abbreviations into the basic ACT ONE constructs. The following abbreviations have been used :

(1) STRING OF / SET OF constructs : String and Set are predefined types in ACT ONE. However, a simple notation for generic strings and sets does not exist. This is introduced by these abbreviations. In the case of STRING, the notation

```
type <name> is STRING OF <element type> endtype
```

is an abbreviation for

```
type <name> is <new name> renamedby sortnames <name> for String endtype
type <new name> is String actualizedby <element type>
     using sortnames <element type> for Element Bool for FBool endtype
```

The case of SET OF is similar.

(2) TUPLE construct : this construct corresponds to the well-known concept of "record". The abbreviation has the following form :

```
type <name> is TUPLE <constructor> COMP
     <element 1>   : <type 1> ,
     . . .
     <element n>   : <type n> endtype
```

The type named <name> has n elements, each of a defined type. The <constructor> is a function that constructs a value of type <name> from the values of n elements. The corresponding definition in basic ACT ONE is :

```
type <name> is <type 1>, . . . <type n>
     sorts <name>
     opns <constructor>   : <type 1>, . . . <type n> -> <name>
          <element 1>     : <name>                   -> <type 1>
          . . .
          <element n>     : <name>                   -> <type n>
     eqns forall x1 : <type 1>, . . . xn : <type n>
          ofsort <type 1>
                 <element 1> ( <constructor> (x1, ... xn)) = x1
                 . . .
          ofsort <type n>
                 <element n> ( <constructor> (x1, ... xn)) = xn endtype
```

(3) ONE OF construct : this construct is similar to the well- known concept of a "variant record" or "discriminant union". The abbreviation

```
type <name> is ONEOF <type 1>, ... <type n> endtype
```

means that a value of type <name> must belong to one of the n alternatives. With each alternative i is associated a type named <type i>. The types associated with different alternatives are not necessarily different from one another. Boolean functions of the form IS<altern i> are introduced to determine for a given value to which alternative it belongs. The strict typing rules of ACT ONE also require the definition of conversion functions which allow the conversion between the type <name> and each of the variant types <type i>. In the following definition, they take the form <name i> and <conv i>, respectively. The above ONEOF construct is an abbreviation for the following definition in basic ACT ONE :

```
type <name> is <type 1>, . . . <type n>, Boolean
     sorts <name>
     opns Is<altern 1>: <name>  -> Bool
          . . .
```

```
        Is<altern n>: <name>  -> Bool
        <name 1>    : <type 1> -> <name>
        . . .
        <name n>    : <type n> -> <name>
        <conv 1>    : <name>  -> <type 1>
        . . .
        <conv n>    : <name>  -> <type n>
eqns
        forall x1 : <type 1>  ofsort Bool
                Is<altern 1>    ( <name 1> (x1))     = True,
                Is<altern 2>    ( <name 1> (x1))     = False,
                . . .
                Is<altern n>    ( <name 1> (x1))     = False
                . . .
        forall xn:<type n>  ofsort Bool
                Is<altern 1>    ( <name n> (xn))     = False,
                . . .
                Is<altern n-1> ( <name n> (xn))      = False,
                Is<altern n>    ( <name n> (xn))     = True
        forall x1:<type 1>   ofsort  <type 1>
                <conv 1>        ( <name 1> (x1) )    = x1
                . . .
        forall xn:<type n>   ofsort  <type n>
                <conv n>        ( <name n> (xn) )    = xn endtype
```

3.3. Translation of primitive ASN.1 types

The primitive types of ASN.1 can be translated into the following types in Lotos :

INTEGER : NaturalNumber, plus some additional axioms to handle negative numbers
BOOLEAN : Boolean
BIT STRING : BitString
NumericString, PrintableString, TeletexString, T61String,
VideotexString, VisibleString, IA5String, GeneralString,
GraphicString, GeneralizedTime, UTCTime, OCTET STRING : OctetString

3.4. Translation of ASN.1 composite types

The following paragraphs describe the translation of the ASN.1 composite types into Lotos data types using the abbreviations defined in Section 3.2.

CHOICE : an ASN.1 CHOICE is translated into an ONEOF construct where each alternative of the choice corresponds to a variant type. For example, the ASN.1 definition

Pdu ::= CHOICE { user IA5String,service Integer }

is translated into

type Pdu is ONEOF IA5String, Integer endtype

The names of the boolean and conversion functions, called "Is<altern i>" and "<conv i>", respectively in Section 3.2, are chosen to be equal to the names of the ASN.1 alternatives. Therefore the following is a valid Lotos process :

```
process xxx [gate]: noexit :=
      gate ?s:IA5String ;   gate ! Pdu_user (s) ;
      gate ?p:Pdu;
         ( [Isuser (p)]              -> gate ! user (p); stop
           [ ] [not Isuser (p)]      -> gate ! service (p); stop ) endproc
```

SEQUENCE / SET : the ASN.1 sequence or set can be translated in a straightforward manner into the TUPLE abbreviation defined in Section 3.2. For example, the ASN.1 definition

```
pair ::= SEQUENCE { user IA5String,service Integer }
```

is translated into

```
type pair is TUPLE pair COMP user : IA5String, service : Integer endtype
```

Therefore the following is a valid Lotos process :

```
process xxx [gate]: noexit :=
      gate ?s:IA5String;  gate ? i:Integer;  gate ! pair (s, i) ;
      gate ?p:pair;  gate ! user (p);  gate ! service (p); stop endproc
```

SEQUENCE OF and **SET OF** : these ASN.1 constructs are directly translated into the abbreviations STRING OF and SET OF, respectively, defined in Section 3.2. (Note : the system described in Section 4 also translates the SET OF construct into an ACT ONE string; a comment indicates that the order of the elements does not have any significance).

OPTIONAL : the case that an element of an ASN.1 SEQUENCE or SET is defined as OPTIONAL can be translated in several ways. In an approach which is conceptually simple, an element of a SEQUENCE or SET which is declared of type "<type> OPTIONAL" is translated into an ACT ONE type of the form "ONEOF <type>, Not_present" where "Not_present" is a type predefined for this purpose. However, this approach has the disadvantage that additional conversion functions must be used (see definition of the ONEOF abbreviation in Section 3.2).

Another approach simply adds an additional boolean component to the TUPLE for each optional element of the SEQUENCE or SET. This component may have the name "<element>_IsPresent" and indicates whether the value of the component called "<element>" has a meaningful value or not. This approach has also been used for the translation of ASN.1 into Estelle [Boch 89, Hase 87]. For example, the ASN.1 definition

```
pair ::= SEQUENCE { user IA5String OPTIONAL, service Integer }
```

is translated into

```
type pair is TUPLE pair COMP user_IsPresent : Bool,
      user : IA5String, service : Integer endtype
```

Integer constants : ASN.1 allows the definition of mnemonic names for integer constants, as in the example

```
Status ::= Integer {OK (0), too_high (1), too_low (2)}
```

This can be easily represented in ACT ONE by the introduction of additional constant operators. The example above would be translated into

```
type Status is Integer
        opns OK          : -> Integer
              too_high : -> Integer
              too_low  : -> Integer
        eqns ofsort Integer
              OK = 0, too_high = succ(0), too_low = succ(succ(0)) endtype
```

Other features : ASN.1 allows embedded type definitions, such as

```
Pdu ::= SEQUENCE OF SEQUENCE  { first      SET OF INTEGER,
                                second SEQUENCE {IA5String, Integer}
```

In Lotos, it is necessary to introduce names for all the intermediate types included in the definitions and to provide separate type definitions for each of them. This requires the introduction of new names for these intermediate types. It is difficult to obtain new nmemonic names automatically. However, by selecting appropriate automatically generated names, one still can obtain readable Lotos specifications, such as the following which corresponds to the ASN.1 definition given above :

```
type Pdu is STRING OF new_sequence_1 endtype
type new_sequence_1 is TUPLE new_sequence_1 COMP
        first : new_set_of_1, second : new_sequence_2 endtype
type new_set_of_1 is SET OF Integer endtype
type new_sequence_2 is TUPLE new_sequence_2 COMP
        new_comp_1 : IA5String, new_comp_2 : Integer endtype
```

4. An ASN.1 support system for Lotos

We have developed an ASN.1 support system for Lotos based on the translation approach described in Section 2, and providing for a ASN.1-to-Lotos translation similar to the one described in Section 3. The system has essentially two components : (1) an ASN.1-to-Lotos translator, and (2) a generator of value translation modules.

The ASN.1-to-Lotos translator translates a given PDU definition written in ASN.1 into a set of Lotos type definitions, which are intended to be used within a complete protocol specification to be written in Lotos. When provided with the same ASN.1 definition as input, the generator generates a C program, in the following called "value translation module", which translates between the ASN.1 encoded form of PDU's and the corresponding value expressions written in Lotos, based on the type definitions generated by the ASN.1-to-Lotos translator, as shown in Figure 1. It is therefore possible to combine this value translator module with a conventional Lotos interpreter which interprets the protocol specification, as shown in Figure 2, in order to obtain a system which behaves according to the protocol specification, including the ASN.1 coding and decoding of the PDU's.

As Figure 1 shows, a value translation module contains a number of different software components executing different functions. The translation of a value between the different representations proceeds through an intermediate representation, which is an internal data structure of the form of a tree, and is used by most software components.

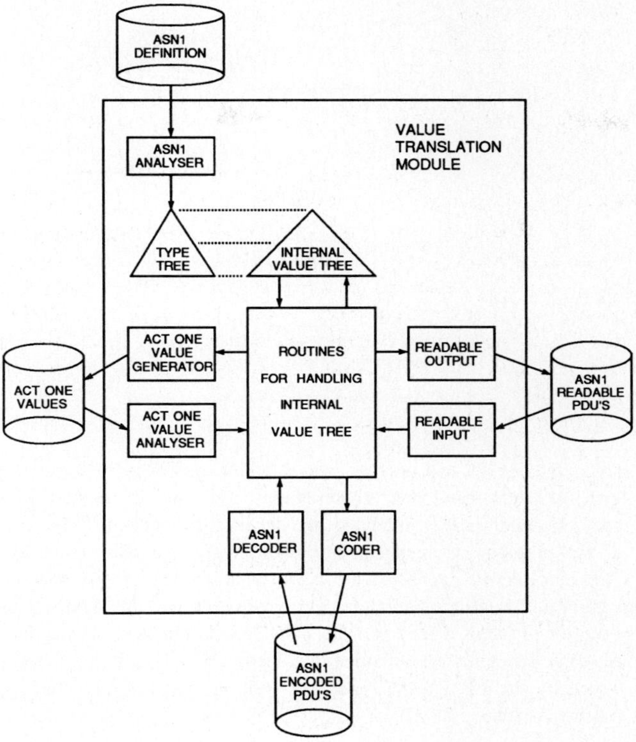

Figure 1 : Internal structure of the Value Translation Module.

(a) The ASN.1 coder and decoder software components are generic modules which convert between the ASN.1 coded and the internal form, for any given ASN.1 definition. These components, as well as the routines for handling the internal value trees, use the information in the "type tree", which is an internal representation of the ASN.1 definition, obtained through the ASN.1 analyser component. All these components were originally developed as a generic ASN.1 support tool for OSI Application protocol implementation and testing [Boch 86b].

(b) The figure also shows software components providing a conversion of the PDU values into the readable ASN.1 value notation (presently not implemented), as provided by the NBS ASN.1 support tool [NBS].

(c) The conversion into Lotos is provided by two other components. The ACT ONE value generator component is a generic software module which uses the information in the "type tree" to generate the ACT ONE representation for the given internal value tree. It takes into account the translation performed by the ASN.1-to-Lotos translator.

(d) The component called "ACT ONE value analyser" is the only non- generic component of the value translation module. It is specifically generated for a given ASN.1 definition, as shown in Figure 3.

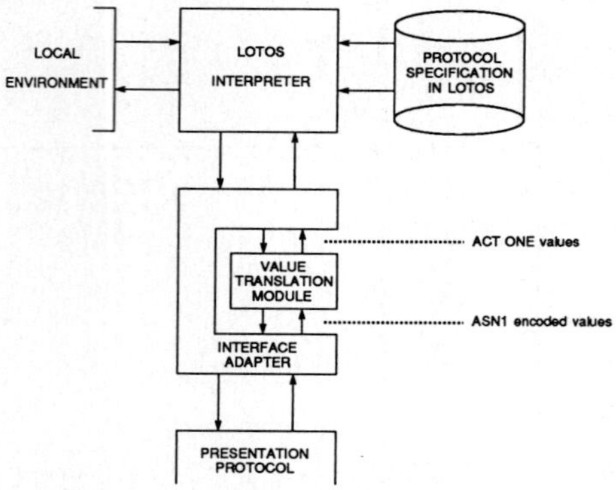

Figure 2 : Utilisation of combined ASN1 and Lotos tools.

Figure 3 shows the ASN.1-to-Lotos translator which proceeds in two steps through an intermediate form of Lotos using the abbreviations discussed in Section 3.2. The resulting ACT ONE type definitions are intended to be incorporated into the complete Lotos specification of the protocol in question. The same type definitions are also read by the generator module in order to generate the corresponding ACT ONE value analyser, to be integrated into the value translation module. The generation of this analyser proceeds in two phases. The generator program, based on the ASN.1 definition and corresponding ACT ONE type definitions, first generates syntax rules in a form suitable as input to the second phase, which is performed by the LEX/YACC compiler writing tools, which translate these syntax rules into a parser (written in C) of ACT ONE value expressions for the given type definitions.

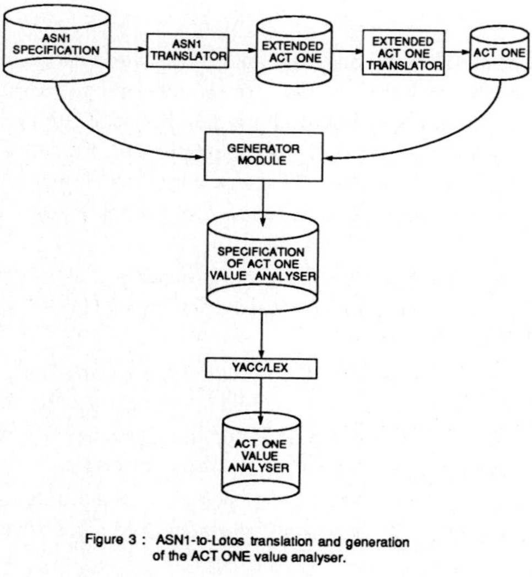

Figure 3 : ASN1-to-Lotos translation and generation
of the ACT ONE value analyser.

We have used this approach and the described ASN.1 tools for two preliminary experiments with the Association Control protocol (ACSE) and the File Transfer, Access and Management protocol (FTAM). In both cases, the resulting ACT ONE specifications of the PDU's were quite lengthy and not particularly readable. However, the representation in the abbreviated notation described in Section 3.2 is fairly similar to the original ASN.1 definitions. The following numbers indicate the size of the different specifications (in octets) :

	ASN.1	abbr. notation	ACT ONE
ACSE :	7400	9400	3500
FTAM :	22000	34000	150000

5. Conclusions

Since ASN.1 is widely used for the definition of OSI Application layer protocols, but only addresses a part of the rules that must be defined in protocol specifications, it is important that these existing definitions can be related to a complete formal protocol specifications which may be written in Lotos or another formal description technique. This paper presents such an approach based on a translation from ASN.1 into Lotos data types.

It is also argued that an abbreviated notation for commonly used data structures be defined for the Lotos language [Scol 87]. Such abbreviations are also useful for defining the ASN.1 translation.

The proposed ASN.1-to-Lotos translation scheme is discussed in some detail. Based on that translation scheme, a tool has been built which allows the automatic conversion between ASN.1 encoded Application layer PDU's and corresponding value definitions compatible with existing Lotos interpreters. The structure of the tool is described. Preliminary experience shows that the form of the PDU definitions obtained in the abbreviated notation described in Section 3.2 is similar to the original definitions in ASN.1; the resulting definitions in ACT ONE, however, are much too lengthy to be readable. We have no experience yet with the writing of complete protocol specifications in Lotos based on the PDU definitions.

Further experience is needed with this approach in relation with the following questions :

(a) How easily can the Lotos data type definitions, obtained from the given ASN.1 definition, be integrated into a complete formal protocol specification written in Lotos ?

(b) Are the resulting tools for the support of Lotos and ASN.1 encoding sufficiently flexible and efficient for use in protocol validation, protocol implementation and/or protocol testing ?

AKNOWLEDGEMENTS

The authors would like to thank Changsheng He and Richard Hankins for building the translators between ASN.1 and Lotos with abbreviations, and Lotos with abbreviations and Lotos, respectively. Thanks also for good suggestions and help from Daniel Ouimet. This work was partly supported by the Natural Sciences and Engineering Research Council of Canada, and the Ministry of Education of Quebec.

References

[Alve 87] "Formal Methods Applied to Protocols: A Framework for the Underlying Concepts of Communications Protocols", Report no.4 to the Alvey Directorate, February 1987.

[ASN1 C] ISO IS 8825, "Information Processing - Open systems Interconnection - Basic Encoding Rules for Abstract Syntax Notation One (ASN.1).

[ASN1] ISO IS 8824, "Information Processing - Open systems Interconnection - Specification of Abstract Syntax Notation One (ASN.1).

[Azco 87] A. Azcorra, "Conversion rules to produce an ACT-ONE specification", European Strategic Program Of Research And Development In Information Theory, SEDOS/119.12, October 1987.

[Boch 86b] G.v.Bochmann, M.Deslauriers and S.Bessette, "Application layer protocol testing and ASN.1 support tools", Proc. IEEE GLOBECOM Conf., Houston, Dec. 1986, pp. 767-771.

[Boch 87c] G.v.Bochmann, "Usage of protocol development tools: the results of a survey" (invited paper), 7-th IFIP Symposium on Protocol Specification, Testing and Verification, Zurich, May 1987.

[Boch 89] G.v.Bochmann and D. Ouimet, "Implementation support tools for OSI application layer protocols", in preparation.

[Boch 89e] G.v. Bochmann, et al., "Object-oriented databases : Modelling and specification of applications in the field of network management", Report for research contract CRIM/BNR, April 1989.

[Bolo 87] T. Bolognesi and E. Brinksma, "Introduction to the ISO Specification Language Lotos", Computer Networks and ISDN Systems, vol. 14, no. 1, pp.3- , 1987.

[Budk 87] S. Budkowski and P. Dembinski, "An introduction to Estelle : a specification language for distributed systems", Computer Networks and ISDN Systems, vol. 14, no. 1, pp. 25- , 1987.

[Ehri 85] H. Ehrig and B. Mahr, Fundamentals of Algebraic Specifications 1, Springer Verlag, 1985.

[Hase 87] T.Hasegawa, et al., "Translator from protocol specification based on Estelle and ASN.1 to Ada", Technical Report on Information Network of IECE of Japan, IN87-74, 1987.

[Loto 87] ISO DIS8807 (1987), "LOTOS: a formal description technique".

[Miln 80] R.Milner, "A calculus of communicating systems", Lecture Notes in CS, No. 92, Springer Verlag, 1980.

[NBS 85] National Bureau of Standards, "Formal Description of the ISO 8073 Transport Protocol", May 1985.

[NBS] ASN.1 support tools developed at NBS, Gaithersburg, US.

[Sara 87] R. Saraca and P.A.J. Tilanus, "CCITT SDL : Overview of the language and its applications", Computer Networks and ISDN Systems, 13 (1987), pp. 65-74.

[Scol 87] ISO 97/21 N1540, "Potential enhancements to Lotos", 1986.

Protocol Specification, Testing, and Verification, IX
E. Brinksma, G. Scollo and C.A. Vissers (Editors)
Elsevier Science Publishers B.V. (North-Holland)

Compilation of LOTOS Data Type Specifications

Dietmar Wolz
Paul Boehm

Technische Universität Berlin
Fachbereich Informatik (20)
Institut für Software und Theoretische Informatik
Franklinstraße 28/29, Sekr. FR 6-1
D-1000 Berlin 10

Berlin, May 1989

Abstract

In this paper we present a compiler for the data type part of the ISO language LOTOS. The compiler translates equational specifications into code of the abstract lazy term rewriting machine LATERM and subsequently into executable programs.

The resulting program implements term rewriting very efficiently and may be used as a prototypical and first implementation of the specified software.

The abstract machine LATERM is based on implementation methods for functional languages like LML and Miranda. It allows the standard call-by-value as well as a lazy-evaluation strategy and is optimized for equational specifications. Furthermore it can use sharing and strictness analysis.

The compilation of data type specifications into LATERM instructions is performed in 3 steps: the transformation into a canonical term rewriting system, the generation of function definitions with case expressions for pattern matching, and the generation of a LATERM instruction sequence for each function definition. Finally the LATERM instructions are macro-expanded into assembler code.

We will describe the instruction set and the operational semantics of the abstract machine. In the final sections we discuss performance and implementation issues and will compare the efficiency of LATERM based compilation with existing interpretation based approaches.

1 Introduction

Algebraic data type specifications are of increasing importance in the field of formal description and design of software systems. They are used to specify algorithms and data structures independently of special hardware and programming languages or operating systems. Their exact mathematical semantics makes them a sound basis for software design, verification, and implementation.

LOTOS [Br 88], a specification language for for the design of protocols and distributed systems, uses algebraic specifications for the formal description of data types. This part of LOTOS is based on ACT ONE [EM 85], a specification language for the structured design of data types with equational axioms and initial semantics.

LOTOS specifications are mainly used for the formal design of a system or a protocol and are not directly executable due to the abstractness of the language concepts.

But nevertheless a subclass of LOTOS specifications may be executed by interactive interpretation or by compilation into machine code. Execution helps verifying and testing the design, and by using LOTOS to LOTOS transformation concepts reducing the abstractness, it is feasible to derive an efficient and prototypical implementation of the specified software.

We present in this paper a new approach for the execution of the data type part – compilation into abstract machine code for the *lazy* term rewriting machine LATERM.

LATERM (LAzy TErm Rewriting Machine) [Wo 89] is an abstract machine for efficient term rewriting. The machine was developed based on implementation methods for functional languages, i.e. LML [Au 87] and Miranda.

LATERM combines techniques of functional program compilation with lazy term rewriting. Compared with abstract machines for functional programming languages it produces faster and simpler code, because no higher order functions have to be compiled. Furthermore any distinction of operating symbols in constructors and non-constructors is not required.
It has following major advantages to typical interpretation approaches for term rewriting systems: it uses a more general strategy, and the term rewriting process is speeded up by factors.
The machine LATERM can operate in different modes. It may perform term rewriting with the strategies:

- call-by-value,
- lazy-evaluation with graph reduction,
- lazy-evaluation with environments.

In [Wo 89] the machine with all operation modes is fully defined. Techniques of following abstract machines have been incorporated: FAM [Ca 83], G-machine [Jos 87,Au 87], and TIM [Fa 87].

In this paper we will present only the third mode, *environment based lazy-evaluation*, a technique similar to [Fa 87].

Algebraic specifications are compiled into executable code in several steps:
First a specification has to be transformed into a term rewriting system, and based on this into a set of function definitions.
The resulting functions definitions are translated into LATERM instructions. These are finally macro-expanded into assembler code of ordinary computers, e.g. SUN or VAX workstations.

Figure 1: Compilation phases

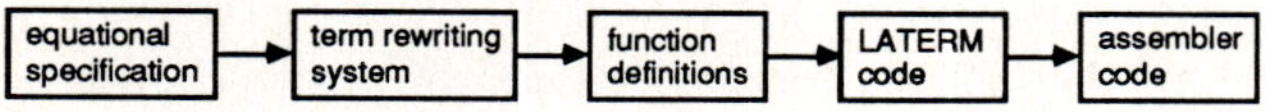

We describe the transformation of an equational specification into a term rewriting system briefly in section 2 and state the requirements, that have to be fulfilled by the term rewriting system. Function definitions with case expressions are introduced in section 3. In section 4 the abstract machine LATERM and its operational semantics is defined. Section 5 contains the translation of function definitions into LATERM code. In sections 6 we discuss implementation issues and give some first performance results.

REMARK

This version of the compilation is only defined for algebraic specifications with *unconditional* equations. An extended version for conditional equations is being prepared.

2 Translation of equations into function definitions

2.1 Translation of equations into term rewrite rules

There are several techniques for the transformation of an algebraic specification into a term rewriting system.
One approach is orienting all equations and substituting equality signs by arrows. More sophisticated techniques use Knuth-Bendix-Completion.

LATERM compilation does not define or require any specific technique to derive term rewrite rules. Any set of rewrite rules with following properties will be suited:

- left-linearity,
- terminating derivation sequences must have unique normal forms,
- left hand sides shall not be single variables,
- the rewriting system has to be stable [Hue 79].

In fig. 2 we give an example for an algebraic specification: STRING with an equality operation *eql*. We obtain a term rewriting system by reading the equations (1) to (10) as rewrite rules from left to right.
All properties mentioned above are satisfied.

Figure 2: Example: Equational specification STRING

$$
\begin{array}{lll}
\text{sorts:} & \multicolumn{2}{l}{char, string, bool} \\
\text{opns:} & a, b: & \rightarrow char \\
 & true, false: & \rightarrow bool \\
 & and: & bool\ bool \rightarrow bool \\
 & empty: & \rightarrow string \\
 & ladd: & char\ string \rightarrow string \\
 & eql: & string\ string \rightarrow bool \\
 & eqc: & char\ char \rightarrow bool
\end{array}
$$

$$
\begin{array}{rll}
\multicolumn{3}{l}{eqns:\ x, y \in X_{char};\ s, t \in X_{string};\ b \in X_{bool}:} \\
and(true, b) & = b & (1) \\
and(false, b) & = false & (2) \\
eql(ladd(x, s), ladd(y, t) & = and(eqc(x, y), eql(s, t)) & (3) \\
eql(ladd(x, s), empty) & = false & (4) \\
eql(empty, ladd(x, s)) & = false & (5) \\
eql(empty, empty) & = true & (6) \\
eqc(a, a) & = true & (7) \\
eqc(a, b) & = false & (8) \\
eqc(b, a) & = false & (9) \\
eqc(b, b) & = true & (10)
\end{array}
$$

2.2 Translation of term rewrite rules into function definitions

All rules $l_1 \rightarrow r_1, \ldots, l_m \rightarrow r_m$ defining an operation symbol k [1] are combined into one function definition $\$k[v_1, \ldots, v_n] = ce$.
$[v_1, \ldots, v_n]$ is a list of variables, ce is a case expression semantically equivalent to $r_1, \ldots, r_m$. ce selects an applicable rule, and calls the corresponding right hand sides.

In fig. 3 the function definitions for the specification STRING are given.

Figure 3: Example: Function definitions for the specification STRING

$$
\begin{array}{llllll}
\$and\ [x_1, x_2] = case\ x_1 & [true\ []: & x_2, & & & (1) \\
 & false\ []: & false\ ] & & & (2) \\
 & otherwise: & and(x_1, x_2) & & & \\
\$eql\ [x_1, x_2] = case\ x_1 & [ladd\ [x_3, x_4]: & case\ x_2 & [ladd\ [x_5, x_6]: & \$and(\$eqc(x_3, x_5), \$eql(x_4, x_6)) & (3) \\
 & & & empty\ []: & false\ ] & (4) \\
 & & & otherwise: & eql(x_1, x_2), & \\
 & empty\ []: & case\ x_2 & [ladd\ [x_3, x_4]: & false & (5) \\
 & & & empty\ []: & true\ ] & (6) \\
 & & & otherwise: & eql(x_1, x_2)] & \\
 & otherwise: & eql(x_1, x_2) & & & \\
\$eqc\ [x_1, x_2] = case\ x_1 & [a\ []: & case\ x_2 & [a\ []: & true & (7) \\
 & & & b\ []: & false\ ] & (8) \\
 & & & otherwise: & eqc(x_1, x_2), & \\
 & b\ []: & case\ x_2 & [a\ []: & false & (9) \\
 & & & b\ []: & true\ ] & (10) \\
 & & & otherwise: & eqc(x_1, x_2)] & \\
 & otherwise: & eqc(x_1, x_2) & & &
\end{array}
$$

[1] These are all rewrite rules having k at the outermost occurrence of the left hand side of the rule

Within the case expressions all occurrences of operating symbols are marked whether they construct data or have to be evaluated further.
Symbols to be evaluated are prefixed by a '$' sign.

In term rewriting systems the set of operators generally can't be divided in disjoint sets of constructors and non-constructor operations. Some operations may construct and manipulate data depending on the given arguments (e.g. the succ operation in an succ/pred INTEGER specification).
Hence all operation symbols in case expressions are assumed to be non constructors, unless they are occur after an *otherwise* or if they have no defining rules.
otherwise clauses handle the case, that no rule is applicable.

See [Wo 89] for the exact definition of the translation of rewrite rules and the operational and denotational semantics of function definitions.

Figure 4: syntax of function definitions

$fdefs$	::=	$[fdef_1, \ldots, fdef_n]$	(function definition list)
$fdef$	::=	$\$k\ vs = ce$	function definition)
ce	::=	$case\ v\ \ [(k_1\ vs_1 : ce_1), \ldots, (k_n\ vs_n : ce_n)]\ \ otherwise : r$	
		$\mid r$	(case expression)
r	::=	$v \mid k \mid \$k$	
		$\mid k(r_1, \ldots, r_m) \mid \$k(r_1, \ldots, r_m)$	(rule term)
t	::=	$k \mid \$k$	
		$\mid k(t_1, \ldots, t_m) \mid \$k(t_1, \ldots, t_m)$	(term)
vs	::=	$[v_1, \ldots, v_n]$	(variable list)

3 Lazy term rewriting

For a selection of a suitable evaluation strategy for function definitions (generated from a equational specification) one has to take into account following requirements:

- The number of reduction steps should be as small as possible;
- execution time and memory allocation for the whole reduction sequence should be minimal.

A term to be rewritten may contain several redexes. [2] A reduction strategy defines which redex has to be rewritten in the next step. The most common reduction strategies are leftmost innermost and call by need [Hue 79].

Existing implementations of algebraic specifications [Ge 88,He 88,Kap 86] usually use leftmost innermost strategy. This strategy requires additional strategy information to control the reduction. If this strategy information is not provided the rewriting would often not terminate for non-noetherian rewriting systems.

A redex in a term is called needed, if in any reduction sequence, ending in a normal form, that redex or one of its descendants is rewritten. The call by need strategy guarantees that only needed redexes are rewritten. So all time spent in rewriting these redexes is never wasted. A disadvantage of the call by need strategy is, that it requires strongly sequential term rewriting systems [Hue 79].

LATERM uses a strategy called lazy rewriting. Lazy rewriting means, that the function definitions generated from the specification are evaluated lazily [Jo 87].
The advantage of this strategy is, that most unnecessary reductions are avoided and the class of term rewriting systems is less restricted.

Lazy evaluation combines outermost evaluation with sharing of argument expressions and lazy constructors. By lazy constructors we mean that constructor arguments are assumed to be left uneval-

[2] occurrences of reducible subterms

uated.
Using the lazy rewriting strategy the produced code from a function definition reduces a term only to its head normal form (HNF). A HNF of a term is a term which cannot further be rewritten on the outermost level (even though subterms may be further rewritable). Thus for an term to become completely rewritten, all subterms must also be rewritten to HNF. We say, an occurrence in a term is stabilized if the subterm at this occurrence is in HNF. Evaluation of an expression representing a subterm means stabilizing this subterm.

During the rewriting process, it can't be decided in all cases, if a function application passed as an argument to a function, will be reduced later on. So it is necessary to find suitable representations of unevaluated expressions, whose reductions are deferred.

One approach is to use combinator graphs as representations of the unevaluated expressions. In this case the expressions can be evaluated by graph rewriting. If no strictness information is provided this method works similar to an interpreter for algebraic specifications reducing graphs (representing subterms) passed as arguments to functions.
We have implemented this algorithm as one LATERM operating mode.

In the following sections we will concentrate on a more promising and efficient method – *environment based lazy evaluation.*

The concepts of this new [3] technique are derived from the machine TIM [Fa 87].

A difference to lazy graph reduction is that all terms produced during the rewriting process are no longer represented as graphs in the heap. Only the just stabilized components of the rewritten term are build on the heap. Unevaluated arguments [4] are represented as closures (suspensions), consisting of a code stream for the evaluation of each argument [5] and an argument frame with pointers to the assignments of the local variables.

Using this method it is impossible to check whether a rewrite rule is matching in an occurrence without evaluation of the subterm representing expressions corresponding to the pattern occurrences of the rule. But we avoid the useless construction of the right hand sides of the rewrite rules and can take advantage of information derived by strictness analysis.

4 The LATERM machine

In order to define an efficient execution model for the function definitions (generated from an equational specification) we have developed the stack based abstract machine LATERM. LATERM-code of each function definition consists of two parts:

1. matching code to determine the applicable rewrite rules for given arguments;

2. code for the function bodies (corresponding to the right hand sides of the rewrite rules).

The matching code could test each pattern in turn to see whether it matched the argument. In practice it is more efficient to merge these tests into a single matching tree.
All arguments for the function code are expected to be on top of the stack. During the matching process arguments are evaluated and the arguments of the results are pushed on the stack. So the stack afterwards contains a list of all variable bindings needed by the code for the function body.

To perform lazy evaluation these variable bindings have to be copied from the stack into a heap-frame if the evaluation of the body is suspended. The code for the function body consists of function calls corresponding to the operation symbols contained in the body.

[3] The method is new only for lazy evaluation, for strict evaluation there are implementations, e.g. the SECD-machine [La 64] and the FAM machine [Ca 83,Ca 84]

[4] Arguments representing subterms which are not in HNF

[5] The rewriting of the represented subterm to a HNF

4.1 The LATERM machine state

A state in the abstract machine LATERM is a 6-tuple $\langle o, I, f, D, A, H \rangle$ where

o is the output produced from the machine. It consists of a sequence of constructors representing the normal form of the input term. For example, for the normal form term $a(b(c,d)), e$ the produced output is the list [a,b,c,d,e]. With a lazy evaluation strategy we get an output even if the calculation does not terminate.

I is the LATERM-code stream currently being executed.

f is a frame pointer which addresses the current frame.

D is a dump used to save the current frame pointer at recursive function calls.

A is the argument stack. Arguments are pointer to objects in the heap. There are two kinds of objects, constructor objects and closures. An object consists of two components. The first is either a constructor or a code stream [6] , the second is a frame pointer to a frame containing the arguments of the object.

H is the heap: a mapping from heap labels to objects and argument frames. The objects and frames in the heap represents the term reduced so far. Objects representing already stabilized occurrences in this term contain constructors, the other objects contain instruction sequences to perform the stabilizing of the represented occurrence when they are called.

4.2 Operational semantics

The produced code for a function definition with the function symbol $\$k$ can be subdivided in two parts. First an applicable rewrite rule is determined by evaluating arguments corresponding to pattern occurrences of rewrite rules matching the constructor symbols at the outermost occurrence of the already evaluated arguments. Secondly, if a matching rule was found, the code for the right hand side of the rule is executed, else a new constructor node of the resulting term is build containing the constructor symbol k corresponding to $\$k$.

The selected code expects his arguments on the stack. Also all arguments of the just stabilized subterms have to be directly accessible by the stack, so they are pushed on the stack after the stabilizing.

The code for the right hand side r of the rewrite rule has to be evaluated lazily. Only the function at the outermost occurrence of r is called, the evaluation of the arguments is deferred until later.

- It is necessary to prevent the multiple evaluation of arguments. The solution of this problem is to avoid copying objects for the evaluation of an argument (sharing). LATERM works exclusively with pointers, it never copies objects in the heap. After the evaluation of an argument the object representing the unevaluated argument has to be overwritten by the root node of the result. So eventually existing other pointers to the evaluated object can profit from the evaluation.

- If an argument needs to be evaluated later, the corresponding code can't access its arguments from the stack. So it is necessary, to add to the code a pointer to a frame containing the arguments. Therefore the code for r first copies the needed part of the stack into a new generated frame in the heap. The current frame pointer f is adjusted to point to this frame and the code for r always uses f to access its arguments. The closures being build for later evaluation of an argument contain the code for this evaluation and the current frame pointer f.

[6]In an implementation the code stream is represented by a code label

The left hand sides of the transition rules defines the conditions which must be satisfied before a rule can be applied, e.g rule 9

$$\langle o, \textbf{print\_node} : I, f, D, a : A, H[a \mapsto (k, f_k)]\rangle \Rightarrow \langle o \mathbin{+\!\!+} [k], I, f, D, a : A, H\rangle$$

is applicable only if the first instruction in the instruction stream is *print_node* and the stack contains an argument a which points to an constructor object (k, f_k) in the heap.

The right hand sides of the rules determines the changes of the machine state, e.g in rule 9 the *print_node* instruction is removed from the instruction stream and the constructor symbol k is appended to the output. An argument (object pointer) that occurs only in the right hand side of a transition rule is considered to be new and unique, e.g a in rule 1. LATERM states that do not match any rule are considered to be run time errors.

Figure 5: LATERM state transition rules

1. $\langle o, \textbf{new\_const}\ \ t : I, f, D, A, H\rangle \Rightarrow \langle o, I, f, D, a : A, H[a \mapsto (t, nil)]\rangle$
   (a selects an unused object)
2. $\langle o, \textbf{new\_node}\ \ t\ \ n : I, f, D, a_n : \cdots : a_1 : A, H\rangle \Rightarrow \langle o, I, f, D, a : A, H[a \mapsto (t, f_t), f_t \mapsto (a_1, \ldots, a_n)]\rangle$
   (a selects an unused object, f_t selects an unused frame)
3. $\langle o, \textbf{get\_arg}\ \ n : I], f, D, a_0 : \cdots : a_n : A, H]\rangle \Rightarrow \langle o, I, f, D, a_n : a_0 : \cdots : a_n : A, H\rangle$
4. $\langle o, \textbf{update}\ \ n : I, f, D, a : a_0 : \cdots : a_n : A, H[a \mapsto (k, f_k)]\rangle \Rightarrow \langle o, I, f, D, a : a_0 : \cdots : a_n : A, H[a_n \mapsto (k, f_k)]\rangle$
5. $\langle o, \textbf{unpack} : I, f, D, a : A, H[a \mapsto (k, nil)]\rangle \Rightarrow \langle o, I, f, D, a : A, H\rangle$
6. $\langle o, \textbf{unpack} : I, f, D, a : A, H[a \mapsto (k, f_k), f_k \mapsto (a_1, \ldots, a_n)]\rangle \Rightarrow \langle o, I, f, D, a_n : \cdots : a_1 : A, H\rangle$
7. $\langle o, \textbf{slide}\ \ n : I, f, D, a_0 : \cdots : a_n : A, H\rangle \Rightarrow \langle o, I, f, D, a_0 : A, H\rangle$
8. $\langle o, \textbf{pop\_args}\ \ n : I, f, D, a_1 : \cdots : a_n : A, H\rangle \Rightarrow \langle o, I, f, D, A, H\rangle$
9. $\langle o, \textbf{print\_node} : I, f, D, a : A, H[a \mapsto (k, f_k)]\rangle \Rightarrow \langle o \mathbin{+\!\!+} [k], I, f, D, a : A, H\rangle$
10. $\langle o, \textbf{init} : I, f, D, A, H\rangle \Rightarrow \langle [\,], I, nil, [\,], [\,], empty\_heap\rangle$
11. $\langle o, \textbf{select}\ \ [k_1, \ldots, k_n]\ \ [I_1, \ldots, I_{n+1}] : I, f, D, a : A, H[a \mapsto (k_i, f_k)]\rangle \Rightarrow \langle o, I_i \mathbin{+\!\!+} I, f, D, a : A, H\rangle$
    (if k_i is not in $[k_1, \ldots, k_n]$ then $I_i := I_{n+1}$)
12. $\langle o, \textbf{if\_code}\ \ n\ \ I_{then}\ \ I_{else} : I], f, D, a_0 : \cdots : a_n : A, H[a_n \mapsto (I_a, f_I)]\rangle \Rightarrow \langle o, I_{then} \mathbin{+\!\!+} I, f, D, a_0 : \cdots : a_n : A, H\rangle$
13. $\langle o, \textbf{if\_code}\ \ n\ \ I_{then}\ \ I_{else} : I], f, D, a_0 : \cdots : a_n : A, H[a_n \mapsto (k_a, f_k)]\rangle \Rightarrow \langle o, I_{else} \mathbin{+\!\!+} I, f, D, a_0 : \cdots : a_n : A, H\rangle$
14. $\langle o, \textbf{take\_frame}\ \ n : I, f_0, D, a_n : \cdots : a_1 : A, H\rangle \Rightarrow \langle o, I, f, D, A, H[f \mapsto (a_1, \ldots, a_n)]\rangle$
    (f selects an unused Frame)
15. $\langle o, \textbf{push\_code}\ \ I_c : I], f, D, A, H]\rangle \Rightarrow \langle o, I, f, D, a : A, H[a \mapsto (I_c, f)]\rangle$
16. $\langle o, \textbf{push\_arg}\ \ n : I, f, D, A, H[f \mapsto (a_1, \ldots, a_n, \ldots)]\rangle \Rightarrow \langle o, I, f, D, a_n : A, H\rangle$
17. $\langle o, \textbf{save\_frame} : I, f, D, A, H\rangle \Rightarrow \langle o, I, f, f : D, A, H\rangle$
18. $\langle o, \textbf{restore\_frame} : I, f_0, f : D, A, H\rangle \Rightarrow \langle o, I, f, D, A, H\rangle$
19. $\langle o, \textbf{call\_arg}\ \ n : I, f, D, a_0 : \cdots : a_n : A, H[a_n \mapsto (I_a, f_I)]\rangle \Rightarrow \langle o, I_a \mathbin{+\!\!+} I, f_I, D, a_0 : \cdots : a_n : A, H\rangle$

Figure 6: LATERM macros

20. $\langle o, \textbf{stabilize\_arg}\ \ n : I, f, D, A, H\rangle \Rightarrow \langle o, if\_code\ \ n\ \ [call\_arg\ n, update\ n]\ \ [get\_arg\ n] : I, f, D, A, H\rangle$

21. $\langle o, \mathbf{print} : I, f, D, a : A, H[a \mapsto (k, nil)]\rangle \quad \Rightarrow \langle o, print\_node : I, f, D, A, H\rangle$

22. $\langle o, \mathbf{print} : I, f, D, a : A, H[a \mapsto (k, f_k), f_k \mapsto (a'_1, \ldots, a'_n)]\rangle \Rightarrow$

$$\langle o, print\_node : unpack : stabilize\_arg\ (n-1) : print : \cdots : stabilize\_arg\ 0 : print : pop\_args\ n : I, f, D, a : A, H\rangle$$

5 Compiling function definitions into LATERM code

In this section we describe an algorithm to translate a list of function definitions produced by earlier phases of the compilation process into LATERM machine code.

The compilation is divided in 5 compilation schemes:

G $[[fdefs]]$ is used to build the global environment δ from the list of function definitions $fdefs$. δ binds the definitions to the operation symbols of the transformed TRS.

M $[[t]]$ produces code to perform the rewriting of the given term t to its normal form. First LATERM is initialized with the instruction *init*. The machine starts with an empty output, a code sequence I_0 ++ $[get\_arg\ 0, print]$ and empty frame, dump, stack and heap. I_0 is produced from scheme R for stabilizing t, the instruction *print* prints and stabilizes recursively the whole resulting term. The machine halts when a normal form of t is reached.

F $[[\$k\ [v_1, \ldots, v_n] = ce]]\ \ \delta$ is the scheme producing code for stabilizing a (sub)term which has $\$k$ as its outermost symbol. A local environment γ is build, where every variable v_i is bound to the integer $i-1$. This environment contains the stack positions which are needed from the translated code of the function definition body *ce* to access the arguments of a function call. The code for *ce* is given by the scheme C.

The code given by F expects the arguments [7] corresponding to the variables v_i pushed on top of the stack. This arguments are replaced on the stack by a pointer to the stabilized term.

C $[[case\ \ v\ \ [(k_1\ vs_1 : ce_1), \ldots, (k_n\ vs_n : ce_n)]\ \ otherwise : r]]\ \ \delta\ \ \gamma\ \ d$ gives code that performs the selection of an applicable rewrite rule. This code first stabilizes the subterm bound to the variable v with the instruction *stabilize_arg*.

stabilize_arg checks whether the argument is already stabilized. Then the argument is pushed on the stack (*get_arg*), otherwise the corresponding code is called (*call_arg*) and a pointer to the result is rewritten to the stack position of the argument (*update*).

Then the selection is performed with the instruction *select*, which chooses the code corresponding to the matching constructor k_i at the stabilized occurrence in the term.

If there is no match, the code for the otherwise expression r produced by scheme D is executed, else first the stabilized term is unpacked on the stack (*unpack*). This means, that the top node pointing to the root node is popped from the stack and the direct subterms of this term are pushed on the stack. The local environment is extended for every case to bind the new variables from the lists vs_i to the stack positions of the subterms under the stabilized occurrence. d is the current stack offset, used to calculate the stack positions needed for the argument access. Then the code corresponding to the matching constructor k_i is executed.

C $[[r]]\ \ \delta\ \ \gamma\ \ d$ produces code for the right hand side r of a rewrite rule. C is only called for the whole rule side, subterms of r are handled from scheme R.

If r consists only of a single variable, the corresponding argument term is stabilized (*stabilize_arg*), then the arguments are eliminated from the stack (*slide*).

If r is a symbol of arity 0, the arguments are eliminated from the stack (*pop_args*). Afterwards, if the symbol is a constructor, a new node of the resulting term is build (*new_const*). If it is a function symbol, the code for the function is executed.

[7] pointer to subterms under the position of $\$k$ in the term

In all other cases a frame on the heap (*take_frame*) is being build containing all arguments of the function on the stack, including the arguments unpacked on the stack after stabilizing an argument. The current frame pointer f is adjusted to point to this frame.

If r is a constructor term $k(r_1, \ldots, r_n)$ the rest of the code is produced from scheme R. Otherwise if r is a function application $\$k(r_1, \ldots, r_n)$ the code for function $\$k$ is executed after the code for the arguments r_i produced by scheme R. C is only called for the whole rule side, subterms of r are handled from scheme R.

D $[\![r]\!]$ d produces code for the otherwise expression r. Superfluous arguments are deleted from the stack (*pop_args*) and a new constructor node (*new_const* or *new_node*) is build on the heap.

R $[\![r]\!]$ δ γ b produces code for the subterms of the right hand rule sides. If r is a single variable, the the corresponding argument in the current frame (pointed by f) is pushed on the stack (*push_arg*).

If r is a constructor term $k(r_1, \ldots, r_n)$ or k, a new node of the resulting term is build on the heap (*new_node*) after the code for the arguments r_i produced recursively by scheme R was executed.

The produced code for function applications depends on strictness information contained in the environment ψ. ψ gives for every operation symbol k a list of boolean values. The n-th boolean in this list is true iff the operation is strict in the n-th argument. The argument b of the scheme corresponds to this strictness information. If there is no strictness information available, ψ gives as default always false.

First we want to discuss the non-strict case (b = false):

For a function application $\$k(r_1, \ldots, r_n)$ or $\$k$ a new closure is build on the heap (*push_code*). This closure contains the current frame pointer and the code produced by scheme R for the application the strict case (b = true).

And in the strict case (b = true):

After the code for the arguments r_i was executed, the current frame pointer f is saved (*save_frame*), the code for function $\$k$ is executed and finally f is restored (*restore_frame*).

The presented compilation schemes would generate infinite instruction sequences for recursive function definitions. We assume that in practice labels are used rather than generate copies of code.

After the LATERM code generation several optimizations can be done, e.g. the instruction calls *pop_args* 0, *take_frame* 0 and *slide* 0 can be eliminated.

Notation

In this paper we represent lists using the SASL notation for lists [Bi 88] and use the standard list operations defined in fig 7. [] denotes the empty list and the list constructing operator : associates to the left. The environment combining operator $\oplus$ is defined by $\gamma \oplus \{I \mapsto x\} = \lambda I'.((I' = I) \longrightarrow x, \gamma\ I')$ and by its associativity.

Figure 7: auxiliary functions

$[\,] +\!\!+\ xs$	$= xs$	(concatenation of two Lists)
$(x : xs) +\!\!+\ ys$	$= x : (xs +\!\!+\ ys)$	
$(x : xs)!0$	$= x$	(list-index, (n-1)th element of a list)
$(x : xs)!(n+1)$	$= xs!n$	
$\#\,[\,]$	$= 0$	(length of a list)
$\#\,(x : xs)$	$= 1 + \#xs$	
$getenv\ \ (v : vs)\ \ n\ \ \gamma$	$= getenv\ \ vs\ \ (n+1)\ \ (\gamma \oplus \{v \mapsto n\})$	(builds an environment)
$getenv\ \ [\,]\ \ n\ \ \gamma$	$= \gamma$	

Figure 8: LATERM compilation rules (environment based evaluation)

1. M $[\![t]\!]$ $=[init] +\!\!+ (\mathsf{C}\ [\![t]\!]\ \ (\mathsf{G}\ [\![fdefs_E]\!]\ \ \delta_{arid})\ \ \gamma_{arid}\ \ 0)$
$+\!\!+\ [get\_arg\ 0, print]$

2. $\mathsf{G}\,[\![\,[\,]\,]\!]\ \delta \quad = \delta$
3. $\mathsf{G}\,[\![(\$k\ vs = ce) : fdefs]\!]\ \delta \quad = \mathsf{G}\,[\![fdefs]\!]\ \ (\delta \oplus \{\$k \mapsto [\![\$k\ vs = ce]\!]\})$
4. $\mathsf{F}\,[\![\$k\ vs = ce]\!]\ \delta \quad = \mathsf{C}\,[\![ce]\!]\ \delta\ (getenv\ \ vs\ \ 1\ \ \gamma_{arid})\ \ (arity\ \$k)$
5. $\mathsf{C}\,[\![case\ \ v\ \ [(k_1\ vs_1 :\ ce_1), \ldots, (k_n\ vs_n :\ ce_n)]\ \ otherwise :\ r]\!]\ \delta\ \gamma\ d$
$$= [stabilize\_arg\ (d - \gamma\ v), select\ \ [k_1, \ldots, k_n]$$
$$[\,[unpack] +\!\!+\ \mathsf{C}\,[\![ce_1]\!]\ \delta\ \ (getenv\ vs_1\ d\ \gamma)\ \ (d + \#vs_1), \ldots,$$
$$[unpack] +\!\!+\ \mathsf{C}\,[\![ce_n]\!]\ \delta\ \ (getenv\ vs_n\ d\ \gamma)\ \ (d + \#vs_n),$$
$$\mathsf{D}\,[\![r]\!]\ d]\,]$$
6. $\mathsf{C}\,[\![\$k]\!]\ \delta\ \gamma\ d \quad = [pop\_args\ d] +\!\!+ (\mathsf{F}\,[\![(\delta\ \$k)]\!]\ \delta)$
7. $\mathsf{C}\,[\![\$k(r_1, \ldots, r_n)]\!]\ \delta\ d \quad = [take\_frame\ \ d] +\!\!+ (\mathsf{R}\,[\![r_1]\!]\ \delta\ \gamma\ \ (\psi\ \$k)!1) +\!\!+ \cdots$
$$+\!\!+ (\mathsf{R}\,[\![r_n]\!]\ \delta\ \gamma\ \ (\psi\ \$k)!n) +\!\!+ (\mathsf{F}\,[\![(\delta\ \$k)]\!]\ \delta)$$
8. $\mathsf{C}\,[\![k]\!]\ \delta\ \gamma\ d \quad = [pop\_args\ d, new\_const\ k]$
9. $\mathsf{C}\,[\![k(r_1, \ldots, r_n)]\!]\ \delta\ \gamma\ d \quad = [take\_frame\ \ d] +\!\!+ (\mathsf{R}\,[\![k(r_1, \ldots, r_n)]\!]\ \delta\ \gamma\ true)$
10. $\mathsf{C}\,[\![v]\!]\ \delta\ \gamma\ d \quad = [stabilize\_arg\ (d - \gamma\ v), slide\ d]$
11. $\mathsf{D}\,[\![k]\!]\ d \quad = [pop\_args\ (d + 1), new\_const\ \ k]$
12. $\mathsf{D}\,[\![k(v_1, \ldots, v_n)]\!]\ d \quad = [pop\_args\ (d - n + 1), new\_node\ \ k\ \ n]$
13. $\mathsf{R}\,[\![\$k]\!]\ \delta\ \gamma\ true \quad = [save\_frame] +\!\!+ (\mathsf{F}\,[\![(\delta\ \$k)]\!]\ \delta) +\!\!+ [restore\_frame]$
14. $\mathsf{R}\,[\![\$k(r_1, \ldots, r_n)]\!]\ \delta\ \gamma\ true \quad = (\mathsf{R}\,[\![r_1]\!]\ \delta\ \gamma\ \ (\psi\ k)!1) +\!\!+ \cdots$
$$+\!\!+ (\mathsf{R}\,[\![r_n]\!]\ \delta\ \gamma\ \ (\psi\ k)!n)$$
$$+\!\!+ [save\_frame] +\!\!+ (\mathsf{F}\,[\![(\delta\ \$k)]\!]\ \delta) +\!\!+ [restore\_frame]$$
15. $\mathsf{R}\,[\![\$k]\!]\ \delta\ \gamma\ false \quad = push\_code\ \ (\mathsf{F}\,[\![(\delta\ \$k)]\!]\ \delta)$
16. $\mathsf{R}\,[\![\$k(r_1, \ldots, r_n)]\!]\ \delta\ \gamma\ false \quad = push\_code\ \ ((\mathsf{R}\,[\![r_1]\!]\ \delta\ \gamma\ \ (\psi\ k)!1) +\!\!+ \cdots$
$$+\!\!+ (\mathsf{R}\,[\![r_n]\!]\ \delta\ \gamma\ \ (\psi\ k)!n) +\!\!+ (\mathsf{F}\,[\![(\delta\ \$k)]\!]\ \delta))$$
17. $\mathsf{R}\,[\![k]\!]\ \delta\ \gamma\ b \quad = [new\_const\ \ k]$
18. $\mathsf{R}\,[\![k(r_1, \ldots, r_n)]\!]\ \delta\ \gamma\ b \quad = (\mathsf{R}\,[\![r_1]\!]\ \delta\ \gamma\ \ (\psi\ k)!1) +\!\!+ \cdots$
$$+\!\!+ (\mathsf{R}\,[\![r_n]\!]\ \delta\ \gamma\ \ (\psi\ k)!n) +\!\!+ [new\_node\ \ k\ \ n]$$
19. $\mathsf{R}\,[\![v]\!]\ \delta\ \gamma\ b \quad = [push\_arg\ \ (\gamma\ v)]$

6 Conditional equations

In most cases the transformation of abstract into executable specifications is rather complicated if the applicability of rewrite rules can't be restricted. Properties like confluence or termination are much easier to achieve with conditional rewrite systems. For this reason we currently prepare an extended version of the LOTOS datatype specification compiler for conditional equations.

The extension of our methods to conditional rewrite systems without extra variables in the conditions or in the right sides of the rules is straightforward. In this case we use an evaluation method called lazy conditional rewriting. In order to determine the applicability of a rewrite rule the substitution instances of both sides of the conditions simultaneously have to be reduced until normal forms are reached or the stabilized parts of the instances are different.

Code for the lazy evaluation of the conditions is inserted between the matching code and the code for the function bodies.

For oriented conditions [8] we often can permit extra variables in the condition without loosing the reductivity of the rewrite system. E.g. the oriented condition in

$$split(x, l) = (l_1, l_2) \Leftarrow sort(ladd(x, l)) = append(sort(l_1), ladd(x, sort(l_2)))$$

[8] in every substitution instance of the right hand side r of the condition every non-variable occurrence of r is stabilized.

(the definition of quicksort) means operationally that we can normalize $split(x, l)$ and then match the result with (l_1, l_2) to obtain the complete binding of the variables l_1 and l_2.

In all other cases with extra variables goal solving is needed for checking the applicability of an rewrite rule. A completion procedure has to transform the system in such a way that not all solutions of a condition need to be found at rewrite time. In this case we can use incomplete but more efficient methods like narrowing [Be 89].

Narrowing is the natural extension of reduction to incorporate unification. It consists in applying the minimal substitution to an expression in order to make it reducible, and then to reduce it. The minimal substitution is found by unifying the expression by the left hand side of a rewrite rule. A step of narrowing can also be followed by a sequence of reductions leading to an irreducible form.

For the extension of LATERM to perform narrowing we have to add a backtrack mechanism and an unification algorithm. Similar to reduction there exist several evaluation strategies (lazy narrowing, basic narrowing, etc., see [Pad 88]).

7 Implementation of LATERM

There are two different approaches for the implementation of the instruction set of the LATERM term reduction machine, instructions can be compiled into machine code or can be interpreted by a simulator.

Interpretation generally lacks efficiency, but can be used for testing purposes or performance analysis and further helps understanding the operational semantics of LATERM. An experimental LATERM simulator written in C-PROLOG was developed at the Techn. Univ. Berlin.

Much more efficient is the generation of machine code for real machines. This can be achieved by compiling the instructions into

- intermediate abstract code, e.g. M-Code [Jos87], which is transformed further,
- "C" programs (other languages may also be suited for this purpose), or directly into
- assembler code for common computers.

Although the first two alternatives have the advantage of hardware independence they are of minor interest in the case of LATERM. Neither the compilation of equational specifications into LATERM instructions nor the instructions itself are difficult to implement and most instructions are just a short sequence of assembler statements. The direct generation of assembler statements allows optimal usage of the processor, its registers, the memory, etc. and results in more efficient code.

7.1 Macro-expansion of LATERM code

In [Wo 89] the transformation of all LATERM instructions in Motorola 68020 assembler code is defined based on macro-expansion.

For each LATERM instruction an assembler macro is defined. The result of the compilation of algebraic specifications, a sequence of LATERM instructions, is interpreted as a sequence of macro calls. These macro calls together with the macro, register and memory definitions are subsequently processed by a standard macro assembler.

Fig. 9 illustrates this technique and shows the structure of the generated code. For the formal definition we refer to [Wo 89].

Figure 9: LATERM macro expansion/structure of generated assembler code

```
*   external procedures
        xref        initgarb                          initialize garbage collector
        xref        printnod                          print node
                    ...
*   definition of heap and stack areas
                    ...
*   register definitions
                    ...
        as          equu        a3                    argument stack pointer
*   macro definitions
                    ...
        getarg      macro                             getarg (n) instruction
                    move.l      4*\1(as),-(as)        copy argument n on top of stack
                    end
                    ...
*   typical LATERM instruction sequence
                    ...
        getarg(2)   expanded to     move.l      4*2(as),-(as)
        getarg(3)   expanded to     move.l      4*3(as),-(as)
                    ...
```

The Motorola 68020 processor was chosen because this processor is well suited for the execution of LATERM code, its instructions are well documented, and it is used in high performance workstations.

The code generation can easily be modified for other processors of comparable type (VAX, NS32000).

The usage of macros instead of subroutines produces more lengthy code but the resulting program is much more efficient. All overhead of subroutine calls is avoided, and instruction-prefetch queues and program caches of modern processors can be used in an optimal way. The overhead of subroutine calls is not negligible, all register have to be saved and restored, and each call interrupts the prefetch queue and forces reloading.

The code generation defined in [Wo 89] can additionally be optimized using peep-hole optimization and standard optimization features of the assembly phase.

7.2 Memory management and garbage collection

Most LATERM instructions generate and manipulate objects in the allocated heap memory. These objects may be representations of terms, frames, closures or other data depending on the operating mode of LATERM.

During the execution of compiled large algebraic specifications, huge amounts of intermediate objects will typically be generated. Generation and access of these objects are the most frequently used operations and have to be implemented in an optimal way.

All heap objects are structured similar to vector application nodes [Jos 87].
This technique gives a good and efficient memory utilization and can be used, contrary to the situation of most applicative languages, because equational specifications used within LOTOS don't have any higher order objects.

Unfortunately garbage collectors based on linked lists of free memory nodes and mark-scan algorithms aren't compatible with this approach.

The LATERM garbage collector therefore is based on a copying and compacting algorithm. This type of garbage collection is also used for the implementation of LML [Au 87].

The heap memory is divided in two partitions. One partition holds all nodes during the execution of LATERM instructions, the other is used only during the process of garbage collection. The garbage collector is activated when there is an overflow of the first heap partition. The intermediate result and all active heap objects are copied in the second partition with simultaneous translation of addresses.

The main advantages of this approach are:

- new objects can easily and efficient be generated by incrementing the actual top of heap pointer,
- nodes of different size are handled in the same way,
- during the copying process tree-like structured heap objects are compacted, i.e. related nodes are created physically adjacent.

7.3 First performance results

Compiled LATERM code gives a performance improvement of a factor of 50-100 to interpreters for term reduction systems written in "C" and over 300 compared with PROLOG interpreters. On a SUN 3/160 LATERM code achieves over 100000 term reductions per second with innermost strategy and about 40000 for full lazy evaluation.

The main reasons are:

- all pattern matching is done by precompiled jump tables,
- in most cases the generation of the right hand sides of reduction rules is not necessary, and is substituted by instruction sequences,
- lazy-evaluation avoids unnecessary reductions and finds short reduction sequences,
- any interpretation overhead is avoided.

Laterm code works similar to compiled LML code. It is faster because of optimization of LATERM w.r.t term rewriting systems and because no functions of higher types have to be considered. This simplifies memory management and the instructions itself.

7.4 Compilation example

Let us consider the data type specification STRING shown in fig. 2 and the corresponding function definitions of fig. 3.

To demonstrate the advantages of the lazy evaluation of LATERM code, we will extend this specification by two operations $s1, s2 : \rightarrow$ *string* and following equations:

$$s1 \;= ladd(a, s1) \qquad (11)$$
$$s2 \;= ladd(a, ladd(b, ladd(a, empty))) \qquad (12)$$

Equations (1) to (12) are read as rewrite rules from left to right. Again all required properties mentioned in section 2 are fulfilled.

Please note, that this extension is no enrichment [EM 85] of the data type STRING and that the constructed term rewriting system is not noetherian.

All implementations for term rewriting systems based on leftmost innermost strategy could not evaluate the term $eql(s1, s2)$, the comparison between the strings $s1$ and $s2$.

The lazy evaluation strategy of LATERM reduces $eql(s1, s2)$ to the correct result $false$.

The function definitions for $s1$ and $s2$ are:

$$\$s1\;[\,] \;= ladd(a, \$s1) \qquad (11)$$
$$\$s2\;[\,] \;= ladd(a, ladd(b, ladd(a, empty))) \qquad (12)$$

The LATERM code produced by the compilation of all function definitions is shown in fig. 10. Fig. 11 contains the executed code sequence for the reduction of the term $eql(s1, s2)$, figure 12 is an illustration of several LATERM machine states during this execution.

Figure 11: Execution sequence for *eql*(*s*1, *s*2)

I_{main}: *init, push_code* $I_{\$s1}$, *push_code* $I_{\$s2}$,
$I_{\$eql}$: *stabilize_arg* 1, *if_code* 1 ... , *call_arg* 1,
$I_{\$s1}$: *new_const a, push_code* $I_{\$s1}$, (picture 1)
new_node ladd 2, (picture 2)
update 1, (picture 3)
select [*ladd, empty*] [I_3, I_4],
I_3 : *unpack*, (picture 4)
stabilize_arg 2, *if_code* 2 ... , *call_arg* 2,
$I_{\$s2}$: *new_const a, new_const b, new_const a, new_const empty*,
new_node ladd 2, *new_node ladd* 2, *new_node ladd* 2,
update 2, (picture 5)
select [*ladd, empty*] [I_5, I_6],
I_5 : *unpack, take_frame* 6, (picture 6)
push_code I_8, *push_code* I_9,
$I_{\$and}$: *stabilize_arg* 1, *if_code* 1 ... , *call_arg* 1,
I_8 : *push_arg* 3, *push_arg* 5
$I_{\$eqc}$: *stabilize_arg* 1, *if_code* 1 ... , *get_arg* 1,
select [*a, b*] [I_{10}, I_{11}]
I_{10} : *unpack, stabilize_arg* 0, *if_code* 0 ... , *get_arg* 0,
select [*a, b*] [I_{12}, I_{13}]
I_{12} : *unpack, pop_args* 2, *new_const true*,
update 1,
select [*true, false*] [I_1, I_2],
I_1 : *unpack, stabilize_arg* 0, *if_code* 0 ... , *call_arg* 0,
I_9 : *push_arg* 4, *push_arg* 6,
$I_{\$eql}$: *stabilize_arg* 1, *if_code* 1 ... , *call_arg* 1,
$I_{\$s1}$: *new_const a, push_code* $I_{\$s1}$, *new_node ladd* 2,
update 1,
select [*ladd, empty*] [I_3, I_4],
I_3 : *unpack, stabilize_arg* 2, *if_code* 2 ... , *get_arg* 2,
select [*ladd, empty*] [I_5, I_6],
I_5 : *unpack, take_frame* 6, *push_code* I_8, *push_code* I_9,
$I_{\$and}$: *stabilize_arg* 1, *if_code* 1 ... , *call_arg* 1,
I_8 : *push_arg* 3, *push_arg* 5,
$I_{\$eqc}$: *stabilize_arg* 1, *if_code* 1 ... , *get_arg* 1,
select [*a, b*] [I_{10}, I_{11}],
I_{10} : *unpack, stabilize_arg* 0, *if_code* 0 ... , *get_arg* 0,
select [*a, b*] [I_{12}, I_{13}],
I_{13} : *unpack, pop_args* 2, *new_const false*,
update 1,
select [*true, false*] [I_1, I_2],
I_2 : *unpack, pop_args* 2, *new_const false*,
update 0,
slide 2, *get_arg* 0, *print, print_node*

Figure 10: LATERM code for specification STRING

I_{main} = [*init, push_code* $I_{\$s1}$, *push_code* $I_{\$s2}$]
++ $I_{\$eql}$ ++ [*get_arg* 0, *print*]
$I_{\$and}$ = [*stabilize_arg* 1, *select* [*true, false*]
[I_1, I_2]]
$I_{\$eql}$ = [*stabilize_arg* 1,
select [*ladd, empty*] [I_3, I_4]]
$I_{\$eqc}$ = [*stabilize_arg* 1,
select [*a, b*] [I_{10}, I_{11}]]
$I_{\$s1}$ = [*new_const a, push_code* $I_{\$s1}$,
new_node ladd 2]
$I_{\$s2}$ = [*new_const a, new_const b*,
new_const a, new_const empty,
new_node ladd 2, *new_node ladd* 2,
new_node ladd 2]

I_1 = [*unpack, stabilize_arg* 0, *slide* 2]
I_2 = [*unpack, pop_args* 2, *new_const false*]
I_3 = [*unpack, stabilize_arg* 2,
select [*ladd, empty*] [I_5, I_6]]
I_4 = [*unpack, stabilize_arg* 0,
select [*ladd, empty*] [I_6, I_7]]
I_5 = [*unpack, take_frame* 6, *push_code* I_8,
push_code I_9] ++ $I_{\$and}$
I_6 = [*unpack, pop_args* 4, *new_const false*]
I_7 = [*unpack, pop_args* 2, *new_const true*]
I_8 = [*push_arg* 3, *push_arg* 5] ++ $I_{\$eqc}$
I_9 = [*push_arg* 4, *push_arg* 6] ++ $I_{\$eql}$
I_{10} = [*unpack, stabilize_arg* 0,
select [*a, b*] [I_{12}, I_{13}]]
I_{11} = [*unpack, stabilize_arg* 0,
select [*a, b*] [I_{13}, I_{12}]]
I_{12} = [*unpack, pop_args* 2, *new_const true*],
I_{13} = [*unpack, pop_args* 2, *new_const false*]

Figure 12: Illustration of the LATERM state during the execution

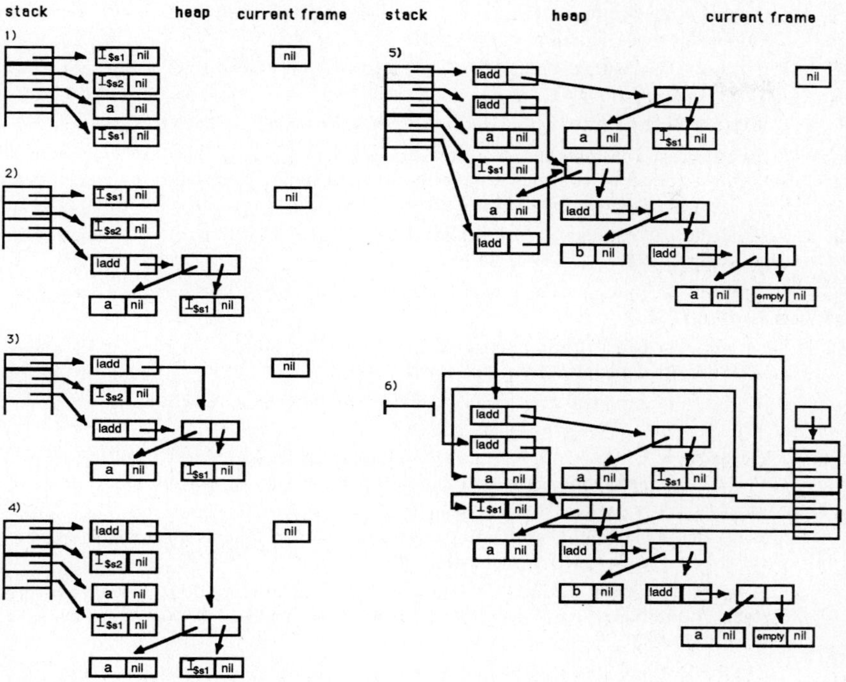

8 Conclusion

The paper outlines a new approach to the implementation of equational specifications of abstract data types.

Equational specifications are transformed in several steps into code of an abstract lazy term rewriting machine – LATERM –, that can efficiently be mapped on machine instructions sequences of ordinary computers.

LATERM incorporates newest techniques used in abstract machines for functional languages like LML (Lazy ML) and is designed and optimized towards fast execution of a wide class of data type specifications.

The main features of LATERM are: lazy reduction strategy, usage of sharing and strictness analysis, frame-based data structures, and evaluation of non-constructor based specifications.

The paper gives details of the compilation scheme and the operational semantics in terms of mathematical definitions, and illustrates the concepts by the compilation of a simple data type specification.

Work is going on to extend the machine to handle conditional equations by means of normal-form reduction and narrowing and to integrate it in the LOTOS toolset which is under development by the Esprit/Lotosphere project.

References

[Au 87] L. Augustsson: Compiling Lazy Functional Languages, Part 2. *PhD thesis, Chalmers Tekniska Högskola, Göteborg, Sweden*, 1987

[Be 89] H.Bertling, H.Ganzinger: Completion-Time Optimization of Rewrite-Time Goal Solving. *RTA 89, Chapel Hill*, 1989

[Bi 88] R. Bird; P. Wadler: Introduction to Functional Programming. *Prentice-Hall*, 1988

[Br 88] E. Brinksma (Ed.): Information processing systems - Open systems interconnection - LOTOS - A formal description technique based on the temporal ordering of observational behavior. *International Standard, ISO 8807*, 1988

[Ca 83] L. Cardelli: The Functional Abstract Machine. *TR-107*, AT&T Bell Laboratories Technical Report, 1983

[Ca 84] L. Cardelli: Compiling a Functional Language. *ACM Symp. Lisp and Functional Programming*, 1984

[Ei 89] Peter van Eijk (Ed.), Chris Vissers, Michel Diaz: The Formal Description Technique LOTOS. *North-Holland ISBN 0 444 87267 1*, 1989.

[EM 85] H. Ehrig; B. Mahr: Fundamentals of Algebraic Specification 1. *Springer EATCS Monographs on Theor. Com. Sci.*, 1985

[Fa 86] J. Fairbairn; S. C. Wray: Code Generation Techniques for Functional Languages. *Proc. of the ACM Symposium on Lisp and Functional Programming, Boston*, 1986

[Fa 87] J. Fairbairn; S. C. Wray: Tim: A Simple, Lazy Abstract Machine to Execute Supercombinators. *Functional Programming Languages and Computer Architecture, Springer, Lecture Notes in Computer Science 274*, 1987

[Ge 88] A.Geser, H.Hussmann, A.Mueck: A Compiler for a Class of Conditional Term Rewriting Systems. *Conditional Term Rewriting Systems, Springer, Lecture Notes in Computer Science 308*, 1988

[He 88] T.Heuillard: Compiling Conditional Rewriting Systems. *Conditional Term Rewriting Systems, Springer, Lecture Notes in Computer Science 308*, 1988

[Hue 79] G. Huet, J.J. Levy: Call by Need Computations in Non Ambiguous Linear Term Rewriting Systems. *Rapport INRIA n.359*, 1979

[Jo 87] S. L. P. Jones: The Implementation of Functional Programming Languages. *Prentice-Hall*, 1987

[Jos 87] T. Johnsson: Compiling Lazy Functional Languages, Part 1 *PhD thesis, Chalmers Tekniska Högskola, Göteborg, Sweden*, 1987

[Kap 86] S. Kaplan: A Compiler for Conditional Term Rewriting Systems *Report*, U. de Paris-Sud, Centre d'Orsay, 1986

[La 64] P. J. Landin: The Mechanical Evaluation of Expressions. *Computer Journal 6, S. 308-320*, 1964

[Pad 88] P.Padawitz: Computing in Horn Clause Theories. *Springer EATCS Monographs on Theor. Com. Sci.*, 1988

[Wo 89] D. Wolz: Theoretische Grundlagen der Compilation algebraischer Spezifikationen und Termersetzungssysteme. *Bericht-Nr. 89-xx*, Technische Universität Berlin, Fachbereich 20, 1989

Invited Presentation:

Open Distributed Processing

Protocol Specification, Testing, and Verification, IX
E. Brinksma, G. Scollo and C.A. Vissers (Editors)
Elsevier Science Publishers B.V. (North-Holland)
IFIP, 1990

Open Distributed Processing (ODP)

J.J. van Griethuysen*
Convener ISO/IEC JTC1/SC21/WG7

The need for distributed processing

Information is the basis for the successful operation of any enterprise. It captures the purpose, resources and objectives of the enterprise. Information may, in detail, be about the location of things of concern to the enterprise, but it is just as important to consider the location of the information itself. A piece of information available at the wrong location is of no benefit to the organization, and may even represent a liability. Above all, uncontrolled inconsistency represents a threat to the enterprise.

To fulfil organizational aims, information may need to be moved from one location at which it is available to another where it is needed so that decisions can be taken. The location of the information will, of course, also be influenced by the location of the information storage and information processing activities which make up the information systems supporting the enterprise. Reasons for this include that information will often be

* replicated against failure;
* distributed to enable timely access;
* processed in parallel, for example to allow the rapid solution of large problems;
* copied to different groups within the management of the enterprise.

The complete collection of information needed by an enterprise will therefore normally be distributed. This distribution of information systems is a necessary consequence of constraints arising from the real world.

---

* PHILIPS International B.V.
Corporate Automation - TMS
Eindhoven - The Netherlands

The main purpose of the standardization of open distributed processing is to allow this process to take place in a consistent and reliable way while using a distributed or heterogeneous collection of equipment.

An information infrastructure

One of the basic requirements of human society is information. To do what we must or want to do, we need knowledge. It has become impossible for each of us individually to acquire this by trial and error only. Therefore, we must gain our knowledge from others. Thus, **information** may be defined as: *any kind of knowledge about things, facts, concepts, etc., that is exchangeable among users*. In order to make exchange of information possible, it must be represented in communicable forms; for example, written or spoken language, data, signals.

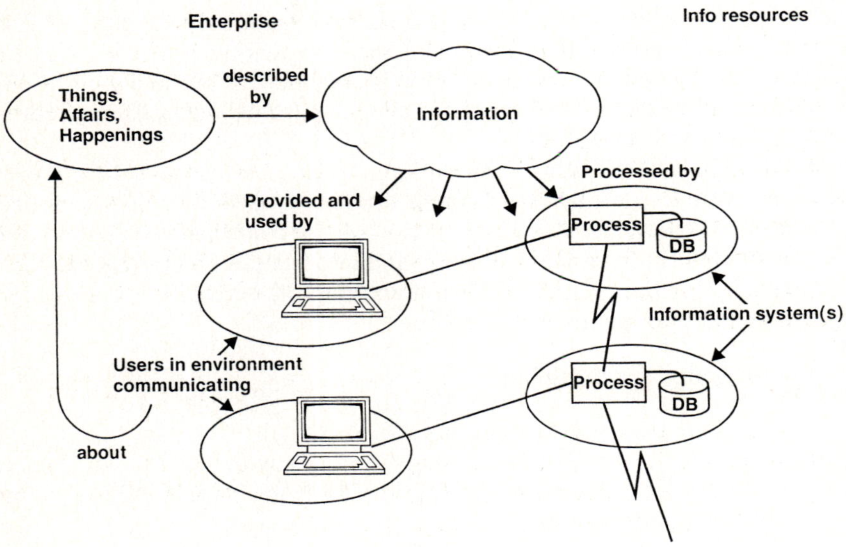

Figure 1 - An information infrastructure with interconnected information systems.

From the viewpoint of information exchange and information manipulation, three groups of aspects may be discerned within this enterprise system:

1. *About which* is the information:
   the **things and affairs** of an enterprise

2. *For which* is the information:
   the **users**

3. *With which* is the information exchanged and manipulated:
   the **information system(s)**.

These groups of aspects may overlap. It is quite possible that a person or enterprise unit may use an information system and at the same time may be something about which information is required. In the same way it is possible that information is required about the information system itself. The "binding" element among these is the information itself. This basic information infrastructure is shown in figure 1.

In this context, an **information system** is defined as: *a system to help users in remembering and exchanging information*.

In some literature, the term "information system" is used to refer to the information system as defined above, together with the activities and behaviour of the enterprise the information system serves.

We follow ISO terminology [1], and limit the term "information system" to the component used for information exchange. The sole objective of an information system is to store, process, and provide information. The ways in which users deal with information and carry out the activities of the enterprise belong to an enterprise system of which the information systems form a part.

A gross architecture for interconnected information systems.

In information exchange, an information provider ("sender") and an information user ("receiver"), not necessarily different, will always be involved. The exchange of information must cope with three important problems:

* provider and user are not at the same location; a *distance gap* must be bridged (*communication function*);

* provider and user are not dealing with the information at the same time instant; a *time gap* must be bridged (*memory function*).

This exchange of information must be co-ordinated and the information must be kept reliable during the exchange process. Moreover, some information can be derived from other information. This yield a third basic function of an information system: the *processing function*.

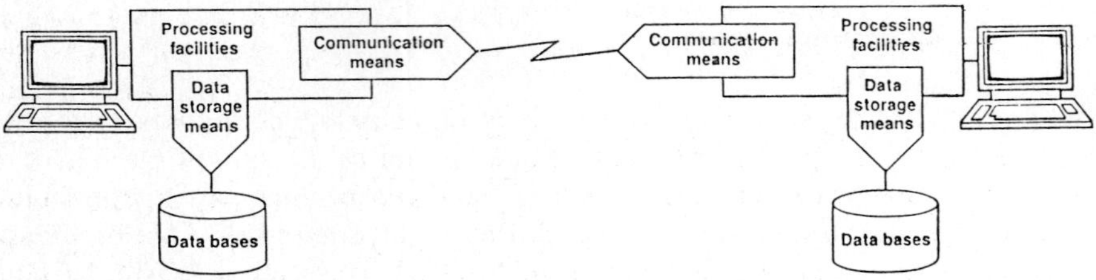

Figure 2 - A gross architecture for interconnected information systems.

The functionalities of modern networks of information processing facilities can be subdivided into these three categories yielding a gross architecture as shown in figure 2. The user interfaces are represented here as terminals. The figure assumes the interconnection of only two information systems. In reality this may be many more.

The distribution problem.

Modern information technology provides the users with complex networks of information processing facilities. These facilities make it possible to interact with them in a seemingly independent way. However, at all times the information in such systems must reflect a truthful description of the things and affairs relevant to the enterprise. Moreover, this information must be available only to authorized people and they must be able to rely on the information being there whenever they need it. For an enterprise applying a network of interconnected information facilities, the distribution problem therefore is:

> *How to keep the information reliable and secure when it is dispersed all over a network of interlinked information processing facilities.*

This is for the enterprise not so much a computer-technical problem, although the computer technology should provide adequate functionalities.

Kinds of distribution

From a user's point of view four kinds of distribution seem relevant:

* Information is needed at several places: *distribution of use*,
* Information is kept at several places: *distribution of storage*,
* Information is processed at several places: *distribution of processing facilities*,
* Information is "owned" at several places: *distribution of authority*.

Why distribution of use ?
We need information to do our jobs and we need it at the places where we do our jobs. Moreover, the same information may be needed for several jobs.

Why distribution of storage ?
Distribution of storage may be needed as a replication against failure. Another reason is ease of storage or ease of access: the information is kept at the place where the most manipulations take place. This may differ for different groups of information.

Why distribution of processing facilities ?
Several reasons can be listed. Replication against failure is one. Possibilities of dedicated processing facilities for dedicated kinds of processing functions and parallel processing are others. Sharing costly facilities is a reason also.

Why distribution of authority ?
Exchange of information is communication of knowledge about situations of an enterprise. The authorities responsible for the described situations often decide who may have this information. They "own" the information. Considering all information available in the network of information processing facilities, many such authorities may own their own sets of information.

Communication (often) crosses boundaries of autonomy within an enterprise. This is even more so if the facilities are used to exchange information among enterprises (E.g. electronic data interchange - EDI).

The objective of Open Distributed Processing seen from the enterprise side therefore is:

Keep information reliable in a distributed environment.

This involve to keep the information correct, that is, good enough, complete enough, and up to date enough. It also necessitates to keep the information secure, that is, available for authorized use and protected against unauthorized use, accidental loss, corruption, and destruction.

Openness in distributed processing

A distributed system may extend over a heterogeneous collection of facilities and equipment. Heterogeneity may be manifest as:

* equipment heterogeneity (e.g. to support a multi-vendor procurement policy);
* operating systems heterogeneity (e.g. because of a multi-vendor procurement policy);
* computational heterogeneity (e.g. because of use of different programming languages, database languages etc.);
* authority heterogeneity (e.g. where cooperation between separate jurisdictions is to be supported);
* application heterogeneity (e.g. where it is desired to integrate otherwise separate applications of information processing to perform a single task).

Heterogeneity means that the facilities and equipment may be of different origin, belong to different families of equipment, follow different internal architectures, etc. In order to overcome the obvious problems with heterogeneity, each individual component of a distributed system must exhibit a consistent and predictable behaviour to other components independent of equipment, implementation technology, management authority, etc. associated with the components. They are "open" to components of heterogeneous origin.

Openness is the quality that a distributed system possesses when it is not required that all its components must be of the same manufacturer/vendor, follow the same software technology, use one operating system, etc. *Open* distributed processing, therefore, allows exchange of information among a wide range of information processing facilities.

Five viewpoints on Open Distributed Processing

So far the aspects of distributed processing have been discussed from a point of view of an enterprise. Other viewpoints also are of interest. Five classes of viewpoints have been identified as focuses of concerns that are thought to be relevant to open distributed processing. Each kind of viewpoint allows modelling and reasoning about an ODP system to be oriented to a particular area of concern (figure 3).

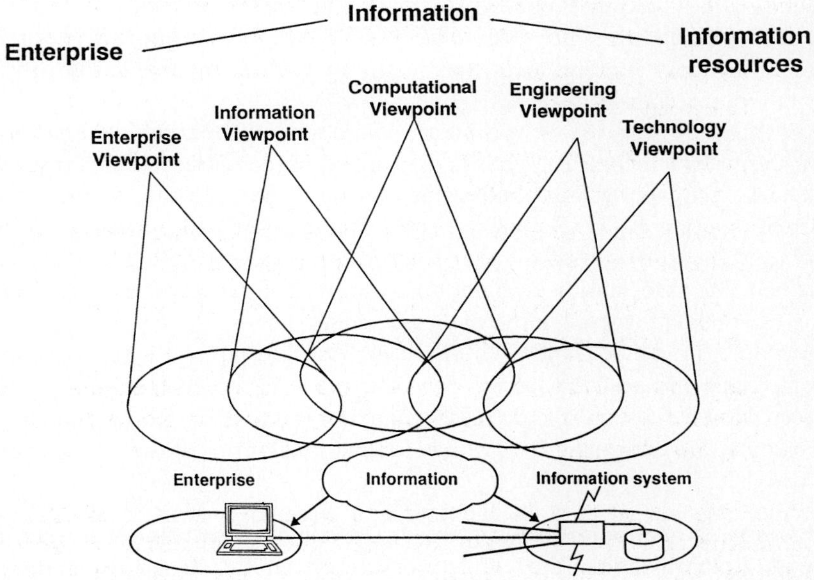

Figure 3 - Viewpoints on open distributed processing.

The purpose of the viewpoints and aspects is to provide a framework of abstractions - by partitioning the concerns to be addressed when describing all facets of an ODP system, the task is made simpler. In addition, this framework of abstraction should help in the placement of boundaries upon ODP standardization.

Informally, a viewpoint leads to a representation of the system and its use with emphasis on a specific concern. More formally, the resulting representation is a set of abstractions of the system, where the abstraction is a description that recognizes some distinctions, those relevant to the concerns at hand and ignores others, those not relevant to the concerns.

What viewpoints to choose?

The opposite of an enterprise viewpoint is to consider the computer technology side. These two kinds of viewpoint view the system from opposite ends of a spectrum of possible viewpoints:

The **enterprise viewpoints** see the distributed processing in terms of what it is required to do for the enterprise concerned. The model from this viewpoint captures business requirements that justify and orientate the design of the distributed processing system.

Note that the enterprise viewpoints are *not* addressing the complete enterprise itself; they view a technical system in the context of the enterprise that it serves.

The enterprise viewpoints concentrate on user aspects relevant to distributed information systems. The enterprise units that support and participate in the distributed processing system under consideration are explicitly identified and described. The information domains and resources of the enterprise are visible, as are the people involved in the enterprise units.

Enterprise models describe people, user interfaces of the systems, system actions, goals and policies. Design decisions made in the enterprise viewpoint concern what the system is to do rather than how it is to do it. Requirements are expressed at the enterprise level purely in functional terms of the enterprise.

The **technology viewpoints** concentrate on the technical artifacts (realized components) from which the distributed processing system is built. It must model the hardware and software that comprise the local operating systems, the input/output devices, storage, points of access to communication services, etc.

In effect, these two viewpoints delimit the design space given to the distributed application designer: ie. *what it is for* (enterprise viewpoints) and *with what* (technology viewpoints).

The other three classes of viewpoints in the spectrum are about the *structure* and *behaviour* of distributed processing.

The **information viewpoints** concentrate on information, and information exchange aspects of distributed processing systems. Information structures and information flows are modelled. The rules and constraints that govern manipulation and management of information are identified. These are modelled in terms of information structures, the relationships and constraints between them, and information flows. Both manual and automated aspects of information processing are taken into account. The resulting models results in a "specification" for what must be achieved by distributed processing system. This viewpoint is of great relevance to ODP, since it specifies *what information* may be exchanged through the distributed processing systems, and *where* and *when* this exchange must take place.

The **computational viewpoints** involve the operation and computational characteristics of the distributed processing system, and the processes which change the information. They concern the structuring of applications so that they are independent of the computer systems and networks on which they run. They yield a computational model of the information representations and manipulations identified in the information viewpoint, resulting in specifications of the required data structures, application processes and the communications between them.

The **engineering viewpoints** view a distributed processing system in terms of the engineering necessary to support the distributed nature of the processing. They are concerned with the provisions and assurance of desired characteristics such as performance, dependability and distribution transparency. They could be considered models of how to "engineer" the distributed processing system identified in computational viewpoints. They should allow the definition of families of system components and reveal how to organize them to achieve the desired characteristics.

Models in the engineering viewpoints define families of system building blocks and explain how to interconnect and organize them. Engineering level decisions concern trade-offs between quality attributes such as performance, dependability and scaling.

The five classes of viewpoints described here are *not* to be treated as a model for a multi-layer implementation of ODP systems. Neither are the various viewpoints to be taken as *equivalent* to phases in the design process. There is no implied *sequence* in the viewpoints.

The viewpoints represent a *pragmatic*, not a *fundamental*, positioning of concerns. It is believed that a "minimum sufficient set" of viewpoints has been identified. However, this will best be tested by their use in the continuing work of WG7, and changes to this set of viewpoints might be required in the light of this further experience.

Summary table of the viewpoints

Viewpoints	**Disciplines**	**Areas of concern** (as relevant to the distributed system)	**What is specified**
Enterprise	Enterprise operation Users and Management Ergonomics Social sciences	User Interfaces Human & social issues Management & finance Legal concerns	User requirements
Information	Knowledge-representation Information Modelling	Information Models Information Structure Information Flows	Conceptual Design and Specifications
Computational	Data Modelling Software engineering	Data Models Application and process design and development	Software Design and development
Engineering	Operating systems, database systems, communication systems	Distributed system infrastructure Application Support	Infrastructure building blocks
Technology	End-products of relevant disciplines	Technological constraints	Realized components

Where Open Distributed Processing is used

Within information processing, the field of application of distributed processing is virtually unlimited. Any task which requires more than one application process to accomplish is within the scope of the work. The field of application therefore covers basically all fields within information processing. Examples of fields of application to which ODP standards could be applied are listed below. All of these utilize some form of data exchange. This could range from information communication (data, voice, video) to the interchange of storage media. This list is not meant to be exhaustive:

* Office Systems;
* Industrial/Process Control Systems;
* Command and Control Systems;
* Integrated Data/Text/Voice/Image Systems;
* Home Entertainment/Automation;
* Business Data Interchange Systems;
* Banking Systems;
* Engineering Development Systems;
* Research Systems;
* Automated Testing Systems;
* Medical Systems;
* Image Processing;
* Information Services.

Distributed processing is important not only within each field of application, but also as a bridge between them. Many organizations already have information systems that use distributed processing to support a variety of functions. For example, a manufacturing company may have a distributed word processing system in the administration department, a network of CAD workstations in the design shop and an automated factory. There are organizational advantages to be gained from the integration of these separate functions into a single, large scale, distributed system oriented towards achieving maximum effectiveness for the company.

Coordination and cooperation are necessary between separate organizations as well as within a single organization. Electronic trading, for example, leads to distributed systems spanning traders, customers and banks. This level of integration is much harder, since no single authority can control the entire activity of the system. Instead ways must be found to maximize the ability of independent authorities to interwork, without jeopardizing their concerns and interests.

ODP standards

In order to make it possible to build a network of information processing facilities that can fulfil the goals of Open Distributed Processing we need common concepts, and overall architectures for such systems. Moreover, we need in our information systems functionalities to preserve the meaning of information in distributed environments.

One of the ways to reach such common agreement and get facilities that can be interlinked is the development of a common set of standards for Open Distributed Processing (ODP). However, this also implies coordination between standards activities for such subjects as data definition & use, and data processing, storage and communication activities.

The information on the design choices and configuration representing the information processing and storage resources of the enterprise, together with the ODP standards, describe how the information systems within the enterprise are to operate. Several areas of concern have been identified which can be looked at from the viewpoints of users (enterprise), information management, software engineering, and the computer hardware engineering. Figure 4 identifies some major areas for this.

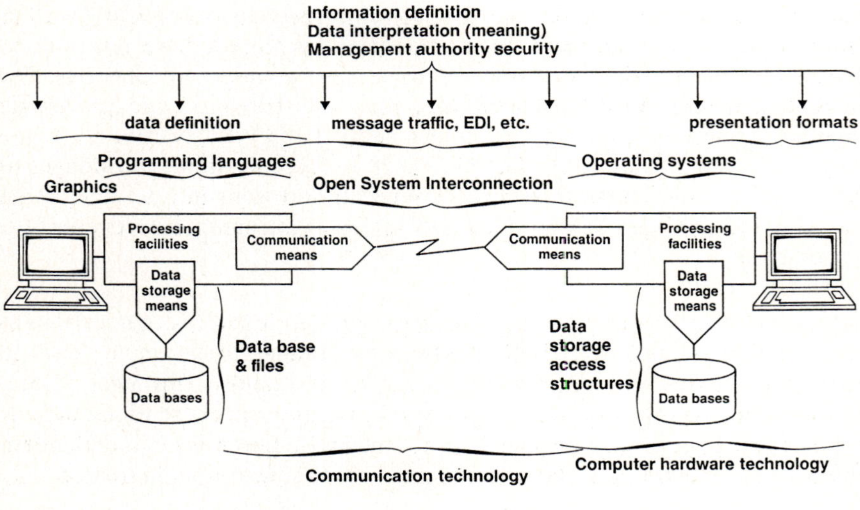

Figure 4 - Areas of concern for open distributed processing standards.

The areas are grouped in four levels: from top to bottom, the enterprise level, the external presentation or user level, the software technology level and the hardware technology level.

At the enterprise level the main areas are: information definition, concepts for information infrastructure and system architectures, and key issues for management, authorizing, control and security of information.

At the external presentation level the main areas are data definition, format definition for messages, etc., standard naming and coding, user directed protocols for communication, and user languages.

At the software technology level the main areas are (internal) communication, storage and processing protocols, standard software interfaces and programming languages.

At the hardware technology level the main areas are hardware interfaces and interconnection standards.

Basic Reference Model of Open Distributed Processing

The ISO work on Open Distributed Processing is about standardization of distributed processing architecture and external linkage, so that coherent systems can be constructed from heterogeneous and re-usable components, and multiple processing systems. This includes:

* common definitions of concepts and terms for distributed processing
* a generalized model of distributed processing using concepts and terms
* a general framework for identifying and relating together open distributed processing standards

The purpose is to enable separate standards groups to develop a coherent set of specific standards for open distributed processing.

ODP will be coordinated with OSI (Open Systems Interconnection) for its communications interconnection, as well as with standards work for data storage aspects, and aspects of security and management of information and information systems. In order to achieve this, the Basic Reference Model of ODP will:

* model distributed processing in terms of components, the services they support, their environment and the interactions between them

* identify levels of abstraction at which the services and interactions can be described

* classify the boundaries between components and identify the points of interaction associated with them

* identify generic functions performed by distributed systems

* show how the elements of the model can be combined to achieve ODP

It defines levels of abstraction at which services and interactions can be defined in other standards, generalizing the concepts of service and protocol defined in the OSI Reference Model.

The place of the Reference Model in the field of standardization is shown in figure 5.

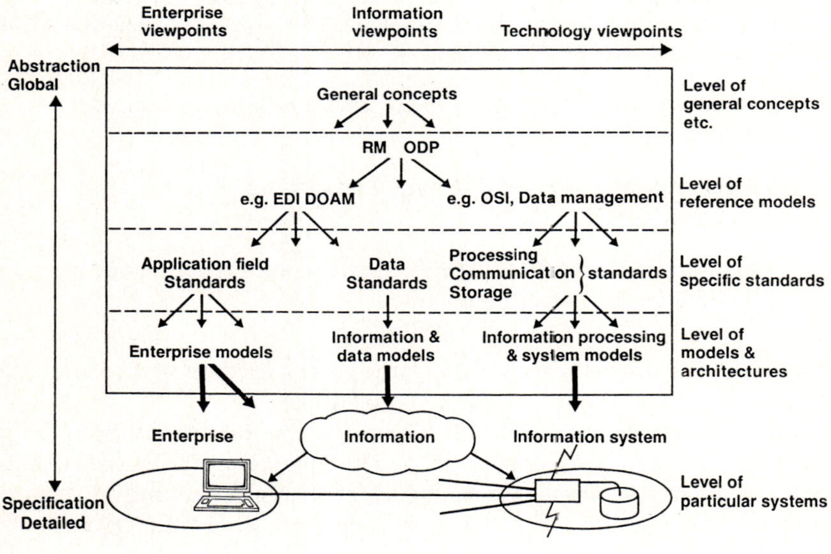

Figure 5 - Place of the Basic Reference Model of Open Distributed Processing.

The Dutch standards organization NNI acts as the Secretariat for the Working Group 7 of ISO/IEC JTC1/SC21 which is charged with the development of the Basic Reference Model of Open Distributed Processing. A proposal for the first part of the reference model will be available at the end of 1990, the complete model is expected to be ready in 1995.

The significance of the new work is demonstrated by the fact that 17 countries (National Bodies) and 7 international groups (Liaison Organizations) are participating in the work.

References

[1] ISO/IEC,
Concepts and Terminology for the Conceptual Schema and the Information Base,
Report No. ISO/IEC TR9007,
International Standardization Organization (ISO),
Central Secretariat, Geneva, Switzerland, 1987

Session 5:

Transition System Applications

Protocol Specification, Testing, and Verification, IX
E. Brinksma, G. Scollo and C.A. Vissers (Editors)
Elsevier Science Publishers B.V. (North-Holland)

Verification Results for ISO FTAM Basic Protocol

R. Lai(*), T.S. Dillon(*), K.R. Parker(%)

(*) Department of Computer Science
La Trobe University
Melbourne, Victoria, Australia.

(%) Division of Information Technology
CSIRO
Melbourne, Victoria, Australia.

This paper presents the results of verifying the ISO File Transfer, Access and Management, FTAM against the deadlock freeness property. There are two protocols specified for FTAM : the basic protocol and the error recovery protocol. The basic protocol consists of two protocols : the Basic File Protocol and the Bulk Data Transfer Protocol. Only the results of verifying the Basic protocol are described in this paper. The Formal Description Technique used is Numerical Petri Nets (NPN), an extension of Petri Nets. The verification technique used is reachability analysis. The behaviour of the protocol is analysed using an automated analysis tool, PROTEAN, developed at Telecom Australia.

1. INTRODUCTION

ISO DIS 8571 [6] defines a file transfer service and protocol, File Transfer, Access and Management (FTAM) [8]. It provides sufficient facilities to support file transfer, and establishes a framework for access and file management. It controls the transfer of whole files or parts of files between end-systems. File manipulation facilities are also included for setting and changing file attributes and for creating and deleting files.

The protocol is available within the application layer [1] of the reference model [4]. The service defined is of the category "Specific Application Service Element". It is supported by Common Application Service Element (CASE) [5], presentation layer and session layer.

The Formal Description Technique (FDT), Numerical Petri Nets(NPNs), an extension of Petri Nets is used for the formal specification of FTAM. The nets were then analysed using an automated tool, PROTEAN. This paper describes the results of verifying the Draft International Standard (DIS) FTAM Basic Protocol against the deadlock freeness property.

2. FTAM SERVICES AND PROTOCOLS

FTAM supports two services: Reliable File Service (RFS) and User Correctable File Service (UCFS). For RFS, the user states its quality of service requirements, but has no awareness of error recovery, delegating such considerations to the service provider.

For UCFS, the user has primitives available for error recovery and transfer management. Users have the ability to choose from amongst a number of styles of error management, depending on the application's requirements.

Two protocols were specified in [6]. They are the basic protocol, which supports the UCFS and the error recovery protocol which supports the RFS.

3. BASIC PROTOCOL

The basic protocol, sub-divided into basic file protocol and bulk data transfer protocol, supports the following functions:

a) representation of the UCFS primitives as a sequence of Protocol Data Units (PDUs) for transmission by the CASE and presentation services;

b) grouping, when appropriate, of the representations of logically separate service primitives as distinct data values in a single request service primitive;

c) ensuring the progress of the protocol.

4. BASIC PROTOCOL MODEL

The operation of the protocol is modelled by the interaction of two file protocol machines (FPMs). The two FPMs communicate by means of the services available at their CASE boundary.

File service user "A" is the initiator and file service user "B" is the responder. A block diagram of this model is shown in figure 1.

5. NUMERICAL PETRI NETS

Numerical Petri Nets (NPNs) [12], originally developed by Symons [10], is one of the many extensions of Petri nets [9].

NPNs consist of the following extensions added to Petri Nets :

a) Tokens can have attributes of several types;

b) The association of global variables with the net;

c) The transition enabling conditions refer not only to the tokens in the input places but also to the global variables;

d) The firing of a transition not only removes tokens from the input places and insert tokens into the output places but it may change the values of the global variables.

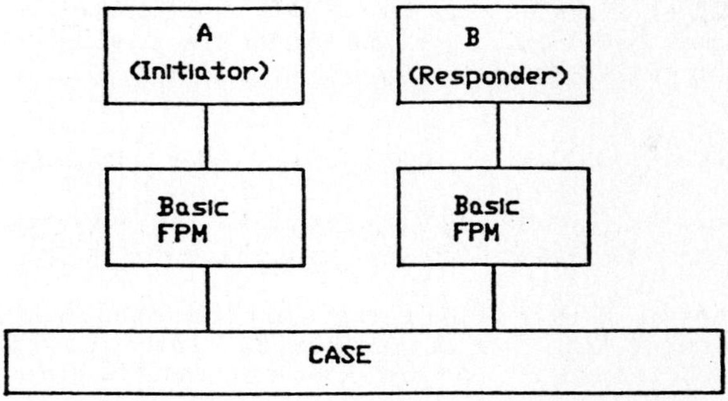

Figure 1. Basic Protocol Model

6. MODELLING OF BASIC PROTOCOL

The NPNs are viewed as modelling the operation of the Basic Protocol Machine. Each service provided by the machine is specified via a separate net. Hence, places represent ports through which data are sent/received and global variables represent states [2]. Predicates are used to govern the conditions of the transition firings.

The model mainly uses 12 places. Their meanings are as followings :

Place	Description
ucfsA	UCFS user of initiator
ucfsinA	Input port for UCFS provider of initiator
Apduout	PDU output port for UCFS provider of initiator
caseA	Input port for CASE provider of initiator
Bpsduin	PSDU input port for UCFS provider of responder
Bpduin	PDU input port for UCFS provider of responder
ucfsB	UCFS user of responder
ucfsinB	Input port for UCFS provider of responder
Bpduout	PDU output port for UCFS provider of responder
caseB	Input port for CASE provider of responder
Apsduin	PSDU input port for UCFS provider of initiator
Apduin	PDU input port for UCFS provider of initiator

where PDU means Protocol Data Unit,
and PSDU means Presentation Service Data Unit.

The Annex of [6] forms an integral part of that standard. In the event of a discrepancy becoming apparent in the protocol described in the body of the standard and the protocol described in the Annex, the Annex is to take precedence. These NPN specifications were based on the Annex as the definitive specifications.

Wherever possible, nomenclature used in the Annex is followed.

The modelling of the services provided by the Basic protocol is given in [7]. To illustrate how this is done, the formal specification of the FTAM regime establishment is described here.

6.1 Informal Specification of FTAM Regime Establishment

a) Initiator - On receiving an F-INITIALIZE request service primitive from the UCFS user while in an "closed" state, the entity shall:

i) construct an F-INITIALIZE request PDU, then ADD the PDU constructed on an A-ASSOCIATE request, and enter the "initialize pd" state, if the F-INITIALIZE request primitive is acceptable, otherwise;

ii) issue a F-INITIALIZE confirm primitive with a result more severe than a warning to the UCFS user and thereafter cease to exist.

b) Responder - On receiving an F-INITIALIZE request PDU on A-ASSOCIATE indication while in an "closed" state, the entity shall :

i) issue an F-INITIALIZE response PDU indicating an error and thereafter cease to exist if the entity is incapable of establishing FTAM regime, otherwise;

ii) issue an F-INITIALIZE indication primitive to the UCFS user and thereafter enter the state "f initialize pd".

c) Responder - On receiving an F-INITIALIZE response service primitive from the UCFS user while in an "f initialize pd" state, the entity shall construct an F-INITIALIZE response PDU and send it on an A-ASSOCIATE response. If there is no indication of failure in the F-INITIALIZE response, it enters the state "initialized"; otherwise it ceases to exist.

d) Initiator - On receiving an F-INITIALIZE response PDU on an A-ASSOCIATE confirm while in the state "initialize pd", the entity shall issue an F-INITIALIZE confirm service primitive to the UCFS user and enter the state "initialized" if the PDU indicates success; otherwise issue one indicating failure and thereafter cease to exist.

6.2 Formal Specification of FTAM Regime Establishment

There are 16 transitions which are described in table 1. No additional variables and predicates are required. The NPN diagram is shown in figure 2.

The specifications in section 6.1 are modelled as follows :

Specification	Modelling Transitions
6.1.a	Finirq
6.1.a.i	Ainirq,Aassrq
6.1.a.ii	np1Finirq
6.1.b	Bassin,Binirq
6.1.b.i	np5Binirp
6.1.b.ii	Finiin
6.1.c	Finirp,Binirp,Bassrp,np3Bassrp
6.1.d	Aasscf,Ainirp,Finicf,np2Finicf

7. VERIFICATION TECHNIQUE

The verification method used is reachability analysis [11]. The total system is analysed by considering every possible sequence and thus every possible state of the total system from given initial conditions. In Petri Nets, the relationship between states is given by the Reachability Graph (RG). The main problem with RG is that it gets very big and unmanageable as the complexity of the system modelled increases, and thus very tedious.

8. PROTOCOL VERIFICATION TOOL

The automated tool to verify the FTAM protocol was developed at Telecom Australia. It is called the PROTocol Emulation and ANalysis or PROTEAN. There are graphics facilities for display of nets and reachability graphs.

PROTEAN is a menu-driven system, with on-line help and simple error messages. It has two parts. The first is the NPN Analyzer Program, which handles the NPNs and the generation of the reachability set. The second is a collection of programs which helps the user detect maloperations in the protocol using the results from the first stage.

A detailed description of PROTEAN is given in [3].

9. VERIFICATION RESULTS

Due to the complexity of the protocol, the verification was done in three parts : basic file protocol, bulk data transfer protocol and basic file protocol under grouping control.

References are made in this section to predicates and actions defined in the ISO 8571/4 FTAM DIS Annex.

9.1 Basic File Protocol

The RG revealed that there are 2 deadlocks.

Deadlock 1 :

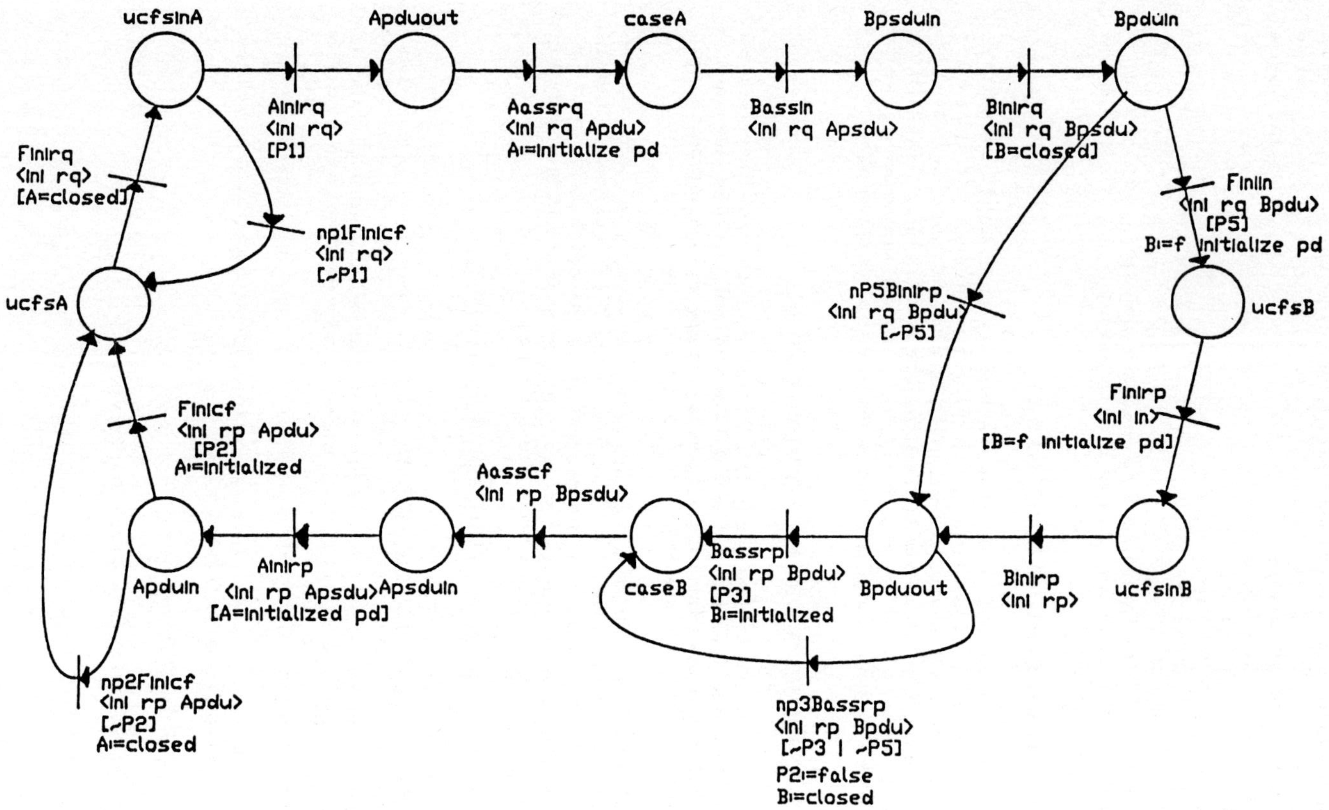

NPN for FTAM Regime Establishment

Figure 2.

This happens after an Open response PDU has been received by the initiator whenever P4 is true. The initiator enters the state "selected" after issuing a F-open confirm primitive. The F-read or F-write request can not be issued as it requires the initiator to be in state "dxfridle".

Deadlock 2 :

This happens after an Open response PDU has been received by the initiator when P4 is false, and P10 and P11 are true. It enters the state "p altin pd", waiting to receive an P-alter-context indication primitive. But the responder does not issue an P-alter-context request primitive under such conditions.

On page 110 of part 4 of [6], it reads as follows :

```
14:   P4            F-OPNCF[8] => SELECTED
     P4 & ~P10:    F-OPNCF => DXFRIDLE
     ~P4 & P10:    [15] => P-ALTIN-PD
```

If it were to read as follows,

```
14:   ~P4           F-OPNCF[8] => SELECTED
     P4 & ~P10:    F-OPNCF => DXFRIDLE
     P4 & P10:     [15] => P-ALTIN-PD
```

and the model was verified again, deadlock 1 and 2 disappeared. It seemed that the deadlocks were caused by typographical errors in the specifications rather than design problem in the protocol.

9.2 Bulk Data Transfer Protocol

There were 3 deadlocks uncovered in this part.

Deadlock 1 :

This happens after the F-write PDU has been received by the responder which subsequently enters state "wrt-symin-pd". When a P-sync-minor indication is received by the responder, it does not issued a P-sync-minor response primitive; whereas the initiator is waiting for a P-sync-minor confirm primitive to proceed further; and hence there is a deadlock.

On page 124 of part 4 of [6], it reads :

```
31:          [49],[27] => WRITE
```

If it were to read as :

```
31:          [49],[27],PSYMRP => WRITE
```

and the model was verified again, the deadlock disappeared.

Deadlock 2 :

It happens after a P-sync-minor response primitive has been issued by the initiator and it enters the state "read", while the responder is in state "rea symcf pd". The responder then receives a Restart request PDU which causes it to change state to "f rrestart pd". It subsequently never returns to a state in which P-sync-minor confirm primitive can be received.

The same situation happens when the responder receives a Cancel Data request PDU while in state "rea symcf pd".

The RG reveals them as deadlocks. However, the protocol can still progress under these conditions. These appear more likely to be protocol errors (as specified in 6.1 of part 4 of [6]) rather than deadlocks.

Deadlock 3 :

It happens when a Cancel data request PDU is received by the responder while in states in which the responder is also capable of receiving F-cancel request from the user. An F-cancel indication is issued to the user and the state is changed to "f cancel pd". However, because the F-cancel request has been received, the state is changed to "cancel pd". The F-cancel response primitive cannot be received from the user as it requires the state to be "f cancel pd", and hence there is a deadlock.

This problem happens vice versa at the initiator's side.

This reveals a concurrency problem when two events are allowed to happen at the same time.

9.3 Basic File Protocol under Grouping Control

There are 3 deadlocks uncovered in this part of verification.

Deadlock 1 :

It happens when a grouped PDU is being processed by the responder. The responder is in state "initialized", "selected", "dxfridle" or "dxfridle rec" to receive a grouped PDU. It enters state "f group pd" after the last PDU has been processed. During this period, the responder is capable of receiving other PDUs. This is where things can go wrong.

In the text of the FTAM standard, it requires the responder to enter state "grouping requests" and the initiator to enter state "grouping responses" immediately after Begin-group PDU has been processed. Such deadlocks disappear when the text specifications are followed instead of the Annex. This shows an inconsistency problem between the text and the Annex, leading to a deadlock, if the Annex takes precedence.

Deadlock 2 :

This is caused by the processing of the F-end-group response primitive by the responder. There were no specifications for predicates P17 and P19 being false. The responder then remains at state "grouping" and, hence, no other request PDU can be received by the responder thereafter.

On page 114 of part 4 of [6], it reads :

```
33:             [39],
     P17:       => INITIALIZED
     P19:       [10],
     ~P11:      => DXFRIDLE
     P11:       P-ALTRQ => P-ALTCF-PD
```

If it were to read as follows :

```
33:             [39],
     P17:       => INITIALIZED
     ~P17:      => SELECTED
     P19:       [10],
     ~P11:      => DXFRIDLE
     P11:       P-ALTRQ => P-ALTCF-PD
     ~(P17&P19): => SELECTED
```

and the model was verified again, the deadlock disappeared.

Deadlock 3 :

This is caused by the processing of End-group response at the initiator's side. It is required to issue a confirm primitive to the user for each of the PDUs (statment 37). On condition that P19 & P10 are true, it enters the state "p altin pd". However, on receiving a P-alter-context indication primitive, an F-open confirm primitive cannot be issued as it has already been issued.

The text specification does require the Open response PDU to be reserved for further processing. This is another example of inconsistency between the text and the Annex.

10. CONCLUSIONS

The ISO DIS FTAM basic protocol has been analysed against the deadlock freeness property. A number of inconsistencies, which produced deadlocks in the NPNs model, have been found in the FTAM DIS. These problems have been communicated to the ISO FTAM group. They should not be present in the FTAM international standard.

The most tedious part of the work was in analysing the RG. The RG was very big for the Bulk Data Transfer protocol. The analysis was made practical by the use of PROTEAN which is found to be an useful tool. However, there are also limitations in PROTEAN. The capabilities of PROTEAN will be improved in future developments [3].

The major part of the work was in the formal specification and analysing the RG. The running of the PROTEAN tool requires minimal effort. With the uses of systematic protocol engineering methods and automated tool, we have shown the analysis of a complex communication protocol, like FTAM, is feasible.

ACKNOWLEDGEMENTS

We want to thank Telecom Australia Research Laboratories for the use of their PROTEAN software, and the staff there for their helpful comments, in particular, J. Billington.

REFERENCES

1. P.D. Bartoli, "The Application Layer of the Reference Model of Open Systems Interconnection", Proceedings of the IEEE, vol. 71, no. 12, pp. 1404-1407, December, 1983.

2. J. Billington, "Specification of the Transport Service using Numerical Petri Nets", Second International Workshop on Protocol Specification, Testing and Verification, ed. C. Sunshine, IFIP, Idyllwild, California, May, 1982.

3. J. Billington, G.R. Wheeler and M.C. Wilbur-Ham, "PROTEAN: A High-level Petri Net Tool for the Specification and Verification of Communication Protocols", IEEE Transactions on Software Engineering, Vol. 14, No. 3, March 1988.

4. J.D. Day, and H. Zimmerman, "The OSI Reference Model", Proceedings of the IEEE, vol. 71, no. 12, pp. 1334-1340, IEEE, December, 1983.

5. ISO DIS 8649, "Information Processing Systems - Open Systems Interconnection - Common Application Service Elements (CASE)"

6. ISO DIS 8571, "Information Processing Systems - Open Systems Interconnection - File Transfer Access and Management - Parts 1,2,3 and 4", Draft International Standard, ANSI, New York, 1986.

7. R. Lai, "Formal Specification and Verification of ISO FTAM Protocol", Draft PhD Thesis, Department of Computer Science, La Trobe University, Australia, 1989.

8. D. Lewan and H.G. Long, "The OSI File Service", Proceedings of IEEE, Vol. 71, no. 12, pp. 1414-1419, December, 1983.

9. J.L. Peterson, Petri Nets Theory and the Modelling of Systems, Prentice-Hall, Englewood Cliffs, N.J., 1981.

10. F.J.W. Symons, "Modelling and Analysis of Communication Protocols using Numerical Petri Nets" PhD Thesis, Department of Electrical Engineering Science and Telecommunications, University of Essex, May, 1978.

11. S.T. Vuong and D.D. Cowan, "Reachability Analysis of Protocols with FIFO Channels", SIGCOM'83 Symposium, Communications Architectures and Protocols, ACM, pp. 49-57, March, 1983.

12. G.R. Wheeler, "Numerical Petri Nets - A Definition", Telecom Australia Research Laboratories Report 7780, Telecom Australia Research Laboratories, May, 1985.

Transition	Description of Event	Input/ Output Place	Input/ Output Token	Transition Condition/ Operation
Finirq	F-initialize request primitive issued by ucfs user	ucfsA/ ucfsinA	ini rq/ ini rq	A=closed
np1Finicf	F-initialize confirm primitive issued to ucfs initiator on condition P1 is false	ucfsinA/ ucfsA	ini rq/ ini cf	˜P1
Ainirq	Addition of Initialize request PDU to PSDU by ucfs provider of initiator	ucfsinA/ Apduout	ini rq/ ini rq Apdu	P1
Aassrq	A-assoicate request primitive issued by ucfs provider of initiator	Apduout/ caseA	ini rq Apdu/ ini rq Apsdu	/ A:=initialize pd
Bassin	A-assoicate indication primitive issued to ucfs provider of responder	caseA/ Bpsduin	ini rq Apsdu/ ini rq Bpsdu	
Binirq	Receipt of Initialize request PDU by ucfs provider of responder	Bpsudin/ Bpduin	ini rq Bpsdu/ ini rq Bpdu	B=closed
Finiin	F-initialize indication primitive issued to responder	Bpduin/ ucfsB	ini rq Bpdu/ ini in	P5/ B:=f initialize pd
Finirp	F-initialize response primitive issued by responder	ucfsB/ ucfsinB	ini in/ ini rp	B=f initialize pd
Binirp	Addition of Initialize response PDU to PSDU by ucfs provider of responder	ucfsinB/ Bpduout	ini rp/ ini rp Bpdu	
np5Binirp	Addition of Initialize response PDU to PSDU by ucfs provider of responder on condition P5 is false	Bpduin/ Bpduout	ini rq Bpdu/ ini rp Bpdu	˜P5/ P2:=false

Bassrp	A-associate response primitive issued by ucfs provider of responder	Bpduin/ caseB	ini rp Bpdu/ ini rp Bpsdu	P3/ B:=initialized
np3Bassrp	A-assoicate response primitive issued by ucfs provider of responder on condition P3 is false	Bpduin/ caseB	ini rp Bpdu/ ini rp Bpsdu	˜P3 | ˜P5/ B:=closed; P2:=false
Aasscf	A-assoicate confirm primitive issued to ucfs provider of initiator	caseB/ Apsduin	ini rp Bpsdu/ ini rp Apsdu	
Ainirp	Receipt of Initialize response PDU by ucfs provider of initiator	Apsduin/ Apduin	ini rp Apsdu/ ini rp Apdu	A=initialize pd
Finicf	F-initialize confirm primitive issued to ucfs user	Apduin/ ucfsA	ini rp Apdu/ ini cf	P2/ A:=initialized
np2Finicf	F-initialize confirm primitive issued to ucfs user on condition P2 is false	Apduin/ ucfsA	ini rp Apdu/ ini cf	˜P2/ A:=closed

Description of NPN Specification of FTAM Regime Establishment

Table 1.

Protocol Specification, Testing, and Verification, IX
E. Brinksma, G. Scollo and C.A. Vissers (Editors)
Elsevier Science Publishers B.V. (North-Holland)

Automated Verification of Equivalence of Protocol Machines

Teruo Higashino+, Kiyoshi Ninomiya++, Tomohisa Kimoto+,
Ken'ichi Taniguchi+ and Masaaki Mori+++

\+ Dept. of Information and Computer Sciences, Faculty of Engineering Science,
Osaka University, Toyonaka, Osaka 560, Japan
++ Information Systems Division, Daikin Industries Ltd., Kitaku, Osaka 530, Japan
+++ Dept. of Management Science, Faculty of Economics,
Shiga University, Hikone, Shiga 522, Japan

ABSTRACT

A protocol machine is described as an automaton with a finite state control and a finite number of registers whose values are integers. We define that two protocol machines M1 and M2 are equivalent if and only if the output sequences of M1 and M2 are the same for any input sequence. M1 and M2 are equivalent if, for some predicate Ψ which represents a relation between the states and the values of the registers of M1 and M2, (A)Ψ is an invariant and (B)for any reachable states of M1 and M2, any values of the registers satisfying Ψ at those states and any input, M1 and M2 emit the same outputs. We have developed a program for verifying that (A) and (B) hold for given M1, M2 and Ψ. Our program prints out the useful information to succeed in the proof of the equivalence of given protocol machines even if the proof of the equivalence failed. Using this program, we proved that two machines of HDLC procedures are equivalent.

1. Introduction

In this paper, an abstract model of a protocol machine is introduced and a technique to mechanically prove the equivalence of protocol machines is proposed. Verification examples are also illustrated.

An abstract model of a protocol machine is an automaton with a finite state control and a finite number of registers whose values are integers. For example, suppose that a protocol machine transmits a data received from the upper layer to another protocol machine. In this case, the transmission action is regarded as an input symbol, say "T", and the binary representation of the data received from the upper layer, say "d", is regarded as its parameter. The automaton reads T(d) as an input, and then emits the received data "d" as an output to another protocol machine. The registers are used to hold the data for the retransmission and the sequence number, and so on, where each data and sequence number are treated as integers. The automaton is defined as a *Mealy machine*. That is, the next state, the next values of the registers and the output are determined depending on the current state, the current values of the registers and the current input. To determine the next state, the next values of the registers and the output, the automaton only uses the operators "+, -, =, <, ≤, ≥, >, and, or, ⊃, not". Hence, the next values of the registers and the output must be defined as the linear combinations of the current values of the registers and the values of the input parameters. This model is powerful enough to specify protocol machines formally. In Section 2, we introduce the automaton and explain its moves.

In Section 3, we define the equivalence of protocol machines formally. We regard a sequence of actions as an input sequence, and we define that two protocol machines are equivalent if and only if the output sequences of the protocol machines are the same for any input sequence. If two protocol machines are equivalent, the protocol machines are interchangeable. Otherwise, some troubles may arise such that a replaced protocol machine cannot communicate with the protocol machine with which the original protocol machine can communicate. Theoretically and also practically, it is an interesting problem to decide whether given protocol machines are equivalent or not. Several notions of equivalences for communicating processes such as observational equivalence and the algorithms for verifying their equivalences have been studied [1]-[6]. But, so far, few methods to prove the equivalence of output sequences of protocol machines have been reported.

In general, it is undecidable whether two protocol machines are equivalent or not. Therefore, in Section 4, we give a sufficient condition for two protocol machines to be equivalent, and also, we propose a procedure to verify that given two protocol machines satisfy this sufficient condition.

In this paper, a predicate which is a logical combination of some linear inequalities on integers is called a *P-sentence* (see Section 2). The sufficient condition for M1 and M2 to be equivalent is that for some P-sentence $\Psi(q,r,\mathbf{x_n},\mathbf{z_m})$ where q and r are variables representing the states of two protocol machines M1 and M2, respectively, and $\mathbf{x_n}$ and $\mathbf{z_m}$ are variables representing the values of the registers of M1 and M2, respectively, the following conditions (A) and (B) hold:

(A) Ψ is an invariant, that is, $\Psi(s,t,\mathbf{u_n},\mathbf{v_m})$ is true for any reachable states s, t and values $\mathbf{u_n}$, $\mathbf{v_m}$ of the registers.

(B) For any reachable states s and t, any values[1] of the registers satisfying Ψ at states s and t, and any input, M1 and M2 emit the same outputs.

In this paper, we prove the equivalence of the protocol machines M1 and M2 using the following method:

(1) A verifier (the person who wants to prove the equivalence of M1 and M2) chooses a P-sentence Ψ.

(2) For M1, M2 and Ψ, verify that above conditions (A) and (B) hold.

(3) If the verification of (2) succeeds, then M1 and M2 are equivalent. Otherwise, find another P-sentence Ψ', and carry out (2) and (3) again. If the verification of (2) fails for several times, terminate this process. This means that the proof of the equivalence of M1 and M2 fails but not that M1 and M2 are not equivalent.

Since Ψ is described as a P-sentence, and since the next values of the registers and the outputs are described as the linear combinations of the current values of the registers and the values of the input parameters, the verification of (2) can be carried out mechanically for given M1, M2 and Ψ.

In Section 4, a procedure is presented for verifying that M1, M2 and Ψ satisfy the sufficient conditions (A) and (B). This procedure checks whether several integer linear programming problems have no integer solution. In Section 5, a program which implements the procedure is explained and the verification procedure is illustrated. Even if the verification of (2) failed, our program prints out the useful information about what P-sentence Ψ should be used in order to succeed in the verification of (2). In Section 6, we explain the result of the proof that two protocol machines corresponding to the secondary stations of HDLC procedure [9] are equivalent.

2. Protocol Machine Model

In this section, we define an abstract model of a protocol machine which we will consider throughout this paper.

[*Definition 2.1*]

A term which consists of integers, variables whose values are integers and operators "+" and "-" is called a P-term. []

Since we abbreviate "$x+x$" as "$2x$" in this paper, a P-term with variables $x_1,x_2,\ldots,x_n$ is described as a linear combination "$a_0+a_1x_1+a_2x_2+\ldots+a_nx_n$" where a_0, a_1, ... and a_n are constant integers (a P-term with no variables is reduced to a single integer a_0).

[*Definition 2.2*]

A P-sentence is defined inductively as follows:

(A) If t and s are P-terms, then $t=s$, $t<s$, $t\leq s$, $t\geq s$ and $t>s$ are P-sentences.

(B) If α and β are P-sentences, then "(α) and (β)", "(α) or (β)", "(α) $\supset$ (β)" and "not(α)" are also P-sentences. []

For example, "$3x+2y$" is a P-term, and "($x\geq y+2$) and ($y=z-1$)" is a P-sentence. The semantics (values) of P-sentences with no variables are defined using the usual semantics of the operators "+, -, =, <, ≤, ≥, >, and, or, ⊃, not". For example, the value of the P-sentence "($3+5\leq 10$) or ($7=2$)" is true.

In this paper, we describe a protocol machine as an automaton with a finite state control and a finite number of registers whose values are integers. The automaton is a *Mealy machine*. The names of the actions of a protocol machine such as "the transmission of a packet", "the reception of a packet" and "the

---

[1] In general, for reachable states s and t, there exist some unreachable values $\mathbf{u_n}$ and $\mathbf{v_m}$ of the registers such that $\Psi(s,t,\mathbf{u_n},\mathbf{v_m})$ is true. Condition (B) requires that the outputs of M1 and M2 must be the same even for such unreachable values of the registers.

reception of a control signal from the timer" are treated as the *input symbols* of this automaton. The number of the input symbols is finite. Each input symbol may have a finite number of parameters called *input parameters*. The values of the input parameters are integers. The pair of an input symbol and its parameters are treated as the *input* to the automaton. If "A" is an input symbol and $p_1,p_2,...,p_j$ are the values of its input parameters, then the input is denoted as $A(p_1,p_2,...,p_j)$. For each input symbol "A", let $|A|$ denote the number "j" of its parameters. Let n and d be constant positive integers. The constant n means the number of the registers. The outputs of the automaton are represented as d-tuples $[e_1,e_2,...,e_d]$ of integers. For each automaton, the constants n and d must be specified.

For example, suppose that whenever a protocol machine receives a packet from another protocol machine, it delivers the packet to the upper layer and it sends a reset signal to the timer. In this case, we consider that (1)the reception action is an input symbol, (2)the packet received is its parameter and (3)if the constant d is 3, then the output is the 3-tuple $[e_1,e_2,e_3]$ corresponding to the triplet of "the packet delivered to the upper layer", "the reset signal to the timer" and "the null string to another protocol machine (since there is no data transmitted to another protocol machine by the reception action)".

A protocol machine is described as a directed graph called a *transition diagram*. The directed graph illustrated in Fig. 1 is an example of the transition diagram. The vertices in the transition diagram correspond to the states of the automaton. The edges in the transition diagram represent the transitions of the automaton. Each edge in the transition diagram is labeled. The next state, the next values of the registers and the output are determined depending on the current state, the current values of the registers and the current input. The label of each edge $s \to s'$ is represented by the 4-tuple $\langle A,c(\boldsymbol{x_n},\boldsymbol{y_j}),\delta(\boldsymbol{x_n},\boldsymbol{y_j}),\rho(\boldsymbol{x_n},\boldsymbol{y_j})\rangle$ where $\boldsymbol{x_n}$ and $\boldsymbol{y_j}$ represent the variables $x_1,x_2,...,x_n$ and $y_1,y_2,...,y_j$, respectively, and the first component "A" is an input symbol. The variables $\boldsymbol{x_n}$ represent the current values of the registers and the variables $\boldsymbol{y_j}$ represent the values of the input parameters for "A". The constant n is the number of the registers and $j=|A|$ holds. The second component $c(\boldsymbol{x_n},\boldsymbol{y_j})$ of the label is a P-sentence with variables $\boldsymbol{x_n}$ and $\boldsymbol{y_j}$. The third component $\delta(\boldsymbol{x_n},\boldsymbol{y_j})$ of the label is the n-tuple $[\delta_1(\boldsymbol{x_n},\boldsymbol{y_j}),\delta_2(\boldsymbol{x_n},\boldsymbol{y_j}),...,\delta_n(\boldsymbol{x_n},\boldsymbol{y_j})]$ where each $\delta_i(\boldsymbol{x_n},\boldsymbol{y_j})$ is a P-term with variables $\boldsymbol{x_n}$ and $\boldsymbol{y_j}$ and the n-tuple $\delta(\boldsymbol{x_n},\boldsymbol{y_j})$ is used to specify the values of the registers after the transition specified by the edge. The fourth component $\rho(\boldsymbol{x_n},\boldsymbol{y_j})$ of the label is the d-tuple $[\rho_1(\boldsymbol{x_n},\boldsymbol{y_j}),\rho_2(\boldsymbol{x_n},\boldsymbol{y_j}),...,\rho_d(\boldsymbol{x_n},\boldsymbol{y_j})]$ where each $\rho_i(\boldsymbol{x_n},\boldsymbol{y_j})$ is a P-term with variables $\boldsymbol{x_n}$ and $\boldsymbol{y_j}$ and the d-tuple $\rho(\boldsymbol{x_n},\boldsymbol{y_j})$ is used to specify the output of the transition. There may exist two or more edges $s \to s'$ and $s \to s''$ whose labels are $\langle A,c_1(\boldsymbol{x_n},\boldsymbol{y_j}),\delta_1(\boldsymbol{x_n},\boldsymbol{y_j}),\rho_1(\boldsymbol{x_n},\boldsymbol{y_j})\rangle$ and $\langle A,c_2(\boldsymbol{x_n},\boldsymbol{y_j}),\delta_2(\boldsymbol{x_n},\boldsymbol{y_j}),\rho_2(\boldsymbol{x_n},\boldsymbol{y_j})\rangle$, respectively. If there exist such edges, it is assumed that "$\sim\exists \boldsymbol{x_n},\boldsymbol{y_j}[c_1(\boldsymbol{x_n},\boldsymbol{y_j})$ and $c_2(\boldsymbol{x_n},\boldsymbol{y_j})]$" is true.

Let s and $\mathbf{v_n}$ be the current state and the current values of the registers, respectively. Let $A(\mathbf{p_j})$ be the current input to the automaton. If (1)there is an edge $s \to s'$ in the transition diagram whose label is $\langle A,c(\boldsymbol{x_n},\boldsymbol{y_j}),\delta(\boldsymbol{x_n},\boldsymbol{y_j}),\rho(\boldsymbol{x_n},\boldsymbol{y_j})\rangle$ and (2)the value of $c(\mathbf{v_n},\mathbf{p_j})$ is true where $c(\mathbf{v_n},\mathbf{p_j})$ is obtained by substituting the values $\mathbf{v_n}$ and $\mathbf{p_j}$ for the variables $\boldsymbol{x_n}$ and $\boldsymbol{y_j}$ in $c(\boldsymbol{x_n},\boldsymbol{y_j})$, then the protocol machine enters the state s' (s' is called the next state). As the output, the d-tuple $\rho(\mathbf{v_n},\mathbf{p_j})$ of integers is emitted. The values of the registers after the transition are given by the n-tuple $\delta(\mathbf{v_n},\mathbf{p_j})$ of integers ($\delta(\mathbf{v_n},\mathbf{p_j})$ is called the next values of the registers). For the automaton, the initial state and the initial values of the registers must be specified.

For the current state s, the current value $\mathbf{v_n}$ of the registers and the current input $A(\mathbf{p_j})$, if there is no edge $s \to s'$ with label $\langle A,c(\boldsymbol{x_n},\boldsymbol{y_j}),\delta(\boldsymbol{x_n},\boldsymbol{y_j}),\rho(\boldsymbol{x_n},\boldsymbol{y_j})\rangle$ such that $c(\mathbf{v_n},\mathbf{p_j})$ is true, then the next state, the next values of the registers and the output are undefined. Note that, in our model, the output is defined if and only if the next state is defined.

[*Example 2.1*]

The directed graph illustrated in Fig. 1 is the transition diagram for a protocol machine named M1. M1 is a simplified model of the sender which communicates using BSC procedure [8]. M1 has four states s_1, s_2, s_3 and s_4. State s_1 denotes the situation where (1)M1 starts the transition at this state or (2)M1 has received the *ack* signal and it can transmit a new packet. State s_2 denotes the situation where M1 has already transmitted a packet and it is waiting for receiving the *ack* or *nak* signal. State s_3 denotes the situation where M1 has received the *nak* signal and it must retransmit the *latest packet*. State s_4 is the final state. M1 has two registers R1 and R2. Register R1 is used to hold the number of transmission and R2 is used to hold the latest packet. The initial values of the registers R1 and R2 are both 0's. There are three input symbols

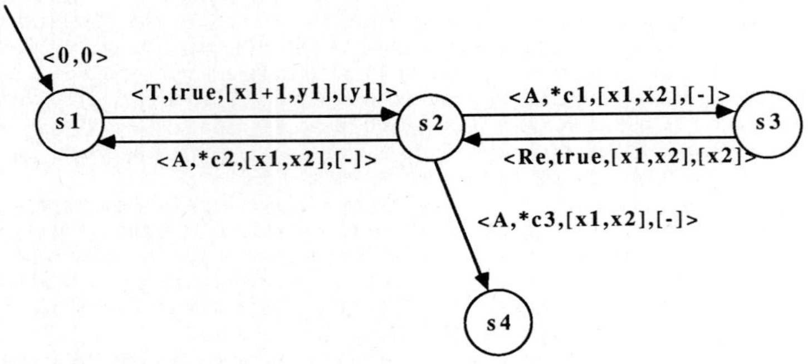

(Here, |T|=1, |Re|=0 and |A|=1 hold.
The variables x1 and x2 represent the values of R1 and R2, respectively.
The variable y1 represents the value of a parameter for T (or A).
The initial state is s1.
The initial values of R1 and R2 are <0,0>.
Abbreviations :
*c1 = (y1=0)
*c2 = ((x1<10) and (y1=1))
*c3 = ((x1=10) and (y1=1)))

Fig. 1 Protocol Machine M1

"T", "Re" and "A" which denote the transmission, retransmission and reception, respectively. The input symbol T has one input parameter and $T(p_1)$ denotes the transmission of the packet whose binary representation is equal to the integer p_1. The input symbol A has also one input parameter. A(1) and A(0) denote the reception of the *ack* and *nak* signals, respectively. The output of M1 is the 1-tuple $[e_1]$ where e_1 is equal to the binary representation of the packet transmitted to the receiver. M1 emits no output if the fourth component of the label is [-]. M1 starts to transmit a packet at the initial state s_1. M1 transmits a new packet if M1 has received the *ack* signal. M1 retransmits the latest packet if M1 receives the *nak* signal. M1 reaches the final state s_4 and halts when M1 has transmitted ten new packets and it receives the *ack* signal. []

Let s_1 and $[v_1,v_2]$ be the current state and the current values of the registers R1 and R2, respectively. Let $T(p_1)$ be the current input to M1. There exists an edge $s_1 \rightarrow s_2$ whose label is $<T,true,[x_1+1,y_1],[y_1]>$. Since the second component of the label is "true", the transition specified by this label is executed regardless of the values of v_1, v_2 and p_1. The next state is s_2. According to the third component $[x_1+1,y_1]$ of the label, the next values of the registers R1 and R2 are modified to v_1+1 and p_1, respectively. And the value "p_1" of the input parameter is transmitted to the receiver according to the fourth component $[y_1]$ of the label.

Suppose that M1 is in state s_2 and input symbol A is applied. In this case, there are three edges $s_2 \rightarrow s_3$, $s_2 \rightarrow s_1$ and $s_2 \rightarrow s_4$ from state s_2 where the first components of these edge labels are A's. Let $[v_1,v_2]$ be the current values of the register R1 and R2, and let p_1 be the parameter for A. If v_1, v_2 and p_1 satisfy the second component *c1 of the label of edge $s_2 \rightarrow s_3$, that is, if "$p_1=0$" is true, then the next state is s_3, and the next values of R1 and R2 are v_1 and v_2, respectively. M1 emits no output for this transition. If v_1, v_2 and p_1 satisfy the second component *c2 (or *c3) of the label of edge $s_2 \rightarrow s_1$ (or $s_2 \rightarrow s_4$), then the next state is s_1 (or s_4). If v_1, v_2 and p_1 do not satisfy the disjunction (*c1 or *c2 or *c3) of the three conditions *c1, *c2 and *c3, then the next state is undefined.

3. Equivalence of protocol machines

In order to define the equivalence of protocol machines, we transform a given transition diagram into another transition diagram called *C-transition diagram* ("*C*" means *Completely specified*).

A C-transition diagram is constructed from the original transition diagram by adding a new state s_0 called

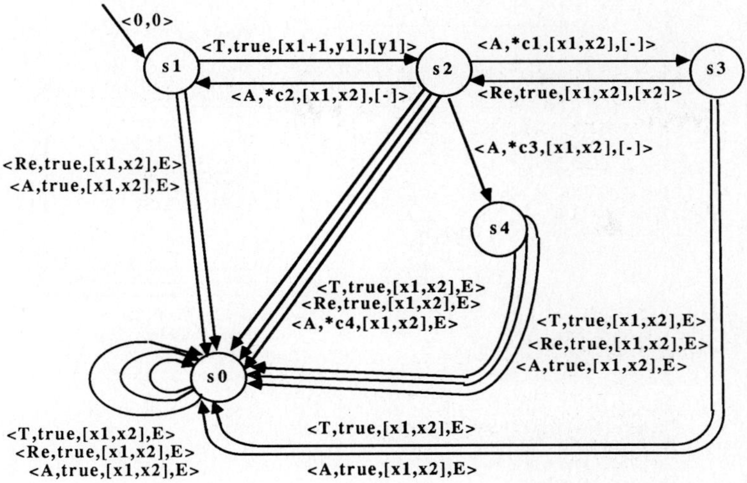

(Here, state s0 is the error state.
E is a special value for the output.
Abbreviation :
*c4 = not(*c1 or *c2 or *c3))

Fig. 2 C-transition Diagram for Protocol Machine M1

the *error state* and some edges to state s_0. In general, the transitions are not defined completely in a transition diagram. That is, the next state, the next values of the registers and the output may be undefined for the current state s, the current values $\mathbf{v_n}$ of the registers and the current input $A(\mathbf{p_j})$. In the corresponding C-transition diagram, the new transitions are introduced for such s, $\mathbf{v_n}$ and $A(\mathbf{p_j})$ as follows:

(1)The next state is the error state s_0.

(2)The next values of the registers are the same as the current values $\mathbf{v_n}$.

(3)The output is a special value "E" where E denotes a d-tuple of integers not used in the original protocol machine.

If a protocol machine has entered the error state s_0, the state of the protocol machine is permanently the error state s_0, and the values of the registers are not changed. The output is always "E" for any transition.

In a C-transition diagram, the transitions are defined completely for any state, any values of the registers and any input.

For example, the directed graph in Fig. 2 is the C-transition diagram corresponding to the transition diagram in Fig. 1. Let s_2 and $[v_1,v_2]$ be the current state and the current values of the registers R1 and R2, respectively. Let $A(p_1)$ be the current input to M1. If v_1, v_2 and p_1 do not satisfy the disjunction (*c1 or *c2 or *c3) of the conditions *c1, *c2 and *c3 in Fig. 1, then the next state is undefined. Then, the new edge $s_2 \rightarrow s_0$ is added to the C-transition diagram in Fig. 2 whose label is <A,not(*c1 or *c2 or *c3), $[x_1,x_2]$,E>.

In this paper, protocol machines whose transitions are described as C-transition diagrams are called the corresponding *C-protocol machines* for the original protocol machines. The corresponding C-protocol machine can be constructed mechanically from any original protocol machine.

Let $\alpha_1 \cdot \alpha_2 \cdots \alpha_k$ be an *input sequence* to the C-protocol machine M where each α_j is an input. If M reads α_i and emits β_i as the output, we say that $\beta_1 \cdot \beta_2 \cdots \beta_k$ is the *output sequence* for the input sequence $\alpha_1 \cdot \alpha_2 \cdots \alpha_k$. Let $\rho(M,\omega)$ denote the output sequence which has been emitted when M has read the input sequence ω. Let the outputs β_i and γ_i be the d-tuples $[\beta_{i1},\beta_{i2},\ldots,\beta_{id}]$ and $[\gamma_{i1},\gamma_{i2},\ldots,\gamma_{id}]$, respectively. We write $\beta_i=\gamma_i$ if

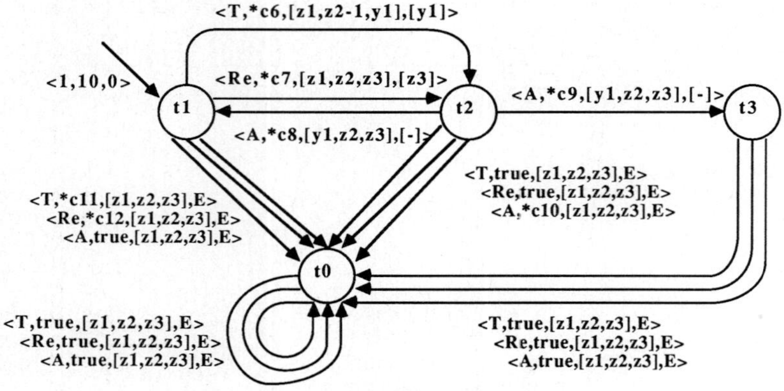

(Here, the variables z1, z2 and z3 represent the values of R'1, R'2 and R'3, respectively.
The variable y1 represents the value of a parameter for T (or A).
The initial state is t1.
The initial values of R'1, R'2 and R'3 are <1,10,0>.
State t0 is the error state.
E is a special value for the output.

Abbreviations :

*c6 = (z1=1)
*c7 = (z1=0)
*c8 = (((z2>0) and (y1=1)) or (y1=0))
*c9 = ((z2=0) and (y1=1))
*c10 = not(*c8 or *c9)
*c11 = not(*c6)
*c12 = not(*c7))

Fig. 3 C-transition Diagram for Protocol Machine M2

and only if all $\beta_{i1}=\gamma_{i1}$, $\beta_{i2}=\gamma_{i2}$,...and $\beta_{id}=\gamma_{id}$ hold. Let β and γ be the output sequences $\beta_1 \cdot \beta_2 \cdots \beta_k$ and $\gamma_1 \cdot \gamma_2 \cdots \gamma_k$, respectively. We write $\beta=\gamma$ if and only if all $\beta_1=\gamma_1$, $\beta_2=\gamma_2$, ... and $\beta_k=\gamma_k$ hold.

Let $\sigma(M,\omega)$ and $\delta(M,\omega)$ denote the state and the values of the registers, respectively, when the C-protocol machine M has read the input sequence ω from the initial state.

[*Definition 3.1*]

Let M1 and M2 be protocol machines such that the sets of the input symbols of M1 and M2 are the same and the outputs of M1 and M2 are both d-tuples of integers for some "d". We say that M1 and M2 are equivalent if and only if $\rho(M1',\omega)=\rho(M2',\omega)$ holds for any input sequence ω where M1' and M2' are the corresponding C-protocol machines for M1 and M2, respectively. []

Since a C-protocol machine can simulate any two-counter machine and a two-counter machine can simulate any Turing machine [7], *Proposition 3.1* follows.

[*Proposition 3.1*]

It is undecidable whether two protocol machines are equivalent or not. []

[*Example 3.1*]

Let M2 be a protocol machine communicating with the protocol machine M1 in *Example 2.1*. The C-transition diagram of M2 is illustrated in Fig. 3. State t_1 denotes the situation where (1)M2 starts the transition at this state, or (2)M2 can transmit or retransmit a packet at this state. State t_2 denotes the situation where M2 has already transmitted a packet and it is waiting for receiving the *ack* or *nak* signal. States t_3 and t_0 denote the final state and the error state, respectively. M2 has three registers R'1, R'2 and R'3. M2 transmits a new packet if M2 is in state t_1 and the value of the register R'1 is 1. M2 retransmits the latest packet if M2 is in state t_1 and the value of the register R'1 is 0. The register R'2 is used to hold "10-k" where "k" denotes the number of transmission. The register R'3 is used to hold the latest packet for the retransmission. []

In Section 4, we propose a technique for mechanical verification of the equivalence of protocol machines. To explain the idea of our technique, we use M1 and M2 whose C-transition diagrams are illustrated in Fig. 2 and Fig. 3 although it may be obvious that M1 and M2 are equivalent.

4. A Sufficient Condition for Equivalence

Let M1 and M2 be C-protocol machines such that the sets of the input symbols for M1 and M2 are the same and the outputs of M1 and M2 are both d-tuples of integers (note that for any input sequence ω, transitions of M1 and M2 are both defined). Let n and m be the numbers of the registers of M1 and M2, respectively. To simplify the formulation, we use integers for the names of the states of M1 and M2 from here on[1]. First, we give a sufficient condition for M1 and M2 to be equivalent.

[*Definition 4.1*]

The tuple $<\sigma(M1,\omega),\sigma(M2,\omega),\delta(M1,\omega),\delta(M2,\omega)>$ of the states and the values of the registers of M1 and M2 is called the *reachable VAL* for the input sequence ω. Let *Rvals*(M1,M2) denote the set of the reachable VAL's for all input sequences. That is,

Rvals(M1,M2)=$\{<\sigma(M1,\omega),\sigma(M2,\omega),\delta(M1,\omega),\delta(M2,\omega)> \mid \omega$ is an input sequence$\}$.

We also define the set of the reachable states as follows:

Rstates(M1,M2)=$\{<\sigma(M1,\omega),\sigma(M2,\omega)> \mid \omega$ is an input sequence$\}$ []

[*Definition 4.2*]

Let $\Psi(q,r,x_n,z_m)$ be a P-sentence where q and r are variables representing the states of M1 and M2, respectively, and x_n and z_m are variables representing the values of the registers of M1 and M2, respectively[2]. The P-sentence $\Psi(q,r,x_n,z_m)$ is an invariant for M1 and M2 if and only if the value of $\Psi(s,t,\mathbf{u_n},\mathbf{v_m})$ is true for any reachable VAL $<s,t,\mathbf{u_n},\mathbf{v_m}>$ in *Rvals*(M1,M2). []

In this section, a tuple $<s,t,\mathbf{u_n},\mathbf{v_m}>$ (where s and t are integers representing the states of M1 and M2, respectively, and $\mathbf{u_n}$ and $\mathbf{v_m}$ are the n-tuple and the m-tuple of integers, respectively) is called a VAL. If a VAL $<s,t,\mathbf{u_n},\mathbf{v_m}>$ is not a reachable VAL, the VAL is called an unreachable VAL. If the value of $\Psi(s,t,\mathbf{u_n},\mathbf{v_m})$ is true for a VAL $<s,t,\mathbf{u_n},\mathbf{v_m}>$, then we say that the VAL $<s,t,\mathbf{u_n},\mathbf{v_m}>$ satisfies the P-sentence Ψ. For an input sequence ω and an input α, $<\sigma(M1,\omega\cdot\alpha),\sigma(M2,\omega\cdot\alpha),\delta(M1,\omega\cdot\alpha), \delta(M2,\omega\cdot\alpha)>$ is called the *next VAL* for the reachable VAL $<\sigma(M1,\omega),\sigma(M2,\omega), \delta(M1,\omega),\delta(M2,\omega)>$ and the input α.

An edge pair is a pair of edges of M1 and M2 where the first components of these edge labels are the same. Let $s\to s'$ be an edge of M1 whose label is η. And let $t\to t'$ be an edge of M2 whose label is φ. Suppose that the first components of the labels η and φ are both A's. Then, the edge pair is denoted by $\{s\overset{\eta}{\to}s',t\overset{\varphi}{\to}t'\}$. If M1 has two edges whose first components of these labels are B's and M2 has three edges whose first components are B's in their C-transition diagrams, then there are six edge pairs where the first components of the labels of the edges in the edge pairs are both B's. For a given edge pair $\{s\overset{\eta}{\to}s',t\overset{\varphi}{\to}t'\}$, the pairs $<s,t>$ and $<s',t'>$ of the states are called a *current node pair* and a *next node pair*, respectively.

[*Proposition 4.1*]

Let $\Psi(q,r,x_n,z_m)$ be a P-sentence as in *Definition 4.2*. If the following two conditions (A) and (B) hold, then M1 and M2 are equivalent.

(A) The P-sentence $\Psi(q,r,x_n,z_m)$ is an invariant for M1 and M2.

(B) For any edge pair $\{s\overset{\eta}{\to}s',t\overset{\varphi}{\to}t'\}$ such that $<s,t>$ is in *Rstates*(M1,M2),

$$\forall x_n,y_j,z_m[\Psi(s,t,x_n,z_m) \text{ and } \{c1(x_n,y_j) \text{ and } c2(z_m,y_j)\} \supset \{\rho1(x_n,y_j)=\rho2(z_m,y_j)\}]$$

holds. Here, η is the 4-tuple $<A,c1(x_n,y_j),\delta1(x_n,y_j),\rho1(x_n,y_j)>$ and φ is the 4-tuple $<A,c2(z_m,y_j),\delta2(z_m,y_j),\rho2(z_m,y_j)>$.

(Proof) Let ω be an input sequence and suppose that the output sequences of M1 and M2 are the same for ω. Let $<s,t,\mathbf{u_n},\mathbf{v_m}>$ be the reachable VAL for ω (if ω is the null sequence, then the output sequences for ω are trivially the same). For the reachable VAL $<s,t,\mathbf{u_n},\mathbf{v_m}>$ and an input $A(\mathbf{p_j})$, there exists an edge pair

---

[1] For example, we use integers 0,1,..,4 for states $s_0,s_1,...,s_4$ in Fig. 2, respectively.

[2] Since, in this section, we use integers for the names of the states, q and r are variables whose values are integers. Hence, $\Psi(q,r,x_n,z_m)$ is a P-sentence.

$\{s \xrightarrow{\eta} s', t \xrightarrow{\varphi} t'\}$ to define the next VAL $<s',t',\mathbf{u'}_n,\mathbf{v'}_m>$ and the outputs. That is, there exists an edge pair $\{s \xrightarrow{\eta} s', t \xrightarrow{\varphi} t'\}$ where η is the 4-tuple $<A, c1(\boldsymbol{x}_n, y_j), \delta 1(\boldsymbol{x}_n, y_j), \rho 1(\boldsymbol{x}_n, y_j)>$ and φ is the 4-tuple $<A, c2(z_m, y_j), \delta 2(z_m, y_j), \rho 2(z_m, y_j)>$ and the value of "$c1(\mathbf{u}_n, \mathbf{p}_j)$ and $c2(\mathbf{v}_m, \mathbf{p}_j)$" is true. Since condition (A) holds and the value of "$c1(\mathbf{u}_n, \mathbf{p}_j)$ and $c2(\mathbf{v}_m, \mathbf{p}_j)$" is true, the value of "$\Psi(s,t,\mathbf{u}_n,\mathbf{v}_m)$ and $c1(\mathbf{u}_n, \mathbf{p}_j)$ and $c2(\mathbf{v}_m, \mathbf{p}_j)$" is also true. Since condition (B) holds, the value of "$\rho 1(\mathbf{u}_n, \mathbf{p}_j) = \rho 2(\mathbf{v}_m, \mathbf{p}_j)$" is true. That is, the outputs of M1 and M2 are the same, and then, the output sequences of M1 and M2 are the same for any input sequence $\omega \cdot A(\mathbf{p}_j)$. This completes the proof that M1 and M2 are equivalent. []

Note that *Proposition 4.1*(B) requires that the outputs for the current input $A(\mathbf{p}_j)$ must be the same even for an unreachable VAL $<s,t,\mathbf{u}_n,\mathbf{v}_m>$ satisfying Ψ if $<s,t>$ is in *Rstates*(M1,M2). In general, it is undecidable whether two conditions (A) and (B) in *Proposition 4.1* hold or not. Thus, we propose a technique only to verify mechanically that two conditions (A) and (B) hold.

[*Definition 4.3*]

Let $\Psi(q,r,\boldsymbol{x}_n,z_m)$ be a P-sentence. Let $\{s \xrightarrow{\eta} s', t \xrightarrow{\varphi} t'\}$ be an edge pair where η is the 4-tuple $<A, c1(\boldsymbol{x}_n, y_j), \delta 1(\boldsymbol{x}_n, y_j), \rho 1(\boldsymbol{x}_n, y_j)>$ and φ is the 4-tuple $<A, c2(z_m, y_j), \delta 2(z_m, y_j), \rho 2(z_m, y_j)>$.

(I)If the following statement is true, then $\{s \xrightarrow{\eta} s', t \xrightarrow{\varphi} t'\}$ is called an *edge pair* of *type I for* Ψ.

$$\forall \boldsymbol{x}_n, y_j, z_m [\Psi(s,t,\boldsymbol{x}_n,z_m) \supset \text{not}\{c1(\boldsymbol{x}_n, y_j) \text{ and } c2(z_m, y_j)\}]$$

(II)If $\{s \xrightarrow{\eta} s', t \xrightarrow{\varphi} t'\}$ is not an edge pair of type I for Ψ and the following statement is true, then $\{s \xrightarrow{\eta} s', t \xrightarrow{\varphi} t'\}$ is called an *edge pair of type II for* Ψ.

$$\forall \boldsymbol{x}_n, y_j, z_m [\Psi(s,t,\boldsymbol{x}_n,z_m) \text{ and } \{c1(\boldsymbol{x}_n, y_j) \text{ and } c2(z_m, y_j)\}$$
$$\supset \{\Psi(s',t',\delta 1(\boldsymbol{x}_n, y_j), \delta 2(z_m, y_j)) \text{ and } \rho 1(\boldsymbol{x}_n, y_j) = \rho 2(z_m, y_j)\}]$$

(III)If $\{s \xrightarrow{\eta} s', t \xrightarrow{\varphi} t'\}$ is neither an edge pair of type I nor that of type II, then $\{s \xrightarrow{\eta} s', t \xrightarrow{\varphi} t'\}$ is called an *edge pair of type III for* Ψ. []

For any P-sentence $P(\boldsymbol{w}_n)$ with variables $w_1, w_2, \ldots, w_n$, it is decidable whether $\forall w_1, w_2, \ldots, w_n [P(\boldsymbol{w}_n)]$ is true or not [7]. Therefore, for given P-sentence Ψ and edge pair, we can determine the type of the edge pairs. Let $Nextnodes_{[\Psi]}$(M1,M2,$<s,t>$) be the set of the next node pairs of the edge pairs of type II for Ψ whose current node pairs are $<s,t>$. That is,

$$Nextnodes_{[\Psi]}(M1,M2,<s,t>) = \{<s',t'> \mid \{s \xrightarrow{\eta} s', t \xrightarrow{\varphi} t'\} \text{ is an edge pair of type II for } \Psi\}.$$

For example, for state s_1 in the protocol machine M1 in Fig. 2 and state t_1 in the protocol machine M2 in Fig. 3, there are five edge pairs $\{s_1 \xrightarrow{<T,\ldots>} s_2, t_1 \xrightarrow{<T,\ldots>} t_2\}$, $\{s_1 \xrightarrow{<T,\ldots>} s_2, t_1 \xrightarrow{<T,\ldots>} t_0\}$, $\{s_1 \xrightarrow{<Re,\ldots>} s_0, t_1 \xrightarrow{<Re,\ldots>} t_2\}$, $\{s_1 \xrightarrow{<Re,\ldots>} s_0, t_1 \xrightarrow{<Re,\ldots>} t_0\}$ and $\{s_1 \xrightarrow{<A,\ldots>} s_0, t_1 \xrightarrow{<A,\ldots>} t_0\}$ whose current node pairs are $<s_1,t_1>$.

Let Ψ_0 be the following P-sentence:

$$\Psi_0(q,r,x_1,x_2,z_1,z_2,z_3) = [(x_1+z_2=10) \text{ and } (x_2=z_3) \text{ and } (q=s_1 \supset z_1=1) \text{ and } (q=s_3 \supset z_1=0)]\,. \quad (4\text{-}1)$$

(Here, q and r are variables representing the states of M1 and M2, respectively. The variables x_1 and x_2 represent the values of the registers R1 and R2 of M1, respectively. The variables z_1, z_2 and z_3 represent the values of the registers R'1, R'2 and R'3 of M2, respectively[1].)

For this P-sentence Ψ_0, the following (1)~(4) hold.

(1)$\{s_1 \xrightarrow{<T,\ldots>} s_2, t_1 \xrightarrow{<T,\ldots>} t_0\}$ and $\{s_1 \xrightarrow{<Re,\ldots>} s_0, t_1 \xrightarrow{<Re,\ldots>} t_2\}$ are the edge pairs of type I for Ψ_0.

(2)$\{s_1 \xrightarrow{<T,\ldots>} s_2, t_1 \xrightarrow{<T,\ldots>} t_2\}$, $\{s_1 \xrightarrow{<Re,\ldots>} s_0, t_1 \xrightarrow{<Re,\ldots>} t_0\}$ and $\{s_1 \xrightarrow{<A,\ldots>} s_0, t_1 \xrightarrow{<A,\ldots>} t_0\}$ are the edge pairs of type II for Ψ_0.

(3)There exists no edge pair of type III for Ψ_0 whose current node pairs are $<s_1,t_1>$.

(4)$Nextnodes_{[\Psi_0]}(M1,M2,<s_1,t_1>) = \{<s_2,t_2>,<s_0,t_0>\}$ holds.

Let $<s_1,t_1,[u_1,u_2],[v_1,v_2,v_3]>$ be a reachable VAL satisfying Ψ_0. For any input, the next node pair is either $<s_2,t_2>$ or $<s_0,t_0>$. The next VAL satisfies Ψ_0 and the outputs are the same, since there exist no

[1] In our formulation, we use integers for the names of the states. Here, s_1 represents integer 1, and s_3 represents integer 3.

edge pair of type III for Ψ_0.

[*Proposition 4.2*]

Let Ψ be a P-sentence and assume that $\Psi(s_I,t_I,\mathbf{u_{In}},\mathbf{v_{Im}})$ is true where s_I and t_I are the initial states of M1 and M2, respectively, and $\mathbf{u_{In}}$ and $\mathbf{v_{Im}}$ are the initial values of the registers, respectively. If the following procedure *Equivalence* prints out the message "*Success*", conditions (A) and (B) in *Proposition 4.1* hold, and then M1 and M2 are equivalent.

Procedure *Equivalence*(M1,M2,Ψ);
    $S \leftarrow \{<s_I,t_I>\}$;   /* First, $<s_I,t_I>$ is not marked */
    while *there exists a pair of states in S which is not marked* ***do***
        begin
            Let <s,t> *be a pair of states in S which is not marked.*
            if there exists an edge pair of type III for Ψ *whose current node pair is* <s,t>
                then begin *print(Failure)*; *halt* ***end***
                else begin $S \leftarrow S \cup Nextnodes_{[\Psi]}$(M1,M2,<s,t>);
                        /* If a new pair of states <s',t'> is appended to *S*, <s',t'> is not marked */
                        Mark the pair of states <s,t> ***end***
        end;
    print(Success); *halt*
end.

(Proof)By using induction of the length "k" of an input sequence ω, we prove that

(I) $\Psi(\sigma(M1,\omega),\sigma(M2,\omega),\delta(M1,\omega),\delta(M2,\omega))$ is true, and

(II) $<\sigma(M1,\omega),\sigma(M2,\omega)>$ belongs to *S* (the value of variable *S* when the procedure terminates with *Success*).

Basis: Let ω be the null sequence. The reachable VAL for ω is $<s_I,t_I,u_{In},v_{Im}>$ and then $\Psi(s_I,t_I,u_{In},v_{Im})$ is true from the assumption of *Proposition 4.2*. Hence, property (I) holds. Since $<\sigma(M1,\omega),\sigma(M2,\omega)>$ is $<s_I,t_I>$ and $<s_I,t_I>$ belongs to *S*, then the property (II) holds.

Induction: Suppose that (I) and (II) hold for any input sequence ω whose length is k. Let $<s,t,\mathbf{u_n},\mathbf{v_m}>$ be the reachable VAL for ω and let $\{s \xrightarrow{<A,..>} s', t \xrightarrow{<A,..>} t'\}$ be the edge pair to define the next VAL $<s',t',\mathbf{u'_n},\mathbf{v'_m}>$ and the outputs for the reachable VAL $<s,t,\mathbf{u_n},\mathbf{v_m}>$ and an input $A(\mathbf{p_j})$. From the hypothesis (II) of the induction, the pair of states <s,t> belongs to *S*. Since the procedure *Equivalence* prints out the message "*Success*", there exists no edge pair of type III whose current node pair is <s,t>. Since the edge pair to define the next VAL is either type II or type III, $\{s \xrightarrow{<A,..>} s', t \xrightarrow{<A,..>} t'\}$ is an edge pair of type II for Ψ. Hence, by the definition of the edge pairs of type II, property (I) holds for the input sequence $\omega \cdot A(\mathbf{p_j})$ whose length is k+1. Since <s',t'> belongs to $Nextnodes_{[\Psi]}$(M1,M2,<s,t>) by the definition, <s',t'> also belongs to *S*. That is, property (II) holds for the input sequence $\omega \cdot A(\mathbf{p_j})$ whose length is k+1.

By the discussion above, it is proved that properties (I) and (II) hold for any input sequence ω. From property (I), it follows that condition (A) of *Proposition 4.1* holds. Property (II) shows that $S \supseteq$ *Rstates*(M1,M2) holds. Since there exists no edge pair of type III whose current node pair belongs to *S*, and hence to *Rstates*(M1,M2), any edge pair whose current node pair belongs to *Rstates*(M1,M2) is either type I or type II. Therefore, condition (B) of *Proposition 4.1* holds. The equivalence of M1 and M2 follows from *Proposition 4.1*. []

Let n_1 and n_2 be the numbers of states of M1 and M2, respectively. If we can assume that the numbers of edges from states in the C-transition diagrams of M1 and M2 are at most constants (not depending on n_1 and n_2), and that the type of a given edge pair is determined within a constant time (not depending on n_1 and n_2), then the time complexity of the procedure *Equivalence* is $O(n_1 \cdot n_2)$.

For two protocol machines M1 and M2 in Fig. 2 and Fig. 3 and the P-sentence Ψ_0 described in (4-1), the procedure *Equivalence* prints out the message "*Success*". In Section 5, a way to find such a P-sentence Ψ_0 is explained.

5. Program for Verifying Equivalence

We have developed a program which executes the procedure *Equivalence* in *Proposition 4.2*. This program is developed on SUN3-60 produced by Sun Micro Systems, Ltd..

In the program, we must determine the types of edge pairs, and hence, we must check for a given P-sentence $P(\boldsymbol{w_n})$ with variables $w_1,w_2,\ldots,w_n$ whether $\forall w_1,w_2,\ldots,w_n[P(\boldsymbol{w_n})]$ is true or not. Since "$\forall w_1,w_2,\ldots,w_n[P(\boldsymbol{w_n})]$" is equivalent to "$\sim\exists w_1,w_2,\ldots,w_n[Q(\boldsymbol{w_n})]$" where $Q(\boldsymbol{w_n})$ is the P-sentence "not($P(\boldsymbol{w_n})$)", "$\forall w_1,w_2,\ldots,w_n[P(\boldsymbol{w_n})]$" is true if and only if $Q(\boldsymbol{w_n})$ is unsatisfiable. The P-sentence $Q(\boldsymbol{w_n})$ can be transformed into the disjunctive normal form "$Q_1(\boldsymbol{w_n})$ or $Q_2(\boldsymbol{w_n})$ or ... or $Q_k(\boldsymbol{w_n})$" where each $Q_j(\boldsymbol{w_n})$ is a conjunctions of some linear inequalities. $Q(\boldsymbol{w_n})$ is unsatisfiable if and only if all $Q_1(\boldsymbol{w_n})$, $Q_2(\boldsymbol{w_n})$, ... and $Q_k(\boldsymbol{w_n})$ are unsatisfiable. By regarding each linear inequality in $Q_j(\boldsymbol{w_n})$ as a constraint of an integer linear programming problem, we can check whether its integer linear programming problem has no integer solution. By using this method, it can be checked whether "$\forall w_1,w_2,\ldots,w_n[P(\boldsymbol{w_n})]$" is true or not. To save the computation time, our program regards the integer linear programming problem as a linear programming problem on real numbers and it checks whether its linear programming problem has no real solution. This method fails to prove the equivalence when there exists a real solution. However, there may be the cases such that no integer solution exists. Therefore, in order to decrease the possibilities of the

(1)*P-sentence* Ψ? <u>true</u>

$\langle s_1,t_1\rangle$

$\downarrow \quad \langle T, (z_1=1), [[x_1+1,y_1], [z_1,z_2-1,y_1]], [[y_1], [y_1]]\rangle$

$\langle s_2,t_2\rangle$

$\downarrow \quad \langle A, (y_1=0), [[x_1,x_2], [y_1,z_2,z_3]], [[-], [-]]\rangle$

$\langle s_3,t_1\rangle$

$\downarrow \quad \langle Re, \text{not}(z_1=0), [[x_1,x_2], [z_1,z_2,z_3]], [[x_2], E]\rangle$

$\langle s_2,t_0\rangle$

The outputs are not the same !!

$\{(q=s_3 \text{ and } r=t_1) \supset z_1=0\}$ should be contained in the invariant. ---(a)

(2)*P-sentence* Ψ? $\underline{\{(q=s_3 \text{ and } r=t_1) \supset z_1=0\}}$

$\langle s_1,t_1\rangle$

$\downarrow \quad \langle T, (z_1=1), [[x_1+1,y_1], [z_1,z_2-1,y_1]], [[y_1], [y_1]]\rangle$

$\langle s_2,t_2\rangle$

$\downarrow \quad \langle A, (y_1=0), [[x_1,x_2], [y_1,z_2,z_3]], [[-], [-]]\rangle$

$\langle s_3,t_1\rangle$

$\downarrow \quad \langle Re, (z_1=0), [[x_1,x_2], [z_1,z_2,z_3]], [[x_2], [z_3]]\rangle$

$\langle s_2,t_2\rangle$

The outputs may not be the same !!

$\{(q=s_3 \text{ and } r=t_1) \supset x_2=z_3\}$ should be contained in the invariant. ---(b)

(3)*P-sentence* Ψ? $\underline{\{(q=s_3 \text{ and } r=t_1) \supset (z_1=0 \text{ and } x_2=z_3)\}}$

$\langle s_1,t_1\rangle$

$\downarrow \quad \langle T, (z_1=1), [[x_1+1,y_1], [z_1,z_2-1,y_1]], [[y_1], [y_1]]\rangle$

$\langle s_2,t_2\rangle$

$\downarrow \quad \langle A, (y_1=0), [[x_1,x_2], [y_1,z_2,z_3]], [[-], [-]]\rangle$

$\langle s_3,t_1\rangle$

Ψ may not be an invariant !!

$\{(q=s_2 \text{ and } r=t_2) \supset x_2=z_3\}$ should be contained in the invariant. ---(c)

(4)*P-sentence* Ψ? $\underline{\{(q=s_3 \text{ and } r=t_1) \supset z_1=0\} \text{ and }}$
$\underline{\{((q=s_2 \text{ and } r=t_2) \text{ or } (q=s_3 \text{ and } r=t_1)) \supset x_2=z_3\}}$

:

Ψ may not be an invariant !!

$\{(q=s_1 \text{ and } r=t_1) \supset x_2=z_3\}$ should be contained in the invariant. ---(d)

(5)*P-sentence* Ψ? $\underline{\{(q=s_3 \text{ and } r=t_1) \supset z_1=0\} \text{ and } \{x_2=z_3\}}$

:

$\{(q=s_2 \text{ and } r=t_2) \supset ((z_2=0 \supset x_1\geq 10) \text{ and } (z_2=1 \supset x_1\geq 9))\}$ should be contained in the invariant. ---(e)

(6)*P-sentence* Ψ? ....

:

$\{(q=s_1 \text{ and } r=t_1) \supset ((z_2=1 \supset x_1\geq 9) \text{ and } (z_2=2 \supset x_1\geq 8))\}$ ---(f) should be contained in the invariant.

(7)*P-sentence* Ψ? ....

:

$\{(q=s_3 \text{ and } r=t_1) \supset ((z_2=0 \supset x_1\geq 10) \text{ and } (z_2=1 \supset x_1\geq 9))\}$ ---(g) should be contained in the invariant.

(8)*P-sentence* Ψ? $\underline{\{(q=s_3 \text{ and } r=t_1) \supset z_1=0\}}$
$\underline{\text{and } \{x_2=z_3\} \text{ and } \{x_1+z_2\geq 10\}}$

:

$\{(q=s_2 \text{ and } r=t_2) \supset ((z_2=0 \supset x_1\leq 10) \text{ and } (z_2=1 \supset x_1\leq 9))\}$ should be contained in the invariant. ---(h)

(9)*P-sentence* Ψ? ....

:

$\{(q=s_1 \text{ and } r=t_1) \supset ((z_2=1 \supset x_1\leq 9) \text{ and } (z_2=2 \supset x_1\leq 8))\}$ should be contained in the invariant. ---(i)

(10)*P-sentence* Ψ? ....

:

$\{(q=s_3 \text{ and } r=t_1) \supset ((z_2=0 \supset x_1\leq 10) \text{ and } (z_2=1 \supset x_1\leq 9))\}$ should be contained in the invariant. ---(j)

(11)*P-sentence* Ψ? $\underline{\{(q=s_3 \text{ and } r=t_1) \supset z_1=0\}}$
$\underline{\text{and } \{x_2=z_3\} \text{ and } \{x_1+z_2=10\}}$

$\langle s_1,t_1\rangle$

$\downarrow \quad \langle Re, (z_1=0), [[x_1,x_2], [z_1,z_2,z_3]], [E, [z_3]]\rangle$

$\langle s_0,t_2\rangle$

The outputs are not the same !!

$\{(q=s_1 \text{ and } r=t_1) \supset \text{not}(z_1=0)\}$ should be contained in the invariant. ---(k)

(12)*P-sentence* Ψ? $\underline{\{(q=s_3 \text{ and } r=t_1) \supset z_1=0\} \text{ and }}$
$\underline{\{x_2=z_3\} \text{ and } \{x_1+z_2=10\} \text{ and }}$
$\underline{\{(q=s_1 \text{ and } r=t_1) \supset \text{not}(z_1=0)\}}$

Success: The two protocol machines are equivalent !!

Fig. 4 A way to find a P-sentence Ψ necessary to prove the equivalence of the protocol machines failure, our program transforms a given P-sentence of the form "$\xi>\lambda$" into that of "$\xi\geq\lambda+1$". This program was applied for several verification examples and the proofs of the equivalence were succeeded for their verification examples.

Even if the proof of the equivalence failed by using our program, our program prints out the useful information for proving the equivalence of given protocol machines. For example, a procedure to verify that two protocol machines M1 and M2 in Fig. 2 and Fig. 3 are equivalent is illustrated in Fig. 4. Suppose that, first, there is no information for proving the equivalence of M1 and M2. Then, "true" is specified as Ψ in Fig. 4(1). Our program chooses an edge pair $\{s_1 \xrightarrow{\langle T,...\rangle} s_2, t_1 \xrightarrow{\langle T,...\rangle} t_2\}$ and determines the type of edge pair $\{s_1 \xrightarrow{\langle T,...\rangle} s_2, t_1 \xrightarrow{\langle T,...\rangle} t_2\}$. Since $\{s_1 \xrightarrow{\langle T,...\rangle} s_2, t_1 \xrightarrow{\langle T,...\rangle} t_2\}$ is an edge pair of type II for Ψ, our program finds another edge pair whose current node pair is $\langle s_2,t_2\rangle$. $\{s_2 \xrightarrow{\langle A,...\rangle} s_3, t_2 \xrightarrow{\langle A,...\rangle} t_1\}$ is an edge pair of type II for Ψ. Since $\{s_3 \xrightarrow{\langle Re,...\rangle} s_2, t_1 \xrightarrow{\langle Re,...\rangle} t_0\}$ is an edge pair of type III for Ψ (because the outputs of M1 and M2 are $[x_2]$ and E, respectively), our program prints out the message "The outputs are not the same !!". Our program finds that $\{s_3 \xrightarrow{\langle Re,...\rangle} s_2, t_1 \xrightarrow{\langle Re,...\rangle} t_0\}$ must be an edge pair of type I if M1 and M2 are equivalent, and it prints out the message "$\{(q=s_3$ and $r=t_1) \supset z_1=0\}$ should be contained in the invariant." (see Fig. 4(a)).

In Fig. 4(2), $\{(q=s_3$ and $r=t_1) \supset z_1=0\}$ is specified as Ψ. Since $\{s_3 \xrightarrow{\langle Re,...\rangle} s_2, t_1 \xrightarrow{\langle Re,...\rangle} t_2\}$ is an edge pair of type III, the message "$\{(q=s_3$ and $r=t_1) \supset x_2=z_3\}$ should be contained in the invariant." is printed out (see Fig. 4(b)). Since $\{s_2 \xrightarrow{\langle A,...\rangle} s_3, t_2 \xrightarrow{\langle A,...\rangle} t_1\}$ is an edge pair of type III for the P-sentence Ψ in Fig. 4(3), and since the outputs are both [-]'s, our program prints out the message "Ψ may not be an invariant !!". Since the statement of (II) in *Definition 4.3* for this edge pair is reduced to "$y_1=0 \supset x_2=z_3$", the value of "$y_1=0 \supset x_2=z_3$" must be true at states s_2 and t_2 for arbitrary values of y_1, x_2 and z_3. If the conjunction of the P-sentence Ψ in Fig. 4(3) and "$\{(q=s_2$ and $r=t_2) \supset x_2=z_3\}$" is specified as a new P-sentence Ψ, then $\{s_2 \xrightarrow{\langle A,...\rangle} s_3, t_2 \xrightarrow{\langle A,...\rangle} t_1\}$ becomes an edge pair of type II for the new Ψ. Thus, our program prints out the message "$\{(q=s_2$ and $r=t_2) \supset x_2=z_3\}$ should be contained in the invariant." (see Fig. 4(c)). Similarly, the message of (d) in Fig. 4 is printed out. From the messages of (b), (c) and (d) in Fig. 4, we could find that "$x_2=z_3$" may be an invariant. Then, the P-sentence of Fig. 4(5) is specified as Ψ. From the messages (e), (f) and (g) in Fig. 4, we could find that "$x_1+z_2\geq 10$" may be an invariant. Then, we construct Ψ as in (8). Similarly, from the messages (h), (i) and (j) in Fig. 4, we construct Ψ as in (11). And, from the message (k), we construct Ψ as in (12). Then, our program prints out the message "*Success*: The two protocol machines are equivalent !!".

There exist several P-sentences such that our program prints out the message "*Success*" for M1 and M2. For example, for the P-sentence Ψ_0 described in (4-1), our program also prints out the message "*Success*". But we cannot always find a P-sentence Ψ such that the procedure *Equivalence* of *Proposition 4.2* prints out the message "*Success*" for M1, M2 and Ψ in general even if M1 and M2 are equivalent and there exists such a P-sentence Ψ. However, from experiments, we are sure that we could find such a P-sentence Ψ in most case by using our program. In Fig. 4, it takes about 10 to 30 seconds on SUN3-60 to obtain the messages (a),(b),...,(k) from the P-sentences in Fig. 4(1)~(11). It also takes about 60 seconds to prove that two protocol machines are equivalent for the P-sentence in Fig. 4(12). The number of the checks of unsatisfiabilities of linear programming problems is 22 for the P-sentence in Fig. 4(12).

6. Verification Example

We proved the equivalence of two protocol machines M_a and M_b which are secondary stations of HDLC procedure [9]. The protocol machine M_a is an abstract model of a protocol machine which is produced by a computer maker. Another machine M_b is produced by us where the number of the states of M_b is less than that of M_a.

The numbers of the input symbols for M_a and M_b are 12. These symbols represent "starting command", "the transmission (or reception) of I (or RR or RNR) frame", "the reception of SNRM (or DISC or invalid) frame" and "the occurrence (or removal) of the busy situation".

M_a has four registers R_1, R_2, R_3 and R_4. Register R_1 denotes the send state variable (the sequence number of the next in sequence I frame to be transmitted). Register R_2 denotes the lowest_unacked state variable (the minimum number of the sequence numbers of I frames which have been transmitted, but which have been unacknowledged). Register R_3 denotes the outstanding I frame number (the number of the I frames which have been transmitted, but which have not been acknowledged). Register R_4 denotes the receive state variable (the sequence number of the next in sequence I frame to be received). M_a has 11 states. By these states, M_a can decide whether M_a can transmit a frame with Final bit set to "1" and whether it is in the busy situation.

M_b has four registers R'_0, R'_1, R'_2 and R'_4. Registers R'_1, R'_2 and R'_4 denote the send state variable, the lowest_unacked state variable and the receive state variable, respectively. M_b does not have a register corresponding to register R_3 of M_a because the outstanding I frame number is equal to the difference between the values of registers R'_1 and R'_2. M_b has only 7 states. In order to reduce the number of states, M_b has an additional register R'_0. Register R'_0 stores the difference between the number of the receptions of the frames with Poll bits set to "1" and that of the transmissions of the frames with Final bits set to "1".

First, the conjunction of the four equalities representing the relations between registers R_1, R_2, R_3, R_4, R'_1, R'_2 and R'_4 described above was specified as the P-sentence Ψ. Then, our program successively printed out the eight P-sentences representing the relations between the states of M_a and M_b and the value of register R'_0. For the P-sentence Ψ which consists of the conjunction of the four equalities described above and these eight P-sentences, the verification of the equivalence of M_a and M_b succeeded. For this P-sentence Ψ, our program took about 30 minutes to prove the equivalence, and the program repeatedly checked about 1200 times whether the linear programming problems have no real solution.

7. Conclusion

In this paper, we describe a technique to prove the equivalence of the protocol machines mechanically. Let I_1 and I_2 be the sets of the input symbols of M1 and M2, respectively. In this paper, it is assumed that $I_1 = I_2$ holds. In general, many facilities are represented in a communication protocol, and only some of them are implemented when a protocol machine is developed. Then, even if two protocol machines are developed for the same communication protocol, the facilities of M1 and those of M2 may be different. For example, let M1 be an extended model of M2. Then $I_1 \supseteq I_2$ holds. For this case, our technique can be also applied. That is, by using our technique, we can prove that the output sequences of M1 and M2 are same for any input sequence ω such that all input symbols in ω belong to I_2. If the proof succeeds and only input symbols in I_2 are applied to M1, then M2 can be replaced by M1.

We are now studying a technique to prove safeness and liveness properties mechanically in our model [10].

References

[1] R. Milner : "A Calculus of Communicating Systems", Lecture Notes in Computer Science 92, Springer-Berlag (1980).

[2] S.D. Brookes and W.C.Rounds ; "Behavioural Equivalence Relations Induced by Programming Logics", Proc. ICALP 83', Lecture Notes in Computer Science 154, pp.97-108, Springer-Berlag (1983).

[3] R. De Nicola : "Extensional Equivalences for Transition Systems", Acta Informatica, Vol. 24, pp.211-237 (1987).

[4] P.C. Kanellakis and S.A. Smolka : "CCS Expressions, Finite State Processes, and Three Problems of Equivalence", Proc. 2nd Ann. ACM Symp. Principles of Distributed Computing, pp.228-240 (1983).

[5] T. Bolognesi and S.A. Smolka : "Fundamental Results for the Verification of Observational Equivalence : a Survey", Proc. 7th. Int. Conf. on Protocol Specification, Testing, and Verification, pp.165-179 (1987).

[6] K. Rea and R. de B. Johnston : "Automated Analysis of Discrete Communication Behavior", IEEE Trans. Software Eng., Vol. SE-13, No. 10, pp.1115-1126 (1987).

[7] J.E. Hopcroft and J.D. Ullman : "Introduction to Automata Theory, Languages, and Computation", Addison-Weslay (1979).

[8] IBM : "IBM Binary Synchronous Communications", IBM N:GA27-3004-1 (1969).

[9] ISO : "Data Communication -High level Data Link Control Procedures-" ISO 3309 & 4335 (1979).

[10] T. Kimoto, T. Higashino, K. Taniguchi, M. Mori and K. Ninomiya : "A Method for Verifying Error Recoverability of Two Protocol Machines", Proc. Tech. Group Information Networks, IEICE Japan, Rep. IN88-80, in Japanese (1988).

Protocol Specification, Testing, and Verification, IX
E. Brinksma, G. Scollo and C.A. Vissers (Editors)
Elsevier Science Publishers B.V. (North-Holland)

INCLUDING A QUEUE IN A FORMAL-DESCRIPTION-DRIVEN PROTOCOL PERFORMANCE ANALYSIS

Jan GUSTAFSSON and Harry RUDIN

IBM Research Division, Zurich Research Laboratory, Säumerstrasse 4,
8803 Rüschlikon, Switzerland
hr@ibm.com

Several investigators have considered the problem of analyzing the performance of a communications protocol direct from its formal description. These earlier analyses have been made for the saturated case, i.e., when there is an over-abundance of offered traffic. If a **queue** is added to create a waiting line for the incoming traffic, we show here that direct analysis can also be made. Results and limitations are discussed.

1. INTRODUCTION

There are a number of reasons for describing communication protocols formally. First among these is the promise of unambiguous interpretation by those parties who must implement compatible versions of the same protocol. The potential of identification of logical errors in a protocol at an early stage in the design, semi-automated implementation of the protocol, and semi-automated testing of the protocol are other reasons. Another possibility is using the formal protocol specification, directly, to help estimate the performance of a protocol. This paper describes a development in this last vein; new is the addition of a **queue** or **waiting line** to the analysis.

Those familiar with the finite-state model of a queue and the finite-state-machine representation of a protocol might conclude that the inclusion of a queue is a trivial exercise. This is not the case; difficulties arise from the clash of the anonymity of the messages in the queueing model with the specific identification of the semantic content of messages in the formal protocol model. We will return to this point later.

1.1 The Problem

The potential utility in making direct use of the formal protocol specification is avoidance of the usual preliminary step of making a model of the protocol and then using methods of traffic and queueing theory to analyze the model. A number of previous investigators have pursued this goal; none have included a queue in their analysis.

1.2 Past Work

Included here are the studies most relevant to the performance analysis of computer-communication protocols. More general references can be found in (Rudin85).

In 1978, Gouda suggested using a manual, graphical reduction technique to estimate the delay of communication protocols (Gouda78). His work is similar to that of Beizer who was instead interested in predicting program running time (Beizer70).

The first automated technique appeared in 1981, when Bauerfeld described automatic generation of a simulation program for estimating protocol performance. The simulator is derived directly from the formal specification (Bauerfeld81).

Here we use a finite-state-machine based model of the underlying protocols, but sometimes Petri networks are suggested for the analysis of communications protocols. Razouk and Phelps have made a performance analysis using Petri networks (Razouk84) based on a convenient system-status description formulated by Zuberek (Zuberek80).

Returning to the finite-state-machine description of the underlying protocol, Rudin published a numerical approach (Rudin83) in 1983, following this with a substantially more efficient algorithm in 1984 (Rudin84). Also in 1984, Kritzinger took the same model and, having made a number of assumptions, applied methods of closed, multiclass, multichain queuing networks. His approach sheds light on the performance of multiple copies of multilayer protocols competing with one another for processor cycles (Kritzinger86). A sample application may be found in (Engelbrecht85).

One can choose to assume that all elapsed-time specifications in the protocol have values drawn from a negative-exponential distribution. If this is done, a continuous time Markov-chain analysis can be made as shown by Molloy (Molloy82) and by Gravey and Dupuis (Gravey86). The shortcoming of this approach is that **all** time values must have a negative exponential distribution and this is often a bad assumption: for timeout values, as one example.

The representation of time in a formal protocol specification is itself an interesting issue. Early work is summarized in (Rudin85). Bochmann and Vaucher (Bochmann88) have suggested how time — and branching probabilities — might be added to the three most popular, standardized languages for the formal description of protocols, SDL, Estelle, and LOTOS.

Recently, Demitrijevic and Chen, (Demitrijevic88) have found a more efficient algorithm for analyzing the performance of protocols specified in terms of finite-state machines.

One can also analyze protocol performance on the basis of an algebraic description of the protocol. In this connection the reader is referred to (Nounou84) and (Barghouti86).

After this review of past work we now turn our attention to the first protocol we have studied. Our formal description is in terms of finite-state machines. In the ideal case this description would be given to us. To it we add the descriptions of the traffic source and a queue which serves as the interface between the source and the protocol proper. This queue has the capability of storing messages which the protocol cannot immediately transmit, thereby smoothing the message flow but potentially introducing delay. It is this combined system which we wish to analyze.

2. THE PROTOCOL MODEL

Figure 1 shows a finite-state-machine representation for a very simple — and not very practical — data-link level protocol. Incoming messages are queued before transmission to the receiver. Only one message can be outstanding, i.e., in effect there is a window size of one. Messages can be corrupted or lost in transmission to the receiver which generates the appropriate positive or negative acknowledgement. These acknowledgements can also be corrupted or lost during transmission back to the transmitter. A timer for retransmission takes care of the case where either the message or its acknowledgement is lost.

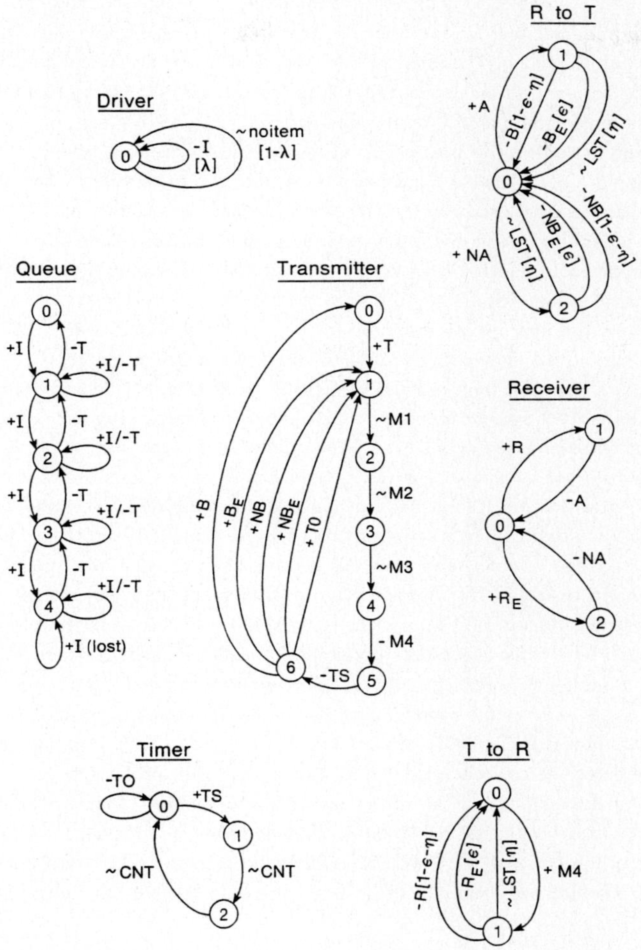

FIGURE 1

Data-link-level protocol specification. Single message outstanding, message length = 4, queue size = 4.

The protocol is modeled as seven processes. We assume that the processes run synchronously, all advancing a single time unit at each tick of an implied system clock. The "time unit" is thus the smallest time increment which is resolved. In the example shown in Figure 1 this was chosen to be the time required to move the smallest information unit (an acknowledgement, for example) from one process to another.

The "-" sign in the "-I" in Figure 1 means that a message is generated, or sent to another process. The source of traffic (messages) is the single-state process labeled "Driver" at the top left. There are two arcs labeled "-I" and "~noitem". At each time unit, either the arc "-I" is executed with some probability λ — representing the arrival of a message — or the inactive "noitem" arc is executed — representing that there was no arrival — with the remaining probability, 1 - λ. For most of the numerical calculations here, we assume the former (arrival) probability, λ, to be 0.1, corresponding to the arrival of a message every tenth time interval, on the average.

This message is sent to the next process, the queue, where it is accepted, represented by an arc labeled "+I". The "+" indicates reception of the message. The queue stores messages for later transmission by the transmitter. These messages are intended for the receiver and ultimately reach the receiver via another process labeled "T to R". The message is received by the receiver which appropriately generates a positive or negative acknowledgement. The channel "R to T" returns the acknowledgement to the transmitter which retransmits the appropriate message in the case of a negative acknowledgement or timeout, transmits a new message, or remains idle if the queue is empty.

Communication between the processes uses the "rendezvous" synchronization model — also used in the LOTOS specification language; see, for example, the tutorial on LOTOS by Bolognesi and Brinksma (Bolognesi87). How rendezvous synchronization works is best explained with reference again to Figure 1. Specifically, let us look at the communication between the queue and the transmitter. In the idle condition, the transmitter is in state 0. It cannot progress further until it receives a message of type "T" from the queue. As soon as there is a message in the queue, then the two transitions "-T" in the queue and "+T" in the transmitter are executed simultaneously. The transmitter can then proceed with transmission. A message length of 4 time units is modeled with the transition of three inactive arcs ("M1", "M2", "M3") followed by the generation of "M4", indicating completed sending of the message. Sending the message "TS" to the timer process starts the timer.

In the "T to R" channel, reception of the message (actually, reception of the last segment of the message) is indicated by the arc "+M4". Following this action, three events are modeled: a lost message "~LST", occurring with probability η, a transmission error "-R_E", with probability ε, or an error-free transmission "-R", with probability 1 - ε - η. The numerical value for the probabilities of message loss or message transmission-error are properties of the channel and should be calculated or measured. Here, for a numerical example, both ε and η are assumed to be 0.005, leaving 0.99 for the probability of perfect transmission.

The receiver simply generates a positive acknowledgement "-A" or a negative acknowledgement "-NA", depending on the case. These two acknowledgements, in turn, can be corrupted, lost, or returned error-free to the transmitter by the return channel "R to T". Erroneous transmission of a positive acknowledgement is modeled by the event "-B_E with probability ε, loss by "~LST" with probability η, and successful transmission by "-B". Similarly, erroneous transmission of a negative acknowledgement is modeled by the event "$-NB_E$", loss by "~LST", (again with probabilities ε and η) and successful transmission by "-NB". Arbitrarily, the same probabilities for loss and error have been assumed for the forward and backward channels.

In the case of error-free reception of a positive acknowledgement, the transmitter tries to fetch a new message from the queue. In all other cases — including timeout indicated by reception of the message "TO" from the timer — the previous message is retransmitted.

Note that multi-way synchronization (or rendezvous) can be modeled. For example, the arcs in process Queue labeled "+I/-T" indicate that at the same time a message is transferred from the queue to the transmitter, the driver can transfer a new message to the queue.

3. DETERMINING DELAYS

We assume here that we want to calculate the average delay between two events, usually the average time between the arrival of a message at the queue and the time the transmitter receives a positive acknowledgement for that message.

The dynamic behavior of the system can be described as a sequence of global states. A global state is a specification of the states of each of the component processes — in the present case, seven.

Calculation of performance proceeds in three steps. The first step is calculation of the global-state probabilities, the probabilities that the system is in each of the possible global states. The second step is calculation of **conditional delays**, one for each of the reachable global states determined from the computation in the first step. The conditional delay is the delay which a newly arrived message would experience if it arrived with the protocol in the specified global state. Finally the conditional delays have to be added together, each weighted by the probability of the respective global states, and possibly normalized, to give the desired average delay.

3.1 Step 1: Finding Global-State Probabilities

We represent this problem as a discrete-time, finite Markov chain. The one-step transition probabilities for this chain $p_{j,i}$, can be calculated from the transition probabilities of the individual processes. Due to the nature of the arrival process (there is a non-zero probability of a new message arriving during each discrete time slot), the chain can be seen to be irreducible and aperiodic. It thus follows (Kemeny60) that the chain possesses a unique equilibrium distribution.

There are several methods for finding the equilibrium distribution for such a Markov chain. Here, a particular initial global state is assumed with probability one. The probability distribution for the state of the chain at time $t+1$ (t = 0,1,2, ...) can be then determined by repeated application of the equation

$$P_i(t+1) = \sum_j P_j(t) \bullet p_{j,i} \ .$$

That is, the distribution at time $t+1$ is calculated in terms of the distribution at time t. Since our chain is irreducible and aperiodic, this procedure will always converge to the unique equilibrium distribution (Kemeny60). This process is carried out until transients die out and the equilibrium distribution is approached. We use a termination condition that compares the largest absolute difference between two successive iterations and stops when this difference falls below the value of a "precision parameter".

For the protocol of Figure 1 there are only a small number of global states, specifically, 65. For a more complicated protocol or for a protocol with a large queue size, the number of states could become enormous. We plan to investigate various techniques for reducing the size of the global-state space explored and the effects of this on the calculation's accuracy.

As the reader can imagine, the calculation involves the handling of many vectors, or lists, of global states, transition probabilities, global-state probabilities, conditional delays, etc. One also wants to convert from the states of the individual processes to the corresponding global state and vice versa. For these reasons a high-level language with advanced list-processing capabilities was selected, specifically, Common LISP. A reference is the book by Winston and Horn (Winston89).

3.2 Step 2: Finding Conditional Delays

Knowing the steady-state probabilities of all reachable global states, it remains to calculate the average delay between sets of global states which represent various situations. Usually we are concerned with response time. We take this to be the time between a new message arrival at the queue and the time a positive acknowledgement for that message is received at the transmitter.

Straightforward introduction of a labeled test message would require modification of the formal protocol specification, a measure we would like to avoid. We are able to avoid this modification by making use of the following procedure.

First, we can imitate the behavior of the arrival of a new "test" message by associating the global-state probability as determined above with the global state which would result if the states of all processes other than the Queue process are fixed but the state of the Queue process is advanced by one (i.e., by the arrival of one message). We cannot do this for the global states where the queue is already full because the arrival of a message in these states means a queue overflow or message loss. The sum of the probabilities of these (queue full) states is simply the probability of queue overflow: this is a performance figure which is of interest to us.

The above calculation gives us the probabilities for all possible starting global states for the ensuing calculation of the conditional delays in the tree of paths starting at each of those global states and terminating when the appropriate positive acknowledgement reaches the transmitter.

Here again, we see a result of the mixing of unlabeled messages in the queue (anonymous except that we need somehow to take the test message into account) and labeled messages in the protocol specification. In effect, we need to identify the positive acknowledgement of a specific message for the termination of the paths starting at a specific global state. An effective method here is recalculating the global-state transition probabilities for this second step of the calculation after setting the arrival probability for a new message to zero. Doing this, the desired terminating global state is simply that for which all component processes are in their zero state; i.e., a positive acknowledgement has just been accepted by the transmitter and since there are no more messages to be transmitted, this positive acknowledgement must be for the test (last-added) message.

For the protocol of Figure 1, where only a single message may be outstanding, this method is exact. For other protocols this may not be the case. For example, we have also analyzed a protocol with window size of two, that is, two messages may be transmitted before an acknowledgement is received. For this case we would calculate an inaccurate value of delay because we would ignore the additional delay which might be indirectly introduced by messages enqueued after the test message but whose positive acknowledgement was received before that of the test message. It is also possible that the acknowledgement of the test message is not the last to be returned to the transmitter, causing an inflated delay value.

Thus the calculation of the conditional delay starting in some particular global state i is given by

$$T_i = \sum_{j=1}^{N} (P_{\text{path}\, j}) \bullet (D_{\text{path}\, j}) \ ,$$

where $D_{\text{path}\, j}$ is the delay from the given state i to the terminating state along path j, $P_{\text{path}\, j}$ is the probability of following that particular path, and N is the number of paths in the tree rooted at global state i.

The tree of paths rooted in a particular global state may not be finite. Again a terminating algorithm must be found: once the probability of a path drops below a parameterized value, the path is no longer considered.

3.3 Step 3: Finding the Average Delay

Finally, the average delay T_{avg} is given by the weighted sum of the conditional delays;

$$T_{\text{avg}} = \sum_i (P_i) \bullet (T_i) \ ,$$

where T_i is the conditional delay for global state i and P_i is the probability of being in that state i.

For the protocol of Figure 1, we exclude those messages which are lost through queue overflow from the delay calculation, i.e., the average delay must be normalized. The probability of the set of global states for which incoming message experiences delay is $1 - P_{\text{loss}}$ where P_{loss} is the probability of the queue being full or of a message being lost. Thus, in our case,

$$T_{\text{avg}} = \frac{1}{1 - P_{\text{loss}}} \bullet \sum_i (P_i) \bullet (T_i) \ .$$

4. SAMPLE RESULTS

We have used these techniques to analyze three data-link level protocols. The first, with a single message outstanding, is that of Figure 1. The second is a protocol with window size of two and the third is a go-back-N protocol (Lin84). Only the first is discussed here.

Figure 2 shows several performance measures as a function of the probability of message arrival in the driver; the larger this probability, the more traffic offered to the protocol. The uppermost curve in Figure 2 is the utilization of the "T to R" channel. As the traffic increases, the utilization rises, asymptotically approaching 50 percent. 50 percent is the maximum because of the nature of the protocol and assumed message length: the protocol requires a minimum of eight time units to transmit a message in the forward direction and to receive an acknowledgement in the reverse direction. The forward channel is only occupied during four of these eight time units.

The average delay, from message arrival at the queue to the reception of a positive acknowledgement for it at the transmitter, has a value of somewhat over eight for light

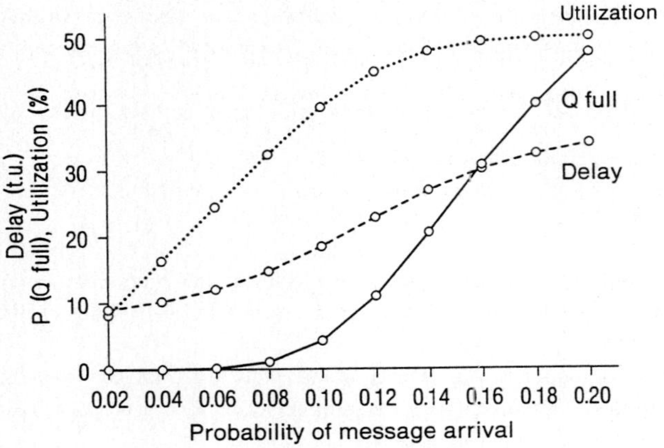

FIGURE 2
Varying the arrival probability. Average delay, forward channel utilization, and blocking or full-queue probability as a function of message arrival probability.

traffic. The value of slightly more than eight time units results from the fact that sometimes several transmissions are required because of errors or losses in the channels. As Figure 2 shows, the average delay grows — because of longer waiting times in the queue — as the offered traffic increases. Finally, with buffer capacity of only four messages, the queue cannot handle all the offered traffic and so the probability of the queue being full, i.e, the probability of a newly arriving message being lost, also increases with offered traffic.

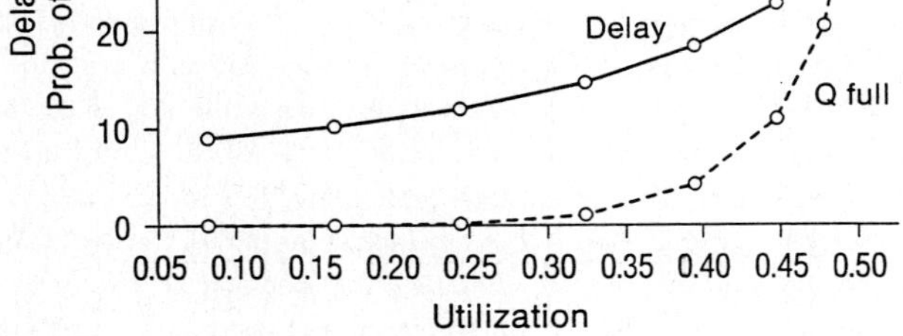

FIGURE 3
Average delay and blocking probability as a function of channel utilization.

Figure 3 shows the probability of the queue being full (i.e., message overflow) and average delay growing as a function of the utilization. Delay is expressed in terms of time units. Note again that saturation occurs with a utilization of the "T to R" channel of 50 percent.

Figure 4 shows the probability density function, the probability of the delay being equal to various numbers of time intervals. For the message loss and corruption probabilities in both the forward and reverse channel equal to one-half of one percent, somewhat over twenty percent of the messages experience the minimum delay of eight time units. A smaller peak in probability occurs with a delay of 16 time units, i.e., two transmission cycles.

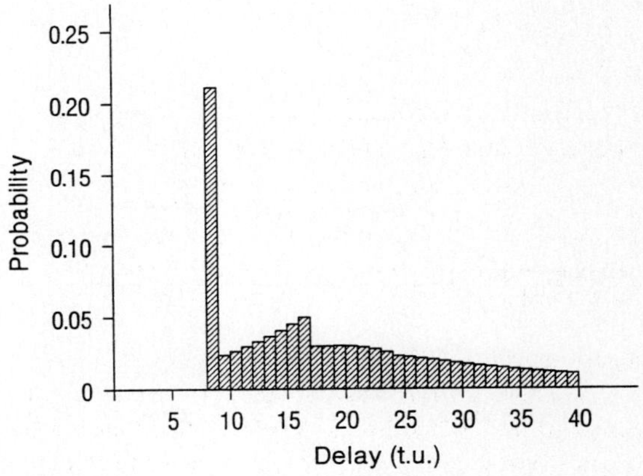

FIGURE 4
Probability density function of delay

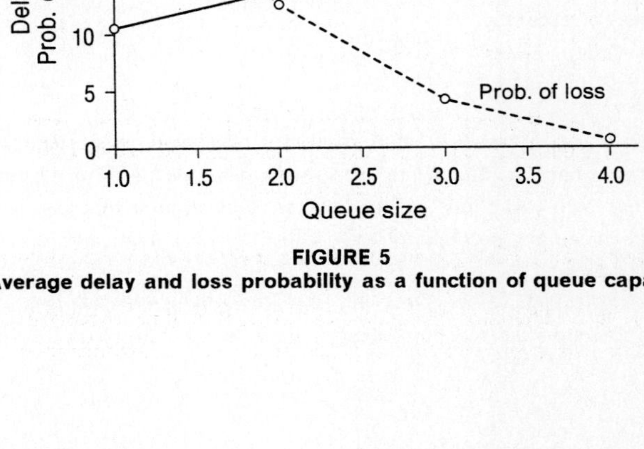

FIGURE 5
Average delay and loss probability as a function of queue capacity.

It is interesting to vary the queue size, holding the message arrival probability fixed at 0.1. Results are shown in Figure 5 for the average delay and probability of loss, i.e., the probability of the queue being full. The probability of loss decreases with increasing queue capacity but the average delay increases, both as one would qualitatively expect.

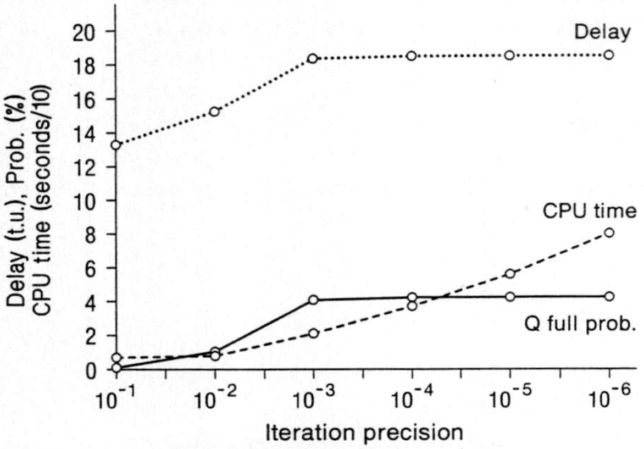

FIGURE 6
Varying the precision of the calculation.

As mentioned earlier, we have included a provision for adjusting the accuracy with which the computations are made. Figure 6 shows curves obtained when the parameter which terminates the iterative global-state calculation is reduced. The smaller this parameter, called iteration precision in Figure 6, the more iterations made, the higher the accuracy, and the greater the computer time required to carry out the computation. The average delay and the overflow probability become stable with an iteration precision of about 0.0001. A continually growing demand for the precision results in increasing computation time, as also shown in Figure 6. The calculations were made on an IBM RT/125 work station.

For the protocol of Figure 1, there are only 65 global states. For the range of precision shown in Figure 6, all of these global states were explored but their probabilities found with varying degrees of accuracy.

5. CRITIQUE

One of the main objectives of this analysis is that of determining protocol performance directly from a formal specification. While the specifications of the three protocols we have examined are of our own invention, we made a serious attempt to observe our evolving design of these specifications, particularly with regard to the influence of the analysis technique on the specification.

The pure finite-state machine is a very limiting abstraction; this is the main reason for going to extended finite-state-machine abstractions as in the case of CCITT's SDL

(Belina89) or ISO's Estelle (Budkowski87). Here, we have also been constrained by this abstraction and were forced to resort to various techniques to avoid extensive modification of the formal protocol specification in order to make the analysis. It is probably safe to say that had we been given finite-state descriptions of the protocols, we would have had to make some modifications to them in order to be able to carry out the analysis. For example, the specification of timers is awkward.

Earlier, we mentioned the problems which arise when the notion of unlabeled messages — as in the queue model — is mixed with that of labeled messages — as in the formal specification of the protocol. In the protocol of Figure 1 this was not too much of a problem; in the case where there is a window size of only two messages outstanding, the problem reaches awkward proportions. The measurement problem, i.e., specification of when to start measuring delay and when to stop in terms of sets of global states, had also to be solved on an ad hoc basis. We have not found a method applicable to the general case.

6. CONCLUSIONS

We are yet some distance away from being able, automatically, to predict performance directly from a given formal specification. Some of the limitations we experienced in this analysis are listed above. The limitations are admittedly significant.

Nevertheless, we have been able to make a relatively effective analysis. There are many protocols which are difficult to analyze when combined with a queue. We hope that we may have opened the door to a new technique for analyzing such situations directly from a protocol's formal description.

7. ACKNOWLEDGEMENT

We thank Günter Karjoth and Heinrich Müller for their help with Common LISP and Werner Bux, Felix Closs, Steve Fuhrmann, and Mehdi Nassehi for discussions and suggestions. We also thank three anonymous reviewers for their comments.

REFERENCES

Barghouti86- N. Barghouti, N. Nounou, and Y. Yemini, "An interactive protocol development environment," Proc. Sixth IFIP Workshop on Protocol Specification, Testing, and Verification, G. Bochmann and B. Sarikaya, Eds., Gray Rocks, Montreal, Canada, June 10-13, 1986, (North-Holland, Amsterdam), pp. 63 - 69.

Bauerfeld81- W. L. Bauerfeld, "Description, verification, and performance prediction of computer network protocols", Proc. INWG/NPL Workshop on Protocols, Vol. 1, Teddington, England, May 27-29, 1981, pp 253-269.

Beizer70- B. Beizer, "Analytical techniques for the statistical evaluation of program running time," Proc. Fall Joint Computer Conference, 1970, pp. 519 - 524.

Belina89- F.Belina and D. Hogrefe, "The CCITT-Specification and Description Language SDL", Computer Networks and ISDN Systems, Vol. 16, No. 4, March, 1989.

Bochmann88- G. v. Bochmann, "Adding performance aspects to specification languages", Proc. Eighth IFIP Symposium on Protocol Specification, Testing, and Verification, Atlantic City, NJ, June 7 - 10, 1988 (North-Holland, Amsterdam), pp. 19 - 31.

Bolognesi87- T. Bolognesi and E. Brinksma "Introduction to the ISO specification language LOTOS", Computer Networks and ISDN Systems, Vol. 14, No. 1, pp. 25 - 59, 1987.

Budkowski87- S. Budkowski and P. Dembinski, "An introduction to Estelle: a specification language for distributed systems", Computer Networks and ISDN Systems, Vol. 14, No. 1, pp. 3 - 23, 1987.

Demitrijevic88- D. D. Demitirijevic and M.-S. Chen, "An integrated algorithm for probabilistic protocol verification and evaluation", IBM Research Report, RC13901, August 4, 1988. (To be published in the Proceedings of IEEE INFOCOM'89, Ottawa, Canada, April, 1989.)

Engelbrecht85- J. Engelbrecht, P. Kritzinger, and H. Rudin, "Predicting protocol performance from a meta-implementation," Proc. Fifth Workshop on Protocol Specification, Testing, and Verification, M. Diaz, Editor, Moissac-Toulouse, France, June 10-13 1985, (North-Holland, Amsterdam, 1985), pp. 349 - 362.

Gouda78- M. G. Gouda, "Protocol machines: towards a logical theory of communication protocols," Ph.D. thesis, University of Waterloo, Ontario, Canada, Jan. 1978 (see especially Chapter 11.)

Gravey86- A. Gravey and A. Dupuis, "Performance evaluation of two mutual exclusion distributed protocols via Markovian modeling," Proc. Sixth IFIP Workshop on Protocol Specification, Testing, and Verification, G. Bochmann and B. Sarikaya, Eds., Gray Rocks, Montreal, Canada, June 10-13, 1986, (North-Holland, Amsterdam), pp. 335 -346.

Kemeny60- J. G. Kemeny and J. L. Snell, Finite Markov Chains, (D. Van Nostrand, Princeton, NJ), 1960.

Kritzinger86- P. Kritzinger, "A performance model of the OSI communication architecture", IEEE Trans. Commun., Vol. COM-34, No. 6, pp. 554 - 563, June, 1986.

Lin84- S Lin, D. J. Costello, and M. J. Miller, "Automatic request error-control schemes", IEEE Communications Magazine, Vol. 22, No. 12, Dec., 1984, pp. 5 - 17.

Molloy82- M. K. Molloy, "Performance analysis using stochastic Petri nets," IEEE Trans. Computers, Vol. C-31, No. 9, pp. 913-917, Sept. 1982.

Nounou84- N. Nounou and Y. Yemini, "Algebraic specification-based performance analysis of communication protocols", Proc. Workshop on Protocol Specification, Testing, and Verification, IV, Skytop, Pennsylvania, June 1984, (North-Holland, Amsterdam, 1985), pp. 541 - 560.

Razouk84- R. R. Razouk and C.V. Phelps, "Performance analysis using timed Petri nets", Proc. Fourth Workshop on Protocol Specification, Testing, and Verification, Skytop, Pennsylvania, June 1984, (North-Holland, Amsterdam, 1985), pp. 561 - 576.

Rudin83- H. Rudin, "From formal protocol specification towards automated performance prediction," Proc. Workshop on Protocol Specification, Testing, and Verification, III, Rüschlikon, Switzerland, May 1983, (North-Holland, Amsterdam, 1983), pp. 257 - 269.

Rudin84- H. Rudin, "An improved algorithm for estimating protocol performance", Proc. Fourth Workshop on Protocol Specification, Testing, and Verification, Skytop, Pennsylvania, June 1984, (North-Holland, Amsterdam, 1985), pp. 515 - 525.

Rudin85- H. Rudin, "Time in formal protocol specifications", Proc. GI/NTG Conference on Communication in Distributed Systems, Karlsruhe, West Germany, March 11-15, 1985, pp. 575 - 587.

Winston89- P. H. Winston and B. K. P. Horn, "LISP", (Addison-Wesley Publishing Co., London), Third edition, 1989.

Zuberek80- W. M. Zuberek, "Timed Petri nets and preliminary performance evaluation", Proc. 7th Annual IEEE Symposium on Computer Architecture, May 6 - 8, 1980, pp. 88 - 96.

Session 6:

Tool Environments

Protocol Specification, Testing, and Verification, IX
E. Brinksma, G. Scollo and C.A. Vissers (Editors)
Elsevier Science Publishers B.V. (North-Holland)

On Executable Specifications, Validation, and Testing of MAC-level Protocols

Paweł Gburzyński* and Piotr Rudnicki†

Department of Computing Science
The University of Alberta,
Edmonton, Alberta, Canada T6J 2H1

Abstract
Numerous tools for specifying protocols have been proposed in the literature, e.g. Estelle, Lotos. These approaches are aimed at providing general-purpose specification methods for distributed computations. In this paper, we consider a limited class of distributed computations, namely medium access control level protocols for local area networks. We present LANSF—a software environment for specifying and emulating MAC-level protocols. The specification language is based on C; essentially protocols are described (programmed) in C with the assistance of numerous standard data types. The heart of LANSF is an event-driven emulator that models communication phenomena in physical distributed systems at the medium access control level. The software package can be (and already has been) applied to various areas of protocol design, e.g. prototyping, investigating the protocol performance, verification, validation, and testing. The modelling package, runnable under the 4.2 and 4.3 BSD versions of UNIX[1], is available from the authors upon request.

1 Introduction

Medium access control level protocols form an interesting subclass of distributed computations. They are distinguished from higher-level protocols by the direct contact with physical media. Certain events occurring in physical channels are not under immediate control of the protocol software, e.g. the propagation time of a signal is an intrinsic hardwired property of the channel. Another example of such an event is a collision of two or more transmissions in a channel. A collision is not generated explicitly by the protocol program: its occurrence is due to the nature of the channel. For CSMA/CD protocols, the ability of a station to detect collisions is a critical prerequisite. Therefore, a sound specification system for this type of protocols must take into account the physical properties of the underlying communication media. The experience of the present authors indicates that expressing the nature of a physical channel in general-purpose specification systems as LOTOS[1] or Estelle[2] poses a serious challenge and seems to be impractical.

LANSF is built around a model of the communication channel [8]. This model is implemented as a data type which offers a number of functions corresponding to physical operations performed on communication media by physical stations. These are: starting a packet transmission, finishing or aborting the transmission, and sensing the state of the channel. The software part of the protocol defines the behaviour of stations by describing how they interact with the channels. This description takes the form of a collection of interrupt-driven processes. The code of a process is a C function. A process function can perform numerous standard operations (processed by LANSF), in particular, it can execute operations from the data type describing communication channels.

*Supported in part by NSERC Grant No. OGP9183. email: pawel@alberta.UUCP.
†Supported in part by NSERC Grant No. OGP9207. email: piotr@alberta.UUCP.
[1] UNIX is a trademark of AT&T Bell Laboratories.

Protocols specified in LANSF can be executed which is achieved by modelling the time flow. For a channel, it means that an activity initiated by a station on the channel will propagate to all "places" of the channel in time dependent on its geometry and propagation speed. Besides channels, there are other sources that generate timed events, e.g. the "outside world" of the network which provides it with packets to be transmitted. The execution of a protocol consists in accepting the packets from the outside and emulating their transmission and reception—according to the protocol. The system models the propagation of signals in the channels.

Originally, LANSF was designed as a tool for investigating the performance of LAN protocols. During numerous experiments that we have carried out with our system we have noticed that actually LANSF offers much more. For some protocols it was important to assert certain local properties of stations, e.g. in some collision protocols [9, 11, 12] a packet should not be allowed to collide more than once. It turned out to be quite easy and natural to incorporate such assertions into the protocol specification. This was due to the modular structure of the protocol programs: the behaviour of each station is defined independently of the behaviour of the other stations. This definition consists of a set of processes, each process executing a certain logically separable collection of functions.

The possibility of adding new processes without affecting the dynamic structure of the existing ones allows us to program dedicated monitoring functions. For example, assume that we want to determine the distribution of the number of stations involved in a single collision in Ethernet. A natural way of solving it in LANSF is to program a separate process monitoring events in the carrier. As another example, let us consider a token ring protocol with multiple tokens. We would like to assert that the tokens are passed correctly and are never lost. To achieve this goal, we can define a process that does nothing else but tests dynamically a certain Boolean formula which involves variables belonging to different stations. Let us note that in such circumstances LANSF offers a serious advantage over real, physical implementations. Namely, it allows us to express and test assertions that would be impossible or difficult to verify in the physical system.

The rest of this paper is organised as follows. In section 2 we introduce the language tools for interfacing the protocol with the network backbone. Section 3 briefly presents the protocol definition language. These two sections serve as an introduction to section 4 which discusses the tools for testing and validating protocols during emulation. The discussion is centered around an example of a variant of the token ring protocol.

2 The Network Environment

In this section, we briefly describe how LANSF emulates the hardwired elements of the physical system. The full semantics of this part of LANSF is given in [8].

2.1 Network configuration: links, ports, stations

A physical distributed system which can be modelled in LANSF consists of a number of *stations* interconnected via communication channels called *links*. The simplest link can be viewed as a single and uniform signal passing medium: a signal (an *activity*) entered into any place of the link propagates with a certain speed to all other places. LANSF models several types of communication media (links) including unidirectional fibre-optic lines. Links are visible to stations via *ports*. A station can be equipped with a number of ports and thus connected to a number of links. The distance between any two ports connected to the same link is given in the link distance matrix (supplied as part of the input data).

For example, a bus-type network, e.g. *Ethernet* [13], consists of a single link and a number of stations, each station having a single port to the link. A ring network, e.g. *Token Ring* [14], is built of a number of stations and the same number of links. Each station is connected to exactly two links. In a star-type network with a central station there are n stations and $n-1$ links. The central station is connected to every link, while the other stations have only one port each.

The physical system operates according to the communication protocol which gives the rules that govern the behaviour of stations. From the viewpoint of implementation, the protocol is described by a distributed program specifying the code and data structures of the physical processes that are executed by the stations. The physical processes communicate by inserting signals into ports (and thus into the underlying links) and sensing events at the ports.

2.2 Time and distances

Time in LANSF is discrete: natural numbers are used to denote time instants. The interval between two consecutive time instants is called the *Indivisible Time Unit* (*ITU*).

The information sent by stations through links is organised into finite sequences of *bits* called *packets*. A station knows the transmission speed of each of its ports—the number of *ITU*'s required to transmit a single bit. Different ports may have different transmission speeds.

Entries in the link distance matrix are also expressed in *ITU*'s. Each entry specifies the number of *ITU*'s required to propagate a signal between some two ports.

2.3 The station structure

Only a part of the station structure is predefined by LANSF. The following attributes of this structure are essential: `id` — the station's identifier, `ports` — the list of ports accessed by the station, `packet_queue` — the queue of packets to be transmitted, `current_packet` — the buffer for the packet to be transmitted next, and `process_list` — the list of processes executed by the station. The station structure can be extended by the protocol specification, i.e. non-standard attributes can be added to the station structure.

2.4 Activity Interpreters

An *activity interpreter* (*AI* for short) emulates an active element of the hardwired part of the network environment. The following *AI*s are built into LANSF: the *client*, the *link AI*, the *timer*, and the *signaler*. They are implemented as data types and are visible as collections of functions and data. The protocol is specified as a distributed program (a set of processes) that calls these functions and references the data.

*AI*s generate events which can be sensed by processes. A process suspends itself by executing `return`. Before doing so, it may specify events which can wake it up in the future, by calling the following function:

```
wait_event (s, e, a)
```

The parameters identify:

- `s` — the *AI* expected to generate the waking event; it can be: `CLIENT`, `TIMER`, `SIGNAL`, or a port *AI* determined by the port identifier.
- `e` — the (waking) event appropriate for *s*.
- `a` — a user-defined integer value.

The operation `wait_event` is implemented in the *AI* responsible for the generation of the event. A process may execute a number of wait requests before it eventually goes to sleep (suspends itself). The function `wait_event` returns to the process and the process is continued until it executes `return`. Then the process is suspended and will be resumed only when one of the awaited events takes place. Multiple wait requests executed before `return` are collected on a list. When the process is restarted due to the occurrence of one of the awaited events, its entire wait list is cleared.

On the occurrence of one of the events awaited by a process, the process function is called and the corresponding value of `a` is returned in global variable `the_action`. Variable `the_action` is meant to identify the entry point of the process.

2.4.1 The timer

The timer *AI* provides each process with a clock that allows the process to measure time intervals. The global variable `current_time` defined by the timer tells the time (in *ITU*'s) since the beginning of the protocol execution. A process can set up an alarm clock by issuing a `wait_event` request to the timer. This request specifies the time delay. When the specified time interval elapses, the timer generates an event that wakes up the process.

2.4.2 The client

The client *AI* is a *daemon* that provides stations with packets to be transmitted. The packet arrival process is defined in the input data to the client. The arriving packets are queued at the sending stations. Whenever a station is ready to transmit the next packet it calls the function:

```
int    get_packet (min, max, frm)
int    min, max, frm;
```

The three parameters of `get_packet` denote the minimum and maximum packet length, and the length of the frame information, respectively. All these lengths are specified in bits. The function returns `0` if the packet queue is empty. In such a case, the process can wait for a `MESSAGE_ARRIVAL` event which is generated by the client whenever a new packet is queued at the station. Otherwise, the station's packet buffer `current_packet` is assigned a new value.

The packet buffer is emptied by calling:

```
release_current_packet ()
```

after a successful transmission. Packets are addressed to stations. Upon reception of a packet, the process at the receiving station calls the function:

```
accept_packet (packet, port_id)
PACKET   *packet;
int      port_id;
```

to notify the client that its packet has been processed. The two functions listed above are used in calculating the performance measures of the protocol. They also provide some rudimentary means for asserting the protocol consistency, e.g. it is an error to attempt to acquire a new packet for transmission before releasing the previous one.

2.4.3 Link

The link *AI* includes a collection of port *AI*s. A process can interact with a link via a port only: the port must be defined at the station to which the process belongs. This interaction consists in inserting activities into the port and sensing events at the port. The role of the link *AI* is to transform activities into events.

Starting and terminating activities

There are two kinds of activities that a station can insert into a link: packet transfers and jamming signals. An activity can be started and then terminated or aborted which is modelled by the following functions:

```
start_transfer (port_id, packet)
int      port_id;
PACKET   packet;
```

By calling `start_transfer` the station starts transmitting a packet (which is described by the contents of structure `packet`) on port `port_id`. The transfer continues until the station terminates the transmission by either `stop_transfer` or `abort_transfer`.

```
stop_transfer  (port_id)
abort_transfer (port_id)
int     port_id;
```

Function **stop_transfer** is used when the entire packet has been successfully transmitted. The second function aborts the transfer of a partially sent packet, e.g. after a collision.

The timer is used to determine when the packet has been entirely transmitted. There is a convenient alias (a C macro) for **start_transfer** which automatically sets up the timer for the time delay corresponding to the total length of the transmitted packet:

```
transmit_packet (port_id, packet, eot_action)
int      port_id, eot_action;
PACKET   packet;
```

The following two functions control the emission of jamming signals.

```
start_jam (port_id)
stop_jam    (port_id)
int     port_id;
```

With **start_jam**, the station starts sending a jamming signal which is emitted until the station calls **stop_jam**. The following alias can be used to start a jam and, at the same time, set up the timer for the jam length.

```
emit_jam (port_id, jam_length, eoj_action)
int     port_id, eoj_action;
TIME    jam_length;
```

Port events

Below we list the symbolic constants representing valid port events and give informal explanation of their meaning. The formal semantics of these events is contained in [8].

- SILENCE — The event occurs at the beginning of the nearest silence period heard at the port. If no activity is heard on the port when the request is issued, the event occurs immediately.
- ACTIVITY — The event occurs when SILENCE does not.
- COLLISION — The event occurs when a collision is heard on the specified port.
- BOJ — The event occurs when the beginning of a jamming signal is heard, preceded by a period of silence or by a transfer.
- EOJ — The event is triggered by the end of a jamming signal followed by a silence period or by a transfer attempt.
- EOT — The event occurs when the end of a successful packet transmission is heard on the port.
- MY_PACKET — The event occurs when the station hears the beginning of a packet for which the station is the receiver.
- END_MY_PACKET — The event occurs when the station hears the end of a packet for which the station is the receiver.

Port inquiries

Besides awaiting various port events, stations are also able to perform port (link) inquiries. The station processes need not remember the history of past events: they can inquire the port *AI*s. The history of past link activities is archived by the link *AI*. A process can inquire a port about the last: beginning or end of an activity, collision, end of a successful transfer, beginning or end of a jamming signal.

2.4.4 Signaler

Processes of the same station can pass signals among themselves. A signal is generated by a process through calling

```
internal_signal (signal_id)
int signal_id;
```

A process awaits a signal by calling **wait_event** with SIGNAL as the first parameter and the signal identifier as the second parameter. Passing a signal takes no emulated time.

2.5 Implementation notes

The present sequential implementation of LANSF is driven by a centralised event manager which controls the flow of time. The manager communicates (internally) with the *AI*s, inspects their events, and computes the next event to occur. Then the timer's variable `current_time` is set to the time of this event. If there is a process awaiting the event, the event manager wakes up the process. When the process eventually goes to sleep, the event manager takes over and selects the next event to occur. While a process is active, the time does not flow, thus, it is possible that two or more events occur at the same time. In such a case, the actual order of their service is determined at random. The flow of the emulated time in LANSF is defined formally in [8].

The implementation includes a number of auxiliary functions which serve the following purposes: generating random numbers, error handling, memory management, and user interface. The most important feature of the LANSF user interface is a window-oriented dynamic display toolbox. This collection of functions offers monitoring tools similar to sophisticated debugging systems (see [5]).

3 Protocol Definition Language

This section presents the syntax of the LANSF protocol definition language (the full description is given in [5]). The language is simply C extended with the operations and data structures described above. We assume that the syntax and semantics of C is known: we will restrict ourselves to the LANSF-specific aspects of the protocol definition language.

The protocol specification is contained in a C file and defines a number of processes. The code of a process is given as a C function; its data area consists of the station's attributes and global variables. The protocol file must also contain the declaration of the startup function `in_protocol` which initialises variables, reads the protocol-specific input, and, most importantly, creates and then starts the processes.

A single station may run an arbitrary number of processes. For example, in the case of the Ethernet protocol, it is convenient to have two processes at a station, namely the transmitter and the receiver. The code of a process (the process function) can be shared by a number of actual processes. For example, in Ethernet, all transmitters share the same process function.

3.1 Creating processes

A process is created by the following function:

```
new_process (code, version)
int  (*code)(), version;
```

The first argument is a pointer to the function representing the process code. The function pointed to by `code` will be called whenever the execution of the process is resumed. The global integer variable `process_version` will then contain the value of `version` with which the process has been created. The purpose of `version` is to distinguish multiple processes sharing the same code at the same station. For example, let us look at the following fragment of `in_protocol` for Ethernet:

```
for (i = 0; i < n_stations; i++) {
  the_station = id_to_station (i);
  new_process (transmitter, 0);
  new_process (receiver, 0);
}
```

Variable `n_stations` tells the number of stations in the network. The stations are identified by numbers `0..n_stations-1`. The function `id_to_station` maps station identifiers into pointers to the corresponding data structures. Two processes are created for each station: their codes being defined by the functions `transmitter` and `receiver`. The declarations of these functions must be included in the protocol file.

3.2 The process environment

The environment of a process is described by the contents of variables `the_station`, `the_action`, `the_process_version`, `the_packet`, and `the_port`. Variable `the_station` is a pointer to the station at which the process has been created. (Note that in the above example, the value of `the_station` changes with each turn of the loop in order to create a pair of processes at each station in the network.) The integer variable `the_action` is used to identify the entry point of the process. Before the process puts itself to sleep, it issues a sequence of wait requests (2.4). Each wait request identifies an event awaited by the process and specifies an integer value that will be returned via `the_action` when the process is awakened by this event. Immediately after a new process is created, it is started with the value of `the_action` equal `0` (constant `INITIALIZE`). The variables `the_packet` and `the_port` are used by LANSF to pass additional information to the process for certain types of events (see examples below).

3.3 The process code

The code of a process is a C function. The tools provided by LANSF facilitate specification of interrupt-driven processes. The most pragmatic way of organising a process code is to make it a single `switch` statement controlled by the value of `the_action`. For example, consider the receiver part of an Ethernet station.

```
receiver () {
  switch (the_action) {
    case INITIALIZE :
      wait_event (BUS, END_MY_PACKET, END_OF_PACKET);
      return;
    case END_OF_PACKET :
      accept_packet (the_packet, BUS);
      wait_event (TIMER, 1, INITIALIZE);
      return;
  }
}
```

Immediately after the receiver is created, it is awakened (i.e. the function `receiver` is called) with the value of `the_action` equal `INITIALIZE`. Then, the process issues a wait request to the port *AI* (`BUS` identifies the only port of the station) for the event corresponding to the reception of a packet. The event `END_MY_PACKET` is triggered when the end of a packet addressed to the station is heard at the port. In such a case, the process will be restarted with `the_action` equal `END_OF_PACKET`. The environment variable `the_packet` carries information about the received packet. Having accepted the packet, the process starts expecting the next one. However, before doing that, it has to sleep for a short period of time in order not to sense the same `END_MY_PACKET` event again (as we have already mentioned, the time does not flow when a process is active).

The process structure suggested above can be seen as a description of a finite-state machine. Namely, each entry of the switch statement corresponds to a state. Transitions between states are defined by wait requests (calls to `wait_event`). In a given state, the process issues a sequence of wait requests that specify the transitions from this state. The chosen transition is determined by the occurrence of the earliest event from those specified in the wait requests. Then, the value of `the_action` indicates the new state.

4 Assertions

Originally, LANSF was designed as a tool for modelling communication protocols. The built-in notion of time allows us to compute performance measures of the modelled protocol. LANSF offers a number of functions to collect performance statistics. Several protocols have been been investigated from this point of view and the results have been published [3, 4, 6, 7].

LANSF has appeared to be very helpful in the process of protocol design. At the design stage of a protocol, the issue of its correctness comes before the performance. Correctness proofs of realistic protocols can be quite complex. The experience of numerous users indicates that experimenting in LANSF facilitates the process of constructing such proofs. The properties of protocols that we want to verify can be turned into Boolean expressions and programmed in LANSF as assertions.

In the process of protocol design, LANSF plays the role of a fast prototyping environment. This environment is more flexible than the physical implementation. Testing the LANSF prototype of a protocol is simple, and it is easy to modify the prototype, should the testing expose a design error. Some global conditions that cannot be tested in a physical implementation can be programmed and examined in LANSF.

4.1 Token ring

To illustrate how LANSF can be used for protocol testing, we will discuss a variant of a token ring protocol. In a ring-type network, stations and links form a circular structure so that each station is directly connected with two immediate neighbours via two ports. Each station receives information on one (input) port and transmits on the other (output) port. A special packet (the token) is circulated among the stations. If the station receiving the token has no data packet to be transmitted, it immediately passes the token on its output port. In the opposite case, the station stops the token and passes the data packet instead. Having completed the transmission of the data packet, the station passes the token.

In the presented version of the protocol, a station may only transmit one data packet per each acquisition of the token. A station detecting a data packet addressed to itself receives the packet and removes it from the ring. Other data packets are passed around until they reach their proper destinations. In our model, each of the two station ports is serviced by a separate process. The processes communicate by passing signals. The input port is denoted by `LEFT_PORT` and the output port by `RIGHT_PORT`. The amount of time elapsing between the reception of the first bit of a packet and passing that bit on the output port is determined by the length of the packet header (variable `hdr`). The code of the two processes is listed below.

```
left_port_process () {
  switch (the_action) {
    case INITIALIZE:
      if (the_station->id == 0) {
        /* Station 0 creates the token.                              */
        make_token ();
    case GOT_TOKEN:
        /* Inform the transmitter that it is allowed to transmit. */
        internal_signal (TRANSFER_PERMITTED);
        the_station->packets_passed = 0;
    case WAIT_FOR_SILENCE:
        /* Wait until the packet disappears from the port.           */
        wait_event (LEFT_PORT, SILENCE, WAIT_FOR_PACKET);
        return;
      }
    case WAIT_FOR_PACKET:
      wait_event (LEFT_PORT, ACTIVITY, RECEIVING_PACKET);
      return;
    case RECEIVING_PACKET:
      /* Buffer the packet until it is known what to do with it.  */
      the_station->buffer = *the_packet;
      wait_event (TIMER, hdr, HEADER_RECOGNIZED);
      return;
    case HEADER_RECOGNIZED:
      if ((the_station->buffer).type == TOKEN_PACKET)
```

```
        continue_at (GOT_TOKEN);
      if (my_packet (&(the_station->buffer))) {
        /* A packet addressed to this station.                    */
        wait_event (LEFT_PORT, EOT, PACKET_RECEIVED);
        return;
      }
      /* A packet addressed to somebody else - pass it.           */
      internal_signal (PACKET_TO_PASS);
      assert (the_station->packets_passed < n_stations,
        "Unfair token passing");
      the_station->packets_passed++;
      continue_at (WAIT_FOR_SILENCE);
    case PACKET_RECEIVED:
      /* Receive the packet.                                      */
      accept_packet (the_packet, LEFT_PORT);
      continue_at (WAIT_FOR_SILENCE);
  }
}
```

Station 0 is responsible for creation of the token packet (function **make_token** is not listed here). Whenever an activity is sensed on the left port, the process buffers the incoming packet until it recognises the header. If the incoming packet is addressed to the station, it is accepted and removed from the ring. Otherwise, a signal is sent to the right-port process. If the packet is the token, the right-port process is restarted by the signal TRANSFER_PERMITTED—and now it is allowed to transmit a data packet. Otherwise, the packet must be relayed to the next station in the ring. This action is also performed by the right-port process which, in this case, is awakened by the signal PACKET_TO_PASS.

```
right_port_process () {
  switch (the_action) {
    case INITIALIZE:
      /* Wait for a signal from the right port process.          */
      wait_event (SIGNAL, TRANSFER_PERMITTED, TRANSMIT_OWN_PACKET);
      wait_event (SIGNAL, PACKET_TO_PASS, TRANSMIT_OTHER_PACKET);
      return;
    case TRANSMIT_OWN_PACKET:
      if (get_packet (min, max, hdr+trl) == YES) {
        /* Transmit own packet.                                  */
        transmit_packet (RIGHT_PORT, the_station->current_packet,
                                             PACKET_TRANSMITTED);
        return;
      } else {
    case PASS_TOKEN:
        /* Pass the token.                                       */
        transmit_packet (RIGHT_PORT, the_station->buffer,
          TOKEN_PASSED);
        return;
      }
    case TOKEN_PASSED:
    case TRANSFER_COMPLETED:
      stop_transfer (RIGHT_PORT);
      continue_at (INITIALIZE);
    case PACKET_TRANSMITTED:
      stop_transfer (RIGHT_PORT);
      release_current_packet ();
```

```
      wait_event (DELAY, spc, PASS_TOKEN);
      return;
    case TRANSMIT_OTHER_PACKET:
      transmit_packet (RIGHT_PORT, the_station->buffer,
                                                    TRANSFER_COMPLETED);
      return;
  }
}
```

Whenever the station acquires the token, the right-port process checks whether there is a data packet awaiting transmission, and if so, it transmits the data packet and then passes the token preceded by a packet space. Packets addressed to other stations are relayed on the right port—in the same way as the token packet.

4.2 Local assertions

The code of a LANSF process is sequential. The well-known technique of assertions can be employed to terminate the program if an abnormal condition arises. There is a standard function

```
assert (boolean_expression, string)
int boolean_expression;
char *string;
```

that serves this end. If `boolean_expression` evaluates to false (0), the emulation is aborted and `string` is printed out.

This simple technique proved valuable in debugging the specifications of several collision protocols based on passing virtual tokens [9, 11, 12]. The common property of these protocols is that the station possessing the token is allowed to collide at most once, before it transmits successfully. This property can be expressed in terms of local variables of a process and then turned into an assertion.

In the `left_port_process` of our token ring protocol, we use an assertion to make sure that the number of packets relayed by a station between two consecutive acquisitions of the token is less than the number of stations in the network (see action `HEADER_RECOGNIZED`). We may interpret it as a locally perceived fairness. The condition of this assertion may seem intuitively obvious; however, it need not be so in more refined versions of the protocol, e.g. when there are multiple tokens and/or the behaviour of stations is not identical.

4.3 Global assertions

Some properties of protocols are not locally verifiable. In the example from the previous section, the asserted property expresses only the fairness as perceived by a single station. It may happen that there are numerous transmissions that are not seen by the station, and thus the network can be globally unfair. In order to ensure the global fairness we have to assert that each station obtaining the token will pass it to the immediate successor. In this particular case, it is possible to add some information to the token, so that upon its reception the station can locally test where the token comes from. However, such a solution is "impure" as it involves an otherwise unwarranted modification of the protocol. LANSF offers tools, called *observers*, to separate the concerns: it is not necessary to modify the protocol to express and test global assertions.

4.3.1 Observers

In LANSF we can have processes that are not associated with any specific stations. These processes are called *observers* and their code is programmed in a way similar to station processes. However, there exist operations that can be performed only by regular processes (`wait_event`, `continue_at`) and not by observers, and vice versa (`inspect`, `timeout`).

Observer processes are created analogously to regular processes. The following function is used to create an observer:

```
new_observer (code)
int (*code)();
```

An observer is able to react to certain actions of regular processes. The following operation allows an observer to await a certain moment in the emulation when the event manager is about to restart an ordinary process:

```
inspect (s, p, v, a, ma)
STATION *s;
int (*p)(), v, a, ma;
```

where

- s — is a pointer to structure STATION or symbolic constant ANY.
- p — is a pointer to a process code or ANY.
- v — is a process version number or ANY.
- a — is an action of the regular process p or ANY.
- ma — is an integer identifying an action of the observer that calls inspect.

The function is analogous to wait_event in ordinary processes. It specifies the condition upon which the observer process can be awakened. The value of ma is fully analogous to the third parameter of wait_event; it specifies the observer action to be taken when the condition specified by the first four parameters occurs.

A regular process specifies its waking conditions in terms of events at ports, timer interrupts, client events, or signals. An observer can be restarted by the event manager, just before the manager is to wake up a regular process. The waking conditions of an observer are specified in terms of the environment variables of a regular process. If the event manager is about to restart a regular process and the values of the environment variables of the process match the corresponding parameters of a previously executed inspect, the observer is awakened first, with the global variable the_observer_action set to the corresponding value of ma.

The symbol ANY used in place of one or more of the first four parameters of inspect has a special meaning—it stands for an arbitrary value. In such a case, any actual value of the corresponding environment variable matches the parameter. This actual value is returned in the corresponding environment variable (the_station, the_process_code, the_process_version, the_action) which is available to the observer when it is restarted.

An observer can set an alarm clock by using the function:

```
timeout (delay, ma)
TIME delay;
int  ma;
```

where delay gives the number of *ITU*'s the alarm clock is to be set for. If the time elapses without an interrupt then the observer will perform the action ma.

A somewhat similar notion of an observer was proposed by Groz [10]. However, in that approach, the observer processes were unrestricted and allowed to reference local variables of regular processes. In our case, observers are clearly separated from the protocol and perceive it as a finite state machine. If a protocol process wants to be observable, it has to exhibit its operations in actions. This apparent restriction forces a careful design of the protocol structure.

The suggested way of organising the code of an observer is the same as for an ordinary process, i.e. a single switch statement controlled by the value of the_observer_action.

4.3.2 Examples of Observers

Let us consider an observer that detects the violation of the global fairness in the token ring. We would like to test whether the token packet is always passed to the immediate successor of the station currently having the token. Each station on the ring is identified by the_station->id which is an integer number in the range 0..n_stations-1. We assume that these identifiers are assigned in such a way that the successor of a station i is numbered $(i+1)\bmod$ n_stations.

```
fairness_observer   () {
  switch (the_observer_action) {
    case INITIALIZE:
      last_token = NONE;
    case RESUME:
      inspect (ANY, left_port_process, ANY, GOT_TOKEN, VERIFY);
      return;
    case VERIFY:
      assert ((last_token == NONE) ||
        ((last_token + 1) % n_stations == the_station->id),
          "Unfair token passing");
      last_token = the_station->id;
      resume_at (RESUME);
  }
}
```

Immediately upon creation, the observer process is awakened with **the_observer_action** equal **INITIALIZE**. The process sets a local variable and waits until any **left_port_process** is to be awakened at **ANY** station with the value of **the_action** equal **GOT_TOKEN**. Then the observer examines whether the token has been passed from the immediate neighbour of its new recipient, and if not, the unsatisfied assertion terminates the emulation. Note that testing the property locally at each station would require modification of the protocol code, which does not seem to be a good practice.

As another example, let us take the same protocol in which we would like to test that token is never lost nor duplicated. In this case no local assertion can help, unless each station can access local data of any other station.

```
token_observer   () {
  switch (the_observer_action) {
    case INITIALIZE:
      inspect (ANY, left_port_process, ANY, GOT_TOKEN, VERIFY);
      return;
    case VERIFY:
      inspect (the_station, right_port_process, ANY, TOKEN_PASSED, INITIALIZE);
      inspect (ANY, left_port_process, ANY, GOT_TOKEN, DUPLICATE_TOKEN);
      timeout (token_passing_timeout, LOST_TOKEN);
      return;
    case DUPLICATE_TOKEN:
      excptn ("Duplicated token");
    case LOST_TOKEN:
      excptn ("Token has been lost");
  }
}
```

(The standard function **excptn** aborts the emulator and prints out the parameter string.)

The observer process is awakened whenever a station gets the token. The first **inspect** at the observer action **VERIFY** describes the correct continuation of the protocol, i.e. the corresponding **right_port_process** passing the token. If **ANY** other station gets the token before that event occurs, the observer will terminate the emulation. The case of the lost token is recognised when the token received by a station is not passed before **token_passing_timeout** elapses. The order in which the **inspect** statements are listed is important: they are tested also in this order. The first condition matched by the the environment of the process to be awakened will be effective: the observer action specified in it will be executed. When an observer is restarted, its inspect list is cleared and the observers' waking conditions have to be specified anew.

5 Conclusions

We have presented a software system for specifying MAC-level protocols. The specification is executable: it can be translated into a program that emulates the physical network. The emulator is based on an accurate model of a communication channel with a formally defined semantics. Besides providing a convenient environment for investigating the performance of protocols, the system offers some tools for protocol testing and validation. The software package presented in this paper has been used for designing new protocols, examining their performance, and testing their properties. LANSF turned out to be helpful in the process of finding proofs of protocol correctness.

References

[1] T. Bolognesi and E. Brinksma. Introduction to the ISO specification language LOTOS. *Computer Networks and ISDN Systems*, 14:25–59, 1987.

[2] S. Budkowski and P. Dembinski. An introduction to ESTELLE a specification language for distributed systems. *Computer Networks and ISDN Systems*, 14:3–23, 1987.

[3] W. Dobosiewicz and P. Gburzyński. Ethernet with segmented carrier. In *Proceedings of Computer Networking Symposium*, pages 72–78, Washington, DC, Apr. 1988. IEEE.

[4] P. Gburzyński and P. Rudnicki. A better-than-Token protocol with bounded packet delay time for ethernet-type LAN's. In *Symposium on the Simulation of Computer Networks*, pages 110–117, Colorado Springs, Co., Aug. 1987. IEEE.

[5] P. Gburzyński and P. Rudnicki. *LANSF — A Configuarble System for Modeling Communication Networks, version 1.4.* The University of Alberta, Department of Computing Science, TR 88-19, Edmonton, 1988.

[6] P. Gburzyński and P. Rudnicki. Modeling low-level communication protocols: A modular approach. In *Proceedings of the 4th International Conference on Modeling Techniques and Tools for Computer Performance Evaluation*, pages 89–108, Palma de Mallorca, Spain, 1988. Universitat de les Illes Balears.

[7] P. Gburzyński and P. Rudnicki. A note on the performance of ENET II. *IEEE Journal on Selected Areas in Communications*, 7:424–427, Apr. 1989.

[8] P. Gburzyński and P. Rudnicki. On formal modelling of communication channels. In *IEEE INFOCOM'89*, pages 143–151, 1989.

[9] P. Gburzyński and P. Rudnicki. A virtual token protocol for bus networks: Correctness and performance. *INFOR*, 1989. (Accepted).

[10] R. Groz. Unrestricted verification of protocol properties on a simulation using an observer approach. In *Proceedings of the IFIP WG 6.1 6th Workshop on Protocol Specification, Testing, and Verification*, pages 255–266. North-Holland, June 1986.

[11] W. Kiesel and P. Kuehn. A new CSMA/CD protocol for local area networks with dynamic priorities and low collision probability. *IEEE Journal on Selected Areas in Communications*, 1(5):869–876, 1983.

[12] M. Ríos and N. Georganas. A hybrid multiple-access protocol for data and voice-packet over local area networks. *IEEE Trans. on Computers*, 34(1):90–94, Jan. 1985.

[13] J. Schoch et al. Evolution of the Ethernet local computer network. *IEEE Computer*, Aug. 1982.

[14] W. Stallings. A tutorial on the IEEE 802 Local Network Standard. In R. Pickholtz, editor, *Local Area & Multiple Access Networks*, pages 1–30. Computer Science Press, 1986.

Protocol Specification, Testing, and Verification, IX
E. Brinksma, G. Scollo and C.A. Vissers (Editors)
Elsevier Science Publishers B.V. (North-Holland)
IFIP, 1990

LOTOS Tools based on the Cornell Synthesizer Generator

Peter van Eijk

University of Twente
The Netherlands
mcvax!utrcu1!pve

ABSTRACT

This paper describes how the Cornell Synthesizer Generator, a system for constructing language-based editors, was used to construct a variety of interactive tools for the specification language LOTOS. Two examples are discussed in detail. One is an editor for the full LOTOS language, incorporating static semantics checks as well as a 'menu'-function, which allows investigation of the dynamic behaviour of a specification. The other is a tool that supports interactive equivalence proof by transformation. For presentation purposes only a CCS version of this tool is treated.

1. Introduction

We have implemented interactive tools for the specification language LOTOS [ISO1988] by using the Cornell Synthesizer Generator (CSG) [Teitelbaum1989]. Most interactive tools can be seen as editors. In an editor the user issues commands to navigate through, manipulate or view the edit-object. For example, the edit-object of a conventional text editor is a sequence of lines of characters. In a database system the edit-object is an entire database and can be accessed through a database query language. Tools that support a specification language operate on expressions in this language and on objects that denote the semantics of these expressions (as in a programming language: the program, its execution state and assertions). The CSG generates language specific editors from a high level language specification. Editor specifications are written in a formalism (SSL) that is based on attribute grammars. Our research concerns the possibilities and limitations of using the CSG for the generation of interactive tools for LOTOS and related languages.

The problem addressed here is the following. We want tools that we can trust (i.e. are correct). We want new tool functionality in these tools and we want that fast (i.e. yesterday). The traditional approach is implementing tools in a regular programming language. This approach has the disadvantage that there is a large distance between the description of functions and their implementation, and between the semantical objects and the available data structures to express them in. This leads to software that is hard to change and error prone. The approach discussed here is to make high-level descriptions of tool functions that can be translated automatically into tools. This has the following advantages. The closer the (executable) description of tools is to the semantics of the language they support, the more confidence we can have in the correctness of these tools. Automatic generation of tools also allows for rapid prototyping of tool functions, so that their usefulness can be evaluated quickly.

This paper is organised as follows. Section 2 gives a very brief overview of specification languages such as LOTOS, including their semantic model. Section 3 elaborates on possible functions of LOTOS tools that can be used in a design process based on LOTOS. Section 4 discusses the Cornell Synthesizer Generator and how it can be applied to create tools. Elaborate examples of tools are given in section 5. The first example is an editor for the full LOTOS language, with static semantics checking as well as dynamic analysis functions. The second example is a proof assistant tool to support equivalence proofs through transformation. For prototyping purposes this tool was first developed for CCS, one of the languages on which LOTOS is based. This is also the presented version. The section concludes with a few other example tools and some ideas for the design of a new editor.

2. LOTOS and CCS

LOTOS (Language Of Temporal Ordering Specification) is a language developed for the formal specification of communication protocols and services. It was developed by ISO for the work on Open Systems Interconnection and is now international standard IS8807. LOTOS is based on Milner's CCS (Calculus of Communicating Systems) [Milner1980]. Its data type structure is based on the abstract data type language ACT ONE [Ehrig1985]. An overview of LOTOS, including specifications and theory, can be found in [Eijk1989]. A tutorial on LOTOS can also be found in [Bolognesi1987].

In process algebraic approaches, such as LOTOS and CCS, the emphasis is on describing systems as behaviours. A behaviour is a sequence of events and event-offers. An event is the result of a *synchronous* interaction of behaviours. A behaviour is described by a behaviour expression. A behaviour expression can be composed by combining atomic event-offers and by combining other behaviour expressions with the choice, parallel, enable, disable etc. operators. Behaviour expressions can also be named and parameterised.

Semantically, a behaviour expression denotes a *transition system* of states and transitions (corresponding to events) between states. At each state of the behaviour a number of events are possible. The set of these events is called the *menu* of that state. If no events are possible, the state is a *deadlock* state. All possible sequences of events form the tree of behaviour, also called the *communication tree*. Each node in the tree is a state, and each edge corresponds to an event, which is possibly parameterised with values. The communication tree is an important concept that is the basis of a number of tools.

Different specifications can have the same externally observable behaviour. The typical example in the protocol field is a service as opposed to the protocol that should deliver the service. The service only describes, for example, that a certain event on one side is followed by an event on the other side. The protocol also describes *how* this is done. One aspect of *verification* is proving the equivalence of two specifications. The strong semantical foundations of LOTOS give a theory that describes when two specifications are equivalent in a certain sense. A number of these equivalence relations are discussed in [Brinksma1988, Brinksma1988b, Milner1980]. These equivalence relations do not only have a use in the proof of correctness of a specification, as in the previous protocol example. They can also serve as the basis for correctness preserving transformations for restructuring specifications. In addition to the communication tree, this is another important concept for tools.

3. Functions of LOTOS Tools

The purpose of tools is to support a design process, based on LOTOS, from specification to implementation. After making a formal specification of a system in LOTOS, subsequent steps of this process are aimed at verifying it, refining it and adding implementation decisions.

We distinguish between an external structure and an internal structure of tools. The external structure is the functionality as perceived by the user. For a user a tool is a bundle of functions with an appropriate user interface. These functions are motivated by the supporting role they play in the design process. The internal structure of tools is their implementation. It is based on a description of the tool functions in terms of a definition of the supported language, in our case LOTOS. The theme of this paper is to investigate how close an implementation of tool functions can be to their description.

Functions of tools can be grouped according to two broad phases in a design process. The first group of functions supports the construction and analysis of specifications. Here we find functions that support the editing of specifications and the checking of properties such as syntax and static semantics, functions for the static analysis (e.g. datatype and process structure browsing), and functions for the dynamic analysis of behaviour (e.g. walking through and unfolding of the communication tree of the behaviour, also called simulation). The second group of functions supports the implementation, refinement and correctness proof of specifications. Characteristic of these functions is that they relate specifications to each other. Examples include comparing a service to a protocol specification, or transforming a specification into a differently structured one. This involves test generation and checking, symbolic manipulation, transformation by equivalence laws, and proof assistance.

Existing tools for full LOTOS include the simulator Hippo [Eijk1989b] and the Ottawa simulators [Logrippo1988]. A transformation tool, LOLA, is discussed in [Quemada1989]. A system for equivalence checking of basic LOTOS expressions is described in [Bolognesi1989].

The central problem in tool design is to find functions that are meaningful to a user *and* can be implemented. For new functions this problem is not trivial. The user does not know what will be useful new functions, and the tool builder does not know if they can be implemented. For a decision to invest considerable resources in tool development, this is a poor basis. It would be much better if prototype versions that allow early evaluation of proposed new tool functions can be developed quickly.

4. Using the Cornell Synthesizer Generator

The Cornell Synthesizer Generator (CSG) is an example of an *environment generator*. An environment generator takes a (formal) description of a language and functions on objects in this language and yields an *environment* of functions for users working with the language. For example, a programming environment for Pascal allows users to edit, compile and run their programs with one tool. Work on environment generators is itself a challenging task, especially if we want efficient realisations of tool functions with a good user interface. Good environment generators also enable rapid evaluation of the usefulness of tool functions and increase the confidence in the correctness of the implementation of these functions.

As has been explained in the introduction, most interactive tools can be seen as editors. For tools supporting a specification language the most natural model appears to be *language-based* editors. In these the edit-object is an expression in a specific language, and the commands of the editor can be tailored to this language. In the CSG the edit-object is a derivation tree with respect to the grammar of the supported language. Edit operations work on the *selection*, which is always positioned at a node of this derivation tree. The CSG generates such editors from a description of the language and tool functions. The input language of the CSG is called SSL and is described in [Teitelbaum1984, Teitelbaum1989b, Teitelbaum1989]. An editor can be fully described in SSL. SSL is based on attribute grammars. An editor specification in SSL describes the abstract syntax of the edit-object, attributes, functions on attributes, and attribute rules with respect to the edit-object, concrete syntax for the input of text and for the display of the edit-object, and structural edit operations. The attributes can for example be used to compute and display error messages and other informatives, to generate a translation of the edit-object into code, and to compute different semantical views of the edit-object.

A generated editor maintains a consistently attributed edit-object. What makes this approach feasible for interactive tools is that CSG generated editors employ algorithms for *incremental reevaluation* of the attributes. This means that a small change of the edit-object incurs only the necessary computation to reestablish a consistent attribuation.

How can we describe the language and tool functions in SSL? In this section we will illustrate this with parts of the CCS editor specification. A (computer) language definition consists of syntax, static and dynamic semantics, and a model on which the dynamic semantics is based. Here we illustrate how each of these components is described in SSL.

In the following table the *syntax* of our CCS behaviour expressions is given. *B* stands for an arbitrary behaviour expression, and *id* denotes an identifier.

Inaction	NIL
Summation	*B* + *B*
Composition	*B* | *B*
Instantiation	*id*
Action	*id*?; *B*
	id!; *B*
(tau)	i; *B*
Restriction	res *id* in *B*
Relabelling	*B* with for *id* -> *id*

From this we derive the abstract syntax and the concrete syntax. The abstract syntax, as expressed in SSL, is given in the following table. In the abstract syntax all terminal symbols that serve solely for parsing purposes, such as keywords and parentheses, are omitted.

```
bexp   :   Nil()
       |   Sum( bexp bexp )
       |   Com( bexp bexp )
       |   Use( id )
       |   Quest( id bexp )
       |   Exclam( id bexp )
       |   Internal( gate bexp )
       |   Res( id bexp )
       |   Relab( bexp id id ) ;
```

Here `bexp` is a nonterminal (called *phylum* in SSL), described as an enumeration of production rules, separated by vertical bars. Each production rule is labelled with an *operator* name (as it is called in SSL). The operator name differentiates between production rules that have the same right hand side.

Derivation trees with respect to the abstract grammar (and expressions denoting them) are called *terms* in SSL. As phyla are also used to denote attribute types, terms can also correspond to attribute values. In SSL a term can even be used as an attribute value and at the same time as a derivation tree.

In addition to the abstract syntax there is also a *concrete syntax,* which describes a textual representation of the edit-objects. It is used for input and modification of (selections of) the edit-object. The concrete syntax is used to parse input text. The parse tree is then attributed to give an abstract syntax term. The *display* of edit-objects is governed by *unparsing* schemes. These describe the formatting and layout of a term. Attributes may be included in the unparsing. For example, the unparsing can include a string-valued *error* attribute, which contains an error message. This is used in the following fragment.

An example of a *static semantics* condition in CCS is that for every process instantiation a defining occurrence exists. In an attribute grammar this condition can be checked by constructing an attribute `procenv`, which is a list of all process identifiers, and passing the attribute to every instantiation. In pseudo-SSL this is described as follows.

```
Use(id) { error = if id ∈ procenv then ""
                                 else "{id not declared}" ;}
```

This is an attribute rule for the operator `Use`, where the attribute `error` contains a message indicating if `id` is contained in the attribute `procenv`, i.e. if it is defined. `error` will be displayed next to the display of `id`. In the example we used mathematical notation instead of SSL functions. The SSL facility for defining functions over terms is effectively a side-effect free, applicative, language. It is not discussed further here.

The *dynamic semantics* of CCS describes the possible actions of a behaviour expression through an 'inference system.' Based on this we can define the previously mentioned *menu* of a behaviour expression. Chapter 4 of [Eijk1988] shows how this definition can be transformed into a 'constructive' definition. In this way we can compute for each `bexp` an attribute `menu` as a function of the menus of the constituent behaviour expression(s). An example is the following attribute rule.

```
bexp: Sum( bexp bexp) { bexp$1.menu = bexp$2.menu ∪ bexp$3.menu;}
```

`bexp$1.menu` denotes the attribute `menu` of the first `bexp` in this rule (counting starts at 1 and includes the left hand side). For a sum of behaviour expressions, it is the union of the menu of the operands. The hard case for the menu computation with attributes is the occurrence of a behaviour instantiation. For this we need another important facility of SSL, viz. *attribution expressions*, which allows *any* term, e.g. an attribute value, to be attributed. The attribute `procenv`, as used here is a list of `(id, bexp)` pairs, and represents all process definitions. The menu of a behaviour instantiation is computed by looking up the corresponding behaviour expression in the `procenv`, and computing the synthesized attribute `menu` of that term, using an attribution expression.

Derived from the *dynamic semantics* are equivalence laws, which state equivalences between two behaviour expressions. An example of an equivalence law for CCS is:

`g?;i;B = g?;B` *(tau1)*

Equivalence laws can be implemented using SSL's *transformations*. Transformations are structural editing commands that can be invoked by the user when the selection matches a certain pattern. The selection is then replaced by the expression that is computed from the transformation rule. The example equivalence law is translated as follows:

```
transform bexp
    on "tau1l" Quest(s, Internal(i, b)) : Quest(s, b)
```

It defines that the command `tau1l` is enabled whenever the selection is at a `bexp`, matching the left hand side of the law. In general the left hand side can contain arbitrary patterns with variables (here `s`, `i` and `b`), and the right hand side can contain arbitrary expressions over these variables, possibly involving attributes. Both sides can contain multiple occurrences of the same variables.

For another approach to implementing dynamic semantics we refer to the communication tree editor in the section on example editors.

To complete the discussion of the CSG we briefly mention a few other facilities. First, it is essential that a language-based editor can handle 'incomplete' objects, e.g. that arise as the result of removing a subterm. In the CSG this is handled by defining for each phylum a *completing term,* which represents an empty subterm. Edit-objects with completing terms can still be fully attributed. In the editors that we will discuss this implies that functional analysis can also be done on incomplete specifications. Second, an interface to C-code exists through which the edit-objects can be accessed to add functions that cannot be described conveniently in SSL. Finally, the user interface can be generated for video display terminals and the multi window systems X and SunView. In the latter user interfaces, a mouse can be used to make selections in edited objects and to invoke edit operations and other commands.

5. Example Editors

In this section we discuss some of the editors that were produced using the CSG. Our first example is an editor to support static and dynamic analysis of specifications in full LOTOS. The second example shows how verification through transformation can be done and what its limitations are. The presented version of this tool is for the CCS language. With less detail we discuss two other editors. One has a communication tree rather than a behaviour expression as its main edit-object, the other is an editor for the derivation of canonical testers [Brinksma1988, Brinksma1988b]. The experiences with the existing editors are the basis for the design of a new editor that we propose to work on. We conclude the section with a few statistics.

5.1. Full LOTOS - Static and Dynamic Semantics Checking

The full LOTOS editor is a tool for the construction and analysis of specifications. It allows only syntactically correct edit-objects. Violations of the static semantics are displayed as comments. Other information can be displayed on demand through a variety of mechanisms. Figure 1 gives a screen dump of the full LOTOS editor. The display shows part of a specification based on the two slot buffer in annex C.2.4.4 of the LOTOS standard [ISO1988]. The two slot buffer consists of the parallel composition of two one slot buffers, with the appropriate gates connected. Each of the one slot buffers cycles between accepting a value on one gate and presenting it on the other gate.

```
buffer.lot

behaviour
hide middle
 in
buffer [input, middle]
 |[midle(*-E UNDEFINED GATE-ID *) ]| buffer [middle, output]
where
  process buffer[input, output] : noexit :=
  input ?x : nat ; output !x ; buffer [input, output]
  endproc (* buffer *)
endspec (* two_slot_buffer *)

Positioned at behaviour_expression      let         id-choice
gate-choice          par||      par|||      par|[...]|          hide
>>          [>       ||         |||         |[...]|    []        ->
i;          communication;
```

Figure 1. A screen of the full LOTOS editor.

From top to bottom the screen contains a title bar with the name of the specification, a line (now empty) for system messages, a window on the specification itself where the selection of the editor is displayed in reverse video, the horizontal scroll bar, and a help pane that displays the phylum (`behaviour_expression`) of the current selection and the transformations on it that are enabled. The vertical scroll bar is on the right hand side. The transformations here are structural editing operations. For example, applying the transformation `i`, in the lower left corner, would change the selection

```
buffer [middle, output]
```

to

```
i; buffer [middle, output].
```

To the left of the selection an error message is displayed. The gate identifier `midle` is mispelled, and the resulting error message is appended to it, enclosed in comment brackets. Note the proximity of the error message to the identifier. The error message itself is not editable, and selecting it will also select the term to which it refers. As the result of incremental evaluation, editing to correct the identifier will almost immediately cause the error message to disappear. Other informatives, such as the 'functionality' of a behaviour expression and the sort of a value expression, can be displayed in the same way (see figure 2 after `!x`).

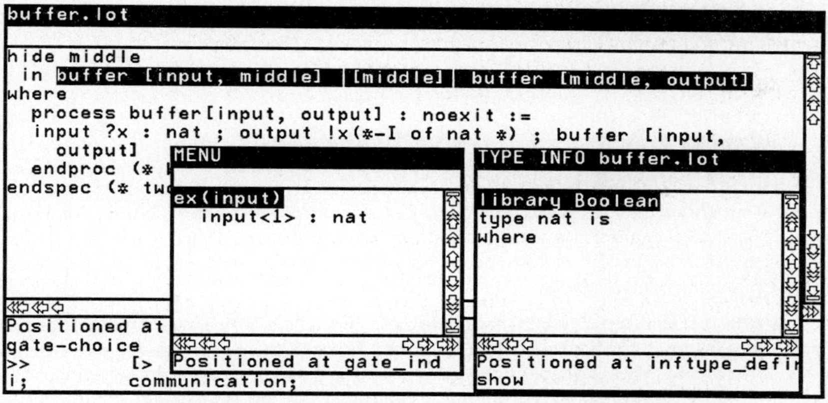

Figure 2. The full LOTOS editor: data type browser and menu.

Figure 2 shows the result of the commands that display the *menu* and the data type browser. These results are edit-objects themselves, and are displayed in separate windows. In the editor, the *menu* command displays the menu of the selected behaviour expression, which is, as explained, the set of possible events of the initial state of that behaviour expression. It shows an external event on gate `input`, with one parameter of sort `nat`. The data type browser shows that the specification contains the type `nat` and imports the type `Boolean` from the library. Selecting the transformation `show` will give the complete contents of the type. There is a comparable browser for processes, but it is not shown.

The implementation of the menu function is done in a way comparable to that sketched in the description of the CSG. The data type and process browsers are implemented as windows on synthesized attributes of the specification. A minor amount of fiddling in C-code is needed to pass those attributes to the right windows. We have also worked on an editor that has an expansion command comparable to that of the CCS editor discussed below, and an interface to an abstract data type interpreter written in C.

The LOTOS editor is in daily use at our department. People prefer it over non-interactive static semantics checkers. After the LOTOS editor has come into use, only one minor error was discovered. Furthermore, making this tool has uncovered a number of mistakes and unclarities in the language definition.

5.2. CCS - Equivalence Proofs by Transformation

The CCS editor discussed here is a tool for verification by transformation. The transformations are applications of laws that preserve a certain kind of equivalence. The language is CCS according to Milner, without value passing. The example is also very simple. We have worked with editors for more complex languages on larger examples, but a presentation of these would be too big for this paper.

A number of equivalences and congruences are defined over CCS behaviours. For such equivalences and congruences a number of laws can be derived. These laws are the basis for our transformations. For each law B1 = B2, where B1 and B2 are CCS behaviours, and = a congruence relation, we implement two transformations:

l: B1 → B2, the left-to-right rewrite rule, and
r: B2 → B1, the right-to-left rewrite rule.

In our example we will employ observation congruence and we will use the laws

```
g?;i;B = g?;B                  (taul)
g!;i;B = g!;B                  (taul)
p is defined as B then p = B   (ide)
```

and the *expansion theorem*, which 'normalizes' behaviour expressions to a sum of events. The laws and transformations are named as they appear in the appendix of Milner's book. For example `taull` is law *taul* applied as a rewrite rule from left to right, and `ider` is law *ide* applied from right to left. If these transformations are the only editing operations used, the edit-object can only be changed into an equivalent one.

The example is taken from [Milner1980] chapter 2. It models a binary semaphore, such as can be used for realising exclusive access to a resource. Through transformation we prove that it exhibits the desired behaviour. Events on the gates `p` and `v` model the access to the semaphore, which is controlled by the process `s`. `p1` and `p2` are the 'users' of the semaphore, and their critical section is expressed by the events on the gates `read1` and `write1`, etc. Figure 3 gives the complete specification. The screen structure is exactly the same as in the full LOTOS editor.

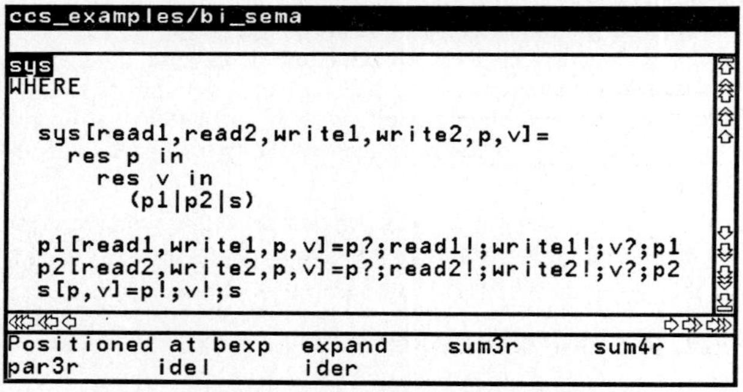

Figure 3. A binary semaphore in the CCS editor.

After applying the transformation `expand` on the selection, the screen looks as in figure 4. Note that internal steps are labelled (for user convenience) with the gates they originated from.

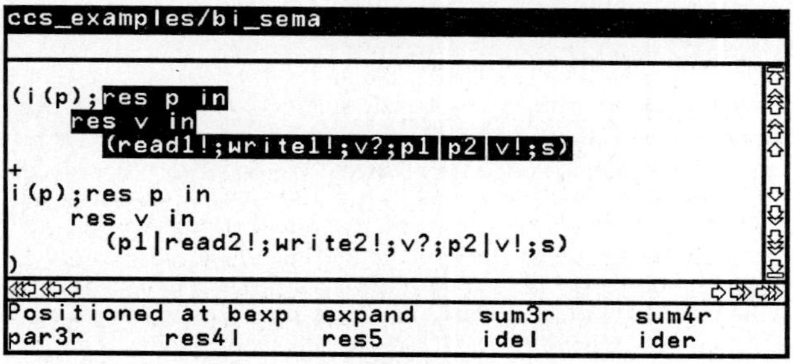

Figure 4.

The expansion command 'brings out' the events. Doing this three times more yields figure 5.

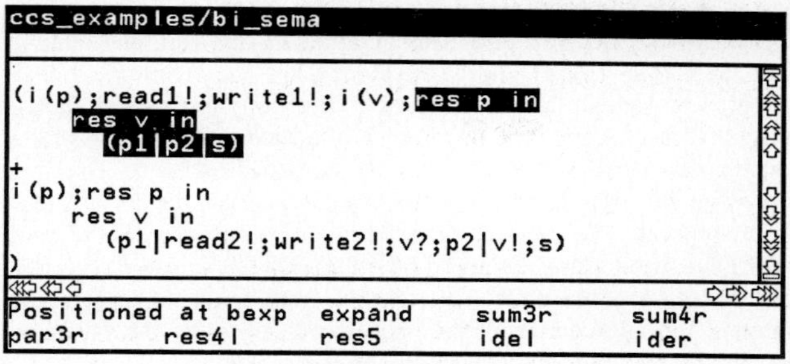

Figure 5.

Now the selection is identical to the original definition of sys, and we can apply ider. This together with the same sequence of transformations on the second branch gives figure 6.

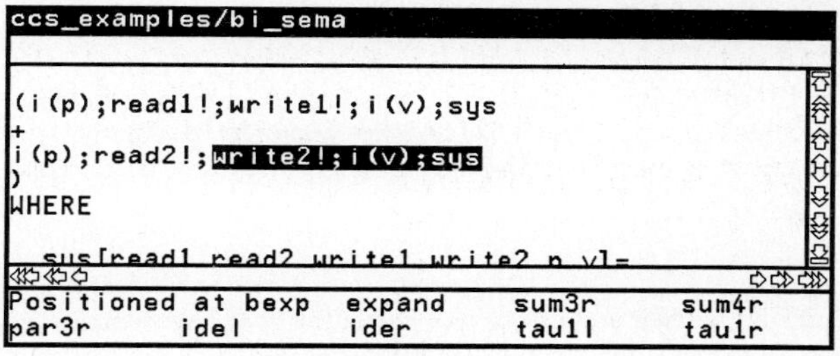

Figure 6.

At this point the transformation taul1 is enabled, which expresses that, under observational congruence, the internal step has no significance here. Applying this transformation on both branches yields figure 7. It shows that the semaphore only allows exclusive access to the resource.

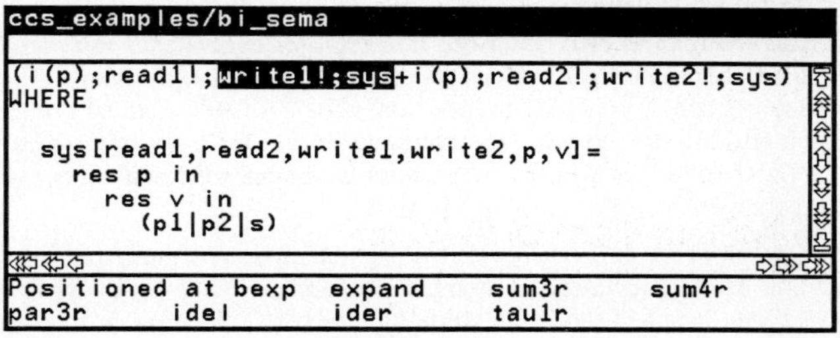

Figure 7.

All equivalence laws can be expressed as transformations in SSL. There are two problematic cases. Laws with conditions (such as *ide*) are implemented with transformations that are no-ops if the conditions are not satisfied. It would be more convenient if the CSG would allow such conditions in the definition of transformations. The transformations that are not applicable will then not be shown in the help pane. The second problem arises with laws that 'add' information in one direction, such as in `NIL = res b in b!;p`. We can handle this by prompting the user in an extra window for this information, in this case `b` and `p`.

In our experience, the approach taken here can also be applied to other languages, such as CCS with value passing, LOTOS and LOTOS subsets. Additional transformations may have to be added to invoke expression evaluation.

A session with the CCS tool is characterised by repeated applications of `expand`, alternated with reductions such as `taull` and `ider`. `Expand` eliminates parallelism, the resulting internal steps are removed by the tau laws, and `ider` folds back the expanding tree. Interestingly, only a small subset of the equivalence laws are needed. The first obstacle in scaling up this approach is that we have to do the state folding by hand. A multiple occurrence of a state or substate has to be found, turned into a definition with a new name and replaced by the name, all by hand. The limit of what we were able to do is proving the alternating bit protocol equivalent to the service, and you have to know the answer to succeed. We have some experience in automating the state matching. Chapter 5 of [Eijk1988] describes a tool doing this for the LOTOS subset *llv*. Alternated applications of an llv editor and this tool made the alternating bit proof much smoother. Our current research considers extending the approach with automatic application of the tau laws. This is comparable to LOLA [Quemada1989], although that is not an interactive tool.

The CCS tool is most suitable for the elimination of parallelism. Through this, a constraint or process oriented specification can be transformed into a more state machine oriented specification. For a discussion of these specification styles see [Vissers1988]. The strength of an interactive tool is that this can be done on a *part* of the specification.

It remains a disadvantage of the tool that an equivalence proof is *done*, rather than registered and checked. It is cumbersome to backtrack from a mistake. An alternative approach is to make the *proof* itself the edit-object, as is done in some of the CSG demonstration editors and in [Dybvig1985]. A proof is probably an order of magnitude larger than the specification it concerns, however.

5.3. Other Examples

The example editors have a specification as their edit-object. An alternative is to have a *model* of the specification as the edit-object, for example the communication tree. Edit operations can then 'unfold' the tree. The advantages of this approach are that it allows easier exploration of the behaviour, and that it more resembles a simulator. It is less suitable for analysis of parts of specifications and during modification of a specification. It also does not allow behaviour investigation by equational transformation, as in the CCS editor. Our main use of the communication tree editor is as a 'thinking' model for our simulators.

In [Brinksma1988, Brinksma1988b] a theory is described that explores equivalence relations for *testing*. A test case distinguishes between specifications that are not (testing) equivalent. The *canonical tester* of a specification contains exactly all the test cases for it. The canonical tester editor employs a constructive algorithm for deriving canonical testers. The edit-object is a specification in a subset of LOTOS (basic LOTOS). On an arbitrary behaviour expression a command can be invoked to give its canonical tester in a separate window.

Our plan for a new LOTOS editor involves a strong relation with an automatic analyser. The editor should allow the application of the equivalence law transformations, including the expansion theorem. Furthermore, along the lines laid out in the discussion of the CCS editor, it should be possible to select an arbitrary behaviour expression and feed this through an automatic expansion and reduction tool. This allows a very controlled removal of parallelism, through which a specification can be selectively restructured.

5.4. Sizes and Other Numbers

The statistics we present here are based on a SUN 3/60 with 8 Mbytes of memory and release 2.0 of the CSG. The LOTOS editor is generated from approximately 20.000 lines of SSL and 3000 lines of C. A number of different versions can be generated from this though. The C lines are mostly variations on code of the editor itself. Reading and fully checking a 1974 line specification (of which approximately ⅓ are comment lines) of the OSI Transport Service, which uses a standard library, takes 323 seconds of processor time and a maximum of 7.3 Mbytes of data space. In our environment this is considered usable.

The CCS editor is generated from 1341 lines of SSL (no C-code). Working through the complete example as presented takes 5 seconds of processor time and a maximum of 392 Kbytes of data space.

The development times of the editors range from days to weeks, as for the CCS editor, to a few months for a first LOTOS editor, to a year or more for the full LOTOS editor. Adding new tool functions has usually been a matter of days or weeks.

6. Conclusion

We have shown the viability of making fully functional tools through the use of environment generators such as the CSG. It appears that the full LOTOS editor described in section 5 is one of the first cases of a fully functional, automatically generated, language based editor that is in regular use.

From the software engineering standpoint it is not only important that tools can be made, but also that they can be made in a *systematic* way. The CSG provides a convenient framework to do this, because tool functions can be expressed in SSL on a fairly high level of abstraction, and a neat interface is possible to implementations of tool functions that cannot be expressed in this way. Furthermore we feel that this approach fulfills our goals of rapid prototyping.

Our case studies indicate what can be made in this way, which is also of interest to people not directly involved in tool construction. The challenge ahead is to explore new tool functionality, rooted in sound theory, and ways to implement and use it.

7. Acknowledgements

The editors mentioned were mainly produced by Axel Belinfante, Erik Slotboom and Jan Tretmans. Tim Teitelbaum's group at Cornell University provided us with rapid fixes to our bug reports. Jan Tretmans and other members of the IPS group made valuable suggestions for improving this paper.

References

Bolognesi1987.
T. Bolognesi and H. Brinksma, "Introduction to the ISO Specification Language LOTOS," *Computer Networks and ISDN Systems*, vol. 14, pp. 25-59, 1987.

Bolognesi1989.
T. Bolognesi and M. Caneve, "Equivalence Verification: Theory, Algorithms and a Tool," in *The Formal Description Technique LOTOS*, ed. P.H.J. van Eijk et al., pp. 303-326, North-Holland, Amsterdam, 1989.

Brinksma1988.
H. Brinksma, "A Theory for the Derivation of Tests," in *Proceedings of the eighth international conference on protocol specification, testing and verification*, ed. S. Aggarwal, pp. 63-74, North-Holland, Amsterdam, 1988.

Brinksma1988b.
H. Brinksma, "On the Design of Extended LOTOS," Ph.D. Thesis, Twente University of Technology, Enschede Netherlands, 1988.

Dybvig1985.
R. K. Dybvig and Bruce T. Smith, "A Semantic Editor," *SIGPLAN Notices*, vol. 20, no. 7, pp. 74-82, July 1985.

Ehrig1985.
H. Ehrig and B. Mahr, *Fundamentals of Algebraic Specification 1,* Springer-Verlag, Berlin, 1985.

Eijk1989.
P.H.J. van Eijk, C. A. Vissers, and M. Diaz (eds), *The Formal Description Technique LOTOS - Results of the ESPRIT/SEDOS Project,* North-Holland, Amsterdam, 1989.

Eijk1988.
Peter van Eijk, "Software Tools for the Specification Language LOTOS," Ph.D. Thesis, Twente University of Technology, Enschede Netherlands, 1988.

Eijk1989b.
Peter van Eijk, "The Design of a Simulator Tool," in *The Formal Description Technique LOTOS*, ed. P.H.J. van Eijk et al., North-Holland, Amsterdam, 1989.

ISO1988.
ISO, "Information processing systems - Open Systems Interconnection - The definition of the specification language LOTOS," International Standard ISO/IS 8807, 1988.

Logrippo1988.
L. Logrippo, A. Obaid, J. P. Briand, and M. C. Fehri, "An Interpreter for LOTOS, A specification Language for Distributed Systems," *Software - Practice and Experience*, vol. 18, no. 4, pp. 365-385, April 1988.

Milner1980.
R. Milner, "A Calculus of Communicating Systems," *Lecture Notes in Computer Science*, vol. 92, Springer-Verlag, 1980.

Quemada1989.
J. Quemada, S. Pavon, and A. Fernandez, "Transforming LOTOS Specifications with LOLA - The Parameterised Expansion," in *Formal Description Techniques - Proceedings of the FORTE 88 Conference*, ed. K. J. Turner, pp. 45-54, North-Holland, Amsterdam, 1989.

Teitelbaum1984.
T. Teitelbaum and T. W. Reps, "The Synthesizer Generator," *SIGPLAN*, vol. 19, no. 5, pp. 42-48, May 1984.

Teitelbaum1989b.
T. Teitelbaum and T. W. Reps, *The Synthesizer Generator Reference Manual: Third Edition,* Springer-Verlag, New York, 1989.

Teitelbaum1989.
T. Teitelbaum and T. W. Reps, *The Synthesizer Generator - A System for Constructing Language-Based Editors,* Springer-Verlag, New York, 1989.

Vissers1988.
C. A. Vissers, G. Scollo, and M. van Sinderen, "Architecture and Specification Style in Formal Descriptions of Distributed Systems," in *Proceedings of the eighth international conference on protocol specification, testing and verification*, ed. S. Aggarwal, pp. 189-204, North-Holland, Amsterdam, 1988.

Protocol Specification, Testing, and Verification, IX
E. Brinksma, G. Scollo and C.A. Vissers (Editors)
Elsevier Science Publishers B.V. (North-Holland)

A Semantics-Based Verification Tool for Finite-State Systems*

Rance Cleaveland † Joachim Parrow ‡ Bernhard Steffen §

Abstract

The Concurrency Workbench is an automated tool that caters for the analysis of concurrent finite-state processes expressed in Milner's Calculus of Communicating Systems. Its key feature is its scope: a variety of different verification methods, including equivalence checking, preorder checking, and model checking, are supported for several different process semantics. One experience from our work is that a large number of interesting verification methods can be formulated as combinations of a small number of primitive algorithms. The Workbench has been applied to examples involving the verification of communications protocols and mutual exclusion algorithms and has proven a valuable aid in teaching and research. We will present the architecture of the Workbench and illustrate the verification methods through some simple examples.

1 Introduction

This paper describes the Concurrency Workbench [7], a prototype tool for the automatic verification of finite-state processes. Automated verification tools are practically motivated: the development of increasingly complex distributed computer systems requires increasingly complex verification techniques to guarantee correctness, and the increase in detail rapidly becomes unmanageable without computer assistance.

The analysis of concurrent systems relies heavily on the underlying formal semantics of processes, about which there is as yet no consensus. One goal in the design of the Workbench is to incorporate several different verification methods, as well as process semantics, in a modular fashion. This means that each method may be applied to different semantic models, yielding a spectrum of techniques for reasoning about processes. The versatility of the Workbench has many advantages: it facilitates a comparison between many aspects of formal verification, it supports mixed verification strategies which use more than one method, and it makes the system easily extensible. This versatility contrasts with existing automated tools, which typically embody a particular semantics and a particular form of verification. Examples of such systems include Aldébaran [10], AUTO [2], CESAR [25], EMC [4], and Winston [20]. For a survey of systems for the verification of communication protocols see [1].

In order to achieve this flexibility the algorithms in the Workbench are partitioned into three *layers*. The first layer manages interaction with the user and also contains the basic definition of process semantics in terms of labeled transition graphs. The second layer provides transformation algorithms on transition graphs. These algorithms enable the user of the Workbench to change the semantic model of processes. The third layer features several basic

*Research supported by Science and Engineering Research Council grant GC/D69464
†Computer Science Department, MAPS, University of Sussex, Falmer, Brighton, BN1 9QH, ENGLAND
‡Swedish Institute of Computer Science, Box 1263, S-164 28 Kista, SWEDEN
§Computer Science Department, University of Edinburgh, The King's Buildings, Edinburgh EH9 3JZ, SCOTLAND

analysis algorithms for establishing whether a process meets a specification. Depending on the algorithm used, a specification may either be another process (describing the desired behavior) or a formula in a modal logic expressing a relevant property.

The distinction between these three layers is one of the main achievements of the Workbench. In particular, the combination of various graph transformations with the analysis algorithms yields a wide spectrum of verification algorithms, and yet the underlying code is small and structured. As the layers are implemented independently of one another, the system is easy to maintain and extend.

The Workbench has been successfully applied to verification of communication protocols, notably the alternating bit protocol and the CSMA/CD protocol [24], and mutual exclusion algorithms [30]; it has also been used to debug the Edinburgh Computer Science Department's electronic mailing system. Furthermore, it is a valuable instrument in education, in industries as well as in universities, and is being investigated as a tool for analyzing communications protocols by Swedish Telecom and by Hewlett-Packard.

The remainder of the paper is organized as follows. In the next section we describe the conceptual structure of the workbench, and give an overview of the different verification methods. Section 3 presents the syntax and basic semantics of processes, and Section 4 some of the transformations on transition graphs. Sections 5 through 7 illustrate the basic verification methods, Section 8 mentions some additional features of the Workbench, and Section 9 contains our conclusions and directions for future work.

2 The Architecture of the Workbench

2.1 The Interface Layer

An overview of the Workbench is presented in Figure 1. The user interacts with a *command interpreter* in the interface layer, which invokes the appropriate parts of the other layers and presents analysis results. Each verification method is implemented as one command, which may require parameters in the form of processes and modal formulas. A *parser* transforms the concrete syntax of such parameters into an abstract syntax in the form of parse trees, which can be stored in a small *data base*. There is also a package defining the *basic semantics* of processes. Following [21], each process yields a labeled transition graph which describes its behavior in terms of visible communication events and internal, or τ, events. A description of the syntax and semantics of processes can be found in Section 3.

2.2 The Semantics Layer

The semantics layer consists of algorithms for transforming the transition graphs generated by the interface layer. For example, the *observation* transformation extends the transitions by absorbing internal τ-events into visible events; thus the resulting graphs do not record the timing of internal computations in the corresponding processes. The *deterministic* transformation makes the graphs deterministic in the usual sense of the word: the resulting graphs do not record nondeterministic choices. The *acceptance* transformation yields deterministic graphs augmented with deadlock potentials in the form of acceptance sets. These transformations, and some minor variations, are described in Section 4.

The semantics layer refers to processes represented as transition graphs rather than processes in the abstract syntax. Thus, future changes of the particular syntax will not require changes in this layer.

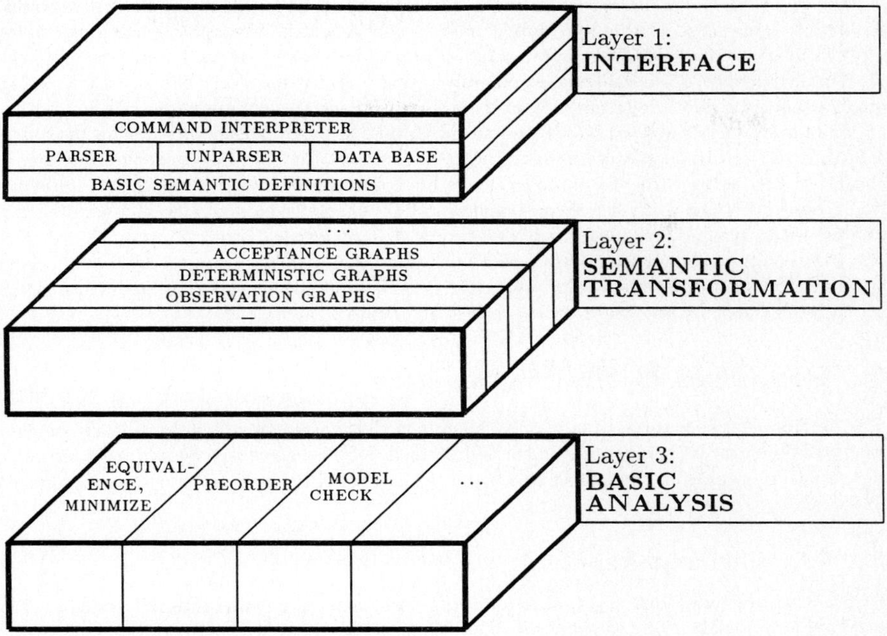

Figure 1: Overview of the Workbench

2.3 The Analysis Layer

The Workbench features three main verification methods for proving that processes meet their specifications, and the analysis layer contains the corresponding basic analysis algorithms. In the first method, specifications are themselves processes that describe precisely the high-level behavior required of an implementation. The corresponding algorithm determines whether two processes are *equivalent* in the sense of having the same behavior. This algorithm can also be used to *minimize* a process, i.e. compute an equivalent process with a minimal number of states. A definition of equivalence and a brief account of the algorithm can be found in Section 5.

The second method also uses processes as specifications, but these specifications are treated as minimal requirements to be met by implementations. In this approach specifications can be annotated with "holes" (or "don't care" points); an implementation satisfies one of these *partial* specifications if it supplies at least the behavior demanded by the specification while filling in some holes. The method relies on an ordering relation, or *preorder*, between processes: a process A is "more defined than" a process B if A has the same behavior as B except for the holes in B. The preorder algorithm determines if a process is more defined than its specification in this sense. A definition of the preorder and an account of the algorithm can be found in Section 6.

The third method involves the use of a modal logic, the propositional (modal) mu-calculus. Assertions formulated in this logic are viewed as specifications; examples of such assertions are "there are no deadlocks" or "every action of type a is always followed by an action of type b". The logic exhibits a considerable expressive power. As further described in Section 7, the *model checking* algorithm determines whether a process satisfies an assertion.

The basic analysis algorithms are polymorphic; that is, they work equally well on the different kinds of transitions graphs supplied by the semantics layer. For instance, the equivalence algorithm computes CCS strong equivalence on transition graphs. If applied to observation graphs then this equivalence corresponds to CCS observation equivalence on the original graphs; if the graphs have been made deterministic it corresponds to trace equivalence. Observation congruence and testing (failures) equivalence can also be computed by first choosing appropriate transformations and applying the general equivalence checking algorithm. Analogous results hold for the other basic analysis algorithms.

3 Processes in the Workbench

This section describes the syntax of the Calculus of Communicating Systems (CCS), which is used to define processes, or *agents*, in the Workbench. We also show how agents are interpreted as transition graphs. In the rest of this paper we assume the reader to have some familiarity with CCS.

3.1 Actions and Agents

CCS agents are built from a set of *actions* containing a distinguished internal action τ. The external actions, also called *communication events*, are divided into input events and output events. We use $a, b, \ldots$ to range over actions. If a is an input event then $\overline{a}$ is the *complementary* output event; intuitively these represent input and output on the port a. As in pure CCS we consider only communication events without value parameters. Agents are defined using the following operators from [21]:

Nil	Termination
$\perp$	Divergence (or *bottom*, "hole", or "don't care")
$a.$	Prefixing by action a; unary prefix operator
$+$	Choice; binary infix operator
$\mid$	Parallel composition; binary infix operator
$\backslash L$	Restriction on (finite) set of actions L; unary postfix operator
$[f]$	Relabeling by f, which maps communication events to communication events; unary postfix operator

We use $p, q, \ldots$ to range over agents. Relabeling functions are written as a sequence of renamings; for example $p[a_1/b_1, a_2/b_2]$ is the agent p with b_1, b_2, $\overline{b_1}$ and $\overline{b_2}$ renamed to a_1, a_2, $\overline{a_1}$ and $\overline{a_2}$, respectively.

Finally, we assume a set of *agent identifiers* (called *Constants* in [21]). An identifier A may be *bound* to an agent p, written $A \stackrel{\text{def}}{=} p$, where p may itself contain A. This enables recursively defined agents. For example, the following bindings constitute a definition of a buffer of capacity n.

$$\begin{array}{lcl} \mathrm{BUF}_n & \stackrel{\text{def}}{=} & \mathrm{BUF}_n^0 \\ \mathrm{BUF}_n^0 & \stackrel{\text{def}}{=} & in.\mathrm{BUF}_n^1 \\ \mathrm{BUF}_n^i & \stackrel{\text{def}}{=} & in.\mathrm{BUF}_n^{i+1} + \overline{out}.\mathrm{BUF}_n^{i-1} \quad \text{for } i = 1, \ldots, n-1 \\ \mathrm{BUF}_n^n & \stackrel{\text{def}}{=} & \overline{out}.\mathrm{BUF}_n^{n-1} \end{array}$$

Here BUF_n^i represents a buffer of capcity n currently holding i items. The following agent, CBUF_n, is a composite implementation of BUF_n using n buffers of capacity 1 (here $n \geq 2$).

$$\text{CBUF}_n \stackrel{\text{def}}{=}$$
$$(\,\text{BUF}_1[a_1/out]\,|\,\underbrace{\cdots\,|\,\text{BUF}_1[a_i/in, a_{i+1}/out]\,|\,\ldots}_{i=1,\cdots,n-2}|\,\text{BUF}_1[a_{n-1}/in]\,)\setminus\{a_1,\ldots,a_{n-1}\}$$

Finally the partially specified buffer PBUF_n acts as BUF_n as long as the environment never attempts to store more than n items; otherwise its behavior is undefined.

$$\begin{array}{lcl}
\text{PBUF}_n & \stackrel{\text{def}}{=} & \text{PBUF}_n^0 \\
\text{PBUF}_n^0 & \stackrel{\text{def}}{=} & in.\text{PBUF}_n^1 \\
\text{PBUF}_n^i & \stackrel{\text{def}}{=} & in.\text{PBUF}_n^{i+1} + \overline{out}.\text{PBUF}_n^{i-1} \quad \text{for } i = 1,\ldots,n-1 \\
\text{PBUF}_n^n & \stackrel{\text{def}}{=} & in.\bot + \overline{out}.\text{PBUF}_n^{n-1}
\end{array}$$

3.2 Transition Graphs

Agents are given an operational semantics defined in terms of *transition relations*, $\stackrel{a}{\longrightarrow}$, where a is an action. Intuitively, $p\stackrel{a}{\longrightarrow}p'$ holds when p can evolve into p' by performing action a; in this case, p' is said to be an *a-derivative* of p. The transition relation is defined inductively on the basis of the operators. Thus $a.p\stackrel{a}{\longrightarrow}p$, and $p+q\stackrel{a}{\longrightarrow}p'$ if either $p\stackrel{a}{\longrightarrow}p'$ or $q\stackrel{a}{\longrightarrow}p'$. The agent $p|q$ behaves like the interleaving of p and q with the possibility of complementary actions synchronizing, yielding a τ-action. $p\setminus L$ behaves like p with the exception that no actions in L are allowed, while $p[f]$ behaves like p with actions renamed by f. A formal account of this semantics is found in [21]. We also define a *divergence* predicate on agents: agents with an unguarded occurrence of $\bot$ (i.e. with a $\bot$ not within the scope of an action prefixing operator) are considered divergent.

The Workbench adopts *transition graphs* as models of agents. The transition graph of an agent p contains a set of nodes, where each node corresponds to an agent. There is one distinguished node, called the root node, which corresponds to p itself. Edges are labeled by actions; there is an edge labeled by a with source node n and target node n' if $p\stackrel{a}{\longrightarrow}p'$ holds of the corresponding agents. A node is *divergent* if the corresponding agent is divergent. Each node additionally carries a polymorphic *information* field, the contents of which vary according to the semantic transformations or analyses being performed on the graph.

Figure 2 contains examples of transition graphs. Divergent nodes are represented by unfilled circles, and other (convergent) nodes by filled circles. The root node is indicated by an unlabeled arrow.

4 Transition Graph Transformations

As indicated previously, various transformations on transition graphs are used in conjunction with basic analysis algorithms, yielding a variety of verification methods. We briefly describe some of the transformations here.

4.1 Observation Graphs

The transition graphs as described in Section 3.2 faithfully represent τ actions, and hence the "timing behavior", of agents. Many verification methods require this information; however, others do not, and to cater for these the Workbench includes an algorithm for computing

a) The transition graph for BUF_n, the buffer of capacity n. The graph has $n+1$ nodes.

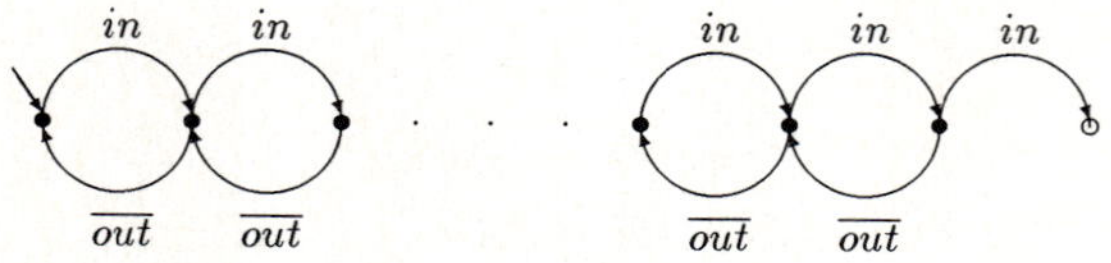

b) The transition graph for PBUF_n, which has one additional divergent node.

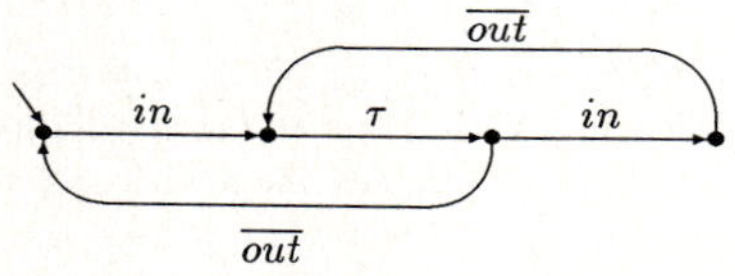

c) The transition graph for CBUF_2, the composite buffer of capacity 2.

Figure 2: Examples of transition graphs.

observation graphs. These are based on the notion of *experiment relations*, which are defined as follows.

$$n \stackrel{\varepsilon}{\Longrightarrow} n' \text{ if } n(\stackrel{\tau}{\longrightarrow})^* n'$$
$$n \stackrel{a}{\Longrightarrow} n' \text{ if } n \stackrel{\varepsilon}{\Longrightarrow} \stackrel{a}{\longrightarrow} \stackrel{\varepsilon}{\Longrightarrow} n'$$

Thus $\stackrel{\varepsilon}{\Longrightarrow}$ is defined as the transitive and reflexive closure of $\stackrel{\tau}{\longrightarrow}$, and $\stackrel{a}{\Longrightarrow}$ is defined in terms of relational products of $\stackrel{\varepsilon}{\Longrightarrow}$ and $\stackrel{a}{\longrightarrow}$. These relations allow τ actions to be *absorbed* into communication events, so that information as to the precise amount of internal computation is concealed.

The observation graph transformation takes a transition graph and modifies the edges to represent the $\stackrel{a}{\Longrightarrow}$ and $\stackrel{\varepsilon}{\Longrightarrow}$ relations instead of the $\stackrel{a}{\longrightarrow}$ and $\stackrel{\tau}{\longrightarrow}$ relations. It uses well-known techniques for computing the product of two relations and the transitive and reflexive closure of a relation. Figure 3 indicates the nature of the transformation (for clarity, we have omitted the ε-edges resulting from the reflexive closure of $\stackrel{\tau}{\longrightarrow}$).

The transformation takes time that is polynomial in the size of the graph. Surprisingly, in most cases the subroutine for transitive closure accounts for more than 80 per cent of the execution time when determining observation equivalence.

A slight variation of the observation transformation, called the *congruence* transformation, yields observation graphs that additionally record the possibility of initial τ-actions. Such graphs are suitable for determining observation congruence [21] and weak precongruence [29].

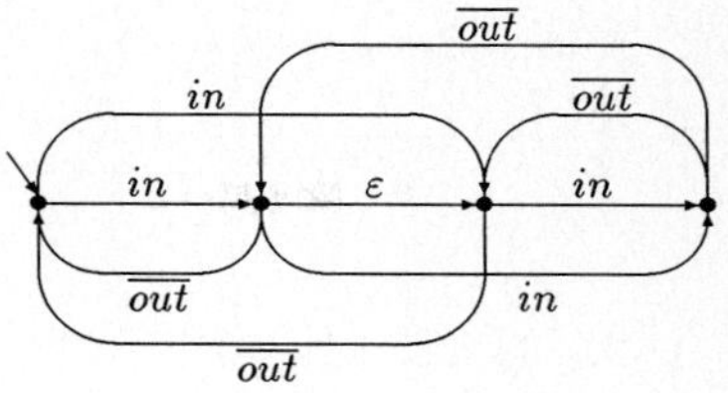

Figure 3: The observation graph corresponding to CBUF$_2$.

4.2 Deterministic Graphs

The strong and observation equivalences and preorders distinguish agents on the basis of the exact points during their executions where nondeterministic choices are made. Accordingly, the graphs mentioned in sections 3.2 and 4.1 faithfully record each time a agent makes such a choice. However, other equivalences and preorders, like the *may* preorders and equivalences [11] and ordinary trace (language) equivalence, do not require such detailed accounts of the choice structure of agents. In order to cater for these equivalences the Workbench includes an algorithm for transforming graphs into *deterministic* graphs (also called *Dgraphs*), which are graphs having no τ-derivatives and at most one a-derivative for any action a. As a simple example, the transition graph

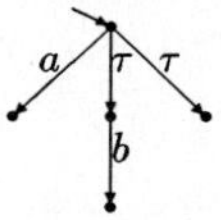

is transformed to

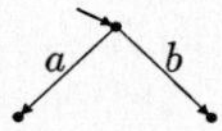

As another example, the deterministic graph of CBUF$_2$ is precisely the transition graph of BUF$_2$. The algorithm for computing deterministic graphs is well-known from automata theory (see e.g. [14]). In general, this transformation has an exponential complexity, owing to the fact that it is theoretically possible to have a node in the deterministic graph for each subset of nodes in the original graph. Our experience, however, indicates that the number of nodes is usually smaller than the number of nodes in the original graph.

4.3 Acceptance Graphs

The deterministic graphs do not contain information pertinent to the deadlock properties of agents. Some verification methods, notably methods based on the *testing* ([11]) and *failures* ([13]) equivalences and preorders, require this information, but still do not require the detailed information concerning choice structure present in observation graphs. The appropriate transition graphs for these equivalences are *acceptance* graphs (also called *Tgraphs*); these are deterministic graphs whose nodes additionally contain deadlock and divergence information encoded as *acceptance sets.* The acceptance set $n.acc$ of a node n is a set of sets of actions: each member of $n.acc$ is a set of actions, representing an obligation to be able to continue from n with any action in the set. For example,

has the acceptance graph

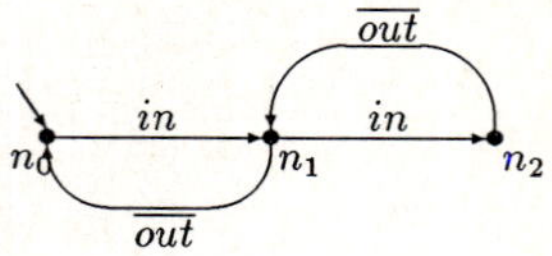

$$
\begin{aligned}
n_0.acc &= \{\{in\}\} \\
n_1.acc &= \{\{in, \overline{out}\}\} \\
n_2.acc &= \{\{\overline{out}\}\}
\end{aligned}
$$

Figure 4: The acceptance graph for CBUF$_2$.

where only the root node has a nontrivial acceptance set:

$$\{\emptyset, \{b\}\}$$

Each element in the acceptance set corresponds to a stable state (a state from which no internal action is immediately possible) in the original graph; such an element contains precisely the actions that are immediately possible from the stable state. In the example, the two elements of the acceptance set correspond to the possibilities of the original graph to evolve unobservably along the right branch (where no further action is possible) or the middle branch (where only b is possible). Note that $\{a\}$ is not a member of the acceptance set since the original graph cannot evolve into a state where only a is possible. The acceptance sets in the other nodes contain only the empty set. As another example, Figure 4 shows the acceptance graph resulting from the transformation of CBUF$_2$.

Acceptance sets also encode information pertinent to divergence. A node in the original graph which is reachable from a *globally divergent* node (a node which can either evolve through internal actions to a divergent node, or is on an infinite path of internal actions) is characterized by an empty acceptance set of corresponding acceptance graph nodes.

A closely related kind of graph, the *must* graph (also called *STgraph*), is appropriate for the must equivalence and preorder ([11]). Must graphs are like acceptance graphs, except that a node reachable from a globally divergent node has no outgoing edges. The algorithm for generating acceptance and must graphs is described in [6].

5 Equivalence Checking

The first basic analysis within the Workbench involves checking for equivalence between two agents. As indicated in Section 2, our approach is to convert the agents to transition graphs of the appropriate type and then apply a general equivalence algorithm.

5.1 Definition of the Equivalence

Let G_1 and G_2 be transition graphs with node sets N_1 and N_2, respectively, let $N = N_1 \cup N_2$, and let $\mathcal{C} \subseteq N \times N$ be an equivalence relation reflecting a notion of "compatibility between information fields."

Definition 5.1 A *$\mathcal{C}$-bisimulation* on G_1 and G_2 is a relation $\mathcal{R} \subseteq N \times N$ such that $\langle m, n \rangle \in \mathcal{R}$ implies that:

1. if $m \xrightarrow{a} m'$ then $\exists n' : n \xrightarrow{a} n'$ and $\langle m', n' \rangle \in \mathcal{R}$, and
2. if $n \xrightarrow{a} n'$ then $\exists m' : m \xrightarrow{a} m'$ and $\langle m', n' \rangle \in \mathcal{R}$, and
3. $\langle m, n \rangle \in \mathcal{C}$.

Two graphs are said to be $\mathcal{C}$-equivalent if there exists a $\mathcal{C}$-bisimulation relating the root nodes of the graphs.

5.2 Derived Equivalences

Many interesting equivalences turn out to be instances of $\mathcal{C}$-equivalence combined with graph transformations. Let U denote the universal relation, i.e. $U = N \times N$. Then a U-bisimulation is a bisimulation in the sense of Milner [21] and U-equivalence is strong equivalence in CCS. Also, observation equivalence corresponds to U-equivalence on observation graphs, observation congruence to U-equivalence on congruence graphs, and trace (or may) equivalence to U-equivalence on deterministic graphs. For must and testing (failures) equivalence define $\langle m, n \rangle \in \mathcal{A}$ to hold exactly when $m.acc$ and $n.acc$ are compatible, i.e. each element of $m.acc$ is a superset of an element of $n.acc$, and vice versa. Then two graphs are must equivalent if their associated must graphs are $\mathcal{A}$-equivalent, and they are testing (failures) equivalent if their associated acceptance graphs are $\mathcal{A}$-equivalent [6].

As an example, for any particular n it is the case that BUF_n and CBUF_n (see Section 3) are both observation and testing equivalent.

5.3 The Algorithm

Our algorithm is adapted from one presented in [17]. It works by attempting to find a $\mathcal{C}$-bisimulation relating the root nodes of the graphs. To do so, it maintains a *partitioning* of the nodes in G_1 and G_2, the graphs under consideration. A partitioning is a set of *blocks*, where each block is a set of nodes such that each node is contained in exactly one block. Such a partitioning naturally induces an equivalence relation on the nodes of the graphs: two nodes are related precisely when they are in the same block.

The algorithm starts with the partition containing only one block and successively refines this partition. It terminates when the roots of the two graphs end up in different blocks (in which case the graphs are not equivalent) or the induced equivalence relation on the nodes becomes a $\mathcal{C}$-bisimulation (in which case the graphs are $\mathcal{C}$-equivalent).

The time and space complexities of this algorithm are $O(k * \ell)$ and $O(k + \ell)$ respectively, where k is the number of states, and ℓ is the number of transitions, in the two graphs. A marginally more efficient algorithm appears in [22]; however, there is not yet enough evidence to suggest that this algorithm is appreciably faster in practice. In any event, this complexity is not a limiting factor; tests with the Workbench have shown that the time consumed by this algorithm is only a small fraction of the total time spent when computing observation equivalence. Most of the time is consumed in the graph transformations.

One final interesting point is that the algorithm can be trivially modified to determine the coarsest $\mathcal{C}$-bisimulation on the nodes of a single graph. This can be used to transform a graph into a $\mathcal{C}$-equivalent one which has a minimum number of states: first compute the coarsest $\mathcal{C}$-bisimulation and then collapse each block in the final partition into a single node.

6 Preorder Checking

The second basic analysis within the Workbench involves checking a preorder between two agents. This is done in a way similar to equivalence checking; after converting the agents to transition graphs we then apply a general preorder algorithm. The algorithm is based upon the following generalization of the notion of equivalence introduced in Section 5.1.

6.1 Definition of the Preorder

Let G_1 and G_2 be transition graphs with (disjoint) node sets N_1 and N_2, let $N = N_1 \cup N_2$, and let $\mathcal{C} \subseteq N \times N$ be a preorder reflecting a notion of "ordering on information fields" (in general a preorder is a transitive and reflexive relation). Also let $\mathcal{P}_a \subseteq N$ and $\mathcal{Q}_a \subseteq N$ be predicates over N, where a ranges over the set of actions. Intuitively, $\mathcal{P}_a$ and $\mathcal{Q}_a$ determine the states from which a-transitions must be matched.

Definition 6.1 A $\mathcal{C}$-*prebisimulation* between G_1 and G_2 is a relation $\mathcal{R} \subseteq N \times N$ such that $\langle m, n \rangle \in \mathcal{R}$ implies that:

1. if $n \in \mathcal{P}_a$ then [if $m \xrightarrow{a} m'$ then $\exists n' : n \xrightarrow{a} n'$ and $\langle m', n' \rangle \in \mathcal{R}$], and
2. if $m \in \mathcal{Q}_a$ then [if $n \xrightarrow{a} n'$ then $\exists m' : m \xrightarrow{a} m'$ and $\langle m', n' \rangle \in \mathcal{R}$], and
3. $\langle m, n \rangle \in \mathcal{C}$.

The $\mathcal{C}$-preorder is defined by: $G_1 \sqsubseteq_{\mathcal{C}} G_2$ if there exists a $\mathcal{C}$-prebisimulation relating the roots of the two graphs. Note that when $\mathcal{P}_a = \mathcal{Q}_a = N$ and $\mathcal{C}$ is an equivalence relation, then a $\mathcal{C}$-prebisimulation is just a $\mathcal{C}$-bisimulation.

6.2 Derived Preorders

Many interesting preorders turn out to be instances of the $\mathcal{C}$-preorder combined with graph transformations. Let U denote the universal relation on N and $\Downarrow a$ the *local convergence* predicate on a; $n{\Downarrow}a$ holds if n is not globally divergent and cannot be triggered by means of an a-action to reach a globally divergent state. For details of this predicate see [27, 29]. Now many interesting preorders can be constructed as instances of the $\mathcal{C}$-preorder:

- The bisimulation divergence preorder [27, 29] results by setting:

$$\mathcal{P}_a = N, \mathcal{Q}_a = \{n | n{\Downarrow}a\} \quad \text{and} \quad \mathcal{C} = \{\langle m, n \rangle | \text{ for all } a{:}\, m{\Downarrow}a \Rightarrow n{\Downarrow}a\}.$$

  This defines the strong version of the divergence preorder. The weak version, $\lesssim$, where τ-actions are not observable, can be obtained from the corresponding observation graphs.

- The may, must and testing preorders require the transformation of graphs into deterministic, must, and acceptance graphs, respectively. Then these relations are the following instances of the general preorder [6].
  - The may preorder: $\mathcal{P}_a = N$, $\mathcal{Q}_a = \emptyset$, and $\mathcal{C} = U$.
  - The must preorder: $\mathcal{P}_a = \emptyset$, $\mathcal{Q}_a = \{m | m.acc \neq \emptyset\}$, and $\langle m, n \rangle \in \mathcal{C}$ holds exactly when either $m.acc = \emptyset$, or both $m.acc$ and $n.acc$ are nonempty and each element in $n.acc$ is a superset of some element in $m.acc$.
  - The testing preorder: $\mathcal{P}_a = N$, $\mathcal{Q}_a = \{m | m.acc \neq \emptyset\}$, and $\mathcal{C}$ is defined as for the must preorder.

As an example, we can establish the following.

$$\mathrm{PBUF}_n \underset{\sim}{\sqsubset} \mathrm{BUF}_m, \text{ for all } m > n$$

Here PBUF_n is used as a partial specification that is satisfied by all BUF_m for $m > n$. Partial specifications like this can be used to express that two agents, although not equivalent, may be used interchangeably in certain contexts. As an example, assume that we have a transport protocol with sender entity SENDER and receiver entity RECEIVER, interconnected through ports L with a medium MEDIUM. The desired service of the protocol is SERVICE; a verification that the protocol is correct is to determine

$$\mathrm{SERVICE} \quad \approx \quad (\mathrm{SENDER}|\mathrm{RECEIVER}|\mathrm{MEDIUM})\backslash L \tag{1}$$

(where $\approx$ is observation equivalence). Further assume that the protocol strictly uses the medium as a one-place buffer: when this buffer contains an item no attempt will ever be made to place another item in the buffer. We then expect (1) to hold also when MEDIUM is replaced by BUF_m for any $m > 1$, since all these buffers behave identically in this context. One way to prove this is to first prove that

$$\mathrm{SERVICE} \quad \underset{\sim}{\sqsubset} \quad (\mathrm{SENDER}|\mathrm{RECEIVER}|\mathrm{PBUF}_1)\backslash L \tag{2}$$

From $\mathrm{PBUF}_1 \underset{\sim}{\sqsubset} \mathrm{BUF}_m$ for all $m > 1$ we get

$$(\mathrm{SENDER}|\mathrm{RECEIVER}|\mathrm{PBUF}_1)\backslash L \quad \underset{\sim}{\sqsubset} \quad (\mathrm{SENDER}|\mathrm{RECEIVER}|\mathrm{BUF}_m)\backslash L \tag{3}$$

and from (2), (3), and the transitivity of $\underset{\sim}{\sqsubset}$ we get

$$\mathrm{SERVICE} \quad \underset{\sim}{\sqsubset} \quad (\mathrm{SENDER}|\mathrm{RECEIVER}|\mathrm{BUF}_m)\backslash L \tag{4}$$

If we further assume that SERVICE contains no divergent states, it follows from [29] that

$$\mathrm{SERVICE} \quad \approx \quad (\mathrm{SENDER}|\mathrm{RECEIVER}|\mathrm{BUF}_m)\backslash L$$

The same technique is equally applicable to other equivalences. The methodology of introducing "don't care" states in order to get partial specifications could also be useful within a stepwise refinement strategy.

6.3 The Algorithm

The algorithm for computing the $\mathcal{C}$-preorder works by attempting to find a $\mathcal{C}$-prebisimulation relating the roots of the graphs. In contrast to Section 5.3, however, preorders cannot be represented by partitions. We obtain an appropriate representation by annotating every node n with a set of nodes considered to be "greater" than n.

In principle, the preorder algorithm proceeds in the same way as the equivalence algorithm. It starts by considering all states to be indistinguishable, i.e. every node is annotated with the set of all nodes N. Then it successively refines the annotation of each node until the root node of G_1 no longer is in the annotation of the root node of G_2 (in which case $G_1 \not\sqsubseteq_{\mathcal{C}} G_2$) or the annotations determine a $\mathcal{C}$-prebisimulation (in which case $G_1 \sqsubseteq_{\mathcal{C}} G_2$).

The time and space complexities of this algorithm are $O(k^4 * \ell)$ and $O(k^2 + \ell)$, respectively, where k is the number of states, and ℓ is the number of transitions, in the two graphs. The loss of efficiency compared with the equivalence algorithm is due to the fact that we cannot use the same compact representation of relations as in Section 5.3.

7 Model Checking

The third basic analysis within the Workbench is based on model checking [3, 4, 5, 9, 28], in which specifications are written in an expressive modal logic, the *propositional (modal) mu-calculus.* The Workbench can check whether an agent meets such a specification.

7.1 Definition of the Logic

The formulas, or propositions, of the logic are described by the following grammar:

$$
\begin{array}{rcl}
\Phi & ::= & tt \mid \mathit{ff} \mid X \\
& \mid & \neg\Phi \mid \Phi \vee \Phi \mid \Phi \wedge \Phi \mid \Phi \Rightarrow \Phi \\
& \mid & \langle a\rangle\Phi \mid [a]\Phi \mid \langle .\rangle\Phi \mid [.]\Phi \\
& \mid & B \ \mathit{arg\text{-}list} \\
& \mid & \nu X.\Phi \mid \mu X.\Phi
\end{array}
$$

In the above, X ranges over propositional identifiers; these can be bound to formulas in the same way as agent identifiers can be bound to agents. Also, a ranges over actions, B over names of user-defined macros, and *arg-list* stands for a list of actions and/or formulas that B requires in order to produce a proposition. In $\nu X.\Phi$ and $\mu X.\Phi$ all free occurrences of X must be positive.

These formulas are interpreted with respect to nodes in transition graphs. The formulas tt and ff hold of every node and no node, respectively. A propositional identifier is interpreted with respect to an environment binding identifiers to propositions: a node n satisfies X if it satisfies the formula to which X is bound in the environment. The connectives $\neg, \vee, \wedge$, and $\Rightarrow$ have their usual meanings.

The modal operators $\langle a\rangle$, $[a]$, $\langle .\rangle$ and $[.]$ make statements about the edges from a node. A node n satisfies $\langle a\rangle\Phi$ if it has an a-derivative satisfying Φ, while n satisfies $[a]\Phi$ if *all* its a-derivatives satisfy Φ. In the case that n has no a-derivatives, n trivially satisfies $[a]\Phi$. In $\langle .\rangle\Phi$ and $[.]\Phi$, the "." should be thought of as a "wild-card" action; n satisfies $\langle .\rangle\Phi$ if it satisfies $\langle a\rangle\Phi$ for some a, while it satisfies $[.]\Phi$ if it satisfies $[a]\Phi$ for all a.

A macro can be thought of as a function that accepts arguments, which may be either actions or formulas, and returns a proposition. The formula B*arg-list* is then interpreted as the proposition returned by B in response to *arg-list.*

Formulas of the type $\nu X.\Phi$ and $\mu X.\Phi$ can be understood as "Φ, where X is bound to Φ". Since X may occur in Φ they represent *recursive formulas.* Formally they correspond to infinite conjunctions and disjunctions in the following sense. Let Φ_0 be the proposition tt, and define Φ_{i+1} to be the proposition $\Phi[\Phi_i/X]$, namely, the proposition obtained by substituting Φ_i for free occurrences of X in Φ. Then a node satisfies $\nu X.\Phi$ if it satisfies all the Φ_i. Also let $\hat{\Phi}_0$ be the proposition ff, and let $\hat{\Phi}_{i+1}$ be defined as $\Phi[\hat{\Phi}_i/X]$. Then a node satisfies $\mu X.\Phi$ if it satisfies one of the $\hat{\Phi}_i$. As a trivial example, $\nu X.X$ holds of any node while $\mu X.X$ never holds.

7.2 Derived Logics

Applying the model checking algorithm to graphs generated by the different graph transformations yields different interpretations for the modal operators. For instance, model checking with observation graphs causes the modal operators to be insensitive to τ-actions, but also makes it difficult to formulate liveness properties since $n \xrightarrow{\varepsilon} n$ holds for every node n in an observation graph.

The recursive formulas add a tremendous amount of expressive power to the logic (see e.g. [9, 26]), since they allow the description of safety and liveness properties. However, such formulas are in general difficult to understand. We have found that the most effective way to use the model checker is to choose a collection of intuitively well-understood operators and then define these operators as macros. For example, it is possible to define the operators of the branching time temporal logic CTL [4]. Examples include the following:

$$\begin{aligned} \mathit{Henceforth}(\Phi) &= \nu X.(\Phi \wedge [.]X) \\ \mathit{Eventually}(\Phi) &= \mu X.(\Phi \vee (\langle . \rangle tt \wedge [.]X)) \end{aligned}$$

Thus *Henceforth*(Φ) holds of n if Φ holds of every node reachable from n, while *Eventually*(Φ) holds of n if along every path leading from n there is a node satisfying Φ. In CTL, these operators are written $AG\Phi$ and $AF\Phi$ respectively.

As an example, consider the graph corresponding to CBUF_2 in figure 2. It is possible to show that it is deadlock-free as follows. Define the macro *Deadlock* by

$$\mathit{Deadlock} = \neg \langle . \rangle tt$$

This proposition is true of states that cannot perform any actions. For any particular n the model checker can establish that CBUF_n satisfies the formula

$$\mathit{Henceforth}(\neg \mathit{Deadlock})$$

where *Henceforth*() is the macro defined above; therefore CBUF_n never deadlocks.

7.3 The Algorithm

Our model checking algorithm comes from [5]; we shall not describe it here. The complexity of the algorithm is in general exponential in the length of the formula being checked, although for large classes of formulas the algorithm is well-behaved. A precise characterization of this complexity is still under investigation. Other algorithms include the tableau-based approach in [28], and a semantics-based algorithm in [9]. An automated proof system for a subset of the logic is described in [18].

8 Other Features of the Workbench

The Workbench includes other facilities for examining the behavior of agents. In addition, as a result of its modular structure it is relatively easy to extend. This section describes some of these facilities and extensions.

8.1 State Space Analysis

The Workbench includes a variety of ways of analyzing the state space of an agent. In addition to commands for computing transitions and derivatives, there are features for determining which states are deadlocked and for computing sequences of experiments that lead to deadlocked states. These types of analyses are traditionally found in automatic verification tools, and will not be discussed in this paper.

8.2 Equation Solving

The equation solving feature of the Workbench [23] is used to solve equations of type $(A|X)\backslash L = B$ where A, B and L are given. The method is useful within a top-down or stepwise refinement strategy: if a specification (B) and parts of an implementation (A) are known, solving such an equation amounts to constructing a specification of the missing submodules. The method works by successively transforming equations into simpler equations, in parallel with the generation of a solution. These transformations can be performed automatically by the system according to certain heuristics, or the user can apply them interactively. The tool has been used for the generation of a receiver in a communication protocol, where the overall service, medium, and sender are known.

8.3 Experimental Extensions

Two extensions to the system have been implemented and are being investigated. In the first, the model of computation has been extended to include a restricted form of *value passing*. In its "pure" form, CCS does not provide for the association of values to communication events, although it is possible to encode the passing of values by associating a unique event name to an event/value pair. In the case of infinite value domains, however, this leads to syntactically infinite agents. In [16], an alternative encoding is proposed, in which the infinitely many data values are represented schematically. Using the resulting transitional semantics, bisimulation equivalences can be defined in such a way as to correspond exactly to the bisimulation equivalences in full CCS. This result entails a decision procedure for *data-independent* agents, i.e. agents which communicate data values but do not perform any computations or tests on the values. The decision procedure has been implemented in the Workbench [19].

An interface has also been built between the Workbench and the Extended Model Checker (EMC), which is a tool for checking the satisfiability of temporal logic (CTL) formulas. CTL differs from the logic in Section 7 in that the view of processes is different: in CTL there are no communication events, and states can be distinguished by atomic propositions. EMC has successfully been applied to verification of nontrivial pieces of hardware. The integration with the Workbench was achieved by defining a translation from labeled transition graphs to the type of structures analyzed by EMC [15].

9 Conclusion

In this paper we have presented an overview of the Concurrency Workbench. We have shown that it is possible to supply a variety of algorithms for deducing the correctness of processes based on a variety of different process semantics. This has been achieved through a strict separation between the semantic models of processes and the basic algorithms used to analyze them. The modularization makes the Workbench relatively easy to extend, although it slightly impairs efficiency.

There are a variety of directions for future work on the Workbench. One involves extending the kinds of value-passing that are supported. Another involves the computation of *distinguishing formulas* [12]. At present, when processes are found not to be equivalent, no indication is given as to why. One way to convey this information is to give a modal formula satisfied by one process but not the other. Work is also underway on a graphical interface.

Another possible area of investigation involves *compositional reasoning* [3]. The parallel composition of two processes usually entails a combinatorial explosion in the size of the state space of the resulting process. One means of coping with this is to verify the parallel components separately in a way that implies the correctness of the composite process. The preorder has been investigated in this respect [29]; one possibility is to implement this in a way similar to the equation-solving tool in Section 8.2. It is also conceivable to extend the model checker to check formulas compositionally, using techniques developed by Stirling [27].

We close with some facts about the development of the Workbench. The implementation (in Standard ML under Unix) was begun by Parrow in 1986; the early versions featured mainly an observation equivalence checker and the equation solver. Since 1987 the Workbench has been developed jointly by the three of us, and we arrived at the current modular structure in 1988. The implementation now (1989) comprises approximately 10,000 lines of code, and runs on Vax, Sun, and Macintosh computers. The project has consumed more than 5 man-years of effort.

Acknowledgements

We are grateful to Matthew Hennessy, Robin Milner, and Colin Stirling for initiating and managing the Workbench project. Also, many thanks to Lennart Beckman, Jo Blishen, Michael Mendler, Kevin Mitchell, Fredrik Orava, Björn Pehrson, and David Walker for many helpful suggestions concerning the implementation of the Workbench and/or the presentation in this report.

References

[1] Bochmann, G. "Usage of Protocol Development Tools: The Results of a Survey." In *Proceeding of the Seventh IFIP Symposium on Protocol Specification, Testing, and Verification*, 1987, North-Holland.

[2] Boudol, G., de Simone, R. and Vergamini, D. "Experiment with Auto and Autograph an a Simple Case Sliding Window Protocol." Inria Report 870, July 1988

[3] Clarke, E.M. "Compositional Model Checking." In *Proceedings of the REX Summer School/Workshop*, Noordwijkerhout, the Netherlands, 1988.

[4] Clarke, E.M., Emerson, E. and Sistla, A.P. "Automatic Verification of Finite State Concurrent Systems Using Temporal Logic Specifications." *ACM Transactions on Programming Languages and Systems*, v. 8, n. 2, 1986, pp. 244-263.

[5] Cleaveland, R. "Tableau-Based Model Checking in the Propositional Mu-Calculus." University of Sussex Technical Report 2/89, March 1989.

[6] Cleaveland, R. and Hennessy, M.C.B "Testing Equivalence as a Bisimulation Equivalence." To be presented at the Workshop on Automatic Verification Methods for Finite State Systems, Grenoble 1989.

[7] Cleaveland, R., Parrow, J and Steffen, B. *The Concurrency Workbench: Operating Instructions*, University of Edinburgh, Laboratory for Foundations of Computer Science, Technical Note 10, September 1988.

[8] DeNicola, R. and Hennessy, M.C.B. "Testing Equivalences for Processes." *Theoretical Computer Science*, v. 34, 1983, pp. 83-133.

[9] Emerson, E.A. and Lei, C.-L. "Efficient Model Checking in Fragments of the Propositional Mu-Calculus." In *Proceedings of the First Annual Symposium on Logic in Computer Science*, 1986, pp. 267-278.

[10] Fernandez, J.-C. *Aldébaran: Une Système de Vérification par Réduction de Processus Communicants.* Ph.D. Thesis, Université de Grenoble, 1988.

[11] Hennessy, M.C.B. *Algebraic Theory of Processes.* MIT Press, Boston, 1988.

[12] Hillerström, M. *Verification of CCS-processes.* M.Sc. Thesis, Computer Science Department, Aalborg University, 1987.

[13] Hoare, C.A.R. *Communicating Sequential Processes.* Prentice-Hall, London, 1985.

[14] Hopcroft, J. and Ullman, J. *Introduction to Automata Theory, Languages and Computation.* Addison-Wesley, Reading, 1979.

[15] Jonsson, B., Kahn, A., and Parrow, J. "Implementing a Model Checking Algorithm by Adapting Existing Automated Tools." SICS Research Report, 1989. In preparation; to be presented at the Workshop on Automatic Verification Methods for Finite State Systems, Grenoble 1989.

[16] Jonsson, B. and Parrow, J. "Deciding Bisimulation Equivalences for a Class of Non-Finite-State Programs." In *Proceedings of the Sixth Annual Symposium on Theoretical Aspects of Computer Science*, 1989. Lecture Notes in Computer Science 349, pp. 421-433. Springer-Verlag, Berlin, 1989.

[17] Kanellakis, P. and Smolka, S.A. "CCS Expressions, Finite State Processes, and Three Problems of Equivalence." In *Proceedings of the Second ACM Symposium on the Principles of Distributed Computing*, 1983.

[18] Larsen, K.G. "Proof Systems for Hennessy-Milner Logic with Recursion." In *Proceedings of CAAP*, 1988.

[19] Lee, C.-H. "Implementering av CCS med värdeöverföring." SICS Technical Report 1989 (in Swedish).

[20] Malhotra, J., Smolka, S.A., Giacalone, A. and Shapiro, R. "Winston: A Tool for Hierarchical Design and Simulation of Concurrent Systems." In *Proceedings of the Workshop on Specification and Verification of Concurrent Systems*, University of Stirling, Scotland, 1988.

[21] Milner, R. *Communication and Concurrency.* Prentice Hall 1989.

[22] Paige, R. and Tarjan, R.E. "Three Partition Refinement Algorithms." *SIAM Journal of Computing*, v. 16, n. 6, December 1987, pp. 973-989.

[23] Parrow, J. "Submodule Construction as Equation Solving in CCS." In *Proceedings of the Foundations of Software Technology and Theoretical Computer Science*, Lecture Notes in Computer Science 287, pp. 103-123. Springer-Verlag, Berlin, 1987.

[24] Parrow, J. "Verifying a CSMA/CD-Protocol with CCS." In *Proceeding of the Eigth IFIP Symposium on Protocol Specification, Testing, and Verification*, 1988, North-Holland, pp 373-384.

[25] Richier, J., Rodriguez, C., Sifakis, J. and Voiron, J.. "Verification in XESAR of the Sliding Window Protocol." In *Proceedings of the Seventh IFIP Symposium on Protocol Specification, Testing, and Verification*, 1987, North-Holland.

[26] Steffen, B. "Characteristic Formulae." In Proceedings ICALP, 1989.

[27] Stirling, C. "Modal Logics for Communicating Systems." *Theoretical Computer Science*, v. 49, 1987, pp. 311-347.

[28] Stirling, C. and Walker, D.J. " Local Model Checking in the Modal Mu-Calculus", In *Proceedings TAPSOFT* 1989, Lecture Notes in Computer Science 351, pp 369-383, Springer Verlag 1989.

[29] Walker, D.J. "Bisimulation Equivalence and Divergence in CCS." In *Proceedings of the Third Annual Symposium on Logic in Computer Science*, 1988, pp. 186-192.

[30] Walker, D.J. "Analysing Mutual Exclusion Algorithms Using CCS." University of Edinburgh Technical Report ECS-LFCS-88-45, 1988.

Protocol Specification, Testing, and Verification, IX
E. Brinksma, G. Scollo and C.A. Vissers (Editors)
Elsevier Science Publishers B.V. (North-Holland)
IFIP, 1990

A Software Environment for OSI Protocol Testing Systems

R. I. Chan, B. R. Smith, G. Neufeld, S. T. Chanson,
W. B. Davis†, S. T. Vuong, H. L. See, S. Chan

Department of Computer Science
University of British Columbia
Vancouver, B. C., Canada
V6T 1W5

† IDACOM Electronics Ltd.
4211 – 95th Street
Edmonton, Alberta, Canada
T6E 5R6

Abstract

A general protocol testing system should be able to support conformance testing, testing during development, passive monitoring, or performance testing at any OSI protocol layer. A conceptual architecture of a protocol testing environment based on the OSI reference model is presented here. Protocol entities are implemented within the environment such that their behaviour can be observed and controlled in a straightforward manner. Many events are observable, and the flexibility and degree of control that test functions can exercise facilitates a wide range of protocol testing capabilities. The paper also presents the design of a particular implementation of this environment, the OSI Protocol Testing Environment (OSI PTE).

1. Introduction

The growth in computer communications and networking has caused a worldwide increase in the effort being expended to implement communications protocols. This has led to a greater emphasis on the testing of protocol implementations and on the development of protocol testing systems and tools [Bochmann 87].

A cooperative research project, currently being undertaken by the University of British Columbia and IDACOM Electronics Ltd., is endeavoring to develop a portable OSI (Open Systems Interconnection [CCITT 88a]) protocol testing system [Davis 88]. The system will be capable of testing – whether formal conformance testing [ISO 88], testing during development, passive monitoring, or performance testing – protocol implementations at any OSI protocol layer, while meeting high performance criteria. The primary components of this system are a set of custom VLSI circuits [Anderson 89], and a special-purpose software environment called the OSI Protocol Testing Environment (OSI PTE).

The test system will contain implementations of all OSI protocols that it will be capable of testing. These implementations must be structured in a manner that allows the ability to observe and/or control at different points within the protocol stack. This ability is central to all forms of protocol testing, and is especially important in order to provide the wide range of protocol testing capabilities that are required for the UBC-IDACOM tester. The OSI PTE provides such structuring, allowing testing of single- or multi-layer protocol implementations at any level of the OSI protocol stack. It is felt that this system is more powerful and flexible than most of the earlier test systems [Ansart 82, Rayner 82, Linn 83, Lonc 85, Rafiq 85, Austermuehl 86].

The OSI PTE is a realization of the OSI Reference Model (OSI RM) [CCITT 88a] that has been designed to support general protocol testing. Within the environment, a protocol implementation executes as an *entity* that passes *events* back and forth to other entities. To support testing, events are made visible to any testing functions that require observation capabilities. Testing functions, and other software components such as user-defined test programs, are also realized within the OSI PTE.

The next section of this paper introduces the OSI PTE and outlines a conceptual architecture of the environment. Section 3 describes how entities and events are represented. The services that are provided by the OSI PTE are described in sections 4 and 5 : event posting, the most important of these services, in section 4, and additional services in section 5. Section 6 presents some closing thoughts and conclusions.

2. Conceptual Architecture

In the OSI RM, entities at adjacent layers access each other through Service Access Points (SAPs) using Abstract Service Primitives (ASPs). This model of inter-layer communications is also used in the OSI PTE. In addition, the OSI PTE includes some extensions to the OSI RM in order to meet the unique requirements of protocol testing.

An *entity* is a basic execution unit in the OSI PTE. The OSI PTE entity concept is an extension of that defined in the OSI RM as two types of entities are defined: *protocol entities* and *test entities*. Entities interact by posting *events* to other entities; ASPs are represented by events.

Figure 1 illustrates the composition of the OSI PTE. Arrows represent the flow of events between entities: solid arrows indicate normal event flow between protocol entities, while dashed arrows indicate event flow to/from the test entities. Test entities interact with the normal (solid arrow) event flow by observing events, generating events, or intercepting events. Test entities may be configured in many ways, and for simplicity they are represented collectively in Figure 1.

The following sections describe the key conceptual components of the OSI PTE.

2.1 Protocol Entities

Protocol entities are analogous to OSI RM entities. They are implementations of supported protocols in execution. Each protocol entity resides within one of the seven OSI protocol layers. If several sub-layers exist within an OSI protocol layer, each sub-layer may be implemented in the OSI PTE as a separate entity. A protocol entity provides services to protocol entities at the layer above, and utilizes services made available by protocol entities at the layer below. The only means of communication between protocol entities at adjacent layers is by ASPs through SAPs.

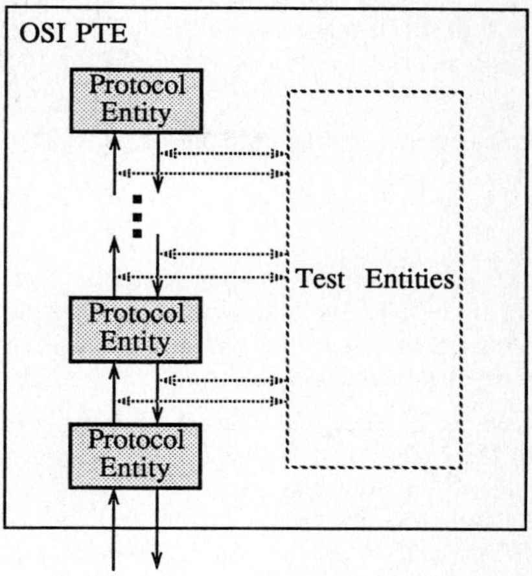

Figure 1 – The OSI PTE

2.2 Test Entities

Test entities are user test programs which utilize the protocol entities to control and observe the implementation under test (IUT). They are given observation and control capabilities that are not made available to protocol entities. They may observe, alter, or intercept events that are passed between protocol entities, or generate events and pass them to a protocol entity. Test entities need not reside within any particular OSI protocol layer; they may be specified to span several protocol layers and simultaneously interact with several protocol entities.

Test entities may operate as *service users*, or *observers*, or both (see Figure 2). Service user test entities are specified to be the normal recipients of ASPs and operate as though they

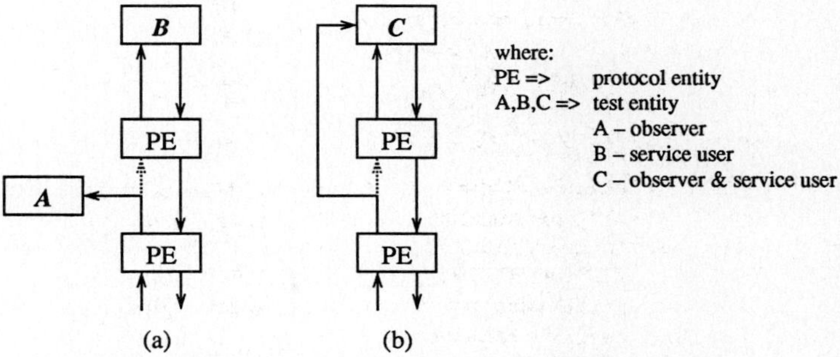

Figure 2 – Observation and Service User Test Entities

are protocol entities. They are useful for conformance testing purposes, *e.g.* implementation of a lower tester. Observer test entities are specified to observe, alter, or intercept ASPs normally destined for some other entities. This mode is useful for diagnostic testing or monitoring purposes.

A test entity may also control protocol entities through direct manipulation of their internal state variables.

2.3 Events

Events are one-way interactions between two entities based on the OSI concept of ASPs. To a protocol entity, an event is an indication that some processing has to be done. To a test entity, an event is a unit of processing that it may observe, intercept, or alter. A protocol entity is not aware of any test entity interaction with the events that it sends or receives.

With protocol testing requirements in mind, the concept of events in the OSI PTE has been extended to include Protocol Data Unit (PDU) events, timer events, state change events and protocol error events (see Figure 3). The additional events are accommodated by defining seven event interfaces for a protocol entity, instead of the two (ASP up and down) normally defined for an OSI entity. These extra event interfaces allow some important internal protocol entity events to be exposed to test entities in a controlled fashion.

Abstract Service Primitive Events

Figure 3 illustrates the relationships between a protocol entity and its ASP interfaces. The (N)-ASP Down service corresponds to request and response ASPs received from an entity at the layer above. The (N-1)-ASP Up service corresponds to indication and confirmation ASPs received from an entity at the layer below. A protocol entity also generates (N)-ASP Up events to the layer above and (N-1)-ASP Down events to the layer below.

Protocol Data Unit Events

Events pertaining to Protocol Data Units may be grouped into PDU Up events for decoded PDUs being received and PDU Down events for encoded PDUs to be transmitted. Since these are internal events, they are normally received by the entities that generate them.

Making these events external allows the test entities to interface with the protocol entities through PDUs in addition to ASPs, and gives more flexibility to the test entities for monitoring or generating PDUs. A test entity may observe SDUs or decoded PDUs depending on

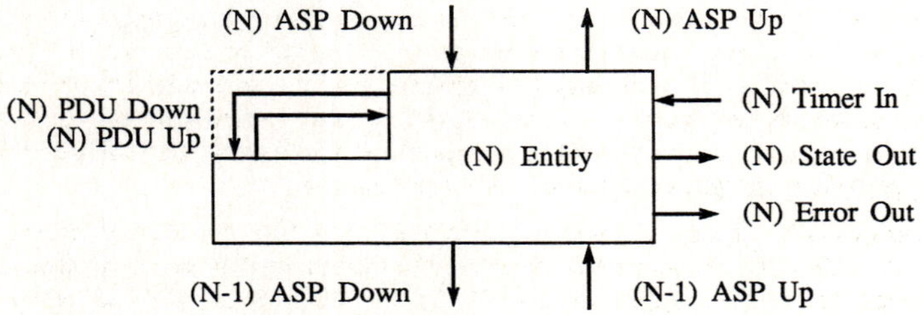

Figure 3 – Event Interfaces for an Entity

whether it observes ASP Up (DATA indication) events or PDU Up events. Similarly, a test entity may transmit SDUs or encoded PDUs depending on whether it generates ASP Down (DATA request) events or PDU Down events.

Timer Events

A Timer In event represents the expiry of a timer that has previously been set by the entity. Making these events observable allows the test entities to be aware of time-outs within the protocol entities that they control or monitor. Timer In events are generated by the OSI PTE's timer manager, which is not considered to be an OSI PTE entity. Therefore, setting a timer is not an event, only a timer expiry is.

Test Management Events

The last two event types (State Out and Error Out) are generated by the protocol entities strictly to provide additional points of observation for test entities. A State Out event is generated whenever the internal state of a protocol entity changes. An Error Out event is generated whenever a protocol violation is detected or some other error condition arises within the protocol entity. Like PDU events, the normal destination of both of these types of events is the entity which generated them. However, as these events have no effect on the operation of the protocol, a protocol entity usually takes no action when they occur.

3. Realization of Entities and Events

Based on the conceptual architecture presented in the previous section, an implementation of the OSI PTE has been designed. This section presents the high level architecture of the OSI PTE in terms of the major data structures used to represent protocol entities and events.

3.1 Entities

The protocol entities are constructed such that there is a clear separation between their data areas and their code areas. All variables used globally within the protocol entities are placed in control blocks. All subroutines using these global variables take a pointer to a control block as one of their parameters. The separation between code and data allows multiple instances of a protocol entity to be created.

The software that composes a protocol entity consists of one or more state machines and a set of support routines. The state machine is driven by incoming events and makes use of the underlying support routines to carry out actions appropriate to its current state. The state machine and the support routines interact through parameters and through variables located within the set of control blocks specified for the entity.

The separation of support routines from state machine routines allows test entities and protocol entities to share a significant portion of the code necessary to carry out protocol operations. A test entity may be created simply by specifying a new state machine, which may also make use of the support routines. Test entities may either share control blocks with the protocol entities or create their own private copies of the control blocks. Additional data areas and support routines may also be defined for the test entities.

An entity maintains a separate *Connection Control Block* (CCB) for each connection under its control. A CCB contains connection-specific information such as state variables and protocol parameters for the connection. The CCBs for all connections within an entity are collected together into a *connection table*. Each connection is assigned a *connection identifier* which serves as an index into the connection table. The size of each protocol entity's connection table is configurable during system initialization.

Each entity has an associated *Entity Variable Area* (NVA) which contains variables global to all connections. An NVA contains entity-specific information such as default parameter values for initializing a connection. Variables necessary for layer management within an entity are also contained in the NVA. In particular, the NVA contains a pointer to the entity's connection table and a variable indicating the table's size.

3.2 Events

The state machine of each entity acts on events that it receives. Each event type defined in the system is represented by an *event identifier* and an associated *Event Parameter Area* (EPA). An EPA is a control block which contains the parameters to be passed between two entities during an interaction. The receiving entity uses the event identifier to determine the structure of the EPA and the action necessary to process the event.

3.3 Entity Entry Points

When an event is posted to an entity, the OSI PTE invokes that entity through a PTE entry point. Each entity has one or more entry points, and each entry point may handle one or more of the seven types of OSI PTE event interfaces (ASP up, PDU down, *etc.*). There are 4 parameters associated with each entry point:

- a pointer to the entity's NVA,
- a connection identifier,
- an event identifier, and
- a pointer to the event parameter area.

This information is sufficient for the entity state machine to process the event.

4. Event Posting

In being an environment in which entities execute, the OSI PTE provides a set of services that are used by the entities during execution. The primary service provided is *event posting*, the act of passing an event from one entity to another.

4.1 Entity Table

For control purposes, a certain amount of information is maintained for each active entity in the system. There is an *Entity Control Block* (NCB) associated with each active protocol entity. All NCBs are kept in the *entity table*, which is indexed by each entity's *entity identifier.*

An NCB contains a pointer to the entity's private data area (the NVA) and a set of *post vectors*, one for each type of event interface. A post vector contains the address of the entity's entry point for that type of event interface, and a set of test entity entry point addresses.

The relationships between these data structures are depicted in Figure 4.

4.2 The PostEvent Service

When an entity posts an event, it makes use of the *PostEvent* service of the OSI PTE. PostEvent requires five parameters:

- identifier of the entity that the event is being posted to,
- identifier of the connection to which the event pertains,
- event interface type,
- event identifier, and
- event parameter area pointer.

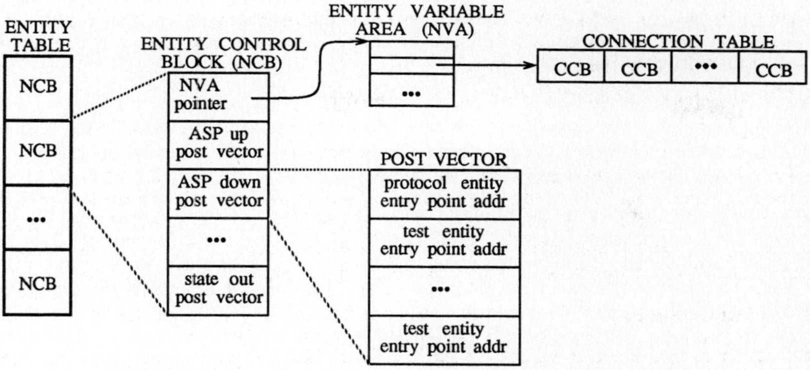

Figure 4 – Entity Data Structure Relationships

Based on the entity identifier and event interface type, PostEvent can locate the appropriate post vector within the entity table, and thereby identify the entity entry point to be invoked. The remaining PostEvent parameters, along with the NVA pointer (obtained from the entity table), are passed to the entity entry point.

The act of posting an event is implemented as a direct procedure call to the destination entity, *i.e.* all entities within the OSI PTE are implemented within a single process. Because procedure calls are used, entity invocations are nested. Whenever an entity posts an event, control is passed to the entity to which the event is posted. While the invoked entity processes the event, processing within the invoking (posting) entity is suspended.

In keeping with the definition of events being one-way interactions between two entities, the request/confirm and indication/response pairs of ASP events are implemented as separate procedure calls. There are no additional meanings attached to the return from an event procedure call other than the fact that the invoked entity has completed processing the event. In particular, the invoked entity does not use the EPA it received to pass information back to the invoking entity.

Performance was a key consideration during the design and implementation of the OSI PTE. For this reason, all entities coexist within a single process and direct procedure calls are employed for event posting. This minimizes the overhead associated with event posting, primarily by eliminating the context switching that would be required in a multi-process implementation. With a single processor, events within a protocol stack are processed sequentially, and the operation of the system is essentially synchronous.

It should be noted that the semantics of PostEvent allow porting of the environment to a multi-process system in which entities are realized as separate processes and event posting is realized using message passing. This change could be made with minimum impact on the protocol implementations.

After an entity posts an event, the receiving entity (or an observing test entity) may post events back to the original posting entity. In effect, the posting entity is invoked again through indirect recursion [Clark 85]. An entity must therefore ensure that it is in a consistent state before posting any events, otherwise subsequent (recursive) invocations of the entity may not operate correctly. In most cases, state consistency can be achieved by delaying the posting of events until the very last moment in the processing of an incoming event.

4.3 Test Entity Interaction

Recall that a post vector contains a set of test entity entry point addresses in addition to the address of a protocol entity entry point. In fact, the PostEvent service invokes each of these test entities before invoking the normal intended protocol entity. In this way, each test entity observes events as they are posted to protocol entities.

The test entities are given three additional control capabilities: they can alter events, they can forward events immediately, and they can intercept events. Event parameter areas are always passed by address; it is therefore a simple matter for a test entity to change a value in the EPA before it is passed to the protocol entity. Forwarding is used if the test entity wishes to regain control after the protocol entity has completed processing the event; there is an OSI PTE service that permits this. Similarly, there is an OSI PTE service that allows the test entity to prevent the PostEvent service from invoking the normal protocol entry point; this effectively intercepts the event. These capabilities allow the designer of test entities to exercise a wide range of control over the test system.

When designing protocol implementations, there are two implications of this test entity interaction scheme that must be kept in mind. First, due to test entity interference, the length of time that the next entity may take to process an event is not predictable. Therefore, entities may be unable to make accurate timing estimations in regards to the events being posted. Timing assumptions can be minimized by setting all relevant timers before posting any events. Second, as indicated before, it is possible that the test entity will post an event back to the entity that posted the original event (indirect recursion); entities must be prepared for this occurrence.

5. Additional PTE Services

Besides event posting, the OSI PTE provides several additional services. This section highlights other major services.

5.1 System Control

As stated earlier, the entire OSI PTE resides within a single process. Processing within the OSI PTE is driven by external events including the following.

- frame arrival.
- time-out notification.
- user test input.
- application service request.

There is a *dispatcher* within the OSI PTE which translates these external events into internal events.

A frame arrival event is generated by the physical layer hardware, via the operating system, and causes the dispatcher to post a DATA service indication event to the data link layer. Time-out notifications are generated by the operating system; each of these is processed by a *timer manager* (see section 5.5) within the dispatcher, which posts a Timer In event to the appropriate entity. User test input is forwarded to a test entity for further processing. Application service requests are also generated by the user (test operator), and are posted to the application layer by the dispatcher.

For each internal OSI PTE event generated by the dispatcher (in response to an external event), the entity invoked by the dispatcher may invoke other entities to carry on the processing. Due to the procedure call characteristics of event posting, the dispatcher does not regain control until the initial event is completely processed by all entities involved.

5.2 System Configuration

Services are provided to configure entities within the OSI PTE. Essentially, these services manage the entity table, registering entity entry points in post vectors. There are services to create and delete entities, and to begin and end observation by a test entity.

The service that creates protocol entities simply allocates a new entity control block in the entity table. The entity's NVA address is recorded, as are the address of its entry points for each event interface (type of event). Deletion of an entity is accomplished simply by removing the appropriate NCB.

For a test entity to begin observation, it must specify the protocol entity and event interface(s) that it wishes to observe. The OSI PTE modifies the appropriate post vector to add the test entity's entry point. This entry point is removed when a test entity wishes to end observation of a protocol entity.

5.3 Data Buffering

The test system hardware deals with received data and data for transmission using special buffer formats. There are two different types of buffers: *transmit buffers* contain encoded PDUs ready for transmission, and *receive buffers* contain received PDUs ready for decoding. Each type of buffer is fixed in length, and a PDU is thus represented by a list of one or more buffers.

The OSI PTE maintains a global pool of free buffers, from which both transmit and receive buffers are allocated. To hide knowledge of buffer formats from protocol implementations, OSI PTE service routines are provided to insert and retrieve data from transmit and receive buffers. Additional services are provided to queue PDUs, and to handle PDU manipulations such as segmentation, concatenation, separation, and reassembly.

The buffering mechanism has been designed to eliminate or minimize data copying in the system. A PDU passed between layers is represented only by a pointer to a list of buffers. The buffer structure also allows for efficient recording of PDUs, again by eliminating the need for copying.

5.4 PDU Decoding

Since decoding is a common operation, the OSI PTE provides a special purpose PDU decoder. A set of rules for parsing the fields (tokens) of a PDU is specified in a *decoder program*. Besides indicating how a PDU should be decoded, a decoder program also indicates the format of the decoded PDU. The decoded format is stored in a *token buffer*; space for the token buffer is generally allocated in a protocol entity's NVA or CCB.

The decoder accepts a list of receive buffers representing a PDU, a decoder program, and a pointer to a token buffer. It decodes the fields (tokens) of the PDU, and fills in the token buffer. The decoder function has been designed for future implementation in hardware.

5.5 Timer Management

The timer management portion of the OSI PTE interfaces with the operating system to provide services that start, stop, suspend, and resume timers. To start a timer, an entity specifies the timer type and duration, and the connection to which the timer applies. A timer identifier is assigned by the OSI PTE when the timer is started. The stop, suspend, and resume services make use of this identifier.

All timer related functions are handled by the *timer manager*, a part of the dispatcher. When a timer expires, the timer manager determines which entity started the timer, and posts a Timer In event to that entity. The timer type is used as the event identifier; there is no event parameter area associated with the event.

6. Conclusion

The key feature of the OSI PTE is the powerful observation and control capabilities that are provided to test entities. These capabilities, and the flexibility with which a set of test entities may be configured, lead to a very general protocol tester. Adding to the generality of the UBC-IDACOM tester is its support for testing at any OSI protocol layer. Testing may be performed at one layer only, independently at multiple layers, or cooperatively at multiple layers.

Given the OSI PTE and a set of protocol implementations, protocol entities and test entities can be specified to do a wide range of protocol testing. For conformance testing, protocol entities are used to provide underlying communications services to the SUT, while test entities are configured to act as the lower tester (for remote, distributed, or coordinated testing), active ferry [Zeng 88], or active ferry clip† [Zeng 89]. If desired, testing can be performed by implementing an error generator test entity for use with a protocol entity as a reference implementation. Test entities can be defined to realize passive testing and monitoring functions such as triggering, filtering, event recording, and event reporting (logging) [Davis 88]. Test entities can also be specified to count and time ASP and PDU events for performance testing purposes. Note that implementation of test entities related to protocol *P* is eased by the existence of support routines (*e.g.* encoding/decoding functions) in the protocol implementation for *P*.

Efficiency has been a major consideration because there are performance requirements that must be met in a protocol tester capable of testing at multiple layers. For this reason, the entire OSI PTE has been implemented within a single process in order to eliminate the overhead of context switching.

A special purpose test language has been designed for the specification of test entities. One of its major design goals is to facilitate the translation from TTCN (the Tree and Tabular Combined Notation [ISO 88]), but as it is based on a general-purpose programming language, it also allows specification of more general testing functions.

At the University of British Columbia, a prototype of the OSI PTE has been implemented on a UNIX-based workstation, and protocol implementations have been completed up to the session layer. Work is underway to port the environment onto an IDACOM portable protocol tester, and to expand the set of protocol implementations to include the message handling protocols (X.400 [CCITT 88b]).

† The ferry clip approach is able to realize all of the abstract test methods proposed by ISO for conformance testing [ISO 88].

Acknowledgments

The authors would like to acknowledge the financial support given to the UBC-IDACOM Project by the Natural Sciences and Engineering Research Council of Canada, and by IDACOM Electronics Ltd. of Edmonton, Canada.

References

[Anderson 89]
C. Anderson and R. Ito, "Architecture and Design of VLSI Hardware for Protocol Testing," UBC-IDACOM Technical Report, Department of Computer Science, University of British Columbia, January 1989.

[Ansart 82]
J. P. Ansart, "GENEPI / A – A protocol independent system for testing protocol implementations," *Protocol Specification, Testing, and Verification*, C. Sunshine (ed.), North-Holland, 1982.

[Austermuehl 86]
B. Austermuehl, "MHTS/400 – Testing Message Handling Systems," *Protocol Specification, Testing, and Verification VI*, B. Sarikaya and G. v. Bochmann (eds.), North-Holland, 1986.

[Bochmann 87]
G. v. Bochmann, "Usage of Protocol Development Tools: The Results of a Survey," *Protocol Specification, Testing, and Verification VII*, H. Rudin and C. West (eds.), North-Holland, 1987.

[CCITT 88a]
CCITT Recommendation X.200, "Reference Model of Open Systems Interconnection for CCITT Applications," 1988.

[CCITT 88b]
CCITT Recommendation X.400, "Message Handling Systems: System Model – Service Elements," 1988.

[Clark 85]
D. D. Clark, "The Structuring of Systems Using Upcalls," Proc. 10th ACM Symposium on Operating Systems Principles, December 1985.

[Davis 88]
W. B. Davis, "Architecture and Design of a Portable Protocol Tester," invited paper, International Workshop on Protocol Test Systems, Vancouver, October 1988.

[ISO 88]
ISO DP 9646, "OSI Conformance Testing Methodology and Framework," July 1988.

[Linn 83]
R. J. Linn and J. S. Nightingale, "Some Experience with Testing Tools for OSI Protocol Implementations," *Protocol Specification, Testing, and Verification III*, H. Rudin and C. West (eds.), North-Holland, 1983.

[Lonc 85]
Brigitte Lonc, "GENEPIX: A Portable Version under UNIX of the OSI Protocol Tester GENEPI," *Protocol Specification, Testing, and Verification V*, M. Diaz (ed.), North-Holland, 1985.

[Rafiq 85]
O. Rafiq *et al.*, "Towards an Environment for Testing OSI Protocols," *Protocol Specification, Testing, and Verification V*, M. Diaz (ed.), North-Holland, 1985.

[Rayner 82]
D. Rayner, "A System for Testing Protocol Implementations," *Protocol Specification, Testing, and Verification*, C. Sunshine (ed.), North-Holland, 1982.

[Zeng 88]
H. X. Zeng *et al.*, "New advances in ferry testing approaches," *Computer Networks and ISDN Systems*, volume 15, number 1, 1988.

[Zeng 89]
H. X. Zeng, S. T. Chanson, and B. R. Smith, "On Ferry Clip Approaches in Protocol Testing," to appear in *Computer Networks and ISDN Systems*.

Session 7:

Verification by State Space Exploration

Protocol Specification, Testing, and Verification, IX
E. Brinksma, G. Scollo and C.A. Vissers (Editors)
Elsevier Science Publishers B.V. (North-Holland)

Validating SDL Specifications: an Experiment

Gerard J. Holzmann

AT&T Bell Laboratories
Murray Hill, New Jersey 07974

Joanna Patti

AT&T Bell Laboratories
Naperville, Illinois 60540

ABSTRACT

This paper describes a method for validating specifications written in the CCITT language SDL. The method has been implemented as part of an experimental validation system. With the experimental system we have been able to perform exhaustive analyses of systems with over 250 million reachable composite system states. The practicality of the tool for the analysis of substantial portions of AT&T's 5ESS® Switch code is now being studied.

1. Introduction

A particularly effective and well understood technique for validating systems of extended finite state machines is reachability analysis. With this method a validation program exhaustively forces the system into all states that are reachable by a series of execution steps, starting from a single known initial system state. For each reachable system state the program then verifies the observance of a predefined set of correctness criteria, such as the absence of deadlocks and unspecified receptions. Variants of this technique have been in use for over ten years [e.g. Zaf '77].

Without too much programming effort this technique can be used to analyze systems generating in the order of 100,000 reachable system states. Larger systems are problematic for almost all existing validation methods. The CPU-time and storage requirements quickly become prohibitive [Holz '90]. The basic complexity of the search algorithms, of course, can not be changed. The complexity can be expressed as the number of system states that has to be generated, inspected and stored to perform a completely exhaustive search. The amount of time that must be spent in each basic operation of the algorithm, however, can be reduced substantially with a few, relatively simple, programming tricks.

In a well-tuned system the most expensive operations of the search are all storage related: storing states, comparing two states, computing a hash value for states. With moderate programming effort other operations can be optimized sufficiently to have a smaller impact on the run time. An attempt to replace the traditional storage techniques with less time consuming ones proves to be exceptionally rewarding. The exhaustive search technique can gain one to two orders of magnitude in power, measured as the maximum number states that effectively can be analyzed on a machine with a given size and speed. The method and its rationale are fully described in [Holz '88] and [Holz '90].

We now have almost two years of experience with this new method, which was named *supertrace*. The scope and performance of supertrace have been documented and the software has meanwhile been made available by AT&T, for non-commercial use. A mild challenge to protocol designers, posed by the first author after the development of supertrace, has been to find protocols of true practical significance that, because of their size, still can not be validated exhaustively. This challenge, of course, did not go unanswered for very long.

In this paper we will focus on the application of supertrace to a large problem of unquestionable practical significance: SDL code that is being developed for a telephone switching system. Where applicable we refer to other documents for more information about supertrace, the validation languages *Argos* and *Promela* used by supertrace, and the specification language SDL.

2. Telephone Switching: the 5ESS Switch

AT&T's 5ESS Switch contains over three million lines of code. The largest part of the software is written in the programming language C. The switch, however, contains not only a substantial amount of code, it also uses a large amount of concurrency. A substantial portion of the switch software (approximately 10%) is therefore written in the CCITT specification language SDL. SDL was specifically designed for the specification of distributed systems, in particular for telephone switching systems [e.g. Jilek '84, Lippold '85, Bennett '86].

SDL is used in the 5ESS Switch to implement the call processing aspects of the business and residential customer features (BRCS), ISDN call processing, and it is used for the implementation of the operator administration features. About 10% of the 5ESS Switch software developers at AT&T write their code exclusively in SDL. Before the SDL code is run in the switch it is translated into C, which is then run under the control of a special purpose real-time executive system called FEX (Feature Execution system) that provides the proper SDL semantics.

2.1. Reasons for Using SDL

SDL is well suited to handle the multiplicity of features that is required to implement BRCS services. The BRCS software is structured into a series of independent SDL processes, with each feature corresponding to one or more processes. The interactions between the different features are simple intraprocess message communications [Bennett '86]. The decision to use SDL has several additional benefits:

- The structure of the language mimics the way people tend to think about how telephone service works. For this application it is more natural to use SDL than a procedural language like C.
- The language can support stepwise refinement: the code passes easily from a system engineer to a code designer, without changes in format. The system engineer, for instance, can concentrate on the message passing level of feature development, and pass the design on to the code developer for refinement.
- The formalism of SDL supports a mechanical translation of specifications into Finite State Machine (FSM) models coded in C. The code generated in this way implicitly enforces a structure that makes the feature logic more evident.
- SDL is an internationally supported language, often used and required by AT&T's customers.
- Since the feature code can be sub-divided into a series of separate FSMs, teams of code designers can conveniently work in parallel.

2.2. Existing Support Tools

Two versions of SDL are supported for the 5ESS Switch development: SDL/GR and SDL/PR. SDL/GR is the familiar graphical form of SDL; SDL/PR is the textual, program form, equivalent. The existing SDL tools support mainly the front-end of the development process. There is an editor for creating SDL/GR graphs, with some syntax checking built in. There are tools for translating specifications from SDL/GR into SDL/PR and back, and there is a tool for translating SDL/PR into C. There is also a report generator and an SDL simulator. So far, however, each tool still accepts a slightly different set of SDL constructs. The ultimate goal is of course to provide a tool set supporting one consistent set of language constructs, and providing a range of capabilities.

The SDL simulator is the most recent addition to the support tools. It has proven invaluable in debugging fresh designs. But simulation, like testing, can never prove the absence of errors with any measure of reliability.

SDL is an extended FSM language, enhanced with general primitives for exchanging data through asynchronous message passing. It can in principle be translated into any other FSM based language. One such language is *Argos*, developed as a standard protocol validation language, which has been used since 1983 to implement a series of protocol analyzers of increasing power and performance [Holz '87a]. 'Supertrace,' is merely the latest entry in this series. The question we are trying to answer is: Can the method employed by supertrace be used for the analysis of SDL code, rather than *Argos*, and in particular can it cope with the complexity of the SDL code that runs in the 5ESS Switch?

3. The Experimental System

3.1. Overview

Figure 1 illustrates the experimental system that is being studied for the validation of SDL code.

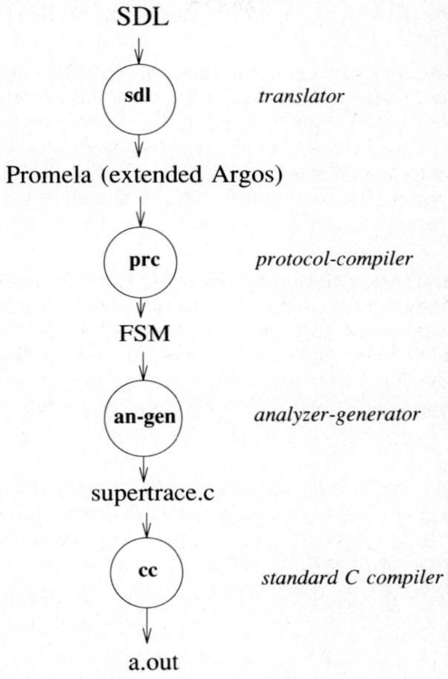

Figure 1 – Experimental Validation System

After a series of translations, this system derives an executable protocol analyzer that can perform an exhaustive validation of the original SDL specification. At present, the validation is based on an intermediate model in a validation language. The construction of the experimental validation system required substantial changes in the validation language *Argos*. Rather than patch the changes into the existing language, it was decided to design a new language that can support SDL features, while maintaining the elegance and simplicity of the initial design. The new language is called *Promela*, short for Protocol Meta Language. Features supported by *Promela*, that were not in *Argos*, include:

- The dynamic creation of processes and message channels.
- An arbitrary number of message parameters.
- Multiple data types (bit, byte, short, int).
- Facilities for using externally defined C functions, linked in by the C compiler.

With the new language, a new supertrace analyzer-generator was written that also supports some features not found in the original system:

- Detailed source level tracebacks.
- A rubber state vector.

The rubber state vector is a logical extension of the original state vector model [Holz '87b, '88]. A rubber, rather than a static, state vector allows for dynamically growing or shrinking systems. Most other features of the original supertrace software have been preserved. The support of a rubber state vector, however, did lower the effective performance by a factor of approximately two.

3.2. Supertrace Performance, a brief review

By measurement we can determine that the speed of supertrace software is dominated the calculation of hash values for state vectors: the only fundamental storage operation that cannot easily be replaced.[1] The hash function used in the current implementation can process approximately 1 million bytes (Mbytes) per second on a DEC-VAX-8550 (running the Unix® Operating System), or about 5 Mbytes per second on a large IBM 3090 computer (running Amdahl's UTS® operating system).

The state vector in supertrace contains compacted runtime values of all state information relevant to the system being validated: contents of queues, values of all local and global variables, control flow states for all running processes etc. The above performance figures mean that a system with a state vector of 100 bytes can be analyzed at a constant, and predictable, speed of 60,000 reachable states per second of CPU time on the larger machine, independent of the total size of the state space being constructed. Since the runtime requirements are with good approximation a linear function of the length of the state vector, the performance can also be expressed as: 6 million state-bytes per second.

The algorithm that achieves this performance was published [Holz '88]. Source code for the complete validation system shown in Figure 1 is available for non-commercial use, i.e. to universities. This revised implementation of the supertrace software, incurs a time penalty (a factor of roughly two) for the usage of the rubber state vector. Nevertheless, we know of no other algorithm with a better measured performance and coverage of the target state space for large systems. Supertrace, then, seems an appropriate tool for tackling the job of formally validating large protocol systems.

4. First Results

The system illustrated in Figure 1 has been in use since the middle of 1988. At the time of writing the system is used on a daily basis by a team of developers, and it works as advertised: it quickly finds the bugs in the interactions of concurrent modules. The errors found correspond to unexpected interleavings of events, unspecified receptions, unexecutable code, or even complete system deadlock. The largest modules analyzed so far contain over 10,000 lines of SDL. It translates into a validator of over 100,000 lines of C, which produces a state space of over 250 billion reachable system states when run. The initial choice for a pre-processor and a redefined validation language does, however, have some drawbacks that will have to be remedied. The first drawback is that error tracebacks produced by the analyzer generated are source level tracebacks through the *Promela* source, not the original SDL sources. The second drawback is that a translation from SDL source to analyzer in three separate steps can introduce clumsy code that may unnecessarily complicate and slow down the final validations.

The new system we are developing, to remedy these drawbacks, is depicted in Figure 2 below.

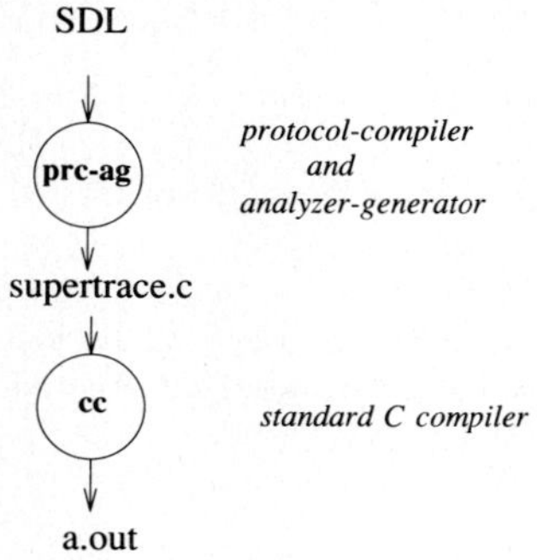

Figure 2 – Target Validation System

In the target system, the first three programs of the experimental system will be replaced by a single

1. The calculation is necessarily part of all validators based on reachability analysis, but in traditional systems there are also other, more time-consuming, operations to perform.

program that reads SDL specifications and produces an optimized analyzer generator, with source level traceback capability directly into the original SDL files.

5. Problem Areas

The problems we have encountered in the derivation of an analyzable model from SDL specifications in most cases have to do with the possibilities that SDL offers to circumvent the language proper. We will discuss those cases in the next few sections. One other problem is temporary. It is caused by an incompleteness in the version of the SDL language currently supported by our tools. The destination of a message in SDL can be any process. If the process is unambiguously named, there can be no confusion. There is, however, also a facility for defining a hierarchy of SDL processes in SDL blocks. Within that context it is possible to define message 'paths,' a sequence of processes that can act as a processing pipeline, transferring messages along the path towards their destination. A message, for instance, can be sent to a generic destination 'NEXT,' where it depends on the hierarchy, and the current process's place within that hierarchy, what the destination of the message is. Hierarchy specifications and message destinations such as 'NEXT' are not yet within the scope of the experimental system.

5.1. Open Coded Tasks

The contents of some SDL statements, such as tasks and decisions, is not subject to any language rule. A task may contain C, Pascal, Fortran, or a James Joyce novel. Clearly, there cannot be any method for validating the contents of SDL tasks unless some further rules are imposed. The simplest rule is that the code in declarations, tasks, and decisions is compatible with the target language of the SDL translator, which in our case is *Promela*. In the experimental system the SDL translator can also optionally hide code that is not compatible with the target language, and produce a non-deterministic model that will be validated exhaustively (i.e. for all possible effects of the hidden code on the visible code).

An example can illustrate this process. Consider the following specification in SDL/PR format.

```
BLOCK B2;
    PROCESS P1;
        STATE ST1;
            INPUT M2;
                TASK 'x = y+1';
                NEXTSTATE ST2;
            INPUT M5;
                DECISION 'x<y';
                (TRUE): NEXTSTATE ST2;
                (FALSE): NEXTSTATE ST1;
                ENDDECISION;
        STATE ST2;
            INPUT M5;
                OUTPUT M4;
                NEXTSTATE ST1;
    ENDPROCESS;
ENDBLOCK;
```

Example 1 – SDL/PR fragment.

The task and decisions in this example conform to both C and *Promela* syntax, so it can be translated into a literal *Promela* model, which may look like as follows.

```
proctype P1() of { byte[2] }
{    byte _msg;
ST1:
     if
     :: SELF?M2 ->
          x=y+1;
          goto ST2
     :: SELF?M5 ->
          if
          :: (x<y) -> goto ST2
          :: (!(x<y)) -> goto ST1
          fi
     fi;
ST2:
     SELF?M5 ->
          ENVIRON!M4(SELF);
          goto ST1
}
```

Example 2 – Promela version.

The message buffer through which processes of type P1 receive their input is accessible through the (local) name SELF. The destination of the output generated is by default ENVIRON. Note that within SDL the identity of a sender (i.e. SELF) is tagged onto each message transmitted and is available to the receiver, in a local variable named SENDER.

If the user of the validator chooses to hide the contents of the tasks and decisions, the following model would be produced.

```
proctype P1() of { byte[2] }
{    byte _msg;
ST1:
     if
     :: SELF?M2 ->
          goto ST2
     :: SELF?M5 ->
          if
          :: (1) -> goto ST2
          :: (1) -> goto ST1
          fi
     fi;
ST2:
     SELF?M5 ->
          ENVIRON!M4(SELF);
          goto ST1
}
```

Example 3 – Promela version – hidden tasks and decisions.

The decision after the reception of a message M5 in state ST1 is now a nondeterministic one: both branches are considered executable and the execution paths that can follow either choice will be traced. Note that in Examples 1 and 2 the decision is forced by the possible values of variables x and y. Even in those cases though, it is still possible for x and y to have different relative values, for different execution paths that lead to the decision point. In that case the two possible decision clauses may still be validated, depending on the execution histories. With the model from Example 3, however, coverage of both clauses is guaranteed (though maybe not always desired). Hiding tasks therefore increases the complexity of the systems to be validated: though the number of statements per process is reduced, the number of permissible paths increases substantially. It does however allow us to perform validations even for incompletely specified systems, or for systems that rely heavily on portions of code that are written in a target language other than SDL (or *Promela*).

It is still possible to write SDL code that cannot be hidden or translated. It is, for instance, valid in SDL to use non-SDL code to dynamically evaluate the destination of a message transmission:

```
OUTPUT message TO 12**3 + Fortran_routine()*6;
```

The expression that produces the destination is not compatible with C or *Promela*. In cases like these, therefore, the translator will modestly have to admit defeat and flag an error.

5.2. Uninterpreted Decisions

There is another problem associated with the conversion of explicit SDL into non-deterministic *Promela* decisions in the validation models. Consider the following SDL code fragment.

```
DECISION (x);
(3):NEXTSTATE ST2;
(y):NEXTSTATE ST1;
ENDDECISION;
```

Example 4 – SDL Decision, implicit 'ELSE'

If 'x==3' the first clause is to be executed, if 'x==y' the second. If, however, 'x!=3 && x!=y' the decision clause is to be skipped. The general translation of this code into *Promela* therefore looks as follows.

```
if
:: (x == 3) -> goto ST2
:: (x == y) -> goto ST1
:: (x != 3 && x != y) -> skip
fi
```

Example 5 – Promela Decision, explicit 'ELSE'

The 'if' statement in *Promela* blocks if none of its clauses is executable.[2] If the decision is hidden from view, this becomes:

```
if
:: (1) -> goto ST2
:: (1) -> goto ST1
:: (1) -> skip
fi
```

Example 6 – Promela Decision, explicit 'ELSE', uninterpreted decision

From the SDL specification it can not be determined if the implied 'else' clause can ever be executed. In Examples 1 and 2 the two clauses in the decision form a complete set: '(x<y && !(x<y))' is always unexecutable. However, Examples 4 and 5 show that it is not always that clear. If tasks are hidden from view the analyzer may report errors caused by choices that would be unexecutable in reality. In the last example it may even cause a violation of implied SDL syntax: there is a path through the transition that does not specify a next state. To see how the problem can be avoided, consider the following example.

```
DECISION (a);
(0):NEXTSTATE ST2;
(1):NEXTSTATE ST1;
ENDDECISION;
```

Example 7 – SDL Decision, implicit but unintended 'ELSE'

Only the programmer knows in this case if variable 'a' can ever have any other value than 0 or 1. The only prudent choice for the analyzer generator is to consider also the third possibility where '(a<0||a>1)', which is in accordance with SDL semantics. The designer can avoid the confusion by using the SDL keyword 'ELSE' in all cases where it is known that the 'implicit else' should be ignored:

2. The *Promela* 'if' statement is mainly used as a synchronization mechanism.

```
DECISION (a);
(0):  NEXTSTATE ST2;
ELSE: NEXTSTATE ST1;
ENDDECISION;
```

Example 8 – SDL Decision, explicit 'ELSE'

5.3. Open Systems

Another problem that had to be dealt with in the experimental system was that many SDL applications are not self-contained. They are meant to run in an environment of other processes that is not specified. Supertrace, however, was designed to perform an exhaustive validation for all possible behaviors of a 'closed' system, i.e. a system in which all processes are specified. Performing a validation of an open system for all possible behaviors of the environment is almost always undesirable: a malicious environment can disrupt the best designed system. Note for instance that a phone system need not be designed for customers who can generate two off-hook signals in sequence, without an intermediate on-hook. Not only does it increase the complexity of the analyses to generate and validate all possible nonsensical behavior of the environment, the results of such an analysis can not be of much interest to the designer.

The best solution to this problem, from the validator's point of view, is to ask the designer of the partial system to supply a dummy SDL specification of the (expected) behavior of the environment, for instance as a special SDL process definition. The validator can than exhaustively analyze the system under the given constraints to the environment. The validation in these cases, however, will be no more reliable than the accuracy of the environment specification, which is usually no more than a quick guess.

Another solution is to extract the expected behavior of the environment directly from the model that the designer provides. This is risky, but at least self-contained: it assumes that the assumptions inherent to the original SDL design are correct, and validates for any logical inconsistencies that remain. Precisely those errors are of primary interest to the designer. In a validation of this type, all message interactions with the environment are labeled 'free.' The label means that those interactions (i.e. the reception or the transmission of a message) are always considered to be executable and have no effect. In other words: wherever the original design claims that a message from the environment may arrive, supertrace will validate for the possibility that such a message will arrive, and it will check the consequences of that event. If in Example 2 message M5 would be labeled 'free,' the model generated would change as follows.

```
proctype P1() of { byte[2] }
{    byte _msg;
ST1:
     if
     :: SELF?M2 ->
          x=y+1;
          goto ST2
     :: (1) ->    /* input of free message M5 */
          if
          :: (x<y) -> goto ST2
          :: (!(x<y)) -> goto ST1
          fi
     fi;
ST2:
     (1) ->
          ENVIRON!M4(SELF);
          goto ST1
}
```

Example 9 – Free messages

Note that in the above example (following the simulated reception of free message 'M5') both paths through the decision in state 'ST1' are always validated, while the path following the reception of message 'M2' is only validated if there is at least one scenario in which the message 'M2' can arrive in state 'ST1.' The translator can determine, without user assistance, for some messages that they should be set 'free.' This is the case for messages that are sent but not received and for messages received but not sent. Other messages will have to be provided by the user in a special file that contains a list of message names. This so-called 'freelist' is then used by the analyzer generator to label the additional messages.

5.4. Modeling Timeouts

SDL has a facility for specifying any number of timers. A timer can be set or reset, thus enabling or disabling a timeout. Timers are traditionally a difficult concept to handle in a validation system. The validation, after all is meant to establish the self-consistency of a specification *irrespective* of timing considerations, that is independent of the relative speeds of processes and independent of possible transmission delays of messages. That means that in its full generality a validation of this type must consider the timeout as a possibility that is either present or absent, never as a true probability or even as a conditional probability that depends on the relative timings in the system.

It is quite feasible, though also quite pointless, to consider all possible consequences of an ill-set timer, for instance a timer that fires immediately when set. The purpose of the timer, however, is to recover from potential deadlock, for instance a deadlock caused by message loss. In the experimental system, therefore, a 'timeout' is an action that only becomes executable in, what otherwise would be, a deadlock state. This heuristic has proven to be very successful in avoiding the tracing of non-errors caused by unlikely timer behavior, and finding the remaining logical errors. A timer 't0' in an SDL process, for instance, is modeled in the experimental system by a *Promela* process as follows:

```
proctype t0() of { byte[2] }
{    byte SENDER;

     do
     :: SELF?SET,SENDER
     :: SELF?RESET -> SENDER = 0
     :: timeout ->
          if
          :: ( SENDER) -> SENDER!11,SELF; SENDER = 0
          :: (!SENDER) -> skip
          fi
     od
}
```

Example 10 – Model of an SDL Timer in Promela

The timer can be set or reset, in accordance with the SDL specification. When a timeout becomes executable (using the heuristic rule above) the appropriate timeout message is sent only if the timer is currently set. The analysis is still independent of timing considerations, but does take a reasonable subclass of timer behaviors into account.

5.5. Non-Standard Correctness Criteria

By default, the validation system will check for the completeness of the specification submitted to it: absence of unspecified receptions, absence of deadlocks, absence of improper terminations (i.e. reaching an endstate with not all processes in their final state or in the final state with one or more residual messages in their input buffers). On request (a command line option) the system can also check for the possibility of buffer overrun, or for the presence of non-progress loops, or unexecutable code. With a little more work the system can also verify the observance of any user-specified correctness criterion, phrased as the reachability or unreachability of system states, or the observance of specific system properties. At present we have no formalism for describing such correctness criteria. Though this is potentially the most valuable type of validation that the system can perform, it is also, at least in the experimental system, the least utilized. In practice, in most cases we have seen so far, the basic test for the absence of deadlocks suffices.

6. Non-Technical Considerations

Until now, validation by any other means than simulation or code-walkthroughs by committees of experts was infeasible in 5ESS Switch development. The supertrace software, used in tandem with the existing SDL Simulator, can improve the quality of the code, by finding also the errors that can not be found by manual inspection.

Still, it is not a foregone conclusion that a seasoned SDL designer will accept the new tool, however promising it might appear. Programmers are accustomed to the traditional coding cycle, (edit, compile, run, debug). However, not all SDL designers are necessarily programmers. It is perhaps a strength of SDL that designs can be comfortably created using just pen and paper. The use of sophisticated support tools for the design and analysis of SDL designs needs to be well publicized, formally taught, and promoted, before it can be truly successful. Our aim is to change the coding cycle into: editing, formal analysis, compilation, and conformance testing. At first this may seem needlessly clumsy and involved to the user. It requires, for instance, a rigorous use of SDL and a well-developed abstraction of the environment in which a new application, or feature, is to be used. The body of code that makes up the environment in a telephone switch is very large and difficult to comprehend in any detail. The effort involved may therefore be substantial at first. Part of our job is therefore to show potential users that the extra overhead to the design process can pay off.

7. Summary

The experimental system for validating SDL specifications has been in operation since the middle of 1988. It supports a large fraction of the language, e.g. including SAVE, and CREATE, but not process hierarchies and procedures. The experience we have gained with this system will guide us in the development of the target system: a one step analyzer generator for SDL specifications. Experience so far shows that we cannot expect to be able to validate any arbitrary SDL specification. With some reasonable precautions, however, validation will be feasible. The precautions should guarantee that the non-SDL portions of a design do not redefine or affect the interactions that are written in SDL proper.

With the experimental system we have been able to complete analyses of over 250 million reachable composite system states. This gives reason to be moderately optimistic about the capability of the system to tackle the tasks for which it is being designed, again if some reasonable constraints on the size of the models to be validated are placed.

The target SDL validation system is scheduled to be operational by the end of 1989.

8. References

[Bennett '86], Bennett, R.L., Lindner, J.A., Michelsen, R.W. and Rypka, D.J., "SDL in 5ESS Switching System Development," *Proc.*, Sixth International Conference on Software Engineering for Telecommunication Switching Systems, Eindhoven, the Netherlands, 14-18 April, 1986.

[Jilek '84], Jilek, E. R., "Implementation of SDL/PR in a Digital Switching System," *Proc.*, IEEE Global Telecommunications Conference, Atlanta, Ga. November 26-29, 1984.

[Lippold '85], Lippold, T. T., "Programming Call Processing Directly in SDL," *Proc.*, National Communication Forum, 1985.

[Holzmann '87a], "Automated protocol validation in '*Argos*,' assertion proving and scatter searching," *IEEE Trans. on Software Engineering*, Vol. 13, No. 6, June 1987, pp. 683-697.

[Holzmann '87b] Holzmann, Gerard J. "On Limits and Possibilities of Automated Protocol Analysis," *Proc.* VII-th Workshop on Protocol Specification, Testing, and Verification, Zurich, 1987, North-Holland Publ. Co., Amsterdam, pp. 339-346.

[Holzmann '88] Holzmann, Gerard, J., "An Improved Protocol Reachability Analysis Technique," *Software, Practice & Experience*, pp. 137-161, Feb. 1988.

[Holzmann '90] Holzmann, Gerard, J., "Algorithms for Automated Protocol Validation" , to appear, *AT&T Technical Journal*, Jan/Feb. 1990.

[SDL '87], "Special issue on the CCITT language SDL," *Computer Networks and ISDN Systems*, Vol. 13, No. 2, pp. 65-134, 1987.

[Zafiropulo '77] Zafiropulo, P., *A new approach to protocol validation*, Int. Conf. on Communications, June 1977, Chicago.

Protocol Specification, Testing, and Verification, IX
E. Brinksma, G. Scollo and C.A. Vissers (Editors)
Elsevier Science Publishers B.V. (North-Holland)

Dynamic State Exploration in Quantitative Protocol Analysis

Dragomir D. Dimitrijevic[$1]
Mon-Song Chen[@]

Polytechnic University[$]
IBM T. J. Watson Research Center[@]

ABSTRACT

This paper extends the dynamic state exploration technique used in an integrated probabilistic protocol verification and evaluation procedure [7] . The extension reduces the complexity from $O(n^2m)$ to $O(n^3)$, where n and m are the numbers of generated states and explored transitions, respectively. Additional properties of the technique are also analyzed to further enhance the verification and evaluation procedure. The procedure based on this technique is unique in that (1) it evaluates the importance of states in the course of global reachability graph (GRG) generation, (2) it, based on the importance of states, explores only the most interesting subset of states, and (3) it computes important reliability and performance measures such as Mean Time To Unknown and Confidence Level, which is the probability sum of checked scenarios, and uses them as the stopping criteria. The procedure is demonstrated using the call establishment phase of X.75 protocol.

1. INTRODUCTION

Correctness of protocols is the key to cost effective communication networks. Reachability analysis is useful in protocol verification because it can verify a large set of correctness properties [1] such as boundness, state ambiguities freeness, deadlock freeness, etc., and can easily be automated. However, complete reachability analysis in general is very difficult because of the state space explosion problem. Partial verification [2] is thus an attractive alternative.

The justification of partial verification and evaluation is that a protocol needs only be as reliable as other parts of the communication systems, e.g., hardware. It is observed [3 – 5] that transitions in most protocols have highly unbalanced probabilities, e.g., successful message transmission vs message corruption. Thus the majority of states and transitions in a typical protocol have negligible probabilities and need not be verified or evaluated.

The probabilistic approach [5], which is of the type of partial verification, is attractive in that it attempts to quantify the extent of a partial verification. The probabilistic approach assumes that transitions in Global Reachability Graph (GRG) can be assigned with independent probabilities. Then, a GRG in essence is a discrete state Markov chain,

[1] This work was partially supported by Foldes Fellowship Foundation at Polytechnic University.

and the probabilities of states or sequences of transitions can be evaluated. This quantitative nature facilitates certain dynamic search procedure, most likely the Best-First search, in guiding the verification and evaluation of only the most important subset of states. Compared to the random walk model in [2], this approach in some sense is more efficient because it never checks the same scenario more than once.

A major issue in this approach is the excessive computation when a global reachability graph has cycles. In [3, 6], a cyclic graph is converted to acyclic by unfolding cycles to large but finite sets of series of transitions. This is not desirable because states in a cycle, after unfolding, need be checked multiple times. In addition, the approach gives only an approximation even when a cyclic GRG is not particularly large.

A new dynamic state exploration technique is introduced and used in an integrated probabilistic protocol verification and evaluation [7]. This paper extends the technique and reduces the complexity from $O(n^2m)$ to $O(n^3)$, where n and m are the numbers of generated states and explored transitions, respectively. Additional properties of the technique are also analyzed to further enhance the verification and evaluation procedure. The procedure based on this technique is unique in that (1) it evaluates the importance of states in the course of GRG generation, (2) it, based on the importance of states, explores only the most interesting subset of states, and (3) it computes important reliability and performance measures such as Mean Time To Unknown and Confidence Level, which is the probability sum of checked scenarios, and uses them as the stopping criteria. The procedure is demonstrated using the call establishment phase of X.75 protocol.

The paper is organized as follow. The model is described in the next section. In Section 3, the theory and properties of the new computational technique are described. The procedure is demonstrated using the call establishment phase of X.75 protocol as an example in Section 4. Section 5 contains the conclusion.

2. THE MODEL

The ***Global Reachability Graph (GRG)*** is a set nodes and directed edges representing states and transitions, respectively, i.e., GRG = { S, E }, where S = { s_i } is the set of states and E = { e_{ij} } is the set of edges. For simplicity and without loss of generality, we assume that there is at most one directed edge from s_i to s_j , i.e., e_{ij}. (Note: multiple transitions from s_i to s_j can always be transformed to a single transition.) An independent transition probability p_{ij} is assigned to transition e_{ij}. Probabilities of the transitions out of each state must sum to one. In essence, GRG is viewed as a discrete state ***Markov chain.***

A ***Path*** in GRG is a sequence of consecutive transitions. The probability of a path is the product of the probabilities of its constituent transitions. A special state, s_1, is chosen as the ***initial state***. A ***Scenario*** is a path that has s_1 exclusively as its initial and final states. A protocol is ***Correct*** if all its scenarios do not have any undesirable property.

When only a subset of scenarios can be verified, slight modification to GRG is introduced for the ease of discussion. A virtual state, which is referred to as the ***unknown state*** and is denoted as s_u, is added to a partially generated GRG. The state represents all states that have not been generated. All unexplored transitions are made destined to s_u. The probabilities of transitions entering s_u are chosen so that probabilities of outgoing transitions from any state sum to one. In this convention, the definition of a scenario is extended: a ***checked*** scenario is a path that has s_1 exclusively as its starting and ending states; an ***unchecked*** scenario is a path that starts from s_1 and ends at s_u.

A protocol is considered ***acceptable*** if a significant and quantifiable subset of scenarios are correct. Two most interesting acceptance criteria are the ***Confidence Level***, which is the sum of probabilities of all checked scenarios and denoted as P_c, and ***Mean Time To Unknown (MTTU)*** , which is the average operation time before any unchecked scenario occurs.

Let V_i be the average number of visits to s_i in a scenario. Let $\hat{V}_i$ be an approximation to V_i when GRG is partially explored, and clearly $\hat{V}_i \leq V_i$. Let t_i be the mean holding time of s_i . Since only unchecked scenarios can visit s_u and each such scenario visit s_u exactly once, $\hat{V}_u$ is equal to P_u, which is the sum of probabilities of unchecked scenarios. Hence,

$$P_c = 1 - P_u = 1 - \hat{V}_u \tag{1}$$

The average length of a scenario or ***Turnaround time***, denoted as T, is

$$T = \sum_i V_i t_i \geq \hat{T} = \sum_i \hat{V}_i t_i \tag{2}$$

Let $\hat{T}_c$ and $\hat{T}_u$ be the average length of a checked and unchecked scenario, respectively, when GRG is partially explored. Averaging over every possible number of checked scenarios before an unchecked scenario, an exact expression for MTTU is

$$MTTU = \sum_{i=0} P_u P_c^i (i\,\hat{T}_c + \hat{T}_u) = \frac{P_u \hat{T}_u + P_c \hat{T}_c}{P_u} = \frac{\sum_i \hat{V}_i t_i}{P_u} \tag{3}$$

V_i's are also useful in computing other important performance measures. For example, the stationary state probability of s_i, denoted as π_i, is

$$\pi_i = \frac{V_i t_i}{T} \sim \frac{\hat{V}_i t_i}{\hat{T}} \quad (4)$$

Another example is that the average number of times that a transition, say e_{ij}, takes place in a scenario is $V_i\, p_{ij}$. If sufficient insight to the nature of each transition is available, then many performance measures such as the throughput in the number of packet receptions per second can be computed.

This formulation is insensitive to the specific protocol specification techniques, such as Finite State Machines (FSM) or Petri Net, so long as GRG can be generated as a directed graph. To illustrate how GRG is generated, we discuss an example when a protocol is specified as a set FSM's, synchronous as well as asynchronous.

In a synchronous model, the time for a local transition to take place is one clock cycle. Exactly one local transition in each local FSM fires in each clock cycle, and a combination of one local transitions from each local FSM forms a global transition. Thus the time for a global transition to take place is also one clock cycle, and the probability of a global transition is the product of probabilities of its constituent local transitions. The mean holding time of, or the average duration per visit to, each global state is one clock cycle, i.e, $t_i = 1$ for all i.

In an asynchronous model, the time for a local transition to take place is assumed to be an exponentially distributed random variable. Hence, local transitions are assigned with their average exponential rates, instead of probabilities. A global transition is one of the local transition from one of the constituent local states of the originating global state. The rate of a global transition is thus the rate of the corresponding local transition. The mean holding time of a global state is the reciprocal of the total rate of all outgoing global transitions from the global state. The probability of a global transition is the ratio of its rate to the total rate of all outgoing global transitions from the same global state.

3. THE THEORY

Since the probabilistic approach attempts to explore only the most important subset of states, GRG generation procedure should not follow either Depth-First nor Breadth-First rules. It should be of the Best-First type and guided by the "importance" of states. Because both P_c and MTTU can be computed from V_i, it is reasonable to use V_i as the measure of importance of s_i. Then a desirable Best-First exploration procedure can be outlined as:

1. Initialize the set of generated but unscanned states, U , as $U = \{s_1\}$
2. Find the state s_i such that $V_i \geq V_j$ for $\forall j \in U$

3. Scan s_i by exploring all outgoing transitions from s_i. If a transition leads to a state which has not been generated yet, the state is added to U.
4. Update V_i's and GRG and remove s_i from U, and
5. If the stopping criteria are met, such as P_c and $MTTU$ are larger than the pre-specified tolerance thresholds, stop. Otherwise, go to step 2.

The above procedure needs repeatedly compute V_i's in the course of GRG generation. To compute V_i, let ***walk(k)*** be a path that starts from s_k and ends upon first visit to s_1. *Walk*(k) can be viewed as a ***semi-scenario*** in that it ends upon visiting s_1, but does not have to start from s_1. The probability of a *walk*(k) is the product of the probabilities of its constituent transitions. Let X_{kl} be the average number of visits to s_l in a *walk*(k). By definition, $V_i = X_{1i}$.

X_{kl} can be solved as follows. When $k = l$, there is one visit to s_l before any transition is made. After one transition, two situations are considered separately. If the next state is the initial state s_1, then the *walk* terminates according to definition. Otherwise, the additional visits to s_l on average in the subsequent part of a *walk*(k) is identical to X_{jl}. Hence, X_{kl}'s satisfy the following set of linear equations

$$X_{kl} = \sum_{j \neq 1} p_{kj} X_{jl} + \delta_{kl}\,, \quad \text{for } \forall k,\ l \tag{5}$$

For a given matrix of transition probabilities, X_{kl} and the interesting performance and reliability measures defined in the previous section can be computed in general in $O(n^3)$ complexity, where n is the number of states. This approach, however, is inadequate for the proposed Best-First search, because the overall complexity to explore n states over n iterations would be $O(n^4)$. What is needed is a different form of recursion, which is compatible to the nature of the guided search, i.e., iterative and simultaneous GRG generation and evaluation of X matrix.

Consider the situation that X_{kl}, $\forall k,\ l$, are known when a subset of m transitions, which are members of the set E_m, are explored. Let them be denoted as $X_{kl}^{(m)}$. Let $X_{kl}^{(m+1)}$ be the values of X_{kl} after exploring (m+1) transitions, which are members of E_{m+1} and $E_{m+1} = E_m + \{e_{st}\}$. The issue is then to find an expression for $X_{kl}^{(m+1)}$ in terms of the known $X_{kl}^{(m)}$ and p_{st}.

The difference between $X_{kl}^{(m+1)}$ and $X_{kl}^{(m)}$ is due to the new *walk*(k)'s that go through the new transition, i.e., e_{st}, at least once. A *walk*(k) that goes through e_{st} exactly once must start from s_k, reach s_s, go over e_{st} to s_t, and then, without going over e_{st} again, visit s_l before termination. In general, a *walk*(k) that goes through e_{st} exactly r times must

1. start from s_k and reach s_s without passing through e_{st},
2. go over e_{st} to s_t,

3. reach back to s_s without going over e_{st},
4. repeat steps 2 and 3 exactly $(r - 1)$ times, and
5. finally, without going over e_{st} again, visit s_l at least once after leaving s_t .

We argue, and will prove it later, that the additional visits to s_l due to the new *walk*(k)'s that go over e_{st} exactly r times on average is $X_{ks}^{(m)} p_{st} (p_{st} X_{ts}^{(m)})^{r-1} X_{tl}^{(m)}$. Therefore, $X_{kl}^{(m+1)}$ can be computed as

$$X_{kl}^{(m+1)} = X_{kl}^{(m)} + X_{ks}^{(m)} p_{st} \left(\sum_{r=1}^{\infty} \left(p_{st} X_{ts}^{(m)} \right)^{r-1} \right) X_{tl}^{(m)} \tag{6}$$

Define ***loop gain*** to be $p_{st} X_{ts}^{(m)}$ and denoted as G_{ts} . If $G_{ts} < 1$, then

$$X_{kl}^{(m+1)} = X_{kl}^{(m)} + X_{ks}^{(m)} \frac{p_{st}}{1 - p_{st} X_{ts}^{(m)}} X_{tl}^{(m)} \tag{7}$$

Loop gain G_{ts} is the probability of a path that starts from s_t and ends upon first visit to e_{ij} . Hence, if $G_{ts} = 1$, then any path leaving s_t will always return to s_t via e_{st} without visiting s_1. That is a ***livelock.***

We now prove the correctness of the recursive formula (7).

Lemma 1: Let E_m be the set of m explored transitions that give the known $X_{kl}^{(m)}$. Let E_{m+1} be the set of (m + 1) explored transitions that give $X_{kl}^{(m+1)}$ and $E_{m+1} = E_m + \{e_{st}\}$. Then formula (7) is correct.

Proof: From definition, we have

$$X_{kl}^{(m)} = \sum_{\substack{i \neq 1 \\ e_{ki} \in E_m}} p_{ki} X_{il}^{(m)} + \delta_{kl} , \quad \text{for } \forall k,\ l \tag{8}$$

and

$$\begin{aligned} X_{kl}^{(m+1)} &= \sum_{\substack{i \neq 1 \\ e_{ki} \in E_{m+1}}} p_{ki} X_{il}^{(m+1)} + \delta_{kl} \\ &= \sum_{\substack{i \neq 1 \\ e_{ki} \in E_m}} p_{ki} X_{il}^{(m+1)} + \delta_{ks} p_{st} X_{tl}^{(m+1)} + \delta_{kl} , \quad \text{for } \forall k,\ l \end{aligned} \tag{9}$$

The proof shows that formula (7) satisfies equations (8-9). By substituting formula (7) for $X_{il}^{(m+1)}$ and $X_{tl}^{(m+1)}$ on the right-hand side of equation (9), **RHS**, we have, for all k, l,

$$\mathbf{RHS} = \sum_{\substack{i\neq 1\\ e_{ki}\in E_m}} p_{ki}\left(X_{il}^{(m)} + X_{is}^{(m)}\frac{p_{st}}{1-p_{st}X_{ts}^{(m)}}X_{tl}^{(m)}\right)$$

$$+\,\delta_{ks}p_{st}\left(X_{tl}^{(m)} + X_{ts}^{(m)}\frac{p_{st}}{1-p_{st}X_{ts}^{(m)}}X_{tl}^{(m)}\right) + \delta_{kl}$$

$$= X_{kl}^{(m)} - \delta_{kl} + \left(X_{ks}^{(m)} - \delta_{ks}\right)\frac{p_{st}X_{tl}^{(m)}}{1-p_{st}X_{ts}^{(m)}}X_{tl}^{(m)} \tag{10}$$

$$+\,\delta_{ks}p_{st}\frac{X_{tl}^{(m)}}{1-p_{st}X_{ts}^{(m)}} + \delta_{kl}$$

$$= X_{kl}^{(m)} + X_{ks}^{(m)}\frac{p_{st}}{1-p_{st}X_{ts}^{(m)}}X_{tl}^{(m)}$$

Since both sides of equation (9) are the same after applying formula (7), the proof is completed.

Lemma 2: $X_{kl}^{(0)} = \delta_{kl}$.

Proof: This is directly from equation (5) because all transition probabilities are zeros.

Theorem 1: Computation of X_{kl} in the Best-First search procedure can be done as follows. Initialize $X_{kl}^{(0)}$ to δ_{kl}. Use equation (7) to compute $X_{kl}^{(m+1)}$ from $X_{kl}^{(m)}$ for $m = 0, 1, \ldots$.

Proof: The theorem is a direct result of Lemmas 1 and 2.

During the course of exploration, the dimension of matrix X increases with the number of generated states. In general, the complexity of using formula (7) to update X_{kl} for $\forall k,\ l$, in exploring one transition is $O(n^2)$, where n is the number of states generated at the time. There are special cases, however, in which the complexity in exploring one transition is one order of magnitude less, i.e., $O(n)$. For example, in exploring transition e_{st}, if s_t is either not generated before or is generated but not yet scanned, then only n elements of X matrix need to be updated. The n elements are X_{kt} for $\forall k$. This is because $X_{tl} = 0$ for $\forall l$ unless s_t is generated and scanned. Thus, according to formula (7), $X_{kl}^{(m+1)} = X_{kl}^{(m)}$ for $\forall k$ and $l \neq t$. Nevertheless, the overall complexity for the procedure to generate n states and explore m transitions is in general still $O(n^2m)$. This is significantly better than $O(n^4)$, particularly when the transition matrix is sparse.

It is interesting to note that the reciprocal of recursion (7) can easily be derived from equation (7), as shown in the next theorem.

Theorem 2: Let $X_{kl}^{(m)}$, $X_{kl}^{(m+1)}$, E_m, E_{m+1} , e_{st}, and p_{st} be defined as in Theorem 1. A reciprocal recursion of formula (7) is

$$X_{kl}^{(m)} = X_{kl}^{(m+1)} - X_{ks}^{(m+1)}\frac{p_{st}}{1+p_{st}X_{ts}^{(m+1)}}X_{tl}^{(m+1)} \tag{11}$$

Proof: Two special cases of formula (7) when $l = s$ and when $k = t$ are

$$X_{ks}^{(m)} = \frac{X_{ks}^{(m+1)}}{1 + p_{st}X_{ts}^{(m+1)}}, \text{ for } \forall k \tag{12}$$

$$X_{tl}^{(m)} = \frac{X_{tl}^{(m+1)}}{1 + p_{st}X_{ts}^{(m+1)}}, \text{ for } \forall l \tag{13}$$

Equation (11) can be derived by substituting equations (12-13) into formula (7).

This technique can be enhanced so that only a complexity of $O(n^3)$ is needed to explore n states over n iterations. The idea is to modify the technique so that it takes only a complexity of $O(n^2)$ to explore all outgoing transitions of a state, instead of $O(n^2)$ per transition. This is done as follows. Conceptually s_s is viewed as a combination of two ***sub-states***, as depicted in Figure 1, one receives all incoming transitions of s_s, denoted as s_s^r, and one generates all outgoing transitions of s_s, denoted as s_s^t. Then e_{js} and e_{sj} are also represented as e_{js^r} and e_{s^tj}, respectively, for all j. The two sub-states are connected by a directed transition from s_s^r to s_s^t, i.e., $e_{s^rs^t}$, with a probability of one.

If s^r is not reachable from any other state, which is the case when $e_{s^rs^t}$ is not explored yet, exploration of each e_{s^tj} affects only n elements, i.e., X_{s^tl} for all l. Hence, if the procedure explores e_{s^tj} for all j before $e_{s^rs^t}$, the complexity of exploring all outgoing transitions of s_s is $O(n^2 + d_sn) = O(n^2)$, where d_s is the number of outgoing transitions of s_s .

Theorem 3: Let X_{kl}^{-s} and X_{kl}^{+s} be the values of X_{kl} before and after outgoing transitions of s_s are explored, respectively. Then

$$X_{kl}^{+s} = X_{kl}^{-s} + X_{ks}^{-s} \frac{\sum\limits_{j\neq 1} p_{sj}X_{jl}^{-s}}{1 - \sum\limits_{j\neq 1} p_{sj}X_{js}^{-s}} \tag{14}$$

Proof: Let $X_{kl}^{(s)}$ be the values of X_{kl} after all e_{s^tj} for all j, but not $e_{s^rs^t}$, are explored. Since s_s^t is not reachable by any other state before $e_{s^rs^t}$ is explored, $X_{kl}^{(s)} = X_{kl}^{-s}$ for $k \neq s^t$ and all l. And, $X_{s^tl}^{(s)} = \sum_{j\neq 1} p_{s^tj}X_{jl}^{-s}$ since exploration of each e_{s^tj} adds $p_{s^tj}X_{jl}^{-s}$ to $X_{s^tl}^{-s}$. Then, from equation (7),

$$\begin{aligned} X_{kl}^{+s} &= X_{kl}^{(s)} + X_{ks^r}^{(s)} \frac{1}{1 - X_{s^ts^r}^{(s)}} X_{s^tl}^{(s)} \\ &= X_{kl}^{-s} + X_{ks}^{-s} \frac{\sum\limits_{j\neq 1} p_{s^tj}X_{jl}^{-s}}{1 - \sum\limits_{j\neq 1} p_{s^tj}X_{js^r}^{-s}} = X_{kl}^{-s} + X_{ks}^{-s} \frac{\sum\limits_{j\neq 1} p_{sj}X_{jl}^{-s}}{1 - \sum\limits_{j\neq 1} p_{sj}X_{js}^{-s}} \end{aligned} \tag{15}$$

During the course of a partial exploration, it is useful if the errors of $\hat{V}_i$'s, i.e., $V_i - \hat{V}_i$, can be bounded. The following theorem provides a simple upper bound.

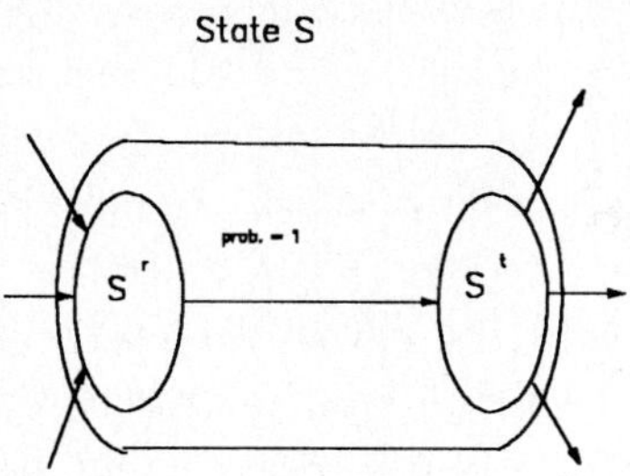

Figure 1. Decomposition of state s.

Theorem 4:

$$V_i - \hat{V}_i \leq P_u \frac{1}{1 - \hat{X}_{iu}} \hat{X}_{ii} \tag{16}$$

Proof: Let X'_{kl} be the values of X_{kl} when a fictitious transition with probability one from s_u to s_i is added to the set of explored transitions that gives $\hat{X}_{kl}$. Then

$$X'_{1i} = \hat{X}_{1i} + \hat{X}_{1u} \frac{1}{1 - \hat{X}_{iu}} \hat{X}_{ii} \,. \tag{17}$$

Since all unexplored transitions are assumed to lead directly to s_i, $X'_{ki} \geq X_{ki}$ for all k. Then,

$$V_i - \hat{V}_i \leq X'_{1i} - \hat{X}_{1i} = \frac{P_u \hat{X}_{ii}}{1 - \hat{X}_{iu}} \tag{18}$$

because $\hat{X}_{1u} = P_u$, as defined in equation (1).

4. EXAMPLES

The proposed procedure has been applied to the Alternating Bit protocol [7] and the call establishment phase of X.75 protocol, which will be described next in this section.

The specification in [8] is taken as the input to the procedure. The same specification has also been studied in [9] and shown that the complete GRG contains 1576 states and 3456 transitions, and each of the two channel queues has at most 8 control messages.

There are eight different control packets in the specification: Call Request (CAR), Call Confirm (CAC), Clear Request (CLR), Clear Confirm (CLC), Interrupt (INT), Interrupt Confirm (INC), Reset Request (RER), and Reset Confirm (REC).

GRG is modelled as an asynchronous Markov chain. The transition rates are computed as follows. The average reception rate is computed from the average time for a control packet to be transmitted and processed. By assuming all control packets have the same length, the reception rates of all control packets are identical. Two different reception rates are used. Case 1 assumes the rate is 17241, which is derived from the environmental parameters of 10 MIPS processor, 1 Mb/s communication link, 100 instructions to process each packet, and 48 bits packet length. (Note that $1/17241 = 48/1000000 + 100/10000000$.) Case 2 assumes the rate is 1000, which is from the parameters of 1 MIPS processor, 1 Mb/s communication link, 1000 instructions to process each packet, and 48 bits packet length. These two cases are listed in Table 1.

Transmissions of request packets are determined by independent arrival processes. Their rates are different because they have different protocol meanings. The assumptions are as follows. For each CAR there is eventually a matching CLR. There are more CAR and CLR than INT and RER. There are more INT than RER. For each request, i.e., CAR, CLR, INT, and RER, there is a matching confirm, i.e., CAC, CLC, INC, and REC. Unlike request packets, generation of a confirm packet is conditioned on reception and processing of a triggering request packet, instead of driven by an independent arrival process. In addition, when conditions are satisfied, the rate of transmitting a confirm packet is the same as the common reception rate, because they involves the same time--transmission and processing time. Hence, transmission rates of all confirm packets are made the same as the common reception rate. Several sets of transmission rates are used and listed in cases a-e in Table 1. Notice that cases a-c must go with case 1, and cases d-e must go with case 2.

	Reception (+)		Transmission (–)				
Case	1	2	a	b	c	d	e
CAR	17241	1000	1	10	100	10	100
CAC	17241	1000	17241	17241	17241	1000	1000
CLR	17241	1000	1	10	100	10	100
CLC	17241	1000	17241	17241	17241	1000	1000
INT	17241	1000	2.7e-4	2.7e-4	2.7e-4	10	100
INC	17241	1000	17241	17241	17241	1000	1000
RER	17241	1000	1.6e-5	1.6e-5	1.6e-5	10	100
REC	17241	1000	17241	17241	17241	1000	1000

Table 1. Different cases of transition rates

To evaluate the efficiency of the procedure, results for different tolerance thresholds on P_u for the case 1-c are shown in Table 2. The first column is the exponent of the pre-specified tolerance threshold on P_u The second column is the actually achieved P_u. The turnaround time T is shown in the third column, which is useful in computing MTTU. The numbers of generated states (ngs), scanned states (nss), and explored global transitions (ngt) are shown in columns 3-5, respectively. It can be observed that T converges rapidly, after only 89 scanned states and 164 explored transitions.

1.0e-n	Pu	T	ngs	nss	ngt
1	5.51351e-2	0.0098966	38	12	48
2	8.82625e-3	0.0100024	58	28	92
3	4.58827e-4	0.0100452	70	36	114
4	9.12557e-5	0.0100476	80	50	143
5	9.97836e-5	0.0100478	89	59	164
6	9.96921e-7	0.0100478	102	67	187
7	9.74510e-8	0.0100478	113	84	220
8	9.13295e-9	0.0100478	129	92	249
9	7.93117e-10	0.0100478	148	109	289
10	9.40656e-11	0.0100478	161	120	314
11	8.89343e-12	0.0100478	182	136	352
12	8.96663e-13	0.0100478	192	149	376
13	9.55741e-14	0.0100478	216	167	420
14	9.99020e-15	0.0100478	266	190	502
15	9.12058e-16	0.0100478	317	224	620
16	9.94152e-17	0.0100478	347	253	705
17	9.68097e-18	0.0100478	402	289	817
18	9.42223e-19	0.0100478	426	312	867
19	9.25781e-20	0.0100478	450	338	921
20	9.24755e-21	0.0100478	465	358	957

Table 2. Results for case 1–c with different tolerances on P_u

The Best-First procedure is more effective when transition probabilities are more unbalanced, since the major portion of probability mass is condensed in a smaller subset of states. To see this effect, the procedure is applied to several different sets of rates and two different tolerance thresholds on P_u. The results are summarized in Table 3. In cases, 1-a, 1-b, and 1-c, because the common reception rate is much larger any transmission rate, the transition probabilities are highly unbalanced and the procedure is very effective, i.e., generates less than 500 states and 1000 transitions to satisfy $P_u \leq 10^{-21}$. In cases 2-d and 2-e, independent transmission rates are assumed the same and are 1% and 10% of the common reception rate, respectively. Hence transitions probabilities in GRG are less unbalanced, and the procedure is less effective. The procedure needs generate about 700 states and explore about 1500 transitions to make P_u close to 10^{-7} and 10^{-4} for cases 2-d and 2-e, respectively.

Assumptions	Pu	T	ngs	nss	ngt
1 – a	9.93044e-20 9.51102e-21	0.999835 0.999835	412 470	277 330	822 998
1 – b	9.42870e-20 9.85973e-21	0.100042 0.100042	428 455	310 337	867 928
1 – c	9.25781e-20 9.24755e-21	0.0100478 0.0100478	450 465	338 358	921 957
2 – d	9.96920e-8 5.02834e-8	0.0677286 0.0677286	639 669	473 500	1452 1515
2 – e	9.83830e-5 4.72117e-5	0.00998821 0.00998865	592 649	449 500	1337 1472

Table 3. Results for different sets of transition rates

It is interesting to note that throughout all cases the number of messages in each of the two channels is no more than 5, and the probability of having 5 messages in a channel ranges from 10^{-6} to 10^{-25}.

5. CONCLUSION

This paper extends the dynamic state exploration technique used in an integrated probabilistic protocol verification and evaluation procedure [7] . The extension reduces the complexity from $O(n^2m)$ to $O(n^3)$, where n and m are the numbers of generated states and explored transitions, respectively. Additional properties of the technique are also analyzed to further enhance the verification and evaluation procedure. The procedure based on this technique is unique in that (1) it evaluates the importance of states in the course of GRG generation, (2) it, based on the importance of states, explores only the most important subset of states, and (3) it computes important reliability and performance measures, such as Mean Time To Unknown and Confidence Level, and uses them as the stopping criteria. The procedure is demonstrated using the call establishment phase of X.75 protocol.

REFERENCES

[1] Sajkowski, M., "Protocol Verification Techniques: Status Quo and Perspectives," Protocol Specification, Testing, and Verification, IV, Y. Yemini, R. Strom, and S. Yemini (Editors), Elsevier Publishers B.V. (North-Holland), 1985, pp 697-720.

[2] West, C., "Protocol Validation by Random State Exploration," Protocol Specification, Testing, and Verification, VI, B. Sarikaya, and G. Bochmann (Editors), Elsevier Publishers B.V. (North-Holland), 1986.

[3] Rudin, H., "An Improved Algorithm for Estimating Protocol Performance", Protocol Specification, Testing, and Verification, IV, Y. Yemini, R. Strom, and S. Yemini (Editors), Elsevier Publishers B.V. (North-Holland), 1985, pp 515-525.

[4] Kritzinger, P.S., "Analyzing the Time Efficiency of A Communication Protocol", Protocol Specification, Testing, and Verification, IV, Y. Yemini, R. Strom, and S. Yemini (Editors), Elsevier Publishers B.V. (North-Holland), 1985, pp 527-539.

[5] Maxemchuk, N.F., and Sabnani, K., "Probabilistic Verification of Communication Protocols," Proceeding of Protocol Specification, Testing, and Verification, 1987.

[6] Rudin, H., and West, C.H., "A Validation Technique for Tightly Coupled Protocols," IEEE Transactions on Computers, July 1982., Vol 31, No 7, pp 630-636.

[7] Dimitrijevic, D.D. and M-S. Chen, "An Integrated Algorithm for Probabilistic Protocol Verification and Evaluation," Proceeding of INFOCOM'89.

[8] Vuong, S.T. and D.D. Cowan "Protocol Validation Via Resynthesis and Decompositon: The X.75 Packet Level as an Example", Journal of Telecommunication Networks, Vol.2, Summer 1988, pp. 153-176.

[9] Frish, I.T., A. Kershenbaum, and M.J. Post, "Network Management and Control of Protocols", Proc. of the IEEE GLOBECOM-88, Nov.1988.

Protocol Specification, Testing, and Verification, IX
E. Brinksma, G. Scollo and C.A. Vissers (Editors)
Elsevier Science Publishers B.V. (North-Holland)

Parallel Protocol Verification: The Two-Phase Algorithm

Maria C. Yuang and A. Kershenbaum

Bell Communications Research, Piscataway, N. J.
Department of EECS, Polytechnic University, Brooklyn, N.Y.

Protocol verification detects the existence of logic errors in protocol design specifications. Various verification approaches have been proposed to deal with the state space explosion problem resulting from the reachability analysis. This paper proposes a parallel protocol verification algorithm, called the Two-Phase algorithm, in an attempt to provide a maximum of verification with a minimum of state space. Rather than compose all communicating Finite State Machines (FSMs) into a large global reachability tree, the Two-Phase algorithm constructs a local expanded tree for each FSM augmented with external information. The first phase of the algorithm performs the expanded tree construction, and the second phase performs error detection based on the constructed expanded trees. This algorithm allows verification for all FSMs to be executed in parallel. Moreover, the algorithm requires smaller run-time and fewer explored states. To quantify the reduction in state space, the paper also gives experimental results on several realistic protocols, including the Call Set-Up and Termination phases of the CCITT X.25 and X.75 protocols.

1. Introduction

Traditional approaches to protocol design have involved informal specification and verification by "walk throughs" or scenario analysis. Such *ad hoc* methods not only lead to ambiguities but also result in errors in every stage of the protocol development life cycle. This causes time-consuming redesign or recoding. This problem is exacerbated by the ever increasing complexity of the communication protocols. To overcome these ambiguities and complexities, formal specification and verification [2,10] have been developed. Three models [11] have been used successfully to approach this problem. This paper employs the Finite State Machine (FSM) approach [1,4,16] within the state transition model.

Protocol verification detects the existence of logic errors in protocol design specifications. Various verification approaches have been proposed to deal with the state space explosion problem resulting from the conventional reachability analysis [16]. Our previous survey [14] classified these verification approaches into five categories: (a) closed covers [5], (b) modified reachability analysis [13], (c) divide-and-conquer [7,12,15], (d) partial state exploration [8,9], and (e) localized approach [3,6]. Among them, the localized approach was deemed the most promising. Formerly, approaches (in (a)-(d)) considered an execution of all processes as a whole. The localized approach, however, considers N executions of N processes separately [3]. That is, instead of creating one large global reachability tree, a local expanded tree for each individual FSM is constructed and augmented with external information. Based on the local expanded trees, protocol verification is performed.

Based on the localized approach, Kakuda, et al. [6] proposed a verification algorithm (called the KWN algorithm, hereinafter). Compared to the reachability analysis, the KWN algorithm can detect all logic errors with smaller run-time and state space. However, The algorithm has three major drawbacks. First, the algorithm constructs expanded trees for all FSMs on a back-and-forth-among-processes (or ping-pong) basis, instead of in an independent and parallel fashion. The construction is very time-consuming. This problem is exacerbated for protocols with more than two processes. Second, the expanded trees are constructed by a fairly complex procedure involving lots of tree searching and copying. Third, because the employed external information is insufficient to discover equivalent states at an earlier time, the algorithm produces many repeated states and redundant constructions. To overcome these drawbacks, this paper proposes a parallel protocol verification algorithm, called the Two-Phase algorithm.

The Two-Phase algorithm constructs the expanded tree in the first phase and performs error detection in the second phase. By separating verification into two phases, this algorithm allows verification for all processes to be accomplished in parallel. Moreover, the algorithm employs a simple method of the construction of the expanded tree and a new piece of external information. The algorithm thus requires smaller run-time and fewer explored states.

In this paper, Section 2 overviews the Two-Phase algorithm. Section 3 gives definitions of terms used in this paper. Section 4 describes the first phase (the expanded tree construction phase), and Section 5 describes the second phase (the error detection phase) of the algorithm. Section 6 provides experimental results on several realistic protocols. Finally, advantages and limitations are discussed in Section 7.

2. Algorithm Overview

The Two-Phase algorithm constructs the expanded tree for each process in the first phase, and performs error detection in the second phase. By separating error detection from expanded tree construction, the algorithm allows verification for one process to be totally independent from verification for other processes. Verification of all processes can be accomplished in parallel. That is, to perform protocol verification for N processes, N copies of the Two-Phase algorithm can be run simultaneously in an N-processor parallel machine (see Figure 1).

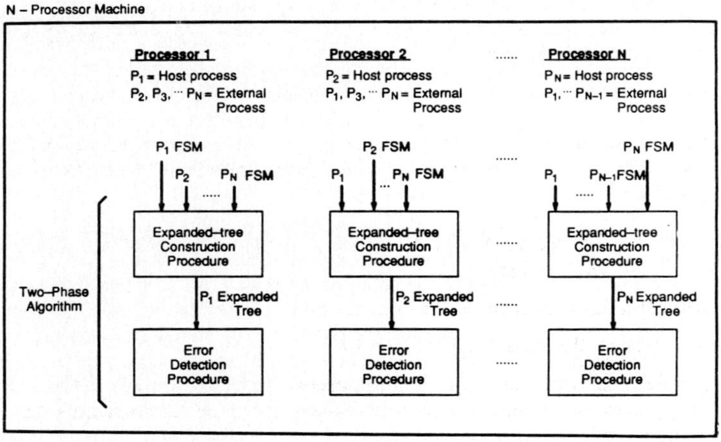

Figure 1. Parallel protocol verification for N processes: the Two-Phase algorithm.

The process being verified is called the *host process*, and all other processes are called *external processes*. Obviously, a two-process protocol always has one host process and one external process. The expanded tree consists of nodes and links. Links are the same as transitions in

FSMs. A node is composed of a state and two-set external information. A state is uniquely identified by a two-part name, say $s.v$, where s represents the state visited in the traversal of the corresponding FSM, and v is an ordinal number identifying a particular visit to state s during the construction of the expansion tree. For example, states $s.0$ and $s.1$ represent the first and second visits to state s of the FSM, respectively. The first set of external information, called the least state pair, consists of the *least state* and its associated output channel. The least state represents the last state in the external process that must have been reached. The second set, called the synched set, consists of the *synched states* and their associated input channels. A synched state represents the first state in a possible execution path of the external process' FSM that will be eventually reached (see Figure 2).

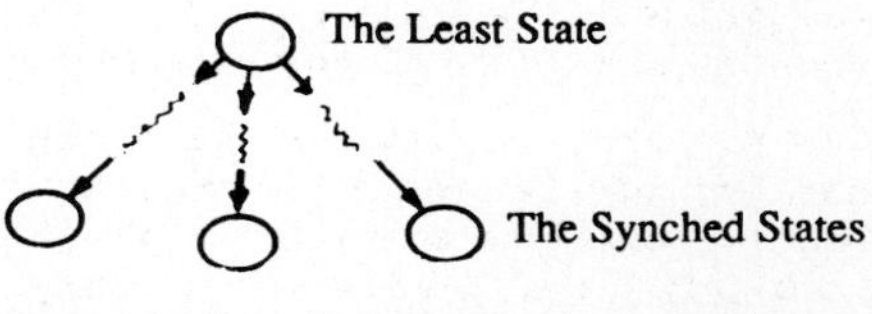

Figure 2. The least state and synched states in the external process' FSM.

The first phase of the algorithm constructs the expanded tree for the host process. Starting from the initial state of the host process, the tree is expanded, one state at a time, by adding all of the state's exit transitions onto the tree. For each transition, a new state is generated and the two-set external information is computed according to the L/S (Least state/Synched states) algorithm to be discussed in Section 4.1. The construction of the expanded tree terminates from a given state when either the further generation from this state only results in the repetition of a state already generated, or the further generation is not possible (e.g. errors). The termination rules are formally described in the T/E (Termination/Error) algorithm to be discussed in Section 4.2.

The second phase performs error detection upon the completion of the first phase. Protocol errors, such as deadcode, deadlocks, and channel overflows, can be easily detected by the simple "look-through" of the expanded tree. Unspecified receptions are detected by a two-rule procedure to be discussed in Section 5.2.

3. Definitions

Communication protocols can be modeled as communicating FSMs consisting of processes and channels between the processes. This model assumes FIFO and error-free channels.

[Definition 1]

A protocol system is defined as N FSMs $\{m_1, m_2, ..., m_N\}$. Each FSM m_i is defined by a quadruple $(S_i, o_i, M_i, succ)$, where

1. S_i represents a finite set of states of process i.
2. $o_i \in S_i$ represents the initial state of process i.
3. M_i represents the messages from and to process i, i.e. $M_i = M_{ij} \cup M_{ji}$, where M_{ij} represents the messages sent from process i to process j, and M_{ji} represents the messages sent from process j to process i.
4. $succ$ is a partial function mapping, where $succ : S_i \times M_{ij} \rightarrow S_i$ and $S_i \times M_{ji} \rightarrow S_i$, from the states and messages of m_i to the states of m_i. In other words, $succ(s,x)$ specifies the transitional state from state s after transmitting or receiving message x. If $succ(s,x)=t$, s is called the from_state of transition x, denoted as from_state(x)$=s$, and t is called the to_state of transition x, denoted as to_state(x)$=t$. If $succ(s,x)=t$ and $succ(t,y)=r$, transition x is called an entry transition of state t, and y an exit transition of the state.

[End of Definition 1]

In this FSM model, each process or FSM is represented by a directed labeled graph with nodes and edges representing states and transitions, respectively. Figure 3 shows a protocol example with two processes P_1 and P_2. In the figure, circles denote states, arrows denote transitions. A minus sign "-" shows a transmission transition while a plus sign "+" shows a reception transition. Initially, both processes are at their initial states - state 0. P_1 can only send message 2 to P_2 and then enters state 1. P_2 enters state 2 upon receiving message 2, etc.. As shown in P_1 of Figure 3, since $succ(1,+4)=3$, states 1 and 3 are the from_state and to_state of transition +4, respectively. Besides, transition +4 is an entry transition of state 3, and transition +3 is the exit transition of state 3.

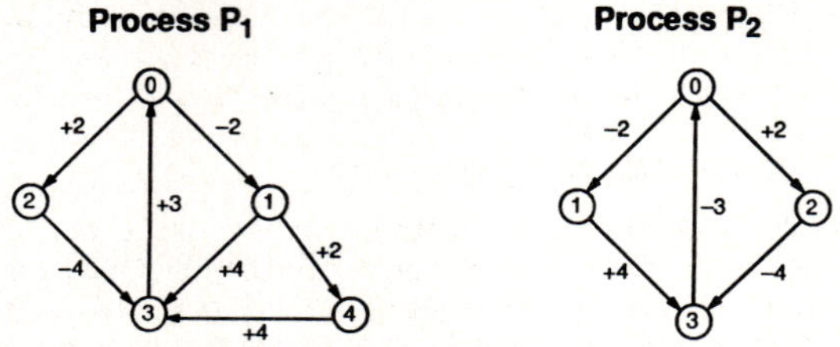

Figure 3. Protocol example 1.

[Definition 2]

In a multi-processor parallel machine (see Figure 1), if the expanded tree for process i is constructed by processor i, process i is called the *host process* of processor i, and all other processes are called the *external processes* of this processor.

[End of Definition 2]

As shown in Figure 1, the input to the expanded tree construction procedure of the algorithm for host process i is the FSMs of host process i and all external processes $1,..,i-1,i+1,..,N$. For the convenience of illustration, $N-1$ external process' FSMs are shown in acyclic form. Some definitions for acyclic FSMs are given next.

[Definition 3]

In a process' acyclic FSM,

1. if $succ(s,x_1)=t_1, succ(t_1,x_2)=t_2,..., \text{and } succ(t_{k-1},x_k)=s'$, then $succ(s,X)=s'$, where X is the path after s and before s', consisting of all states and messages between states s and s'.

2. First_sent(X) is defined to be the first transmission message within path X. First_rcv(X) is the first reception message within path X. Sent_msgs(X) is defined to be the complete sequence of transmission messages within path X. Rcv_msgs(X) is the complete sequence of reception messages within path X.

3. If Q and C are two sequences of messages, then $Q \subseteq C$ iff every message in Q is in C and the sequence of messages in Q is the same as that in C. Notice that messages in Q do not have to be contiguous in C.

4. If Q and C are two sequences of messages and $Q \subseteq C$, then $C-Q$ is defined to be a new sequence of messages comprised of messages in C but not in Q.

[End of Definition 3]

In figure 4(b), for example, within a path $P= 0.0\xrightarrow{-2}1.0\xrightarrow{+4}3.0\xrightarrow{-3}0.1$, First_sent($P$)=2, First_rcv($P$)=4, Sent_msgs($P$)={2,3}, and Rcv_msgs($P$)={4}. Assume $C=\{4,2\}$, and $Q=$Rcv_msgs(P). Then, $Q \subseteq C$, and $C-Q=\{2\}$. Next, we define the expanded tree for the case of protocols with only two processes. For the convenience of illustration, protocols with two processes are assumed throughout the rest of the paper.

[Definition 4]

The expanded tree of the host process P_x is a directed labeled acyclic tree composed of an ordered pair (V, E) where $V=\{n_i \mid i=1,...,M\}$ represents M *nodes*, and E represents $M-1$ *links* specifying the function *succ* defined before. Each *node i* (i = the node number) is defined as a tuple $(s.m, L_i, Y_i)$, where

1. $s.m$ denotes the state, where s represents the state visited in the traversal of the FSM, and m is an ordinal number that identifies a particular visit to state s during the expanded tree construction. State s in the FSM is called the *corresponding state* of state $s.m$.

2. $L_i = (l_i, C_{Oi})$ is the *least state pair* of node i, where

   i. l_i denotes the least state in the external process for state $s.m$. The *least state* in external process P_y for state s in host process P_x is defined as the last state in external process P_y that must have been reached before state s in host process P_x is reached. (Notice that this least state is the same as the "last state" defined in the KWN algorithm.)

   ii. C_{Oi} denotes the output channel for node i when the host process is at state $s.m$ and the external process is at state l_i.

3. $Y_i = [y_{ik}, C_{Iik}]_{k=1,W}$ (W = a finite number) is the *synched set* of node i, where

   i. y_{ik} denotes the kth synched state in the external process for state $s.m$. A *synched state* in external process P_y for state s in host process P_x is defined as the first state in a possible path of the external process P_y's FSM that will eventually be reached and *synchronized* with state s. A state t in P_2 is said to be *synchronized* with state s in P_1 iff (1) all messages transmitted by P_1 before state s is reached have been received by P_2 before state t is reached, and (2) all messages received by P_1 before state s is reached have been sent by P_2 before state t is reached.

   ii. C_{Iik} denotes the input channel for node i when the host process is at state $s.m$ and the external process is at state y_{ik}.

[End of Definition 4]

Notice that, in Definition 4, the input channel for the least state and the output channels for the synched states are not included in a node. This is because they are always empty for the case of two-process protocols. This can be easily seen from the definitions of the least state and synched states.

The notation for the expanded tree is set up as follows (see Figures 4(a) and 4(d)). For links, transition names are labeled next to the arrows. For nodes, ovals denote states. The number at the upper-left corner of an oval denotes the node number. The pair in parenthesis, "( )", denotes the least state pair. The pairs surrounded by "[ ]" and combined by "+" denote the synched set. A "?" within the least state pair indicates that the least state pair cannot be computed. This indicates an error, and the expanded-tree construction from this node thus terminates.

In Figure 4(d), for example, state 1.0 and external information $L_2=(0.0, 2)$ and $Y_2=[2.0,\varnothing]+[4.0, 2]$ compose node 2. In other words, when P_2 is at state 1.0, P_1 must have reached state 0.0 and P_2's output channel contains message 2. This is because message 2 sent by P_2 may or may not be received by P_1. Besides, this node has two synched states, 2.0 and 4.0, in the synched set. The P_2's input channel for synched state 2.0 is empty, and the input channel for synched state 4.0 contains message 2. This is because when P_2 is at state 1.0, P_1 will eventually progress to either state 2.0 or state 4.0 after receiving message 2.

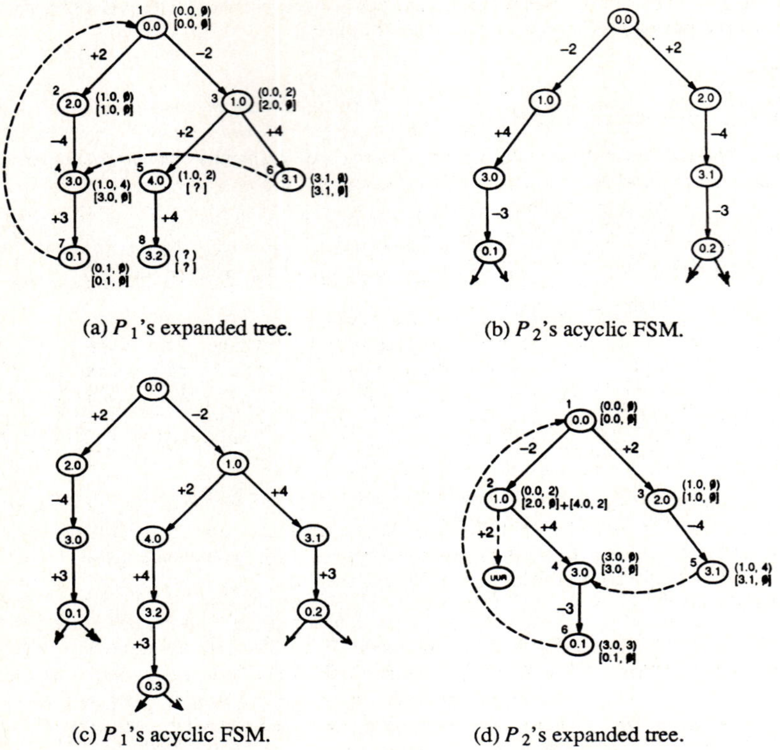

Figure 4. Protocol verification for protocol example 1.

[Definition 5]

1. Two states (or least states, or synched states) $s.m$ and $t.n$ are *equivalent*, denoted as $s.m \sim t.n$, iff $s = t$.

2. Two input channels C_{Iij} and C_{Ikl} (or output channels C_{Om} and C_{On}) are said to be *equivalent*, denoted as $C_{Iij} = C_{Ikl}$ (or $C_{Om} = C_{On}$), if the sequences of messages within these two channels are the same.

3. Assuming that $L_i = (l_i, C_{Oi})$ and $L_j = (l_j, C_{Oj})$, then L_i and L_j are said to be *equivalent*, denoted as $L_i \equiv L_j$, iff $l_i \sim l_j$ and $C_{Oi} = C_{Oj}$.

4. Assuming that $Y_p = [y_{p\,i}, C_{Ipi}]_{i=1,N}$ and $Y_q = [y_{qj}, C_{Iqj}]_{j=1,M}$, then Y_p is said to be an *improper subset* of Y_q, denoted as $Y_p \subseteq Y_q$, iff (i) $N \le M$, (ii) for every $i, 1 \le i \le N$, there exists a j, $1 \le j \le M$, such that $y_{p\,i} \sim y_{qj}$ and $C_{Ipi} = C_{Iqj}$.

5. Assuming that $Y_p = [y_{p\,i}, C_{Ipi}]_{i=1,N}$ and $Y_q = [y_{qj}, C_{Iqj}]_{j=1,M}$, then Y_p and Y_q are said to be *equivalent*, denoted as $Y_p \equiv Y_q$, iff $Y_p \subseteq Y_q$ and $Y_q \subseteq Y_p$.

[End of Definition 5]

For example, in Figure 4(a), according to Definition 5.1, 3.1 ~ 3.0. According to Definitions 5.3 and 5.5, $L_7 \equiv L_1$ and $Y_6 \equiv Y_4$.

4. The First Phase

4.1 External Information - L/S Algorithm

The computation of the external information after making a transmission transition differs from that after making a reception transition. When the host process progresses from an old state to a new state due to the "transmission" of message x, the least state of the new state remains the same as the least state of the old state. Message x is added into the output channel for the new state. The synched states are those states to which the external process progresses after message x has been received; all messages transmitted by the external process beforehand are added into the input channel for the new state.

On the other hand, if the host process progresses from an old state to a new state due to the "reception" of message x, the least state of the new state is the state to which the external process progresses after message x has been transmitted; all messages received beforehand are deleted from the output channel for the new state. If the computed output channel is empty, the synched set is the same as the least state pair for the new state. Otherwise, the computation of the synched set is the same as that for the transmission case described above.

When the computation of the least state pair produces multiple least state pairs, the new node is split into multiple nodes and each of them owns one least state pair. The computation of the synched set for each new nodes can be similarly computed. When the computation of the least state pair fails, a flag associated with each node i, called Term_flag$_i$, is set to be "DL (Deadlock) + DC (Dead Code)".

In the following, the L/S (Least state/Synched set) algorithm formally gives the computation of the external information. Table 1 lists used variables and functions.

Variables	Definitions	Domain of values
Term_flag$_i$	Termination flag for node i	= NULL/DL+DC
First_sent(X)	The first transmission message within path X	message name
Rcv_msgs(X)	The complete sequence of reception messages within path X	{message name + etc.}
Sent_msgs(X)	The complete sequence of transmission messages within path X	{message name + etc.}

Table 1. The variable table for the L/S algorithm.

[L/S Algorithm]

[Part A]

If the host process progresses from an old node $(s.n, L_i, Y_i)$, where $L_i=(l_i, C_{Oi})$ and $Y_i=[y_{ia}, C_{Iia}]_{a=1,W}$, to a new node $(t.m, L_j, Y_j)$, where m is the next occurrence of state t, due to the transmission of message x, and $succ(s,-x)=t$, then

1. $L_j=(l_j, C_{Oj})$, where $l_j=l_i$ and $C_{Oj}=C_{Oi}+x$, where "+" is the message concatenation operator.

2. $Y_j=[y_{jb}, C_{Ijb}]_{b=1,Z}$ is determined as follows:

   case i. If, in the external process' acyclic FSM, there exists p $(p>0)$ paths $X_k, k=1,..,p$, after state l_j and before state $s'_k, k=1,..,p$ such that

Rcv_msgs(X_k)=C_{Oj}, $k=1,..,p$, then (1) $Z=p$, (2) $y_{jk}=s'_k$, $k=1,..,p$, and (3) $C_{Ijk}=$ Sent_msgs(X_k), $k=1,..,p$.

case ii. Otherwise, set Y_j = "UNKNOWN".

[Part B]

If the host process progresses from an old node $(s.n, L_i, Y_i)$, where $L_i=(l_i, C_{Oi})$, and $Y_i=[y_{ia}, C_{Iia}]_{a=1,W}$, to a new node $(t.m, L_j, Y_j)$, where m is the next occurrence of state t, due to the reception of message x, and $succ(s,+x)=t$, then

1. $L_j=(l_j, C_{Oj})$ is determined as follows:

   case i. If, in the external process' acyclic FSM, there exists only a path X after state l_i and before the to_state of the first transmission message such that First_sent(X)=x and Rcv_msgs(X) $\subseteq C_{Oi}$, then $l_j=$ to_state($-x$) and $C_{Oj}=C_{Oi}-$ Rcv_msgs(X).

   case ii. If, in the external process' acyclic FSM, there exist p paths X_k, $k=1,..,p$ $(p>1)$ after state l_i and before the to_state of the first transmission message in each path such that First_sent(X_k)=x and Rcv_msgs(X_k) $\subseteq C_{Oi}$, $k=1,..,p$, then first create p least state pairs such that $l_{jk}=$ to_state($-x$) and $C_{Ojk}=C_{Oi}-$ Rcv_msgs(X_k), $k=1,..,p$. Second, split node j into p nodes, numbered $j, j+1, ..., j+p-1$, or state $t.m, t.(m+1), t.(m+2), ..., t.(m+p-1)$, such that $l_{j+k-1}=l_{jk}$ and $C_{O(j+k-1)}=C_{Ojk}$, $k=1,..,p$. The computation of the synched set being applied to the original node j will be applied to every node $j+k-1, k=1,..,p$.

   case iii. Otherwise, L_j = "UNKNOWN" and Term_flag$_j$="DL+DC".

2. $Y_j=[y_{jb}, C_{Ijb}]_{b=1,Z}$ is determined as follows:

   case i. If $C_{Oj}=\varnothing$, then $Y_j=L_j$. (i.e. the synched set has only one synched state, and the synched set is the same as the least state pair).

   case ii. Otherwise, follow the procedures in Part A.2.

[End of Algorithm]

As shown in Figure 4(d), P_2 moves to state 1.0 from state 0.0 due to the transmission of message 2. According to A.1 of the L/S algorithm, the least state of state 1.0 remains 0.0, and the output channel contains message 2. In addition, there are two paths, $X_1=0.0\overset{+2}{\rightarrow}2.0$ and $X_2=0.0\overset{-2}{\rightarrow}1.0\overset{+2}{\rightarrow}4.0$, in P_1's acyclic FSM (see Figure 4(c)). According to A.2 of the L/S algorithm, states 2.0 and 4.0 are two synched states, and the input channel for synched state 2.0 is empty, and the input channel for synched state 4.0 contains message 2.

On the other hand, due to the reception of message 4 (see Figure 4(d), P_2 moves from state 1.0 to state 3.0. According to B.1.i, the least state of state 3.0 is 3.0, and the output channel is empty. This is because P_1 will progress to state 3.0 after message 2 has been received and message 4 has been transmitted. Finally, according to B.2.i, since $C_{O4}=\varnothing, Y_4=L_4=[3.0,\varnothing]$.

4.2 Tree Termination - T/E Algorithm

The T/E (Termination/Error) algorithm determines the termination of the expanded tree construction from a given node. The algorithm consists of three rules: the Termination Rule, the Merge Rule, and the Error Rule. The Termination Rule determines equivalent nodes. If nodes are equivalent, the expansion can be performed from either node. The Merge Rule determines subset-relation nodes. That is, the expansion needs to be performed only from node B, if the construction from node A only results in being a subset of the construction from node B. Finally, the Error Rule determines impossible construction when errors are encountered and the least state cannot be computed.

[T/E Algorithm]

1. **Termination Rule**
   A node $(s.n, L_i, Y_i)$ is called a *precursor of type* $t1$ of another node $(t.m, L_j, Y_j)$, and the second node is said to be *marked* $t1$, if $t.m \sim s.n$ and $L_j \equiv L_i$. When a node is marked $t1$, the construction from this node terminates.

2. **Merge Rule**

   A node $(s.n, L_i, Y_i)$ is called a *precursor of type* $m1$ of another node $(t.m, L_j, Y_j)$, and the second node is said to be *marked* $m1$, if $t.m \sim s.n$ and $Y_j \subseteq Y_i$. When a node is marked $m1$, the construction from the node is said to be merged to the construction from its precursor of type $m1$.

3. **Error Rule**

   A node $(s.n, L_i, Y_i)$ is marked $e1$ if Term_flag_i = "DL+DC". When a node is marked $e1$, the construction from this node stops.

[End of Algorithm]

In Figures 4(a) and 4(d), a curved dashed arrow links a node to its precursor of type $t1$ or $m1$. For example, in Figure 4(a), according to the Termination Rule, node 1 (state 0.0) is a precursor of type $t1$ of node 7 (state 0.1). According to the Merge Rule, node 4 (state 3.0) is a precursor of type $m1$ of node 6 (state 3.1). Therefore, the construction of the expanded tree from nodes 7 and 6 terminate. Finally, according to the Error Rule, node 8 (state 3.2) is marked $e1$ because Term_flag_8="DL" (Deadlock) (explained later).

4.3 Tree-Construction Procedure

The Tree-Construction Procedure starts from the expanded tree with only the initial node (0.0, (0.0,∅),[0.0,∅]) (assuming that the initial state of an FSM is 0). The tree is expanded, one node at a time, by adding all exit transitions of the corresponding state onto the tree. A child node is created for each transition. The least state pair and the synched set are computed according to the L/S algorithm. The termination of the construction from this newly created node is determined by the T/E algorithm. The construction of the expanded tree terminates when all expandable nodes are expanded. Table 2 lists variables used by the Procedure.

Variables	Definitions	Domain of values
Term_flag_i	Termination flag for node i	= NULL/DC/DL
Node_queue	The FIFO queue of expandable nodes	= EMPTY/NOT_EMPTY
Etr_num(s)	The number of exit transitions of state s	> 0
Node_num	The next available node number	> 0

Table 2. The variable table for Tree-Construction Procedure.

[Tree-Construction Procedure]

Initialize Node_num=1;
Initialize Node_queue to have initial node (0.0, (0.0,∅), [0.0,∅]);
Initialize the expanded tree to have root node (0.0, (0.0,∅), [0.0,∅]);
while (Node_queue="NOT_EMPTY") **do**
{ Dequeue the first node i $(s.n, L_i, Y_i)$ from Node_queue;
  for Each exit transition x_k, $k = 1, .., Etr\_num(s)$, of the corresponding state s
  do {Create a node with state $t.m$, if $succ(s, x_k) = t$ and m is the next occurrence of state t;
    Add the node onto the expanded tree as a child node of node i;
    Assign Node_num to this child node, say j;
    Node_num ← Node_num+1;
    Compute the least state pair and the synched set for node j;
    if Any of the rules in the T/E algorithm can be applied to node j
      then Mark node j;
      else Add node j into Node_queue; };
  if There exists at least one child node c of node i such that Term_flag_c="NULL"
    then for Those child nodes with Term_flag = "DL+DC" **do** Term_flag = "DC";
    else for Those child nodes with Term_flag = "DL+DC" **do** Term_flag = "DL";
};

[END].

4.4 Example

The protocol example shown in Figure 3 has logic errors. The expanded trees for processes P_1 and P_2 are shown in Figures 4(a) and 4(d), respectively. In the following, we give a step-by-step illustration of the construction of the P_1's expanded tree (Figure 4(a)). In this example, P_1 is the host process and P_2 is the external process. The construction starts from the initial node 0.0.

1. Initialize Node_num=1, Node_queue to have initial node (0.0, (0.0,∅), [0.0,∅]), and the expanded tree to have root node (0.0, (0.0,∅), [0.0,∅]).

2. Dequeue node 1 from Node_queue.

3. Since node 1's corresponding state 0 in P_1's FSM has two exit transitions, $succ(0,+2)=2$ and $succ(0,-2)=1$, two links and two child nodes are added onto the expanded tree (0.0 $\xrightarrow{+2}$ 2.0 and 0.0 $\xrightarrow{-2}$ 1.0). These two nodes are assigned as node 2 and node 3, respectively. Increment Node_num (=4).

4. Compute the external information, and we get $L_2=(1.0,\varnothing)$, $Y_2=[1.0,\varnothing]$, $L_3=(0.0,2)$, and $Y_3=[2.0,\varnothing]$.

5. Since $L_1 \not\doteqdot L_2 \not\doteqdot L_3$ and $Y_1 \not\doteqdot Y_2 \not\doteqdot Y_3$, nodes 2 and 3 are not marked. Add nodes 2 and 3 into Node_queue.

6. Dequeue node 2 from Node_queue.

7. Since node 2's corresponding state 2 has one exit transition, $succ(2,-4)=3$, one link and one child node are added onto Expanded_tree (2.0 $\xrightarrow{-4}$ 3.0). This node is assigned as node 4. Increment Node_num (=5).

8. Compute the external information, we get $L_4=(1.0,4)$ and $Y_4=[3.0,\varnothing]$.

9. Since $L_4 \not\doteqdot L_1 \not\doteqdot L_2 \not\doteqdot L_3$ and $Y_4 \not\doteqdot Y_1 \not\doteqdot Y_2 \not\doteqdot Y_3$, node 4 is not marked. Add node 4 into Node_queue.

10. Dequeue node 3 from Node_queue.

11. Since node 3's corresponding state 1 has two exit transitions, $succ\,(1,+2)=4$ and $succ\,(1,+4)=3$, two links and two child nodes are added onto the expanded tree ($1.0 \xrightarrow{+2} 4.0$ and $1.0 \xrightarrow{+4} 3.1$). These two nodes are assigned as node 5 and node 6, respectively. Increment Node_num (=7).

12. Compute the external information, and we get $L_5=(1.0,2)$, $Y_5=$"UNKNOWN", $L_6=(3.1,\varnothing)$, and $Y_6=[3.1,\varnothing]$.

13. Since $L_5 \not\equiv L_1 \not\equiv L_2 \not\equiv L_3 \not\equiv L_4$ and $Y_5 \not\equiv Y_1 \not\equiv Y_2 \not\equiv Y_3 \not\equiv Y_4$, node 5 is not marked. Add node 5 into Node_queue. However, since $Y_6 \equiv Y_4$, node 6 is marked $m1$ and the construction from node 6 terminates.

14. Dequeue node 4 from Node_queue.

15. Since node 4's corresponding state 3 has one exit transition, $succ\,(3,+3)=0$, one link and one child node are added onto the expanded tree ($3.0 \xrightarrow{+3} 0.1$). This node is assigned as node 7. Increment Node_num (=8).

16. Compute the external information, and we get $L_7=(0.1,\varnothing)$ and $Y_7=[0.1,\varnothing]$.

17. Since $L_7 \equiv L_1$, node 7 is marked $t1$. The construction from node 7 terminates.

18. Dequeue node 5 from Node_queue.

19. Since node 5's corresponding state 4 has only one exit transition, $succ\,(4,+4)=3$, one link and one child node are added onto the expanded tree ($4.0 \xrightarrow{+4} 3.2$). This node is assigned as node 8. Increment Node_num (=9).

20. Compute the external information, and the computation fails. Node 8 is thus marked $e1$. Since node 8 is the only child node of node 5, Term_flag_8="DL".

21. Since Node_queue is empty, the construction terminates.

5. The Second Phase

5.1 Detection of Deadcode, Deadlocks and Channel Overflows

Deadcode, deadlocks, and channel overflows are detected by examining the expanded tree generated in the first phase. Deadcode may occur in two different situations. A *Dead State/Transition* (DST) represents a deadcode situation in which a state can never be reached, and consequently, none of its exit transitions will be executed. A *Dead Transition* (DT) represents another deadcode situation in which, although the from_state of a transition is reachable, this transition can never be executed. Throughout the expanded tree, if all nodes to which the host process progresses after the same transitions have been fired are flagged "DC", this transition is considered as a DT. For a given state s, if all its nodes throughout the expanded tree, $s.0, s.1, ..$, are flagged "DC", this state and all its exit transitions are considered as a DST. Moreover, if a state which appears in the FSM but is absent from the expanded tree, this state and all its exit transitions are considered as a DST.

Deadlocks are detected by the presence of nodes flagged "DL". For example, in Figure 4(a), a deadlock is detected at node 8. Channel overflows are detected by the presence of nodes in which the outbound channel within the least state pair has the number of messages exceeding a predefined number (buffer size). In figure 4(a), if the buffer size is two, channel overflows will not be detected.

5.2 Detection of Unspecified Receptions

An unspecified reception is a reception that is executable but not specified in the FSM. It may occur in two different situations: Unconditional Unspecified Reception (UUR), and Conditional Unspecified Reception (CUR). A UUR represents a situation in which the reception of the first message in the channel is not specified at a state and no further transmission from this state can be made. UUR is considered as a severe logic error since once the system is in this situation, the system is blocked forever. A CUR represents another situation in which the reception is not specified at a state, but from this state and through transmission transitions, the process can move to another state at which the reception of the message is specified. As opposed to UUR, CUR is often considered as a warning (depending on how the system is defined). UUR and CUR are detected by two rules: the Induction Rule, and the Propagation Rule.

When two processes transmit messages at the same time, causing a collision, then the reception of the other message by a process should be specified both before and after the process' message has been transmitted. For example, if P_1 sends message m to P_2 at state s_1 and enters state s_2 and P_2 sends message n to P_1 at state t_1 and enters state t_2, then P_1 should be able to receive message n at either state s_1 or state s_2. In other words, both $succ(s_1,+n)$ and $succ(s_2,+n)$ should be specified. A similar statement applies to the reception of message m in P_2. Therefore, if only $succ(s_2,+n)$ is specified in P_1's FSM, the Induction Rule detects a CUR for $succ(s_1,+n)$. Whereas if only $succ(s_1,+n)$ is specified, the Propagation Rule detects a CUR or UUR for $succ(s_2,+n)$. For the convenience of illustration, we only provide the detection of the CURs of a single reception message. The detection of the CURs of a sequence of messages can be similarly applied.

[Induction Rule]
Search through the expanded tree for a reception message $+n$ such that $succ(s.x,+n)=d.y$ and the output channel of node $d.y$ is $m_1+m_2+\cdots+m_p$ where $p \geq 1$, then $succ(\text{from\_state}(-m_i),+n)=$"CUR", for $i=1,..,p$, are created and detected.

[End of Induction Rule]

[Propagation Rule]
Search through the expanded tree for a reception message $+n$ such that $succ(s.x,+n)=d.y$. If there exists a path X after state $s.x$ and before state $t.r$, such that $succ(s.x,-m_1)=t_1$, $succ(t_1,-m_2)=t_2$, ..., $succ(t_{q-2},-m_{q-1})=t_{q-1}$, and $succ(t_{q-1},-m_q)=t.r$, where $q \geq 1$, and $t.r$ has only reception exit transitions, then (1) if $succ(t_i,+n)$ does not exist, create $succ(t_i,+n)=$"CUR", for $i=1,..,q-1$ and $q \geq 2$, and (2) if $succ(t.r,+n)$ does not exist, create $succ(t.r,+n)=$"UUR".

[End of Propagation Rule]

In Figure 4(d), according to the Propagation Rule, the reception of message +2 should also be specified at state 1.0, thus $succ(1.0,+2)=$"UUR" is created and detected. The Induction Rule is illustrated in another example given in Figure 5. This figure shows an expanded tree. Three straight dotted-line transitions are created after these two rules are applied. According to the Induction Rule, the reception of message 3 should be specified both before and after message 2 is transmitted. Since $succ(1.0,+3)$ does not exist on the expanded tree, CUR is created and detected. According to the Propagation Rule, if message 3 can be received at state 2.0, the message can also be received after any number of transmissions have taken place. Thus, since $succ(4.0,+3)$ and $succ(5.0,+3)$ do not exist on the expanded tree, a CUR and a UUR are created and detected, respectively.

6. Experimental Results

To quantify verification state space required by the reachability analysis, the KWN algorithm, and the Two-Phase algorithm, we implemented these three algorithms and conducted experiments on several realistic protocols. The numbers of states and transitions of each protocol are listed in Table 3. The numbers of explored states using the reachability analysis, the KWN algorithm, and the Two-Phase algorithm are shown in Table 4. These experimental results

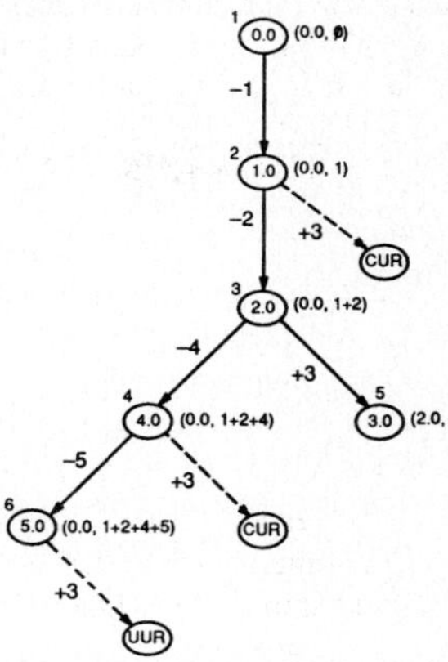

Figure 5. UUR/CUR detection using the Induction and Propagation Rules.

show that the Two-Phase algorithm requires much fewer explored states than that using the reachability analysis and the KWN algorithm.

	P_x states	P_x transitions	P_y states	P_y transitions
Simple Data Transfer	8	12	8	12
X.25 Call Set-Up/Clearing	7	22	7	21
X.75 Call Set-Up/Clearing	12	69	12	69
Modified BISYNC	68	174	68	174

Table 3. The states and transitions of experimented protocols.

State Space	Reachability Analysis	KWN Algorithm	Two-Phase Algorithm
Simple Data Transfer	42	37	18
X.25 Call Set-Up/Clearing	111	78	17
Modified BISYNC	292	280	172
X.75 Call Set-Up/Clearing	1534	438	46

Table 4. The numbers of explored states for experimented protocols in Table 3.

7. Advantages and Limitations

Compared to other approaches, most notably the KWN algorithm, the Two-Phase algorithm has five advantages. First, the algorithm allows verification for all processes to be executed in a parallel fashion. Moreover, the algorithm employs a simple tree construction procedure. The algorithm thus requires smaller run-time. Second, the algorithm employs a new piece of external information, "synched state", and the "Merge" operation. This, in turn, allows more states to be combined to avoid redundant tree construction. The algorithm thus requires fewer explored states. For example, our experimental results showed that the total numbers of explored states for verifying the X.75 protocol using the reachability analysis, the KWN algorithm, and the Two-Phase algorithm are 1534, 438, and 46, respectively. Third, since the number of explored states is reduced, the algorithm allows protocol designers to manually analyze protocols if necessary. Whereas the manually examining of a huge global reachability three is often impossible. Fourth, the algorithm can detect all logic errors. Finally, there are no restrictions on the number of processes and the number of messages of the protocols to be validated.

However, the algorithm has two limitations. First, different procedures for detecting different types of logic errors are required during the execution of the second phase. However, this is not a serious drawback since the generation of the expanded trees in the first phase takes most of the time of protocol verification. Thus, running several different procedures for detecting different errors in the second phase does not significantly affect the overall performance.

Second, extra memory space is required for keeping track of the external information (e.g., synched state). However, in fact, in the real implementation, when the computation of these synched states results in larger numbers of synched states than a predefined buffer capacity, we terminate the computation of synched states. This termination will not affect any subsequent tree construction. The lack of synched states for that node only makes the Merge operation from or to that node impossible. With only the least state information, this node becomes the same as a state on the expanded tree used by the KWN algorithm.

8. Conclusions

This paper proposed a parallel protocol verification algorithm, called the Two-Phase algorithm, in an attempt to provide a maximum of verification with a minimum of state space. The algorithm constructs the expanded trees in the first phase and performs error detection in the second phase. By separating expanded tree construction from error detection, the algorithm allows verification for one process to be totally independent from verification for other processes. This, in turn, allows verification of all processes to be accomplished in parallel. This parallelism tremendously reduces the run time for verifying protocols with higher numbers of processes. In addition, the algorithm employs a simple tree construction procedure and a new piece of external information, "synched states", the algorithm thus requires fewer explored states. We finally showed experimental results on several realistic protocols to quantify the reduction in verification state space.

9. Acknowledgments

The authors would like to especially thank Dr. A. L. P. Chen, Dr. C. H. Chow, Dr. I. Frisch, and Dr. M. Koblentz for their giving valuable comments and suggestions.

References

[1] G. V. Bochmann, "Finite State Description of Communication Protocols," Computer Networks, Vol. 2, Oct. 1978, pp. 361-372.

[2] G. V. Bochmann and C. A. Sunshine, "Formal Methods in Communication Protocol Design," IEEE Trans. on Communications, Vol. COM-28, No. 4, April 1980, pp. 624-631.

[3] D. Brand and P. Zafiropulo, "On Communicating Finite-State Machines," Journal of the ACM, Vol 30, No. 2, April 1983, pp. 323-342.

[4] A. Danthine, "Protocol Representation with Finite State Models," IEEE Trans. on Communications, Vol. COM-28, No. 4, April 1980, pp. 632-643.

[5] M. G. Gouda, "Closed Covers: To Verify Progress of Communicating Finite State Machines," IEEE Trans. on Software Engineering, Nov. 1984, Vol. SE-10, No. 6, pp. 846-855.

[6] Y. Kakuda, Y. Wakahara, and M. Norigoe, "A New Algorithm For Fast Protocol Validation," Proc. IEEE COMPSAC, 1986, pp. 228-236.

[7] S. Lam and A. Shankar, "Protocol Verification via Projections," IEEE Trans. on Software Engineering, Vol. SE-10, No. 4, July 1984, pp. 325-342.

[8] F. Lin, P. Chu, and M. Liu, "Protocol Verification Using Reachability Analysis: The State Space Explosion Problem and Relief Strategies," Proc. ACM SIGCOMM, Aug. 1987.

[9] N. F. Maxemchuk and K. Sabnani, "Probabilistic Verification of Communication Protocols," Protocol Specification, Testing, and Verification, VII, pp. 307-320, North-Holland, 1987.

[10] P. M. Merlin, "Specification and Validation of Protocols," IEEE Trans. on Communications, Vol. COM-27, No. 11, Nov. 1979, pp. 1671-1680.

[11] "Communication Protocol Modeling," Edited by Carl A. Sunshine, Artech House.

[12] S. T. Vuong and D. D. Cowan, "A Decomposition Method for the Validation of Structured Protocols," Proc. IEEE INFOCOM, April 1982.

[13] S. T. Vuong, D. D. Hui, and D. D. Cowan, "VALIRA - A Tool for Protocol Validation Via Reachability Analysis," Protocol Specification, Testing, and Verification, VI. North-Holland, 1986.

[14] M. C. Yuang, "Survey of Protocol Verification Techniques Based on Finite State Machine Models," Proc. NBS Computer Networking Symposium, 1988, pp. 164-172.

[15] P. Zafiropulo, "Protocol Validation by Duologue-Matrix Analysis," IEEE Trans. Commun. COM-26, 8(August, 1978), pp. 1187-1194.

[16] P. Zafiropulo, et al., "Towards Analyzing and Synthesizing Protocols," IEEE Trans. on Communications, COM-28, 4(April, 1980), pp. 651-661.

Session 8:

Temporal Logic Applications

Protocol Specification, Testing, and Verification, IX
E. Brinksma, G. Scollo and C.A. Vissers (Editors)
Elsevier Science Publishers B.V. (North-Holland)

VERIFYING SAFETY AND DEADLOCK PROPERTIES OF NETWORKS OF ASYNCHRONOUSLY COMMUNICATING PROCESSES

Fredrik Orava

Swedish Institute of Computer Science
P.O. Box 1263
S-164 28 KISTA
SWEDEN

email (uucp): fredrik@sics.se

Abstract

We present a method for specifying and verifying networks of non-deterministic processes that communicate by asynchronous message-passing. The method handles safety and deadlock properties. Networks are specified in an operational manner by transition systems. We say that the specification A *implements* another specification B if every safety and deadlock property true of A is also true of B. We establish a proof rule for verifying that A implements B in this sense. The proof rule is based on simulation between the states of A and B. We illustrate the method by applying it to the alternating bit protocol.

1. INTRODUCTION

The importance of formal specification and verification in the design of distributed systems is now commonly recognized. A formal specification gives an unambiguous description of the intended behavior of a system, and can be used to verify that the design is correct before it is implemented.

A specification method suitable for distributed systems should allow abstraction from irrelevant details, and modular composition of a specification of a large system from specifications of its components. For example, using OSI-terminology, given the (N-1)-service and the (N)-protocol, it should be possible to verify that their composition fulfills the requirements of the (N)-service.

A class of specification and verification methods that achieve this are based on *traces*, sequences of interactions between systems ([CH81], [MC81], [BM82], [MCS82], [NDGO86]). Many of these approaches specify a system by its finite traces. However, the set of traces of a system does not capture some aspects of its behavior, such as properties related to deadlock and termination. To illustrate this point, consider two processes: The first process outputs an a and then deadlocks. The second process is non-deterministic and may initially be deadlocked or it may output an a and then deadlock. These two processes have the same set of traces, namely $\{\langle\rangle, \langle a\rangle\}$ although the second process has a potential deadlock (here $\langle\rangle$ denote the empty sequence).

Extensions of the trace model for synchronously communicating networks usually include information on potential deadlocks after a sequence of communication events. An example of such a model is the failure model ([BHR84]). A process is deadlocked if it can not accept more input or provide more output that matches the requirements of the environment. The difference compared with our model is that we consider asynchronously communicating processes, thus our network can not cause deadlock by refusing input.

Our method for specification and verification is based on finite traces. In addition, we specify deadlock properties by designating certain traces as *quiescent*. After performing a quiescent trace, the execution of a system is suspended until more input arrives ([Mi84], [Jo85], [Jo87]). In a formal sense, when the execution of a system is suspended this is either an intended behavior (i.e. a type of termination) or an unintended behavior (which we call deadlock). By reasoning about quiescent traces, it is possible to verify deadlock and termination properties. For example, consider again the two processes mentioned above. The first process only has the quiescent trace $\langle a \rangle$, whereas the second process has the two quiescent traces $\langle\rangle$ and $\langle a \rangle$.

We use *transition systems* ([Pl81],[MP81]) to specify the set of traces and quiescent traces of networks in an operational style. We define an implementation ordering between specifications. Intuitively, a specification A implements another specification B if everything A can do is allowed by B. Formally, A implements B if the set of traces and quiescent traces of A are subsets of the set of traces and quiescent traces of B. We present a rule on transition systems for establishing this implementation relation. The rule is based on a simulation between the states of the two transition systems. This method is related to the bisimulation technique, originally suggested in [Pa81] and later elaborated in the context of SCCS ([Mi83]).

The treatment of transition systems and simulation relations in this paper is adopted from [Jo87]and [LT87]. In the works by Back and Mannila ([BaMa82]), by Chen and Hoare ([ChHo81]), and by Misra and Chandy ([MiCh81]), networks are represented by traces. As we pointed out above, such models can not describe deadlock properties of networks. For networks that can always accept input, Misra and Chandy ([MiCh84]) used the idea of quiescent traces to model liveness properties. Jonson ([Jo85],[Jo87]) formalized this idea and included infinite traces and properties related to fairness. In an earlier paper Misra, Candy and Smith ([MCS82]) proposed an extension to the trace model by adding conditions under which a trace must be extended. Their model is closely related to ours; it does not contain infinite traces and as such can not represent fairness properties. Their specification method is different from ours, and a proof involves reasoning about sequences of actions, whereas a proof with our method only involves reasoning about individual actions.
In summary, the contributions of this paper are:

(i) a simple model of asynchronously communicating processes, and

(ii) a method to decide whether an implementation conforms to a specification. The correctness criteria involve safety properties including absence of deadlock.

In the next section we define transition systems as a means of specifying networks. In section 3 we define composition of transition systems. This operation corresponds to parallel execution of a set of networks. In section 4 we present a rule for proving that a transition system specifying a network implements another transition system. The proof rule is shown to be sound. We apply our methods to the alternating bit protocol in section 5. Finally, in section 6 some concluding remarks are made.

2. SPECIFYING NETWORKS BY TRANSITION SYSTEMS

We will use *transition systems* to formulate specifications of networks. A transition system has a set of *states* and a set of *transitions* between the states. A state consists of values of internal variables, contents of message buffers, etc. To specify deadlock properties of networks, we designate some states of the transition systems as *resting.* The intuition is that a transition system in a resting state is blocked until it receives more input. The resting states of a transition system thus describe the allowed deadlocks and terminations.

Communication events can occur simultaneously with transitions. There are two types of communication events: *input events* and *output events.* We also consider *silent events* which label transitions which merely update the state.

We represent a transition system as a set of *labeled guarded commands* of the form:

$$g \xrightarrow{e} [\tilde{y} := \tilde{v}]$$

where the guard, g, is a boolean expression, $\tilde{y}$ is a subset of the local variables of the network, $\tilde{v}$ is a set of value expressions, and e is an event. The intuition of such a labeled guarded command is that when the guard g is true, then the transition system may perform a computation step, which assigns the values of $\tilde{v}$ to the variables $\tilde{y}$. The computation step is labeled with an event e. Events can be of two types:

(i) Internal events denoted by τ.

(ii) Communication events denoted by *ch(m)*, where *ch* is an input channel or an output channel and m is a message possibly dependent on state variables. The intended meaning is that the network receives or transmits the message m via the channel *ch*.

Definition. A transition system is a tuple $\langle I, O, \tilde{x}, \Phi, G\rangle$where

- I is a set of *input events* , not containing the silent event τ.
- O is a set of *output events* , not containing the silent event τ.
- $\tilde{x}$ is a set of *state variables* $\{x_1, \ldots, x_n\}$.
- Φ is an *initial predicate* over the state variables.
- G is a set of *labeled guarded commands.* □

Definition. Let N be the transition system $\langle I, O, \tilde{x}, \Phi, G\rangle$.

- A *state*, σ, of N is an assignment of values to $\tilde{x}$. The evaluation of the expression *exp* relative to the assignment σ is denoted $\sigma(exp)$.
- A *transition* of N is a labeled transition

$$\sigma \xrightarrow{e} \sigma'$$

  such that there is a labeled guarded command $g \xrightarrow{e} [\tilde{y} := \tilde{v}]$, where we write $\tilde{y}$ for $y_1, \ldots, y_n$ and $\tilde{v}$ for $v_1, \ldots, v_n$, in G, for which $\sigma(g)$ is true and σ' differs from σ only in the values of $\tilde{y}$, i.e. $\sigma'(u) = \sigma(v_i)$ if $u = y_i$ and $\sigma'(u) = \sigma(u)$ otherwise. If e is of type output and depends on state variables, then e is interpreted according to σ.
- A transition $\sigma \xrightarrow{e} \sigma'$ is *enabled* in state σ. □

Let N be the transition system $\langle I, O, \tilde{x}, \Phi, G\rangle$. We define the *resting states* of N to be the states in which no transition labeled with an output or silent event is enabled. We represent resting states by a predicate $\mathcal{R}_N$ over the state variables in N such that $\sigma(\mathcal{R}_N)$ is true if and only if σ is a resting state of N. The predicate $\mathcal{R}_N$ can be obtained as the conjunction of the negation of the guards for each guarded command labeled with an output or silent event.

It will be convenient to consider communication events as instantaneous events. It will also be convenient to assume that when two processes communicate, an output event in one process is equivalent with an input event in the other process. However, these two assumptions contradict the asynchronous nature of communication: when a message is transmitted it may not be received until later. In order to resolve this conflict we follow [Mi84], [Jo85], [Jo87] and regard the reception of a message by a process to occur when the message is transmitted by the sending process. The message is not necessarily received immediately at the destination, but it is bound to be received at the destination at some later moment. It follows that the occurrences of input events are controlled by the environment of the process rather then by the process itself. Hence, in each state of the process all input events must be enabled. This requirement is formalized as follows:

For each state σ and input event e
there is a state σ' such that $\sigma \xrightarrow{e} \sigma'$ is enabled

The standard way to achieve this is to use a state variable, buf_{ch}, for each input channel ch and include

$$true \xrightarrow{ch(d)} [buf_{ch} := buf_{ch} \bullet d]$$

in G. Here $buf_{ch} := buf_{ch} \bullet d$ means appending d to the end of buf_{ch}. In this command as in the following we consider d to be implicitly universally quantified; formally this command represents a set of commands (one for each possible value of d).

We now define the *denotation* of a transition system. This denotation will be used in the next section where we define the implementation relation. The denotation of a transition system is the set of traces, i.e. sequences of communication events a transition system may perform, together with the set of quiescent traces, i.e. sequences of communication events after which the transition system may reach a resting state.

Definition. Let N be the transition system $\langle I, O, \tilde{x}, \Phi, G\rangle$. A *computation* of N is a finite sequence of transitions

$$\sigma^0 \xrightarrow{e_1} \sigma^1 \xrightarrow{e_2} \cdots \xrightarrow{e_n} \sigma^n$$

which fulfills conditions (i) and (ii) below. If the computation also fulfills condition (iii), then the computation is a *quiescent computation.*

(i) *Initialization.* The first state of the sequence, σ^0, satisfies Φ.
(ii) *State to state sequencing.* Each transition $\sigma^{i-1} \xrightarrow{e_i} \sigma^i$ is a transition of N.
(iii) *Quiescence.* The last state of the sequence, σ^n, satisfies $\mathcal{R}_N$. □

Definition. Let $N = \langle I, O, \tilde{x}, \Phi, G\rangle$be a transition system.

(i) A *trace* (*quiescent trace*) of N is the sequence of communication events (i.e. non-τ events) in a computation (quiescent computation) of N.
(ii) The *denotation* of N, denoted by $[N]$, is the tuple $\langle I(N), O(N), T(N), Q(N)\rangle$, where
$I(N) = I$, the set of input events of N
$O(N) = O$, the set of output events of N
$T(N)$ is the set of traces of N
$Q(N)$ is the set of quiescent traces of N □

Note that the set of quiescent traces, $Q(N)$, is included in the set of traces, $T(N)$. Intuitively, $T(N)$ represents safety properties such as; "the event a is always preceded by the event b" or "messages are delivered in the same order as they were received". The properties that can be expressed in this way are safety properties, with the notable exception of deadlock properties. The set of quiescent traces, $Q(N)$, represents termination or deadlock properties such as "the network may deadlock after the sequence of events s".

Example. (Buffer) A buffer receives sequences of input along channel α and transmits the received inputs along channel β, preserving the ordering of items. The communication events of the network are of the form $\alpha(d)$ and $\beta(d)$ with d taken from some set of values. A state of the transition system specifying the buffer corresponds to the sequence of messages received at α but not yet transmitted at β. We use the following notation for finite sequences:

- $\langle\rangle$ denotes the empty sequence.
- $s \bullet d$ denotes the result of adding the element d to the end of the sequence s.
- $tl(s)$ denotes the result of deleting the first element of the sequence s.
- $hd(s)$ denotes the first element of the sequence s.

Input events:	$\alpha(d)$
Output events:	$\beta(d)$
Variables:	buf
Initialization:	$buf = \langle\rangle$
Commands:	$true \xrightarrow{\alpha(d)} [buf := buf \bullet d]$
	$buf \neq \langle\rangle \xrightarrow{\beta(hd(buf))} [buf := tl(buf)]$

Figure 2.1: *Specification of a buffer.*

The resting condition, $\mathcal{R}$, for the buffer of figure 2.1 is $buf = \langle\rangle$, i.e. the network can only halt in a state such that all messages received along α are transmitted along β.

3. COMPOSITION OF SPECIFICATIONS

A specification N is intended to specify the externally observable behavior of a network. To be able to investigate the resulting externally observable behavior of a network built from subnetworks, we define an operation, called *parallel composition* of transition systems.

Assume that we are specifying a network consisting of communicating subnetworks. The subnetworks are interconnected by *internal channels* and communicate by sending messages via these channels. Channels of the subnetworks that are not connected to other subnetworks are referred to as *external channels*; via these channels the network communicates with the environment. The output of a message by one subnetwork into an internal channel is an input of some other subnetwork. Thus, communication via the internal channels are internal events of the composed network, and communication via the external channels are external (observable) events of the composed network. This leads to the following operation on the transition systems: The parallel composition of the transition systems $N_1, \ldots, N_k$ yields a new transition system N. A state of N is a tuple, whose components are states of the transition systems $N_1, \ldots, N_k$. A transition of N is either an action of one component N_i, or it is an action where two components participate in a communication event. In the latter case the transition affects the states of both participating components in N. The event in such a joint transition is internal to the network N, and should as such no longer be observable from the outside of the transition system. We achieve this by replacing these communication events by the silent event τ. To ensure that internal channels interconnect only two processes, and to ensure that all local variables are unique, we need to define the concept of a set of transition systems being compatible.

Definition. The transition systems $N_i = \langle I_i, O_i, \tilde{x}_i, \Phi_i, G_i \rangle$for $i = 1, \ldots, k$ are *compatible* if the following holds whenever $i \neq j$:

- $O_i \cap O_j = \emptyset$,
- $I_i \cap I_j = \emptyset$, and
- $\tilde{x}_i \cap \tilde{x}_j = \emptyset$, i.e. all variable names are distinct. □

Definition. Let $N_i = \langle I_i, O_i, \tilde{x}_i, \Phi_i, G_i \rangle$ for $i = 1, \ldots, k$ be compatible transition systems. Define $IE = (\cup_i O_i) \cap (\cup_i I_i)$ to be the set of *internal events*. The *parallel composition* of $N_1, \ldots, N_k$, denoted $(N_1 \| N_2, \ldots, \| N_k)$ is the transition system $N = \langle I, O, \tilde{x}, \Phi, G \rangle$, where

$O = \cup_i O_i - IE$, i.e. the set of external output events of N.
$I = \cup_i I_i - IE$, i.e. the set of external input events of N.
$\tilde{x} = \tilde{x}_1 \cup \ldots \cup \tilde{x}_k$.
$\Phi = \Phi_1 \wedge \ldots \wedge \Phi_k$.
G is obtained from $T_1, \ldots, T_k$ as follows:

(i) If $e \in IE$, then e is an event internal to N but external to two subsystems N_i and N_j. Let

$$g_i \xrightarrow{e} [\tilde{y}_i := \tilde{v}_i] \text{ and } g_j \xrightarrow{e} [\tilde{y}_j := \tilde{v}_j]$$

be labeled guarded commands in G_i and G_j respectively. Then there is a labeled guarded command in G of the form

$$g_i \wedge g_j \xrightarrow{\tau} [\tilde{y}_i := \tilde{v}_i, \tilde{y}_j := \tilde{v}_j]$$

(ii) Transitions with external (i.e. $e \in I \cup O$) or silent (i.e. $e = \tau$) events are not synchronized. Thus each labeled guarded command with an external or silent event in G_i is also a labeled guarded command in G. □

Remember that a network must always be prepared to accept input. Thus, a composite network is in a resting state if and only if all subnetworks are resting, i.e.

$$\mathcal{R}_N = \mathcal{R}_{N_1} \wedge \ldots \wedge \mathcal{R}_{N_k}$$

It can be proved that the denotation, $\langle I(N), O(N), T(N), Q(N) \rangle$, of the parallel composition N of the transition systems $N_1, \ldots, N_k$ can be obtained from the denotations $\langle I(N_i), O(N_i), T(N_i), Q(N_i) \rangle$of $N_1, \ldots, N_k$ as follows.

$O(N) = \cup_i O(N_i) - IE$
$I(N) = \cup_i I(N_i) - IE$
$T(N) = \{ s \backslash IE \ : \ s \in (\cup_i E(N_i))^* \ \wedge \ s|E(N_i) \in T(N_i) \ \text{ for all } i \}$
$Q(N) = \{ s \backslash IE \ : \ s \in (\cup_i E(N_i))^* \ \wedge \ s|E(N_i) \in Q(N_i) \ \text{ for all } i \}$

where we have used the following notation:

- $E(N)$ denotes the union of input and output events of the transition system N.
- $s|E$ denotes the maximal subsequence of s containing only events in E.

- $s \backslash E$ denotes the result of deleting the events in E form s.
- E^* denotes the set of finite sequences of events in E.

For this result to hold it is essential that the networks involved always can accept input.

4. CORRECTNESS OF IMPLEMENTATION

In this section we present a rule for proving that an implementation correctly implements a specification. We use transition systems to express both implementations and specifications, and view the implementations as less abstract (or more concrete) specifications. We are interested in verifying only the observable behavior of an implementation. Thus, it is the set of traces and quiescent traces of a transition system that reflects the interesting properties of a network. We will use the convention that an implementation correctly implements a specification if everything the implementation can do is allowed by the specification. This leads to the following correctness criterion: Let N_1 and N_2 be two transition systems. We say that N_1 *implements* N_2 if every (quiescent) trace of N_1 is, when restricted to the set of communication events of N_2, also a (quiescent) trace of N_2. This is formalized in the definition below.

Definition: Let N_1 and N_2 be transition systems. We say that N_1 *implements* N_2 if the following holds:

(i) $I(N_2) \subseteq I(N_1)$,
(ii) $O(N_2) \subseteq O(N_1)$,
(iii) $T(N_1)|E(N_2) \subseteq T(N_2)$, and
(iv) $Q(N_1)|E(N_2) \subseteq Q(N_2)$ □

Requirement (iii) states that N_1 can only perform sequences of communication events that are also sequences of communication events of N_2. Requirement (iv) states that N_1 can only halt after a sequence of communication events if N_2 can halt after the "same" sequence (i.e. the sequence restricted to the set of communication events of N_2). That is, all deadlocks of the implementation must also be deadlocks of the specification. This implies that a property true of traces (quiescent traces) of N_1 also is true of traces (quiescent traces) of N_2.

We now present a proof rule on the transition systems for proving that N_1 *implements* N_2. The main idea is to find a simulation relation between the states of N_1 and the states of N_2. The rule is based on related verification methods in [Jo87] and [LT87].

Definition. Let N_1 and N_2 be transition systems with $I(N_2) \subseteq I(N_1)$, and $O(N_2) \subseteq O(N_1)$. A *simulation relation* $\mathcal{S}$ is a relation between the states of N_1 and the states of N_2 such that

(i) for each initial state σ_1^0 of N_1 there is an initial state σ_2^0 of N_2 such that $\mathcal{S}(\sigma_1^0, \sigma_2^0)$ holds.

(ii) whenever $\mathcal{S}(\sigma_1, \sigma_2)$ holds and $\sigma_1 \xrightarrow{e} \sigma_1'$ is a transition of N_1, then either
  (a) $e \in E(N_2)$ and there exists a state σ_2' of N_2 such that $\sigma_2 \xrightarrow{e} \sigma_2'$ is a transition of N_2 such that $\mathcal{S}(\sigma_1', \sigma_2')$ holds, or
  (b) $e \notin E(N_2)$ and $\mathcal{S}(\sigma_1', \sigma_2)$ holds. We refer to this case as N_2 doing a *null transition.*

□

Definition. A simulation relation $\mathcal{S}$ between the states of N_1 and N_2 is *quiescence preserving* if the following holds:

for all states σ_1 in N_1, if $\mathcal{S}(\sigma_1, \sigma_2)$ and σ_1 is resting then σ_2 is resting.

□

Rule	For proving N_1 *implements* N_2.
(i)	Check that $I(N_2) \subseteq I(N_1)$ and $O(N_2) \subseteq O(N_1)$
(ii)	Find a *simulation relation* $\mathcal{S}(\sigma_1, \sigma_2)$, between the states of N_1 and N_2.
(iii)	Check that the simulation relation $\mathcal{S}$ is *quiescence preserving*.

Proof of soundness. (Sketch) Given a quiescence preserving simulation relation $\mathcal{S}$ between the states of N_1 and N_2, we can by induction conclude that for each computation C_1 of N_1 there exists a computation C_2 of N_2 that simulates C_1 step-by-step. By induction on the length of C_1 we conclude that for each computation C_1 of N_1 with the sequence of communication events $s \in T(N_1)$ there is a corresponding computation C_2 of N_2 with the sequence of communication events $s|E(N_2) \in T(N_2)$. By an analogous reasoning we conclude that the same holds for the quiescent computations of N_1. □

Example. As an example we shall prove that the parallel composition of two buffer networks yields a new buffer network. A transition system that specifies a buffer network, with input channels α and output channel β, was given in figure 2.1. We shall now show that if we compose this buffer network with a buffer network with input channels β and output channel δ we get a buffer network with input channels α and output channel δ. We specify the second buffer network in analogy with the buffer network in figure 2.1 and obtain their parallel composition according to the rules in section 3 as the transition system *B2* below.

Input:	$\alpha(d)$	
Output:	$\delta(d)$	
Variables:	buf_1, buf_2	
Initialization:	$buf_1 = buf_2 = \langle\rangle$	
Commands:	$true \xrightarrow{\alpha(d)} [buf_1 := buf_1 \bullet d]$	(G1)
	$buf_1 \neq \langle\rangle \xrightarrow{\tau} [buf_2 := buf_2 \bullet hd(buf_1), buf_1 := tl(buf_1)]$	(G2)
	$buf_2 \neq \langle\rangle \xrightarrow{\delta(hd(buf_2))} [buf_2 := tl(buf_2)]$	(G3)

Figure 4.1: *The parallel composition B2, of two buffer networks*

The resting condition for *B2* is obtained as the conjunction of the resting conditions for the two components, i.e. $\mathcal{R}_{B2} = [buf_1 = buf_2 = \langle\rangle]$. We shall prove that the transition system given if figure 4.1 *implements* the transition system *SS*, with the resting condition $\mathcal{R}_{SS} = [buf = \langle\rangle]$, below.

Input:	$\alpha(d)$	
Output:	$\delta(d)$	
Variables:	buf	
Initialization:	$buf = \langle\rangle$	
Commands:	$true \xrightarrow{\alpha(d)} [buf := buf \bullet d]$	(S1)
	$buf \neq \langle\rangle \xrightarrow{\delta(hd(buf))} [buf := tl(buf)]$	(S2)

Figure 4.2: *A specification SS, of a buffer network*

According to the proof rule for the implementation relation, we must find a quiescence preserving simulation relation $\mathcal{S}$ between the states of *B2* and *SS*. The simulation relation $\mathcal{S}$ is given by:

$$buf \quad = \quad buf_2 \quad \bullet \quad buf_1$$

It is a simple exercise to verify that $\mathcal{S}$ is a simulation relation. We must verify the following cases:

(i) For the initial states we get $\langle\rangle = \langle\rangle \bullet \langle\rangle$ which is true.

(ii) To check that $\mathcal{S}$ is preserved by each transition of *B2* we see that the transition (G1) is simulated by (S1), (G2) by a null transition of *SS*, and the transition (G3) is simulated by (S2). In order to do this we must verify the following implications:

$$[buf = buf_2 \bullet buf_1] \Rightarrow [buf \bullet d = buf_2 \bullet (buf_1 \bullet d)] \qquad (G1)$$
$$[buf = buf_2 \bullet buf_1 \ \wedge \ buf_1 \neq \langle\rangle] \Rightarrow [buf = (buf_2 \bullet hd(buf_1)) \bullet tl(buf_1)] \qquad (G2)$$
$$[buf = buf_2 \bullet buf_1 \ \wedge \ buf_2 \neq \langle\rangle] \Rightarrow [tl(buf) = tl(buf_2) \bullet buf_1] \qquad (G3)$$

It remains to check that $\mathcal{S}$ is quiescence preserving. We must verify that whenever $\mathcal{S}$ holds between a state of *B2* and a state of *SS* and $\mathcal{R}_{B2}$ is true then also $\mathcal{R}_{SS}$ is true. We must prove that:

$$[buf \quad = \quad buf_2 \ \bullet \ buf_1 \quad \wedge \quad buf_1 = buf_2 = \langle\rangle] \Rightarrow [buf = \langle\rangle]$$

which follows immediately. We have now verified that the requirements of proof rule above are fulfilled, and can conclude that *B2 implements SS*.

To show the completeness of the proof rule above we must show that if the transition system N_1 *implements* the transition system N_2 then there exists a simulation relation between the states of N_1 and N_2. However, this is not in general the case. To guarantee the existence of a simulation relation, we require the transition system N_2 to be *deterministic*. A transition system N is deterministic if it has only one initial state, no guarded commands labeled with silent events, and at most one transition of the form $\sigma \xrightarrow{e} \sigma'$ for each state σ and communication event e.

The above requirement is necessary to guarantee the uniqueness of a computation with respect to the sequence of communication events. Requiring N_2 to be deterministic means that there exists only one computation of N_2 corresponding to each trace of N_2. The proposition below is a slight modification of a similar result in [Jo87]. The proof can be found in [Or88].

Proposition. Let N_1 and N_2 be two transition system. If N_1 *implements* N_2, and N_2 is deterministic then the premises of the proof rule hold. □

5. VERIFICATION OF THE ALTERNATING BIT PROTOCOL

To illustrate the use of our verification method we specify and verify the alternating bit protocol (AB-protocol) ([BSW69]). The AB-protocol is a simple data link protocol, which guarantees error-free one way communication across a faulty medium. The AB-protocol is a standard example for which correctness proofs in various styles have been given frequently in the literature ([Bo78], [BK84], [La83], [Pa85], [Jo85]).

5.1 Protocol architecture.

The architecture of the AB-protocol is shown in figure 5.1. The protocol consists of four components: a *Sender*, a *Receiver*, and two *media*. The components are connected with each other and with the environment via six channels. A user can access the AB-protocol via the input channel X and the output channel Y.

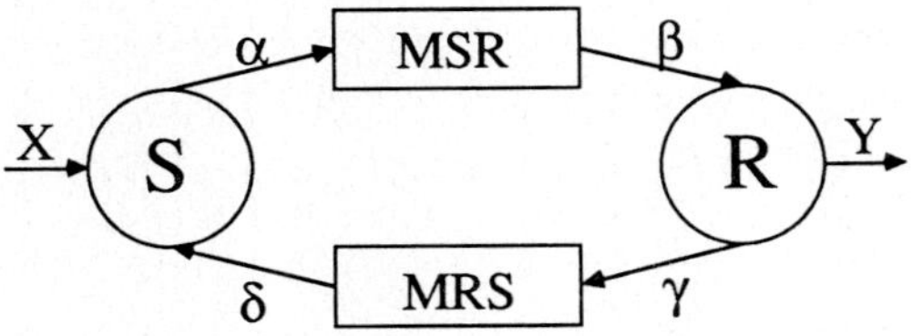

Figure 5.1: *The architecture of the alternating bit protocol*

5.2 Service specification.

The service specification of the AB-protocol is the service of an unbounded FIFO queue. Each message received on X is delivered on Y in the same order as received. In the service specification we use a buffer variable buf to model the unbounded input channel of the protocol. The resting condition for the service specification is: $\mathcal{R}_{SS} = [buf = \langle\rangle]$.

Input events:	$X(d)$	
Output events:	$Y(d)$	
Variables:	buf	
Initialization:	$buf = \langle\rangle$	
Commands:	$true \xrightarrow{X(d)} [buf := buf \bullet d]$	(S1)
	$buf \neq \langle\rangle \xrightarrow{Y(hd(buf))} [buf := tl(buf)]$	(S2)

Figure 5.2: *Service specification.*

5.3 Protocol specification.

The protocol specification consists of a sender, S, a receiver, R, and two media, *MSR* and *MRS*. The operation of the protocol is as follows. The sender accepts messages to be transmitted on channel X. When it has a message to send it adds a one bit sequence number to the message and transmits the message to the medium *MSR* via the channel α. The sender then awaits an acknowledgement with the same sequence number on the channel δ from the medium *MRS*. When an acknowledgement with the correct sequence number is received the procedure is repeated with the sequence number inverted. A transition system specifying S is given in figure 5.3. The resting condition is: $\mathcal{R}_S = [buf_X = \langle\rangle \wedge buf_\delta = \langle\rangle \wedge a = s]$.

Input events:	$X(d), \delta(n)$
Output events:	$\alpha(\langle d, n\rangle)$
Variables:	$buf_x, buf_\delta, a, s, r$
Initialization:	$buf_x = \langle\rangle, \quad buf_\delta = \langle\rangle, \quad s = a = 0$
Commands:	$true \xrightarrow{X(d)} [buf_x := buf_x \bullet d]$
	$true \xrightarrow{\delta(n)} [buf_\delta := buf_\delta \bullet n]$
	$buf_x \neq \langle\rangle \wedge s = a \xrightarrow{\tau} [r := hd(buf_x), s := \overline{s}, buf_x := tl(buf_x)]$
	$s \neq a \xrightarrow{\alpha(\langle r, a\rangle)} [NOP]$
	$buf_\delta \neq \langle\rangle \xrightarrow{\tau} [a := hd(buf_\delta), buf_\delta := tl(buf_\delta)]$

Figure 5.3: *Specification of the sender.*

The receiver acknowledges all messages from *MSR* with unexpected sequence numbers by transmitting the sequence number of the next expected message to the *sender* via *MRS*. Each message with a sequence number different from the preceding one is transmitted via channel Y. The specification is given in figure 5.4, $\mathcal{R}_R = [buf_\beta = \langle\rangle]$.

Input events:	$\beta(\langle d, n\rangle)$
Output events:	$Y(d), \gamma(n)$
Variables:	$buf_\beta, \quad Next$
Initialization:	$buf_\beta = \langle\rangle, \quad Next = 0$
Commands:	$true \xrightarrow{\beta(\langle d,n\rangle)} [buf_\beta := buf_\beta \bullet \langle d, n\rangle]$
	$hd(buf_\beta) = \langle d, Next\rangle \xrightarrow{Y(d)} [buf_\beta := tl(buf_\beta), Next := \overline{Next}]$
	$hd(buf_\beta) = \langle d, n\rangle \wedge n \neq Next \xrightarrow{\gamma(Next)} [buf_\beta := tl(buf_\beta)]$

Figure 5.4: *Specification of the receiver.*

The media, *MSR* and *MRS* are potentially infinite buffers. Each medium can lose but not reorder messages. Corruption of messages can be taken into account by assuming the existence of some mechanism that will discard corrupted messages and thereby modeling corrupted messages as loss. Specifications of the media are given in figure 5.5 and 5.6. The resting conditions are: $\mathcal{R}_{MSR} = [buf_\alpha = \langle\rangle]$ and $\mathcal{R}_{MRS} = [buf_\gamma = \langle\rangle]$ respectively.

Input events:	$\alpha(\langle d, n\rangle)$
Output events:	$\beta(\langle d, n\rangle)$
Variables:	buf_α
Initialization:	$buf_\alpha = \langle\rangle$
Commands:	$true \xrightarrow{\alpha(\langle d,n\rangle)} [buf_\alpha := buf_\alpha \bullet \langle d, n\rangle]$
	$buf_\alpha \neq \langle\rangle \xrightarrow{\tau} [buf_\alpha := tl(buf_\alpha)]$
	$hd(buf_\alpha) = \langle d, n\rangle \xrightarrow{\beta(\langle d,n\rangle)} [buf_\alpha := tl(buf_\alpha)]$

Figure 5.5: *Specification of medium MSR.*

Input events:	$\gamma(n)$
Output events:	$\delta(n)$
Variables:	buf_γ
Initialization:	$buf_\gamma = \langle\rangle$
Commands:	$true \xrightarrow{\gamma(n)} [buf_\gamma := buf_\gamma \bullet n]$
	$buf_\gamma \neq \langle\rangle \xrightarrow{\tau} [buf_\gamma := tl(buf_\gamma)]$
	$hd(buf_\gamma) = n \xrightarrow{\delta(n)} [buf_\gamma := tl(buf_\gamma)]$

Figure 5.6: *Specification of medium MRS*

5.4 Verification.

We shall now prove that the network consisting of the four components S, R, MSR and MRS satisfies the specification SS. The first step towards this goal is to construct the parallel composition $(S \| MSR \| R \| MRS)$ denoted *PS*. This is done, by applying the rules in the definition of the parallel composition operation, below. The resting condition for the composition is obtained as the conjunction of the resting conditions for S, R, MSR and MRS, i.e.:

$$\mathcal{R}_{PS} = [buf_X = \langle\rangle \wedge buf_\delta = \langle\rangle \wedge s = a \wedge buf_\beta = \langle\rangle \wedge buf_\alpha = \langle\rangle \wedge buf_\gamma = \langle\rangle]$$

Input events:	$X(d)$	
Output events:	$Y(d)$	
Variables:	$buf_\alpha, buf_\beta, buf_\gamma, buf_\delta, s, a, Next$	
Initialization:	$buf_\alpha = buf_\beta = buf_\gamma = buf_\delta = \langle\rangle, s = a = Next = 0$	
Commands:	$true \xrightarrow{X(d)} [buf_x := buf_x \bullet d]$	(G1)
	$buf_x \neq \langle\rangle \wedge s = a \xrightarrow{\tau} [s := \overline{s}, r := hd(buf_x), buf_x := tl(buf_x)]$	(G2)
	$s \neq a \xrightarrow{\tau} [buf_\alpha := buf_\alpha \bullet \langle r, a\rangle]$	(G3)
	$buf_\alpha \neq \langle\rangle \xrightarrow{\tau} [buf_\alpha := tl(buf_\alpha)]$	(G4)
	$hd(buf_\alpha) = \langle d, n\rangle \xrightarrow{\tau} [buf_\alpha := tl(buf_\alpha), buf_\beta := buf_\beta \bullet \langle d, n\rangle]$	(G5)
	$hd(buf_\beta) = \langle d, Next\rangle \xrightarrow{Y(d)} [buf_\beta := tl(buf_\beta), Next := \overline{Next}]$	(G6)
	$hd(buf_\beta) = \langle d, n\rangle \wedge n \neq Next \xrightarrow{\tau} [buf_\beta := tl(buf_\beta), buf_\gamma := buf_\gamma \bullet Next]$	(G7)
	$buf_\gamma \neq \langle\rangle \xrightarrow{\tau} [buf_\gamma := tl(buf_\gamma)]$	(G8)
	$hd(buf_\gamma) = n \xrightarrow{\tau} [buf_\gamma := tl(buf_\gamma), buf_\delta := buf_\delta \bullet n]$	(G9)
	$buf_\delta \neq \langle\rangle \xrightarrow{\tau} [a := hd(buf_\delta), buf_\delta := tl(buf_\delta)]$	(G10)

Figure 5.7: *Parallel composition $(S\|MSR\|R\|MRS)$, of the sender, receiver and the two media.*

We now prove that *PS implements SS*. The proof is divided into two main steps: we first establish a simulation relation, $\mathcal{S}$, then we prove that whenever $\mathcal{S}$ holds between two states σ_{PS} and σ_{SS} in PS and SS respectively, and $\sigma_{PS}(\mathcal{R}_{PS})$ holds then also $\sigma_{SS}(\mathcal{R}_{SS})$ holds. That is, a resting state of *PS* can only be simulated by a resting state of SS. To establish $\mathcal{S}$, we must first establish an invariant over the states of *PS*. The invariant consists of three parts:

(I1)	$\{a = s\} \Rightarrow \left\{\begin{array}{c} s = Next \\ a = Next \end{array}\right\}$
(I2)	$buf_\delta \bullet buf_\gamma \in a^* Next^*$
(I3)	$buf_\beta \bullet buf_\alpha \in \langle d, \overline{Next}\rangle^* \langle r, \overline{s}\rangle^*$

The first invariant, (I1), relates the sequence numbers of the sender to the sequence number of the receiver. The second and third invariants, (I2) and (I3), relate the sequence numbers of the receiver and the sender to the contents in the message buffers.

Proof. We first prove that I1, I2 and I3 are invariants over *PS*. To do this we must verify that I1, I2 and I3 are preserved by all transitions of *PS*. We omit the details, but as an illustration, we prove that the labeled guarded command G2 does not alter the truth of the invariants. G2 deletes one element from buf_x and updates the variables s and r. We must prove the following implication:

$$\left\{\begin{array}{c} (a = s) \Rightarrow \left\{\begin{array}{c} s = Next \\ a = Next \end{array}\right\} \\ s = a \\ buf_\beta \bullet buf_\alpha \in \langle d, \overline{Next}\rangle^* \langle r, \overline{s}\rangle^* \end{array}\right\} \overset{G2}{\Longrightarrow} \left\{\begin{array}{c} buf_\beta \bullet buf_\alpha \in \langle d, \overline{Next}\rangle^* \\ s \neq a \end{array}\right\}$$

The simulation relation, $\mathcal{S}$, is given by:

$$buf = \textbf{ if } (Next = s) \textbf{ then } buf_x \textbf{ else } r \bullet buf_x$$

This relation relates buf with the state of PS. The buffer buf contains the sequence of messages received at X but not yet delivered at Y. We must prove that $\mathcal{S}$ satisfies the requirements of a simulation relation. For the initial states we get: $\langle\rangle = \langle\rangle$, which is true. It remains to verify that whenever PS can perform a computation step, then this computation step can be simulated by a computation step of SS preserving $\mathcal{S}$.

G1 is simulated by S1 and G6 is simulated by S2. The rest of the transitions in PS are simulated by null transitions of SS. We must prove, for each transition in PS that changes a variable in $\mathcal{S}$, that this transition and the simulating transition in SS preserve the truth of $\mathcal{S}$. We omit the details, but as an illustration we verify that G1 is simulated by S1. G1 adds one element to buffer buf_x. We must verify that $\mathcal{S}$ holds regardless of the values of s and $Next$. We have two cases:

(i) $Next = s$. In this case we must verify the following implication:

$$\{\, buf = buf_x \,\} \Rightarrow \{\, buf \bullet d = buf_x \bullet d \,\}$$

(ii) $Next \neq s$. In this case we must verify the following implication:

$$\{\, buf = r \bullet buf_x \,\} \Rightarrow \{\, buf \bullet d = r \bullet buf_x \bullet d \,\}$$

The last step in the proof is to verify that $\mathcal{S}$ is quiescence preserving, i.e. resting states of PS can only be simulated by resting states of SS. We must prove that if $\mathcal{S}$ holds between two states σ_{PS} and σ_{SS} of PS and SS respectively, and $\sigma_{PS}(\mathcal{R}_{PS})$ = true, then $\sigma_{SS}(\mathcal{R}_{SS})$ = true. We verify this by proving the implication:

$$\{\mathcal{R}_{PS} \wedge \mathcal{S}\} \Rightarrow \mathcal{R}_{SS}$$

As a matter of fact, the truth of the above implication is not dependent on all the conjunctions in $\mathcal{R}_{PS}$. As is shown below, only the conjuncts $buf_x = \langle\rangle$ and $s = a$ are needed. To prove the implication above we must verify that:

$$\left\{ \begin{array}{c} buf = \textbf{ if } (s = a) \textbf{ then } buf_x \textbf{ else } r \bullet buf_x \\ buf_x = \langle\rangle \\ s = a \end{array} \right\} \Rightarrow \{\, buf = \langle\rangle \,\}$$

Thus we have proven that $\mathcal{S}$ fulfills the requirements of a quiescence preserving simulation relation and can conclude that *PS implements SS*.

6. CONCLUSION

We have presented a method for specification and verification of non-deterministic processes that communicate by asynchronous message-passing. The method is based on traces and have the following features:

(i) Operational specification. The specification of a network as a transition system has the form of an abstract program. With this approach, the operational intuition often helps to convey the meaning of a specification.

(ii) Our verification method is based on the operational intuition of simulations. We say that a transition system, N_1, *implements* another transition system, N_2, if we can find a simulation relation between the states of N_1 and N_2. Our verification method captures safety properties and absence of deadlock. Note the difference from bisimulation, e.g. in CCS ([Mi83]), where two processes are considered as equal if there exists a bisimulation between the states of the processes, i.e. in our terminology; the processes implement each other.

We only consider the finite behavior of processes, and can not model divergence or properties related to fairness. Furthermore, we do not distinguish between deadlock and normal termination, both are modelled as resting states of transition systems. However, when proving that the transition system N_1 *implements* the transition system N_2, we can view the resting states of N_2 as normal termination. If we can find a quiescence preserving simulation relation between the states of N_1 and N_2, then we can be sure that N_1 will not halt in any state other than the states prescribed by N_2.

7. REFERENCES

[BM82] R.J.R. Back, H. Mannila: "A refinement to Kahn's semantics to handle non-determinism and communication." *Proc. ACM SIGACT-SIGOPS Symp. on principles of Distributed Computing,* 1982, pp. 111-120

[BHR84] S.D. Brookes, C.A.R. Hoare, A.W. Roscoe: "A theory of communicating sequential processes." *ACM Journal 31,* **3** (1984), pp. 560-599

[BK84] J. Bergstra, J. Klop: "Verification of an alternating bit protocol by means of process algebra." Centrum voor Wiskunde en Informatica, Amsterdam, 1984

[Bo78] G. Bochmann: "Finite state descriptions of communication protocols." *Computer Networks* **2** (1978), pp. 361-372

[BR84] S.D. Brookes, A.W. Roscoe: "An improved failure model for communicating sequential processes." In S.D Brokes, A.W. Roscoe G. Winskel eds. *Proc. Seminar on Concurrency, 1984, Lecture Notes in Computer Science* **197**, Springer-Verlag, 1985, pp. 281-305

[BSW69] K. Barlett, R. Scantleburry, P. Wilkinson: "A note on a reliable full-duplex transmission over half-duplex links." *Comm. ACM 5,* **12** (1969) pp. 260-261

[CH81] Z.C. Chen, C.A.R. Hoare: "Partial correctness of communicating sequential processes." *Proc. IEEE 2nd International Conf. on Distributed Computing Systems,* 1981

[Ho85] C.A.R. Hoare: *Communicating Sequential Processes,* Prentice-Hall, 1985

[Jo85] B. Jonsson: "A model and proof system for asynchronous networks." *Proc. 4th ACM Symp. on Principles of Distributed Computing,* 1985, pp. 49-58

[Jo87] B. Jonsson: "Modular verification of asynchronous networks." *Proc. 6th ACM Symp. on principles on Distributed Computing,* 1987, pp. 152-166

[LT87] N.A. Lynch, M.R. Tuttle: "Hierarchial correctness proofs for distributed algorithms." *Proc. 6th ACM Symp. on principles on Distributed Computing,* 1987, pp. 137-152

[MP81] Z.M Manna, A. Pnueli: "The temporal framework for concurrent programs." In Boyer, More eds. *The Correctness Problem in Computer Science,* Academic-Press, 1981, pp. 215-274

[Mi84] J. Misra: "Reasoning about networks of communicating processes." INRA Advanced Nato Study Institute on Logic and Models for Verification an Specification of Concurrent Systems, La Colle sur Loup, France, 1984

[MC81] J. Misra, K.M. Chandy: "Proofs of networks of processes." *IEEE Trans. on Software Engineering SE-7,* **4** (1981), pp. 417-426

[MCS82] J. Misra K.M. Chandy, T. Smith: "Proving safety and liveness of communicating processes with examples." *Proc. ACM SIGACT-SIGOPS Symp. on Principles of Distributed Computing,* 1982, pp. 201-208

[Mi80] R. Milner: *A Calculus for Communicating Systems, Lecture Notes in Computer Science,* **92**, Springer-Verlag, 1980

[Mi83] R. Milner: "Calculi for synchrony and asynchrony." *Theor. Computer Science, 3,* **25** (1983), pp. 267-311

[NDGO86] V. Nguyen, A Demers, D. Gries, S Owicki: "A model and temporal proof system for networks of processes." *Distributed Computing 1,* **1** (1986), pp. 7-25

[OH86] E.R Olderog, C.A.R Hoare: "Specification oriented semantics for communicating processes." *Acta Informatica, 1* **23**, (1986), pp. 9-66

[Or88] F. Orava: "Specification and Verification in SDL", Licentiate thesis, ISSN 0283-0574, Computer System Dept., Uppsala University

[Pa81] D. Park: "Concurrency and automata on infinite sequences." *Proc. 5:th GI Conf. on Theoretical Computer Science 1981, Lecture Notes in Computer Science* **104** Springer-Verlag, 1981, pp. 245-251

[Pa85] J. Parrow: "Fairness Properties in Process Algebra with Applications in Communication Protocol Verification", Ph.D thesis, ISSN 0283-0574, Computer Systems Dept., Uppsala University

[Pl81] G.D. Plotkin: "A structural approach to operational semantics." DAIMI FN-19, Computer Science Dept., Aarhus University, 1981

Protocol Specification, Testing, and Verification, IX
E. Brinksma, G. Scollo and C.A. Vissers (Editors)
Elsevier Science Publishers B.V. (North-Holland)

Extensions of Temporal Logic for Counting with Applications to Model Verification

Robert P. Kurshan
AT&T Bell Laboratories

Shlomit S. Pinter
Yale Univ., New Haven, CT*

Baruch Solomon
Technion, Haifa Israel

Abstract

A class of extensions of the Linear-time Propositional Temporal Logic ($LPTL$) is presented, with application to verification of distributed systems. The class of new logics, TL^n, constitute an infinite hierarchy of logics each of which is more expressive than $LPTL$. The logic TL^n is defined in terms of new operators $\boxed{k}$ *Until-k*, $\boxed{k}$ *Forever-k* and $\textcircled{k}$ *Next-k*, (for any natural number $k \leq n$); these introduce the notion of counting modulo k. For example, $\boxed{k}\, f$ is true on a sequence σ provided f is true on every k-th tail of σ. Given a TL^n formula f, we construct a Büchi automaton $\mathbf{U}_f$ which is a model generator for f. (The language defined by $\mathbf{U}_f$ is precisely the set of models of f.) The construction of $\mathbf{U}_f$ introduces a new technique, based upon an idea of Choueka for comparing languages. As in $LPTL$ ($\equiv TL^1$), the time complexity for constructing $\mathbf{U}_f$, as well as a decision procedure for f, are each one exponent in the size of f.

The inability to "count modulo n" is a (well-known) major weakness of $LPTL$, especially relative to applications involving the analysis of communication system behavior involving sequence numbers. While this was overcome by Wolper's ETL, it did not produce a temporal syntax for such counting (but rather subsumed counting in arbitrary regular expressions). The present extensions specifically extend a temporal syntax to counting modulo n. Accordingly, the class of logics TL^n, with a decision procedure and model generation no more complex than that of $LPTL$, is thought to provide a natural and useful extension to $LPTL$.

1 Introduction

This work investigates a class of extensions of Linear time Propositional Temporal Logic ($LPTL$). $LPTL$ is widely accepted as a specification language for concurrent systems ([HO81], [MP81], [OL82] and [HO83]), since it has the benefit of high level language structure on the one hand, and mathematical precision on the other. Common applications of temporal logic to concurrent program verification include deductive inference [MP81], [HO81], [OL82], model-checking [CE81], [CES83] and model generation [WVS83]. This paper focuses upon model generation for the class of logics TL^n. Specifically, given a formula f in TL^n, an explicit construction is given for a Büchi automaton [Bu62] $\mathbf{U}_f$

*On sabbatical leave from the Dept. of Electrical Engineering, Technion — Israel Institute of Technology.

which accepts exactly those sequences which are models for f. The construction of $\mathbf{U}_f$ is one exponential in the size of f.

It was proved by Wolper in [W82] that the *even* property is not expressible in $LPTL$. This property states that a certain proposition is *true* in every second state of a sequence. It follows that many basic properties of distributed systems such as those pertaining to flow-control, cannot be expressed in $LPTL$. Instead of the temporal operators $Next$, $Until$ and $Forever$ in TL^n we present three groups of new operators: $\textcircled{k}$ (*Next-k*), $\lfloor k \rfloor$ (*Until-k*) and $\boxed{k}$ (*Forever-k*), where $k \leq n$ is a natural number. The $\lfloor k \rfloor$ and $\boxed{k}$ operators are special forms of the known temporal operators, with the difference that they do not refer to every state of a sequence like $Until$ and $Forever$ do, but to every k-th state. The operators $\lfloor k \rfloor$ and $\boxed{k}$ have a notion of counting modulo k, which allows, for example, expression of the *even* property. (A related notion for automata accepting (finite) strings is presented by McNaughton and Papert [McNP71]. Its relation to temporal logic, is presented in [Th79]).

The new logic TL^n, defined in terms of the new operators (above) for $k \leq n$, while more expressive than $LPTL$, is less expressive than the existing extension of $LPTL$ known as ETL [W82], which is proved to be as expressive as the language of $\omega-regular\ expressions$. Nevertheless, TL^n may be considered syntactically attractive, in that TL^n formulas have the intuition of $LPTL$ formulas, and in addition they are natural to use where counting (modulo n), or scheduling policies are needed. (In ETL, non-$LPTL$ expressions are represented by a right linear grammer of the regular expressions.) Furthermore, although there are an infinite number of operators in TL^n (as in ETL), there are only three different types of operators.

To demonstrate the difference of the two methods we express the property "b must be true in some even state and a should be true in all even states that precedes it". In order to express this property in ETL we need first to come up with the following grammer.

$$V_0 \rightarrow v_1 v_2 V_0 \quad V_1 \rightarrow v_4 V_1 \quad V_0 \rightarrow v_3 V_1 \quad V_0 \rightarrow V_2 \quad V_2 \rightarrow v_5 v_6 V_2$$

Where the V_i, for $i = 0, 1, 2$ are the non-terminals, with V_0 as the initial non-terminal. The v_j, for $j = 1, 2, 3, 4, 5, 6$ are the terminals letters. The next step is to assign formulas to the terminal letters and temporal operators to the non-terminals. Here we use Γ_0 and Γ_2 for the non-terminals V_0 and V_2 respectively, a for v_1, t for v_2, v_4, and v_6, b for v_3, and $\neg b$ for v_5. Where the formula t is used for every proposition (a, b) or its negation. The ETL formula which expresses the desired property is:

$\Gamma_0(a,\ t,\ b,\ t,\ \neg b,\ t) \wedge \neg\Gamma_2(a,\ t,\ b,\ t,\ \neg b,\ t)$. The same property is written as $a \lfloor 2 \rfloor b$ in TL^n, where it is interpreted over a sequence σ as: $\exists i \geq 0 \ \ [tail_{2i}(\sigma) \models b \ and \ \forall j[\ 0 \leq j < i \rightarrow (tail_{2j}(\sigma) \models a)]]$ where $tail_k(\sigma)$ is the suffix of σ starting from its k-th state, for $k \geq 0$.

The simplicity of TL^n can be exemplified further in expressing the following safety property which is not expressible in $LPTL$. "Something good (a) will happen every n-th state infinitely often" (for some natural n). This is expressed with the formula $\boxed{n}\,(\Diamond_n\, a)$ where $\Diamond_n\, a \equiv true \lfloor n \rfloor\, a$. The Round Robin discipline between three processes a, b and c requires that the order in which the processes get their turn is pre-defined, and will repeat itself for each state n, $2n, \ldots$ for some $n \geq 3$. The following TL^n formula express this property: $\boxed{n}\,(a \wedge \textcircled{1} b \wedge \textcircled{2} c)$ for $n \geq 3$.

The construction of a model generator for a TL^n formula introduces a new technique and is uniform for all "eventualities" and for all formulas. This gives a particularly simple construction of a decision procedure, facilitating an efficient implementation of the algorithm. The "non-eventuality" part of the formula is modeled through the "tableau" technique for deciding satisfiability, similar to that used for branching time temporal logic, described in [BMP81, CE82, EH82, FST84], and that of $LPTL$ described by Manna and Wolper in [MW84]. For the "eventuality" part in contrast to the constructions of [WVS83] for ETL and [ES84] for CTL formulas, we present a simpler construction motivated by the "flag" construction of Choueka [Ch74]. It consists of a product of 2-state automata, one for each eventuality, coupled with a cyclic automaton, with one state for each eventuality. A 2-state automaton notifies the need for fulfillment of the respective eventuality condition, while the cyclic automaton ensures the satisfaction of all the needed eventualities.

The algorithm for constructing a model generator of a given formula is divided into three stages. In the first two stages respectively we generate the transition graph and then alter it by a recursive procedure which removes edges and states in order to eliminate all non-satisfiable eventualities, similar to [Wo82]. These two stages constitute a decision procedure for TL^n: a TL^n formula is satisfiable iff the initial state of the derived graph is not eliminated. The resulted graph generates the set of all the models of the formula and all the sequences generated have the property that every *finite* string generated is a prefix of some model of the formula. In the last stage we construct a Büchi automaton whose language is equal to the set of all the models of the formula.

The time and space complexities of the decision procedure and the construction of a model generator for a TL^n formula, like those for $LPTL$ and ETL, are one exponential in the size of the input formula.

We demonstrate how TL^n may be used for model verification. This has applications to protocol verification [HO80] and hardware circuit analysis [FST84],[GK87]. In these applications we specify a system (defining, say, a protocol or circuit) as a finite state machine. Partial correctness of the system is cast in terms of verifying that the system performs a variety of "tasks", defined by respective TL^n formulas. A system S *performs* a task f provided each execution of S satisfies f. Given a system S and a task f, let $\mathbf{U}_{\neg f}$ be the Büchi automaton (as above) whose language $\mathcal{L}(\mathbf{U}_{\neg f})$ is the set of all models of $\neg f$. Then S performs f iff the set of executions of S, $\mathcal{L}(S)$ satisfies $\mathcal{L}(S) \cap \mathcal{L}(\mathbf{U}_{\neg f}) = \phi$ (as in [WVS83] for ETL). This emptiness may be tested in time which is linear in the size of S.

2 System and Task Description

Concurrent systems such as communicating protocols and digital circuits may be defined in term of finite number of communicating state machines running concurrently. One such model is the *s/r model of coordinating processes* [Ku85]. The s/r model is a discrete-event model of concurrently coordinating entities, with the semantics of automata on ω-languages. In this model, a "system" is defined by a collection of Moore-like state machines. State transitions in each component machine are enabled by conditions on the output of the various component machines. These enabling conditions, or "transition predicates", are represented by Boolean functions of the outputs of the component machines. Under the Boolean operations of *and, or* and *negation*, these transitions predicates generate a Boolean algebra. Through this Boolean algebra, one may readily compute the single state machine which represents the system operating concurrently: for k component machines, its state space is the cartesian product of the respective state spaces of the component machines, and the transition predicate associated with the product machine state transition $(v_1, v_2, ..., v_k) \rightarrow (w_1, w_2, ..., w_k)$ is the k-fold (Boolean) *and* of the k respective transition predicates associated with the component machine state transitions $v_i \rightarrow w_i$ for $i = 1, 2, ..., k$. While it may be defined more generally, for the purpose of this paper we define the *language* of a state machine P, denoted by $\mathcal{L}(P)$, to be the set of all sequences of states of P derived from respective executions of P.

Specifically, we define an *execution* $c = (v_0, v_1 ...)$ of a state machine P with states V

to be an infinite sequence over V such that: $v_0 \in I$, the set of initial *states* of P, and for every $i \geq 0$, $(v_i, v_{i+1}) \in E$ the set of edges (state transitions) of P. The set of all executions of P, denoted $\mathcal{L}(P)$, is a subset of V^ω, where V^ω denotes the set of all infinite sequences over V.

Define a *task* $\mathbf{T}$ for a state machine A with set of states V_A to be a set of sequences $\mathbf{T} \subseteq V_A^\omega$.

We say that system A *performs* a task $\mathbf{T}$ iff $\mathcal{L}(A) \subseteq \mathbf{T}$.

In the next section we show how TL^n may be used to specify tasks. A formula in the logic specifies a task by defining a set of models which satisfy the formula.

3 Extensions of the Linear Time Propositional Temporal Logic

A class of temporal logics, TL^n, (for $n > 0$) is defined, where each logic is an extension of $LPTL$. This results in an infinite hierarchy of logics $TL^1 \subset TL^2 \ldots TL^n \subset \ldots$.

The formulas of TL^n are built over a set of atomic propositions $Prop$ using boolean operations and temporal operators $\textcircled{k}$, $\underline{\lvert k\rvert}$, $\boxed{k}$ $(1 \leq k \leq n)$. The formulas are interpreted over linear time structures of the form V, Π, R where V is a set (say, states of a system under consideration), and $\Pi : Prop \to 2^V$ is a mapping which assigns for every proposition in $Prop$ a set of states where the proposition is true. The formulas *true* and *false* correspond to the sets V and ϕ, respectively. $R \subseteq V \times V$ is an assignment of a unique successor to each state. Such structures can be viewed as infinite sequences over the alphabet V, since they can be unwound to an infinite word over V.

Syntactically the formulas of TL^n are build in the same way as the $LPTL$ formulas, where $\textcircled{k}$, $\underline{\lvert k\rvert}$ and $\boxed{k}$ for $k \leq n$ are used instead of the usual $LPTL$ operators.

For the definition of the semantics, define the following operation on infinite sequences. Let $\sigma = (v_0, v_1, \ldots) \in V^\omega$ be an infinite sequence. Then $tail_k(\sigma) = (v_k, v_{k+1}, \ldots)$ is an infinite sequence which is the suffix of σ starting from v_k.

Now define the satisfaction of a TL^n formula f by infinite sequences. Let $\sigma \in V^\omega$, $\sigma = (v_0, v_1, \ldots)$ and let f be some TL^n formula $(\forall n \geq 1)$. Then σ *satisfies* f, denoted $\sigma \models f$, is defined according to the next recursive definition.

- $\sigma \models p$ *iff* $v_0 \in \Pi(p)$ *for any proposition* $p \in Prop$
- $\sigma \models f \vee g$ *iff* $\sigma \models f$ *or* $\sigma \models g$
- $\sigma \models \neg f$ *iff* *not* $\sigma \models f$
- $\sigma \models \textcircled{n} f$ *iff* $tail_n(\sigma) \models f$
- $\sigma \models \boxed{n}\, f$ *iff* $\forall i \geq 0\ [tail_{ni}(\sigma) \models f]$
- $\sigma \models f \underline{\lvert n\rvert}\, g$ *iff* $\exists i \geq 0\ [tail_{ni}(\sigma) \models g \text{ and } \forall j[0 \leq j < i \to (tail_{nj}(\sigma) \models f)]]$

As usual we define $f \wedge g = \neg(\neg f \vee \neg g)$ and $\Diamond_{n} f = true \underline{\lvert n\rvert}\, f$. Intuitively if $n > 1$ the operators $\boxed{n}$ and $\underline{\lvert n\rvert}$ do not refer to every state of a sequence (as $LPTL$ operators), but to every n-th state. For example the operator $\boxed{2}$ refers to every other state of a given sequence. Hence the *even*(a) property which means "a is true in every even state", is expressed by the formula $\boxed{2}\, a$. Indeed:

$$\sigma \models \boxed{2}\, a \;\; iff \;\; \begin{array}{l} \sigma \models a \;\; and \\ tail_2(\sigma) \models a \;\; and \ldots \end{array}$$

The letter a in the formula is a short notation for the property: "The system is in state a". Another example is a formula which specifies that "Eventually every third state of a sequence will be a followed by a b which is followed by a c" is:

$$\Diamond_{1} \boxed{3} (a \wedge \textcircled{1} b \wedge \textcircled{2} c).$$

Remark: We use the strong $\lfloor n \rfloor$ operators, meaning that if σ satisfies the formula $f_1 \lfloor n \rfloor f_2$, then there should exist a place i in σ such that $(v_i, v_{i+1}, ...) \models f_2$. This is called "eventuality property" of the formula, and i is the place where this property is *fulfilled* in σ.

The following statments are used for decomposing TL^n formulas $\forall n \geq 1$, giving the basis for the tableau construction for our new logic. Let f and g be TL^n formulas and $f \equiv g$ means that both formulas are satisfied by the same set of sequences.

T1. $\models \boxed{n} f \equiv f \wedge \textcircled{n}(\boxed{n} f)$

T2. $\models f \lfloor n \rfloor g \equiv g \vee (f \wedge \textcircled{n}(f \lfloor n \rfloor g))$

T3. $\models \neg \textcircled{n} f \equiv \textcircled{n} \neg f$

T4. $\models \neg(f \lfloor n \rfloor g) \equiv [\neg g \lfloor n \rfloor (\neg f \wedge \neg g)] \vee \boxed{n}(\neg g) \equiv (\neg f \wedge \neg g) \vee (\neg g \wedge \textcircled{n} \neg (f \lfloor n \rfloor g))$

T5. $\models \neg \boxed{n} f \equiv true \lfloor n \rfloor \neg f$

Their proof is derived from the semantics of TL^n (see [KPS87]).

4 Task Specification and Verification

There are at least two purposes for building a model generator for a temporal logic formula. One is to synthesize a state machine representation of the formula which is more closely related to a physical system described by the formula than the formula itself [WVS83]. Another is to find an automaton which defines a behavioral property or "task" for a given system. The question of whether the system "performs" the given task may be cast in terms of language containment relative to the respective languages associated with the system and the task.

Letting $\mathbf{T}_f$ denote the task defined by f, we prove that a given system performs $\mathbf{T}_f$ by checking that every execution of the system is a model of f. To implement this language containment check, one may construct the model generator $\mathbf{U}_{\neg f}$ for $\neg f$; the performance of $\mathbf{T}_f$ by a system is then checked by testing that the respective languages associated with $\mathbf{U}_{\neg f}$ and with the system are mutually exclusive [WVS83].

Example: Figure 2.1 describes a system comprised of three component machines: a sender (S) sending messages and two receivers (R_1, and R_2) that accept the messages. The edges are labeled with the associated enabling conditions. Thus, for example, the edge from G_1 to X_1 at receiver R_1 is labeled with $S : S_1$ to indicate that R_1 in its state: Get (G_1), will move to its Wait state (X_1) if the sender is in state S_1 (trying to send to R_1). A label "1" (= true) corresponds to a transition which is always enabled. (Hence, the two transitions of R_1 out of state B_1, are non-deterministic.)

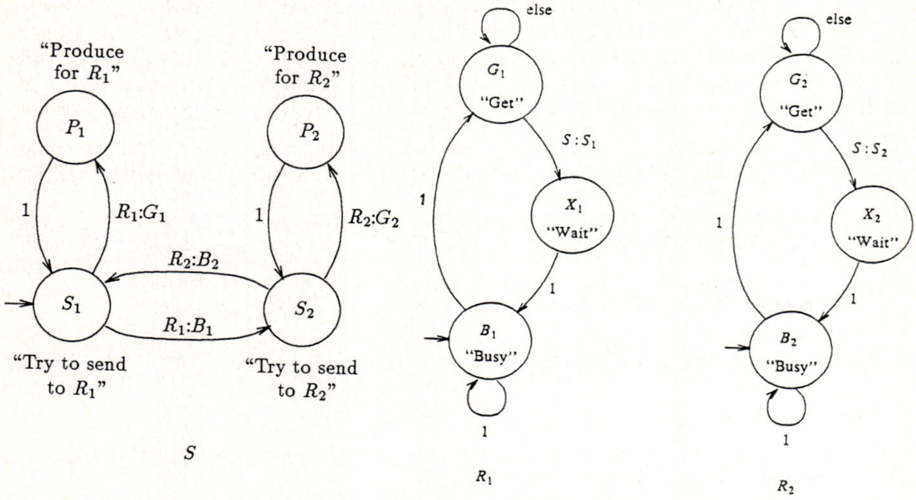

Figure 2.1: A system composed of a Sender S and two Receivers R_1 and R_2.

A possible task for the system is: "If Receiver R_1 will be in his *Get* state (G_1) infinitely often then the Sender will be in state P_1 infinitely often in odd states (serving R_1)." The task is expressed by the TL^n formula $h = \boxed{2}(b \rightarrow \Diamond\!\!\!\!\;2\;\textcircled{1}a)$, where b denotes the property $(R_1 : G_1)$ and a denotes $(S : P_1)$

In this section we give a construction which, for any TL^n formula f produces an ω-automaton $\mathbf{U}_f$, a *model generator* for f, such that the sequences accepted by $\mathbf{U}_f$ are exactly the models of f.

4.1 Tableau Method for TL^n Formulas

The construction of the transition graph is based on a well known technique, which, given a formula f derives the requirements imposed by f on the "current state" of the sequence and the requirements on "the rest of the sequence".

A TL^n formula is *elementary* if it is a propositional formula or it is of the form $\textcircled{1}f$ (note that $\textcircled{n}f \equiv \textcircled{1}(\textcircled{n-1}\,f)$, for $n > 1$). The rest of the formulas are called *nonelementary* and are classified as either α, or β formula, which are decomposed into its subformulas by the α, β-rules listed below:

$$
\begin{array}{lll}
\alpha = f \wedge g & \alpha_1 = f & \alpha_2 = g \\
\beta = f \vee g & \beta_1 = f & \beta_2 = g \\
\beta = f \,\lfloor n \rfloor\, g & \beta_1 = g & \beta_2 = f \wedge \textcircled{n}(f \,\lfloor n \rfloor\, g) \quad \forall n \geq 1 \\
\alpha = \boxed{n}\, f & \alpha_1 = f & \alpha_2 = \textcircled{n}(\boxed{n}\, f) \quad \forall n \geq 1 \\
\beta = \neg(f \,\lfloor n \rfloor\, g) & \beta_1 = \neg f \wedge \neg g & \beta_2 = \neg g \wedge \textcircled{n} \neg(f \,\lfloor n \rfloor\, g) \quad \forall n \geq 1
\end{array}
$$

Given a formula f we define a set $BLOCKS(f) = \{Block_1(f), ..., Block_m(f)\}$ where $Block_i(f)$ are sets of formulas derived from $\{f\}$ by the α, β rules as follows: If $Block_i(f)$ includes an α formula then it includes also the formulas α_1 and α_2. If $Block_i(f)$ includes a β formula then it includes also β_1 and in addition there is $Block_j(f)$ which has the same formulas except that instead of β_1 it has β_2. Blocks that contains local inconsistencies are deleted.

Using the α, β-rules, the equivalence $\textcircled{1}\, g_1 \wedge \textcircled{1}\, g_2 \equiv \textcircled{1}\, (g_1 \wedge g_2)$ and the negation rules a TL^n formula f can be transformed into a logically equivalent form : $f = \vee_i (h_i \wedge \textcircled{1} g_i)$ where h_i are propositional formulas and $g_i \in TL^n$. Hence every $Block_i(f) \in BLOCKS(f)$ corresponds to the conjunction of all the elementary formulas in it, which give a term $h_i \wedge \textcircled{1} g_i$.

For example the set $BLOCKS(g)$ of the formula $g = \Diamond{2}\, \boxed{2}\, \textcircled{1} \neg a$, are:

$$BLOCKS(g) = \{\{\textcircled{2} \Diamond{2}\, \boxed{2}\, \textcircled{1} \neg a,\ \Diamond{2}\, \boxed{2}\, \textcircled{1} \neg a\},\ \{\textcircled{1} \neg a,\ \textcircled{2} \boxed{2}\, \textcircled{1} \neg a,\ \boxed{2}\, \textcircled{1} \neg a,\ \Diamond{2}\, \boxed{2}\, \textcircled{1} \neg a\}\}$$

4.2 Stage 1: the Transition Graph

Given a TL^n formula f we construct a *nondeterministic edge – labeled finite graph* , called the "transition graph", $\mathbf{G'}_f = < S', P^{Prop}, E', s_f >$, where S' is a set of nodes, each one is corresponding to a term represented by a formula g, derived from f, and a set $BLOCKS(g)$, the finite alphabet is P^{Prop} which contains the propositional formulas built over the atomic propositions in $Prop$, the set of edges E' which are labeled with elements in P^{Prop}, and an initial node s_f. The algorithm for constructing $\mathbf{G'}_f$ is as follows:

(1) The node s_f corresponds to the initial formula f.
Define $BLOCKS(s_f)$ as $BLOCKS(f)$.

(2) For a node s in $\mathbf{G'}_f$ look at each $Block_i(s) \in BLOCKS(s)$ described by a term $h_i \wedge \textcircled{1}\, g_i$, where h_i is a propositional formula, $g_i \in TL^n$, and the term does not have inconsistent propositions. Create an edge labeled h_i from the node s to the node corresponding to g_i. If there is no such a node, create a new one. If g_i does not appear in the term, then we refer to it as $h_i \wedge \textcircled{1} true$. If h_i does not appear then the corresponding edge is labeled *true*.

(3) There is only one node corresponding to the formula *true*, denoted by Ω, and there is an edge from Ω to itself labeled by *true*.

Note : If two terms of some node s have the same g_i formula then two parallel edges are drawn between s and the node corresponds to g_i. Thus, every edge in $\mathbf{G'}_f$ which comes out of node s corresponds to $Block_i(s) \in BLOCKS(s)$, for some i, and if no ambiguity arise we use the index of the block as the name of the edge . We also draw parallel edges, for the proposition formula h_i, for each conjunctive close of h_i given in its conjunctive normal form.

Let f be a TL^n formula, then define the *size of* f to be: $|f| = OPS(f) + PROD(f)$ where $OPS(f)$ is the number of TL^n operators in f and $PROD(f)$ is the product of all the indexes used by the operators $\textcircled{n}$, $\lfloor n \rfloor$ and $\boxed{n}$ in f. Including the size of $PROD(f)$ (rather than $OPS(f)$ alone) in the size of f stems from the nature of the TL^n operators. When generating the generalized Fisher-Ladner closure [FL79] of a TL^n formula f, written $FL(f)$, (see [KPS87]) we add that many formulas to the closure.

Theorem 1 *Given any TL^n formula f, the size of its transition graph, $\mathbf{G'}_f$, is $O(2^{|f|})$.*

Proof: Every node of $\mathbf{G'}_f$ corresponds to a subset of $FL(f)$ and hence the maximal size of the graph is $O(2^{|FL(f)|})$. Since one can show that $|FL(f)| = O(|f|)$, the size of $\mathbf{G'}_f$ is exponential in the size of f. □

A *path*, $\psi(s_0) = (s_0, l_0, s_1, l_1, ...)$, in a graph G, starting from a node s_0 is an infinite sequence of nodes and labels of edges such that:

i) $\forall i \geq 0$, $s_i, s_{i+1} \in S$ and $(s_i, s_{i+1}) \in E$ and

ii) $\forall i \geq 0$, l_i labels an edge $(s_i, s_{i+1}) \in E$

The path $\psi(s_0)$ can also be identified by an infinite sequence of its labels $(l_0, l_1, ...)$ or when no ambiguity arise by its sequence of nodes $(s_0, s_1, ...)$. We say that a path $\psi(s) = (l_0, l_1, ...)$ *generates* a sequence $\sigma = (v_0, v_1, ...) \in V^\omega$ if $\forall i \geq 0, v_i \in l_i$. A graph G *generates* an infinite sequence σ over V iff there exists a path $\psi(s_0) = (s_0, l_0, s_1, l_1, ...)$ in G which generates σ.

4.3 Stage 2: the ω-graph

It was observed in [W82, EH82] and [CE82] that in order to show satisfiability of a formula f using the tableau construction (the transition graph in our case), only the satisfiability of eventuality formulas derived from f need to be checked, where all other conditions are satisfied by the construction of the transition graph $\mathbf{G'}_f$. This is so since the conditions for fulfilling an eventuality property may be postponed by the decomposition rules (using the $\textcircled{n}$ operator), thus some paths may never satisfy some of their eventualities.

Let g be a TL^n formula then a formula $g_1 \in Block_i(g) \in BLOCKS(g)$ with the main connective $\mathcal{U}_k$ $(1 \leq k \leq n)$ is called an *eventuality* of g. If no eventuality appears in the decomposition of g then g is called *simple*.

For every edge i, comming out of node s in $\mathbf{G'}_f$ with its corresponding $Block_i(s)$, define the eventuality set $EV_i(s)$ as follows:

$$EV_i(s) = \{ R : R \textit{ is an eventuality in } Block_i(s) \in BLOCKS(s) \}.$$

Remark: If a set $Block_i(s)$ has no eventualities then $EV_i(s) = \phi$.

For example in $g = \Diamond_2 \boxed{2} \textcircled{1} \neg a$, there is only one eventuality $R = \Diamond_2 \boxed{2} \textcircled{1} \neg a \in BLOCK(s_g)$ and $EV_1(s_g) = EV_2(s_g) = \{ \Diamond_2 \boxed{2} \textcircled{1} \neg a\}$

Definition:

i) An eventuality $R = f_1 \mathcal{U}_n f_2$ (for $n \geq 1$) in $Block_i(s) \in BLOCKS(s)$ is *immediately fulfillable for* $EV_i(s)$ if $f_2 \in Block_i(s)$. The edge from s that corresponds to $Block_i(s)$ *immediately fulfills* R *for* $EV_i(s)$.

ii) An eventuality $R = f_1 \mathcal{U}_n f_2$ $(n \geq 1)$ in $Block_i(s_0) \in BLOCKS(s_0)$ is *fulfillable for* $EV_i(s_0)$ on a path $\psi(s_0) = (s_0, l_0, s_1, l_1, ...)$, s.t. $Block_i(s_0)$ corresponds to an edge from s_0 to node s_1 labeled by l_0 **if**

1. It is immediately fulfillable for $EV_i(s_0)$ by the edge labeled with l_0 or
2. There is a node $s_{k \cdot n}$ for $k \geq 1$ on $\psi(s_0)$ and R is fulfillable for $EV_i(s_{k \cdot n}) \subseteq Block_i(s_{k \cdot n}) \in BLOCKS(s_{k \cdot n})$ that corresponds to $l_{k \cdot n}$.

In the construction of a transition graph whenever an eventuality $R = f_1 \mathcal{U}^{n} f_2 \in EV_i(s) \subseteq Block_i(s)$ is not immediately fulfillable for $EV_i(s)$, by the decomposition of the operator *Until* the formula f_1 is satisfied in s and the eventuality R is pushed forward (with the $\textcircled{n}$ operator) to the n-th node through the edge corresponding to $Block_i(s)$.

Next is the elimination step. Let i be an edge from s and i corresponds to $Block_i(s)$. If there is no path from s through i fulfilling every eventuality in $EV_i(s)$ then eliminate edge i. This is followed with the elimination of nodes without successors, and the step is repeated until no edge is eliminated. If the resulting graph is not empty and contains s_f then f is satisfiable and the resulting graph is called an ω-graph $\mathbf{G}_f$. The next two procedures describes the elimination.

Marking Procedure for an Eventuality:

If $R = f_1 \mathcal{U}^{n} f_2$ is an eventuality immediately fulfillable for $EV_j(s) \subseteq Block_j(s)$, then mark s **fulfills** R **for** $EV_j(s)$. For every node s which is marked as fulfilling R find the predecessors of s at distance n. Let v be such a predecessor and i be an edge from v leading to s. For such a pair v and i : If $R \in Block_i(v) \in BLOCKS(v)$ then mark v **fulfills** R **for** $EV_i(v)$. The marking process continues until no new marking occur (no new pair v and i). Note that each marked node is used at most once to propagate the fulfill search for R.

Elimination Procedure:

(1) For every eventuality R in some EV_i mark every edge immediately fulfilling R and its corresponding eventuality set at the corresponding node in $\mathbf{G'}_f$.

(2) Apply the marking procedure for every eventuality that is immediately fulfillable in $\mathbf{G'}_f$.

(3) If at some node s an $EV_i(s)$ of $Block_i(s)$ has an eventuality R and s is not marked as fulfilling R for $EV_i(s)$ then delete edge i and erase the set $EV_i(s)$ from s.

(4) If a node has no successor in the resulting graph, delete this node with its incoming edges. This step is repeated until every node has a successor.

(5) If an edge or a node was deleted then erase early marking (of Step 2) and return to Step 2.

If the resulting graph is not empty denote it as ω-graph $\mathbf{G}_f$.

Theorem 2 *The ω-graph $\mathbf{G}_f$ of a TL^n formula f constructed in this chapter has the following two properties:*

I) Every model of f is generated by $\mathbf{G}_f$.

II) For every node s of $\mathbf{G}_f$ the corresponding formula g is satisfiable in $\mathbf{G}_f$, i.e. there is a path $\psi(s)$ which generates models of g.

For a proof see [KPS87].

The problem now is to build an ω-automaton $\mathbf{U}_f$ from the ω-graph $\mathbf{G}_f$, such that $\mathbf{U}_f$ accepts exactly the set of all the models of f. The difficulty is in the need to pick up only some of the infinite paths generated by the ω-graph. According to our perception, a graph generates infinite sequences and an automaton accepts some of the sequences according to its accepting condition.

4.4 Stage 3: The ω-automaton $\mathbf{U}_f$

Define a *finite edge-labeled edge-final (edge recurring) nondeterministic Büchi automaton*, to be a pair $\mathbf{U} = < G,\ F >$, where G is a nondeterministic edge-labeled finite graph and

$F \subseteq E$ is a set of designated edges of G, called accepting edges. A sequence $\sigma \in V^\omega$ is *accepted* by **U** iff there exists a path starting from s_f in G which generates σ, and traverses some edge in F infinitely often. The class of edge-recurring Büchi ω-automata, like the class of conventional Büchi automata [Ch74] (accepting conditions on nodes) defines the class of all ω-regular languages, although the former are more concise [Ku86].

Given a TL^n formula f a *model generator* for f, $\mathbf{U}_f$, is a finite Büchi ω-automaton that accepts exactly the set of models of f. The ω-automaton $\mathbf{U}_f$ is a product of two components: $\mathbf{U}_f = \mathbf{M}_f \otimes \mathbf{L}_f$. The $\mathbf{L}_f$ part is a local ω-automaton which is derived from $\mathbf{G}_f$. It generates infinite sequences and satisfies the local conditions of the formula (defined by the propositional and temporal operators, except *Until*). The automaton, $\mathbf{M}_f$, is a monitor that makes sure that all the eventualities of the formula f are satisfied whenever they appear in a node on the path which generates a sequence.

4.5 The Local Automaton

In the ω-graph $\mathbf{G}_f$ the same eventuality R can appear in different nodes, say s_1 and s_2. The path $\psi(s_f)$ which passes s_1 and s_2 and satisfies R of s_1 does not imply satisfiability of R in s_2. This follows from the nature of TL^n operators which do not refer to every state of a sequence. Thus, for satisfying an eventuality it is not enough to see that a path traverses an edge that immediately fulfills the eventuality, but the edge has to be at the right distance from the node.

We observe that at most $O(|f|)$ eventualities (together with the different occurrences) can be derived from a formula f and appear in the ω-graph. We denote the maximal number of eventualities, including their different occurrences in $\mathbf{G}_f$ by K. Next we enumerate all the K eventualities of f with a colouring procedure that assigns a colour (number between 1 to K) to each eventuality, R, in every node s, denoted by $c_s(R)$. Also every edge e is assigned a set, $C(e)$, which correspond to the coloured eventualities immediately fulfilled by e. Given a node s and an eventuality R the procedure looks for the same occurrence of R at a distance not grater than $|f|\cdot|S|$.

Colouring Procedure

For every node s of $\mathbf{G}_f$ define a set of nodes :

$$Neighbor^m(s) = \{t \in S \mid \textit{ there is a path with } m \textit{ edges from } s \textit{ to } t\}$$

- For every node s in $\mathbf{G}_f$ do:
  - For every eventuality $R \in EV_i \subseteq Block_i(s) \in BLOCKS(s)$ do:

    Let $R = f_1 \boxed{n} f_2$. If R has no colour in s then it gets a new colour k, i.e. $c_s(R) = k$. For every node $s' \in Neighbor^{i\cdot n}(s)$, $0 \le i \le |f|\cdot|S|$, for every edge $(s',\ j)$ if there is $R \in EV_j \subseteq Block_j(s') \in BLOCKS(s')$, then $c_{s'}(R) = k$, also if $(s',\ j)$ immediately fulfills R then add the colour k to $C((s',\ j))$.

The local ω-automaton $\mathbf{L}_f$ is defined as follows: $\mathbf{L}_f =< \mathbf{G}_f,\ F_L >$ where $\mathbf{G}_f =< S,\ P^{Prop},\ E,\ s_f >$ is the ω-graph of f together with the colouring sets, and the Büchi accepting condition is defined by the set of accepting edges $F_L = \{$ edges which enter simple nodes of $\mathbf{G}_f\}$, where a simple node is a node that corresponds to a simple formula.

4.6 The Monitor

Let $\mathbf{L}_f$ be the local automaton of f. Given an input σ, $\mathbf{L}_f$ traverses a path $\psi(s_f)$. The monitor $\mathbf{M}_f$ ensures that every eventuality which is on the path $\psi(s_f)$ is fulfilled by the path. It uses Büchi acceptance condition defined by a set of accepting edges. The monitor is composed of several automata: 2-states automaton for each coloured eventuality that indicates, at any step, whether that eventuality need be fulfill or not, and a cycle automaton which has a state for each coloured eventuality. The moves of each 2-states ω-automaton depend on the moves of the local automaton, and it pass an accepting edge whenever its eventuality need not be fulfilled. The role of the cycle automaton is to verify that no 2-states automaton is forever in a state where the correspondings eventuality need be fulfilled.

Formally for each coloured eventuality i define $M_i =< \{q_{i_o}, q_{i_f}\}, L_i, \rho_i, q_{i_f}, F_i >$ as follows:

- $L_i \subseteq E \times P^{Prop}$ is the labeling on the edges of M_i.
- q_{i_f} is the initial state of M_i.
- ρ_i is a transition function $\rho_i : \{q_{i_o}, q_{i_f}\} \times L_i \rightarrow \{q_{i_o}, q_{i_f}\}$.
  - $\rho_i(q_{i_o}, D_i) = q_{i_f}$, where $D_i = \{[(s,t),h] | (s, t)$ is an edge in $\mathbf{L}_f$ labeled with h and color $i \in C((s, t))\}$.
  - $\rho_i(q_{i_f}, B_i) = q_{i_o}$, where $B_i = \{[(s, t), h] | (s, t)$ is an edge in $\mathbf{L}_f$ labeled with h, and color $i \in \{c_s(R) | R \in EV_t$ that corresponds to $(s, t)\}$ and $i \notin C((s, t))\}$.
  - $\rho_i(q_{i_f}, \bar{B}_i) = q_{i_f}$, $\rho_i(q_{i_o}, \bar{D}_i) = q_{i_o}$ (where the bar over a set denotes the complement of the set).
- $F_i = \{(q_{i_f}, q_{i_f}), (q_{i_o}, q_{i_f})\}$ and they are called the accepting edges.

The last factor of the monitor is a "cyclic" automaton M_W whose nodes and transitions are structured in a directed cycle. We use W to denote its states and $w_i \in W$ denotes a node in M_W that correspond to the coloured eventuality i. The edges of M_W are directed from w_i to w_{i+1} (indices modulo $|W| = K$) and in addition each node has a self loop. This ω-automaton uses the respective edges of the two-state automata as "flags" to trigger its transitions. From a state w_i the cycle automaton moves to w_{i+1} when the eventuality (flag) automaton M_i is traversing one of the edges in F_i. Otherwise M_W loops in w_i. The initial state of the cycle automaton is w_1 and the only accepting edge is the edge from w_K to w_1.

Now, formally $\mathbf{M}_f = (\otimes_i M_i) \otimes M_W$ where i is an index over all the coloured eventualities.

4.7 The Model Generator

The model Generator, $\mathbf{U}_f$, is a product of the monitor, $\mathbf{M}_f$ and the local automaton $\mathbf{L}_f$. The local automaton reads (or generates) the input sequence and its moves are similar to the moves of $\mathbf{G}_f$. When $\mathbf{L}_f$ traverses an edge satisfying (fulfilling) some coloured eventuality i or the corresponding 2-states ω-automaton M_i is in q_{i_f} (need not fulfill i), M_i will traverse an accepting edge, and the cycle automaton M_W will advance forward if it was in the state waiting for eventuality i to be fulfilled. Whenever the local automaton traverses an edge whose corresponding eventuality set contains an eventuality that is not immediately fulfilled by that edge the corresponding 2-states ω-automaton will traverse a non accepting edge.

Formally $\mathbf{U}_f =< P^{Prop}, Q_1 \times ... \times Q_K \times W \times S, \rho, < q_{1_f}, ..., q_{K_f}, w_1, s_f >, F_U >$ is obtained by taking a product of the local automaton and the monitor, $\mathbf{U}_f = \mathbf{M}_f \otimes \mathbf{L}_f$:

- P^{Prop} is the alphabet,

- $Q_1 \times ... \times Q_K \times W \times S$ is the set of nodes.
- $< q_{1_f}, ..., q_{K_f}, w_1, s_f >$ is the initial node,
- ρ : The transitions (edges) of the product are the tuples of edges of respective components whose proposition formulas (from P^{Prop}) labels are simultaneously satisfied and the edges in the labeling include those traversed by the local automaton. For example the moves of the local automaton together with one of the eventuality automaton (M_i) are: Let $e = (t, s)$ be an edge in $\mathbf{L}_f$ labeled by h.
  - Let (q_{i_o}, q_{i_f}) be an edge in M_i labeled by D_i.
    Then $< ..., q_{i_f}, ..., s > \in \rho(< ..., q_{i_o}, ..., t >, h)$ **if** $[(t, s), h] \in D_i$.
  - Let (q_{i_f}, q_{i_o}) be an edge in M_i labeled by B_i.
    Then $< ..., q_{i_o}, ..., s > \in \rho(< ..., q_{i_f}, ..., t >, h)$ **if** $[(t, s), h] \in B_i$.
  - The traversal of the two other self-loops of M_i are described in a similar way.
- $F_U = (F_M \times E_L) \cup (F_L \times E_M)$ is a Büchi accepting condition, where F_M are the edges in the monitor that correspond to the accepting edge (w_K, w_1) in the cycle automaton M_W, F_L are the accepting edges of the local automata, and E_M and E_L are the monitor and local automaton edges respectively.

For any ω-automata $\mathbf{U}$, let $\mathcal{L}(\mathbf{U})$ denote the language accepted by $\mathbf{U}$.

Theorem 3 *Let f be a TL^n formula. Then a sequence σ satisfied f iff $\sigma \in \mathcal{L}(\mathbf{U}_f)$.*

The proof follows from the above construction. The details may be found in [KPS87].

5 Expressiveness and Complexity

Gabbay, Pnueli, Shelah and Stavi in [GPSS80] proved that $LPTL$ is as expressive as the monadic first order logic of linear orders. In this work we have proposed a new linear time temporal logic. Let $EXPR(LPTL)$ and $EXPR(TL^n)$ denote the set of all the sets of infinite sequences which can be defined by $LPTL$ and TL^n formulas, correspondingly.

Theorem 4 $EXPR(LPTL) \subset EXPR(TL^n)$

Proof: From the syntax any $LPTL$ formula is a legal TL^n formula and hence $EXPR(LPTL) \subseteq EXPR(TL^n)$. In addition the *even* property (a property ,say, p is true in every even state),is expressible in TL^n by the formula $\boxed{2}(p)$, but is not expressible in $LPTL$ (see [W82]). □

Theorem 5 *Given any TL^n formula f, its satisfiability is decidable in exponential time in the size of the formula.*

Proof: By Theorem 1 the algorithm in chapter 4 constructs a transition graph $\mathbf{G'}_f$ in exponential time in the size of f. The construction of $\mathbf{G}_f$ (the elimination procedure), takes polynomial time in size of $\mathbf{G'}_f$ since the satisfiability of an eventuality set is checked in polynomial time in the size of $\mathbf{G'}_f$, and there are at most $2^{|FL(f)|}$ eventuality sets in every node of $\mathbf{G'}_f$. □

Theorem 6 *The size of the model generator and the time, which takes to construct it, are exponential in the size of f.*

Proof: The size of the ω-graph, $\mathbf{G}_f$, which is a the tableau for a TL^n formula f is equal to the size of the transition graph $\mathbf{G'}_f$, whose size is exponential in the size of the formula by Theorem 1. The model generator $\mathbf{U}_f$ is a product of $\mathbf{G}_f$ and the monitor. Since the monitor is of size $O|FL(f)|$ the proof follows. □

6 References

[BMP81] M. Ben-Ari, Z. Manna, A. Pnueli, "The Temporal Logic of Branching Time" 8th ACM Symposium on Principles of Programming Languages, Williamsburg, VA, January 1981, pp. 164-176.

[Bu62] J. R. Büchi, "On a Decision Method in Restricted Second-Order Arithmetic", *Proc. Inter. Congress on Logic, Methodology and Philosophy of Science 1960,* Stanford Univ. Press, 1962, pp. 1-12.

[CE82] E. M. Clarke, E. A. Emerson, "Synthesis of Synchronization Skeletons from Branching Time Temporal Logic", *Proceedings of the Workshop on Logics of Programs,* Yorktown-Heights, NY, Lecture Notes in Computer Science Vol. 131, Springer-Verlag, Berlin, 1982, pp. 52-71.

[CES83] E. M. Clarke, E. A. Emerson, and A. P. Sistla, "Automatic Verification of Finite State Concurrent System Using Temporal Logic", *10th Annual ACM Symp. on Principles of Programming Languages, 1983.*

[Ch74] Y. Choueka, "Theories of Automata on ω-tapes. A Simplified Approach", *J. of Computer and System Sciences.* Vol. 8 (1974), pp. 166-170

[EH82] E. A. Emerson, J. Y. Hailpern,"Decision Procedures and Expressiveness in the Temporal Logic of Branching Time", *14th ACM Symp. on Theory of Computing,* San Francisco, CA, May 1982, pp. 169-180.

[ES84] E. A. Emerson, C. L. Sistla, "Deciding Branching Time Logic", *16th ACM Symp. on Theory of Computing,* Washington, 1984, pp. 14-24

[FL79] M. J. Fischer, R. Ladner, "Propositional Dynamic Logic of Regular Programs", *J. of Computer and System Sciences,* 18(2), 1979, pp. 194-211.

[FST84] A. Fusaoka, H. Seki, and K. Takahashi, "Description and Reasoning of VLSI Circuit in Temporal Logic", *New Generation Computing,* Ohmsha Ltd. and Springer-Verlag, 1984 Vol. 2 pp. 79-90

[GK87] I. Gertner, and R. P. Kurshan, "Logical Analysis of Digital Circuits", *Proceedings of Computer Hardware Description Languages and their Applications,* M. R. Barbacci and C. J. Koomen (eds.) Elsevier Science Publishers B. V. (North-Holland).

[GPSS80] D. Gabbay, A. Pnueli, S. Shelah, and J. Stavi, "The Temporal Analysis of Fairness", *7th ACM Symp. on Principles of Programming Languages,* Las Vegas, 1980, pp. 163-173.

[HO80] B. T. Hailpern, and S. S. Owicki, "Verifying Network Protocols Using Temporal Logic", in *Proceedings and Applications 1980: Computer Network Protocols, and Applications 1980: Computer Network Protocols,* IEEE Computer Society, 1980, pp. 18-28.

[HO81] B. T. Hailpern, and S. S. Owicki, "Modular Verification of Concurrent Programs", in *9th ACM Symposium on Principles of Programming Languages,* Albuquerque, New Mexico, January 1982.

[HO83] B. T. Hailpern, and S. S. Owicki, "Modular Verification of Computer Protocols", *IEEE Transactions on Communications,* Vol. Com-31, No. 1, January 1983.

[KPS87] R. P. Kurshan, S. S. Pinter, and B. Solomon, "Temporal Logic for Counting Modulo n", *AT & T Bell Laboratories,* TM87-0826-17, August 1987.

[Ku85] R. P. Kurshan, "Modeling Concurrent Processes", *Proceedings of the Symp. in Applied Math.* Vol. 31 (1985) AMS pp. 45-57.

[Ku86] R. P. Kurshan, "Complementing Deterministic Büchi Automata in Polynomial Time", *J. of Computer and System Sciences.* to appear.

[McNP71] R. McNaughton, and S. Papert, "Counter-Free Automata", M.I.T. Press, Cambridge, Massachusetts, and London, England. 1971.

[MP81] Z. Manna, and A. Pnueli, "Verification of Concurrent Programs. Part I: the temporal Framework", in *The Correctness Problem in Computer Science* , Academic Press, 1981, pp. 215-273.

[MW84] Z. Manna, and P. Wolper, "Synthesis of Communicating Processes from Temporal Logic Specifications", *ACM Transactions on Programming Languages and Systems",* Vol. 6 (1984), pp. 66-93.

[OL82] S. S. Owicki, and L. Lamport, "Proving Liveness Properties of Concurrent Programs", *ACM Trans. on Programming Languages and Syst., Vol. 4. No 3,* July 1982, pp. 455-495.

[Th79] W. Thomas, "Star-Free Regular Sets of ω-Sequences", *Information and Control* Vol. 42 (1979), pp. 148-156.

[W82] P. Wolper, "Temporal Logic can be more Expressive", *Information and Control* Vol. 56 (1983), pp. 72-99.

[WVS83] P. Wolper, M. Vardi, and A Sistla, "Reasoning About Infinite Computation Paths", *24th IEEE Symp. on Foundations of Computer Science,* Tucson, 1983, pp. 185-194.

Protocol Specification, Testing, and Verification, IX
E. Brinksma, G. Scollo and C.A. Vissers (Editors)
Elsevier Science Publishers B.V. (North-Holland)

AXIOMS OF COMMUNICATION USING TEMPORAL LOGIC WITH PAST

Brigitte PRADIN-CHEZALVIEL, Michel DIAZ

Laboratoire d'Automatique et d'Analyse des Systèmes du C.N.R.S.
7, Avenue du Colonel Roche 31077 Toulouse Cedex, France.

Abstract: This paper shows that it is possible to express different classes of reachability and sequence properties, using simultaneously past and future operators in an integral time temporal logic system.Those properties are then used to express axioms of communication.Different strong and weak levels of behaviours are stated such as messages not lost, not created, ... etc and the relationships between the corresponding properties are given.

1. INTRODUCTION.

Since temporal logic is used to express properties of concurrent programs [PNUE-77], the most currently expressed properties are invariance and reachability properties.

The purpose of this paper is first to express reachability, precedence (weak or strong) and sequence properties with past temporal logic, particular attention being paid to logical events ; then these properties are used to give an axiomatic representation of any message communication. Two sets of axioms are given, depending on the selection of weak or strong precedence properties; the past is used not only to express past properties but also some reachability properties involving simultaneously past and future operators.

Section 2 covers some aspects relating to existing temporal systems based on differences such as the nature of time (linear or branching), the use of an integral time (past ,present and future) and the temporal operators which are used.

A system, ITTL (Integral Time Temporal Logic), is proposed. It uses branching time classical temporal operators (G,H and F,P) and two additional temporal operators, related to the future and the past, called UNTIL and SINCE respectively, whose definitions are given in Section 3.

The important thing is that these properties differentiate the evolutions related to a given timing from those not related to such timing. In fact, a conceptual difference is established between, on the one hand, evolutions which occur within the same instant, where timing does not occur, and, on the other hand, evolutions which occur when a timing event occurs, leading to a different state of affairs for the system.

Thus, some events are not considered as timing events while some others are seen as timing events; note that timing events can be represented by a usual clock time, and also by all events considered as defining a timed behaviour for the global system.

For instance:

1- classical synchronous machines can be regarded as being timed by clock events;
2- asynchronous circuits without unstable states can be viewed as timed by inputs changes;
3- asynchronous circuits with unstable state(s) can be seen as timed by input events but, in this case, going from the unstable state(s) to the corresponding stable state can be considered as an evolution occurring within the same instant.

The work reported here is an extension of this foregoing concept to complex systems. As timing is always related to occurrences of events, the ITTL logic is based on timing events. The latter are supposed to be defined as proposition changes: an event will be defined by the change of proposition p from True to False and another event by the change of p from False to True. For example, it is shown that (p UNTIL q) refers to the instant where proposition q will change from False to True and (p SINCE q) refers to the instant where proposition q has changed from True to False.

Operators SINCE and UNTIL used in this system have been defined to detect state changes. For example (p UNTIL q) formulae may be true on instant t0 only if a change of proposition q from false to true occurs in the future : hence, if q is true at present time t0, it must first be false and then, true again.

This differs from the already published views [SCHW-83] where only the future was considered, or in [KOY-83], [DIAZ-83] where the past was first used. Handling at the same time past and state changes allows easy expression of an interesting set of axioms for communication.

Section 4 presents reachability and sequence properties expressed in this system.

Section 5 presents the application of this temporal logic system to express a set of properties aimed at logically defining possible behaviours of communications in distributed systems.

2. SOME DISCUSSION POINTS.

2 .1 Linear or branching time.

Temporal logic is now used to express properties of the execution sequences of concurrent programs. Two different approaches can be distinguished, depending on the time structure considered [LAMP-80].

The linear time approach allows to study properties that hold for all the execution sequences, since the model is the set of all linear execution sequences generated by the program. Thus, this approach is the right one for formalizing and studying universal properties.

The branching time approach also considers the set of all execution sequences, the difference being that the execution history is considered as a tree: some execution states may have more than one successor. The properties which can be handled involve «necessarily» and «potentially» operators, applied to one or all execution sequences [BEN-83]. Ongoing research often considers a version, using various notations, each modality being duplicated into two different operators:

- an existential operator : EF, EG and EX
- a universal operator : AF, AG and AX.

The existential modalities are evaluated on some execution sequence, and the universal ones are assessed on all execution sequences. The «next» modality (EX and AX) is used in most systems.

Some researchs utilize this approach [CLAR-83], [QUEI-83], [SCHW-83], [CLAR-81] while others [MANN-84], [PNUE-85], [PNUE-86] employ linear time when the properties of interest are universal.

The system used here is an integral branching time system (past,present and future) with regular branching time modalities (F and G for the future, and P and H for the past). This approach has been first used in [DIAZ-83].

2.2 Temporal or modal systems.

Most research works involving past temporal operators such as [SIST-84], [LICH-85], [CAVA-87], consider dual modal systems since present is included in the past and the future.

For example, formulaes (true Until p) and (true Since p) are true at instant t0 if p is true at t0.

The logic system ITTL considered in this paper uses a temporal system according to usual definitions [RESCH-71],[HUGH-68],[CHEL-80] .

Three different notions of time exist : the past, the present and the future.

3. ITTL TEMPORAL SYSTEM.

3.1 Usual definitions of until operator.

Temporal properties of concurrent programs are divided into several classes: safety properties, liveness properties, precedence properties,....

The «Until» operator is specially used to express precedence properties [GABB-80],[MANN-83], but there are two major variants that define this operator in branching time temporal systems.

Let t0,t1,t2,... be one of the sequences of time instants starting at instant t0.

<u>Definition 1</u>

$p\mathcal{U}q$ is true on t0 (denoted $t0 \models p\mathcal{U}q$) iff

$(\forall i \geq 0)\ (ti \models p)$

or $(\exists i \geq 0)\ (ti \models q$ and $\forall j\ (0 \leq j < i \supset tj \models p))$

For example, for formula $p\mathcal{U}q$:

* with Definition 1 precedence properties cannot be expressed between p and q since it may be true even if q never happens.

<u>Definition 2</u>

$t0 \models p\mathcal{U}q$ iff

$(\exists i \geq 0)\ (ti \models q$ and $\forall j\ (0 \leq j < i \supset tj \models p))$

These two definitions appear too weak to handle precedence properties because they cannot easily distinguish between highly different sequences.

For example, for formula $p\mathcal{U}q$:

* with both definitions, this formula is true if q is true, whatever p.

* with definition 2, this formula is not able to distinguish between the following two sequences:

```
q        ~q      ~q
*_________*_______*_____
t0        t1      t2

p∧~q     p∧~q               p∧~q        q
*_________*_____  ...     ___*__________*_____
 t0        t1                ti         ti+1
```

Thus, an «until» operator, (denoted UNTIL) is considered such that:

(p UNTIL q) is true only if there exists at least one sequence (in a branching time) such that:

- q will be true in the future (irrespective of the present time).
- p is true until next change of proposition q from False to True.

3.2 Attempt at a new definition.

One interesting possibility could be stated as follows:

<u>Definition 3</u>

$t0 \models$ p UNTIL1 q iff

$(\exists i > 0)\ (t0 \models p$ and $ti \models q$ and $\forall j (0 < j < i \supset tj \models p \wedge \sim q))$

where t0,t1,t2,.... is a sequence in a branching time context.

The problem is that with this definition, p UNTIL1 q is true on the following sequence:

```
p∧q             q
*_______________*_____
t0              t1
```

As there is no change of proposition q from False to True, this definition does not satisfy our requirement and must be adapted to distinguish this sequence from those where q is changing.

3.3 Definition of until and since operators.

After some attempts, the following definition has been selected and will be used in the sequel.

<u>Temporal UNTIL operator.</u>

$t0 \models$ p UNTIL q iff

$(\exists\ i2 > i1 \geq 0)\ [ti2 \models q$ and $ti1 \models \sim q$ and $\forall j (0 \leq j < i1 \supset tj \models p \wedge q)$ and $\forall j (i1 \leq j < i2 \supset tj \models p \wedge \sim q)]$

```
p∧q        p∧q      p∧~q        p∧~q       q
*___________*________*___________*_________*__
t0                  ti1                   ti2
```

As stated in Section 1, this operator allows us to consider that important instant times are those where q is becoming true. All instants of time where $p \wedge \sim q$ (resp. $p \wedge q$) are true are not distinguished by this operator: they are seen as the same instant when looking at changes of q.
This operator may be expressed using the POT operator of CTL system [QUEI-83]:
$t0 \models p \text{ UNTIL } q \equiv t0 \models \text{POT}(p \wedge q, \sim q \wedge \text{POT}(p \wedge \sim q, q))$

<u>Temporal SINCE operator.</u>
This operator applies to the past.
Let ....,t-2,t-1,t0 be a sequence whose present state is denoted t0, and past states are denoted t-1,t-2,.... .

$t0 \models p \text{ SINCE } q$ iff

$(\exists i2<i1\leq 0)$ [$ti2 \models q$ and $ti1 \models \sim q$ and $\forall j(i1<j\leq 0 \supset tj \models p \wedge q)$ and $\forall j(i2<j\leq i1 \supset tj \models p \wedge \sim q)$]

Similarly, this leads to:

```
q        p∧~q       p∧~q       p∧q       p∧q
*_________*__________*__________*_________*
ti2                  ti1                  t0
```

3.4 Semantics of temporal operators used in ITTL.

Integral Time Temporal Logic (ITTL) is regular temporal logic system Kc extended with UNTIL and SINCE operators : time is considered as a branching time, in the past and in the future.

<u>Syntax.</u>
Primitive symbols are:
- a denombrable set P of propositions: p,q,...
- the operators ~ , ∨ , G , H , UNTIL , SINCE ,
- parenthesis.

Some other operators are defined:
$\wedge$, $\supset$ and $\equiv$: as usual
F : $Fp = \sim G \sim p$ (there exists some future instant where p will be true)
P : $Pp = \sim H \sim p$ (there exists some past instant where p has been true).

<u>Semantics</u>
The propositional variables are either False or True, and propositional calculus operators have the usual meaning.

A model for ITTL is a 3-tuple (T,U,V) where:
T is a set of time instants, also called «worlds»: {ti}.

U is a binary relation defined over members of T, called accessibility relation. This relation defines a partial order on members of T since branching time is considered. Noting U(ti,tj) means «from time instant ti we can access time instant tj».
This relation is transitive but not reflexive.

V is a value assignment satisfying the following conditions:

- $\forall q, \forall ti$ V(q,ti)=1 or V(q,ti)=0

- $\forall p, \forall ti$ **V(~p,ti)=1 if** V(p,ti)=0;
  otherwise V(~p,ti)=0

- $\forall p, \forall q, \forall ti$ **V((p∨q),ti)=1 if** V(p,ti)=1 or V(q,ti)=1;
  otherwise V((p∨q),ti)=0

- $\forall p, \forall ti$ **V(Gp,ti)=1 if**
  $\forall tj$ such that U(ti,tj) V(p,tj)=1;
  otherwise V(Gp,ti)=0 (p will hold every time in the future).

- $\forall p, \forall ti$ **V(Hp,ti)=1 if**
  $\forall tj$ such that U(tj,ti) V(p,tj)=1;
  otherwise V(Hp,ti)=0 (p has hold every time in the past).

The often used rules for $\wedge$,$\supset$,P and F are now given.

- $\forall p, \forall q, \forall ti$ **V((p$\wedge$q),ti)=1 if** V(p,ti)=1 and V(q,ti)=1;
  otherwise V((p$\wedge$q),ti)=0.

- $\forall p, \forall q, \forall ti$ **V((p $\supset$ q),ti)=1 if** V(p,ti)=0 or V(q,ti)=1;
  otherwise V((p $\supset$ q),ti)=0.

- $\forall p, \forall ti$ **V(Fp,ti)=1 if**
  $\exists tj$ such that U(ti,tj) and V(p,tj)=1;
  otherwise V(Fp,ti)=0. (p will hold in some future instant)

- $\forall p, \forall ti$ **V(Pp,ti)=1 if**
  $\exists tj$ such that U(tj,ti) and V(p,tj)=1;
  otherwise V(Pp,ti)=0. (p has hold at some past instant)

- $\forall p, \forall q, \forall ti$ **V((p UNTIL q),ti)=1 if**

a) * V(q,ti)=0 and V(p,ti)=1 and
  {$\exists tj$ such that U(ti,tj) and V(q,tj)=1
  and [$\forall tk$ such that U(ti,tk) and U(tk,tj),
  then V(p,tk)=1 and V(q,tk)=0]};

  or

  * V(q,ti)=1 and V(p,ti)=1 and
  [$\exists tl$ such that U(ti,tl) and V(q,tl)=0
  and { $\forall tm$ such that U(ti,tm) and U(tm,tl),
  then V(p,tm)=1 and V(q,tm)=1 }
  and {$\exists tj$ such that U(tl,tj) and V(q,tj)=1
  and [$\forall tk$ such that U(tl,tk) and U(tk,tj), then V(p,tk)=1 and V(q,tk)=0] }];

b) otherwise V((p UNTIL q),ti)=0;

- $\forall p, \forall q, \forall ti$ **V((p SINCE q),ti)=1 if**

a) * V(q,ti)=0 and V(p,ti)=1 and
  {$\exists tj$ such that U(tj,ti) and V(q,tj)=1
  and [$\forall tk$ such that U(tj,tk) and U(tk,ti),
  then V(p,tk)=1 and V(q,tk)=0];

  or

  * V(q,ti)=1 and V(p,ti)=1 and
  [$\exists tl$ such that U(tl,ti) and V(q,tl)=0
  and { $\forall tm$ such that U(tl,tm) and U(tm,ti),
  then V(p,tm)=1 and V(q,tm)=1 }
  and {$\exists tj$ such that U(tj,tl) and V(q,tj)=1
  and [$\forall tk$ such that U(tj,tk) and U(tk,tl), then V(p,tk)=1 and V(q,tk)=0] }];

b) otherwise V((p SINCE q),ti)=0;

A formula A is *true in a model iff* it is true in all the worlds of the model.
A formula A is *valid iff* it is true in all the models.

4. EXPRESSING PROPERTIES WITH ITTL

4.1 Some simple properties.

Consider first how to express some simple properties that are used in the following paragraphs.

t0 $\models$ True SINCE p (True UNTIL p)

This formula implies that:

p has been True in some past (future) instant t

p is now, (in t0), False or has been False in some past (future) instant t' between t and t0.

t0 $\models$ ~p SINCE p (~p UNTIL p)

This formula states that p is False at present instant t0.

~p SINCE p $\equiv$ ~p $\wedge$ (True SINCE p)

t0 $\models$ [(True SINCE p) $\wedge$ (True UNTIL q)]

This formula expresses that we are at time instant t0 whose particularity is to be «after a change of p from True to False and before a change of q from False to True».

t0 $\models$ [(~p SINCE p) $\wedge$ (~q UNTIL q)]

This formula expresses the same property than the latter and indicates that p and q are False at instant t0.

4.2 Between operator.

t0 $\models$ [(~q SINCE p) $\wedge$ (~p UNTIL q)] noted BETWEEN(p,q)

This formula will be referred to as «between p and q».

Present instant t0 is whithin an interval delimited by changes of p (True to False) in the past, and of q (False to True) in the future; furthermore, in all the instants in this interval p and q are False.

4.3 Reachability.

Two classes of reachability are considered:

p-reachability : reachability concerning past instants.

f-reachability : reachability concerning future instants.

Let us first present different reachability expressions between p and q, whose expressiveness is different. Each of them will be discussed latter.

<u>Note</u> : all properties expressed in this section concern events p and q; they are true if event q for p-reachability, and event p for f-reachability never occur. They must be true at every instant (denoted $\models$).

	f-reachability	p-reachability
potential	$\models$ p $\supset$ Fq	$\models$ q $\supset$ Pp
repetitive	$\models$ Pp $\supset$ Fq	$\models$ Fq $\supset$ Pp
unavoidable	$\models$ (~q SINCE p) $\supset$ Fq	$\models$ (~p UNTIL q) $\supset$ Pp
strict	$\models$ (~q SINCE p) $\supset$ (~p UNTIL q)	$\models$ (~p UNTIL q) $\supset$ (~q SINCE p)

<u>Potential reachability.</u>

Clearly from definitions of F and P, we have:

f-reachability : at each time instant where p is True, there exists at least one path leading to an instant where q will be True.

p-reachability : at each time instant where q is True, there exists at least one path coming from an instant where p was True.

Repetitive reachability.
A notion close to «infinitely often», is now given:
f-reachability : all the sequences starting at an instant where p is True are such that q may be True infinitely often in those sequences.
p-reachability : all the sequences ending at an instant where q is True are such that p may have been True infinitely often in those sequences.

Unavoidable reachability.
f-reachability : all paths starting at an event p lead to an instant where event q will be true.
p-reachability : all paths ending at an instant where event q is true were coming from an instant where event p was true.

Strict reachability.
f-reachability : each occurrence of p is followed by at least one occurrence of q.
p-reachability : each occurrence of q is preceded by at least one occurrence of p.

Relations between these properties.
We can prove easily than:
Strict reach. ⊃ Unavoidable reach. ⊃ Potential reach.
and
Repetitive reach. ⊃ Unavoidable reach.

4.4 Inference of reachability properties.

For potential, repetitive, and unavoidable reachability, inference preserves the reachability property.

One additional condition is necessary for preserving inference for strict reachability, the strongest of the four preceding reachability notions: «between q and r, p is always False» for f-reachability and for p-reachability «between p and q, r is always False».

f-reachability

$$\frac{\models[(\sim q \text{ SINCE } p) \supset (\sim p \text{ UNTIL } q)] \text{ and } \models[(\sim r \text{ SINCE } q) \supset (\sim q \text{ UNTIL } r)] \text{ and } \models[(q \wedge \text{BETWEEN}(q,r)) \supset \sim p]}{\models[(\sim r \text{ SINCE } p) \supset (\sim p \text{ UNTIL } r)]}$$

p-reachability

$$\frac{\models[(\sim p \text{ UNTIL } q) \supset (\sim q \text{ SINCE } p)] \text{ and } \models[(\sim q \text{ UNTIL } r) \supset (\sim r \text{ SINCE } q)] \text{ and } \models[(q \wedge \text{BETWEEN}(p,q)) \supset \sim r]}{\models[(\sim p \text{ UNTIL } r) \supset (\sim r \text{ SINCE } p)]}$$

4.5 Sequence.

What seems interesting is that if the previous notions of strict reachability are associated as follows the notion of sequence between p and q is logically expressible :

$$\text{SEQ}(p,q) \text{ =def= } \models [(\sim p \text{ UNTIL } q) \equiv (\sim q \text{ SINCE } p)]$$

which means that each occurrence of p is followed by one and only one occurrence of q before a possible other occurrence of p, and each occurrence of q is preceded by one and only one occurrence of p after another previous possible occurrence of q (if p or q are not true forever).

Inference of sequence.
As for strict reachability, inference is not always preserved, but this notion of sequence ensures that:

- if SEQ(p,q) and SEQ(q,r)
then there will be the same number of occurrences for p and r.

5. AXIOMS EXPRESSING COMMUNICATIONS.

The aforementioned properties are now used to express two sets of axioms defining possible behaviours of communications in distributed systems. Two potential cases are considered: one uses strong reachability properties, leading to a set of three axioms and the other utilizes weak reachability properties, leading to a set of five axioms. As will be seen, the axioms in both cases fulfil interesting logical relationships that should allow easy and simple descriptions of different levels of axiomatisation based on different communications assumptions.

Let us first suppose the most basic interaction of communication is defined by two events: the first, called r, relates to the request for sending a message; the second, called i, relates to the indication of receipt. Thus the event from true to false of r is meaningful: in other words, the message of the communication user (the request of the sender) has been handled and is sent to the communication provider (the underlying service); then the event from false to true of r means that the request of the user has been accepted and is being prepared before being sent to the service for transmission. Similarly the event from false to true of i means that the message is being passed to the other communication user (indication of a new message to the receiver); the event from true to false of i means that the message has been delivered and another one can be or is being handled. Note that r and i refer to the same message and that only one message is considered by the sender and the receiver at any time.

5.1 STRONG PROPERTIES.

Consider first strong properties. Two axioms A1 and A2 are proposed to define a perfect service provider -a perfect medium- that does not loose nor create messages.

5.1.1. A1: Messages are not lost.

$$\models (\sim i \text{ SINCE } r) \supset (\sim r \text{ UNTIL } i)$$

This axiom, which must hold for any path in the past and in the future, means that *each event r will be followed by at least one event i*, where event r is the event from true to false of r and event i is the event from false to true of i.

It may be seen that the message is not lost but can be duplicated either after having been sent or without having been sent; this is because this axiom is true when i, the corresponding indication, occurs more than once, either after one r or after no r. This formula expresses that i may occur without any previous event r: the medium can create messages. On the other hand, this axiom is false when more than one r appear or when no i appear after one r.

The corresponding allowed sequences are given by the Petri net of Figure 1-a, when place m is empty.

5.1.2. A2: Messages are not created.

$$\models (\sim r \text{ UNTIL } i) \supset (\sim i \text{ SINCE } r)$$

This axiom, which is symmetrical to the previous one, means that *each event i is preceded by at least one event r.*

The duality with axiom A1 implies that messages are not created, but they can be lost.

This formula is also true if many events r occur without the occurrence of any event i: the medium can loose messages.

The corresponding sequences are given by the Petri net of Figure 1-b.

5.1.3 AA: Perfect medium.

$$\models (\sim i \text{ SINCE } r) \equiv (\sim r \text{ UNTIL } i)$$

For any message, *each r is followed by exactly one i and each i is preceded by exactly one r: any communication is defined by a sequence of the couple (r,i).*

This medium cannot neither create nor loose messages. In the sequel, this property will be referred to as SEQ(r,i).

5.1.4 FIFO property.

$$\underline{\text{IF}}\ \text{SEQ}(r1,r2) \wedge \text{SEQ}(r1,i1) \wedge \text{SEQ}(r2,i2) \wedge \models \text{BETWEEN}(r1,i1) \supset \sim i2 \quad \underline{\text{THEN}}\ \text{SEQ}(i1,i2)$$

where IF and THEN define a metaformula.

Given two distinct messages, r1 being sent before r2, the medium being perfect for both, it appears that the FIFO behaviour occurs if i2 cannot be received before i1.

5.2 WEAK PROPERTIES.

Let us now express weaker properties: the medium can loose some messages or create others ones.

5.2.1 a1: No infinite loss of messages.

$\models$ (~i SINCE r) $\supset$ Fi

This property is different from the strong «no loss property» (§5.1.1) because *one or more event r will be followed by at least one event i*: there is no infinite loss of message.

5.2.2 a2: No infinite creation of messages.

$\models$ (~r UNTIL i) $\supset$ Pr

Difference with §5.1.2 is that *one or more event i have been preceded by at least one event r*: messages cannot be created infinitely.

5.2.3 aa: Medium transmits messages.

$\models$(~i SINCE r) $\supset$ Fi $\wedge$ $\models$(~r UNTIL i) $\supset$ Pr

This formula expresses that:

-one or more event r will be followed by at least one event i, and

-one or more event i has been preceded by at least one event r.

This is the expression of a «weak sequence» notion since events r without any consequent i, and events i without any preceding r are not allowed.

5.2.4 a3: No duplication of Request.

$\models$ ~ [(~i SINCE r) $\wedge$ (~i UNTIL r)]

There must be at least one event i between two successive events r.

5.2.5 a4: No duplication of Indication.

$\models$ ~ [(~r SINCE i) $\wedge$ (~r UNTIL i)]

There must be at least one event r between two successive events i.

5.2.6 AA: Perfect medium.

Combining the four precedent properties, a1 to a4, one obtains again the specification of a perfect medium, AA, given in §5.1.3.

5.2.7 Relationships between axioms .

The values of the axioms for some sequences are given in Figure 2-a; their relationships appear in Figure 2-b.

5.2.8 On proving properties.

These axioms can be used to prove properties in different ways. For instance, consider the system given in Fig. 3 where a mutual exclusion is considered [ELL77]. The two users - resp states *pi,ei* and states *di,ei* - can make requests - (when *reqi*) - for the exclusion and the exclusion mechanism is enforced through messages; places *p3* and *q3* represent the critical sections.

The proof may be conducted by taking as an initial state the (partial) state where *p3* and *q3* are true (the corresponding places are marked). Then the verification can proceed towards the past by firing the net transitions backwards.

When a state is reached, as *entCS1*, where a message is received (indications), the axiom furnishes the direction the proof must follow. For instance, if Axiom A2 is used, going backwards means that when receiving a message, there is a set - not empty - of previous states where the message was sent and for all states in this set one or many sendings (requests) have to be considered: in Figure 3, for *entCS1*, this set has two states: either (case 1) *OK2to1* or (case 2) *Signal2to1*.

Applying this method to the system given in Figure 3 proves that mutual exclusion is enforced: going backwards when assuming that mutual exclusion does not hold - *p3* and *q3* being marked at time t0 - leads to inconsistencies with the logical values of *C1* and *C2* and with the control states pi and qi. This is because in case 1, *OK2to1* implies *C2=0* and states *q1* to *q3* imply *C2=1*; in case 2, *Signal2to1* implies *q6=1* which is not possible since the state is *q2* or *q3*. Symmetry completes the proof.

6. CONCLUSION.

The aim of this paper was to show that the use in temporal logic of past operators combined with an event-driven definition of UNTIL appears of interest. It has been shown that it allows expression of some interesting reachability properties. In particular, the sequence notion, often needed when describing behaviours, is easily expressed. Further, this approach leads to the definition of a set of axioms or properties which are easy to write and which can be related together in order to handle different levels of behaviours of communications systems.

This has been made possible by using simultaneously past and future operators which allowed to express the changes of events. Those properties should be of high interest to prove correctness of communications protocols.

An axiomatic definition is under development. A complete methodology is not available in this paper devoted to the expressivness and interest in expressing communication properties.

BIBLIOGRAPHY

[BEN-83] BEN-ARI M., PNUELI A., MANNA Z. «The temporal logic of branching time» Acta Informatica, vol.20, 1983, pp 207-226

[CAVA-87] CAVALLI A., HORN F. «Proof of specifications properties by using finite state machines and temporal logic» IFIP Workshop on Protocols Specification, Verification and Testing, 1987.

[CHEL-80] CHELLAS B.F. «Modal logic: an introduction» Cambridge University Press, 1980.

[CLAR-81] CLARKE E.M., EMERSON E.A. «Design and synthesis of synchronization skeletons using branching time temporal logic» Lecture notes in Computer Science n.131, pp52-71.

[CLAR-83] CLARKE E.M., EMERSON E.A., SISTLA A.P. «Automatic verification of finite state concurrent systems using temporal logic specifications: a practical approach» Tenth ACM Symposium on Principles od Programming Languages, Austin, Texas, January 1983.

[DIAZ-83] DIAZ. M., GUIDACCI DA SILVEIRA G. «Specification and validation of protocols by temporal logic and predicate Petri nets» Proceedings IFIP 1983, pp47-53.

[ELL-77] ELLIS C.A. «Consistency and Correctness of Duplicate Data Base Systems», ACM Symp on Operating System Principles, Nov 1977.

[GABB-80] GABBAY D., PNUELI A., SHELAH S., STAVI J. «On temporal analysis of fairness» Seventh ACM Symposium on Principle of programming Languages, Las Vegas, January 1980, pp 163-173.

[HUGH-68] HUGHES G.E, CRESSWELL M.J. «An introduction to modal logic» Methuen and Co Ltd, London, 1968.

[KOY-83] KOYMANS R., VYTOPIL J., DE ROEVER W. «Real-Time Programming and Asynchronous Message Passing», ACM PODC 1983.

[LAMP-80] LAMPORT L. «"Sometimes" is sometimes "not never"» Proceedings 7th annual symposium on principles of programming languages, Las Vegas, January 1980.

[LICH-85] LICHTENSTEIN O., PNUELI A., ZUCK L. «The glory of the past» Proceedings of Workshop on Logics of Programs, Springer-Verlag, 1985, pp 196-218.

[MANN-83] MANNA Z., PNUELI A. «Proving precedence properties: the temporal way» Automata, languages and programming, Lectures notes in computer science n.154, Springer-Verlag, 1983, pp. 491-512.

[MANN-84] MANNA Z., WOLPER P. «Synthesis of communicating processes from temporal logic specifications» ACM Transactions On Programming Languages and Systems, vol.6, n°1, January 1984, pp 68-93.

[PNUE-77] PNUELI A. «The temporal logic of programs» Proceedings 18th symposium on foundations of computer science, Providence, RI(1977), pp.46-57.

[PNUE-85] PNUELI A. «In transition from global to modular temporal reasoning about programs» Esprit/Lpc advanced school on Current on trends in concurrency, Noordwijkerhout, The Netherlands, June 10-21, 1985.

[PNUE-86] PNUELI A. «Specification and development of reactive systems» Proceedings IFIP 1986, pp845-858.

[QUEI-83] QUEILLE J.P., SIFAKIS J. «Fairness and related properties in transition properties - A temporal logic to deal with fairness» Acta Informatica vol.19, 1983, pp 195-220.
[RESCH-71] RESCHER N., URQUHART A. «Temporal logic» Springer-Verlag, Library of exact philosophy 3, Editor: Mario Bunge, Montréal, 1971.
[SCH-82] SCHWARTZ R., MELLIAR-SMITH P.M., «From State Machines to Temporal Logic», Protocol Specification, Testing and Verification, C. Sunshine Editor, North Holland, 1982.
[SCHW-83] SCHWARTZ J.P. «Quasar, une réalisation du système César: description, spécification et analyse des applications réparties» Thèse de docteur-ingénieur, Université Scientifique et Médicale de Grenoble, Novembre 1983.
[SIST-84] SISTLA A.P., CLARKE E.M., FRANCEZ N., MEYER A.R. «Can message buffers be axiomatized in linear temporal logic?» Information and Control n°63, pp 88-112, 1984.

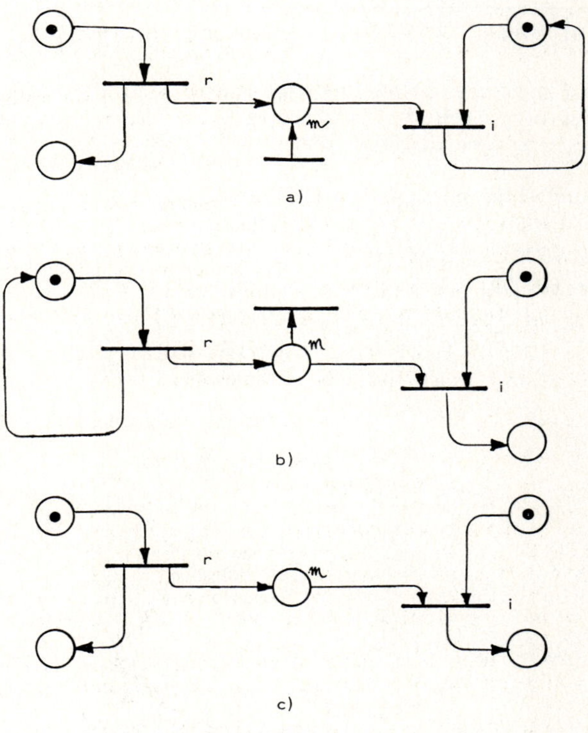

FIGURE 1

a)

some sequences of events	A1	A2	a1	a2	a3	a4	aa	AA
____ r↓__________ i↑_____	T	T	T	T	T	T	T	T
_____ r↓ _________ i↑...i↑__	T	F	T	T	T	F	T	F
____________________ i↑ ...i↑__	T	F	T	F	T	F	F	F
_ r↓...r↓_______________	F	T	F	T	F	T	F	F
___ r↓...r↓__________ i↑_____	F	T	T	T	F	T	T	F
____ r↓...r↓__________ i↑...i↑_	F	F	T	T	F	F	T	F

where

each r↓ is a sequence: a false to true transition of r followed by a true to false transition of r; each i↑ is a sequence: a false to true transition of i followed by a true to false transition of i.

A1 is $\models$(~i SINCE r) $\supset$ (~r UNTIL i)
A2 is $\models$(~r UNTIL i) $\supset$ (~i SINCE r)
a1 is $\models$(~i SINCE r) $\supset$ F i
a2 is $\models$(~r UNTIL i) $\supset$ P r
a3 is $\models$ ~ [(~i SINCE r) $\wedge$ (~i UNTIL r)]
a4 is $\models$ ~ [(~r SINCE i) $\wedge$ (~r UNTIL i)]
aa is (a1 $\wedge$ a2), and AA is (A1 $\wedge$ A2) .

b)

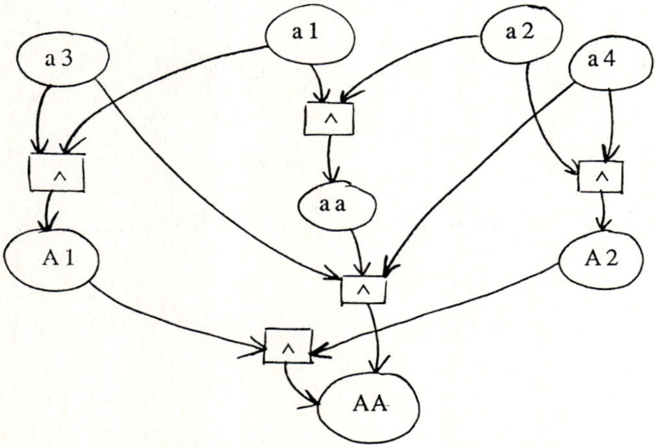

Figure 2

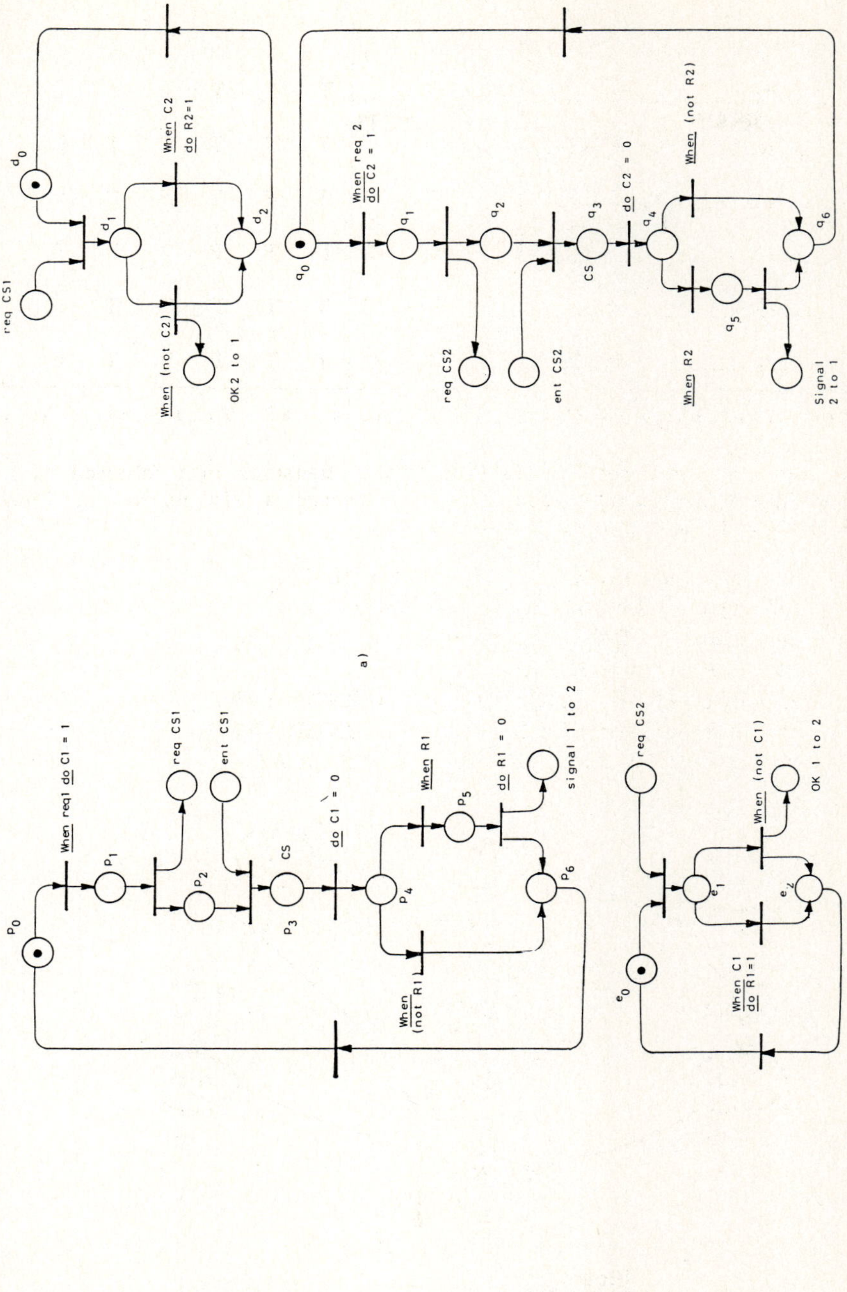

req CS1
d_0
d_1
When C2
do R2=1
When (not C2)
OK2 to 1
d_2
q_0
When req 2
do C2 = 1
q_1
q_2
req CS2
ent CS2
q_3
CS
do C2 = 0
q_4
When (not R2)
When R2
q_5
q_6
Signal
2 to 1
p_0
When req1 do C1 = 1
p_1
req CS1
ent CS1
p_2
CS
p_3
do C1 = 0
p_4
When R1
p_5
do R1 = 0
signal 1 to 2
p_6
When
(not R1)
req CS2
e_0
e_1
When (not C1)
OK 1 to 2
e_2
When C1
do R1=1

a)

FIGURE 3

Author Index